Dec ~~ 30th 1950

EW YORK HERALD TRIBUNE,

Sus ...ram Thom... Is Dead; First ... Explore South Arabia Desert

...end of Lawrence Made 58-Day Trek in '30 After 5 Years of Preparation

Bertram Thomas

BRISTOL, England, Dec. 29 (AP)—The death of Bertram Thomas, explorer and friend of Lawrence of Arabia, was announced today. He was fifty-eight.

Became World Famous

Bertram Thomas became world famous in the early 1930s for his exploration of the vast southern desert of Arabia, which until then no European had crossed. He made the trek with a camel caravan of Bedouins in fifty-eight days, speaking their language and holding strictly to their customs, while gathering the first scientific data of a region which had been a blank spot on the maps of civilization.

Though only thirty-eight, Mr. Thomas was then probably the only man qualified to make the hazardous journey. He had served in the ranks in Belgium in World War 1, and from there was assigned to the Somerset Light Infantry in the Mesopotamian Insurrection. He rose to captain in the service, and was mentioned in dispatches.

Six feet tall, quick at languages and imposing in appearance, he caught the attention of the British government which assigned him to the land that held his imagination throughout his life, Arabia. He was Wazir and Finance Minister to the Sultan of Muscat and Oman from 1925 to 1930 and it was during this time that ...

sometimes five to eight days apart, but he found that there was water in a land thought to be completely arid. He carried a prismatic compass, a sextant and navigational instruments for map making, and along the way he gathered all the scientific data he could.

Caravan Dwindled

He started from the high mountains back of Dhufar on the Arabian shore, halfway down the southeastern coast, with seventy camels and forty guides. Fifty-eight days later he arrived in ...

...

This rule, Mr. Hubbell said, has created "an anxiety neurosis" in the public at large. Actually, he said, there is no necessity for a rule, because instead of either "I shall" or "I will," most people say "I'll," which is a contraction for both forms. And where one does use the uncontracted form, Mr. Hubbell said, "use whichever seems perfectly natural to you and you'll be right."

Who and Whom

As to "who" and "whom," he ...

...

All Previous Mapmakers

BUFFALO, N. Y., Dec. 29 (AP).—A helicopter has proven successful in measuring for the first time the depth of the upper Niagara River rapids.

The district United States Engineer's office, in announcing completion of the last of 252 soundings by helicopter, described the venture as "highly successful." The eight or nine-mile-an-hour cur-...

ARABIA DESERTA

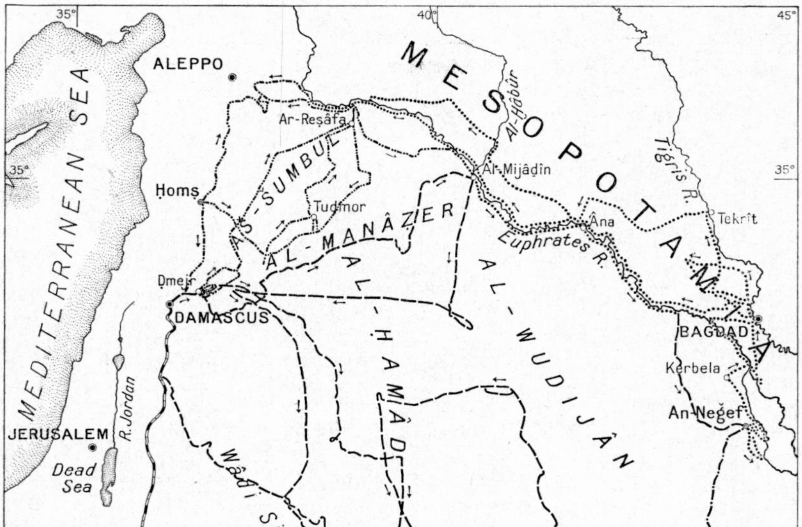

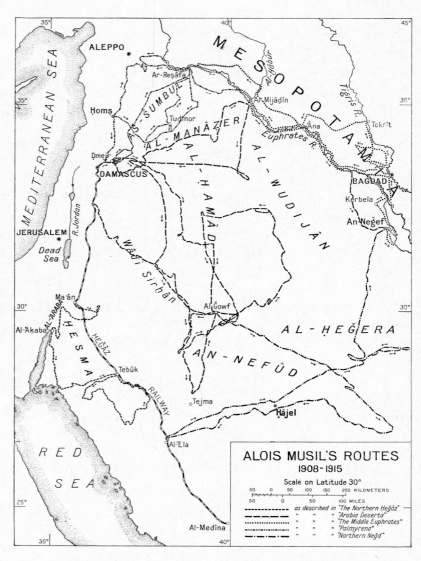

Alois Musil's routes as described in the topographical volumes of the series *American Geographical Society, Oriental Explorations and Studies*: No. 1, *The Northern Ḥeǵâz*, published 1926; No. 2, *Arabia Deserta*, published 1927; No. 3, *The Middle Euphrates* (forthcoming); No. 4, *Palmyrena* (forthcoming); No. 5, *Northern Neǵd* (forthcoming).

AMERICAN GEOGRAPHICAL SOCIETY
ORIENTAL EXPLORATIONS AND STUDIES No. 2.
Edited by J. K. WRIGHT

ARABIA DESERTA

A Topographical Itinerary

BY

ALOIS MUSIL
Professor of Oriental Studies
Charles University, Prague

Published under the Patronage of the
CZECH ACADEMY OF SCIENCES AND ARTS
and of
CHARLES R. CRANE

NEW YORK
1927

THE AMERICAN GEOGRAPHICAL SOCIETY
BROADWAY AT 156TH STREET
NEW YORK, N.Y., U.S.A.

3353

STÁTNÍ TISKÁRNA, PRAGUE, CZECHOSLOVAKIA

TO

CHARLES R. CRANE

WHO HAS MADE POSSIBLE THE PUBLICATION
OF THE RESULTS OF THE AUTHOR'S EXPLORATIONS
OF 1908-1915 AND OF HIS RESEARCHES
IN ORIENTAL GEOGRAPHY, HISTORY, ARCHEOLOGY,
AND ETHNOLOGY

THIS VOLUME

IS GRATEFULLY
DEDICATED

CONTENTS

PART II

Expedition of 1912

LIST OF ILLUSTRATIONS

PREFACE

My explorations in Arabia Petraea in 1896—1902 led me to the northern border of Arabia Felix and to the western border of Arabia Deserta, and awakened in me a desire to carry my studies farther. Since Arabia Deserta attracted me more than Arabia Felix I made up my mind first to penetrate into the former and to remain there for some considerable time in order to draw a map as a basis for historical investigations and to study the life of the inhabitants. As the Rwala tribe is the most powerful in Arabia Deserta, I tried to secure the protection of its head chief, an-Nûri eben Šaʿlân, and to migrate with him like a member of his family. By the grace of God and with the help of my oriental friends I was able to realize my intention, and during 1908 and 1909 I spent many months in mysterious Arabia Deserta.[1]

In drawing the map and in carrying out historical studies of places and roads, I soon discovered that there were some lacunae that made new investigations desirable. To fill in the gaps, in 1912 I explored the southeastern corner of Arabia Deserta and in 1914 I again visited its center.

As will be shown in *Palmyrena,* a forthcoming volume of the present series, I had hoped in 1908 to establish a triangulation net as a skeleton for my topographical map. I soon discovered, however, that in the time at my disposal and without a larger staff it would be impossible to carry out a trigonometrical survey of the whole country which I intended to explore. To have attempted to do so would have jeopardized my entire program of exploration. Consequently I was obliged to base the skeleton of my map upon astronomical determinations of latitude, plane-table surveys, and detailed route traverses only. My latitudes for all the points actually visited by me are reliable, as they were either astronomically determined or directly measured by route traverse from astronomically determined points. My latitudes for points between my routes

[1] Charles M. Doughty, in his noble volumes, *Travels in Arabia Deserta* (2 vols., Cambridge 1888, reprinted 1920, 1923), describes journeyings in a region which was actually the Arabia Felix of the ancient authors. Though his title is apt from the descriptive point of view, it is misleading when regarded in the light of ancient geography.

were determined either by plane-table or from precise topographical descriptions given me by various natives who sketched for me maps of the regions which I could not visit in person. Such positions are of course subject to error, and many of the latitudes thus determined will have to be corrected by such future explorers as are able to carry out astronomical observations.

After some unsuccessful attempts at determining longitudes astronomically, I was obliged to establish my longitudes from plane-table surveys, detailed route traverses, and natives' reports. Although this did not yield results comparable in accuracy with astronomically determined positions, the results proved sufficiently satisfactory, especially in regions where they could be controlled. As we rode on camels only, we soon learned the different rates of march per hour across regions of varying physiographic character. We were able to gain particularly accurate data on the camels' rates of march when traveling for a considerable length of time northward or southward, for then we could check our estimates of distance by the astronomical latitudes. This gave us criteria for plotting route traverses in an easterly or westerly direction far more accurate than one might at first believe possible.

To illustrate my method, I will outline the manner in which I established the longitude of Ḥâjel. In 1915 I had occasion to march east to al-ʿElaʾ,[2] the position of which is definitely known, as it lies on the Ḥeǧâz Railway. On this journey I passed within a few kilometers to the south of Ḥâjel, and, hence, from my route traverse I was able to estimate the difference in longitude between the meridian of this town and that of al-ʿElaʾ. I was able to check the longitude of Ḥâjel on my return journey eastward, in the course of which I passed within a few kilometers to the north of the town. Furthermore, I was also able to check my longitude of Ḥâjel in relation to the meridians of al-Ǧowf, Bagdad, and ar-Rijâḍ. Certain prominent points in the Nefûd were visible on our eastward journey from al-ʿElaʾ to Ḥâjel. Knowing the position of al-Ǧowf — which had been previously determined by me — and the course of the road between that oasis and Ḥâjel as described in detail by Huber,[3] I was able by means of the plane-table to correlate the positions of the points in the Nefûd — and

[2] See the author's forthcoming volume *Northern Neǧd,* which will be published in the present series.

[3] Huber, *Journal* (1891), pp. 49—61.

therefore of al-Ǧowf — with that of Ḥâjel. The Pilgrim Route from al-Kûfa to al-Medîna, as I determined in 1915, runs for hundreds of kilometers in an almost perfectly straight line toward Bagdad. Knowing the angle which this line makes with the meridian of Bagdad and having ascertained the latitudes of many points along it, I was able to plot the course of the Pilgrim Route with considerable accuracy. As, in 1915, I twice traversed the regions between the Pilgrim Route and the meridian of Ḥâjel, I was thus provided with still another check on the longitude of the latter place. Finally, I checked the longitude of Ḥâjel against that of ar-Rijâḍ as determined by Lewis Pelly in 1865,[4] by reconstructing Huber's detailed itinerary between Ḥâjel and ʿAnejza[5] and correlating it with detailed indications of the direction of the route from ʿAnejza to ar-Rijâḍ given me by natives.[6]

My theodolite, six chronometers, and five aneroid barometers were examined before and after my expeditions at the Military Geographical Institute at Vienna, and under the supervision of the Directorate of this Institute the map was drawn and altitudes obtained in 1908 and 1909 determined. The altitudes according to aneroid readings taken in 1912 and 1914-1915 were calculated by Dr. Gustav Swoboda of the State Meteorological Institute at Prague.

The primary motive of my explorations was historical, not cartographical; therefore I tried to collect as many topographical names as possible as a basis for historical researches and in so doing I paid especial attention to the spelling.[7] In transliterating Arabic letters I have used the same signs as in

[4] Pelly, *Wahabee Capital* (1865), p. 177.

[5] Huber, *op. cit.*, pp. 677—710.

[6] Except for the observations of Huber in the region south of the Nefûd, no other explorer's data were of use to me in the construction of my map of Northern Arabia. Where I based my conclusions upon Huber's material I consistently used his original notes (Huber, *op. cit.*) instead of the misleading sketch maps compiled from them in Paris and accompanying the published journal as an atlas. In general, it is difficult to indicate precisely the routes of travelers who have neither determined latitudes by astronomical means nor have made use of the plane-table, especially when these routes have been sketched by others.

[7] A word of caution to cartographers may not be amiss in the matter of the transcribing of place names. I may refer to the following examples of the sort of error that easily occurs. The name of the mountain ʿEnâza, first shown on my preliminary sketch map of northern Arabia published with my *Nord Arabien: Vorbericht über die Forschungsreise 1908—1909* (1909), now appears on maps as "Anazan," "Eneze," or "Aneze." On this same sketch map is drawn a Šeʿîb al-Ḫerr, the lower end of which I followed on April 25-26, 1912 (see Sixtus of Bourbon and Musil, *Nordostarabien, Vorbericht* [1913], p. 12). This name appears on recent maps misspelled "El-Khur" or "El-Khar," which has facilitated its confusion with the neighboring Wâdi ab-al-Ḳûr (Leachman, *Central Arabia* [1914], p. 504). The oasis of al-Bedʿ and the ruins of Ḥawra shown on my preliminary sketch map of the northern Ḥeǧâz (see Musil, *Nördlicher Ḥeǧâz, Vorbericht* [1911]) figure on recent maps as one place, "Beidha el-Hawra," which would mean "The White White." Persons not thoroughly familiar with Arabic geographical place names should never venture to change spellings that have been accurately recorded by explorers in the field, since in doing so they run the risk of destroying one of the bases of historical investigation. The existing maps of northern Arabia reveal so many impossible names that all concerned should beware of increasing their number.

my *The Northern Ḥeǧâz* (New York, 1926), attempting to express every sound by a single letter or a single symbol. The meaning of the different symbols will be found by experts below the title of the accompanying map of Northern Arabia. For the general reader I would point out that *ǧ* is to be read like *g* in gem, *š* like *sh*, *ž* like *z* in azure, *č* like *ch* in chief, *j* like *y* in yoke, and that ʿ is a strong guttural sound. The remaining symbols need not trouble him.

Throughout this work most of the Biblical and Assyrian names have been transliterated consistently with the scheme of transliteration employed for Arabic names. The Biblical forms, therefore, are often somewhat different from those found in the King James version, but the latter may readily be ascertained by reference to the Bible itself. Greek names are in general spelled in their Latin form rather than directly transliterated from the Greek.[8]

References to the Bible are to Rudolf Kittel's second edition of the Hebrew text, Leipzig, 1913. The reader will observe that occasionally these references are at variance with the text of the King James version. These variations are due to the fact that my interpretations of the meaning of the original Hebrew sometimes diverge from that of the translators of the King James version.

Bibliographical references in the footnotes are given in abbreviated form. The full references, with the dates of Arabic and ancient authors, will be found in the Bibliography, pp. 575—584.

The meaning of the majority of Arabic terms used in the text will be evident from the context. Two terms, however, are frequently employed without explanation:

šeʿîb (plural, *šeʿibân*): relatively small watercourse or valley occupied by an intermittent stream.

wâdi (plural, *wudijân*): relatively large watercourse or valley occupied by an intermittent stream.

Arabic botanical terms appearing in the text are listed in the index with brief characterizations and Latin equivalents as far as these have been determined.

A sketch map showing the author's route and indicating the pages in this volume on which the different portions of his itinerary are discussed accompanies the volume.

[8] Exceptions to these general rules governing transliteration are made for those proper names that have acquired conventional English forms, the latter being used to avoid the appearance of pedantry.

To Dr. Isaiah Bowman and other members of the staff of the American Geographical Society I should like to express my grateful appreciation for the facilities extended to me in the publication of this work. I wish also heartily to thank Dr. J. K. Wright, the editor, for his aid in clearing up obscure points and for many valuable suggestions. Special acknowledgment is due to Miss Anna Blechová, Secretary of the Oriental Seminar at Charles University, Prague, for her competent services in preparing the index, and also to the State Printing Establishment (Státní tiskárna) at Prague for its efficient accomplishment of the unusually difficult task of printing a work which not only is in a foreign language but abounds in difficult words and phrases.

PART I

1908—1909

CHAPTER I

ḌMEJR NEAR DAMASCUS TO AL-MIJÂḎÎN ON THE EUPHRATES

In the autumn of 1908* I was camping east-northeast from the settlement of Ḍmejr (37 km. northeast of Damascus)† with the Prince an-Nûri eben Šaʿlân of the Rwala tribe, which belongs to the ʿAneze nation, my object being to explore from his encampment the districts near by as well as those more remote. In the cartographical work I was assisted by Rudolf Thomasberger (called Tûmân) of the Military Cartographical Institute in Vienna, who had charge of all my scientific instruments. My acquaintances in Damascus had hired an ʿAḳejli camel trader, named Mḥammad al-Ḳaẓîb, as a servant for me, and I myself had procured two others, one named Nâṣer eben ʿObejd al-Maṛlûḳ, of al-Žerjitejn, the other Blejhân eben Dûẖi eben Meṣreb, of the Ḳmuṣa subdivision of the Sbaʿa tribe. I had two tents like those used by the ʿAḳejl. The larger one was oblong, the smaller circular; and I had provided seventeen camels to carry enough supplies for ten or fourteen months and to transport our scientific equipment and ourselves. When I was merely exploring in the neighborhood of the camp, these camels grazed with the other herds, sometimes a long way off.

ḌMEJR TO DEKWA

Monday, November 16, 1908. As the camels were about to return from the distant pasture to the watering pool nearer camp, I decided to start on a longer excursion the following day. I had everything ready but had not as yet spoken to the Prince, for he and his son Nawwâf were staying with other clans. Visiting him after his return, I found that he was planning to remove the camp on the morrow to the district south of al-Baṣîri, where he intended to wait for

* The author's explorations in Palmyrena during the autumn of 1908 immediately preceding the expedition narrated in the following chapters (I—XI) are dealt with in *Palmyrena*, a forthcoming volume of the present series.

† A key to the place names mentioned in this volume and which appear on the map of Northern Arabia published in this series is included in the index. See also the index map.

rain. He was not fully decided about his departure, for he wished first to confer with Ršejd eben Smejr, the head chief of the Weld ᶜAli, who was to join us. This news caused me to change my plans. Having bought two additional camel loads of flour, I needed two camels to carry these newly-acquired provisions and two more to carry the four bags of water which I was to take to the new camp at the request of the Prince, who informed me that we should not then be camping near water but in an arid land (*bel-manda*). Hence I could not start on a long excursion with even one of my animals. Besides, the Prince thought I could explore the unknown territory with much greater facility from the nearest camp than from Ḍmejr. I regretted losing my last opportunity to visit the volcanic district of Tlûl al-ᶜIjâṯ; but the Prince, willing to extend his help even in this instance, proposed that we move in a southeasterly direction.

For the past ten days an-Nûri had been going about strongly armed. Besides a dagger and an eight-barreled Gasser revolver with forty-eight rounds of ammunition, he carried 120 Mannlicher sharp cartridges and a carbine. Wondering at this array, I asked him the reason and received this reply: "Brother, it's our habit. We are at war with many a tribe and know not when we may be attacked. I myself must be doubly careful and alert, for I know not when or where the avenger may surprise me. I never sleep alone at night; yet it is for the good of my family, nay, of the whole tribe, that I did what I did." This he said in allusion to his brother and predecessor, Prince Fahad, who had been murdered by a slave at an-Nûri's own order, and to another brother, Mišᶜal, whom he had killed with his own hand. He boasted of having personally killed in fights over 120 men; and yet there he was sitting before me and looking at me with his childlike, sincere eyes!

That afternoon we took a walk with Tûmân to the Ḍmejr al-ᶜAtîže ruins and drew a plan of the local Roman camp. As we were coming back we scented a very repugnant stench blown toward us by the north-northwesterly wind from the gullies adjoining the camp on the northern side. For almost two months there had been pitched at al-Maksûra over four hundred tents, whose tenants made daily trips to these gullies for the purpose of relieving themselves therein privately. When the wind blew from the north we could hardly remain in the camp; we all stuffed our noses and even our mouths, and men as well as women kept their head-cloths pulled up to their eyes. I had noticed the same thing when we were at al-Ṛûṭa, where the vicinity of the camp was watered every other day, a practice which increased the stench so much that many children became sick and in consequence the Prince had moved the camp to the valley of al-ʿAṣejfîr and later to Ḍmejr.

Tuesday, November 17, 1908. At night the thermometer registered a minimum of six degrees below zero (centigrade). I could hardly believe it, but the ice that formed upon the water bags vindicated the truthfulness of the instrument. The first thing in the morning I left with Tûmân for the Roman camp, where we worked for over three hours under difficulties, for a violent, icy, northwest wind kept bending the tape measure and making our hands and fingers numb.

After finishing our work we returned to the tents, to find them fully packed and their tenants plodding in groups to the south. I joined the Prince's troop, which started to the south-southeast at 10.20 A. M. Presently my female camel began to prance as she came up with three whelps, still blind, which were sadly whining for their mother, who had gone with the mistress of the tent and left her offspring to die of hunger. Farther on a camel with a broken leg was writhing in pain; another victim of the fate of death by starvation. It was a disagreeable journey, for the high wind was raising almost opaque masses of dust and sand, the fine grains of which penetrated to our skin and caused an unpleasant tickling sensation, while at the same time the air was so cold that my hands and feet were freezing. I would gladly have walked, but the Prince persuaded me that it was imperative for me to maintain my honor by riding. Indeed, he had even reproached me for walking to Ḍmejr on my visit to the *mudîr* (Turkish governor of a *nâḥije*, or small administrative division). "Thou hast become my brother and Nawwâf's," he said; "thus thou hast also become the sheikh of our tribe, and a sheikh must not go afoot to another camping ground but must ride at the head of his tribe (*salaf*)."

Toward noon, as we reached a rocky territory, the clouds thinned, and I realized the cause of the penetrating cold. All the higher peaks to the north, west, and south were glistening in the enchanting beauty of freshly fallen snow, and the wind was blowing toward us from every direction bringing news of the winter that prevailed near by.

After a while Nawwâf overtook me, riding a light thoroughbred *d̲elûl* (riding camel) with his cousin Mežḥem holding to the saddle from behind, while his mare, tied by the check rein to the camel's girth, was trotting alongside without a rider. Mežḥem, a weak boy about ten years old, had lost his father two years before at the hands of a member of the Šammar tribe who had been camping with him as a neighbor (*ḳaṣîr*). One day Mežḥem's father, Mḥammad, was showing to the neighbor in his tent a new revolver, urging him to try how easily the spring functioned. The Šammari took the proffered weapon and pressed the trigger, whereupon the projectile was shot out and hit Mḥammad in the chest, wounding him mortally. Mḥammad's slaves fell upon the unfortunate neighbor intending to kill him, but an-Nûri and Nawwâf, attracted by his outcries, saved his life.

"Why, it was allowed by God (*amr min allâh*)," they explained, "Allâh had ruled it should happen so, and we should have acted infamously (*ʿajb*), had we permitted our neighbor to be killed by our slaves."

Riding alongside Nawwâf, I was addressed by a strange Arab who announced that he, Ršejd eben Smejr, greeted me. He was the head chief of the Weld ʿAli, whom I had already met in Damascus at the house of the Director-in-Chief of Pilgrimages, ʿAbdarraḥmân Pasha. He was about thirty years old, with a pleasant expression on his rather full face. Exchanging greetings with him, I asked about his health and that of his family; and he in turn told me that, wishing to do me a favor, for my sake he had refused the proposition of an-Nûri to camp south of al-Baṣîri and had likewise persuaded the Prince to go south of the Dekwa volcano, thus giving me an opportunity to explore Tlûl al-ʿIjâṯ. Smiling, I thanked him for his interest and support but hastened to add that the vicinity of al-Baṣîri afforded no extensive pasturage, as the Ḳmuṣa subdivision of the Sbaʿa tribe had been camping there for over a month; whereas the southern half of Tlûl al-ʿIjâṯ had thus far not been visited by camels. And I also mentioned that camping in the territory of enemies and grazing their best meadows and shrubs would prove the chivalrous determination of both chiefs, an-Nûri and Ršejd.

An-Nûri confirmed my words. "By Allâh," he said, "Mûsa speaks the truth and knows that for years I have been feeding my stock upon the lands of his old friends the Ahl aš-Šemâl (Beni Ṣaḫr). During the harvest I camped at Libben, and we and our animals ate all that we found upon their lands and in their villages, for we had no fear of anybody."

"Still thou fearest the inhabitants of the volcanic district of the Ḥawrân, the Ahâli al-Ǧebel, as thou hast admitted, Father of Nawwâf, since thou wouldst not permit me to visit the castle of ar-Raḥba."

"Ahâli al-Ǧebel! they are not decent enemies but malicious robbers who steal out of their dens, running away with their loot the moment they sight us. They have neither courage nor strength to oppose us, and they abandon even their booty just to crawl into their dens."

"Hast thou never sought them out in their cliffs?"

"Twice I have done so, but we lost so many mares, which were not used to the volcanic ground, that our loss exceeded the profit from the booty we carried off."

And Ršejd added: "No Bedouin will wage war in the volcanic gulches. Only the open desert affords the possibility of a decent fight."

Slowly we penetrated into a land that was hardly passable. It was covered with irregular stretches of lava and sand, out of which protruded numerous black, pointed rocks, about ten meters high by one hundred to three hundred meters long, and most of them split perpendicularly, each into two oval parts which together formed an ellipsoid. The ascent over their sharp edges was very difficult for a beast of burden, the inclined planes of the fragments being smooth enough to cause even a camel to slip. Once my beast fell head downwards and it was only through the protection of Allâh, as an-Nûri proclaimed, that I leaped off the saddle without breaking my neck. It was not easy to force my frightened *ḏelûl* to rise.

At 3.30 P. M. we reached a point southwest from the hill of al-Hdejb. The Prince rode ahead to find a suitable camping ground, and presently, signaling me with the white sleeve of his shirt, pointed to a spot where I was to order my camel to kneel. There I was to pitch my tent. He had hardly dismounted from his own animal before he was surrounded by the Arabs, all seeking favorable locations for their tents. At 3.40 I unloaded my baggage, unsaddled my camel, and tying the bridle to her left foreleg allowed her to graze while I sat down by my saddle and awaited the arrival of my companions with the other camels. I was very tired and shivered frightfully from cold. Immediately after the tent was ready I ordered a cup of tea and drank it, but my stomach refused it. I was so violently shaken by the accompanying fever that to get warm I put on all the blankets I had. The fever did not abate, and it was not until midnight that I was slightly relieved. The thermometer registered –6.5° C.

Wednesday and Thursday, November 18 and 19, 1908. Although trembling with cold and exhaustion and hardly able to stand, I had to get up and superintend the loading of my baggage and then plod ahead. A stinging pain afflicted my intestines. Thank God! the chilly wind calmed down and the sun grew appreciably warmer. We started at 10.10 A. M. When the Prince designated a new camping ground as early as eleven o'clock, I could not even unsaddle my camel, and he bade his scribe Ǧwâd do it for me. Nawwâf remained with me till my companions arrived and erected the tent, whereupon I immediately lay down and took the necessary medicines, but I could not fall asleep. All night long I writhed in pain and in the morning felt even weaker than I had felt the evening before; but the internal pains had so far abated that I could take some oaten soup.

In the afternoon Nawwâf came to visit me and stayed late into the night. Again and again he inquired whether I was married and how many children I had; for it was above his comprehension that a healthy man could remain single. He had had four wives already. Three of them had given birth to a son each, and yet he had divorced them all, one after another. The first one, whom he loved best, was the daughter of the assassinated Prince Fahad; she deserted him because she was more attached to her own family than to her husband and son. The second, daughter of the deceased Prince Saṭṭâm, became repugnant to him and so was dismissed from his tent, although she wept bitterly and begged him to keep her. His third wife, a famous beauty and daughter of a minor chief, was also compelled to return to her family, because Nawwâf grew tired of her: *šabeʿet minha,* as he expressed it. The fourth wife, Fhêde, had now lived in his tent two years and as yet had borne him no child. When I wondered at his fickleness in destroying the happiness of Allâh's creatures, of his wives as well as of his sons, he laughed: "Why, with us it is *ʿâde*," he said, "our custom and our habit. How could the son of a prince be satisfied with one wife? What would the warriors say?"

To my inquiry concerning the fate of his sons he answered that they would remain to their third or fourth year with their mothers and then would come to his tent, where his old mother would rear them just as she was already rearing his first-born son Sulṭân. I pitied the children and their mothers for having to live apart, remarking that the women of my land fare much better, because their husbands cannot put them away without sufficient cause. "True," retorted he, "but I pity your men. If one of them finds after a year or two that he does not love his wife and yet is forced to live with her and stay with her all his life, how unhappy he is! Such a burden we could not accept."

He would not concede that women may have equal rights with men. "Lookest thou, brother Mûsa; when the enemy appears and the sound of the battle cry arises, is it the women who rush to the defense? Is it the women who undertake aggressive raids? Is it the women who return with the booty? We keep women to bear us children and to care for our tents. We do not oppress them, but a woman must always be conscious of the fact that man is her master. Thus Allâh has willed; our ancestors observed this order and we likewise observe it. It is our habit, our custom, our law."

"Yet at times your women are braver than you," I replied; "and when you men flee from the enemy it is the women who by words and gestures urge you, nay, force you, to offer resistance; and many of your women can wield a weapon as well as you can."

"Those are but exceptions. The women remind us by their words and gestures of our love, and they promise us a reward. Unwilling to be humiliated by the enemy, we muster up fresh resistance and fight for the women's sake; but the women have never yet saved us from the enemy."

"And, pray, could not a woman be your chief? Do you not esteem more highly than many a chief Turkijje, the widow of Saṭṭâm? Why do you call her children *ʿejâl Turkijje;* why do you not call them *ʿejâl Saṭṭâm?*"

"Turkijje surpasses by the virtue of her intelligence and calm deliberation. We consult her, but I do not think we would subject ourselves to her were she our chief."

"How about ʿÂlija, who led not only the Beni Ṣaẖr but also your warriors against the troops of Ibrâhîm Pasha? She was a woman and you obeyed her."

"That was a long time go."

"It is not so very long ago. The contemporaries of ʿÂlija are still living."

"On that occasion Allâh took from the Arabs a prudent man and substituted a woman, but today we would permit no woman to command us. When I last visited Damascus I learned that the Sultan had granted liberty (*ḥorrijje*) to his subjects; from then on, so they said, women and slaves should be equal to free Arabs. On hearing that, I declared: 'But with us in the desert it will not be so. You settlers may do as you like among yourselves, but do not try to force your freedom upon us in the desert.' It is, indeed, a fine freedom, brother Mûsa, that now prevails among the settlers, where a subordinate officer thinks himself more clever than his commander, as happens, so they say, in Damascus and in Ḥaleb (Aleppo). I should like to see a subordinate chief who would dare to criticize my orders, or who would oppose me while on a war expedition! We were free (*ḥorr*) always and need no new kind of freedom."

The air was very cold, –6° C. I was able to sleep all night, however, and the rest gave me strength.

Friday, November 20, 1908. I was in my tent trying to work when, about ten o'clock, I caught the sound of an agitated cry, "Oh! some riders (*jâ-hla-l-ẖâjl*)!" and hurrying out I saw that the women and girls were running toward the mares, saddling them, and bringing them forward to their husbands and brothers, who threw off their heavy fur coats, fastened on their cartridge belts, and seized their rifles. In less than two minutes the armed warriors were riding off toward the south to repulse some unknown enemy. Which of them would return? But everyone in the camp remained calm and peaceful; no woman cried, no elder offered advice. A few men, left to defend the camp, ascended a cliff to the south with rifles, and I stumbled after them in the hope that I might be able to watch the fray through binoculars. I saw our fighters divide into two bands, the stronger one with the Prince at its head galloping to the south, the weaker one led by Nawwâf to the southwest. Both soon disappeared behind a high wall of rocks extending from the west to the east, and when I could see them no longer I went back to my work.

In the afternoon three men on horseback came with the news that there had appeared in the morning, thirteen kilometers south of the camp, a band of Druses and their tributaries, goat and sheep raisers, who had attacked the herds of Eben Meǧwel. Three warriors who were present had, they said, fought valiantly, and Rašrâš, the son of our neighbor chief ʿAḏûb, and the slave of Prince an-Nûri had shot two of the enemy and seized their horses; but the raiders had nevertheless driven off one herd (*ḳaṭîʿa*) numbering over seventy camels. The guards stationed upon the higher hills, they said, had repeated the alarm cry of the attacked herdsmen, so that the news reached the camp in a few minutes; but as soon as the troop led by the Prince had approached the enemy, who were retreating with the loot about twenty kilometers from the camp, the latter had abandoned the booty and fled to the southeast.

Unable to overtake the raiders, although he urged his followers to top speed, the Prince returned that evening worn out and unsuccessful, cursing the young warriors for not guarding the flocks carefully, as he had ordered them in the morning. Had they obeyed, he grumbled, they would have been able to meet and reward the enemy in a different manner. His son Saʿûd, who was with the young warriors by the grazing camels, attempted to excuse their negligence by pointing out their diligence in guarding the herds for over three weeks, during which time the Ahâli al-Ǧebel had not once come out of their dens; therefore, he said, since it was so cold now, they had assumed that the rascals would not leave their warm dwellings. An-Nûri interrupted his apology with: "A Bedouin depends on neither cold nor heat; he never trusts his enemy but confides solely in himself." What had become of Nawwâf and his troop so late in the night nobody knew. Herdsmen returning from the southwest told of hearing shots, but they had seen nothing in the rugged volcanic land.

Saturday, November 21, 1908. We changed our camp. The tents were struck, loaded, and all the inhabitants and camels were soon plodding along to the south-southeast. As we were starting, at 9.22 A. M., the Prince greeted me but immediately rode off again westward to the chief Ršejd eben Smejr. The weather was cold but calm. Along on my left rode several slaves of the Prince, each of them carrying on his left hand a fowling falcon, which was promptly released whenever the greyhounds scared out a small hare. At 10.52 the Prince signaled to me again with his white sleeve, pointing to a spot where I was to pitch my tent. Standing by his camel, he next showed his nearest immediate relatives where they were to camp; and then he went to his mare, which had been lame since yesterday's ride through the almost impassable district.

After a while I was joined by Nawwâf, who came leading his brown horse by the bridle. As I went to greet him I saw that his clothes were very bloody. He explained curtly that his troop had overtaken the fleeing enemy and fired several shots after them, but that a young ʿAbdelli, who was riding alongside, had been struck at the same time by an enemy's bullet. Leaving the lad to the care of two riders, Nawwâf had pursued the enemy to a point in sight of the first settlement, when he had turned back for fear he might be surrounded. On reaching the wounded ʿAbdelli he had lifted him into his saddle and held him on with his right hand. "The poor ʿAbdelli," he said, "was embracing me, kissing me, and imploring me to lay him on the ground, fearing he could not stand the pain caused by riding on horseback. But how could I do so? He would have frozen if the beasts did not tear him to pieces beforehand. When at night the horses could not go on, we rested, covering the boy with our thin clothing, and ourselves freezing. Oh, brother Mûsa, how I shivered with cold! As soon as the ruddy glow appeared in the east we rode on, and when the sun began to shine we laid the ʿAbdelli on the ground and hurried to the tents of his clan, whence men rode out for him with litters on camelback."

From me Nawwâf went to the tent of his father, where they were examining his exhausted mare. The Prince, four Arabs, and Nawwâf squatted down, and Nawwâf told his adventure again, receiving a rebuke from the Prince for venturing so far. Meantime the women gave drinks of warm salt water to both mares and wrapped them in rugs. The stallion brought back by the men as the booty of one of the Prince's slaves also had some salt water given him and had his wound washed out. He was still carrying the narrow saddle of the Druses, sprinkled with the blood of his former owner, who had been shot from it.

In the evening we determined the latitude with precision. This was no easy task with the thermometer at –4° C.

Sunday, November 22, 1908. I had planned to ascend the volcano of Dekwa for the purpose of drawing a map of the vicinity; but, alas, the air was not so clear as it had been for the last few days, for fine mists were spreading out from east to west and giving a trace of warmth. However, we left at 9.10 A. M. in a northeasterly direction. At first I was overcome by such a weakness that I seemed to see everything about me moving in circles and had to hold tight to my saddle to keep from falling off; but I felt better as we went on. Our way led over the countless sharp edges and smooth planes of lava crags, so dangerous that we had to ride with the greatest care and difficulty. But by eleven o'clock we arrived in safety at the southwestern foot of the volcano of Dekwa, entrusted our camels (Fig. 1) here (at the height of 838 m.) to the slave ʿAbdallâh, and with Tûmân and Blejhân continued to the peak. Climbing cautiously along the southern edge of a covered crater for a full half-hour, we finally reached the top and went to work.

Dekwa, with an elevation of 1016 meters, is the highest volcano of the Tlûl al-ʿIjâṯ territory. On the south, east, and west it is unattached, but on the northern side it sends out a stream of lava about twenty-five meters deep. The northeastern edge of the rounded crater projects to its original height, but the other parts have either sunken in or been gradually eroded away by channels of water. From the west the inner side of the eastern edge resembles a vertical, black, smoky wall, the northern half of which consists of about twenty horizontal layers of soft banded rocks. I noticed plenty of moss in the crevices. Although the air was not yet quite clear, we could see the northern belt of volcanoes from Mount ʿÂde in the east as far as the Ḥalîmt al-Ḳâra cone in the north. Of those in the Tlûl al-ʿIjâṯ district (Fig. 2) we noted in the north aš-Šâmât, Mtejrîčât, and Karawišât; to the south of these, al-Afejḥem; and easterly from this, Umm Iḏen[1] and Mâlḥat al-Ḳronfol, in which the clove tree thrives.

To the southwest of Umm Iḏen we saw the long chain of al-Mintaṯrât and al-Muṭallaᶜ, and to the east of this the

FIG. 1—The author's camel at the foot of the volcano of Dekwa.

small volcano of al-Maḥfûr. To the south of Dekwa was the aš-Šejbe group; east of these Ruṛejla and Ẓerâjer, and to the southeast the semi-circular Estârât al-ᶜÂżer group, with the high Tell al-ᶜÂżer at the southern end. East of the latter were the volcanoes of Ṯlejṯwât; to the south al-Ḫejl and Ẓers,

[1] Jâḳût, *Muᶜǧam* (Wüstenfeld), Vol. 1, p. 356, says that Umm Uḏun is a solitary table-hill in the district of as-Samâwa, whence a black stone is brought for mills. — In Syria the best millstones are made from basalt; therefore it is necessary to seek Umm Uḏun in a volcanic district. This district is found only in the western part of as-Samâwa (the Arabia Deserta of the classics) and here in the northwestern corner is our volcano of Umm Iḏen, which we may identify with the Umm Uḏun of Jâḳût.

and beyond them the white, arid lowland of ar-Raḥba,[2] where in spots we caught sight of the dark river bed of at-Tejs.

East of Dekwa the guide pointed out to me the volcanoes of Umm al-Maᶜᶜâze; south of these Ḳbejjân, Ḫnêfes, and al-Aḳᶜas; and southeast from the last-named the great odd cone of Sejs.[3]

FIG. 2—The Tlûl al-ᶜIjâṯ from Dekwa.

North of Umm al-Maᶜᶜâze could be seen Ammu-r-Rḳejbe and Ab-al-ᶜAjš, and in the northwest the high Tell Makḥûl. The whole district of Tlûl al-ᶜIjâṯ, with its dark blue masses of lava and high, solitary volcanoes, presented a very depressing view.

After we returned to the camp we heard that the enemy had again appeared in the east but had fled before they came within shooting distance. Towards evening Nawwâf visited me; and, as we were chatting together, I told him I had just learned from the negro ᶜAbdallâh that my servants were in the habit of asking his assistance in every service which it was their own duty to perform, that Nawwâf had to do their thinking and acting for them. When I reproached him for not having called my attention to this laziness, he smiled and retorted that a brother must help his brother; whereupon I made an agreement with him according to which he was to assent to their appeals and demands only upon being shown by them a camel stick (*miḥǧân*), which he had given me. This was to be a sign that I knew of their demand and agreed to it; for of course I could not use a written order, as he

[2] During the reign of the Caliph Hišâm the property of ar-Ruḥbe in the Damascus district was usurped by Bekr ibn Nawfal for the benefit of al-Walîd, the son of Yazid (Abu-l-Farağ, *Aġâni* [Bûlâḳ, 1285 A. H.], Vol. 6, p. 133).

Jâḳût, (*op. cit.*, Vol. 2, p. 762) and Abu-l-Faḍâ'il (*Marâṣid* [Juynboll], Vol. 1, p. 465) say that the settlement of ar-Ruḥbe lies at the edge of the volcanic territory of al-Leğa in the administrative district of Ṣarḫad.

[3] Jâḳût, *op. cit.*, Vol. 1, p. 271, writes that there is a water of Usejs to the south of Damascus. — This Usejs must sound in the dialect of the Rwala like Sejs or Sâjes, hence I identify it with our Ḫabra Sejs, east of Damascus.

could neither read nor write. Besides this I asked him to lend me two or three camels to carry my loads whenever we were to change our camp or when I happened to be going on an expedition. My seventeen camels were not sufficient for these things, and I did not intend to buy any more. He willingly promised to grant my wish, saying, "My property is thine, and thy property is mine (*ḥelâli ḥelâlak w ḥelâlak ḥelâli*)."

THE RWALA TRIBE

Nawwâf told me many details about the tribe of Rwala, of which his father an-Nûri was the supreme chief and which he himself would rule in the future.

The Rwala belong to the ʿAneze group called Ẓana Muslim, over whom they exercise control, for the entire group with all its divisions (*ḳabâjel*) acknowledges the priority of Prince an-Nûri eben Šaʿlân.

The Ẓana Muslim consist of the Beni Wahab and the Âl Ǧlâs, the Rwala being a subdivision of the latter.

The Beni Wahab are divided thus:
- al-Ḥsene (their head chief is from the family of Eben Mezjed, called also Eben Melḥem)
- Weld ʿAli, consisting of:
  - Ẓana Mifreǧ (head chief from the family of Eben Smejr)
  - al-Mašṭa (head chief from the family of Eben Ṭajjâr)
  - al-Meṣâlîḫ (head chief from the family of Eben Jaʿîš)

The Âl Ǧlâs are divided into al-Miḥlef and ar-Rwala:
- al-Miḥlef consisting of:
  - al-Ešâǧeʿa, also called Čenhâb, the head chief of which is from the family of Eben Meʿǧel and which contains the following families:
    - Âl Ḥḏâḳ (chief: Nâṣer eben Meʿǧel)
    - al-Belâʿîs (an individual: Belʿâsi)
    - al-Bdûr (chief: Nâfel eben Hejẓâl)
    - al-Ḫlejfât
    - Âl Mhajûb
  - as-Swâlme; families:
    - Âl Ǧandal (from which descends the chief)
    - Âl Milḥâḳ
    - Âl Hlejb
    - al-Furâhde (an individual: Farhûdi)
  - ʿAbdelle; families:
    - Âl Mǧejd (from which descends the chief)
    - al-Ḥreza
    - al-Ḫmesa
    - al-Meṣâḥle
    - al-Kšûš
- The Rwala are divided into *bedâjed*, or clans, as follows: Âl Duṛmân (an individual: Duṛmâni); Âl Murʿaẓ (an individual:

Murʿaẓi); al-Freğe (an individual: Frejği); al-Ḳaʿâžʿa (an individual: Ḳaʿêžʿi). The common ancestor of the Âl Duṛmân and the Âl Murʿaẓ is said to have been Ğamʿân, the son of Muslim. The following are the families and minor subdivisions of these clans:

Âl Duṛmân; families:
- Âl Ḥakše
- Âl Ḥasan
- Âl Derʿân
- aṣ-Ṣwâlḥa
- al-Barâbra

Âl Murʿaẓ; families:
- Âl Šaʿlân (from whom descends the head chief)
- Âl Nṣejr
- Âl Maʿabhel
- Âl Ğâber
- Âl Whejf, or al-Whafa' (an individual: Wejmi)
- Âl Naṣîr
- al-Kbûš
- Âl Rowẓân
- Âl Bnejje
- Âl Ṣabîḥ
- as-Sabte
- al-Ḳaṭâʿa
- al-ʿEleme (an individual: ʿElejmi); subdivisions:
  - ar-Rašde
  - Âl Ḥamad
  - Âl Medhem
  - Âl Ḏwêḫ

al-Freğe; subdivisions:
- Âl Ḥaẓaʿ
- Âl Fleta
- as-Swâḥle
- Âl Ğufjân
- Âl Sumrân
- Âl Huṭlân
- Âl Šaʿêl
- Âl Ğidrân
- Âl Mšêṭ
- Âl Ṣabbâḥ
- Âl Rmâḥ

al-Ḳaʿâžʿa; subdivisions:
- al-Ṛšûm (an individual: Ṛušmi)
- al-Ḥamâmîd (an individual: Ḥammâdi)
- Âl Šḳejr
- Âl Ribšân; families:
  - Âl Ḥnejjân
  - Âl Maʿêrîr
  - Âl Wuḳejd
  - as-Sabʿa
  - Âl Ğerri (an individual: Ğerrâwi)

Âl ʿAwênân (an individual: ʿWênâni)
Âl ʿAǧîl
Âl Slejm
Âl Mšanna (an individual: Mešâne)
Âl Mâneʿ; subdivisions:
Âl Ḳaʿḳaʿ
Âl Dwêrež
Âl ʿAṭijje
al-Čwâṯle (an individual: Čwêṯli)
aš-Šerâṭîn (an individual: Šerṭâni)
Âl Rašîd
Âl Ršejdân

With the Rwala camp al-Kwâčbe (an individual: Kwêčbi) who are believed to belong to the Ḳḥaṭân. They have about 150 tents and are subdivided as follows:

Âl Ṣwejt, consisting of:
al-Mdêṛem; subdivisions:
al-Uklân; families:
Âl ʿObejdân (chief: Ẓabʿân ab-al-Okl)
Âl Smejr
Âl Rabîʿ
al-Ǧwâhle
Âl Solmân
Âl Šǧêr
Âl Rnêm
ar-Ršûd
Âl Wuhejb; families:
Âl Meḥsen (chief: ʿAwdân eben Radhân)
Âl Ǧlejdân („ Zeben eben Ǧlejdân)
Âl Wâdi („ Salmân eben Zejdân)
Al-Ǧirfe, consisting of:
Âl Mǧejbel (chief: ʿAskar âl Kwejčeb)
Âl Ḫomši („ Ṭurḳi aš-Šrejfi)
Âl ʿArẓân („ al-Obejẓ al-ʿArejjeẓ)
Âl Ḫaṭṭâm

IN CAMP OF AN-NÛRI EBEN ŠAʿLÂN NEAR DEKWA

Monday and Tuesday, November 23 and 24, 1908. Our camels were driven to Baḥrat al-ʿAtejbe (Lake of the ʿAtejbe) to be watered. As my herdsman Ḥarrân was to bring water for the next seven days, he had taken Blejhân with him; and, since the way was long from Dekwa to the lake, besides leading through the land of our enemies the Ahâli al-Ǧebel, the men were accompanied by a troop of warriors commanded by Nawwâf. There was not a drop of water in the Prince's tent; indeed, he had sent his servant to us three times for a pitcher of water, but we had none ourselves. In the afternoon his scribe brought me a hare, a present from his master, whose hunter had killed two.

Behind my tent the little boys were practicing with slings. They had gathered a quantity of round pebbles and were throwing them with wonderful precision at the edge of the cliff thirty to forty paces distant. The pebbles whistled through the air and, falling on the ledge, rebounded and flew several feet farther. A pebble released from an Arab sling will fracture the thickest skull. In that country it is easy to see how David could kill Goliath.

Towards evening I was visited by Ṭrâd eben Saṭṭâm, who told me that the wounded ʿAbdelli "*râḥ*, had gone (had died)." The evening and the night were unusually peaceful. There were no cries or curses of herdsmen to break the stillness, nor growls, roars, or gruntings of the camels, for the herds were passing the night by water and did not return till the following Tuesday evening.

Wednesday to Saturday, November 25 to 28, 1908. As I was convalescing but slowly from my recent illness, which had weakened me considerably, I devoted the days to folklore studies: from sunrise until four o'clock in the afternoon I sat in my round tent. In the morning Mḥammad usually brought me some informant, with whom I closeted myself. Often I found it impossible to question him, for he would not answer me until he had told all that was in his mind. He would sit opposite me with his kerchief pulled over his chin and over half of his nose, covering his mouth and nose thus to insure himself against my scent, for only Allâh knew whether my queries might harm him! Resting his left hand on a camel saddle, with the camel stick in his right hand, he would lazily draw pictures on the ground, until all at once he would stop and, with downcast eyes, appear to be sound asleep. Then suddenly he would look keenly at me, draw his eyebrows together, and gaze longingly at the exit of my tent. How gladly would he have disappeared through that exit to avoid the torment of my questions! Only when he was explaining something to his own liking would he show more animation. Then his words would run along like a brooklet whose water at places is absorbed by sand but reappears a little farther on. Talking earnestly and drawing with his stick, he would suddenly come to a dead stop in the middle of a sentence and only after a minute or two would he slowly resume his story. After he reached the end of it, he would continue drawing with the stick, gazing fixedly at it as if he were ashamed of having spoken so long, sitting statue-like, and collecting his wits; for he knew from experience that the real torture was near at hand. Every word he had said I had jotted down, and now he was to be asked to repeat the particular phrases, to explain, to supplement; and he was not used to such a mental strain. He would usually answer in complete embarrassment, would shift from one subject to another, and then deny knowledge of the very facts he had just admitted. Often he would say: "It is unknown among us;" but after a while of his own accord he would begin to talk of things about which he had previously pleaded ignorance. If I asked him to explain some neat phrase he had used, he would assure me that he had forgotten it. At the end of such an ordeal I was usually no less tired than he was; but it was necessary for me so to overcome my feelings that I should not by a word or even by a glance betray my displeasure or impatience. I must not utter a single offending word but must treat my informer like a spoiled child in order to gain his confidence and lead him on to where I wanted him. At the end of it all I must appear very much gratified and thank him for the invaluable information I had been at such pains to extract; otherwise he would fail to come the next day and would scare off others also.

This was always in the morning. Toward evening Nawwâf usually visited me and stayed rather late.

Wednesday night there appeared in the camp three thieves at whom about ten shots were fired, all misses. In the morning nine camels were gone. Thereafter the guard was increased. The thermometer was dropping below zero (centigrade) at night, and, as the watchmen feared they might fall asleep, they kept singing and yelling at each other so boisterously that I was awakened frequently. Arabs do not sleep long at night; usually they lie down after the morning star appears and then remain in their beds till almost noon. The afternoon is spent in visiting.

Saturday morning the entire landscape was covered with frost. A strong west wind caused us a great deal of work, as all the tents had to be fastened anew, ropes doubled, and pegs driven deeper and braced. During the night from Saturday to Sunday no one in the camp slept much. The wind finally became so violent that the slaves of the Prince had to hold down his tent all night long, and the high litters of the women were all carried out in front of the tents for fear they would be damaged by the heavy roofs, plunging about under the lash of the gale. My round tent stood the test well, though several times during the night we had to tighten the ropes and incline the central pole toward the wind; but the oblong tent had to be struck and laid upon the baggage. My fellows had pitched it with the long sides toward north and south instead of toward west and east, as the other Arabs had set theirs, and so the west wind beat on the flank side and loosened the pegs. Finally, as the whole tent was lifted bodily and could not be secured again, the men crawled under it, nestled among the baggage, and waited for dawn.

Sunday, November 29, 1908. The piercing wind continued all day long and, as its fury increased, drove before it huge clouds of sand. Upon my belongings in the round tent it deposited a coat of white sand from four to five centimeters deep, although the tent was closed and stuffed both without and within. The sand was driven along with a peculiar tinkling sound, as if countless metallic leaflets were striking against one another, and it filled everything not hermetically sealed. As the sand-laden blasts increased in power the Arabs lifted the lower portion of the tent walls and thus afforded a free passage to the sand and wind but made it impossible to kindle the fires. No one would leave his tent; even the camels would not go to graze. They knelt, with heads turned toward the east, so that the west wind passed them, while the sand piled up behind them long drifts about four tenths of a meter high, half-covering them. They refused to rise when Ḥarrân and Blejhân urged them, and, when compelled, they knelt down again after a few minutes. It was not until nearly noon that they got up and, still with evident dislike, went to pasture with Ḥarrân constantly tempting them in front and Blejhân driving them from behind. It seemed as if the animals had lost all desire to graze, because of the dismal weather. Shortly before four o'clock in the afternoon the wind ceased and with it the whirling sand. Then a light rain began to fall.

I had worked all day with my informant, a difficult task at any time and especially in such weather; for in the onslaughts of the blasts at times I could not hear my own voice; besides, my fingers were stiff with cold all the while, and I continually had to blow the sand off my notebook and wipe it out of my eyes. The night proved no better, for I was suddenly awakened by a cold liquid spilling over my head and chest. It was raining into the tent!

Monday, November 30, 1908. Glorious was the view of the surrounding hills in the early morning! All the elevations rising above the horizon to the northwest and south almost down to the plain were covered with a snowy mantle, which glistened in the rays of the rising sun like myriads of flashing jewels. Even the valley of al-ʿAṣejfîr, where we had camped before, was covered with snow. The sun soon disappeared, however, and it began to sprinkle again. Toward noon hailstones (*ṛuzlân*) of considerable size began falling and covered the ground to a depth of three centimeters. Nawwâf asked me to go with him to visit his white slave Dammân, one of a large family whose members had from time immemorial been slaves of the Prince's lineage. Dammân and his kin were the only white slaves in the entire tribe, for it had not been feasible to buy a white slave during the last century, although black ones are still being brought by traders from Mecca and al-Medîna for sixty to one hundred *meǧîdijjât* ($54 to $90). Dammân had a gunshot wound in the calf of his right leg. The ball had penetrated through the flesh and emerged on the other side and in time the wound had apparently healed. After a year, however, the leg becoming swollen and extremely painful, they cauterized it with red-hot iron (*kej*), but this gave no relief. Finally they cut it open; whereupon a quantity of blood flowed out, the swelling vanished, and the leg healed again; but, about twenty days before, it had begun to swell again, and now Dammân was unable to stir. We found him in an open tent at a temperature of 6° C, covered with only a shirt and with both nostrils stuffed to protect himself from the harmful influence of the emanations and scents of his visitors. His brother served us with coffee, and his wife implored me to help him, promising to carry out my orders faithfully.

Tuesday, December 1, 1908. The first of December looked in the desert just as it sometimes does at home: a heavy frost covered everything — tents, ropes, perennial plants — and clouds of dense mist hung in the sky. The frost-covered sand had disappeared entirely, and dry stalks crunched under my feet when I stepped on them. The thermometer registered

–6.5° C, and a damp, raw wind penetrated our clothing and coverings. The tent walls were very thin, the ground was cold, and we were unable to build good fires because the camel dung and other fuel were so damp. As if this were not enough, a thick smoke was rising from the fire, hurting both our eyes and our lungs. The Arabs lay about, huddled like porcupines in their fur coats and mantles, knees drawn up to their chins, and they would not move even when called; they would merely respond out of their shells and remain lying, waiting for the air to get warm. The mist became so dense that Tûmân, who had wandered some thirty paces from the tent, could not find it again. When he failed to return after half an hour, I sent out my fellows to search for him and fetch him back.

Wednesday to Friday, December 2 to 4, 1908. Snow fell in the entire vicinity, covering the slopes for several days. The frost was so heavy that everything remained frozen until ten o'clock, and it was almost noon before it warmed up.

On Thursday, the vicinity having been entirely grazed off, we moved our camp. Starting out at ten o'clock to the southeast, we encamped soon after noon between the volcano of Dekwa and the aš-Šejbe group, at an altitude of 719 meters. As it was not very cold, we sat in the open with the Prince for about an hour before the tents were pitched. Toward evening, however, it grew rapidly cooler and the thermometer again fell below zero (centigrade). The air was clear, the moon was shining, and there was no sign of the approach of the longed-for rain.

I decided to undertake another excursion to the district between 33° 30′ and 34° 30′ north latitude, reaching to the Euphrates. No sooner had I mentioned my intention to my servant Mḥammad, than Blejhân approached me and addressed me thus: "May Allâh grant thee a happy evening, O Mûsa. Thou art my master, but permit me to speak out to thee as to a brother." After this introduction he begged me to take him along and to depart immediately, regardless of the advice of the Prince, who, he said, purposely delayed me for fear some harm might befall me. He warned me, however, that, should I not explore the district immediately, it would be impossible to do so after the period of steady rains set in and the Prince had departed for the south. I replied by declaring my readiness for the journey and my intention to discuss the matter with the Prince in the morning. Whether or not I should take Blejhân along I would decide later.

On Friday morning I called on the Prince, who was sitting by the fire with his sons Saᶜûd and al-Ḫafâǧi, the scribe Ǧwâd, and four slaves, while Nawwâf was still lying asleep at the southern side of the fireplace. All rose at my entrance and the Prince proffered me a place of honor at his left. When, after a few words of greeting, I told him that I was about to undertake a new expedition, he tried to induce me to delay but agreed reluctantly when he saw I was bent on leaving immediately. He inquired in what direction I intended to travel and what goal I aimed to reach; and, on hearing of my desire to visit the head chief Fahad and his son Metᶜeb eben Haḏḏâl of the ᶜAmârât tribe, he promised me a letter of introduction to these friends.

"Why, thou and they are enemies!" I exclaimed.

"Yes, O Mûsa. We, as the chiefs of our tribes, are enemies, but as men we are the best of friends. And, by thy life, I say to thee that I love Metᶜeb as I love my sons, for he is a gallant, noble, and sincere man, and, by Allâh, I am speaking the truth."

"Still thou wouldst attack him, perhaps even kill him?"

"At the head of my warriors I spare no one."

Then he ordered his scribe to write letters at once to Fahad and Metᶜeb. I should have liked to leave that very day, but the Prince opposed the plan, pointing out to me the necessity of having a guide, whom he himself wished to provide. He named the negro Ambâr, who was born in the ᶜAmârât tribe and reared among them, having for two years served the chief ᶜAḏûb eben Meǧwel, and was therefore fit to be my guide. The Prince wished to direct him to me, saying that he had no doubt he would accompany me. "Were he my slave I would order him," he declared, "but as he does not belong to me I must negotiate with him." The messenger he sent to Ambâr returned with the information that he had gone hunting but would appear before the Prince toward evening.

Meantime we began to get ready. Blejhân, with a camel and two bags, made a trip for water to the volcano of Umm Iḏen, where several rocky cavities had been filled by the recent rain; the rest of the men prepared the provisions to take on the journey. I reckoned that the trip would last fifteen or at the most twenty days, but when Nawwâf came he urged Mḥammad to carry provisions for twenty-five or thirty days. This we could not do, however, as we did not wish to overburden our beasts unnecessarily. Shortly before evening Ambâr came and informed Mḥammad of his willingness to accompany me on condition that he should have one *meǧîdijje* (90 cents) a day and the privilege of riding my camel; but, having settled with both Nawwâf and the Prince to pay half a *meǧîdijje* a day for the slave accompanying me, I did not as a matter of principle want to accept these conditions of Ambâr, for I knew I could never secure a cheaper guide. Moreover, I reflected that, since Ambâr had left the tribe with which he had grown up, the ʿAmârât might not like to see him again; and, furthermore, Blejhân kept begging me to let him go with me, saying he wanted to see his mother. Finally, after consulting with Nawwâf, I told Ambâr that he might accompany me for half a *meǧîdijje* a day but that he must ride the camel I should assign to him; whereupon he went away displeased.

It was settled that I should be accompanied by Tûmân, Mḥammad, and Blejhân, while Nâṣer and the herdsman were to be left to guard the tent, provisions, and camels. I had dismissed my former herdsman, Ḥarrân, because he was lazy, shunned work, and had not been taking good care of my camels, for, being married, he slept in his father's tent and sometimes left the herd without a guard. Moreover, he was not satisfied with his wages but demanded higher pay and new gifts every week. A better herdsman was found, a Šarâri of the name of Mufaẓẓi, an orphan, still single, who had nothing and was eager to earn something by serving us. When he came with his younger brother to arrange an agreement, I offered him food, the necessary garments, and four *meǧîdijjât* ($3.60) monthly on condition that he would perform his duties faithfully. Mufaẓẓi accepted the offer gladly; for the Bedouins pay their herdsmen only one *meǧîdijje* a month, and, if they starve, their herdsmen starve likewise.

Toward evening Nawwâf came to take me again to his white slave, Dammân, who was writhing in pain. On examining his right leg and finding a good deal of pus in the swelling, I lanced the sore and released over a half liter of the accumulation, to his great relief. I gave him the necessary medicines for the following days and returned with Nawwâf to my tent, where I sat with him late into the night, discussing my coming journey. He agreed to have an eye to my supplies and camels.

Saturday, December 5, 1908. In the morning the ground was frozen hard and covered with a thin layer of frost when we saddled our camels and loaded the baggage. The Prince came to me, gave me all sorts of advice, and told Nâṣer to sew up all the provision bags and not to open any during my absence, since he regarded himself as responsible for my property.

DEKWA TO THE DARB AS-SÂʿI

Having finally loaded my small circular tent, we four started out eastward at 8.30 A. M. (temperature: $-2°$ C). Each of us four rode a camel, and Blejhân also led a fifth camel, which carried the water saddle and the water bags. As the nearest water was 150 kilometers distant, we took with us enough for three or four days. Between the volcanoes of the aš-Šejba group we wound our way, avoiding the sharp black crests and peaks protruding from the ground, and encircling the elliptical basins (*mukmân*) which were surrounded by high lava walls and cliffs. North of the volcano of Rurejla a diversion occurred when a fox (*ab-al-ḥṣejn*) ran across the path. Blejhân greeted it with glee, called it, and, when told not to mind the fox but rather to look for hares since we needed fresh meat, he replied: "A single fox is better than ten hares, because it ensures the happy outcome of our journey. Allâh hath sent us at the start of our journey a fox; that is a sign that nothing ill will befall us, that we shall return in health." This confident prediction filled us with such joy that we urged our camels to a faster pace whenever it was possible.

North of the volcano of Ḳbejjân we came upon the grazing camels of the Freğe and Fleta, subjects of Prince an-Nûri. Blejhân had just been showing me the different shades of the animals and explaining their names, when several herdsmen rushed toward us and demanded that we stop instantly. We ignored them and kept on our way; but their leader Nâṣer, who mistook us for ʿAḳejl camel traders and wished to levy toll, lashed his camel, aimed the barrel of his rifle at my chest, and ordered us to stop. In vain we assured him that he was mistaken. His men cut the rein with which our water camel was tied to Blejhân's saddle, and took it away as booty; and meantime several more herdsmen rushed to the scene, threatening us with daggers in an effort to intimidate us into compelling our camels to kneel. Two of them recognized me, however, and called to their fellows that I was *aš-šejẖ* (the sheikh) Mûsa, whose tent stood by the tent of an-Nûri, and whom both an-Nûri and Nawwâf visited daily. Nâṣer maintained that it was a lie, that we were all ʿAḳejl, and insisted on Blejhân's oath that none of us belonged to that kin; but as my servant Mḥammad came from the ʿAḳejl tribe Blejhân could not swear, therefore the herdsmen considered us fair game. They pulled the contents out of our saddle bags, cut open the sack of provisions, and took away from me my spare camel stick. At last, however, the two prudent herdsmen succeeded in convincing their fellows of the injustice they were doing, and they returned all they had stolen. But Nâṣer, who had taken my stick given me by Nawwâf, declared with laughter that he would return it only to Nawwâf when he was asked to. I assured him that Nawwâf would want that stick and that all the reward he would get would be a good beating with it for humiliating and abusing his prince's neighbor and brother. This threat did not fail of result: Nâṣer called out to me that I might return and take the stick, but he finally came himself and offered it.

From 2.40 to 5.00 P. M. we rested in a basin, where we cooked our supper (at three o'clock the temperature was only 11.3° C); but we could not pass the night there, for the smoke from our fire would have betrayed us, lodged as we were between two enemies. North of us and north of Ab-al-ʿAjš were encamped the Freǧe and Fleta, whereas to the south were hiding the Ahâli al-Ǧebel, their bitterest enemies, who were continually making plundering raids on the Rwala and Sbaʿa tribes and who in general were notorious for their cruelty. Sneaking about, especially at night, they would attack lone travelers, murder them, and escape with the spoils. How easily they could attack and rob us! Therefore by Blejhân's advice we observed the utmost caution, keeping our carbines loaded and within reach all the time. After supper we proceeded in a northeasterly direction toward the volcanoes of Ammu-r-Rḳejbe and Ab-al-ʿAjš. It was a very exciting journey. Holding the loaded carbines on the forward part of our saddles, straining our eyes and ears not to miss the least suspicious sign, we were constantly apprehensive of the presence of enemies and their bullets whenever we made a turn by any cliff or lava ledge. Added to this, the night was bitterly cold, with an icy west wind penetrating to the marrow; so that finally, unable to stay in the saddle any longer, we took refuge by the volcano of as-Sîb behind a few basalt boulders under a dark cliff, where we fastened our camels and lay down on the frozen ground.

Sunday, December 6, 1908. Shivering with cold, we mounted our beasts at 5.28 A. M. and rode to the east-southeast until 6.08, when we found in a small hollow fresh *rûṯe*[3a] and dry grass (annuals, *ḥemri*) on which the camels grazed till seven, while we prepared hot coffee.

At 8.16 we passed the last volcano of the as-Sîb group. West of that point black cliffs stretch to the southeast and the landscape presents a new view. The lava forms low, narrow ridges, between which extend flat vales in which rain water collects in large and small pools. This entire territory east of Tlûl al-ʿIjâṯ is called al-Bowzelijjât. Carved on the larger lava boulders we noted tribal signs and images of various animals. Expecting to discover some writing also, I was scrutinizing the individual rocks when suddenly I heard a shrill war whoop and saw six, ten, twelve riders charging us from their hiding place behind a pile of lava in the vale! There could be no thought of defense. They seized the reins of our camels, forced them to kneel, and jerked us off the saddles. I was stunned by a blow from the butt of a carbine and, before regaining consciousness, was divested of all my clothing. The same thing happened to my companions. Blejhân, who offered resistance, was held by the two men who regarded him and his camel as their booty. With drawn daggers they urged him to tell where our gold was and, getting no answer, beat him in the face with the handles of their daggers until he bled. One of the three marauders who had captured me put the point of his knife on my chest and, pressing it deeper, urged me to tell him where my gold was; when I refused to

3a Latin equivalents and brief characterizations of many Arabic botanical terms appearing in the text are given in the index.

respond and struggled to get free, the second one beat me with his fist in the face until blood sputtered out of my mouth and nose. They robbed us of everything we had and then divided the spoils. They put on our clothes, loaded our bags and baggage upon our camels, and drove them off to the east, ignoring us entirely. Shivering with cold, we hurriedly followed them.

This was perhaps the most wretched hour of my life! I had been wounded and robbed, and this at the very start of my explorations, before I had penetrated the unknown desert that for so many years had lured me. Barefoot, naked, without food or water and without carriers, we could hardly have reached the very nearest camp of the Rwala. I could not and wished not to think of the future. Presently Blejhân whispered to me that these robbers belonged to the Fedʿân tribe, for he recognized two of them. Knowing that the Fedʿân venture on horseback into these remote places only together with large companies of camel riders, and therefore surmising that these horsemen were merely the vanguard of the main body, I wanted to follow them until they met their leader, that I might ask him to return what his men had stolen from me; and I had actually started after them when Mḥammad ran up to tell me that the robber who took away his things belonged to the ʿEbede tribe, for he had seen him at the chief Barǧas's tent when we were visiting there

At this news the first star of hope flickered before me. The ʿEbedi knew of my having formed a friendship with his chief Barǧas and therefore it was his duty to protect me; otherwise he would blacken the face of his chief and consequently be expelled from the tribe. So I called to him:

"O ʿEbedi, mind thou that I am before thy face, under thy protection and thou shalt answer before thy chief Barǧas eben Hdejb for all that hath befallen me and yet shall befall me."

The ʿEbedi stopped, extended his hand to me, and proclaimed to the rest that we were the protégés of his chief and that it would be necessary to return to us all they had appropriated. Then Blejhân joined in, reminding the ʿEbedi that the ʿEbede and Ḳmuṣa were kinsmen, that he belonged to the Meṣreb clan of the Ḳmuṣa and was accompanying us with the knowledge and consent of his head chief Ṛaṯwân eben Meršed, to whose protection we were thus entitled; therefore, in the name of his head chief, he requested them to restore our property. At this the ʿEbedi promptly returned to Mḥammad all he had taken away from him; but the eleven fighters of the Fedʿân sneered and declared that nobody should snatch from them a booty sent by Allâh.

About a quarter of an hour later the Fedʿân suddenly gave a shrill whoop, which brought some twenty-five horsemen galloping toward us. At my request to speak to the commander (*ʿaḳîd*) of this cavalcade, the latter came up to see what I wanted; whereupon I explained under whose protection I was traveling and informed him that he would be held responsible for everything that had befallen us, should he not immediately help us to regain our property. He proved to be Hawwâš eben Ṛâfel of the Ṛubejn clan of the Fedʿân tribe, a prudent man who had already heard of me and knew of my visit to the chiefs Barǧas eben Hdejb and Ṛaṯwân eben Meršed and of my meeting with Metʿeb eben Haḏḏâl; and he appreciated the fact that my friends could do him much harm in the desert. Therefore he summoned the leader of the allied ʿEbede and consulted with him as to what he should do. The latter expressed the belief that he must protect me and my companions, as he could afford to blacken neither the face of his head chief Barǧas nor that of his kinsman Blejhân.

Leaving the leaders to their deliberations, I returned to my fellows, who were crouching by our camels. The father of the robber who had stolen my carbine and my revolver was just demanding that I show him how to handle them, when I heard one of the fighters near me mention the name of Eben Haḏḏâl. Turning toward the man thus addressed, I asked his name.

"Fanar eben Haḏḏâl," he answered.

"O Fanar eben Haḏḏâl," said I gravely, "look thou well at this white revolver. It is destined for Metʿeb, the son of thy head chief. Tell thou him I send word that he shall obtain it from this robber."

No sooner had the father of the robber holding the revolver heard this than he took the weapon and handed it quickly over to Fanar, declaring he did not want the friendship between himself and Metʿeb eben Haḏḏâl to be undermined.

The commanders were still consulting and I was getting anxious about the result. After a while the father of the man who had robbed me and who had walked over to the conference approached me and in silence handed me my carbine.

"Al-ḥamdu lillâh!" I exclaimed loudly. Already I had the carbine, and now the robbers began to strip themselves of my garments and hand them to me, while I in turn lost no time in putting them on as fast as they took them off. Then the chief in command came to me and asked me what else had been taken from me, saying it was his wish to restore everything. Having thus repossessed myself of all my own property, I went over to help poor Tûmân, who had recovered scarcely one-third of his things, because the robbers had given him back only those he asked for. As he did not know Arabic, it was a difficult task for him and Blejhân, and Mḥammad fared no better; with the aid of Hawwâš eben Ṛâfel, however, we eventually got back everything except a few small articles. The chiefs apologized and then rode off westward at the head of their cavalcade, intending to make a raid upon the herds of the Freǧe. I did not see the camel riders; according to Hawwâš they were northeast of us in the flanking valley of Sabᶜ Bijâr. Should the horsemen succeed in obtaining a large booty of camels, they would drive them thither.

At 11.38 we resumed our journey toward the north-northeast. We did not have a drop of water; the thieving riders and their horses had emptied every bag we had, large and small. The nearest certain source of water was the springs of Sabᶜ Bijâr, or Swaᵓ; but we did not want to go there, because the reserves of the Fedᶜân could again attack and rob us. Nothing remained for us, then, but the springs of al-ᶜElejjânijje, almost seventy-five kilometers distant, which were likewise unsafe, since they lay near a route much favored by raiding parties. Nevertheless, we were certain of meeting the enemy at Sbaᶜ Bijâr, whereas at al-ᶜElejjânijje there was a chance of avoiding them, and so we decided to go to the latter place. Thanking Allâh for having liberated us from the hands of the Fedᶜân, we rode through the undulating plain of al-ᶜÎṯa and stopped from 2.05 to 3.20 P. M. to give our camels an opportunity to pasture.

Having not a drop of water, we could not prepare dinner. We all feared thirst. Like my native companions, I knew that a traveler feels most thirsty just at the time when he has no water, whereas he rarely thinks of water when the bags are full. We all implored Allâh to give us a shower even before we reached al-ʿElejjânijje, for, should it rain, Blejhân assured us, we were pretty certain to find water in cavities in the flat rocks. Presently it seemed as if Allâh had heard our prayers, for the sky began to cloud, and here and there we could see long columns of rain. But only a few drops fell where we were.

THE DARB AS-SÂʿI TO THE ŠEʿÎB OF AL-ʿELEJJÂNIJJE

At 5.18 P.M. we crossed the road Darb as-Sâʿi, leading from Damascus to the city of Hît on the Euphrates. We continued on our way until 10.08 and then rested in a rather small basin that was closed on all sides. Barely had we spread out our covers when it began to drizzle, and we pitched the circular tent, under which we could shelter the baggage as well as ourselves. The drizzle kept on all night, but no puddles of water formed anywhere, for the parched earth absorbed all that fell. We suffered so much from thirst during the night that we were glad to suck the water out of the wet canvas of the tent.

Monday, December 7, 1908. Before dawn the drizzling ceased, but a moist, chilly mist filled the air, penetrating even the things we had sheltered from the rain. As we did not want to fold and load the tent while it was wet, we kindled a fire inside to try to dry the roof, and this kept us from starting until 7.55 A.M. We went on over the same rolling plain of Telʿet as-Sâʿi, but a heavy fog made it impossible to see far around us until 8.58, when the fog began to disperse and at intervals the sun appeared. By this time we had reached a rocky terrain in which we discovered several small cavities filled with rain water. Dismounting from our camels, we lay flat on the ground and gratefully lapped up the welcome fluid. Blejhân, who had been surveying the vicinity, also found rain water on a sloping rock in an artificial hollow about two meters in circumference. There were almost three liters of it, enough for our tea. At 9.20 we went on again.

Suddenly, far in the northeast, we sighted a dark spot that was in striking contrast to its dull gray environment. Blejhân, to whom I pointed it out, uttered merely a single word: "*zôl* (a living being)." Soon there were two dark spots and behind these appeared others and still others. It was evident that in front of us was another troop of riders and that they must have seen us just as we had seen them, since we were moving on an elevated plain and especially since we were riding from west to east, whereas they were moving in the opposite direction and had us before them in the full light. A new anxiety now beset us. Were they friends or enemies? If enemies, did they belong to the ʿAneze, or were they subjects of the Ahâli al-Ǧebel returning from a raid? Or were they al-Ḥadedijjîn, known for their cruelty? There were only four of us and at least forty of the strangers; besides, having had no water, we could not hope to offer an effective resistance. Mḥammad urged us to hide, suggesting that the men might not have perceived us; but Blejhân rejected the idea and admonished him to silence. Presently the group of strangers disappeared; then they scaled another height, and we could distinguish that they were riding camels; then they disappeared again. Did they want to surround us or to ambush us? We were greatly agitated. Finally, as we crossed a wide hollow we found the troop waiting for us in a glen. The moment we approached there was a shrill war whoop and their camels galloped towards us.

"Who are they?" I asked of Blejhân. He was silent until they were about twenty meters distant and then answered: "Ẓana Muslim," which meant the kinsfolk of the Rwala and therefore our friends. I immediately called out as loud as I could:

"O Commander, I tender myself under thy protection, I ride in front of thy countenance. I am Mûsa, whose tent adjoins the tent of an-Nûri."

Meantime, however, ten — yes, twenty — hands had seized my camel, forced her to kneel, pulled me off the saddle, and thrust their fingers into my bag. I resisted them with shouts and blows. At last the commander ran up to them and beat them with his camel stick, bawling out:

"Do not steal, ye thieves! do not steal, ye villains! (*lâ jâ ḏâhebîn! lâ lâ jâ šênîn lâ taḏhabû!*)"

From me he ran to my fellows, then rushed back to me to tear the disobedient away from me by force, and at last he succeeded; but none too soon. Those contents of my saddle bag which had not been stolen were scattered all about; even my handy medicine box had been opened, a few vials broken and the others, with the tubes and pills, stolen. The thieves had already run to their camels to hide the loot.

When I called the commander's attention to this, he shouted after them:

"Where is the honest man who would take anything belonging to these men? If he does not return what he hath, let his camels suffer therefor, and his children in the morning and in the evening; so be it that never again shall he see the people of his kin and that he shall find no joy in the world! (*Wên walad al-ḥelâl illi ᶜendah ᶜelḳ liha-r-rabᶜ wa mâ jidi ᶜasâha tasraḥ wa tarawweḥ ᶜala ḥalâlah wa ᶜejâlah wa ᶜasâh mâ jašûf ahlah wa lâ jašûf ẖejr dubb mâ hu ḥajj!*)"

This imprecation he repeated several times, while one after another of his men brought back to us what they had stolen. The commander, Ṣâjer eben Burmân of the Freǧe, begged to be forgiven for the occurrence. He said he had started out thirty-two days before to make a raid against the Sḳûr of the ᶜAmârât, who, as he had been told, were camping by the al-Barrît well six hundred kilometers southeast of the settlement of Ḍmejr. Meanwhile, however, the Sḳûr had left, and while he was scouting for them he himself was observed and pursued and had to return without booty. His men mistook us for camel robbers (*maᶜâjîr*); they thought we had stolen our camels from the Rwala and were now returning with the booty. That, they said, was the reason why they attacked us. When I informed the commander of the danger that threatened his people from the Fedᶜân, who would certainly raid their herds if they had not already done so, he was anxious to depart without delay. Accordingly, he urged his men to lose no time in returning the stolen articles, calling out to them:

"Come hither to me! Every one of ye shall swear that he hath not kept anything."

This helped so much that before long I had received everything that belonged to me. Nevertheless, each man had to take an oath before the commander, who handed him a handful of dry grass (*ḥemri*) which he took in his right hand and said:

"By the life of these stems and by the life of the Lord whom we revere, I hereby declare that I have not taken more than I have returned."

Each man took the oath in this manner, and one of them added:

"I have not taken more than I returned except a few raisins which are now in my belly and which I cannot return; but I am ready to make amends."

When all had taken the oath, the commander thus addressed me:

"Observe, O Sheikh Mûsa, that Ṣâjer eben Burmân's face is white. If still thou art missing anything, lookest thou for it with the other *ʿaḳîd* (commander or leader), ʿArhân eben Bawwâš, who holdeth sway over his five kinsmen." As ʿArhân had disappeared, I called out:

"O ʿArhân, all that I am still missing lies before thee, and shouldst thou not return it, I shall blacken thy countenance before an-Nûri and all the Rwala."

ʿArhân, an old man whose left eye had been knocked out and whose front teeth protruded, came in response to this threat and inquired which of his people had stolen anything from me.

"Who has stolen, I know not," I replied, "but I am still missing many things. Ṣâjer's men have them not, therefore they must be hidden by thee and thy men. Why, thou art hiding my camel stick! Maybe thou hast concealed other things of mine too." At that I seized my *miḥǧan*, which he was holding under the left arm beneath his mantle, and challenged him thus:

"Do thou swear, and let every one of thy men swear as Ṣâjer has done." When he objected, I ordered Mḥammad to search all the bags and saddles and the clothing as well of ʿArhân and his associates. This plan helped. ʿArhân wanted to go away, but I detained him until we recovered everything he had appropriated.

At 11.48 we started northeast to the broad ridge of aṣ-Ṣerijjât.[4]

The ridge, blazing in the rays of the afternoon sun, could be seen from the plain that extends south and west, as well as from all the passes across the ar-Rwâḳ mountain chain to the northeast and north. For this reason we made a detour to the left of the route, seeking protection in valleys as often as possible. The aṣ-Ṣerijjât district is so rocky that many a slope affords but bare ledge. Great was our joy when at

[4] Ḥaǧǧi Ḫalfa (died 1658 A. D.), *Ǧihân numa'* (Constantinople, 1145 A. H.), p. 531, mentions a rocky district of Ṣerijjât, overgrown with terebinths, in the vicinity of the settlement of al-Ḳarjatejn. — The terebinths grow also in our rock channels of aṣ-Ṣerijjât, to the northwest of which lies the settlement of al-Žerjitejn; thus we may identify aṣ-Ṣerijjât with the Ṣerijjât of Ḥaǧǧi Ḫalfa.

1.04 P.M. (temperature: 10.8° C) we found in one of the rocks four cracks filled with water and in such quantity that we did not need to draw from the dangerous wells of al-ʿElejjânijje, from which all raiding parties water their animals.

While my companions filled the bags and watered the camels, I cautiously climbed a rocky ridge to a large pile of stones from which I could overlook the entire vicinity. Through binoculars I examined carefully every spur, every individual boulder, and when I was not certain as to the identity of this or that object I scrutinized it again and again, for it is such spying that insures the safety of the traveler. Having discovered nothing suspicious, I returned to my companions and despatched Tûmân to the stone pile to draw a map of the environs, while the rest of us gathered a little fuel for Mḥammad and led the camels to a small basin full of dry grass and perennials. This done, we followed with Blejhân to the pile of stones, first taking care to discard our dark garments, for dark objects show up more clearly in the desert than does the white color of shirts and kerchiefs. We climbed cautiously upon the flat ridge and then, bending down with our hands extended forward, we ran to Tûmân. There we sat down and examined the country.

We were in the territory of aṣ-Ṣerijjât, which borders on the northwest upon al-Bowlijjât. In that direction Blejhân pointed out to me the wide mountain of Keḥle, the high ar-Rmâḥ, the cone of Ḳalʿat Ṭejr, and east of the latter the grayish table mountain of ʿÂde, which slopes to the south. South of these mountains, and east of us, extended the flattened hills of Ṣwêwînt aš-Šhabaʾ and al-ʿElejjânijje. In the south these become an endless plain whence, a little to the southwest, protrude the low, rugged hillocks of al-Bowzelijjât, and west of these the volcanoes of Tlûl al-ʿIjâṯ. Off to the west stretched the undulating plain of al-Bowlijjât, and also the low ridge Ṭaraḳ abu Dâlje, that runs from southwest to northeast. To the west from our viewpoint the run-off flows to the rain pools, Ḫabâri Sejḳal; to the north and east into the Tudmor marshes; while on the south during torrential rains the water reaches the basin of al-Ǧwejf.

After we had finished our observations we waited until the sun sank low in the west so that we could pass along the ridge of aṣ-Ṣerijjât with greater safety. We started at 4.38, advancing carefully over rough basalt stones and longing for the moon, which is so desirable in the desert. A bright moonlit night is far more welcome to the Bedouins than a sunny day, for in the daytime the Bedouin may be seen from anywhere, whereas in the moonlight he himself can see well ahead and yet the enemy cannot see him.

After struggling long with the clouds which covered the western sky, the moon finally swung herself above them and sailed majestically among the pale stars. Silhouetted against the western horizon, our shadows moved like huge phantoms. Neither we nor our camels uttered the slightest sound. Now and then the sands whispered or a rolling pebble sounded hollowly, but otherwise all was still. Toward seven o'clock a strong icy wind arose from the southwest and we shivered as it penetrated our clothing.

The route became increasingly difficult. We crossed several short gullies and descended a steep bluff before we finally reached the *šeʿîb* of al-ʿElejjânijje, which spreads into a basin dividing the hills of Ṣwêwînt aš-Šhabaʾ from the precipitous wall of al-ʿElejjânijje on the south. Although we preferred to proceed, the cold (temperature: —10° C) compelled us to stop. Again the ground was covered by a frozen crust. At 8.40 we encamped by two boulders, but as they were free from débris only on the northern side they afforded us no protection from the wind and we had to weight down our covers to prevent their being blown away. The facts that the wells of al-ʿElejjânijje were near and the way thereto — often frequented by robbers — close by, made us alert. I slept scarcely half an hour during that night and shivered with cold as perhaps I never had before. After midnight we heard a noise on the route about three hundred paces distant. Blejhân and I listened, wondering what it could be. In a moment it was repeated. I roused Mḥammad and told him to guard the camp and, with carbines ready, Blejhân and I crept in the direction of the noise. Suddenly I discerned about twenty meters in front of me two squat shadows: two wolves running away to the southeast. *Al-ḥamdu lillâh!* they were not human beasts of prey. Satisfied, we returned to the camp, for now we were sure of the absence of men in the vicinity, otherwise the wolves would not have ventured so near us. Toward morning the entire desert became enveloped in a heavy fog which made the cold even harder to bear.

Tuesday, December 8, 1908. We left our location at 6.30

A. M. and toiled through the basin of al-ʿElejjânijje to the east-northeast. At 7.05 we passed to the left of the solitary hill Tell al-Ḳaṭṭâʿât and crossed the valley of ʿAzzâle,[5] which divides the mountains of ʿÂde and Ṣwêwînt aš-Šhabaʾ.

The fog was as thick as a drizzling rain, and the wind remained so strong that we had to look for a place, closed from the west, where we could kindle a fire. After a while we discovered, a little to the southeast of the route, a limestone rock containing several hollows, in one of which we found something dark — a wild swine. Seizing my carbine, I jumped off my camel and cautiously approached the cave; but the beast remained still and there were traces of blood. It had evidently been shot by a hunter — probably a Ṣlubi (or member of the Ṣlejb tribe) — and had died here. The meat would have been very useful to us; but Blejhân insisted that he had never touched the flesh of any animal from which the blood had not been drained and hence he would not touch the flesh of this swine, no matter how good it might taste. Because we did not want to offend him, we rode on without the carcass, the camels prancing in fear of it.

THE ŠEʿÎB OF AL-ʿELEJJÂNIJJE TO THE ŠEʿÎB OF AL-ʿAWÊREẒ

From 8.05 to ten o'clock we rested north of the solitary Tell ʿOrfân under a rocky projection that afforded us a protection from the cold wind (temperature: 5.2° C). The camels grazed while we prepared our breakfast and dinner, and the drizzle continued. Here the basin broadens between the flattened hills of Ṣwêwînt aš-Šhabaʾ and al-Ḥamraʾ on the north and the precipitous wall of ʿAjerât al-ʿElejjânijje on the south. The latter slope exposes two horizontal strata of uneven thickness and solidity. The top stratum, from three to four meters thick and of dark brown hue, rests upon a layer of white limestone from fifteen to thirty meters in thickness. The lower layer seems to be supported by countless grayish-white ribs standing on the plain. By the river bed in the

[5] About the year 640 B. C. in the course of his ninth conquest Asurbanipal (Rassam Cylinder [Rawlinson, *Cuneiform Inscriptions*, Vol. 5, pl. 9], col. 8, l. 118; Streck, *Die Inschriften Assurbanipals*, Vol. 2, p. 73) defeated the nomads between Jarki and Azalla and refreshed his troops at the wells of Azalla in the desert. — I place Jarki in the settlement of Arak, and the wells of Azalla in al-ʿElejjânijje.

Jâḳût, *Muʿǵam* (Wüstenfeld), Vol. 1, p. 315, refers to the water and the valley of al-Aʿzal in the territory of the Beni Kalb. — The valley of ʿAzzâle, where the important watering place of al-ʿElejjânijje is situated, belonged formerly to the tribe of Kalb.

basin are the wells of al-ʿElejjânijje. Three of them are recent, having been excavated not long ago by the Fwâʿre; the extreme eastern one is old and brick-lined, and about ten others are more or less caved in. By noon we had the wells on our right and had arrived at the western edge of the grayish rolling plain called al-Manâẓer.[6] This is closed on the south by a precipitous escarpment that extends from west to east as far as the Euphrates. Southeast of the wells this scarp is known as al-Halba and farther east as Tlejlât al-ʿEleb, al-Ǧiffa, Čabd, al-ʿEḳfân, and Kbûd.

On the plain of al-Manâẓer I saw for the first time the *kalša* plant, which when fresh is eaten by camels with relish. Since it lay here in dry heaps, torn out by wind and scattered around the bushes of *ʿaḏob* and *nejtûl*, our camels went by without noticing it.

Toward two o'clock Blejhân spied a dark moving object before us on the plain. We watched it closely and, seeing that it was a woman gathering fuel, hurried toward her. Several sheep were grazing near by, and an ass brayed a raucous greeting. Evidently the Ṣlejb, the most wretched of men, were camping somewhere near and were concealing their tents from the rapacious Bedouins. I directed Blejhân to make inquiries as to the camping places of the individual clans of the Sbaʿa and ʿAmârât; but he would not approach the woman, for, to an Arab's mind, contact with the Ṣlejb at the beginning of an important journey always brings misfortune.

"*Melḥathom mâ hi zêne* (their salted meal is not favorable)," he said. On a return journey, however, the Ṣlejb do not bring misfortune to the Bedouins; they are ready to stop with them then and do not hesitate to eat their food.

Since Blejhân would not go to ask for the information (*ʿelem*) wanted, I sent Mḥammad to question the woman, while the rest of us went on slowly to wait at a low hill not far off. From there we sighted three small tents concealed in a little *šeʿîb* and saw two men and several children run to meet Mḥammad, who told us on his return that a clan of

[6] Jâḳût, *op. cit.*, Vol. 4, p. 650, and Abu-l-Faḍâ'il, *Marâṣid* (Juynboll), Vol. 3, p. 152, refer to al-Manâẓer in the Syrian desert near the settlement of ʿUrḍ and beside the Euphrates beyond the city of Hît. These are watchtowers built on high places, whence the sentries scoured the distant neighborhood and defended it from enemies. —

The settlement of ʿUrḍ, aṭ-Ṭajjibe of today, lies on the northern frontier of our territory of al-Manâẓer, which also reaches to the Euphrates and forms a natural division between Palmyrena and Arabia Eremos or Arabia Deserta, as-Samâwa of the Arabs. It likewise forms the northern border of Arabia proper.

the Sbaʿa were camping under the hill of al-Halba, that the others were in at-Telîle and in the valley of al-Mijâh, and that the Fedʿân had not yet returned from their raid. Eight days before, according to his information, a large group of the ʿAmârât and ʿEbede had come to the wells of al-ʿElejjânijje and had attacked the Arabs of Eben Hnejjân of the Rwala who were camping in the depression of Sirḥân. This news made us apprehensive lest we might encounter one of these bands.

From 2.35 to 4.40 (temperature at 3.40: 9° C) our camels grazed at the foot of a broad swell, visible from afar, which we intended to cross after the sun was lower. Meanwhile we climbed carefully with Blejhân to a pile of stones near by and concealed ourselves behind it, scanning the distant plains, especially to the southeast, where we vainly hoped to see the grazing camels by the wells of al-Halba. But either no Bedouins were camping there, or else the herds were at pasture farther south on Tlejlât al-ʿEleb. Crossing the swell very cautiously, we hurried to the east. My camel was so saddle-sore that she complained (*rarat*) during the day, but in the evening she uttered not a sound and paced swiftly ahead. We spoke only when it was necessary and then only in whispers. The Bedouins say:

"When thou art on a journey through the inner desert, be thou on the lookout at all times of the day, but in the night keepest thou silence (*bilejl skât wa bnahâr iltifât*)!" At 8.32 we lay down. We were then south of the solitary hill of al-Frej.[7]

Wednesday, December 9, 1908. Starting at 6.20 A. M. we journeyed through a fertile plain covered with a black soil three meters deep, which might be made still more fertile if it could be irrigated regularly. But in this inner part of the desert

[7] The pursuers, from whom the Caliph al-Walîd ibn Jazîd ibn ʿAbdalmalek was fleeing, encamped by the water al-Lu'lu'a and later by the water al-Malîka, whence they despatched a troop to the east of the high, conspicuous hill of al-Frej by the route of Nihja leading to al-Baḫra'. This troop was to surround the camp of al-Walîd in al-Baḫra' (aṭ-Ṭabari [died 923], *Ta'rîḫ* [De Goeje], Ser. 2, p. 1803).—

In the text is printed al-Ḳrej. This is an error, however, for in the vicinity of al-Baḫra' there is no hill of the name of al-Ḳrej. But to the south towers the Tell al-Frej, which is visible from a distance of forty kilometers. The Berlin and Oxford manuscripts (*ibid.*, note q) give Tihja instead of Nihja, an error caused by the misplacement of the word that follows, *tahajja'a*. The correct word is Halba, instead of either Nihja or Tihja. From Ḳulbân al-Halba an old transport route leads to al-Baḫra'. Al-Malîka is identical with the ruins al-Mlêke, northwest of al-Frej.

Jâḳût, *op. cit.*, Vol. 4, p. 378, says that Lu'lu'a and Saʿâde are waters in the desert of as-Samâwa, by which Sejfaddowle camped while in pursuit of the Beni Numejr and ʿÂmer.—

Saʿâde is a water near the volcano of Tell Saʿâda on the southeastern border of the Ḥawrân, whereas Lu'lu'a is a well at al-ʿElejjânijje, so called by the Ṣlejb.

regular rains are rare. The entire plain is full of holes (*ẖabân*) in which are innumerable jumping rodents called *ǧirdi*. *Roṛol*, *ẖuḏrâf*, *šnân*, and *ḳaẓḳâẓ* thrive here. Last year's plants (*eben al-ʿâm*) were ash-gray and parched; the wind was breaking them off, driving them ahead, and piling them up against the stronger ones. Those of the current year (*eben has-sene*) were of a pale yellow color, and these the camels ate greedily. Here and there were seen the bright yellow shrubs of *ʿaḏob* and the blackish *nejtûl*. In lower places, where rain water gathers in larger quantities, throve annuals that were yellow like straw and therefore were called *ḥemri*. Toward the south stood four cones on the long ridge of Ṭaraḳ al-Halba. Southwest from them begins the shallow valley of Sowḥ Murra, which connects in the southwest with the western vale of al-Hejl that ends in the basin of al-Ǧwejf. Another *šeʿîb* of al-Hejl runs off to the northeast from the four cones, and in this are the five wells of al-Halba.

From 8.16 to 9.40 (temperature at 8.40: 5° C) we rested north of the wells of Umm ʿAjẓer; at 10.00 we crossed the shallow river bed of al-Hejl. In the north we sighted seven camels going south. Wishing to inquire concerning a camping ground, we looked about anxiously but in vain for the drivers of these camels and finally conjectured that the beasts had been stolen and left by robbers who had hidden in fear of us. When we came to the camels, Blejhân found by their brands that they did not belong to the tribe of the Sbaʿa; as he did not know, however, whose brands they were, we concluded that raiders or robbers had captured them somewhere in the far south or southwest. After we had ridden about three kilometers farther without seeing anyone, Blejhân wished to go back and drive the camels ahead. When I warned him that I would not consent to his appropriation of the stolen animals, he replied that he did not intend to keep them, but would drive them to any clan to which he found out they belonged and return them to their owner immediately upon request. He said I ought to be glad to have him get the seven gold Turkish pounds ($31.50), as every finder receives one pound as a reward for returning a lost animal. He had already jumped off his camel and was running after the animals, but I called him back, warning him that since we did not know to whom they belonged we might be attacked by their robber owners at night. I feared also that we should be delayed by driving these shy animals and, furthermore, that, if any raiding party should meet us, it would surely surmise from these seven spare animals that we were robbers (*maᶜâjîr*) and would be the more disposed to plunder us. Blejhân came back very unwillingly and grumbled for a long time because he was not permitted to earn seven gold Turkish pounds.

At twelve o'clock we were riding among the ledges of the low ridge of al-Brêḳa, which reaches to the *šeᶜîb* of al-Hejl. Soon after one o'clock hailstones began to fall and we feared a drenching; but the main black cloud rolling above us from the east deviated to the north, where it split on the Abu Riǧmên mountain range that closes Tudmor on that side. After crossing innumerable broad channels that originate in the hilly district of Tlejlât al-ᶜEleb, we stopped from 1.32 to 3.50 P. M. in a hollow where our camels had abundant pasturage. In the north glittered five precipitous walls of the white range of aẓ-Ẓâḥeč. At 4.15 we found ourselves close by the well of Bajjûẓ, near which rises a low cone of the name of ᶜAṭfa Bajjûẓ and to the northeast of which, about four kilometers south of the channel of al-Hejl, is Želîb al-Mḥazzam. The valley of al-Hejl stretches along the southern foot of the rolling plain of at-Telîle and aẓ-Ẓabᶜ, having in its center the wells Ḳulbân al-Hejl.[8] The country was covered with small parched plants (*fwâne*). At seven o'clock we rode through the *šeᶜîb* of al-Ǧiffa, which connects with al-Hejl, and at 8.12 encamped in the first *šeᶜîb* of the group of as-Slejḥîbât, in which is located about six kilometers southwest

[8] During the war between the Beni Numejr of the tribe of Ḳejs and the tribe of Kalb, Zafar ibn al-Ḥarṯ, the Beni Numejr's head chief, attacked a camp at al-Maṣbaḥ in which were many pilgrims; the first assault was in the early morning at Ḥaṣîf, the next at al-Maṣbaḥ. Two men of the tribe of Taṛleb were killed, and after the battle the chief wanted the women to throw the fallen into a well named Kawkab. As soon as Ibn Baḥdal, head chief of the tribe of Kalb, heard of the attack, he hastened to the aid of his tribe and on arriving at Tadmur slew all the followers of the Beni Numejr. In retaliation Zafar attacked the camp of the Beni Kalb at Wâdi al-Ǧujûš and then departed to Ḳarḳîsija'.

According to the Beni Numejr Zafar attacked the camps of the Kalb tribe at Ḥafîr, al-Maṣbaḥ, al-Firs, and al-Iklîl; ᶜAmr ibn Ḥabbâb subdued the members of the same tribe at Ṛwejr aḍ-Ḍabᶜ, al-Hejl, and Ka'âba; and ᶜUmejr ibn al-Ḥabbâb won victories over it at al-Iklîl, Ǧowf, as-Samâwa, and Dehmân (Abu-l-Faraǧ, *Aṛâni* [Bûlâḳ, 1285 A.H.], Vol. 20, pp. 120ff.). —

I look for al-Hejl, where the Kalb tribe was attacked, at Ḳulbân al-Hejl in our valley.

The *Naḳâ'id* of Ǧarîr and al-Aḫṭal (Salhani), p. 360, says:

"The settled members of the tribe of Kalb set out against the camp of their enemies at al-Hejl and slew its inhabitants. They were led by Ḥumejd ibn Ḥurejṯ ibn Baḥdal."

Al-Bekri, *Muᶜǧam* (Wüstenfeld), p. 570, and Naṣr (Jâḳût, *Muᶜǧam* [Wüstenfeld], Vol. 4, p. 742) call an-Nabi a watering place in the territory of the tribe of Taṛleb in al-Ǧezîre; they name it also an-Nubej and look for it to the south between Wâdi Ẓabj and Wâdi al-Hejl, through which it is possible to come from the Euphrates to the districts of al-Urdunn and Ḥomṣ. — The valley of al-Hejl begins south of Tudmor, extends to the northeast, and ends in the lowland Fejẓat Fâẓel south of al-Bišri. The old route through

from Ḳulbân al-Hejl the well Želîb al-Hğejl, famous for its water.

Thursday, December 10, 1908. The night was very damp and so bitterly cold that all our covers and even the water bags froze hard. In the morning I could not touch my blanket or my kerchief because they were so stiff that I should have broken them, and before we could load our water bags we had to build a fire in order to thaw them. Even after sunrise the thermometer still registered only –1° C, and the damp air and raw west wind made it seem still colder. While we were warming our hands and feet by the fire our backs were freezing (temperature at 6.30 A. M.: 0° C).

We did not leave until seven o'clock, when we started on through the shallow valleys of as-Slejḥîbât, all of which originate in the rather low upland Ḥazm Čabd that loomed in the sunlight far to the south, with two solitary hills, Tlêlên ʿAṣejfîrât, standing in the foreground. The western *šeʿîb* of as-Slejḥîbât, where we passed the night, begins at Tell al-Ṛurâb and fills the rain pool Ḫabra Ḥamda. The territory of as-Slejḥîbât, an undulating plain (*feḳâra*) which slopes to the east, is covered with coarse gravel and abounds in moss. The moderate slopes of the valleys were at this season clothed in the parched grass (*ḥemri*), whereas in the glens grew *nejtûl, šîḥ*, with *ḳaẓḳâẓ* on the crests. Whenever the latter grows in bunches, the two-year-old plants glitter as though silvered and afford a pleasant rest to the eye, tired of the monotonous, yellowish-gray color of the *ḥemri*-bedecked surfaces. As we wound along through this country Blejhân cautioned the utmost carefulness, and, when I retorted that

---

this valley led from ar-Raḥba on the Euphrates to Damascus or to Ḥomṣ. Southwest from the lower end of the valley of al-Hejl begin the valleys of aẓ-Ẓbejwât, in which the name Ẓabj is preserved. Since the authors quoted look for an-Nabi south of the Wâdi Ẓabj, the watering place of an-Nabi, or an-Nubej, should be sought south of Ẓbej al-Bustân on the route from Wâdi al-Hejl to Želîb al-Mumbaṭaḥ.

Al-Bekri, *loc. cit.*, names an-Nabi as a high sandy hill in the territory of the Taṛleb tribe. He bases this assertion on the verses of the poet al-Ḳuṭâmi, who belonged to that tribe and who speaks of his fellow tribesmen as moving after sunrise from ʿAtbân to a new camping ground at an-Nabi in the valley of al-Waʿr. The poet ʿAdi ibn Zejd was acquainted with the hill of Nabi al-Bišr. — Al-Ḳuṭâmi's words lead us to the undulating plain southwest of al-Bišri. About seventy kilometers south of the fortress of ar-Raḥba the valley of al-Waʿar joins the valley of aṣ-Ṣwâb. South of the head of Šeʿîb al-Waʿar extends the hilly range Ṭaraḳ ʿElebân, from the name of which, through faulty transcriptions, evolved the name ʿAtbân. Northwest of this range is Želîb al-Mumbaṭaḥ, where, according to Naṣr, we expect to find the waters of an-Nubej. Almost every watering place in the plain is conspicuous, because the Bedouins erect near each as a guide a cairn upon the nearest cone-shaped hill. Near the Želîb (well) al-Mumbaṭaḥ the high cone of Riğm aṣ-Ṣâbûn is the most promiment. It is called the "soap cairn" on account of the *ḳelw* plant, which grows in profusion in its vicinity and the ashes of which are used in the manufacture of soap. Nabi al-Bišr, mentioned by the poet ʿAdi ibn Zejd, a contemporary of the king an-Naʿmân ibn al-Mundir of al-Ḥîra, is probably a faulty transcription for Ṯeni al-Bišr; for no other poet refers to al-Bišr as being in the vicinity of the watering place of an-Nabi, whereas Ṯeni is always connected with al-Bišr. If this is true, the cone of Ṯeni al-Bišr should be sought among the cones of Ğubejlât aṯ-Ṯni, on the southern slope of the range of al-Bišri.

of course no ill could befall us since we were in his native land, he replied:

"Nawwâf goes for his camels to al-ʿErâḳ (Irak, Babylonia) and al-Ǧezîre (Mesopotamia), to aš-Šumbul (Palmyrena) and al-Ṛûṭa (northwestern Neǧd). No tribe can say that only its own members pass through its territory."

Toward noon the valleys seemed to broaden out and we found in them *ribla, ǧerrejd, erbijjân,* and other plants. Suddenly Blejhân whispered: "A rider behind our right saddle bag!" and I looked around to the south in time to see the stranger, who was approaching us very cautiously, disappear as soon as he found that he was discovered. Who was he? Why did he avoid us? A lone rider on horseback never ventures so far as that into the middle of the desert. Who were his companions and where were they? In a little while we noticed a big dust cloud in the south.

"*Zôl!* (living being!)" exclaimed Blejhân; whereupon I compelled my camel to kneel while I examined the cloud of dust through my binoculars. I found it was being raised by about a hundred camels! Was it a herd of loose camels or mounted riders? As I could not see the animals' backs because of the dust, I was trying to get a glimpse of those on the outside where the dust was thinnest, when Blejhân rapped my shoulder and pointed to the north, whence several camel riders suddenly emerged and immediately disappeared again. Would they attack us, or were they friends? Blejhân ran to a stone pile near by to watch their movements, while I was to keep my eye on the camels to the south. Moving my binoculars from north to south, I perceived upon a high level southwest of the dust cloud several dark objects which appeared to be camels at pasture. That looked as if we had to the south only peaceful country and therefore friends; but who were the riders in the north? As we had already been seen, I ordered fire to be built for the purpose of cooking our dinner and of attracting the attention of the camel herdsmen. Barely had our fire emitted the first smoke when there appeared northwest of us a horseback rider followed by a long train of camels carrying tents, provisions, and implements, the property of migrating men of the Sbaʿa.

"*Al-ḥamdu lillâh!*" called out Blejhân from the distance, announcing that these were his kin, migrating into the valley of al-Mijâh.

We stayed from 1.00 to 3.15 P.M. (temperature at 2: 11.8°C), when we moved on northeastward through a flanking valley to a plain where *šidd al-ǧemal* and *nejtûl* grew. Our camels did not touch the latter, however; they like to eat it only during Ḳrân as-Sâbeᶜ, the seventh month (about April), after the rains have removed its bitterness (*jinrasel*). Then it takes the place of *rûṯe* to them — it is to them what meat is to men. Camels fed with *nejtûl* can stand prolonged and hard marches (*taǧri, teḳîm*).

At 4.53 I sighted in the broad valley of al-Murrabaᶜa three tents and several camels. Blejhân immediately went toward them, while our camels were at pasture upon thick *ḥemri*. Ten minutes later he returned with the information (*ᶜelem*) that his own clan was camping in the valley of al-Mijâh and that the Fedᶜân riders, led by Hawwâš eben Ṛâfel, had watered their horses the night before at the wells Ḳulbân al-Hejl. Their raid had been productive of results, for they had captured from the Freǧe clan two large herds of big, strong she-camels (*raᶜîtên čebîra killhen riḥla*). Of course they were pursued (*fazaᶜû*), but they altered their course (*ᶜajjalû*) several times and disappeared. The owner of the nearest tent came along with Blejhân and offered me and mine his tent for the night. I declined, however, as I thought we might sleep more peacefully and safely alone than by those three tents, which, though secluded, were yet visible a long way off. Blejhân would have liked to stay and talk with his relatives, but I cheered him with the thought that the more we hurried the sooner he would meet his mother, whom he loved so dearly and whom he expected to see in the valley of al-Mijâh.

Turning to the east, we rode on fast in a rolling plain until darkness descended, with no stars in the sky. Blejhân altered the course several times, finally declaring that he did not know which direction to follow and proposing to stop and camp. I would not consent, however, and taking my compass I led my men on toward the east — Blejhân, behind me, all the time complaining that we surely were bound in the wrong direction and that the best thing for us as well as for our camels would be to lie down instead of exerting ourselves needlessly. But from what I had noticed as we traveled along, and from the conversation with the owner of the last tent, I had become convinced that Blejhân often deviated from the course; therefore I resolved that henceforth I would have him merely point out the direction that we should follow (*bâb*) and would take the lead myself. The night was again very cold, and, when the west wind began to blow harder, we encamped after all as early as 7.10 in the *še'îb* of al-'Awêreẓ.

THE ŠE'ÎB OF AL-'AWÊREẒ TO CAMP OF THE 'AMÂRÂT NEAR BÎR ĶRÊṬA'

Friday, December 11, 1908. In the morning frost was lying on our coverings, and, when at 6.15 we mounted our animals and proceeded over a flat plain, we were shivering with cold. At 7.10 we came to the river bed Riğlet 'Awâd that winds through a broad dale surrounded by rocky slopes, where we found fresh footprints of a herd of camels. Ascending the slope at the right side in a southeasterly direction, we reached a vast, desolate plain covered with dark flints (*ṣawwân*), where we sought in vain a pasture for our camels.

At 8.30 we sighted far off at our right the solitary hill, Demlûṛ aṣ-Ṣažri, that looms on the left side of the central part of the valley of al-Mijâh. Southeast from us, upon the slope of the broad *še'îb* of al-'Aṭšân, we saw numerous camels grazing and, finding *rûṯe*, *ḥemri*, and *šîḥ* on the northern slope of the *še'îb* we stopped there from 8.50 to 11.35 to let our own camels eat (temperature at 9.15: 8.1° C). Besides, we desired to learn where Blejhân's relatives were camping. Blejhân immediately made a trip to the herdsmen on the opposite side, remarking wisely enough that he who asks does not go astray (*min nišed mâ tâh*). While Mḥammad was kneading dough for bread I gathered fuel — especially *nejtûl* and *šîḥ* — and Tûmân drew a map of the vicinity. Meantime our camels had strayed over to the other pasturing herds, and I had to go after them to drive them back. After a full hour Blejhân returned with the report that the herds we saw were the property of the Raḥama clan of the Sba'a, which was moving to the well of aṣ-Ṣažri in the valley of al-Mijâh, and that with the Sba'a was camping the Ğelâ'îd clan of the Dahâmše, who were kin of the 'Amârât. He said that Fahad Bêč, the head chief of the 'Amârât and Dahâmše, had been dwelling for a long time in his settlement near Kerbela, but that his son Met'eb was said to be camping somewhere on the southern slope of the ridge of al-Bišri. As I wished to visit the latter and could not do so without securing as a guide an ʿAmâri or a Dahmaši, I was glad to learn that the Ǧelâʿîd camp was in the valley of al-Mijâh. In the vicinity of the al-Barrît wells, where the ʿAmârât and Dahâmše usually camped at this season, there was no pasture this year, we were told, because the spring rains had not materialized; consequently many clans of these tribes had joined the Sbaʿa and Fedʿân tribes. Blejhân maintained that we should find the Ǧelâʿîd either at the wells of aṭ-Ṭajjârijje or at those of Warka.

We headed toward the wells of aṭ-Ṭajjârijje, because we had to deviate to the north to go to al-Bišri and had to pass the wells of Warka. At 11.55 we crossed the vale of al-ʿAṭšân and thence followed the multitudinous camel footprints leading to the watering place of aṭ-Ṭajjârijje. In the valley of al-Mijâh we found *ḳejṣûm* and *ʿabla* in profusion: Blejhân told me that horses grazing on the latter were struck with blindness. On the right side of the valley rises a low swell Zemlet al-ʿEḳfân, with a "nose," Ḫašm Kbûd, which falls away precipitously on the north to the plain of Warka. At the northern end of this swell stands the solitary hill Demlûṛ Warka; while far to the north, between the valleys of al-Murabbaʿa and al-Hejl, extends the long, flat ridge Ṭaraḳ ʿElebân. At 1.15 P.M. a strong wind began to blow from the south-southeast, which we found very annoying as we were riding against it.

At 1.52 (temperature at 2.20: 14.5° C) we dismounted from our camels at the wells of aṭ-Ṭajjârijje and rested until three o'clock. There we discovered several tents of the Meṣârbe clan of which Blejhân was a member. One of the tents belonged to his sister's husband, but his mother was camping with his other relatives somewhere at al-Ḳaʿara, whither she had gone two days before from the al-Mijâh valley. The Ǧelâʿîd also, whom I wanted to see, had pitched their tents somewhere between Warka and Wurejč. Hence I gave the order that we should water our camels, take some water along, and then immediately resume our journey in the direction of these wells. Blejhân's brother-in-law and Fejjâẓ, the chief of the Meṣârbe kin, protested, and Blejhân would have liked very much to remain with his sister throughout the night; but I insisted on departing to the northeast, not wishing to waste any time and not finding any pasture for the camels in this vicinity.

The famous valley of al-Mijâh[9] begins east of the hill of at-Tinf and extends to the Ṭaraḳ and Ḫabra az-Zeḳf, always in a northeasterly direction. Along the entire length of this river bed are many old wells, some of them dry, but some alive and containing good water. Of the live wells south of aṭ-Ṭajjârijje are Ḳulbân aṣ-Ṣażri, al-Msejlîtât, al-Ḥeddâğ, and Umm aṣ-Ṣelâbîḫ.

We rode past many filled-in wells, crossed several dams which kept the fertile soil from being washed away, and at 4.10 found a good pasture for the camels in front of one of the dams. We stayed there until 6.52, ascertaining the latitude meanwhile.

On resuming our journey, we proceeded along a dry river bed, zigzagging from one bank to the other. Blejhân would have liked to deviate, now to the west and then to the east, but I would not consent. Without wasting a moment we reached, at 9.02, the wells of Warka, where we found a large camp, at the northern end of which we made our camels kneel. The air was again cold and we longed to build a fire, but we had no fuel. *ʿAḏob* plants were the only things growing in the vicinity, and they were not dry and hence emitted more smoke than heat.

From the camp there came to us the thudding sounds of drums and tambourines, together with the shrill outcries of a man. Blejhân was of the opinion that a diviner (*ṣâḥeb as-sirr*) had perhaps become frenzied by the strains of the drum and tambourine. The diviners (*ahl as-sirr*) are men or women to whom Allâh manifests through his interpreter the secret of the future. Disciples attach themselves to them and play on various instruments, most often on drums or tambourines, until the diviner becomes frenzied and, transformed to a mouthpiece of Allâh's representative, repeats

[9] Toward the end of December, 1108 A. D., Atabeg Ṭoṛtekîn was traveling with valuable gifts from Damascus through the desert of as-Samâwa to Bagdad. On reaching Wâdi al-Mijâh he learned that the Sultan Muḥammad intended to make war against the Franks; therefore he returned to Damascus (Sibt ibn al-Ğawzi, *Mir'ât* [De Meynard], p. 538; Ibn al-Ḳalânisi, *Ḏajl* [Amedroz], pp. 165 f.).

Jâḳût, *Muʿğam* (Wüstenfeld), Vol. 4, pp. 711, 879, following certain authorities, looks for Wâdi al-Mijâh in the desert of as-Samâwa, which belongs to the Kalb tribe between Irak and Syria. According to others, the location of Mijâh is in the territory of the ʿUḏra tribe near Syria, and the valley of al-Mijâh likewise winds through the territory of Beni Nufejl ibn ʿAmr ibn Kilâb in Neğd. —

The valley of al-Mijâh in the desert of as-Samâwa of the tribe of Kalb is surely identical with our Wâdi al-Mijâh, which is crossed by numerous roads that connect Irak with Syria.

his words. The Sbaʿa and ʿAmârât esteem the diviners; the Rwala expel them.

Saturday, December 12, 1908. In the morning I told my companions to kindle a fire, but they declared it was impossible without fuel. So I sent them to the camp, whence they brought back a quantity of half-dry *ʿaḏob* and a little camel dung, with which we warmed coffee. Soon afterwards several Arabs came to visit us, the owner of the nearest tent bringing us a wooden dish full of camel's milk. Learning that there was only one tent of the Ǧelâʿîd at Warka, whereas all the others were at Wurejč, I sent Blejhân to the tent to inquire whether any of the tenants would guide us. Blejhân was not to enter into an agreement with them; that was to be left to Mḥammad. A little while later, however, a youth stopped, who was on his way from the camp at Wurejč to his acquaintances at Warka and who — as the Arabs sitting at our fire told me — was a member of the Ǧelâʿîd. Of his own accord he offered to guide us if we would compensate him with two *meǧîdijjât* (about $1.80) a day; when I failed to answer him, he said he would accompany us for one *meǧîdijje* a day because of his love for me. At this instant Blejhân came in with an elderly man of mischievous countenance and with black teeth, among which were prominent two lustrously white incisors like the fangs of a rapacious animal. He was very repulsive to me. Sitting down in front of me he warmed his bare, dirty knees at the fire, swinging his legs above the blaze in an oscillating fashion, helping himself to our coffee, and spitting constantly into the fire. And this man, by the name of Zejd, had been hired as a guide by Mḥammad for three-quarters of a *meǧîdijje* (68 cents) a day!

Filling our bags with water, we left Warka at nine o'clock. About three kilometers to the north we passed the camp at the wells of Wurejč; still farther on, to the north-northeast of Wurejč, we saw the wells of Ḥomejma, and north of these, on the southern rim of the basin of Fâẓel, the rain well Moḳr Ḳṭajje. All of these are located in the valley of al-Mijâh. Zejd, as well as the other Arabs in Warka, maintained that Metʿeb eben Haḏḏâl was camping at Ḳrêṭaʿ at the southern base of the al-Bišri ridge. For this reason we went in a northerly direction through a plain covered with small black gravel (*ṣawwân*). On our right, east of Warka, towered the solitary Demlûṛ Warka.

At 10.15 we entered the wide valley of al-ʿAṭšân, through which we rode for some time, and then again ascended to the upland on the slopes of which grew *ṣerr* shrubs to the height of about sixty centimeters. At twelve o'clock (temperature: 8.4° C) in a depression we found *rûṯe* and *rimṯ* upon which our camels grazed until 2.10 P. M. The plain is interpenetrated from west to east by numerous almost parallel valleys, which converge with al-ʿAṭšân and al-Mijâh. At 2.30 we rode along the valley of al-Weššâše, where, on the slopes, grow in abundance *ḥemḥem*, *ʿalanda*, *rimṯ*, *muʿassala*, *ṣollejân*, *šaʿrân*, and *ʿefejna*. The last-named plant, cooked in water and applied to a wound, is said to prevent inflammation. In the *šeʿîb* grew sparsely the *baḫatri* with its black heads, and the fragrant *ḳejṣûm* in bunches. After three o'clock we were riding in a wide plain where there was a large growth of dried, scant grass (*ḥemri*), which, though only twenty centimeters high and very sparse, looked like whole fields of ripening grain. But nowhere behind these grainfields loomed the familiar church tower! Dark clouds were now assembling in the sky, and, when at 4.48 the first drops trickled down, we had to stop and pitch the tent. But, alas, it rained only two hours!

Sunday, December 13, 1908. I untied the camels as early as 4.30 A.M., to allow them to pasture, and directed my companions to build a fire and prepare coffee. This order was so welcome that they crawled speedily from under their coverings, warmed themselves (temperature at 6: 2.2° C), and at 6.53 we were again in the saddle, riding northward through the valley of al-Murabbaʿa. This valley begins at Ḥazm Čabd, presently converges with the valley of al-ʿAwêreẓ, winds through the lowland Fejẓat aṣ-Ṣerâjeb, and ends in Fejẓat Fâẓel.[10]

At 10.30 the low, level summit Ṭaraḳ aṣ-Ṣerâjeb was on our right. In al-Murabbaʿa grow *slajča*, which already was entirely black, together with sparse patches of *šğara* and bunches

[10] In the latter part of June, 1316 A.D., Emir Baha'eddîn set out from the city of Ḥama' through Ğeba' to the camp of the head chief Muhanna of the ʿÎsa family. This camp was constructed at al-Murabbaʿa, a full day's march from the settlement of as-Suḫne. Muhanna had been tempted by the Tatars, whereas Emir Baha'eddîn sought to gain him for the Moslems. He returned from al-Murabbaʿa to Damascus, whence he rode to the son of the head chief, who had been camping a short distance from Salamja. Soon afterwards Muhanna was deposed, and his brother Faḍl ibn ʿÎsa was made the head chief. At the end of July the latter arrived from Damascus at his encampment at Tell Eʿda' (Abu-l-Feda', *Muḫtaṣar* [Adler], Vol. 5, p. 302). —

Ğeba' is situated about 110 kilometers to the south-southeast of the city of Ḥama'. The emir therefore went from Ğeba' by the way of Tudmor to as-Suḫne and thence to the valley of al-Murabbaʿa, about seventy kilometers distant. That Abu-l-Feda' should designate the distance of seventy kilometers a goodly day's march is indeed noteworthy. Tell Eʿda' is the Tell ʿAḏa' of the present, about eight kilometers north of Salamja.

of *rûṯe*. The dry branches of this last plant are of a bright grayish-white color, as though made of the finest nickel, and they glisten in the sunlight, giving a pleasant silvery tinge to the monotonous landscape. It is easy to tell from far away where the *rûṯe* grows.

From 11.42 to 1.15 P. M. we rested west of the *riǧm* (pile of stones) of al-Ḥawijje and at 1.30 arrived in the extensive lowland Fejẓat Fâẓel, which receives its moisture from the valley of al-Hejl. This lowland converges with the eastern border of Fejẓat ʿEḏeme. It is covered with a good soil and is thickly overgrown with various kinds of plants, especially *nejtûl, šîḥ, samne, erbijjân, žṭejjen, riǧlet al-ṛurâb, basbâs, kammûl,* and sparse patches of *ṣerr*. To the west appeared several dark belts: the ridge of Abu Riǧmên, the mountain range of aẓ-Ẓâḥeč, and al-Minšâr with the cone ʿOrf aṭ-Ṭajjibe. North of the Fejẓat Fâẓel soars the gray ridge of al-Bišri, rugged with deep gullies, in which Zejd and Blejhân pointed out to me the spots of special interest.

South of al-Bišri the plain forms a gigantic undulation, on which we could see camels and tents. But the tents were still very far off, although they seemed to be immediately in front of us — for it is well known that upon level plains the eye's appraisal of distance is often so deceptive that the traveler thinks the object he sees is only a few paces away, whereas he would follow it almost *ad infinitum*. The lowland Fejẓat Fâẓel was glittering in the gold of the setting sun, when suddenly there appeared in front of us a horseback rider, who stopped, rifle in hand, and scrutinized us; then, having concluded that we were peaceful travelers (*ṭurûš*), galloped toward us, returned our greetings, and touching with bare heels the flanks of his white mare, circled round us at a gallop. He told us that Metʿeb eben Haḏḏâl was encamped south of the well of Ḳrêṭaʿ, he questioned us as to the location of the camps of various tribes and clans, and then departed at a gallop to announce to Metʿeb my contemplated visit. Numerous herdsmen kept driving their herds past on our right and left.

It was dark when we reached the first tents, and it was not until 6.05 P. M. that we dismounted in front of the one designated for Metʿeb's guests. Metʿeb had two tents; in one with five central poles he lived with his family and in the other he received his guests. By the side of the latter we pitched our circular tent, and having ordered announcement of my arrival to be made to Met'eb, who was sitting in the guests' tent by the fire in the center of a large gathering, I awaited his greeting. In a few minutes a man of his kin came to welcome me and to beseech me in the name of the *šujûh*, or head chief, to enter his tent; but I had taken barely five paces before I met Met'eb coming out to meet me. He greeted me cordially and led me into the tent, all present rising at his command and remaining standing until I was seated.

Met'eb sat on my right. With my left hand I leaned on a camel saddle, against the opposite side of which an older chief was also leaning. In front of me was a large quadrangular hole in which blazed an enormous fire. Beyond the fire to the left sat a black slave, and in front of him stood four coffee cans, one of them very large. Behind the negro and around the entire fireplace crowded the Bedouins, warming their bare feet. Another slave brought some fuel and cast it into the fire over the heads of the company. Having greeted all present, I was welcomed individually by all the chiefs, who inquired how I fared. At this the slave who was preparing the coffee rose abruptly, scoured a coffee cup with a dirty rag, took it in his left hand and a smaller coffee can in his right, planted himself before me, and began to pour the coffee into the cup in a thin thread from a considerable height. When the cup was about one-fifth full he handed it to me and stood waiting. Tasting the coffee, I smacked my lips, took a long gulp, glanced at the company, and after three more cautious gulps handed the empty cup to the slave, who filled it twice more. This ceremony of welcome ended, I was free to do as I pleased.

Met'eb having by this time disappeared, I went to my tent, where Tûmân and I ascertained the latitude (temperature at 7: 7.1° C). We had barely finished when in came Met'eb and invited me to supper. Near my place lay a large, flat copper plate covered with thin pieces of bread like pancakes and a heap of camel meat. A slave poured a few drops of water on three fingers of my right hand, whereupon I knelt on my left knee by the plate, reclined backward on my left heel, and, pronouncing the words *bismi-llâh* (in the name of Allâh), began to eat. Tearing small bits off of the bread, I kneaded them with pieces of meat — which Met'eb, who sat next to me, pulled off and threw to me — and put them in my mouth. As soon as I had finished, my companions, who ate with me, rose, and the dish was passed to others. A slave poured a little water upon my hands and someone even proffered me a small handkerchief, so that I could dry them. The others, however, wiped their mouths and hands on the ropes and sides of the tent. After supper Metʻeb seated himself by me, and we gradually became engaged in a whispered conversation on various topics, which promised to go on indefinitely. When I confided to Metʻeb my intention of leaving early in the morning, he deprecated it, insisting that I must remain at least one day more, so that we could become better acquainted and reinforced in our friendship. It was past midnight when I retired to my tent.

THE ʻAMÂRÂT; THE FEDʻÂN; ARRIVAL AT AL-MIJÂḎÎN

Monday, December 14, 1908. The immense undulation, extending from west to east, upon which the camp of the ʻAmârât was established, consists of white limestone similar to alabaster and is covered with coarse sand in which are rooted large bushes of *rimṯ*, often attaining the height of a meter and a half. Bîr Ḳrêṭaʻ is about ten kilometers north-northeast from the camp. It is sixteen *bâʻ* (31 m.) deep, but its water is so dark and bitter that it is unfit for cooking, hence the ʻAmârât were bringing drinking water from the well of al-Ḳebâžeb farther to the northwest on the road of as-Sulṭâni leading from Tudmor to Dejr az-Zôr. Here there is a barrack (*ḳašla*) occupied by three to five gendarmes. The third well, Ḫaẓar al-Maʼ, is at the southern base of the undulation, about thirteen kilometers south from Ḳrêṭaʻ; and five kilometers east-northeast is the fourth well, Želîb Aʻwâjbe.

For breakfast Metʻeb sent us mashed dates immersed in hot butter, with pancakes (*lezâḳi*); and after a while he came and asked how I had slept under the protection of the ʻAmârât tribe. He was about twenty-five years of age, with features that bore a semblance to the Semitic type of the ancient Assyrians. His teeth were white and lustrous, save one in the upper jaw which was prominent by its blackness; he spoke very slowly, ponderously, and calmly, with a sort of lisping affectation. I gave him a nickel-plated Gasser revolver with a hundred rounds of ammunition, which delighted him immensely. When I had inquired of him about the valleys, wells, and ruins in the territory of Šeṯâṯa, where the ᶜAmârât usually encamped, and noted that he stated the directions and distances correctly, I resolved to remain with him until the next morning. Before we separated he told me a great deal about his tribe:

The ᶜAmârât are divided into the Âl Ğebel and ad-Dahâmše. The Âl Ğebel consist of the clans:

al-Ḥeblân
as-Selḳa
aṣ-Ṣḳûr

The head chief of all the Âl Ğebel is Fahad Bêč eben Haḏḏâl, who is a member of the Ḥeblân clan.

The families of the Ḥeblân are:

al-Ṛšûm
Âl Hajjâzaᶜ
Âl Ḥsejn
al-Ḫatârše

The families of the Selḳa, whose chief is ar-Refedi, are:

al-Ḥsene (chief: Eben Tamrân)
al-Meṭârfe („ Eben Wuṭejf)
Âl Mẓejjân („ Eben Daḫîl)
Âl Šemlân

According to some, the Selḳa originally were not affiliated with the Âl Ğebel but associated themselves with them later.

The families of the Ṣḳûr are:

Âl Dahmân (chief: Maṭᶜân eben Ẓelᶜân)
al-Meṣâᶜeb („ az-Zwêl an-Nbejži)
Âl Ğelâl („ Râfeᶜ eben Môžef)
ad-Dleme („ al-Čâseb eben Marzûḳ)

The clans of the Dahâmše, whose head chief is Ğezzâᶜ eben Miğlâd are:

Âl Mḥallaf
az-Zebene
as-Swêlmât

The families of the Âl Mḥallaf are:

al-Mḥejnât (chief: Ab-ar-Rûs)
Âl Šilḫân („ Dahlûs aš-Šelîḫi)
aḏ-Ḏwâjde („ Ṣnajdeḥ aḏ-Ḏâjdi)
Âl ᶜAjjâš („ Ẓâri eben Ẓbejjân)

The families of the Zebene are:

as-Sebâbîḥ (chief: Ğezzâᶜ eben Miğlâd)
aṣ-Ṣruma („ Barğas walad Ṣerem)
al-Ğmejsât („ al-ᶜErbîẓi)

The families of the Swêlmât are:

as-Salâṭîn; subdivided into Âl Mḥejsen (chief: Mešᶜân eben Ṣaber) and al-Wuṭuba (chief: Mešᶜân eben Bakr)
al-Ḥamâṭre („ ᶜAskar al-Ḥmêṭri)
al-Ḥemmel („ Ğhajjem eben Dawwâj)
al-Ğelâᶜîd („ Eben Zuᶜejr)

After ten o'clock the blare of a military trumpet sounded, and, jumping up in surprise to look out, we saw a cavalcade of about thirty riders on mules escorting two officials, who were headed toward Metᶜeb's tent. I learned later that this squad was despatched by the Turkish Government from Dejr az-Zôr to extract from Metᶜeb's tribe everything that had been taken from the Kurds and especially from the soldiers of Ibrâhîm Pasha. It seems that toward the end of 1907 and in the spring of 1908, the Turkish Government had planned to build the Ḥeǧâz railway from al-Medîna to Mecca, a project which the native tribe of the Ḥarb opposed. To humble the tribe, the Government encouraged the notorious Kurdish chief Ibrâhîm Pasha to march with his soldiery upon the sacred Ḥeǧâz and occupy the district through which the roadbed was to be built. Ibrâhîm obeyed and arrived at Damascus with several hundred soldiers sufficiently equipped by the Government; but, as the summer of 1908 was a time of political dissensions in Constantinople, the building of the railway was forgotten, and Ibrâhîm as well. After he had camped several weeks in the meadows west of Damascus, the Government ceased paying him the money necessary for the upkeep of his soldiers and finally instructed him to retire. Ibrâhîm had neither food for his men nor fodder for their horses; hence on his way home he pillaged not only small settlements but even cities; whereupon the Government was obliged to despatch against him the regular army, which Ibrâhîm defeated. He then incited his followers to an uprising. The Government, too weak to subdue the rebellion by its own force, prompted the various tribes dwelling along the Euphrates and Tigris to coöperate with it in an attack on the Kurds. As the Kurds had been enemies of the Arabs from time immemorial, the latter welcomed this governmental solicitation, assailed the western Kurdish tribes, pillaged their villages, and drove off their herds. The downtrodden western Kurds found auxiliaries, however, in the eastern Kurds, who threatened to displace the Mosul government, should their brethren not be compensated for the losses they had suffered; whereupon the Government responded by despatching the regular army in small units into the camps of the Arabs to force them to restore the spoils to the Kurds.

Metᶜeb decried the conduct of the Kurds, but laughed at the disappointment the Government officials would feel when they found nothing among his tribe. He had no other name for his uninvited guests than dogs (*člâb*); still, he had to be a host to them and was obliged to accompany the officials. For this reason I did not see him until towards evening, when he directed Mḥammad to write for me in his name a letter to all the commanders of the raiding and marauding detachments of his tribe, ordering them not to dare to attack or rob me, a friend of his. Not being able to write, he affixed his seal to the sheet. Of course I gave him my thanks, but I was quite aware that the scrap of paper would be of little use to me, since none of the leaders of any ʿAmârât marauding group was capable of reading; and who was there to compel them to believe a letter read by a stranger commanding them to abandon desired booty?

Metʿeb's home was shared by his two younger brothers, eighteen and twenty years old, who showed great respect for him. Although they came secretly into my tent, they left immediately if they saw Metʿeb in the distance. Toward evening a Šammari visited me, offering for sale his carbine (much resembling a Mannlicher) and a precious dagger of central Arabian workmanship, purporting to be the property of the assassinated prince Metʿeb eben ʿAbdalʿazîz eben Rašîd. I should have liked very much to purchase it, but the Šammari demanded one hundred *meǧîdijjât* ($ 90), and I did not have that amount with me. The handle and the scabbard of the dagger were adorned with massive beaten gold and rubies.

Tuesday, December 15, 1908. In the morning we built a fire, prepared breakfast, and loaded our baggage (temperature at 6.15: 1.2° C), Metʿeb coming to say good-by at 7.05 and escorting us a kilometer on our way. We headed first toward the east, later turning to the northeast. The day was very gloomy, a dense fog soaking our clothing with moisture and so obstructing the view that before we had been gone twenty minutes our guide Zejd declared his inability to keep the course and proposed that we return and wait in the tent for the fog to lift. Here again I had to resort to the other alternative of acting as leader myself with the compass to guide me. It was not an easy task, however, on a level plain overgrown evenly with various plants, among them shrubs of *rimṯ*, with *nejtûl* and bunches of dry *ḥemri*. After nine o'clock we were going through *ʿafw* which shoots up in bushes 1.7 meters high. When devoid of foliage, this resembles vines. In the hollows throve *ᶜefejna* and *ṣrêra*.

At eleven o'clock the fog lifted, and we saw at the right the broad basin of al-Ḫôr littered with tents, while about three kilometers to our left, at the wells Bîr ad-Duḫûl, swarmed large flocks of sheep and goats.[11]

From 12.38 to 2.43 P. M. our camels grazed in the vale of ᶜAḳûla, in which are the wells of al-Čawâṯel.[12]

In the depressions of the undulating plain we were traversing grew *slajča, ḫarbaḳa, ǧaᶜada, ᶜalanda, žetâde*, and at places even *hazzaᵓ*, and *ḳaḥᶜûb*. Before us upon a wide swell we saw a large herd belonging to the tribe of Fedᶜân, and near by two other herds of white camels (*maṛâtîr*). The Fedᶜân are famous for breeding white camels, and the *maṛâtîr* herds belonging to the chief of the Rwala are replenished and enlarged almost entirely from the herds of the Fedᶜân. Not feeling certain of finding any more tents farther to the east and wishing to avoid meeting with a marauding party of the Šammar or the Šwâja, we encamped at 5.20 in the proximity of the tents.

The Fedᶜân are subject to the head chief Ḥâčem eben Mhejd. Their clans are:

Âl Mhejd	(chief:	Ḥâčem eben Mhejd)
ar-Rûs	(,,	Ǧedûᶜ eben Karh)
aš-Šmejlât	(,,	Bejrân eben Ḥbejčân)
al-Ḳšûr	(,,	ᶜÂjed walad Dulmi)
Âl Hazbân	(,,	Ḳdejm eben Ǧbejl)
Âl Ḥâzem	(,,	ᶜAwde abu Šerra)
al-Ḳalfân	(,,	Fadṛam eben Ḳalfaᵓ)

[11] Al-Aḫṭal, *Dîwân* (Salhani), p. 124, mentions ad-Daḫûl, al-Huǧûl, Ḏu Ḫijam, and the ridge of aṣ-Ṣarîme. — The Duḫûl of our day lies in the former territory of the Taṛleb tribe, from which the poet al-Aḫṭal was descended. About seventy kilometers to the southwest of ad-Duḫûl begin the hills of aṣ-Ṣerâjeb, which I identify with aṣ-Ṣarîme, because in the dialect the letter *b* is frequently changed into the letter *m*. About sixty kilometers west of aṣ-Ṣerâjeb lies Želîb al-Hǧejl, which surely is identical with al-Huǧûl. The location of Ḏu Ḫijam is unknown to me.

Jâḳût, *Muᶜǧam* (Wüstenfeld), Vol. 3, p. 379, refers to aṣ-Ṣerâ'em as a place where the Beni Tamîm clashed with the ᶜAbs. — This place is to be sought to the southeast of the sandy desert of the Nefûd.

[12] Jâḳût, *op. cit.*, Vol. 4, p. 315, writes that al-Kawâṯel is the name of a place on the frontier of Syria, traversed by Ḫâled on his march from Irak to Syria. Ibn as-Sikkît asserts that al-Kawâṯel is in the territory of the Dubjân along the frontier of the Kalb tribe. — It is noteworthy that Jâḳût, traveling alongside the right bank of the Euphrates in close proximity to the watering place of al-Kawâṯel, had not discovered the location of this famous station. Al-Kawâṯel that lies in the territory of the Ḏubjân, near the wells of Ubajr, is a different watering place.

Abu-l-Faḍâ'il, *Marâṣid* (Juynboll), Vol. 2, p. 517, adds to Jâḳût's account by stating that al-Kawâṯel, or al-Kawâtel as it is also named, is a well-known caravan station on the route from ar-Raḥba to Damascus. — The road from the fortress of ar-Raḥba, near the present city of al-Mijâḏîn, to Damascus leads in a westerly direction past as-Suḫne or Tudmor, and the first station beyond the city of al-Mijâḏîn is al-Čawâṯel.

al-Ḥanâtîš (chief: Nwejrân eben ʿAǧlân)
al-Ḫraṣa
Âl Mǧelli
al-ʿAžâžre („ Mḥammad eben Ḥrejmîs).

The families of al-ʿAžâžre:

Âl Mejs
Âl Ḳrejn
an-Naʿême
Âl Haǧr
Âl ʿAbdallâh

Wednesday, December 16, 1908. The night was so damp that we had to dry our clothing at the fireside in the morning (temperature at 5.30: 4.5° C). While our camels were at pasture, Blejhân made a trip to the nearest tent to inquire as to other camps and brought back a dish full of camel's milk; but he complained that the miserly owner had diluted the milk a half with water. The Fedʿân and the ʿEbede, who owned this camp, were watering their herds at the well of Mâlḥat al-Ṛurr, at the base of al-Bišri. According to the information we got from them, the chief al-Fḳiḳi of the ʿEbede was encamped southwest of ar-Rḥaba — news very pleasing to us, because all robbers avoid him, as they are aware of his persistence in running them down.

At 6.20 A. M. we set out to the east-southeast. Zejd and Blejhân wanted to turn to the south, but I insisted on the easterly course because I judged from the notes of our journey heretofore that we were almost west from al-Mijâdîn and the fortress of ar-Rḥaba. As a rule, a Bedouin knows his way only when he can follow formations visible from a distance; in a level, monotonous plain he is a bad guide. He can point out the direction (*bâb*) perfectly but is not able to hold the course he designates. He states with precision that a certain spot lies to the left or to the right of the spring sunrise, and yet he deviates immediately to the southeast or northeast and changes the course constantly. His saying that he rides or walks between the north and the south may be truthfully conceded. It is because of his ignorance of the value of time that he cannot comprehend why a traveler who has not been reared in the desert refuses to follow him. A Bedouin is accustomed to be led. When the camp is moved, he walks calmly behind the loaded camels which follow the chief, and on war expeditions with a vacant mind he follows the commander (*ʿažîd*), who again is led in most instances by some member of the Ṣlejb tribe, who know the desert best. Leaderless, a Bedouin is as incapable of finding and maintaining his course as is his camel, which becomes desperate when it loses sight of the herd with its leader.

Before us, as we swung along, the eastern sky at the horizon looked as if it were equipped with shutter slats. The individual ribs lay in a horizontal position, glowing a vivid red and penetrated with bluish rays of light. Suddenly the slats closed and all became blue — nay, black. Our camels, trotting to the east, kept swaying their heads and necks like inverted pendulums, and we were swung to and fro with them. Zejd was enveloped up to his head in his old fur coat and mantle, his elevated right hand with which he directed the camel overlapped by the long sleeve of his coat, from which protruded a thick camel stick with a wide and oblong head. The stick swung back and forth in time with the swaying of the camel's head and neck, until in the morning mist it looked as if a bird with a large rump were sitting on the camel, the camel stick forming its neck and head, Zejd's body its body, and his head its rump.

The plain we were traversing was covered with a coarse sand and was somewhat rolling. Far off in the depressions could be seen the reddening bunches of *slajča,* besides *šîḥ, ṣerr, ǧaʿada, žetâde, ʿalanda,* and *ḳaḥʿûb. Nejtûl* was almost entirely absent and *ḥemri* was not plentiful. At 8.15 we sighted at last the castle of ar-Rḥaba with its four-edged corner towers projecting above the plain and the horizon. The plain, known as al-Ḳerâja, rises gradually to the east, culminating in a flat summit parallel with the Euphrates, toward which it falls precipitously. At twelve o'clock, through the gap of an-Neḫṭeb, we caught our first glimpse of the River Euphrates and to the east of it, far below us, the Mesopotamian plain. Everything was enshrouded in a grayish mantle, desolate and lifeless. Even the leaves of the palms lifting their heads above the city of al-Mijâḏîn had a grayish-yellow tinge, the sign of winter and death. North of ar-Rḥaba the sanctuary of aš-Šejḫ Anes rested upon the crest of the bluffs, while to the south protruded two domes of the sanctuaries of aš-Šibli and aš-Šejḫ ʿAli. The descent from the edge down to the hillock upon which the castle of ar-Rḥaba towers was very difficult, because the ground consisted of soft, crumbling stones. Around ar-Rḥaba grew *ṯhâl*, *ʿerž*, and *ʿaḳûl*. We remained below the castle from 12.32 until 3.28 P. M. (temperature at 1 P. M.: 12.2° C).

Ar-Rḥaba was built in the Middle Ages upon a spur which was separated from the western line of bluffs by a deep, wide moat. The solitary hill was once paved on all sides with solid stone, and upon this pavement there was a road leading into the castle. As the material of which the pavement was built has long since become dislocated and has been transported to al-Mijâḏîn, and as the road has disappeared, it was not easy to get up to the castle. I managed, however, to climb the hill and enter the spacious underground vaults built of bricks and thence to get into the courtyard inclosed by ramparts. In the center of the yard is a large house with thick walls, built around an inner yard. Most of the walls are now wrecked and some are entirely carried away. North and west from the foot of the hillock upon which the castle was erected can still be seen a few remnants of the old brick structures and large heaps of earthenware fragments. Here and there freshly-dug holes betray the fact that building material or treasures are still being sought in the ruins.

From ar-Rḥaba we set out northeast through the flood plain to the town of al-Mijâḏîn, which beckoned to us with its minarets and palm trees. We rode among numerous small fields, in which areas thirty meters square are enclosed by earthen walls about ten centimeters high and crisscrossed with shallow irrigation ditches. At 4.38 we encamped southeast of al-Mijâḏîn, near a merchant caravan that was carrying fresh dates from the oasis of Šeṯâṯa to Aleppo. A needy woman offered to sell us fuel — wood and camel dung. Both were very expensive: with fuel for two piasters (nine cents) we barely succeeded in warming our coffee. I ordered our water bags to be filled from the nearest well, where merchant caravans were watering their camels. Then I helped Tûmân calculate the latitude. Mḥammad and Blejhân went to the city to purchase dates. They came back with eight *roṭols* (about 20 kilograms) of dates which they had bought for forty piasters ($ 1.80).

CHAPTER II

AL-MIJÂḎÎN TO ḪABÂRI SEJḲAL

AL-MIJÂḎÎN TO BIJÂR AL-MLOṢI

Thursday, December 17, 1908. The night was so damp that we had to dry our kerchiefs at the fire again. When we left our camping place at six o'clock we could not see beyond a distance of five meters, so dense was the mist. Intending to travel southward to al-Ḳaʿara, we actually headed in that direction, but when an hour later we approached the bluffs enclosing the Euphrates lowland to the west, Zejd and Blejhân insisted that since we had lost the direction we must turn to the southeast and not ascend the heights until after the atmosphere had become altogether clear. Seeing in the plain, however, many footprints left by asses, camels, and sheep — the property of the ʿAḳêdât tribe camping in the vicinity — I followed them, disregarding Zejd's indignant and warning outcries. We made the ascent through the broad gap near the sanctuary of aš-Šibli and went on due south-southwest, until at 9.15 we entered the hollow of al-Ḫôr, where our camels grazed until 11.10 (temperature: 9.5° C) on *nejtûl, samna,* and especially on quantities of *naṣi.*

Crossing the heights of ad-Dečče, at twelve o'clock we descended into the *šeʿîb* of Enṭêbeḫ almost east of the wells of al-Fwêğe, by which stood a few tents of the ʿAḳêdât. At 12.38 P. M. we were in Telʿat Melḥem and at 1.40 passed through the gully of Ab-al-Žâṣem. South of that the *ṣerr* did not thrive well, but the *ḳejṣûm* sprouted in abundance. At two o'clock there appeared to the southeast the height Zemlet aẓ-Ẓulla, at the northwestern base of which is the well of Ğbejb, while at the western base are about thirty wells called Ğibb. All these are shallow and bored in white loam (*fuḫḫar abjaẓ*). The lowland to the east of them is called Fejẓat Ğibb, in the western part of which terminates the *šeʿîb* of aṣ-Ṣlubi, which comes from the well of Ḥomejma. After two o'clock we rode along in the hollow of Ğibb, overgrown here and there with *šîḥ, ḳejṣûm,* and small shrubs of *rimṯ,* and at 2.20 Zejd pointed out to me, in the lower part of the valley of Swêḥel, the wells of ad-Duḫna and ad-Duḫejne, about twenty kilometers distant.

At 3.16 we came upon several spots where *rûṯe* and *šîḥ* were growing and rested there for supper until 4.38 (temperature at 3: 10.8°C). Having enough water, we made some *šâj*, as my companions called the slightly-sweetened water in which a little tea was brewed. The *šâj* with bread tasted good to them, though the water we had brought from al-Mijâḏîn was salty and so polluted with clay that it left in our cups a sediment from a quarter to half a centimeter thick.

Toward evening the western sky presented a gorgeous picture. The level, desolate desert was dark gray, the summit of aẓ-Ẓulla almost black, the horizon beyond glowed a blazing red, while high aloft swam countless clouds like snowy billows, and the great lustrous ball of the sun was setting. Gradually the snowy clouds in the west grew red and those in the east blue; then the bluish tinge spread westward, the desert darkened, the sky became gray, and we were passing amid the glory like the camel riders of Doré's great paintings. I had not thought of Doré for a long time, but here in the desert he came to my mind again. He is right in rendering his characters of the infinite desert as superhuman giants, for there everything that projects above the horizon assumes immense dimensions. A man nearer to the horizon is nearer to heaven, and above the horizon in heaven reigns Allâh, who is greater than all that he has created. Great is Allâh, *allâhu akbar!*

But it was a desolate plain in which we were journeying, and it seemed all the more dreary when the camels' feet occasionally crunched the dry stalks of *šîḥ*, growing here and there in small patches. In one of these spots we encamped at 8.25.

Friday, December 18, 1908. The night had been so bitterly cold and damp that I woke Blejhân as early as 4.30 A. M. and told him to let the camels pasture while we gathered fuel in order that we might warm ourselves. At six o'clock we were in the saddle again and at 7.15 reached the *šeʿîb* of Swêḥel, as the lower part of the *šeʿîb* of aṣ-Ṣwâb is called. We headed to the south-southwest, the valley winding between rocky bluffs fifteen to twenty meters high, cut out of horizontal strata, and the river bed (*baṭḥa*), which was twenty to thirty meters wide and contained many pools of rain water. At 7.25

we crossed the *šeʿîb* of az-Zerḳa, which comes from the south-southeast, while to the east of it stretches the valley of ar-Raṯḳa (or ʿAli), in which are the wells Ḳulbân ar-Raṯḳa, near the Zemlet al-Ḥarîri.

In the *šeʿîb* of aṣ-Ṣwâb we found plenty of *rûṯe, ʿaḳûl, slajča, ṭarfaʾ, nejtûl*, and *ʿerž*, the latter consisting of large bushes full of fruit. Now and then we passed spots where herdsmen had lodged, conducting their camels every fifth day (*ʿala ḫims*) to the watering stations of ad-Duḫna or Ǧibb. On the adjacent heights we saw numerous piles of stones and an unusual number of large, ravenous birds. From nine to 11.20 we spent the time in relaxing, sketching a map of the environs, and cooking peeled wheat (*burṛul*) for dinner.

At 12.25 P.M. we had at our right the *šeʿîb* of al-Waʿar,[13] which comes from Ḥašm Kbûd.

South of al-Waʿar, in the *šeʿîb* of aṣ-Ṣwâb, grows the brownish *sûs* in patches averaging thirty meters in length and six meters in width. At 2.35 we discerned to the southwest the outlets of the three northern *šeʿibân* of ar-Rtej-mijjât. From 3.05 to 9.15 we prepared our supper (temperature at 3.15: 6.8° C) and then we continued riding until 6.17 when we were compelled to encamp. The *šeʿîb* of aṣ-Ṣwâb winds in so many curves between its slippery sides that our camels made hardly any progress. Because parties of marauders like to take the ṛoute through this valley, we kept watch over our animals and baggage throughout the night.

Saturday, December 19, 1908. In the morning we could not kindle a fire, so thoroughly was the fuel soaked with dew. At six o'clock we left our camp and at seven abandoned the valley. From 8.15 to 10.44 our camels grazed about ten kilometers east of the Demlûṛ Ṣwâb; this is a solitary hill south of the *šeʿîb* of an-Naḳš, which converges with the Ṣwâb at the rain well ʿAḳlat Ṣwâb.

Our road lay through a level plain where *nejtûl, rûṯe, šîḥ*, and *ḥemri* grew profusely. In the east of this district the rain water pours into the shallow *šeʿibân* of al-ʿAkâšât and then sinks into the deep valley of ar-Raṯḳa, which is joined

[13] Al-Aḫṭal, *Dîwân* (Salhani), pp. 252, 271; (al-Bekri, *Muʿǧam* [Wüstenfeld], p. 844), alludes frequently to the valley of al-Waʿr in the territory of his tribe.

The poet al-Ḳuṭâmi of the Taṛleb tribe mentions the migration of his kindred to the valley of al-Waʿr (al-Bekri, *op. cit.*, p. 570).

Jâḳût, *Muʿǧam* (Wüstenfeld), Vol. 1, p. 405, refers to the district of al-Awʿâr in the desert of as-Samâwa dominated by the tribe of Kalb. —

Our valley of al-Waʿar, too, runs through the former territory of the Taṛleb and Kalb tribes and through the northeastern corner of the as-Samâwa desert.

on the right by the *šeʿîb* of al-Ḥelḳûm and the short *šeʿibân* of al-Mânʿijjât, extends through the district of at-Trejčijje, and joins the Euphrates south of Abu Čemâl. At two o'clock we noted to the southeast the flat crest of the Ṭâr al-Ḥaẓar, and to the east the Ḫašm al-Medhem and the Ṭaraḳ abu Saʿad, which enclose the valleys of ar-Raṯka and al-Ḳâjem. To the southwest gaped the entrances into the three *šeʿibân* of al-Herijjân, in the central one of which, close to the Ṣwâb, Turki eben Mhejd, the head chief of the Fedʿân, is buried. The plain we were traversing was stony, and the troughs of the several valleys were deep and narrow. The date merchants we met at al-Mijâdîn had told us there had been heavy rains in the vicinity of al-Ḳaʿara; the news, they said, had been brought by the Kubejsât, the nomadic merchants (*ʿala ʿelm al-kubejs tâh al-maṭar*). But with the exception of a few pools in the channel of the Ṣwâb we had found no traces of sufficient rain.

We supped from 3.10 to 4.23 and then continued on our journey until seven, when we had to stop, for, riding as we were on the brink of the deep trough of al-ʿAkâše in a darkness so black that we could not see two meters ahead, we were obliged to trust ourselves entirely to our camels. Having made our laborious descent between the loose boulders into the trough, we did not propose to ascend it the same way.

Sunday, December 20, 1908. At 6.03 A. M. we were again under way, proceeding south in a rolling plain covered with coarse gravel, in a fog so thick that we did not know for a long time where we were. It was not until 7.20 that we sighted an oblong table-shaped ridge off to the right in the limitless haze; whereupon Blejhân shouted:

"That's Ḳârat Naʿağa; we are in the basin Ğûbt al-Ḳaʿara already!" This is the name of a deep basin that was caused by erosion in a level plain. It is about twenty-five kilometers long from east to west, and twenty kilometers wide, and on nearly all sides is enclosed by precipitous cliffs. To the north these cliffs comprise the Ḳârat Naʿağa, to the west the Ḳârat Ḥamma, and to the south the Ḫašm an-Neğîli[14] and al-Ṛarri.

[14] Jâḳût, *op. cit.*, Vol. 4, p. 743, records a place, Neğâl, between Syria and the desert of as-Samâwa of the Kalb tribe. He infers this from a verse in which the poet al-Kuṯejjer mentions Neğâl as a fertile land. —

Our Ḫašm an-Neğîli of the former desert of as-Samâwa rises along the road leading from the desert into the populated districts, and therefore we may identify it with the Neğâl of the poet Kuṯejjer.

To the east the basin is enclosed by Tlûl al-ʿAfâjef and Ṭâr al-Ḥazar, to the northeast by Ḳârt al-ʿEdeme, to the north by al-Marbaṭ. Rain water gathers in the *šeʿîb* of al-Mloṣi, which begins at al-Ḥamâd far to the southwest, north of Ḫabra Ḳṭajje, and is joined on the right along the southern fringe of al-Ḳaʿara by the narrow, deep *šeʿibân* of an-Neğîli, al-Ṛarri, and al-Ḳnêni[15] (with the latter at Ḳulbân Râḥ), and farther on by the *šeʿibân* of al-ʿAğrumijjât, which approach from Tlûl al-ʿAfâjef. Between Ḳârt al-ʿEdeme and al-Marbaṭ there is a deep rain pool, Ṛadîr aṣ-Ṣûfi, in the valley of al-Mloṣi. East of that the valley is called al-Ḥelḳûm.

As Blejhân was not certain whether his mother was camping at the wells of Râḥ or at al-Mloṣi, we turned at 7.40 to the southwest in the direction of the latter wells. Soon afterward we saw herds of camels to the northwest and smoke to the southwest, which made us certain that the Arabs were camping at al-Mloṣi. As we were aware that there was no pasturage at the wells, we stopped from 9.14 to 12.35 to let our animals graze, while we made a map of the vicinity and took off our lice-infested garments, which Blejhân's sister was to wash for us. We reached the camp at 1.30 P. M. The owner of the first tent called to Blejhân to ride westward, where he would find his mother.

[15] I think that the camp of the Carmathians mentioned by aṭ-Ṭabari, *Ta'rîḫ* (De Goeje), Ser. 3, p. 2259, was in al-Ḳaʿara and the vicinity. In the year 906 A. D. the Carmathians, led by Naṣr, plundered Palestine and Syria. Being pursued, they took refuge in the desert and encamped at the watering holes of ad-Damʿâne and al-Ḥâla. The Moslem army, prevented from further pursuit by lack of water, established quarters at ar-Raḥba. The Carmathians made an onslaught from their camp against the settlement of Hît, stormed the town's outskirts at sunrise, pillaged the ships moored there in the river, and after three days retreated with three thousand camels, which carried the booty and especially the wheat into the desert. The marauders had not scaled the walls of the city proper. Afterward a second army was despatched from Bagdad in pursuit of them, but this army also was unable to close upon them, for they had polluted every source of drinking water between their base and the Euphrates. It was not until this second army had obtained from the settlers enough camels and large leather water bags and had arranged a plan with the army quartered at ar-Raḥba, that an offensive was decided upon. Having been informed of this plan, the members of the Kalb tribe, who were in alliance with the Carmathians, assassinated the commander, Naṣr, shipped his head to the commander of the Bagdad army, and then retreated to the territory of the Ṭajj and the Beni Asad, who were camping at ʿAjn at-Tamr. At the watering holes of ad-Ḍamʿâne and al-Ḥâla remained only remnants of the Carmathians, whom the Moslem armies left in peace.

According to Abu ʿAmr (Jâḳût, *op. cit.*, Vol. 2, pp. 391f.) the Ḫâla, or Ḥâla, watering place lies beside the well-known shallow well of al-Ḳnêni, after which the vicinity is called al-Ḳnênijjât. It belonged formerly to the Beni Taṛleb, who were driven out by the Beni Namr, a clan of the Kalb tribe. —

This Ḥâla may be compared with the basin of Ğûbt al-Ḳaʿara, where the name of al-Ḳnêni is preserved. The valley of al-Ḳnêni terminates in this basin at the wells of Râḥ, which may be identified with the wells of al-Ḳnêni. Al-Ḳnênijjât was the name of the five *šeʿibân* coming from the south to the Ğûbt al-Ḳaʿara. The Kalb and the Carmathians were safe in Ḥâla, or Ğûbt al-Ḳaʿara, as long as the army was not provided with all the water necessary for a long march through the desert. I surmise that the watering place of ad-Damʿâne is among the wells of al-Mḥejwer seventy kilometers east of al-Ḥâla. Tell an-Naṣer is south of al-Ḳnêni. Perhaps it derives its name from the leader of the Carmathians.

Jâḳût, *op. cit.*, Vol. 2, p. 598, records that the waters of ad-Damʿâne belonged to the Beni Namr of the Beni Zuhejr ibn Ğannâb, a clan of the Kalb tribe in Syria.

We halted in front of a small, narrow tent alongside of which we pitched my round one, and presently Blejhân's mother came to us, a little, thin, old woman, who had dyed her hair yellow in my honor. Greeting me, she proffered her hand and thanked me for treating her boy so well. The "boy," taller than she was by a head and a half, hugged and kissed her repeatedly; and the old lady, with tears in her eyes and a smile on her lips, complained because I had retained him so long, explaining that only four days ago she had received the tidings that he fared well, but that for more than forty days she had been grieving because she knew not what had become of him.

Even before our tent was up we were besieged by a crowd of curious Arabs who came in throngs to greet Blejhân and in quest of news. They settled nonchalantly by our fire, drank all our coffee, and would even have devoured our supper had I not told my fellows to take it into the tent. While we were endeavoring to ascertain the latitude, they inquired of Blejhân what we were trying to shoot with that instrument; and their interest in us was so persistent that during the night I had to admonish my guests many times to be more quiet, and finally Blejhân had to use both persuasion and force to disperse them. Again and again through the night there fell upon my ears the loving ejaculation of his mother, in whose tent he was lodging: "*Jâ wlejdi,* O, little boy of mine! . . ." Blejhân's father had died while the son was still very young, leaving the mother to rear the children alone. When later her eldest married son had also fallen and the wife had died, she adopted their children and cared for them as well as her own. In front of her tent were kneeling only eight camels, all the property she had. Her younger son was not at home now, having been sent to Šeṯâṯa by others to buy dates. Blejhân had purchased at al-Mijâḏîn a variety of garments for his mother and even for his brother's children and he also gave his mother five napoleons saved from his wages. The new fur coat he bought at al-Mijâḏîn he gave to Nejtûl, the eldest son of his deceased brother, while he himself was contented with his old, torn one.

BIJÂR AL-MLOṢI TO THE PLAIN OF AN-NÂẒRA

Monday, December 21, 1908. Immediately after sunrise I ascended with Tûmân and Zejd to the rocky summit that enclosed the al-Ḳaʿara basin on the side above the wells of al-Mloṣi (Fig. 3), intending from there to sketch a map of the entire vicinity. Our tent was about fifty paces east of the *šeʿîb* of al-Mloṣi,[16] in the channel and on the left bank of

FIG. 3—Rocky hill overlooking Bijâr al-Mloṣi.

which had been bored a number of wells (*ḥesjân*) from two to four meters deep, which were filled with water from twenty to forty centimeters deep. There were deeper wells in the hollow farther to the east.

Above the right bank of al-Mloṣi rises a high, rocky cliff consisting of two horizontal layers of porous sandstone. The upper layer, which is twelve meters thick, is solid; the lower, about twenty meters thick, is very soft and of a blue and red color. Because the lower one does not resist rain and wind as does the solid upper layer, large blocks are frequently torn away from it, splitting and breaking into sand and waste. Thus the upper crust is without foundation at some places,

[16] Al-Aḫṭal (according to al-Bekri, *op. cit.*, p. 538) refers to camping places in the hollows of Malṣ and ʿArʿar. — ʿArʿar is the present valley of ʿArʿar, and Malṣ is surely our al-Mloṣi, as both are in the former territory of the Taṛleb tribe and both are good camping grounds. Al-Aḫṭal, *Dîwân* (Salhani), p. 121, has Ḫabt instead of Malṣ, which is erroneous. Ḫabt as used by al-Aḫṭal denotes the basin of al-Ǧowf, but this basin did not belong to his tribe.

while at others it overhangs, and large boulders break off and roll into the ravine. Because of its multiformity, this rocky cliff, especially in its upper portion, resembles the ruins of an old castle. The ascent is obviously very difficult. Having crawled up on the soft substructure, I discovered spacious caves between it and the upper layer. The walls of the upper layer are almost perpendicular, and at their protected, more accessible points are covered with a multitude of various Bedouin tribal signs and primitive carvings of gazelles, camels, horses, and so on. In the hope of discovering inscriptions also, I crawled from boulder to boulder but found no writing except the thrice-recorded name of ʿAli.

Having climbed to the top of this rocky wall, we saw to the west a boundless, dark gray plain, in which rose only the low, flat crest of ʿAnz al-Mloṣi. To the south were visible the dark gaps of several ravines running to al-Ḳaʿara, the whole looking like a deep bowl specked with many desolate, dark brown areas.

We had barely reached the top when an Arab overtook us and asked what we were hunting for. The evening before, while we were ascertaining the latitude, the Arabs whispered among themselves that I probably was not preparing to shoot but undoubtedly was questioning the spirits as to the whereabouts of buried treasures. All Arabs are imbued with the idea that in al-Ḳaʿara there are many treasures, guarded by spirits; and everybody believed us to be in the quest of them, else why should we have visited the old ruins of ar-Reṣâfa, al-Ḥêr, and ar-Rḥaba? When I walked away from Tûmân (who was busy drawing a map) and began picking up minerals and wrapping each in a paper, the Bedouin begged me to show him what kind of stones I was looking for and to tell him how I should extract the gold. Having finished our work we returned to our tents, accompanied by a crowd of the curious who prayed me to show them what I had wrapped in the papers.

Near my tent I saw several *sulḳân* (dogs and bitches) which the Arabs offered to sell me. Blejhân in a whisper advised me not to buy any of these hounds, for their owners were demanding thrice their worth, and added that his cousin had two *sluḳi* dogs one of which he would be glad to give me. I understood good Blejhân's words but gave him no reply and bought no dog. When he afterwards called my attention three or four times to the advantage of having a good hound (*sluḳi*) I told him to bring forward the dog belonging to his relative to see if it would do. He produced it immediately. The *sluḳi* was not large but lank and very thin, about two years old. Mḥammad, who claimed to be a good judge of hunting dogs, declared that he was *zên* (good); whereupon I decided to accept the gift, and Tûmân immediately made a collar for Ḳaṭṭâf, as the dog was called, so that we could tie him to the tent. In return for the dog, I considered a gift worth two *meǧîdijjât* ($ 1.80) adequate; but when in the evening I asked Blejhân's opinion, he replied coolly that his uncle's son expected from me a present of at least two napoleons, this being the value he placed on the dog. Blejhân was active in the interest of his kin, demanding one *meǧîdijje* for his sister — in point of fact the eldest daughter of his deceased brother — because she had washed two shirts and two handkerchiefs for us; while for her brother Nejtûl, who had guarded our camels, he wanted one *meǧîdijje* and a gift besides. He even begged a revolver for this boy. Still, who could blame him when his kinsmen possessed nothing? In the desert the poor have no easy lot. When Blejhân wanted to obtain camel's milk for my breakfast he had to draw water for over three hours for the camels of the owner, in return for which he was then permitted to milk two camels the next morning. In the middle of December only such as have borne offspring in the summer yield milk, and even these give little because of the scarcity of fresh pasture.

Tuesday, December 22, 1908. I wished to visit the wells of al-Lmât in the valley of Ḥawrân, intending to go from there due west to the hill of at-Tinf. Zejd boasted that he was familiar with every nook south of al-Ḳaʿara; but from past experience I did not believe him and instructed Blejhân to inquire thoroughly as to the route we should take in order to avoid unnecessary deviations in the rugged district.

Before our departure Blejhân's aged mother came to me and, laying her hands on my shoulders, said:

"Behold, O Sheikh Mûsa! my son Blejhân is as near to me as her collar is to the turtle dove. Behold, I take this collar from my neck and lay it upon thy neck." These are the words with which a dying person appoints a guardian for his children. The mother was not sure that she might not depart to Allâh's realms before her son returned again, and implored me to take as much care of him as though I were his guardian.

Starting at 7.10 A. M., we proceeded first in a westerly direction, turning sharply toward the southeast after we had passed the wells of al-Mloṣi. It soon became apparent that neither Zejd nor Blejhân knew the way. It was not possible to maintain the southeasterly course from al-Mloṣi to al-Lmât, because the deep *še'ibân* of an-Neğîli and al-Ṛarri, in which numerous other short gullies converge, proved impassable for our camels. It was necessary first to go around them to the south and then to head for al-Lmât. Before us broadened a dark plain, to the east of which rose the high Tell an-Naṣer. The vegetation of the plain consisted of sparse *wubêra, rûṯe, šîḥ*, small bunches of *'alanda, ša'rân, ḳazḳâẓ*, and *nejtûl.* One unfamiliar with the district is apt to find himself frequently at the brink of a rocky cliff falling away vertically two to five meters to a ledge that slopes down to a fairly wide trough. Unable to descend the precipitous wall, the camels come to a stop and the rider has no choice but to turn about and make a long detour. From the bottom of the trough this formation of horizontal rocks reminds one of modern fortifications. It consists of from two to five strata of varying thickness and solidity, the softer crumbling and covering the base, while the more solid upper layers remain overhanging.

From 11.08 to 11.22 we rested. At 2.45 P. M. we reached the *še'îb* of al-Ṛarri north of the wells Ḳlejbât aš-Šubejče, where we found a small camp (*ferîž*) of the Sba'a. Blejhân had the lead and as the bottoms of the troughs were more level we could maintain our course better than we did before. After skirting the Tell an-Naṣer on the left, we halted from 3.28 to 4.35 to permit our camels to graze. The day was short, the camels were hungry, and during the night we could not release them.

We did not take fodder along for our camels; they had to seek their own food. Even while we were riding they would bend and pick the plants they passed — a habit most unpleasant for us when they were very hungry, for then, after stopping a minute to graze, they would canter on in a jerky fashion of their own, only to come to another stop half a minute later. It was better, therefore, for us to halt at any place affording good pasturage and not try to resume the journey until after the camels had satisfied their hunger. Our cartographical work impelled us to prefer pastures in proximity to heights, but of course the pastures must lie where they were shielded from sight. Besides, we had to have fuel for the preparation of our food, and it was not always easy to fulfil all these requirements at once. How often did we desire to make a sketch map of a vicinity from a hill, but there would be neither pasture nor fuel in the neighborhood! At other times we would find abundant pasture and plentiful fuel, but it would be in a hollow from which we had no outlook. If I did not stop in the first instance, Tûmân was displeased; in the second instance my other companions grumbled; and yet it was imperative to take the utmost care of our camels, for only through their efficiency could we make progress, and they could not give us good service unless they were well fed.

At seven o'clock we passed through the *šeʿîb* of al-ʿAwǧa and at 7.20 lodged for the night in the plain of an-Nâẓra near the vale of al-ʿAčerši.

REGION EAST OF AN-NÂẒRA

Wednesday, December 23, 1908. Starting at 6.12 A. M. we traversed the plain of an-Nâẓra toward the southeast. At our right were the beginnings of the *šeʿîb* of al-ʿObêlijje, which converges with Wâdi Ḥawrân at the wells Ḳulbân ar-Raṭba.

To the southwest we saw before us a precipitous wall with a flat crest, the northern edge of the table-land Ḳârt aš-Šwâwîž. North of it, upon the right side of Wâdi Ḥawrân, a stony plain broadens, forming an extension of an-Nâẓra between Riǧlet aẓ-Ẓulla and Riǧlet aẓ-Ẓaka, both of which unite with Wâdi Ḥawrân, the first northeast of Ḳulbân al-Lmât, the second by the well of aš-Šrejfijje southeast of Ḳlejbât al-Žaʿadijje and Ṛadîr az-Zwejrît. Still farther to the northeast there merge with the vale of Ḥawrân the *šeʿibân* of al-Ḥasne and al-Ḥsejne, which join at Žaltat al-Ḥeǧra. Several kilometers northeast of Žaltat al-Ḥeǧra, which is also called Ḥeǧrat Ḥawrân, are the wells of al-Mḥejwer on the route Darb as-Sâʿi. In its lower part Wâdi Ḥawrân runs almost directly eastward, and by ʿAḳlat Ḥawrân is joined on the right by the *šeʿîb* of al-Halba, and beyond the ʿAḳlat Ḥawrân by the *šeʿîb* of al-Asad with a spring of the same name. About fifteen kilometers west of the Euphrates in the Ḥawrân valley are the rain wells Ṯemâjel as-Seḥel.

The route Darb as-Sâʿi, which terminates at the city of Hît, leads from the wells of al-Mloṣi to the wells of Râḥ and al-Mḥejwer, and traverses the lowland Fejẓat ʿÂmež, through which also winds a valley of the same name. This valley originates in the highland northeast of Ḳârt aš-Šwâwîž, southwest of the solitary mesas of al-Židr and al-Židrên. In the central portion are the rain wells, Mķejr ab-al-Žâṣed and Moķr ᶜÂmež, about fifteen kilometers apart; between them, west of Tlejl aṣ-Ṣaķķâr, is the influx of the short Riğlet az-Zķâķijje in the *šeᶜîb* of ᶜÂmež.[17]

East of the lower portion of this *šeᶜîb* rise the precipitous walls of the Ķârt aṭ-Ṭlejḥa, which enclose on the west the lowland of al-ᶜEmeše. From this lowland, which falls off somewhat to the east, there issue numerous valleys, the northernmost of which, Riğlet al-Bezem, originates where the lowland of ᶜÂmež merges into that of al-ᶜEmeše southwest of Riğm aṣ-Ṣâbûn and Ṛadîr al-ᶜAwağ on the route Darb as-Sâᶜi. Farther to the southeast the Darb as-Sâᶜi leads from Ṛadîr al-ᶜAwağ past Ķsejr Ḫabbâz to the village of al-Kubejsa, west of which are the springs ᶜAjn Zaᶜzûᶜa and ᶜAjn al-Ḥeğijje. The valley of al-Bezem, which comes from west of al-Kubejsa, turns to the east and is joined on the right by the combined Riğlet ab-al-ᶜOfejn, Riğlet aš-Šwa', and Abu Žalta, which originate in the lowland Fejẓat al-ᶜEmeše southeast of Ḫabra ab-ar-Rmam. The Riğlet umm Deḫân winds along the southeastern fringe of Fejẓat al-ᶜEmeše and is joined on the left by the short valley of aṯ-Ṯmejli al-Wasîṭ, and, beyond the oasis of aṯ-Ṯmejl northeast of the solitary cones of aṯ-Ṯadejjên, by a longer valley of aṯ-Ṯmejli, which united with the water of al-Ḫnej[18] joins the Riğlet umm Deḫân to make the *šeᶜîb* of al-Eķêreᶜ. Northwest of the settlement of aṯ-Ṯmejl gushes the naphtha spring of Ab-al-Žîr, west of which is the *želîb* of al-Bwêrde. This well is in the valley of al-Mḥammadi.

PLAIN OF AN-NÂẒRA TO NEAR ḪABRA AZ-ZERĶA; THE ḤAMÂD

To the east-southeast of us numerous paths worn to a considerable depth into the ground by footsteps led toward two solitary hills lying northwest of the well of al-Lmât. The plain through which they pass is dark brown, almost black, and is covered with flints (*ṣawwân*). In the depressions, however, grow *šîḥ*, *žetâde*, *ğirğîr*, *ķaẓķâẓ*, and also here and there *mḥarût*, the roots of which are dug out and baked. Though somewhat bitter, they are nevertheless palatable.

Near al-Mloṣi the Arabs had told us that the chief, Eben Štêwi, was camping at al-Lmât, whereas those whose camps we had passed at al-Ṛarri maintained that he had already

[17] I seek in the plain of ᶜÂmež the camping place of Uᶜâmeķ. Al-Bekri, *Muᶜğam* (Wüstenfeld), p. 113, places Uᶜâmeķ between Mesopotamia and Syria. The poet al-Aḫṭal mentions a defeat of the tribe of Kalb in Uᶜâmeķ. — The ᶜÂmež of our day is the dialect rendering of the classic Uᶜâmeķ, and its location agrees with that claimed by al-Bekri.
Jâķût, *Muᶜğam* (Wüstenfeld), Vol. 1, p. 313, represents Uᶜâmeķ as a valley; al-Aḫṭal and ᶜAdi ibn ar-Riķâᶜ also mention it. It is apparent from these sources that the plain of Uᶜâmeķ, penetrated by numerous valleys that offer abundant pasture, stretches out in the environs of the settlement of ᶜÂna. — ᶜÂna is the nearest larger settlement in the vicinity of our ᶜÂmež.

[18] According to Jâķût, *op. cit.*, Vol. 2, p. 351, al-Ḥinj is located between Irak and Syria, in the desert of as-Samâwa.

left for the valley of al-ʿÎdân. The Arabs likewise reported that the wells of al-Lmât were being utilized by all the raiding parties and brigands that come from the east and southeast, and they said the Sbaʿa camping in al-Ḳaʿara had been informed that a large group of Šammar from Neǧd had started north upon a war campaign. Fearful of meeting this array in the neighborhood of al-Lmât, Blejhân prevailed upon me not to visit these wells unless we should sight the camp of Eben Štêwi from a distance. He proposed that we should not go direct to the mountain of at-Tinf, but detour to ʿAnz al-Mloṣi, where we could replenish our supply of water. Loath to expose myself and my companions to any unnecessary danger, I scanned the route to Ḳulbân al-Lmât very intently. At 10.35 we were barely ten kilometers distant from them but could not as yet see any camels or any smoke rising above a camp. Blejhân maintained that the wells must surely be deserted and that Eben Štêwi had probably left for al-ʿÎdân. Since we could get water at ʿAnz al-Mloṣi and so did not need to go all the way to the wells of al-Lmât, I decided at 10.40 to retreat northwestward.

About an hour later we found six riders directly behind us and, seizing our weapons, turned toward them. One of the unknown pursuers darted ahead of the others and approached us at a gallop, his hair and shirt sleeves flopping in the air and his hand clenching a rifle. Who was he? What did he want? When he came up to us he reined in his mare abruptly and addressed us:

"Who are ye?"

"Those thou seest. Who art thou?"

"He whom thou seest."

At that moment Blejhân recognized in him one of his kindred, a Sbêʿi, and he told us why we had been pursued. Eben Štêwi, it seemed, was indeed camping at al-Lmât, not in the immediate vicinity of the wells, however, but out of sight in a deep basin; that was why we could not see his tents from the northwest. His herds of camels were at pasture in the ravines south of the wells Ḳulbân ar-Raṭba. Although we had seen neither his camels nor his tents, we had ourselves been observed by a sentry who lay hidden behind a pile of stones upon a hill and who, noting our sudden change of direction, gave the alarm; whereupon a cavalcade of horsemen and camel riders had been despatched after us.

On learning the reason for our deflection, the pursuers withdrew, but after a while two riders armed with spears darted up to us. The older man, whose nose had been cut off, touched me with his spear in the back and my camel in the neck, and demanded roughly that we turn about and visit the chief Eben Štêwi.

"Greet thou Eben Štêwi in my name and tell him that I am the man he visited at the wells of al-Bârde," I answered our tormenter; whereupon his companion, after scrutinizing me closely, declared that he knew me, adding that he had escorted Eben Štêwi to my fire, where we had served him with excellent tea. Accordingly, we were allowed to proceed. About a quarter of an hour later, however, still another horseman approached us, who did nothing but ride alongside of Blejhân for some time and inquire about everything that had occurred in the west, north, and east. We, who had come from the west and had visited the north and the east, were able to give him much interesting news, which he wanted to divulge at greater length to his chief.

Toward the north, as we rode on, we noted the black hillock of Tell ʿObejd, lying on the right side of the *šeʿîb* of ʿÛd al-Mrejjeḥ north of the head of the ʿÛd al-Ḳṣejjer. On the right side of Wâdi Ḥawrân, at the place where ʿÛd al-Ḳṣejjer runs into it, projects the cone of Zôr Ḥawrân, south of which is the deep rain well Ṛadîr az-Zwejrît.

At twelve o'clock we were overtaken by a Ṣlubi mounted upon a white ass, who also sought information concerning the camps of the various tribes. Far behind him we noted a migrating family of Ṣlejb. When he had left us I proposed to stop and dine, but Blejhân urged that we go on or else the Ṣlejb would devour all the food. From 12.35 to 2.36 P. M. we were upon a wide elevation from which we had an excellent view. Next we proceeded through a plain overgrown with various perennials, where we sighted about twenty camels. At 5.40 we encamped at the end of the plain, for we had reached a rugged territory through which we could proceed only by daylight. The night was very cold; the ground, our coverings, and even our water bags froze.

Thursday, December 24, 1908. In the morning everything was covered with white frost and we ourselves were shivering with cold when we resumed our journey at 5.47 A. M. After eight o'clock we spied a herd of gazelles and a little while later saw a large herd of camels coming out of a *šeʿîb* in the low, flat Ṭaraḳ al-ʿAnz (or ʿAnz al-Mloṣi). At 8.53 we discovered tents in the valley of al-Mloṣi, and Blejhân turned toward them to inquire after the camps of his kinsmen. This kept us waiting until 11.20, when we went on to the Ṭaraḳ al-ʿAnz, where we were told the tent of Blejhân's mother was located. Our camels grazed along on the *rûṯe, nejtûl, šilwa,* and *šîḥ* plants, while Blejhân took the animal that carried the water bags and rode with it to his mother. He returned at 1.39 P. M. with the bags more than half full, and we kept on our way until 3.16 to the northwest and then stopped in a side gully, where our camels grazed upon *erǧa* (*ǧerrejd* in the dialect of the ʿAmârât), *drejhme, samna, šiḳḳâra, rûṯe,* and *snejsle* plants.

ʿAnz al-Mloṣi, which appears from the south and east like a precipitous rocky wall, forms the edge of the plain into which we entered at 4.24. I shall never forget the overwhelming feeling that gripped me upon passing into this infinite plain called al-Ḥamâd (Fig. 4). Nowhere is there any elevation; everything is flat and level; below is the desert; above, the sky; and between them, man. How small yet how near to the Creator one seems to be! The heavens are near wherever one turns, and it seems as if one must reach them where they touch the earth. My eyes were drawn to the western horizon, where the sun was setting on the limitless sea of plain, immersed in a golden light in which every mean little plant stem glittered like silver. The lowest parts of the horizon were bluish, and above hung clouds like stalactites with rosy centers and purple borders. Above the sun, up to the very dome of the heavens, were transparent clouds that looked as if woven from a multitude of white ostrich feathers with patches of blue sky appearing through them here and there. Gradually the stalactites acquired an olive tinge, the higher ones turning a pale yellow and then orange. Below them the western sky blazed like molten gold, while in the east gray blended with the bluish tint of the south and north. Suddenly the desert became ash-gray except for the last rays of the setting sun. It was Christmas eve.

All at once, above the descending sun, the narrow sickle of a new moon swung into the sky, and Blejhân, lifting his eyes and extending his hands toward it, greeted it thus:

"New Moon, O Master! O Dispenser of Happiness! (*jâ helâl, jâ sajjed, jâ saʿîd!*)"

All this time, enveloped in our mantles and holding our loaded carbines in readiness, we had been clinging close to our camels as they hastened westward with long strides. At 6.05, when they knelt in the valley of Samḥân, we tied their front legs, and ourselves lay down upon the frozen ground. That Christmas eve I shall never forget.

FIG. 4—Plain of the Ḥamâd.

Friday, December 25, 1908. Although we had nearly perished with cold during the night, we dared not kindle a fire in the morning; for we were stopping in the Ḥamâd, and in the early dawn the smoke would have revealed our presence. Shivering with cold (temperature at 7 A. M.: 1.5° C), we rode from 5.15 until 6.53 A. M., when the first rays of the sun appeared. Then we stopped and basked in them until 7.31. We were journeying through the first of the *šeʿibân* of al-Herijjân, where there was no *nejtûl*. At 8.02 we crossed the Sowḥ al-Heri, in which there is the Ṛadîr an-Nâḳa. Another rain pool, Ṛadîr Sabʿ Ḳarṭât, lies in the valley of Samḥân south of the enormous boulder of al-Weli abu Ruẓuma, which the Ṣlejb worship as sacred. The *šeʿibân* of al-Herijjân, originating near the rain pools Ḥabâri Ḥbûb, form shallow, hardly perceptible river beds, with their level surfaces coated with a coarse, black sand in which nothing will grow. Only in the depressions (*rowẓ, rijâẓ*), where more moisture gathers, flourish *nejtûl, rûṯe, ḳaẓḳâẓ, šidd al-ğemal, îd abu ḥmâr, kalša, erbijjân,* and *ḥemri.*

From 9.56 to 11.42 our camels grazed in one such depression. North of us the spirits of the desert were at play, fanning the sand into funnels (*ʿağâğ*), which flew high up and raced madly through the air; while to the south they showed us a lake surrounded with fresh vegetation. Tûmân allowed himself to be deceived by the spirits into recording this lake on the map. The plants and the shrubs on the edge of the water appeared unusually large, from a distance resembling at intervals a group of riders on camels. The temperature was rising; it became almost hot.

At 12.40 P. M. we crossed the *še'îb* of al-Waleǧ, as the beginning of the *še'îb* of aṣ-Ṣwâb is called. This trough originates far to the south, at the Ḫabâri al-Maẓârî' not far to the northeast of the mesa Ḳârt an-Neẓâjem, and on the left is joined by the long *še'îb* of al-Merbâḥ. Between these valleys is the Ḫabra ummu Člâb and to the north of them the Ḫabâri-š-Šîḥijjât. The *še'ibân* of aṣ-Ṣwejbât, running on the left side into al-Waleǧ, gradually deepen, and between them rise swells from four to ten meters in height. Nowhere was there pasturage to be seen, until at three o'clock in the *še'îb* of Berîm al-Bint we found a small patch, on which grew a variety of perennials. There we stopped. The Berîm al-Bint comes from the Ḫabâri Zênât al-Ma' north of the Ḳârt an-Neẓâjem and converges with al-Waleǧ.

The Ḳârt an-Neẓâjem is merely a projection of the long, broad upland of Ḥazm 'Enâza; from it there extends to the north-northwest as far as the hill of at-Tinf a wide, level swell which forms a divide between the Euphrates, the lowland of ar-Raḥba, and the deep basin of al-Ǧwejf on the borders of the Ḥawrân. East as well as west of this divide the desert is almost entirely level, the valleys are broad and shallow, and rain water gathers in many pools. To the north of an-Neẓâjem, upon the western slope of the upland near Tlûl al-Basâtîn, are the Ḫabâri al-Basâtîn and north of them the Ḫabâri Ruḳubân.

At 4.11 we left Berîm al-Bint and at 4.40 passed through the valley of Ḫwejmât, which fills the *ḫabra* of the same name and north of the Ḳulbân al-Msejlîtât enters into the valley of al-Mijâh. Northwest of the Ḫabra Ḫwejmât is the Ḫabra ammu Mwejl, and southwest of that the Ḫabra Leḳṭa. At seven o'clock we encamped. Christmas in the desert of al-Ḥamâd!

Saturday, December 26, 1908. Setting out at 5.15 A.M., we sunned ourselves from 6.55 until 7.30 in the *še'îb* of Leḳṭa. To the northwest rose the dark solitary hill Tell al-Ṛurâb.[19]

[19] Jâḳût, *Mu'ǧam* (Wüstenfeld), Vol. 3, p. 779, refers to a place, Ṛurâb, in Syria. He avers this on authority of the poet 'Adi ibn ar-Riḳâ', a contemporary of the sons and successors of 'Abdalmalek, who mentions the camps between Ṛurâb and al-Ilâha in as-Samâwa. — Al-Ilâha is the Lâha of the present, therefore I identify the Ṛurâb of Jâḳût's day with the Ṛurâb of ours, between which and the height of Lâha the Bedouins like to camp in winter.

Elsewhere (*ibid.*, Vol. 4, p. 32) Jâḳût refers to a place of the name of Ḳubla in the territory of the tribes of Kalb and Kilâb. According to the assertion of a poet, the tribe

To the south-southwest was a mighty swell, running from the south-southeast to the north-northwest and joining on the west with the hill of at-Tinf and on the east with the lower hill of at-Tnejf. At 8.40 we had at the right the Ḫabra Šaʿlân and at the left far to the south the Ḫabra aṣ-Ṣlubijje; and we could see smaller *ḫabâri* scattered about far and wide. Sometimes a plain slopes imperceptibly, forming depressions measuring in some cases from ten to twenty square meters and in other instances several square kilometers, which gather the rain water of the zone. Such a depression in the level desert when filled with water is called a *ḫabra*. The water often runs into another hollow, or even into a third or a fourth, all of them covered with a yellow clay in which nothing can grow. Various plants, however, edge the borders and flourish in the small, shallow grooves through which the water finds its way.

From 10.30 to 12.10 we were in the opening of the valley of al-Mijâh, northeast of the hill of at-Tnejf. Going west-northwest, we reached at 12.50 P. M. the road Darb as-Sâʿi, which we followed westward. By this route a special carrier (*sâʿi*) brought the English mail from Damascus to Bagdad, whence it was sent to al-Baṣra and India. The postmaster who contracted for this delivery from the English Government ordinarily lived in Bagdad and kept six mounted messengers, one of whom left Bagdad for Damascus every eighth day, returning the same way. From Damascus to the settlement of Ḍmejr he used a horse, from Ḍmejr to Hît a camel. At Hît he crossed the Euphrates in a boat and thence rode to Bagdad, in winter upon a camel, in summer upon a horse, because in summer the dangerous flies would have killed the camel. The trip from Damascus to Bagdad took regularly eleven days. A round trip between the two places consumed forty days, for which the messenger received from the contractor three pounds sterling, out of which he had to defray his living expenses. His gross earnings were much larger, however, as he often took along various nomadic merchants (Kubejsât) and camel traders (ʿAkejl) who rode his spare animals or entrusted to him various pieces of baggage to be

of Kalb camped between Ḳurrab and the valleys of ar-Rajjân. — It seems to me that Jâḳût speaks here of the former territory of the Kalb and Kilâb tribes, as is also recorded by al-Hamdâni. Ḳurrab then would be identical with our al-Ḳurâb south of Tudmor and would constitute the northern border of the tribal territory; the southern one would be formed by ar-Rajjân gulches at the northern foot of the Eǧa' ridge just north of Ḥâjel. Formerly the possession of the entire desert of ʿÂleǧ, or the Nefûd, was in the hands of the Kalb tribe.

Abu-l-Faḍâ'il, *Marâṣid* (Juynboll), Vol. 2, p. 386, calls by the name of Ḳubla the entire territory between ar-Rajjân and Ḳurrab.

delivered for them at Bagdad, at Damascus, or at some camp in the desert.

To the north of us appeared the flat, long summit of the Ṭaraḳ az-Zeḳf, at the northern base of which is a large rain pool of the same name, and farther to the south the Ḫabra al-Bowli, likewise filled by rain water. After one o'clock we perceived in the west a thin dust cloud and, a few minutes after, I announced to my escorts:

"There are camel riders in front of us (*ǧejš bwaǧhana*)!"

On the route Darb as-Sâʿi was a large troop on camels. Who could they be, well-wishers or foes? In numbers they were much stronger than we were. Would there be a combat? Distressing thought! Although they were riding slowly, might they not suddenly rush upon us at a gallop? We spied among them several men on foot and two animals bearing heavy loads. Were they a band of marauders returning with loot? To what tribe did they belong? Suddenly one of the men rode out of the group, made his animal execute various fancy turns, and rejoined the group; whereupon Blejhân straightway brought his camel to the front and imitated the movements, saying:

"See thou, Mûsa, they do the *taʿrîẓ*; they are indicating that they are friends."

The strangers proved to be ʿAḳejl, camel traders, on their way from Egypt and Damascus to their families in Bagdad. *Al-ḥamdu lillâh!* One of the men, who had known me in Damascus, approached and informed me that an-Nûri eben Šaʿlân was no longer camping at Tlûl al-ʿIjâṯ, but was in al-Bowzelijjât south of the rain pools of Sejḳal. As we had but little water left, I directed my companions to inquire of the ʿAḳejl about the pools in the neighborhood of the as-Sâʿi route. The ʿAḳejl asserted that no rain pool in the vicinity would be filled with water now, but that we should find enough water to fill our bags and to water our camels in the depressions of the level rocks in the Sowḥ Murra valley west of the Ḫabra aš-Šhami. Immediately Zejd began to boast of his familiarity with the place, but I did not believe him and again directed Blejhân and Mḥammad to obtain complete information. They stayed with the ʿAḳejl so long that they did not catch up with us until two o'clock, as we were riding through the Ḫôr al-Maškûḳa. From 3.30 to 5.05 the camels were at pasture. We encamped as early as 6.10, for the western and northern horizons were becoming obscured by thick, dark clouds, and presently lightning began to play and it began to sprinkle. We put up the round tent, in order to protect the baggage as well as ourselves, but when the shower came it lasted only an hour. Before midnight the sky cleared and it became bitterly cold.

VICINITY OF ḪABRA AZ-ZERḲA TO ḪABÂRI SEJḲAL

Sunday, December 27, 1908. In the morning the tent was frozen so stiff that we had to carry out all the stores and make a fire in it in order to thaw the canvas (temperature at 6 A. M.: 0° C) so as not to break it in folding. Our camels were covered with hoar frost. Starting at seven o'clock we rode in a plain covered with coarse gravel, in which there were small, sparsely scattered patches of thin perennials. To the south we noted a projection of the wide elevation of Ḫašmet az-Zerḳa, in front of which, nearer to us, gleamed the yellow clay of an evaporated rain pool of the same name. South of the Ḫašmet az-Zerḳa and southwest of at-Tinf rise the *šeʿibân* of al-Ḥrejṯât and al-Mdejsîsât, which flow through an almost level tract supplying the rain pools of Merfijje and Ḫarğa and running into the valley of al-Mdejsîs. This valley emerges from the hills Tlûl al-Basâtîn, contributes to the Ḫabra az-Zwejrijje, and winds towards the basin of al-Ǧwejf between the Ṭaraḳ aḏ-Ḏîb on the south and the Ḫašm al-Kbûd on the north.

After 8.30 A. M. we rode into the opening of the *šeʿîb* of aṣ-Ṣowṭ, which terminates in the Ḫabâri Ṯlejǧwât west of the Tell al-Ḳurâb. From 10.28 to 12.16 our camels grazed, but they could not satisfy their hunger, for all the plants in the valley were dead: no rain had fallen in that locality during the past year. At 2.25 we were at the Ḫabra aš-Šḥami and at 2.50 we reached a small basin enclosed by six groups of low hills named Rumâmîn aš-Šḥami. There we found several circular walls, about forty centimeters high, built of stones without the use of mortar and each provided with a narrow entrance. In the middle of one of them was a four-cornered grave (Fig. 5). South of ar-Rumâmîn protrudes the cone Tell Ferîda, and east of that the dark projection of the Ḫašm al-Kbûd, at the eastern base of which are the Ḫabâri al-Ḥûḳ and at the western the Ḫabra Melḥem. From 3.30 to 5.00 we were confined in the swale Sowḥ Murra (Fig. 6), which comes from the Ṭaraḳ al-Halba and converges with the *šeᶜîb* of al-Hejl, as the lower or western part of al-Mdejsîs is called. Zejd and Blejhân searched in vain for pools of rain water. At 7.05 we encamped in a small depression.

FIG. 5—A grave in the hills of Rumâmîn aš-Šḥami.

Monday, December 28, 1908. In the morning all our baggage and coverings were again enveloped in hoar frost and frozen hard. When we started out at 5.57 A. M. we could barely see the heads of our camels, so thick was the moist, frost-laden fog. At seven o'clock we were traversing the *šeᶜîb* of Sabᶜ Bijâr, or Swaʾ,[20] about ten kilometers south of two low cones that have at their base wells of the same

[20] Jâḳût, *op. cit.*, Vol. 3, p. 172, repeats the assertions of different men about the location of Suwaʾ. According to some it is a watering place of the Bahraʾ clan in the desert of as-Samâwa, according to others a valley issuing from the sandy desert of Dahnaʾ.—

The Arab geographers define as as-Samâwa the waste that spreads from the present sandy desert of an-Nefûd in the south almost to Palmyra in the north and from the Euphrates in the east to the eastern base of the Ḥawrân in the west. The assertion that the Suwaʾ valley issues from the Dahnaʾ was made because of the erroneous belief that through the entire length of Arabia, from south to north, winds a valley, in the northern part of which are Ḥâjel, Ḳurâḳir, and Suwaʾ. Though these watering places are a reality, the valley is a mere phantom.

The poet ar-Ruḳajjât, *Dîwân* (Rhodokanakis), p. 89, in telling of his journey from Syria upon a mule to visit his sweetheart in the vicinity of al-Baṣra, mentions that he saw in the order named: the Ḥawrân, al-ᶜAwîr, Sawaʾ, al-Ḳarjatân, and ᶜAjn at-Tamr. —

Al-Ḳarjatân is identical with the present settlement of al-Ḳarjatejn (al-Žerjitejn), and al-ᶜAwîr is identical with the watering place of al-Bârde. South of them is Swaʾ, whence it is possible to see the dark hills of the Ḥawrân.

name. These wells we did not approach for fear of meeting robbers or raiders, for, since they are the only fresh-water pools in a wide territory, they are much frequented by robbers.

From 9.08 to 11.03 our camels grazed on the dry *šîḥ*. At 11.20 we sighted again the high mountain Ǧebel ʿÂde, so prom-

FIG. 6—Valley Sowḥ Murra.

inent in the northwestern Ḥamâd; at 12.40 P. M. we crossed our route of three weeks before (see above, p. 30) in the valley Telʿet as-Sâʿi. On our left we noted two peaks and on our right a space enclosed by a circular stone wall with a grave in the center like the one we had seen at Rumâmîn aš-Šḥami. Blejhân alleged that such graves were relics of the ancient inhabitants of the Ḥamâd and that the Ṣlejb still worshiped them. The district, a rolling plain with numerous rain pools, was very stony, even the hollows being coated with coarse gravel.

To the north rose the snow-covered frontier ridge of ar-Rawâḳ, enveloped in clouds and enriched by the lustrous glitter of its peaks. At our left lay a camping ground that had evidently been occupied but a little while before. There was the deepened fireplace, upon three stones of which a kettle had been placed; heaps of fuel lay about as well as improvised beds of stones and brush, and in places camels had lodged. A short time before, men had been there, perhaps relatives and friends; but now all was silent. We longed for companions. We had water for that day only, and for two days we had been unable to bake bread because we lacked flour. In the camp we could have supplied ourselves with both, inquired the way to the camp of an-Nûri, and rested; but the camp was deserted.

My companions had failed to find rain water in the Sowḥ Murra. Blejhân had admitted his unfamiliarity with this *šeʿîb*, while the guide Zejd, who had boasted that he knew every stone in the region, made no effort to hunt for water but was the first to eat and drink and the last to work at guiding us. He was totally ignorant and yet he staunchly maintained that he had the northern half of Arabia in his palm. Such a guide I had never met before. Every morning I had to rouse him at least ten times; still he would not get up until the camels had left for the pastures and the fire was built or until the baggage had been loaded. He never gathered the fuel but sat contentedly by the fire, hunted for lice, and warmed his dirty feet. Whenever he saw us preparing to load baggage he would immediately begin to pray, though he offered no prayers at any other time. His capacity for deception and greediness knew no bounds.

At 2.35 we found in the plain a small area where *šaʿrân*, *nejtûl*, *šîḥ*, and *ḥemri* were growing, and we remained there until 4.05. After 4.35 we plodded on through narrow strips of basalt and sand. The stones ranged from brown to black and the sand was red (*ǧamharat al-arẓ*). Before five o'clock we had lost the Darb as-Sâʿi, which here traverses the dry beds of vast rain pools, and had crossed innumerable paths leading in all directions. There were watering places to the west and south and pastures to the north and east. With the help of my compass I maintained the westerly course, despite Zejd's attempts to persuade my companions not to follow me but to take one of the paths which would surely bring them to Ḍmejr. Presently the sky darkened and it began to drizzle, so we encamped at 7.05. The rain ceased in a few minutes but was followed by a thick, moisture-laden mist, which, spreading over the desert on the wings of an icy southeast wind, was converted into rime that covered us, our animals, and everything about us.

Tuesday, December 29, 1908. At six o'clock we mounted our camels, although the mist was thickening and descending in infinitesimal icy drops which immediately froze. Blejhân called this mist *čitâm*, declaring that it was neither rain nor fog (*kubejs*). After the mist had settled somewhat the air cleared, and at 8.32 A. M. we perceived a camp to the south and to the northwest large herds of camels drinking from the Ṛadîr aṭ-Ṭarfâwi. Turning in that direction we stopped near the herds at 9.10, and I despatched Blejhân and Zejd with the camels and water bags to a rain pool of the Ḫabâri Sejḳal to water the camels and to inquire after the whereabouts of Prince an-Nûri. Should the Prince's camp be near, Blejhân was not to take water; should he be camping far away, however, he was to fill both the bags. The men had just started when two camel riders arrived, sat down near our fire, and sought to find out where we came from; receiving evasive answers to their questions, they next asked if they might breakfast with us. Pretending to have an insufficient supply of water, we directed them to the camp close by, whereupon they departed.

When Blejhân was on his way back we perceived from a distance that he had filled both the bags, and therefore we concluded that an-Nûri was camping far away. Blejhân, who was sodden with mire, told us he had filled the bags with thin mud rather than water. He said that the water in the rain pool of Sejḳal was only about twenty centimeters deep and was being drawn upon by several thousands of camels, which had trampled in the morass, polluted the water with their excretions, and converted it into thin mud. The whereabouts of an-Nûri's camp he was not able to ascertain. He had heard merely that the Prince had left al-Bowzelijje and headed toward the fort of Burḳuᶜ and the rain ponds of al-Ḫwejmât, bound for the depression of Sirḥân. It was, then, necessary for us likewise to turn southward.

Our journey from the east to the west was now terminated, and our guide Zejd, who was to bring us to Ḍmejr, was at liberty to return home. I had intended to take him to the nearest camp where he could have awaited a courier or some similar opportunity to be conducted to his tribe. But Zejd had acquired such a liking for us that he resolved not to leave us; he wished to serve us in the manner of Blejhân and to defend us from his kinsmen. He had therefore persuaded or intimidated Mḥammad and Blejhân to such an extent that both came to plead for him, appealing to me to keep him in my service and not to discharge him until we reached the oasis of al-Ǧowf, as we might encounter raiders of the

Dahâmše tribe, the enemies of the Rwala, from whom he could liberate us. I objected that on the way to the depression of Sirḥân we might meet with robbers or marauders of the Ahâli al-Ǧebel, Šammar, Šarârât, aẓ-Ẓefîr, or of almost any other tribe, and ordered fourteen *meǧîdijjât* ($ 13.60) to be paid to Zejd for his services.

AT CAMP OF RŠÊD EBEN SMEJR; THE WELD ʿALI

Leaving at 11.25 in a southeasterly direction, we reached at 2.17 P.M. the tent of Chief Ršêd, or Ršejd, eben Smejr (Fig. 7), whom I wanted to question as to the intentions of an-Nûri and to ask for a dependable guide. He came out to meet me with a joyful greeting, praising Allâh that he beheld me alive and well; for he and an-Nûri had received news only a short time before that I had been attacked, robbed, and murdered at the Euphrates by the ʿAmârât.

"*Al-ḥamdu lillâh* that it is not so!" he cried. He told me of his return from Damascus twelve days before and said that two days afterward an-Nûri, persuaded by Nawwâf, had set out toward al-Ǧowf. He thought he could get one of the Freǧe clan, who was camping with his men, to guide me to him. To this man he offered at first six and later eight *meǧîdijjât* ($ 5.40; $ 7.20) to take me to the tent of an-Nûri, but the Freǧi demanded eighteen *meǧîdijjât* ($ 16.20) to be paid immediately, before he would start; and, in addition, stipulated other conditions which influenced me against him. Ršêd sent for another man and later for still a third and tried to negotiate with them, but neither was willing to leave the camp and venture into the unknown, especially since no one could tell when they would be able to return from the south to their camp in the north. Meanwhile the sun was setting. Suddenly arose an outcry of alarm: an enemy had appeared near by! A few minutes later all the fighters were galloping on horseback toward the southwest, where a herdsman had sighted an unknown rider upon a hill. Darkness descended so rapidly, however, that the horses could not make much progress in the volcanic district and the riders returned, none the wiser.

Ršêd eben Smejr was the head chief of the tribe of Weld ʿAli. It is said that formerly the name of the tribe was Âl Wahab and that the tribe was divided into the Âl Nebhân and the Âl ʿAli. The Âl Nebhân are now called Menâbhe and the Âl ʿAli are called Weld ʿAli.

The Menâbhe are subdivided into:
Âl Ḥağğâğ, consisting of the clans of: al-Ḫamâʿle (chief: ʿAnejzân eben Šenn)
al-Fuḳara' („ Muṭlaḳ âl Fežîr)
al-Meṣâlîḫ, comprising the clan of aṣ-Ṣḳara (chiefs: ʿAžîl eben Jaʿîš and Ḥsejn eben Šeḳa')
al-Ḥsene, (chief: Mḥammad eben Melḥem)

The Menâbhe formerly camped southwest of Tejma as far as Ḫajbar. Later a part of them moved north, a circumstance which explains why there are so many camps of the tribe in the vicinity of Tejma as well as northeast of Damascus. The head chief of the Menâbhe in the north is Mḥammad eben Melḥem, in the south Muṭlaḳ âl Fežîr.

The Weld ʿAli are divided into the Weld ʿAli proper, or Ẓana Mifreğ, and al-Âjde, or al-Ajde. Both camp either east of Damascus or near Tejma.

The Weld ʿAli of the north obey the chief Ršêd eben Smejr and consist of the clans:

Âl ʿAwwâẓ (to which Eben Smejr belongs) Âl Mžejbel
al-ʿAṭejfât al-Ğeḏâlme
al-Ğebbâra at-Twâleʿa
aṭ-Ṭlûḥ ar-Rubejlât
ad-Dumğân al-Mrejḫât

The Âjde of the north consist of the clans:
al-Mešâžže, or Mešâdže (head chief: Sulṭân eben Saṭṭâm eben (or âl) Ṭajjâr)
al-Ḥamâmde
al-Mašṭa'

The Weld ʿAli who camp in the south obey the chief Farḥân al-Ajdi. Clans:
Šemlân
Ğrajde
ʿAbâdle

Ršêd advised me to pass the night in his tent and not to depart until the enemy had withdrawn. I accepted the advice and questioned him as to the route we should follow. He described it minutely and offered me such of his supplies as I might need. When I thanked him and assured him that we could get along with the remainder of our supplies, he summoned Mḥammad and made him swear to tell truthfully what we lacked. Finding out that we had no flour, he ordered our flour sack to be brought and filled it with his own hands.

"Shouldst thou be still lacking anything, O Sheikh Mûsa, say so," he admonished me. "Cast off thy modesty! All that is mine is also thine."

"Thy goodness gladdens me," I responded, "and gratitude toward thee hath taken root deep in my heart. How could I hesitate to accept things from Sheikh Ršêd, whose bounty is known in the west and in the east among the settlers and among the nomads of the wide desert?"

To this the gathering in the tent nodded in assent, and each guest, taking hold of his shirt at the breast with two fingers and flapping it, mumbled, "I believe thee, I believe thee."

FIG. 7—Chief Ršêd eben Smejr.

In the evening I directed Mḥammad to close an agreement with the best of the guides, in order that we might get an early start in the morning, and then we lay down by our stores in front of Ršêd's tent.

Wednesday, December 30, 1908. Late in the night there came to Ršêd four warriors of the Ešâǧeʿa clan, who said they had undertaken a robbing raid against the Fedʿân and upon their return found that their families had gone south with an-Nûri. Hurrying to overtake them, they said they had stopped at Ršêd's camp in quest of a company which might likewise be bound south. Ršêd told them promptly that they might travel with us, as we were going to an-Nûri too and were in search of a guide or of companions. The Ešâǧeʿa informed Ršêd that, three days before, there had been seen by the wells of al-ʿElejjânijje a troop of four hundred fighters of the Fedʿân and ʿAmârât, and, when informed of the appearance south and southwest of Ršêd's camp of the unknown rider sighted by the herdsmen, they declared that he was doubtless a spy of that belligerent horde. They added that they would remain at the camp all the next day to see the enemy attack.

Ršêd decided to transfer the camp to the north and unite with the Âl Ḥammad in order to oppose the onslaught more effectively. Therefore he ordered the tents to be folded early in the morning and despatched north with the herds. Having heard from him of the visit of the Ešâğeʿa I sent Mḥammad to them to arrange the time of our departure. I was so confident that they would appreciate the opportunity of traveling in our company that I was greatly surprised to learn that they would accompany us only on condition that we pay each of them four *meğîdijjât* ($ 3.60) and that Blejhân would guarantee that their camels would be restored should we be attacked by the Fedʿân or by the ʿAmârât. I laughed at this demand, saying that it was instigated by the men with whom Ršêd had been negotiating yesterday and that they ought to be glad to be taken along; but both Blejhân and Mḥammad warned me of the perfidy of these four robbers, observing that they could easily take us by surprise at night and plunder us, and hence it would be to our advantage to hire them and thus insure our belongings with a few *meğîdijjât.* They also told me that the men had four good rifles, which would enable us the better to defend ourselves against a smaller band of robbers. Being well aware of the dangers in the neighborhood of the volcanic territory of the Ḥawrân, which is infested by robbers of the Ahâli al-Ğebel, I empowered Mḥammad to offer each of the Ešâğeʿa three *meğîdijjât* ($ 2.70), payable, however, in Prince an-Nûri's tent, and to stipulate that they should sustain themselves on their own provisions, drink their own water, and assist us whenever necessary. We intended to set out after sunset.

Zejḍ was still with us. Shortly before we were to start, however, there arrived in the camp a courier traveling from Damascus to Bagdad. He was using one camel as a mount and leading another and was on the lookout for a companion; therefore he was much pleased to hear that Zejd would go with him as far as al-Ḳaʿara or to the wells of Râḥ. Zejd was to ride the spare camel, which would then go better and faster than if led by the rein.

I talked with Ršêd a long time. He was keenly interested in politics and surprised me with his uncommon knowledge of matters European and Turkish, being versed even in the history of Arabia. He understood exactly the purpose of my work in the desert and urged me to write exhaustively of the Bedouins' relation to the Government, in order that high officials might form a true opinion of their character, needs, customs, and habits and provide for them accordingly.

CHAPTER III

ḪABÂRI SEJḲAL TO AL-BÎẒ IN WÂDI SIRḤÂN

ḪABÂRI SEJḲAL TO AL-ǦWEJF

Bidding a cordial farewell to Chief Ršêd eben Smejr, we left the camp at seven o'clock in the evening and took an east-southeasterly course into the darkening desert. The journey was full of danger. Shortly before sunset all the fighters had sped to the southeast, where a strong cavalcade of the enemy had been seen. Should we encounter it? Where were their camel riders? Were they not, perchance, waiting in reserve at the well of al-Ǧwejf, where we were to water our camels and fill our bags, as the mire brought from the north was not fit to use?

"We beseech thy protection; give us thy veil, O Lord! *sitrak jâ rabb!*" exclaimed Blejhân.

Like ghosts we moved on over the rolling plain of al-ʿÎṯa, riding side by side in single formation, with the camel carrying the water bags following Blejhân's mount, to which she was tied. The cold wind blowing from the snow-bound mountains and slopes was almost unbearable. There was snow on the heights to the west, to the north, and to the south, where it almost touched the plain. The frost made us shiver. We spoke no word but listened and watched the more attentively. About ten o'clock we sighted in a yellowish, glistening, dried-up rain pool the trail of hostile riders. Horses and camels had passed here on their way to the northwest, and only a little while before, too, for the footprints, which Blejhân and our new escorts examined carefully, were quite fresh. Where was the enemy? Suddenly we heard the neighing of a stallion approaching a mare. *Sitrak jâ rabb!* Had one of our camels emitted a sound at that moment, we should have been lost. Several minutes of extreme suspense followed. The neighing was heard from the west, which indicated that the enemy was behind us; therefore we must forge quickly ahead so as to get as far as possible away from them. It was difficult riding because we were traversing the wet ground of rain pools surrounded by strips of almost impassable lava, through which led but few narrow paths; moreover, everything was level and open, and the eye carried far. Had we passed here in daylight the enemy would surely have seen us. Even as it was, the marauders of the Ahâli al-Ğebel might attack us at any moment, for they were crisscrossing the territory we were traversing, either setting out in lust of booty or returning with their spoils. Finally at 1.50 A.M. we reached the first short ravines leading to the basin of al-Ğwejf and encamped east of Ḫabra Drejhmât among high bushes of *šîḥ* and *nejtûl*, in which our kneeling camels almost disappeared.

Thursday, December 31, 1908. At dawn we built a fire of the dry *šîḥ*, prepared our coffee (which our new companions drank up!), and started on at 7.28. We were traversing a rolling plain that sloped to the south and southeast. To the southwest the truncated summit of Sejs extended from west to east; nearer to us to the north of it spread the hillocks of the volcanic group of al-Bowzelijjât; to the south-southeast were the volcanoes of al-Mḥarûṯa and Ṛurâb al-Ḥadâli, and north-northwest of them stood out the colossal boulder Ruẓumat al-Ğwejf. With the exception of these heights, everything was level; in the west and southeast all was dark gray, in the south and east a brilliant white in spots. The view to the north was obscured by a large swell that joins with al-Bowzelijjât.

We were nearing the extensive basin of al-Ğwejf, which is hedged in by white limestone cliffs twenty to twenty-five meters high and contains two wells, much favored by marauding bands because of the cover the depression affords. There might be even now such a band at the wells, or there might be a sentinel sitting behind the high pile of stones heaped upon the rocky cliff directly above. *Sitrak jâ rabb!* Smejjer and Maʿjûb, two of our new companions, turned their fur coats inside out, in order that the white wool might make them less distinguishable, and with their rifles loaded went out to reconnoiter, while we kept on through the bottom of a shallow valley that comes from Ḫabra ummu-r-Rmam and terminates in al-Ğwejf. Presently, at a signal from our spies, I followed them with the utmost caution to a slight elevation near by and, lying flat on my stomach after their example, surveyed the entire landscape with my binoculars but did not discover anything suspicious. Then we went over to the next summit, from which we again scrutinized the country; and this we repeated twice more, until we came to the brink of the hollow. According to a prearranged plan our companions were to descend through the deeper ravines into the basin unless signaled contrariwise, while we were to run down through a deep gully. The soil in the basin is overlain with a soft, white, limy loam in which *ṭarfa* thrives. The wells, which are about ten meters deep and contain water that is clear, transparent, but very salty, are at the south-southeastern end. While I was lying behind piles of stones watching the terrain for any foe that might otherwise have surprised us unaware, with Tûmân sitting near drawing a map, Blejhân and the others reached the wells (at 9.40), watered the camels, washed out the bags, and filled them with the salty water.

AL-ǦWEJF TO AL-ḪWEJMÂT

At 10.25 we mounted a height, which we traversed to the southeast along the base of a mighty swell that runs from Tlûl al-Bowzelijjât to the south. At twelve o'clock a beautiful vista opened before our eyes. West of the swell spread a large plain, covered with limestone gravel, separating the volcanic district of Tlûl al-ʿIjâṯ from the volcanic areas of Ṛurâb al-Ḥadâli and al-Mḥarûṯa. This plain slopes southward in the direction of the oasis of Manḳaʿ ar-Raḥba, where rain water gathers, brought by the valley of at-Tejs, a tributary of which on the left is the *šeʿîb* of Ǧlêṛem. To the northwest the volcanoes of Sejs, al-Bowzeli, and as-Sîb protruded above the horizon. To the south the horizon was obscured by the dark masses of the Ḥawrân; closer to us glistened the somber slopes of al-Mḥarûṯa and Ṛurâb al-Ḥadâli, and east of them gleamed the long range Ṭaraḳ aḏ-Ḏîb; in the east the promontory of Ḫašm al-Kbûd loomed slightly above the flat surroundings, and to the north stretched the undulating plain of al-ʿÎṯa, with innumerable shadowy strips of valleys and ravines. Riding upon the heights, visible from afar, we urged our camels to a quicker pace and sought depressions and hollows as much as possible to avoid being attacked.

My servant and scribe, Mḥammad, feared our new associates, and no wonder. His mother was a slave, his father an ʿAḳejli, and he himself had served the ʿAḳejl, or camel merchants, who made purchases for rich contractors in Bagdad or Damascus, buying camels from the Bedouins and driving them to the marts in Egypt. Under these circumstances Mḥammad had come to regard every Bedouin as a master: it was the Bedouins from whom he bought camels, and it was they who guaranteed that the purchases would not be taken away from him or stolen. That was why he treated our companions as his masters. He supplied them with our water, built fires for them, baked their bread, while they calmly reposed, smoked, and issued orders to him. Although it had been contracted that they should use their own provisions, nevertheless he cooked for them our peeled wheat (*burṛul*), served them our coffee (which he had begged of Ršêd without my knowledge), and offered them everything from our stores that he knew would gratify them. The partners, all of whom were under twenty-five years of age, were well content. It never occurred to them to gather fuel for Mḥammad or to help him at loading or unloading the baggage. When I called Mḥammad's attention to their conduct, urging him not to slave for hired escorts, he replied that everything could be overcome through patience.

After four o'clock we rode along the eastern base of the somber lava area of Ṛurâb al-Ḥadâli[21] in a desolate plain containing innumerable dry *ḫabâri*, upon the edges of which we noted narrow strips of perennials, all dry.

At 9.05 at the head of the valley of as-Saḥîli we found a wide patch of dry *erbijjân*, which our camels ate greedily. On this spot we encamped.

Friday, January 1, 1909. The New Year! *Sitrak jâ rabb!* At 7.05 A.M. we set out and at eight o'clock came to a rather low slope with a large heap of stones (*riğm*) on the top, to which I climbed cautiously to survey the landscape. We feared the Ahâli al-Ğebel, whose own territory was very near. From the *riğm* I could overlook the main outskirts of the volcanic district and also individual volcanoes.

Far to the west glistened the parched lowland of ar-

[21] Jâḳût, *Muʿğam* (Wüstenfeld), Vol. 2, p. 217; Vol. 3, p. 783, writes that al-Ḥadâla' is located between Syria and the desert of as-Samâwa, which belongs to the tribe of Kalb. The poet al-Mutanabbi fled before Sejfaddowle, the master of Aleppo, to Egypt by the route leading west of al-Ḥadâla' and Ṛurrab. —

This al-Ḥadâla' may be but the extinct volcano of our day which rises upon the border of Syria and as-Samâwa. The poet avoided Damascus and took the old route leading from Ḥomṣ by way of Ḫân at-Trâb, al-Ğwejf, Burḳuʿ, and al-Wusâd to Kerak or to Àjla and so to Egypt. He saw Ṛurâb al-Ḥadâli, or al-Ḥadala' as it is called in the dialect of the Weld ʿAli, in the east. Ṛurrab is a poetical transcription of Ṛurâb. The Ḥadala of our time is, in fact, on the northwestern fringe of the desert of as-Samâwa.

Raḥba, which borders Tlûl al-ʿIjâṯ on the southeast and which after excessive winter rains is converted into a large lake. Into this flows the rain water from a great portion of the northwestern Ḥamâd, most of which is contributed by the Wâdi al-Minḳâṭ, approaching from the south-southeast and joined on the left and on the right by numerous *šeʿibân*. On the left, for example, east of ar-Raḥba, above the Ṛadîr al-Žerîn and south of the volcanoes of Aḳren,[22] it is joined by the *šeʿîb* of al-Ṛumâr, which begins far south of the volcano of that name.

Southeast of al-Žerîn, in the channel of al-Minḳâṭ, is the rain pool Ṛadîr al-Bḥejrât, and north of it rises the solitary volcano of Tell umm Iḏen. The valley of as-Saḥîli already mentioned stretches south of this volcano and converges with al-Minḳâṭ north of the Riǧlet al-Ḥaṭîb, which approaches from the south from the lengthy group of Tell al-Mesmaʾ that terminates the northern volcanic district to the north. Upon the highest summit of this group the Ahâli al-Ǧebel keep a sentinel almost constantly, because all the roads crossing from the east to ar-Raḥba can be seen from there.

After nine o'clock we came to the end of the lava area of al-Ḥadala and proceeded through innumerable small and large *ḫabâri* until at 10.28 we stopped at the Ḫabra umm Riǧmên, where our camels grazed until 12.17 P. M. on *šîḥ*, *rûṯe*, *šaʿrân*, and *šnân*, which grew in bushes about sixty centimeters high. Here and there lay long, thick stalks of the parched *kalḫ*, resembling cornstalks. At 1.37 we traversed the wide channel of the shallow valley of the Rîšt ummu Rǧejm, into which merge many *ḫabâri*. The *šeʿibân* of ar-Rijâši have their beginning to the southeast, upon the high ridge of al-Mezâjen.

At 2.12 we noted to the west-southwest the mouth of the *šeʿîb* of al-Ḫaẓeri, which merges with al-Minḳâṭ. It comes from the south side of the volcano of the same name which towers high above the somber environs. To the south of it rise the volcanoes of the an-Neẓâjem group and northeast from them the solitary crater of al-Meḥdeṯ. At 2.45 we were passing through the Rîšt al-Bṛâlijje which stretches in the plain of al-Bṛâlijje and converges with al-Minḳâṭ north of the

[22] Jâḳût, *op. cit.*, Vol. 1, p. 336, mentions an Aḳrun on the basis of a verse of the poet Imrulḳajs. —
The Aḳren of our day is near the road that leads from the oasis of Tejma to Syria. Imrulḳajs was on his way from Tejma to Syria and therefore we may perhaps identify the Aḳrun of his time with the Aḳren of ours.

castle of Burḳuᶜ at Ṛudrân al-Farâdîs. Its channel is nearly level and over a kilometer and a half wide.

After three o'clock we again proceeded through the desolate grayish desert where only small plots bore vegetation. About twelve kilometers to the southwest from our position this plain is bordered by a somber volcanic wall, the base of which is lined by the white channel of al-Minḳâṭ. Farther east near al-Minḳâṭ rises the huge ridge of al-Ḥwênijje, at the northwestern spur of which stands the castle Ḳaṣr Burḳuᶜ. According to the description of the Rwala, this is a diminutive but gloomy rectangular structure, with walls four meters high. I should have liked to visit this easternmost military fortress upon the ancient road from al-Azraḳ past Ḫân at-Trâb to Ḥomṣ, but my companions objected, arguing that in May or June, when we returned from the inner desert to Damascus, Prince an-Nûri would march east of the Ḥawrân and would encamp at Burḳuᶜ; then I should be able to work in safety, but now certain destruction threatened us at Burḳuᶜ.[23]

At 3.10 we discovered a larger level, Rijâẓ ᶜElejjân, overgrown with dried plants, on which our camels grazed until 4.20. My companions proposed a turn to the southeast, where there is a rain pool called al-Ḥefna in the channel of the *šeᶜîb* of Rwêšed abu Ḥefna. They declared it was full of water from which we could fill our bags, as the water drawn at al-Ǧwejf was unfit to drink. Assuredly, our tea prepared with that water was salty and bitter, and the bread and *burṛul* were also unsavory. Besides, all of us, men and animals alike, were troubled with diarrhea. I turned in this direction, but my companions would not follow me, asserting that I was heading straight to the south and would lead them into the impassable *ḥarra* (lava-covered district). Being averse to a deviation on account of an uncertain source of water, I consented that they should designate the direct course and lead us. With great glee and satisfaction they conducted us to the southeast, as they said, but in reality to the south-southeast. I pointed this out to them several times, but they did not believe me, holding that

[23] Abu-l-Feda' (*Tawârîḫ* [Fleischer], p. 130) recorded of our Burḳuᶜ that al-Ajham ibn Ǧabala, the master of Tadmur, erected in the desert a great castle with reservoirs; he was of the opinion that it was the Ḳaṣr Burḳuᶜ.

Jâḳût, *op. cit.*, Vol. 4, p. 927, writes that the Pilgrim Road from Syria to al-Medîna led across the Ṛadîr Wisâde, lying at the outskirts of the Ḥawrân between Jurfuᶜ and Ḳurâḳir. — From what is known of the situation of Ḳurâḳir and Ṛadîr Wisâde it is evident that the unknown Jurfuᶜ is our Burḳuᶜ. This fortress is, in fact, upon the old road that leads from the Ṛadîr al-Wusâd to the north.

Ḥağği Ḫalfa, *Ğihân numa'* (Constantinople, 1145 A. H.), p. 531, places the rain pool of Umm Burḳuᶜ to the north of al-Azraḳ, on the outskirts of the volcanic district of al-Leğa'.

we were going exactly in the middle, between the east and south, and should reach al-Ḥefna in the channel of ar-Rwêšed as straight as a shot. According to the testimony of the Ṣlejb who came to the camp of Eben Smejr, this Ḥefna was full of rain water, but it was uncertain whether the Rwala migrating with an-Nûri had not already drunk up the water. Therefore I was satisfied when in al-Ḥwênijje my companions gradually deviated almost due south.

At 6.47 we arrived at the *šeʿibân* of ar-Rwêšdât, which come from the Ḥazm ʿEnâza. The northernmost, Rwêšed abu-ṭ-Ṭarâfi, connects with the Rwêšed abu Ḥefna, whither my companions were hastening, and under the name of Rwêšed al-Maḳran merges southeast of Ḳaṣr Burḳuʿ with al-Minḳâṭ. When we finally arrived at the channel of al-Minḳâṭ and noted on the right the somber wall of the *ḥarra*, my companions at last became convinced that they had not led us to the southeast but due south, the water we wanted being thus left at Ḥefna in the valley of ar-Rwêšed, far to the east. Having found in the Ḫabâri al-Ḫwejmât a snug camping ground among high bushes of *šîḥ*, we halted there at 8.40.[24]

AL-ḪWEJMÂT TO WELLS OF ḲERÂŽER

Saturday, January 2, 1909 (temperature at 5.30 A. M.: −0.5° C). At 6.35 A. M. we left our camp at al-Ḫwejmât for the south and at 7.58 reached a high *riǧm*, or heap of stones, upon a ridge. Again it was my part to climb up and make observations, but now I did not look so much for enemies as for the camels and fires of our friends. It was just possible that an-Nûri was camping somewhere to the southeast, provided there was water in the Ḫabâri ad-Dwâra; but I could see indications of the presence of our friends neither in that vicinity, nor upon the slopes of the table mountain of al-Ḫarǧa nor in the rolling plain of ar-Rwêšdât.

At 8.10 I was again seated upon my camel, and at 8.40 we saw the first traces of our hoped-for friends in signs that a great number of camels had gone from the northwest to the southeast and had again returned to the northwest, or *vice versa*. It was evident that they had gone from some

[24] Ḥaǧǧi Ḫalfa, *op. cit.*, p. 531, mentions the district of Rwêšdât as one which stretches out opposite Meṛreḳ and has no water except rain water. — Meṛreḳ is an erroneous transcription of Mefreḳ, an important pilgrim station south of Ḏerʿât, toward which turns the road that leads through the city of Boṣra to the oasis of Teǰma. Our district of Rwêšdât spreads in reality to the east of al-Mefreḳ.

camp to the watering places. Where was the camp and where the water holes? My escorts asserted that the camp was certainly situated at the left, therefore to the southeast, and wanted to head in that direction after the migrating tribe; but I held that the site of the camp was at our right — therefore westward; otherwise we should have already noted the trail of the migrating herds and riders on our way from al-Ǧwejf, whereas up to the present time we had not crossed any such traces. From all this I deduced that the main body of the migrating Rwala remained west of our course and that the Prince an-Nûri had despatched only a part of his herds to the watering places of Ḫabâri ad-Dwâra, or az-Zwâri. My associates refused to believe this; hence I declared that, as the supply of salt water from al-Ǧwejf was sufficient for only two more days, it was imperative that we replenish it in the depression of Sirḥân at Ḳerâẑer or at Etra, before that time had elapsed. I said I knew that we should certainly reach these wells in two days' time, whereas we were not at all sure of finding water in any rain pool or *ṛadîr* to the southeast, and we might not meet our friends within the two days. To these valid arguments my associates had to yield.

Great, then, was our rejoicing when at 9.48 we came upon the trail of the migrating Rwala. The footprints pointed from the west-northwest to the south-southeast; therefore they were going in the same direction that we were. We could distinguish quite clearly where the Prince had trodden, surrounded by riders upon horses, and we followed in his tracks.

The country, a lowland with innumerable *ḫabâri*, is hedged in on the west by a somber precipice of lava but rises gradually to the east and forms wide swells and valleys that appear like broad bottoms; *ḫabâri* originate in them, and the superfluous water is conducted away by level troughs to the northwest. To the northwest we saw the volcano of al-Ḫaẓeri and southeast of it the Tell al-Meḥdeṯ, from which a valley of the ṣame name extends to the northeast to al-Minḳâṭ. Almost due west the group of Tlûl al-Ešâǧef ranges in a half-circle open to the east. It is divided from the volcanoes of al-Ǧeṯûm on the south by the upper portion of the ravine of al-Meḥdeṯ. Almost due north of al-Ešâǧef are three volcanoes of the an-Neẓâjem group. Beyond the northernmost and highest volcano of this group rise to the northwest the lower volcanoes of Rṣên and Saʿâda, near which gushes a stream of the same name. Southwest of Rṣên and almost west of the ṣouthern volcano of an-Neẓâjem appears the crater of al-Rumâr, with the group of al-ʿAbd wa Awlâdah to the south of it, and still farther to the south the imposing Tell Mismâr. South of the volcanoes of al-Ǧeṯûm, above the elevated volcanic region, rises the Tlûl Zrejbînât.

From 10 A. M. to 12.20 P. M. our camels grazed in the plain of al-Bṛejla on the remnants left by the herds of the Rwala (temperature at 12: 15° C). From 2.32 to 5.55 we prepared supper at the edge of the volcanic area, drew a map, and calculated the latitude (temperature at 3.40: 16.6° C). Having lost the tracks of our friends on the rocky ledges of a low slope, we headed straight southward, assuming that Prince an-Nûri was likewise compelled by the lack of water to hasten toward the settlement of Eṯra in the depression of Sirḥân. After 6.30 we entered the prolonged lowland Fejẓat ab-al-Ḥṣejn, in which originates the valley of al-Minḳâṭ. This lowland is covered with a yellow clay, overgrown at places, and in its western portion forms the rain pool Ḫabra ab-al-Ḥṣejn to which water is conducted by the *šeʿibân* of ad-Dmejṯât. These come from the southeast, from the mighty ridges Ḥazm ʿAnḳa and az-Zebîbijjât that extend from south to north. The northern *šeʿîb* is called Dmejṯet ummu Ḳṣejr, a name derived from an unpretentious castle in its central portion. At 6.40 we crossed the valley of Dmejṯet ummu Mḥafûr and after seven o'clock that of Dmejṯet ummu Ṭeʿejs, reaching the stony plain of al-Mṛajẓât.

The Ešâǧeʿa wished again to deviate to the east, arguing that we should not recover the trail of our friends if we continued on the southerly course, as they had surely headed to the southeast, east of the Tell al-Heber and Tell Eḳren. Refusing my men permission to follow the Ešâǧeʿa, I also succeeded in persuading the latter to return to us. When I decided on a fit place to camp in the plain of al-Mṛajẓât, Maʿjûb objected, contending that it could be seen far off *(tabʿad)* and was therefore unsafe; hence we turned to the southeast and at 10.25 stopped to rest. We had barely dismounted from our camels when the Ešâǧeʿa gathered a heap of fuel and kindled a big fire, disregarding the fact that it would attract the attention of travelers far to the north and east. They wished to indicate that in the neighborhood of their kinsmen they were safe.

Sunday, January 3, 1919. Setting out again at 6.43 A.M., we noted to the southeast, not far away, the volcano Tell al-Heber and beyond it to the south-southeast another volcano, which the Rwala call Eḳren, while other ʿAneze call it Tell abu Râsên.

Proceeding along the foot of a stony height which sloped up to the eastward and from which we could scan the surrounding country, we saw the group of al-Ešâǧef rising to the northwest, with, to the south of it, the Tlûl al-Ǧeṯûm and al-Ḳarʿ.[25]

To the southeast of al-Ḳarʿ are two large volcanoes of the Ẓrejbînât group. South of Ẓrejbînât extends a somber mountain range, its eastern slopes covered with yellow tracts of sand, which in the light of dawn turned a pinkish hue. The slopes are overshadowed by numerous cone-

FIG. 8—Range of aš-Šâma from the northwest.

shaped summits. This range, with its flat crests and sandy drifts, is called aš-Šâma (Fig. 8). Its northern limits are formed by the Tlûl al-Awtejdât and the *šeʿîb* of al-Ḳaṭṭâmi, the latter being southwest of the Tlûl Ẓrejbînât. The range extends from Tlûl al-Awtejdât[26] to the northwest and at the Ṛadîr al-Wusâd falls away into the *šeʿîb* of Ab-ar-Rmam, which approaches from the Tell Mismâr.

South-southeast of Tlûl al-Awtejdât glimmered the salients of Tlejlât al-Bṛejṯât, east of them the Tlûl aš-Šmesânât, Tlêl an-Naʿejǧ, and Tlêlât as-Saḳḳâr, and northeast of them the high double cone of Žetab aš-Šâma. Over the low southwestern ledges of the Tell al-Heber we noted to the southeast the two-horned Tell Eḳren, and farther to the southeast three volcanoes of al-Ktejfât, also al-Ḥaṭîmi, ʿÂžer, Liss, and the butte-like crater of ar-Rdêʿânijje. From almost all the eastern volcanoes there were spread over the white desert the black areas of former lava flows.

Descending from the slope mentioned above, we came to a lava spur that extended eastward and terminated at the Tell al-Heber, with several small rain pools adjoining it to the northwest and north. The Ešâǧeʿa grumbled because we had chosen to ride in a lava region, thereby exhausting our camels uselessly; but I refused to deviate from a southerly course. After 8.40 we followed a narrow path — called *mutribe* —

[25] Jâḳût, *Muʿǧam* (Wüstenfeld), Vol. 4, p. 62, gives information regarding the valleys of al-Ḳurʿ in the Syrian desert which he says are destitute of vegetation. — Perhaps they are identical with the arid ravines between the individual hills of our Tlûl al-Ḳarʿ.

[26] Jâḳût, *op. cit.*, Vol. 1, p. 114, records that Utejda, or Uṯejda, is located in the territory of the Ḳuḍâʿa tribe in the Syrian desert. —

The Awtejdât of our time is situated in the former territory of the Ḳuḍâʿa tribe near the road that leads from the depression of as-Sirr to Syria, and we may, therefore, identify it with the Utejda of Jâḳût. The road in question left the depression of Sirḥân at the settlement of Čâf and went north past the Ṛadîr al-Wusâd. Jâḳût, *op. cit.*, Vol. 4, p. 927, refers to it when writing of a place called Wisâde situated upon the Pilgrim Road from Syria to al-Medîna at the termination of the mountain range of Ḥawrân, between Burḳuʿ and Ḳurâḳir. Here died in the year 1160 A. D., on his return from the pilgrimage to Mecca, Jûsef ibn Makki ibn Jûsef al-Ḥâreṯi aš-Šâfeʿi abu-l-Ḥaǧǧâǧ, the *imâm ǧâmeʿ* (leader of the prayers at the principal mosque) of Damascus and expounder of the law.

Wisâde must be identical with our Ṛadîr al-Wusâd, as Burḳuʿ is about one hundred kilometers to the north of it, whereas Ḳerâžer is eighty-seven kilometers to the southeast. The Pilgrim Road led through the depression of Sirḥân and across the oasis of Tejma.

between large and small chips of lava with sharp edges, and here in a few minutes we recovered the trail of our friends; for, like ourselves, Prince an-Nûri had not deviated from a southerly course, although he had been camping somewhat farther to the left.

FIG. 9—The Ḫabra ʿAẓâmân from the northwest.

From the top of the lava ridge we beheld before us an extraordinary picture. The western volcanic region looked like a huge, scale-covered dragon lying immovable in repose. His head, the immense volcano of al-Žetab, his scales, and his vertebrae — the volcanoes Tlêlât as-Saḳḳâr — protruded cold and still. His countless feet and shoulders stretched far into the gray eastern desert, and in his dying gasps, his claws — the scattered volcanoes to the east and south, which run parallel to the lava ridges — buried themselves deep into the level plain. Now the dragon was dead; but when he was alive his vertebrae, head, and claws had emitted fire, and his flaming shoulders and glowing feet had burned their way deeper and deeper into the trembling plain.

Among the somber lava ridges were scattered yellowish tracts resembling huge copper platters with decorated rims. These were the *ḫabâri*, or rain pools, at the brims of which the masses of lava ceased as abruptly as if cut off by a human hand. When these *ḫabâri* are filled with water and wreathed with fresh vegetation, they must look superb. Underfoot among the lava stones was a bed of sand in which our camels sank deep at places.

At 9.30 we came to the enormous Ḫabra ʿAẓâmân (Fig. 9). I had been wondering where our *sluḳi* (also pronounced *sulḳi*) Ḳaṭṭâf had been roaming so long. Usually he hovered in the vicinity of the camels looking for hares in the bushes, and

I thought he was occupied in the same manner today. When we had advanced almost to the middle of the rain pool, however, without seeing any trace of him, my companions began to surmise that perhaps he had started up a herd of gazelles somewhere and pursued them. At ten o'clock we reached the southern brim of the *ḫabra* and waited until 12.35, but he had not put in an appearance. Perhaps he had lost our scent or been killed by a wild animal. Greyhounds of the *sulḳân* breed have an undeveloped sense of smell; they are incapable of following a rider's scent. They follow him as long as they can see him, but the moment he passes out of sight they stop, look about for him, and appear not to know what to do until they catch a glimpse of him again. I had often thrown them pieces of flesh and bones and watched them go past the food two or three times without scenting it. In order to find food they have to see it. At night Ḳaṭṭâf would crawl into a waterproof sack and would not come out until we had built a fire. Then he would lazily sit down and warm himself. For a watchdog a *sulḳi* is absolutely unreliable.

Meanwhile the camels were grazing on *rimṯ*, *nejtûl*, and *šîḥ*. I had seen no *ḳaẓḳâẓ*.

At three o'clock we again ascended a high lava ridge to look over the vicinity. Toward the east below us spread the white lowland of Dowḳara, dotted with yellow *ḫabâri*, whither water is conducted by the Še'ibân al-Ğerânijjât and by other valleys. The Ğerânijjât extend from the western slope of az-Zebîbijjât, which stretches upon the eastern horizon from south to north. At Ğerâni abu Ṛadîr there is a rain pool, Ḫaẓar al-Ma'. South of it, in the Ḫabâri az-Zebîbijjât, originates Ğerâni abu 'Âder, and still farther south is Ğerâni abu 'Aǧram, which cuts through the lava field of al-Eḳren. Between the volcanoes of al-Ktejfe and al-Ḫaṭîmi winds the valley of aṭ-Ṭrejf. West of al-Eḳren the ravine of aš-Šaḥam reaches the rain pools; this *še'îb* originates in the southeast at the volcano of al-Mačmen and divides the volcanoes of aẓ-Ẓbâ'ijje, Liss, 'Âžer, al-Mṣella, and al-Ḥenw from those of al-Maṣlûḫ, aš-Šaḥam, Umm Iḏen, and al-Ḫalâd. The volcanoes of al-Ḫalâd, Umm Iḏen, and al-Maṣlûḫ were almost in line to the south of the spot from which we were viewing them. East of them we could see the deep, whitened gulch of the *še'îb* of aš-Šaḥam winding along the east side of the hills Tlûl aš-Šaḥam that stretch in a semicircle, open toward the west; northwest of the end of this valley rose the group of al-Ufejḥem. The high crest of aš-Šâma, with the volcanoes Tlêlât as-Saḳḳâr and Žetab aš-Šâma, obstructed the view to the west.

After 3.48 we were traversing an almost impassable, stony region. The horse tracks pointed straight to the southwest, but the camels had evidently turned to the south-southwest.

Smejjer wanted us to follow the latter prints, saying that they would lead us to the watering places of the Ḳulbân Ḳerâžer, the location of which he knew so well that we need no longer heed the trail of the migrating tribe. He asserted that he could bring us to the water either that night or early the next morning. As we did not have a drop of water and as he assured us firmly that he knew the shorter route, we forsook the riders' trail and took up that of the camels.

From a small flanking gully we came into a lowland where our camels grazed from 4.10 to 5.08. After that we proceeded in the stony, sand-drifted region of the volcanoes of al-Ḫalâd and al-Aḫejẓrât, encamping within it at 9.25 in a tributary gorge of the *šeʿîb* of Abu Ṭarfa.

Monday, January 4, 1909. At 6.45 A.M. we set out to the southwest, proceeding over numerous lava ridges extending from the northwest to the southeast. To the southeast we saw the volcanoes of al-Aḫejẓrât and the long range of hills, aš-Šaḥam, which form the divide between the basin of Dowḳara and the depression of Sirḥân. Southeast of al-Aḫejẓrât the beams of the rising sun caught the crater of al-Maṣlûḫ, which is sunken in on the northwest and to the southeast of which rose the five somber volcanoes of the al-Mačmen group. From these the *ḥarra* reaches farther east to the group of Zellâḳa, which lies almost south of the volcano Umm Wuʿâl. The group Tlûl aš-Šaḥam is merely a projection of the imposing mountain range Ẓelʿ al-Misma', which stretches to the southeast. Between it and the spot from which we were observing the landscape there lies a craggy area of somber lava with occasional layers of yellow sand in the hollows. The western slopes of these hollow places, being naturally protected from the west winds, are covered deeply with the sand, whereas the eastern slopes are absolutely bare. In front of the higher lava boulders also ran out long strips of the sand in which *rimṯ* grew in isolated patches; in the center of the bottoms *ratam*, *šîḥ*, *ṣerr*, *naṣi*, and *firs* flourished.

After 9.30 when we had crossed the Riğlet aš-Šerâri, there opened before us a fine vista. To the west rose the lava region of Farʿat al-Ḳrênijje, through which penetrated the *šeʿibân* of aš-Šerâri and al-Maḳl. The former begins in the north at the water of Ḥağrat Rubbâḫ, between Žetab aš-Šâma and the Tlêl an-Naʿejğ, and runs along the western base of Tlêlât as-Saḳḳâr and the eastern base of Tlejl aṣ-Ṣubûḥ; al-Maḳl originates in Tlûl aš-Šmesânât, fills the Ḫabâri al-Bṛejtât, and in the west swings round the Tell Maḳl. Both enter the valley of Abu Ṭarfa, a wide plain overgrown with *ṭarfa*, along which, on the north and the south, are aligned numerous grim serrated ridges. As a rule, these ridges are fifteen to twenty meters high and at their base forty to seventy meters wide, uneven in length, somber at the top, dark brown upon the slopes, and in almost parallel alignment from the northwest to the southeast, thus resembling a large camp of Bedouins or the huge piles of coal that we are accustomed to see at our railroad stations. My escorts pointed out to me the black peak of al-Maḥâṭ rising above the wells of Ḳerâžer; but what a vast distance still intervened between us and that peak! Serrated ridge after serrated ridge loomed before us.

ḲERÂŽER TO PRINCE AN-NÛRI'S CAMP IN WÂDI SIRḤÂN

Finally, at 11.38, we reached the water. The wells were entirely deserted, quiet, undisturbed; there were merely a few *ṛurâb* (ravens) circling above them. Ḳerâžer has over twenty wells (Fig. 10), all lying on the northeastern margin of the basin, among the black peaks of al-Maḥâṭ and Rabda. Some of the wells are only thirty centimeters deep, others eighty centimeters. The water has a salty flavor. East of the wells are two palmettos.[27]

We intended to water our camels in Ḳerâžer, fill our water bags, and then go on. But whither? Where were our friends? We had gone but a little north from the wells, when I discovered fresh tracks of many horses and soon afterwards the site of a camp — a pretty good sign that an-Nûri had been lodging here and had proceeded westward, as the traces indicated. This surmise was verified by a man who unexpectedly appeared in the southwest from behind a rocky

[27] Ḥâṭim aṭ-Ṭâ'i, *Dîwân* (Schulthess), p. 43, tells of a battle at Ḳurâḳir and of a camping place at Abâ'ir. — In the dialect of the Ahl aš-Šemâl Abâ'ir sounds like Bâjer. It is a well-known watering place about fifty kilometers southwest of our Ḳerâžer, which I identify with the Ḳurâḳir of the poet. Raiding parties of the Ṭajj, the tribal kinsmen of Ḥâṭim, used to ride past Ḳurâḳir, just as bands of the present Šammar do now.

Jâḳût, *Muʿǧam* (Wüstenfeld), Vol. 4, pp. 49f., admits that he is not acquainted with the situation of Ḳurâḳir. He thinks that it is a water or a valley of the Kalb tribe in the desert of as-Samâwa near Irak. Hišâm ibn al-Kalbi reports that the watering place of Ḳurâḳir was claimed by both the Beni al-Ḳejn and the Kalb. He says the disputes were of long duration but were finally concluded by Caliph ʿAbdalmalek, who quoted a verse from the poet an-Nâbiṛa in favor of the tribe of Kalb. —

Jâḳût merely reiterates the older accounts about the road that was followed by Ḫâled ibn al-Walîd to Syria. Ibn al-Kalbi identifies the watering place of Ḳurâḳir, where Ḫâled stopped, with the one that the tribes of Kalb and al-Ḳejn disputed. The Beni al-Ḳejn had their camps in the eastern half of ancient Moab and in the adjoining steppe as far as the depression of Sirḥân, the tribe of Kalb being in possession of the desert that reaches from

spur. Since we had met nobody in the whole journey from the camp of Chief Ršêd eben Smejr to these wells and so had no means of knowing whether this man was likely to be a friend or a spy of a robbing or raiding party, we immediately tied our camels and seized our weapons. The Ešâğeʿa,

FIG. 10—At the wells of Ḳerâžer.

with rifles in hand, hastened to the stranger, while the rest of us remained at our baggage and watched the southwestern approach to the wells. Soon, however, we were reveling in jubilation. The man proved to be a Rwejli — and hence a friend — on his way from one camp to another, and he told us the glad news that the Prince was encamped in the district of al-Bîẓ on the western edge of the depression of Sirḥân. *Al-ḥamdu lillâh!*

Leaving the wells at 12.30 P. M. and following the horse tracks, from a small hillock we presently sighted herds at pasture in the south at the wells Ḳlejjeb umm al-ʿEbi and a large camp to the west. As the camp stretched a long way

Irak likewise to the depression of Sirḥân. Therefore we may seek the watering place of Ḳurâḳir on the boundary between these tribes at the depression of Sirḥân, which then formed, as it does still, a natural division between the raisers of goats and sheep and the Bedouins proper, the camel breeders. Since our watering place of Ḳerâžer is situated at the eastern brim of the depression of Sirḥân, it could have been claimed by both the Beni al-Ḳejn and the Kalb. ʿAbdalmalek could justify his verdict in favor of the tribe of Kalb, with which he was affiliated, by the situation of the watering place at the eastern side of the Sirḥân, in the volcanic desert of ar-Rağla, which had belonged to the Kalb.

Al-Hamdâni, *Ṣifa* (Müller), p. 129, refers to a watering place of Ḳurâḳir on the boundary between the tribes of Kalb and Dubjân, near ʿUrâʿir, and says that the tribes of Kalb and ʿAbs once fought at Ḳurâḳir and ʿUrâʿir. —As the D̠ubjân camped with the Beni al-Ḳejn and to the south of them, al-Hamdâni could correctly say that the watering place of Ḳurâḳir lay between the tribes of D̠ubjân and Kalb. But the watering place of ʿUrâʿir is known to be in the territory of the D̠ubjân tribe, far from Ḳurâḳir. There were, therefore, two battles, which al-Hamdâni confuses, as he does many other things. His accounts of North Arabia are altogether superficial.

from the northwest to the southeast, I decided to enter it at its center. Beneath us spread the depression of Sirḥân, enclosed by precipitous slopes that were dark to the east and white to the west. Between these glistened broad, almost massive areas of white salt, from which protruded grayish, isolated hillocks, while above the entire depression hung a dense veil of dust and sand. At 1.40 we were at the eastern fringe of the depression, which we had to cross. It was hard plodding, for the camels kept sinking from twenty to thirty centimeters deep in a soil consisting of a deposit of lime mixed with salt and forming a veritable salt marsh. Many spots were coated with a fairly thick crust of salt and hence were absolutely bare; but on the higher ground grew *ratam, ḳaṭaf, mṣaʿ, šwaḥwaḥ, ṯellejṯ* (or *fellejf*) *ʿačreš, ḥalfa, ʿerž, zebb aḏ-ḏîḫ, ṯḥama,* and *firs.*

Tired and hungry, we rested from 2.35 to 4.25; besides, the camels needed rest too. Resuming our way, we finally reached the first tents on the western edge of the depression at the foot of the two pyramidal hillocks of al-Ḫ̮ṣejjên. There we learned that the tent of Prince an-Nûri stood at the southeastern fringe of the camp, so we hurried in that direction, meeting now and then with herdsmen of our acquaintance, who gave us pleasant greetings and asked us many questions. But we hastened on toward the large fire which I knew was flaming inside the Prince's tent. At last I sighted the roof of my own tent at the right of his, and presently, stepping over several tent ropes, at six o'clock I dismounted at home, after an absence of thirty-one days. Immediately I was surrounded and warmly embraced, kissed, and welcomed. The Prince thanked Allâh for having conducted me back alive and well; Nawwâf pressed my hand and inquired the reason of my long absence; Saʿûd, Mežḥem, and all my friends, old and young, clasped my hand. They had received news, purporting to be authoritative, that I had fallen near the Euphrates in a battle with the Dlejm. Much affected, I thanked them all and retired to the tent of the Prince to greet him and thank him for protecting my friends and my property in my absence. Everyone came to see me one after another, touched my hand, and welcomed the Sheikh Mûsa. The Prince had intended to migrate the following day; since I had returned, however, he announced that we should wait another day, "that the Sheikh Mûsa might rest."

After I went back to my tent, I helped Tûmân calculate the latitude. Nâṣer told me that the Prince and Nawwâf had come to the tent two or three times every night to urge him to vigilance. Whenever they changed the camp they allotted him two pack camels and ordered the slave Ḥmâr to assist him with the loading and unloading. But he also had bad news in store for me. In our absence our sturdiest camel, for which I had paid ninety *meǧîdijjât* ($ 81), had died of a malady known as *aṭ-ṭejr*. Her nerves became paralyzed, he said, and she could not stand up the second day and died four days later. An-Nûri assured me that he had summoned all the veterinarians and that they had used every means to save her, but to no avail. Nâṣer also said that one of my two breed camels had foaled a young one (*wledǝt*) which, by order of the Prince, he had immediately separated from the mother, as it was inconceivable that the camel could nurse her offspring and carry baggage too. Ǧwâd, the Prince's scribe, informed me that my friend and agent in Damascus, Ḫalîl Fattâl, had handed over to the scribe of Chief Ṛatwân eben Meršed of the Ḳmuṣa tribe all the letters that had come for me in the last two months. Ṛatwân was camping in Palmyrena several hundred kilometers northwest from us; he was bound for the northwest; we were going southeast. An-Nûri consoled me by saying that I could get along in the desert without papers and that the verbal news of happenings in al-Ǧowf or the Nefûd would certainly be of more interest to me than written words of anything that was going on in the far west where my tribe was encamped.

Tuesday, January 5, 1909. Early in the morning Nawwâf came in, and we chatted about many interesting things. When he went away I asked him to send me the negro Ḥmâr, with whom I wanted to talk about various geographical subjects. The elderly Ḥmâr was the most proficient master of topography in northern Arabia and was also well acquainted with the northern portion of Neǧd. Before noon I was inundated with other visitors, and an-Nûri spent most of the afternoon with me hearing all the particulars about my journey. When I came to the depression of Sirḥân in my narrative, I requested him to draw in the sand all the locations, wells, heights, and valleys situated east and west of this depression, and he willingly complied.

CHAPTER IV

WITH PRINCE AN-NÛRI TO AN-NBÂĞ THROUGH THE WÂDI SIRḤÂN

AL-BÎẒ TO THE ḲULBÂN AZ-ZWEJĞA

Wednesday, January 6, 1909. Next morning the tents were loaded to be moved farther to the southeast (temperature at 7: 1.2° C). I was sorry to leave the camp site at al-Bîẓ so soon, for the Prince's tent and mine stood in the shade of wide-spreading *ṭarfa* trees, the neighborhood was covered with the verdant green of *mṣaʿ*, and the stiff *ḥalfa* rushes east and west of the tents made such a dense thicket that the camels could hardly pass through it. The water was plentiful, too, springing out at many places and flowing in short rivulets, and it tasted but slightly of salt; there was no pasture for the camels, however, and hence we had to go elsewhere.

Even before my tent was folded and loaded the Prince had invited me to keep him company on the journey. He led me to a small fire some distance from his tent, where his slave ʿÂmer was preparing sweet black coffee in my pot. His riding camel was kneeling beyond the fire, and he forced my camel to kneel there too. Beside the fire a wooden stand (*markab*) about thirty centimeters high was driven into the sand and upon it sat a falcon with a red cap (*burḳuʿ*) on its head. When the slaves had finished loading all the stores and the Prince's tent, the scribe brought forward a war mare and tied it by the rein to the camel's saddle girth, while an-Nûri took the stand with the falcon, put the bird on the back of the camel's saddle, and thrust the stand into the saddle bag.

At 9.20 we swung into our saddles and proceeded at a swift pace southeastward. Soon we outran all the loaded camels and, accompanied by four slaves and the scribe riding behind, we headed the migrating tribe. A strange dispensation of Allâh, for a Bedouin prince to be riding beside a Czech in the depression of Sirḥân at the head of a big tribe! When I reminded the Prince of this, he replied:

"Allâh has willed it. I never thought I should make friends with a man whose blood is not mine. Do thou not forget me, Mûsa, when thou shalt tread at the head of thy tribe!"

On our way we came to the remnant of a limestone hillock (Fig. 11), about three meters high. Wishing to photograph this witness of advanced erosion, I asked the Prince to stop, which he did willingly. Meantime Nawwâf with his party (Fig. 12) had caught up with us, and we lingered there ten minutes. Hardly were we again in the saddle when a hare darted out from under a bush near us. Instantly the Prince's hound, a *sluḳi*, was after him, and instantly too the Prince untied the falcon's cap, uncoupled the chain from a leather leash, and released the bird with the leash into the air. The falcon circled once, sighted the *sluḳi* and the hare, swooped down upon the hare, pecked him, rose in the air, plunged again, pecked another time, and the prey lay prostrate. Then the Prince upon his camel rushed up to the hare, chased the hound away from it, cut its throat, and, swinging it aloft, tried to entice the falcon back to him. The bird circled a while in the air, then flew down to the Prince and sat upon his hand, waiting for him to tie it, cover its head with the cap, and put it on the camel. A little while afterwards Nawwâf's falcon also hunted down a hare, which Nawwâf offered to me; but I declined it, asking that he have it prepared and then invite me to the supper. I got a *ḥabâra* (bustard) from Ṭrâd, a son of Saṭṭâm, and therefore had plenty of fresh meat for myself.

After 11.20 we had the wells of al-Ǧfêrât aṭ our left, and at one o'clock reached the springs ʿUjûn ʿEḏwânât, where the Prince assigned a space for my tents. We encamped upon a sandy *firs*-covered height, which rose about two meters above a surrounding sandy marsh. In the evening Nawwâf came to take me into the Prince's tent, where we were to have the hares for supper. The Prince sat beside me on his left heel and tossed me pieces of the meat. When I urged him not to forget himself, since he, as our head, must keep strong in order to take care of us all, he replied that he cared most for his best freebooter (*ṛazzâǰ*), that is, his brother Mûsa. He called my scientific expeditions raids (*ṛazw*).

We were to migrate again the next day, but when I happened to say that I had celebrated neither the holidays of my tribe nor the *aẓ-ẓaḥijje* (commemoration of the faithful departed of the last year) holiday of my friends of the desert, the Prince instantly announced that we would celebrate them together and for that reason would remain over the morrow at the same camping place (*nežîm*). That morning, before dawn, he rode out with Saʿûd into the eastern range to hunt and at the same time to look for pasture. When he returned in the afternoon he ordered it announced in the camp that we should remain at the same location over the following day because of an abundance of *šîḥ* and *firs* to the east.

Meantime I had been sketching a map of the regions east of the Ḥawrân as far as the Euphrates and the city of an-Neğef on the east, and south to al-Ğowf, recording upon it the names of all the locations I had learned on my last expedition as well as at Prince an-Nûri's camp. Afterwards Tûmân was to redraw it and make adjustments of the distances and directions. This sketch afforded me an excellent aid in my topographical inquiries made in camp as well as on the march. In the level desert, bare of mountain ranges, prominent heights, or deep valleys, the investigator often lacks a base or starting point from which to enquire further after topographical designations; and the guide usually forgets to remind him that there, in the vast level stretch, may be located a well, a rain pool, etc., or that this or that depression or basin has a particular name of its own. Through this sketch I was likewise enabled to participate in conversations about the camping places or watering places of various tribes and about the directions of roads. I also learned the names of new places, the situation of which I could thus ascertain with greater ease and later verify on my own expeditions. In this manner I came to be independent of the good or the ill will of my guides and could determine whether what they said was correct or not.

Desiring to finish my improvised sketch that day, I worked until late at night; hence Nawwâf, who came for a chat, left early. I paused in the work only for a short while after noon, when I received a visit from Ṣâjer eben Burmân, who commanded the raiding detachment of the Freğe that had robbed us. While telling Nawwâf what had happened, I asked him whether I should present Ṣâjer with a gift for having compelled his associates to restore the stolen articles.

FIG. 11

FIG. 12

FIG. 11—Eroded limestone hillock near al-Bîẓ.
FIG. 12—Nawwâf and his companions; near al-Bîẓ.

"O brother," he answered, "Ṣâjer forced them to do it because of the fear of my father. Whether thou shouldst give him anything or not, by Allâh, I shall not decide. Thy thought is inspired by Allâh, and it is a sin to deprive anyone of a gift."

Ṣâjer offered himself as a guide or companion on my next expedition; but, convincing myself that his knowledge of topography was poor, I presented him with a mantle (*ʿabaʾ*), with which he left, expressing his thanks.

Friday to Tuesday, January 8 to 12, 1909. On Friday morning I handed the sketch over to Tûmân and began to write out a topographical account of my last expedition. I was frequently interrupted, however. Shortly before noon Nawwâf came and begged me to visit a seriously sick warrior and to give medicines to the Chief Fahad. I hoped to be able to do more work the following day, but early Saturday morning I was aroused by the groaning of uncomfortable pack camels that signified our departure.

At 9.30 A.M. Nawwâf stopped for me, and we proceeded along a swampy depression to the southeast. Meantime my men had been repairing my saddle and had put it upon a camel that had never carried anyone before. The saddle did not fit the hump of that animal but rested too high and shifted forward until it seemed as if it would slide down the camel's neck. The animal had instantly sensed that my position was none too secure and strove to throw me off, but she did not succeed. Nawwâf offered assistance and proposed to stop and wait for the slaves following in the rear to come up and secure the saddle again, but I declined, saying that it would be inadvisable to interrupt the journey at the start by disclosing how careless I had been not to notice how my servants had saddled the camel. To the south two *ḥabâri* rose heavily, and Nawwâf darted forward to hunt them down with his falcon. Then the Prince joined me.

The depression of Sirḥân, upon the western fringe of which we were traveling south of ʿUjûn ʿEḏwânât, is about eight kilometers wide from west to east; on the east it is enclosed by the spurs of the lava area of Ẓelʿ al-Mismaʾ, on the west by a slope about twenty meters high which rises toward the west and forms the undulating limestone upland of aṣ-Ṣawwân. West of the ʿUjûn ʿEḏwânât the depression extends far into this upland, and at the southeastern termination of the embayment thus formed are the wells of al-ʿAẓejmât. Southeast of them the Prince pointed out to me the Želîb an-Nuṣrâni and west of it the gulch formed by the *šeʿîb* of Abu Ṭrejfijjât, which extends from the range of ar-Rḥaʾ. South of this *šeʿîb* the precipitous border of the upland

FIG. 13—Wells of Umm Ǧemâǧem.

runs due east as far as the gully of al-Ṛarra, whence it turns almost to the north and narrows the depression of Sirḥân to a width of only one kilometer. In the lowland protrude many hillocks, the remnants of former strata at a higher level.

At eleven o'clock we reached the precipitous western edge of the depression east of the *šeʿîb* of al-Ṛarra, and at 1.30 the Prince selected a new camp site at the wells of Umm Ǧemâǧem (Fig. 13), west of the Ḳulbân al-Ǧarbûʿijje and Umm al-Fanâǧîl.

On Sunday the chiefs of the settlements of Eṯra and Čâf came to greet the Prince and render him tribute. They had brought five camel loads of dates. In these settlements the princely family of Šaʿlân owned more than five hundred date trees, which the settlers leased for one-fifth of the net profits, getting one-fifth of the fruit themselves and the owner four-fifths. Of the current year's fifth they now brought to the Prince one camel load of dates weighing 170 kilograms, and to the family of the deceased Prince Saṭṭâm they brought four camel loads of about the same weight each. The family of Saṭṭâm — or, as it is commonly called, the family of Turkijje, since it is headed by Turkijje, Saṭṭâm's widow — is richer than the family of an-Nûri, because it owns more camels, horses, and slaves; for Saṭṭâm had been a prudent man who provided for the welfare of his progeny (temperature at 7: –1.2° C; at 12: 16° C; at 6.15: 12.5° C).

On Monday Nawwâf went with many fighters to protect the herds of camels at pasture in the southwest between the *šeᶜibân* of al-Ḳarra and al-Ǧeẓîᶜ. As the herds were to stay there over night, I was thus free for two days to devote myself to my writing without interruption. On Monday evening the courier who had been despatched to al-Ǧowf just a week before returned upon a camel, bringing important news, as well as many letters; but I did not wish to examine them until I had finished my topographical account. Tuesday afternoon Mežḥem brought me a *ḥabâra* and the tidings that Nawwâf had returned with the report that the pasturage in the southwest was so poor that we should be compelled to search elsewhere. Poor Arabs! Four long months they had been waiting for abundant rain. Ḥmâr avowed that he had no memory of any such egregiously unfavorable season in thirty years. Where pasturage was abundant water was absent, and where there was water there was no pasturage.

Wednesday, January 13, 1909. During the night it began to drizzle, and the rain continued intermittently throughout the day. Anticipating a visit from Nawwâf, I delved into work early in the morning in order to finish the account of my recent trip before he came. Presently, however, he sent the slave ᶜÂmer accompanying his first-born boy, Sulṭân, who had sprained his left hand, which I was to treat. Later he came himself and immediately began to talk about al-Ǧowf. He confided to me that he had not as yet asked the scribe Ǧwâd to read him the letters brought by the courier and so had no idea of their contents; but he maintained that al-Ǧowf was enshrined deep in his heart.

"Why, Mûsa, with the help of Allâh, could I not found a dominion there like that which Eben Rašîd had founded? If I took possession of the oasis of al-Ǧowf, I could establish myself there with a picked band and, by prudent words, with arms and gold, in a short time I could subjugate the entire northern portion of Arabia. Let Eben Saᶜûd rule in the south."

We were at the height of our conversation when Ṭrâd, the son of Saṭṭâm, entered the tent; but presently they both left, for I had resumed writing while they were still sitting beside me, and Nawwâf took the hint. I could not afford to waste even an hour, for in five months an-Nûri was to leave inner Arabia (*aš-šerḳ*) and again pitch his camp in the north, at the boundary of the settlements (*al-ṛarb*). Before this occurred I had to explore a vast territory, observe the habits, customs, lore, etc., of the Rwala, and collect the greatest possible number of plants. The Prince likewise, that day, respected my seclusion for writing. In the afternoon I heard a woman say to Nâṣer:

"Thy master, the Sheikh Mûsa, is nowhere to be seen. He must either be on a raid or sitting in his tent writing. Is that life?"

Thursday to Thursday, January 14 to 21, 1909. Thursday morning I called in the negro Ḥmâr abu ʿAwwâd and sketched a map from his description of the territory south of Ḥazm Ğelâmîd and west of al-Ğowf. The chief's boys had put up a target and were amusing themselves with a shooting match (temperature at 6.45: 4.8° C; at 2: 9.5° C; at 5.15: 8.2° C).

Friday was *raḥîl*, migration. We set out at eight o'clock and trod over the lava stones which are scattered to a distance of almost five kilometers west of the depression of Sirḥân. Step by step we ascended the "nose" Ḫašm aẓ-Ẓwâjen, which separates the *šeʿîb* of al-Ṛarra from that of al-Ğeẓîʿ. *Firs* and *naṣi* grew upon it. At 9.25 A.M. we crossed the *šeʿîb* of al-Ğeẓîʿ and at ten o'clock reached the southern end of the volcanic district. The precipitous wall of the western upland, which approaches at the "nose" of aẓ-Ẓwâjen to within one kilometer of the eastern volcanic region, curves again to the west and the depression of Sirḥân broadens. In the east the range of Ẓelʿ al-Mismaʾ loomed up conspicuously with both of its higher elevations clearly visible, the southern resembling a camel saddle and called Šdâd, the northern looking like a sharp horn and named Sinn al-Mismaʾ.

ḲULBÂN AZ-ZWEJĞA TO ḲULBÂN AN-NBÂĞ

At eleven o'clock we encamped at the Ḳulbân az-Zwejğa. Toward evening, after a consultation with the Prince and Nawwâf, I discharged my servant Blejhân. Since we returned from our last journey he would not work and abused Mḥammad and Nâṣer so much that both begged me to dispense with him. Frequent admonitions from me had no effect, and he even grew rude to me; hence nothing remained but to pay him his

FIG. 14—Near the Želîb al-Amṛar.

wages and order him to return to his folk. I added eight *meǧîdijjât* ($7.20) to the wages mentioned in our contract, thanked him for his services, and wished him a happy journey. He left me that very evening and lodged in the tent of the orphans of Mḥammad, the brother of an-Nûri.

On Saturday we moved again. After ten o'clock we pushed onward through a marsh that extends about five kilometers to the east to the Želîb al-Amṛar (Fig. 14). At eleven o'clock we came into a lowland bordered on the east by lava and on the south and west by low limestone hills. Besides low palm brush, there grew in the marsh *sḳoṭi* (which horses like), *ṭarfa*, *mṣaᶜ*, *šwaḥwaḥ*, *ḳaṭaf*, *ṯḥama*, *firs*, and *ᶜâḏer*.

To the right, beyond a low slope about five kilometers off our course, are the wells of Umm Ṛuruba, and beyond these yawns the deep gap of the *šeᶜîb* of al-Ḥaṣa', which comes from Ṭâr al-Waḳf in the southwest. From the eastern volcanic district a somber ridge projects like a peninsula toward the south into the depression of Sirḥân. East of it is seen the *še'îb* of al-Esejd, which has its origin at a well of the same name between Tlûl aš-Šaḥam and Ẓel' al-Misma'; still farther east is the *še'îb* of al-'Abed, reaching from al-Misma'. South of the latter

FIG. 15—Ẓel' al-Misma' from the wells of al-'Ejsâwijje.

range, at the eastern margin of the depression, is situated the cone 'Abd al-Ma'âṣer, west of which terminates a *še'îb* of the same name, in which is a deep rocky crevice that is often filled with rain water (such a crevice being known as *žalta*). Hence this ravine is also called Še'îb al-Žalta. At this point the depression of Sirḥân is more than twenty-five kilometers wide and broadens perceptibly to the southeast, where the scarp of the western upland runs to the south and the edge of the lava tract bears off to the east. Southeast of the outlet of Še'îb al-Esejd, within the depression, are numerous low sandy cones, and east of them glitters the brilliant, white, salt-encrusted marsh of Ḥaẓawẓa.

At three o'clock the Prince selected a new site for the camp among the sandy cones just mentioned about four kilometers north of the Ḳulbân al-'Ejsâwijje (Fig. 15). The burdened camels advanced very slowly in the sand and did not reach the camp until late at night when nobody could pitch tents. The following day, Sunday, I was engaged in attending the sick and examining and rewrapping the supplies.

On Monday we moved again. At eight o'clock we headed southeast and at 9.40, when south of the Ḳulbân al-Mḫejẓer (Fig. 16), we turned to the south-southeast.

We could still see Šdâd al-Misma' in the north-northeast and east of it the gap formed by the *še'îb* of al-Fawz, which approaches from the Tlûl al-Mačmen and separates the hilly al-Metâha and al-Esêḥmât from the range of Ẓel' al-Misma'. At the southern base of these heights winds the *še'îb* of al-'Ajli, which conducts rain water from the southeastern portion of the volcanic district. Al-'Ajli, known at its head as Wudej 'Amr and Šaṭnet ar-Rûṭijje, has its beginning between the volcanoes of al-Mačmen, Zellâḳa, and as-Sḫami. On the left it is joined by the *še'ibân* of aš-Šîḥijje and al-Lwejzijje — al-Lwejzijje being the outlet of the Ḥabra al-Ǧîǧ — and also by the *še'ibân* of Ṭawḳa and at-Tarba; on the right it is entered by the *še'îb* of an-Neḳdijje; it terminates between 'Abd al-Ma'âṣer and Tell al-Žalta. East of the latter hill the somber lava recedes still farther to the east, and between it and the depression to the west stretches a rugged, yellowish region, in which lie the channels of the Šeʿibân abu Slêlijjât. On the southeast this region reaches up to the lava spur of Obêržât aẓ-Ẓbâʿ, which consists of cones dull gray to the west but yellowish to the east where they are covered with sand.

At twelve o'clock we came to the shallow wells of Mṛejrât al-Harma, east of the Šeʿibân al-Fkûk, which the Prince had designated as a new camp site. As it was warm and we were to push onward the next day, the slaves had not pitched a tent for even the Prince, and we all encamped among our supplies (Fig. 17).

On Tuesday morning I was aroused by the herdsman Mufaẓẓi, who came to report the loss of one of our camels — the oldest and best-natured of them all, a dark brown riding camel hailing from ʿOmân. With her had disappeared the riding saddle, the leather water bag and the canvas bucket, a tin ladle, and a rope about forty meters in length. We knew immediately who the thief was as soon as we discovered that Blejhân had also disappeared. Not only was he familiar with the places in which we kept various articles but he was well known by everybody as my servant and so could saddle my camel at leisure and fill the water bag at the nearest well. The camel likewise knew him, and he had selected the quietest animal in order that we should not be aroused by any possible grumbling; moreover he had saddled her not at the camp but at a well about two hundred paces distant, whither he had carried the other things. We found he had also appropriated flour and salt belonging to the Prince and had headed toward the northeast. By the tracks I gauged the time of his departure as before midnight. Some of the men wanted to pursue him, but the Prince and I declined. He had long since got beyond the depression of Sirḥân into the rugged volcanic district to the east, where he could easily hide and obliterate his trail. Thus for a time the camel was lost to me, but not permanently; for restitution would have to be made by the head chief Ṛaṯwân eben Meršed, to whom Blejhân was subject and who had vouched for him. As we did not move that day, I sketched a map of the territory north and south of Tejma.

On Wednesday we set out at 8.45 A.M., heading southeasterly. In the southwest we noted the *šeʿîb* of Ḥedreǧ, which has its origin in the convergence of the Riǧlet Sâlem, al-Ḫonṣor, Umm Ǧezûḥ, aẓ-Ẓwejḥijje, and Umm Leben. In its lower part

FIG. 16

FIG. 17

FIG. 16—At the Ḳulbân al-Mẖejẓer.
FIG. 17—Near Mṛejrât al-Harma.

on the right side the precipitous wall of the western upland turns to the southeast and runs out into the depression of Sirḥân. East of the *šeʿîb*, in the hollow, are the wells of Awejseṭ al-Ǧarbaʾ,[28] which at ten o'clock we had on our right (Fig. 18).

FIG. 18—Wells of Awejseṭ al-Ǧarbaʾ.

The sandy, level plain with abundant vegetation on both banks of the shallow mouth of the *šeʿîb* of Ḥedreǧ is named Marabb al-Awejseṭ. We traversed it in a south-southeasterly direction and encamped at 1.10 P. M. Toward evening there was such intense lightning in the southeast that the poor Arabs indulged in cherished hopes of fresh rain water and verdant pastures. In the depression of Sirḥân all the water savors of salt and the pastures are insufficient. The plants are covered with a layer of salt, and the camels have to be watered as often as every third day. Walking in the depression of Sirḥân is difficult for man and beast. The ground is overlain with a crust of salt one to five centimeters thick, beneath which there is often found a deposit of lime dust or sand ten to twenty centimeters deep. Both men and animals sink into it at every step and hence make slow progress.

[28] Al-Muḳaddasi, *Aḥsan* (De Goeje), p. 253, designates al-Ǧarbaʾ as one or two holes *(ṛadîr)* containing evil-smelling water and surrounded by tamarisk brush. — The Ǧarbaʾ of his day was situated on the Pilgrim Road from Syria through the depression of Sirḥân to the oasis of Tejma, and must be identical with the Awejseṭ al-Ǧarbaʾ of our time. At these wells is the termination of the valley of Ḥedreǧ, the channel of which contains holes

Being very tired, we spent Thursday on the same camping ground. Nawwâf was consumed with a flaming desire to reach al-Ğowf at the earliest possible moment and to capture the city and northern half of the former domain of Eben Rašîd;

FIG. 19—Wells of al-Mejseri.

but his father checked him. The latter was waiting for messages from Eben Saʿûd, who was said to be dwelling in al-Ḳaṣîm.

During the last few days I had often discussed with the Prince my desire to enter the region of the oasis of Tejma upon my next expedition. He did not welcome the idea, however, and urged me to postpone the trip, saying that he would likewise be bound in the same direction with his Arabs, as there was no pasture elsewhere, according to information he had received. He realized, nevertheless, that I could not wait for him and yet have time to explore the territory to the east that belonged to the tribes of the ʿAmârât and Dahâmše; therefore he decreed that I should be escorted upon my expedition by the negro Frejḥ, who had joined him from

filled with rain water called by the Arabs *ṛudrân*. As the water of a *ṛadîr* never has a stench, al-Muḳaddasi must have had in mind pools and puddles of ground water.

Neǧd only two years before and who had visited Tejma several times in his previous service under Eben Rašîd.

Friday, January 22, 1909 (temperature at 6.30 A.M.: 2° C; at 4.20 P.M.: 15.2° C). Again we were on the march. At 8.25 A.M. we proceeded southeast in a plain where *ḳaṭaf*, *mṣaʿ*, *firs*, *ʿerž*, *ʿâḏer*, and *saḥam* grew.

To the east on the horizon stretched a ragged range of gloomy volcanic hills named Obêržât aẓ-Ẓbâʿ, in front of which rose the reddish swell of Batra Šâjba, closing the depression of Sirḥân on the east. At the northern base of the lava hills originates the Šeʿîb as-Sendela, at the southern base the Šeʿîb ar-Ršâjde, and still farther to the south the Šeʿîb al-Maʿâreč. The latter approaches from the low crest Ḥazm al-Ṛarâjes, which extends from northwest to southeast and upon the eastern end of which are situated the four volcanoes of aṯ-Ṯâjât that mark the southern boundary of the volcanic district. West of the *šeʿîb* of ar-Ršâjde lie the Ḳulbân Šâjba.

At the outset I rode with a group of youthful warriors, but later the Prince joined me and invited me to accompany him. We discussed the contemplated occupation of al-Ǧowf and the possible complications that might arise in connection with it. I urged the Prince to offer peace to the ʿAmârât and Dahâmše tribes and to ally himself with all his kinsmen, the ʿAneze, against his ancient enemy Eben Rašîd.

At 10.18 we came to the wells of al-Mejseri[29] by which stood two palm trees (Fig. 19). The Prince watered his camel and his horse from my canvas bucket, which was in great demand, and twenty minutes later he and I proceeded on our way.

Southwest of the wells of al-Mejseri ends the Šeʿîb al-Ṛîne, which rises at the eastern base of Berḳ ad-Dûde and Ṭubejž al-Ḥamar, winds through a low plateau Arẓ al-Ṛîne, and in the north forms the boundary of the dark brown, level, desolate desert of al-Bsajṭa and the hillocks of Ḳaṣîmt al-Arnab. At its left converges the *šeʿîb* of as-Sahab, at the head of which are the wells of al-Amrar and with which merge the *šeʿîbân* of Ammu Ṭlejḥa, al-Halba, Ammu Rṭaʾ, and Ammu Ṛẓejje.[30]

[29] Jâḳût, *Muʿǧam* (Wüstenfeld), Vol. 4, p. 715, mentions a place called Majsar, in Syria. — As our al-Mejseri is situated on the Syrian Pilgrim Road, it may be identical with Majsar.

[30] Through the upper portion of the valley of al-Ṛîne leads a route from Syria to Tejma, and in the lower portion runs the road from Syria through Dûmat al-Ǧandalijje to Irak; therefore I identify our al-Ṛîne with the Ṛajna which Jâḳût, *op. cit.*, Vol. 3, p. 832, writes of as a place in Syria, but the exact situation of which was not known to him. In the dialect Ṛajna is identical with Ṛîna, just as Ajla is identical with Îla. I hold that the Amarr which Jâḳût, *op. cit.*, Vol. 1, p. 361, says is situated in the Syrian desert in the direction of the Ḥeǧâz at the northern fringe of the desolate district of Busajṭa, really lies among the wells of al-Amrar, in the upper portion of the valley of al-Ṛîne. The body of Prince Abu-l-Baḳar of the Ṭajj tribe was interred there. Past the wells of al-Amrar leads the road from Syria to the Ḥeǧâz; Busajṭa is not far distant, and in the twelfth and thirteenth centuries of our era the clans of the Ṭajj were camping in the vicinity of these wells.

At 11.30 we were riding along the boundary of the plain of aš-Šubejče.[31]

East of us stretched the depression of Sirḥân, covered with a multitude of low cones. At 12.16 P. M. we arrived at the wells of an-Nbâğ, where we pitched our tents and prepared our supplies for my next expedition.

[31] Jâḳût, *op. cit.*, Vol. 2, p. 853, designates by the name Rawẓat aš-Šubejke, or Rawẓ aš-Šubajk, the lowland adjoining al-Ğowf between Ḳurâḳir, Amarr, and Busajṭa. — Our lowland of aš-Šubejče is indeed situated not far from the middle of the triangle the corners of which are marked by Ḳerâžer, al-Bsajṭa, and the wells of al-Amrar.

CHAPTER V

AN-NBÂĞ TO AL-ĞOWF (DÛMAT AL-ĞANDALIJJE) BY WAY OF UBEJṬ

AN-NBÂĞ TO ṬUʿÛS SEMNÂN

Saturday, January 23, 1909. I supplied myself with provisions for six persons for thirty to thirty-five days and took with me five camels. The negro Frejḥ was to ride his own beast and, like Mḥammad, he was to lead by a rein a camel carrying a load. While my men were loading, I went to bid farewell to the Prince and found him in front of his tent, squatting among the camels and issuing important orders to two Bedouins who were about to set out on speedy camels to al-Ğowf. As soon as he dismissed them they swung upon their mounts and presently disappeared beyond a slope that hedged the camp on the east. They could not trifle with time, for they had orders to reach al-Ğowf before dawn on the morrow and to report to the Prince the following day; and al-Ğowf was 150 kilometers distant. The Prince had despatched two couriers in order to be sure that, in the event of a mishap to one of them, his message would be delivered by the other.

After the men were out of sight the Prince accompanied me to my tent, warning me of the dangers that would be lurking for me and my fellows at every turn on my new expedition.

"Brother," he said, "thou wilt enter a region where there are not only bands of marauders but single robbers who rob and kill as well. My protection will be of no avail to thee, for nobody will ever learn who thy murderers have been. In the neighborhood of Tejma outlaws of the Šarârât, Beni ʿAṭijje, Htejm, Weld Slejmân, and Šammar tribes are roving; nay, even of the Ḥwêṭât at-Tihama; and all these are our enemies. Therefore be on the alert and see thou returnest to thy friends alive and well."

At 8.43 A. M. we left the camp and rode along the western fringe of the depression of Sirḥân toward the southeast. This hollow is a sandy, marshy lowland, above which protrude solitary low hillocks. At 9.20 we reached the southwestern upland, whence we could see to the northeast, looming far above the horizon, the volcanoes Tell ʿAmûd, southwest of them ar-Rḥaʾ and Mečâmen ar-Rḥa, and south of these, nearer to us, the last volcanic hillocks of at-Ṯâjât. West of the latter extended Šeʿîb al-Ḳutb, rimming the white plain of Siḥle Ẓalma on the south and disappearing in the depression of Sirḥân.

From 11.18 to 12.43 P. M. our camels grazed. Then we proceeded among the light grayish hillocks of Ḳaṣîmt al-Arnab, with their low and frequently sandy slopes, in which grow *ʿağram, ẓamrân, rimṯ, ʿarâd, arṭa,* and at intervals even bushes of *ġaẓa;* in the lowland near the Želîb Ḥlejžîm, which we passed at 2.06, we saw fresh *ṯḥama* growing. From 3.40 to 6.05 we stopped almost due southwest of Abraḳ an-Nabč, a sandy hill at the base of which the small oasis of an-Nabč aš-Šerži is situated in the shade of several palm trees. This oasis is also called an-Nabk abu Ḳaṣr, since there is a little half-ruined stone farm (*ḳaṣr*) there. We ate our supper and then rode on until 7.50, when we made camp at the eastern fringe of the sandy *ġaẓa*-covered hillocks of Ḳaṣîmt al-Arnab.

Sunday, January 24, 1909. As early as 4.30 A.M. I aroused my companions and kindled a fire to prepare the coffee so that we could get a good start. Our negro Frejḥ disliked rising early. He maintained that camels need an absolute rest before sunrise and that, even while on raids, everyone rests at this time and does not set out until the sun is up. He also pointed out the danger to which we exposed ourselves by kindling a fire in the darkness of the night. All this he expounded in order to induce me not to start until after sunrise, but he concealed the real reason, which was that he liked warmth immensely and, as the cold is most acute just before dawn, he wished to spend that time in bed or close to a fire (temperature at 5.15: 1° C).

At 6.38 we were in the saddle and riding among low, precipitous hillocks that had been separated from the western uplands by the action of wind, rain, and sand. Because they were composed of horizontal strata of unequal hardness that naturally defy the elements in varying degrees, they showed singular formations. Among them grew *ʿâḏer* in profusion. About three kilometers to the east Frejḥ showed me the Ḳulbân al-Ğerâwi, situated at the bottom of the depression of Sirḥân, which is here over fifteen kilometers wide and closed on the east by the precipitous slope, al-ʿArâjef, of the Siḥle Ẓalma upland. Far to the east protruded on the horizon the wide, white crest of al-Mefrežijje and south of it the broad summits of Ẓahrat al-Farǧa. West of them, stretching down to the depression of Sirḥân, spread the stony plain Arẓ al-Ǧrejmîs. At-Ṯâjât, the southernmost of the volcanoes, were also visible. Southeast of them the southwestern portion of al-Ḥamâd is called al-Bijâẓ.

At 8.40, as we crossed a swampy stretch of the depression of Sirḥân, we noted several palm trees and wells called Šṛajjer. At the south-southwestern fringe of this stretch are situated the wells of ʿArfeǧa and south of them those of al-Mšâš.

From 9.36 to 10.05 we stopped at the Ḳulbân Šṛâr (Fig. 20) to water our camels and fill the leather bags (temperature at 10: 14.4° C). As there was no pasture in that vicinity we proceeded south until 11.06, resting from that time until one o'clock beside the Ḳulbân Ṣbâjḥa (Fig. 21), situated in a deep hollow in the shade of several palm trees between two sandy hillocks overgrown with *ṛaẓa* bushes. Both of the hillocks resembled the big grave mounds of cooler climates over which droop mournful weeping willows or birches. Around them in the hollow we saw here and there bushes of *ʿaǧram, rimṯ,* and *ʿarâd,* the last-named plant much liked by camels. When, therefore, at 4.15 we came upon a profusion of these bushes about thirty centimeters high in the plain of al-Bsajṭa, west of the Ḳulbân Majḳûʿ, we stayed there until 6.08 to let the camels feed (temperature at 4.30: 17° C). At 9.05 we found a camping place southeast of the Ḳaṣâjem ad-Damm near several sandy hillocks overgrown with more mature bushes of *ṛaẓa.* The Bedouins do not permit their camels to graze upon the *ṛaẓa* that grows here, for they say it would cause them to pass bloody urine and soon die of exhaustion.

Monday, January 25, 1909 (temperature at 6 A. M.: 3° C). Starting at seven o'clock, we rode in the desolate plain of al-Bsajṭa, the surface of which consists of coffee-brown layers of gravel. Not a thing grows in the plain except after the recurrent torrents of the *wasm* (Canopus, October) rains when it is covered with tiny *semḥ* plants, the seeds of which many Bedouins use as a substitute for flour. They pick the matured *semḥ,* deposit it in round holes, thresh it with heavy

Fig. 20

Fig. 21

Fig. 20—At the Ḳulbân Šṛâr.
Fig. 21—Ḳulbân Ṣbâjḥa.

sticks, wring it, and separate the pure brown seeds. We crossed numerous paths leading to the southeast, upon which we noted fresh tracks of camels coming from the watering place of Majḳûᶜ.

At 8.25 I caught sight of a rider and almost instantly of another, appearing upon the low crest of al-Ḳnejfd̲ât. Who were they? Were they the scouts of a raiding party? Were they friends or foes? They were moving along the crest southward, visible from afar. Only Bedouins who feel absolutely sure and safe act thus. Either they belonged to a large company of riders, or, as seemed more likely, they were with a body of peaceful Arabs camping somewhere near; for enemy scouts would not have stayed so long on the crest even if they were preceding a strong horde. With our white shirt sleeves we signaled the unknown riders to approach. At first they ignored the summons and it was not until ten o'clock that they descended at a trot from the summit into the plain. As soon as they were within shouting distance, Frejḥ yelled to them.

"If ye be not Rwala, do not come nearer!" Whereupon one of them recognized Frejḥ, called him by his name, and both approached us. They proved to be Rwala of the Ḳaᶜâžᶜa clan, who were camping at al-Eẓâreᶜ and were on the trail of a Šarâri who had been serving with the clan and had deserted the day before after stealing a camel. They had followed his trail to the vicinity of al-Ḳnejfd̲ât, where the track became obliterated in a multitude of fresh camel footprints. The riders and their mounts were thirsty and hungry and had no prospect of returning to their tents before the next evening. We gave food and drink to the men but had none for the horses, as the wells of Mlêḥ, for which we were bound, were still one and a half days off.

West of al-Ḳnejfd̲ât are three large sandy hills, Ṭuᶜûs Semnân, beneath which we rested from 10.15 to 12.10 P. M. (temperature at 12.30: 16°C). These hills form the southwestern edge of the sandy district of Ṛwêṭa Ǧerâd, situated between Ḳulbân Majḳûᶜ to the north, Ḥzejm ar-Rîm to the south, the broad range of al-Ḳnejfd̲ât to the west, and the undulating plain of an-Nhejdejn to the east.

AL-BSAJṬA AND THE REGION TO THE WEST

The desolate plain of al-Bsajṭa has been evolved through the erosion of countless centuries. Long ago it was covered with hills of sandstone, but the wind, rain, and frost gnawed at the surface of the hills until there remained only the more solid internal substances which rigidly defied the ever-moving sand drifting over and burying them. The erosion went on ceaselessly, however. The rain water kept washing out shallow channels, the edges of which would offer resistance to the strong west winds for a time and then would gradually crumble, leaving only the hard cores which could not be eaten away and were covered with sand. Thus were formed the sandy hills called *ṭuᶜûs* or *ḳaṣâjem,* which, scattered over the plain, give it the mournful aspect noted by Arabian poets.[32]

[32] Ḥâtem aṭ-Ṭâ'i, *Dîwân* (Schulthess), p. 44, refers to secret places upon both sides of the desert of Busajṭa.

Al-Bekri, *Muᶜǧam* (Wüstenfeld), p. 178, writes that Busajṭa is a district between the two Ṭajj ranges and Syria.

Jâḳût, *Muᶜǧam* (Wüstenfeld), Vol. 1, p. 626, says that Busajṭa is a district in the desert between Irak and Syria, the boundary toward Syria being formed by the water of Amarr and that to the south by Ḳaᶜbet al-ᶜElem. He says it is a plain covered with small pebbles of various shapes and uninhabitable because devoid of water and pasture. As Abu-ṭ-Ṭajjeb al-Mutanabbi was fleeing from Egypt to Irak, his slave is said to have seen in this plain a strange bull which he took for the tower of a mosque; another traveler had seen an ostrich and called it a palm, a comparison at which his audience made merry. Naṣr says that Busajṭa is a plain between the territory of the tribes of Kalb and Balḳejn beyond ᶜAfar, or Aᶜfar. Others place Busajṭa on the road traversed by the Ṭajj on their way to Syria. —

The common expression that something is situated between Irak and Syria recurs often in Jâḳût. The plain Arẓ al-Ḳîne on the north being in every way similar to the plain of al-Bsajṭa, he is correct in his statement that Busajṭa reaches as far as the water of Amarr. On the west and north of it spread the mighty heights of the territory of aṣ-Ṣawwân, while the southern boundary of the plain is formed by the plateaus of Ṭubejž al-Ḥamar, which therefore are a part of the district of Ḳaᶜbet al-ᶜElem. The wild bull which the slave took for the white tower of a mosque was really the white, or somewhat yellowish, antelope, *Oryx beatrix,* called *baḳar al-maha'* or *baḳar al-waḥš.* The assertions of Naṣr are also correct. In his time (the latter half of the twelfth century) the Balḳejn were camping to the northwest, the Kalb being northeast of Bsajṭa. Aᶜfar, or ᶜAfar as he writes in the dialect, is identical with Ṭubejž al-ᶜAfar, which hedges the plain of Bsajṭa to the west. Whenever the Ṭajj wished to leave their mountain ranges of Aǧa' and Salma to go to Syria, they had to travel past the desert of Busajṭa no matter if they went either straight through the Nefûd desert or along its western boundary.

According to Jâḳût, *op. cit.*, Vol. 4, p. 145, and to Abu-l-Faḍâ'il, *Marâṣid* (Juynboll), Vol. 2, p. 436, south of Busajṭa there spreads the district of Ḳaᶜbet al-ᶜElem. Though it contains no palatable water, it abounds in *naṣi;* hence the Arabs dwell there during the fine spring weather. West of this district, along the route from Tebûk, rises the high mountain al-ᶜElem from which the district derived its name. South of al-ᶜElem is the fresh water of Ṯaǧr. —

It is impossible to ascertain exactly from Jâḳût which is the road from Tebûk. Granting that his informant probably had in mind the road leading from Tebûk along the western boundary of Ḳaᶜbet al-ᶜElem across Busajṭa to Dûmat al-Ǧandal, we must concede that his mountain of al-ᶜElem is our Ǧedᶜân al-Abraḳ, since the traveler coming from Tebûk near this mountain enters a wild plateau made rugged by deep chasms. Ṯaǧr must be identical with the wide valley of Feǧr to the southeast of Ǧedᶜân al-Abraḳ, in which rain water is retained; the substitution of *f* for *ṯ* is very frequent in the dialects. As the ground and dust are salty even the rain water wells Mšâš az-Zhejrijje and al-Ḥâzem, in the valley of Feǧr, are bitter. The *naṣi,* especially when fresh, provides good pasture for sheep and goats. After the heavy winter rains the Arabs camp in the district of Ǧedᶜân knowing well that there they will find good pasture and an abundance of rain water. They cannot camp there during the summer, because the entire district contains not even a single well of spring water. If it does not rain sufficiently for four consecutive years, all the wells, which are supplied with water through underground natural conduits beneath a deep layer of sand, become dry.

To the west al-Bsajṭa borders on the elevated, undulating district of Arẓ al-Ṛîne, which adjoins on the north the plateau of Ṭubejž al-Ḫamar. Several deep valleys cut through the southeastern part of the latter. To the east the *šeʿîb* of aṭ-Ṭrejf divides Ğaʿalat as-Sawdaʾ on the east from the Ḳârt al-Wuʿela and Ğaʿalat aš-Šhabaʾ on the west. Between the two highlands last named winds the gorge Ṯenijjet ammu-r-Rîlân, and along their western base runs the *šeʿîb* of Abu ʿAlda, which has its origin in the Arẓ al-Ṛîne and its termination in Ḫabra ʿAtîḳ. West of the *šeʿîb* of Abu ʿAlda are the mesas of Ḳlûb Ḥamed, al-Ḥmejdân, and Ḳlejb al-ʿAbd, which are divided by the tenijjet (defile) of Umm ʿArâd. From Ḳlûb Ḥamed comes the valley of Umm Ğirfejn, along which are the Ḫabra ummu Mjele, Mowfaʾ, and the water of Moṛejrat al-Fâṭer in the channel of Umm Ğirfejn. Into this channel there also flows the rain water from the *šeʿibân* of Ammu Ğîfejn, Ṛzejwât, and an-Neğîli. The Šeʿîb an-Neğîli begins under the name of al-ʿAṣra in the mountains of an-Neğîli, aš-Šhejba, and al-Mlejsa and has in its lower portion the Ḳulbân al-Mṛejra and al-Bedîʿ, toward which the Šeʿibân al-Ğawraʿa converge. To the west these various valleys are bounded by the wide uplands of ar-Rîše, an-Neğîli, and aš-Šhejba; to the south by Ğedʿân al-Asmar, Sanâm al-Ḫamar, and Sanâm al-ʿAfar.[33] At the eastern base of the last-named mesa is the Ḫabra-l-Muṣâmel, to the northeast of which spreads the basin Nukṛat ar-Ršejdân, which, in turn, reaches as far as Ğaʿalat aš-Šhabaʾ. Within this last is the solitary Tell Ṣejfûr.

The high, dark bluish wall of Ṭubejž al-Ḫamar was clearly visible from Ṭuʿûs Semnân. To the southwest, closer to us, we noted the slopes of the table mountain Ḳârt al-Wuʿela,[34] which is encircled by the *šeʿîb* of aṭ-Ṭrejf.

On the left side of aṭ-Ṭrejf looms the mighty height of Ğaʿalat as-Sawdaʾ which reaches far into the plain of al-Bsajṭa. East of this mesa rises the level crest of an-Nṣejr, the spurs of which reach as far as Ṭuʿûs Semnân.[35]

[33] Al-Bekri, *op. cit.*, p. 113, and Jâḳût, *op. cit.*, Vol. 1, p. 315; Vol. 2, pp. 339, 734, place the mountain of al-Aʿfar in the territory of the Balḳejn tribe in Syria. They attempt to establish this by quoting a verse of the poet Imrulḳajs in which Aʿfar and Ḥamal are mentioned. According to their interpretation Ḥamal is also a mountain in the territory of the Balḳejn tribe, but according to others it is a region at the boundary of the sandy desert of ʿÂleğ. Imrulḳajs, *Dîwân* (De Slane), p. 26, incorrectly spells these place names "Ḫamalaʾ" and "Awğaraʾ." —

All this appears to indicate that Aʿfar and Ḥamal denote a mountainous region in the former territory of the Balḳejn tribe near the sandy desert of ʿÂleğ. This view is further supported by the location of the mountain districts of Ṭubejž al-ʿAfar — thus pronounced in the dialect instead of Aʿfar — and Ṭubejž al-Ḥamar — the dialect here having substituted *r* for the *l* in Ḥamal — the eastern borders of which adjoin extensions of the sandy desert of ʿÂleğ (or Nefûd). That this mountainous region in the past was a possession of the Balḳejn is also indicated by other reports. Imrulḳajs, who saw the two mountains on his way from Tejma to the Ḥawrân, speaks of them as situated side by side. The old route which he followed actually leads between al-ʿAfar and al-Ḥamar, through the valley of Ammu Ğîfejn. Beside it, in the upper portion of the valley, are the ruins of Ḳaṣr al-Kelwa, some filled-up wells, and a rain pond called al-Kelwa.

Al-Muḳaddasi, who knew the district between Tejma and the depression of Sirḥân, intimates (*Aḥsan* [De Goeje], p. 253) that the water of al-Ağwali is so bad that whoever drinks it becomes swollen and is at the point of death. — Al-Muḳaddasi often substitutes *ğ* for *č* (*k*); hence we may read his al-Ağwali as al-Ačwali or al-Akwali and in that word see another derivative of the word Kelwa. The wells at al-Kelwa are filled up, the Bedouins having neglected to clean them, maintaining that the water is not wholesome.

[34] Al-Hamdâni, *Ṣifa* (Müller), p. 179, mentions a Wuʿâl in the territory of the Ḏubjân tribe. — As our Ḳârt al-Wuʿela rises in the territory formerly belonging to the Ḏubjân tribe, we may take it for the Wuʿâl of al-Hamdâni.

[35] Al-Azhari (Jâḳût, *op. cit.*, Vol. 3, p. 140) names Samnân as a place in the desert.

To the south of Semnân gapes the wide and deep dale of Ḫabb al-Ğemal, dividing Ḥazm an-Nṣejr from the western spurs of the hilly district of al-Ḥaršûfijjât. Turning to the east, we gazed into the sandy stretch of Rwêṭa Ğerâd, parallel with which runs the rocky height of Ḥzejm ar-Rîm. The latter, with the hills of al-Ḥaršûfijjât, forms the western and southwestern boundary of the aṭ-Ṭawîl range.

ṬUʿÛS SEMNÂN TO AL-ʿAREJŽ SANDS

Pushing forward upon a stony plain which slopes to the south, we came into the dale of Ḫabb al-Ğemal and a little after two o'clock sighted in the south a band of migrating Arabs, who proved to be subjects of Eben Ğandal in search of better pastures to the north. At 3.22 we encamped near them at the eastern side of the dale, as I wished to hire for a guide one of the Šarârât who were accompanying them (temperature at 4: 18.5° C).

Toward evening I was visited by the chief, Ṣajjâḥ eben Ğandal, who invited me to his tent for a cup of coffee and a grain of salt. He was hostile to Prince an-Nûri, for his family had allied itself with the descendants of the assassinated Prince Fahad and had sworn vengeance on an-Nûri. Ṣajjâḥ, who might have been forty years of age, was much interested in the history of his family and asked me whether it was true that al-Ğowf had formerly belonged to it and if the place was still rightly called Dûmat al-Ğandal or al-Ğandalijje. When I answered in the affirmative and assured him that the old name of al-Ğowf should rightly be Dûmat al-Ğandal, he ordered all present to listen to what the books said and was so gratified by my opinion that he offered me his friendship. For supper dates with camel meat were served to me. After supper he sent to me a young Šarâri with whom Mḥammad had come to an agreement, whereby he would accompany us and protect us from his co-tribesmen for one *meǧîdijje* a day while southbound and three-quarters of a *meǧîdijje* thereafter, when returning north. He was to ride one of my camels. His name was Masʿûd eben ʿWejned aṣ-Ṣbejḥi, and he was affiliated with the esteemed family of Ṣbejḥât of the Ḥlese clan. Taking a seat close to me, he swore to protect us from all the Šarârât. True, the latter lived in peace with Prince an-Nûri and his Rwala, but the individual clans of the Rwala and Šarârât were always at variance. Only ten days before, Ṣajjâḥ eben Ğandal had attacked the camp of the Šarârât and driven off

132 camels. No wonder he cautioned me of the danger that threatened us on the way south and said that none but Allâh could protect us!

Tuesday, January 26, 1909. Besides Masʿûd, we were accompanied by a Šarâri named Mḥammad Râʿi-s-Sabbâra, who wanted to go to Tejma with his two worn-out camels and praised Allâh for sending us his way with our supplies (temperature at 6: 12° C). We left the camp of Eben Ǧandal at 7.18 A. M., going south-southwest. South of the dale rises a district of low, sandy hills, interspersed with larger and smaller swales in which rain water accumulates, promoting the growth of *ḳejṣûm, ǧeṯjâṯ, ǧrajba, mṭi* (also called *ḏaʿlûḳ al-ǧemal*), *niḳd, šaʿrân, ẓaʿ*, and *ẓamrân*. Because of incessant erosion many of the hillocks stand entirely isolated, resembling dilapidated castles. On the unsubstantial horizontal strata of sandstone rest boulders from three to four meters high, which, being insufficiently supported upon the soft lower layer, roll over or lean to one side or balance upon their edges as if hung in the air. This hilly district, called Umm Ǧeṯjâṯ, is hedged in on the south by a somber mesa of the same name that stretches from west to east. Passing through it at 10.40 in the defile Ṯenijjet umm Ǧeṯjâṯ, we rested at its southern base until 11.40.

Accompanied by the guide, Tûmân and I ascended the mesa to sketch a map from the top. To the west-northwest we noted the bare summits of Ǧaʿalat as-Sawdaʾ and Ǧaʿalat aš-Šhabaʾ, divided by the defile Ṯenijjet aṭ-Ṭrejf. Farther to the northwest, beyond the defile Ṯenijjet ammu-r-Rîlân and several sandstone hills, rose the table mountain of al-Wuʿela, beyond which showed the precipitous walls of Ṭubejž al-Ḥamar. East of Ḳârt umm Ǧeṯjâṯ and east of Ḥabb al-Ǧemal spreads the sandy and hilly district of Obêrež aẓ-Ẓijân in some sections covered with great sand drifts; and northeast of that appear al-Ḥaršûfijjât. Southeast of Obêrež aẓ-Ẓijân towers the black mountain of al-Bârde, while south of the latter and south of Ḳârt umm Ǧeṯjâṯ spreads the plain of al-Luṛuf (Fig. 22), which looks as if it were paved with flags of sandstone and is in turn hedged toward the south by a high wall of pinkish sand, al-ʿArejž. In the Luṛuf, as the levels adjoining the sandy desert are called, we found growing in sand-filled hollows *ḥambâẓ, ḳorẓi* (also called *ǧezzûḥ*), *ḫrîṭ, mṭi, metnân, hazzaʾ, ʿarfeǧ, ʿarâd, ẓamrân, naṣi, heǧîne, ʿâḏer, firs*, and *šaʿrân*, which the Šarârât call *ḥaṣâd* (temperature at 12.15: 23° C).

At 12.50 P. M. we observed on the left, at the northern foot of al-ʿArejž, a small camp (*ferîž*) of the Freǧe clan of the Rwala. Our negro Frejḥ turned in there to inquire the way to the next camps of the Rwala, but he had barely disappeared when a Frejği came rushing toward us, assaulted the Šarâri Mḥammad, pulled him off his camel, swung himself into the saddle, and with both camels sped back to his tent. We learned later that the Freğe had the day before attacked the Šarârât at the wells of Ḥdâğân and that in retaliation

FIG. 22—Plain of al-Luṛuf between Ḳârt umm Ğeṯjâṯ and al-ʿArejž.

the latter had at night robbed them of half their camels. As Mḥammad was a Šarâri, the Frejği saw in him an enemy (*ḳowmâni*) and so appropriated his property as booty. As soon as Frejḥ saw the Frejği riding Mḥammad's camel, he ordered him in the name of Prince an-Nûri immediately to surrender both animals to Mḥammad, who was under my protection. The Frejği hesitated a while, but finally submitted, and Mḥammad was allowed to remount his camel and ride merrily on his way.

Soon after two o'clock we began to ascend to the sands of al-ʿArejž, which form the western fringe of the Nefûd desert, but our camels progressed very laboriously. We were presently overtaken by two Rwala, both on one camel. They had been camping in the vicinity of al-Ğowf, had taken part in a raid against the Dahâmše, and were now seeking their relatives encamped somewhere near Tejma. Meantime they wished to rely upon us for protection and food. From 4.08 to six o'clock our camels grazed at the base of a high, sandy hill, while we scaled the top and drew a map of the surrounding district.

REGION WEST OF AL-ʿAREJŽ

To the north we could see the blue hillocks of Umm Ğeṯjâṯ, to the west the two Ğaʿala and the mesa of al-Wuʿela, and northwest of them the swells of Arẓ al-Ṛîne enshrouded in a purple veil. Ḳârt umm Ğeṯjâṯ protrudes to the south like a nose pointing toward an-Naʿağa — this being the name of the western end of the sandy "little vein" al-ʿArejž. Northwest of Ḳârt umm Ǧeṯjâṯ, at the southeast foot of the Ǧaʿalat aš-Šhaba', the Ḫabâri aš-Šiblijjât receive water from the *šeʿîb* of aṭ-Ṭrejf. The southern base of Ǧaʿalat aš-Šhaba' at the Ḫabra al-Ḫsene turns to the southwest; it then describes a curve to the northwest at the solitary hill Tell Ṣejfûr, and encircles the basin of Nuḳrat ar-Ršejdân, in which terminate the valleys of Umm Ǧirfejn and Abu ʿAlda. To the southwest of the Tell Ṣejfûr we saw the outlines of the dark mountain of Ǧedʿân al-Asmar, south of it the Ẕelʿ Sanâm al-Ḥamar, and farther to the south the black cones of the Ẕlûʿ Feǧr, which are paralleled on the east by a *šeʿîb* of the same name. This *šeʿîb* rises almost due west of Sanâm al-Ḥamar at the eastern slopes of the hills along the western foot of which run the Pilgrim Road and the Ḥeǧâz Railway. To the west the watershed of the Šeʿîb Feǧr and its tributaries is formed from east to west by Ẕelʿ Ṣdâr, Ḥawmât, Sanâm al-Ḥamar, Ǧedʿân al-Abraḳ, the plain of al-ʿArejʿerijje, al-Medâfeʿ, and ad-Dabel; to the southwest, south, and southeast by al-Ṛawânem, aẓ-Ẓufejjer, al-Ṛazwân, Lemleme, al-Edêreʿ, al-Bijâẓijje, Berḳat al-Bṛêṯijje, Ḳûr al-Ǧâjfa, al-Ǧerânijjât, and Mlêḥ. The main valley of this entire region leads northeastward from aẓ-Ẓufejjer under the name of Abu Sella; it is joined on the left by the combined *šeʿibân* of Abu ʿArâd and al-ʿÂžer, and east of them by al-Želîbe, in which is the water Mšâš Dâbes. Farther down, Abu Sella takes the name Šeʿîb Feǧr and is joined on the right by the *šeʿibân* of al-Ǧemalên and aẓ-Ẓâḥčijje. At the northeastern foot of the Ẕlûʿ Feǧr, which overlooks the upper course of the Šeʿîb Feǧr on the north, there are the channels Mšâš az-Zhejrijje and Mšâš al-Ḥâzem and farther to the northeast the Ḫabra ʿAǧâǧ and Ḫabra al-Ḥâwi;[36] at the latter the Šeʿîb Feǧr terminates almost in the sands of an-Naʿaǧa.

From the plain of al-ʿArejʿerijje[37] the rain water flows through the channels of Ammu Rǧâm and Fîhat Ḥawmal northwestward into the Ḫabâri ʿAmrât at the western end of the Ṭubejž al-ʿAfar district.

[36] Al-Muḳaddasi, *op. cit.*, p. 253, refers to the water of Ṯaǧr, which gathers in the hollows of the channel and is neither very palatable nor very plentiful.

Jâḳût, *op. cit.*, Vol. 1, p. 919, writes that this water belongs to the tribe of al-Ḳejn and is situated not far from the hillocks of Ḥamal and Aʿfar between Wâdi al-Ḳura' and Tejma. —

The phrase "Ḥamal and Aʿfar" denotes the hilly district of Sanâm al-Ḥamar, or al-Ḥamal, and al-ʿAfar, which encloses the valley of Feǧr on the northwest. This valley lies between the oases of Tejma and Dûmat al-Ǧandal, the latter of which is also often called Wâdi al-Ḳura', or al-Ḳurejjât. The water of Ṯaǧr may be identified with the rain pools of az-Zhejrijje in this valley. Ṯaǧr is either erroneously transcribed from Faǧr, or else, as frequently happens, the *F* has been replaced by *Ṯ*.

The valley of Feǧr terminates in the rain pool of al-Ḥâwi, which I identify with the watering place Ḥawijj, since, according to Jâḳût, *op. cit.*, Vol. 2, p. 373, this likewise once belonged to the Balḳejn tribe.

[37] In al-ʿArejʿerijje we may look for the old ʿUrâʿir.

Al-Aṣmaʿi (Jâḳût, *op. cit.*, Vol. 3, p. 662) places ʿUrajʿira between the two mountain ranges of the Ṭajj tribe and the sandy desert, an opinion which he attempts to establish by the verse of a certain woman of the Beni Murra tribe, who mentions the valley of ʿUrajʿira in connection with the two ranges. But this does not prove that the valley lies between the Aǧa' and Salma ranges. On the contrary, it should be sought in the former territory of the Beni Murra tribe, where the hills that form the border of the plain of al-ʿArejʿerijje are also called by the same name.

Al-Bekri, *Muʿǧam* (Wüstenfeld), p. 658, and Ibn al-Aṯîr, *Kâmil* (Tornberg), Vol. 1, p. 430, seek ʿUrâʿir in the territory of the Kalb tribe, which before the advent of Islam was attacked there by Ḳejs ibn Zuhejr. — It is true that before the advent of Islam the Kalb owned even the territory north of the oasis of Tejma; therefore al-ʿArejʿerijje may be identical with ʿUrâʿir. This supposition is verified by Jâḳût, *op. cit.*, Vol. 1, p. 360, who seeks the bitter water of al-Amrâr in the territory of the Beni Fezâra. Here were said to be the watering places of ʿUrâʿir and Kunajb, so called because of the bitterness of their water. Such bitter water, al-Amarr, was, according to Jâḳût, *op. cit.*, Vol. 1, p. 361, found near the level desert of Busajṭa and thus in the vicinity of al-ʿArejʿerijje.

In the northeastern portion of al-ʿArejʿerijje are the waters Mšâš al-Ğedʿân, aṭ-Ṯhama, and al-Kfûf.

Upon both sides of the lower part of the valley of Feğr, between Sanâm al-ʿAfar on the west, Ḳârt al-Ḫonṣor on the east, Ğaʿalat aš-Šhaba' on the north, and Ḳûr Mleḥ on the south, there extends the somber level of al-Hûğ, which reminds one of al-Bsajṭa, as it too has been created by the erosion of countless ages. South of al-Hûğ and southwest of the sandy hill from which we were making observations we saw peculiar land forms. In the southwest rose the irregular cones of Ḳûr Mlêḥ, beside which are located the wells of the same name, and east of these cones the tabular hills of Ḳûr al-Hawğa, resembling a modern fortress. East of the latter the straight crest of the hill rising above the Mšâš al-Mowt ran from northwest to southeast; beyond it to the south protruded two horns of ʿḤdâğan; farther to the southeast the rocky heights of Ḥelwât and Abu Ṯenijja lifted themselves like a gigantic Gothic castle; and northeast of the mesa of Mšâš al-Mowt peered the solitary table mountain al-Ḫonṣor. Beyond these heights there spread to the east an almost boundless sea of sand, the Nefûd, above which to the northeast the mountain of al-Bârde in the range of aṭ-Ṭawîl loomed like a dark wall (temperature at 5.10: 16° C).

AL-ʿAREJŽ TO AL-MEẒÂHÎR; THE ŠARÂRÂT

While we were upon the sandy hill, Mḥammad Râʿi-s-Sabbâra plucked a quantity of the dry *sobot* straw with which to feed our camels at the next watering place, and before we left we cleaned our carbines and loaded them with sharp cartridges, for we were not certain that the Šarârât would not attack us during the night. Traveling was very difficult. In the pitch darkness of the night we could not avoid quickly enough the steep slopes of the sand drifts and hillocks and so had to make frequent stops and detours. At last, at the foot of a long, steep sand drift, we found ourselves on the fringe of a deep funnel-like hollow which frightened our camels. For a while we could move neither ahead nor backward, but we had to enter the drift and get through it as best we could. It was a hard and dangerous undertaking. I led my camel, but the animal failed to gain solid footing upon the sandy slope and kept slipping and dragging me along, and when finally with great effort I brought her up to the sharp crest of the drift, the edge gave way under me and slid down with me, burying me under the mass of sand. Frejḥ and Mḥammad in rushing to my aid had the same experience. Once freed from the sandy avalanche, we dug steps in the crest upon which the camels could cross to the other side, and when we had them all over in safety, we lay down upon the sand, at 7.48, under a large bush of *raza*. Not one of us prepared a bed — we were too tired for that. In the sand I had lost my watch, the money I carried, and a camel stick.

Wednesday, January 27, 1909. By 6.32 A.M. we were upon our camels' backs, for we had only a little water left and the nearest well was still a long way off. Having learned that the ᶜAzzâm clan of the Šarârât was encamped at the wells of Mlêḥ and was making robber raids against all the Rwala, we decided to get water at al-Hawǧa and so started in that direction.

From the high ᶜArejž we saw to the south, far below us, a black, boundless level from which protruded solitary hills of fantastic shape. Al-ᶜArejž itself consists of innumerable dunes, called *flûḳ*, each one of which stretches in elliptical form from west to east; here and there are higher sand drifts which the Rwala call *ṭuᶜûs* and the Šarârât *barâẖîs*. The elliptical hollows surrounded by the dunes are called *ḳaᶜar*. Each of these hollows is deepest at the western end of the ellipse, where it forms a huge funnel-like pit that reaches down to the solid rock and is called *farše*. Between the hollows, or *ḳaᶜar*, are larger or smaller low sandy flats called *nawâzi*. In these, as in the hollows, *raza, arṭa, soboṭ, ḳaṣbaʾ, ᶜâḏer, ṭubejž,* and *tarba* grow, and in spots even *ᶜarfeǧ, ᶜalḳa,* and *ḥamâṭ,* of which camels are especially fond.

We noticed in the sand the fresh tracks of six ostriches, and upon a near-by sand hill we saw eighteen eagles, while some distance away, hiding behind a bush of *raza*, were two ravens.

"Lookest thou, O Sheikh Mûsa, there, upon that sand hill," exclaimed our guide Masᶜûd, a Šarâri, "those are Rwala, and those two ravens hiding beyond, those are we, the Šarârât."

From 9.02 to 10.12 we let the camels graze upon the large bushes of *raza* at the southern fringe of al-ᶜArejž (temperature at 9.30 : 15.2° C); but from the copper-green bushes of *baᶜêṯrân* south of the *raza* we drove them away, as these are said to be poisonous. Presently we went on through the gloomy plain of al-Hûǧ, which is covered with coarse sandstone gravel where not a plant is to be seen. Farther to the south, however, where al-Hûǧ is somewhat undulating, we found *rimṯ, ṣollejân,* and *baᶜêṯrân* in the short and shallow hollows. According to Masᶜûd, al-Hûğ is the name of the entire country reaching from north of Ṭubejž to the Ḳulbân al-ʿAssâfijje in the south, which, with a similar country called al-Ḥûl that joins it in the south, forms the territory of the Šarârât.

After one o'clock we reached the southern limit of the plain, only to find ourselves confronted by a deep basin from which rise various hills that we had noted from al-ʿArejž. Making the descent with great effort, we skirted at the left the wells Mšâš al-Mowt, the water of which is said to be bitter and unfit to drink. Used by either man or animal, it is said to cause violent dysentery.[38]

Mḥammad Râʿi-s-Sabbâra told us of four secluded wells, Mšâš as-Sluḳe, containing fresh water, and asked Frejḥ and me to accompany him and fill our bags. Turning to the southeast, we reached the wells in about fifty minutes but found no water in them: they were dead. We then turned to the southwest and at 2.48 P.M. reached the Ḳulbân Ḫrâḳân and at three o'clock the Ḳulbân Ḥdâğân, where we found our companions awaiting us and where we remained until 6.26. Even in these wells there was so little water that we were three hours filling our bags and with the remainder could water but two of the camels. Frejḥ and Masʿûd took the others to the northern wells, where they asked the Rwala who were drawing water there to let them take enough for the camels of an-Nûri eben Šaʿlân (temperature at 4: 17.9° C).

In the territory of the Šarârât a burial ground is adjacent to almost every watering place. At the wells of Ḥdâğân we saw a common dog lying upon one of the graves, and Mḥammad Râʿi-s-Sabbâra thought that probably a woman tent keeper was buried there and the dog was guarding her body. He said that dogs frequently are so attached to the women of the tents that they protect their graves for many months against hyenas, which dig the bodies out and claw them. When he was camping once with his clan in the depression of Sirḥân, he said, his wife died there and he buried her in a secluded place. A short time after he migrated his dog disappeared. Three months

[38] Al-Muḳaddasi, *Aḥsan* (De Goeje), p. 253, writes that the two rain pools of Muḫri are sunken in black soil and contain water so salty that it causes diarrhea in men as well as in camels. The name Muḫri (purgative, purging) itself suggests the action caused by the water of these wells, and the results are sure to occur whether one drinks the water, uses it for cooking purposes, or uses it in the kneading of bread. —

This Muḫri is a station on the route from ʿArfeğa to Tejma. As our Mšâš al-Mowt is situated on the same route, we may identify it with Muḫri. Al-Muḳaddasi fails to distinguish a *ṛadîr* from a *mšâš*. A *ṛadîr* never contains salty water, for a heavy rain never washes away much salt and the water in a *ṛadîr* soon evaporates.

later, when he was going with the clan southward through the depression of Sirḥân, his son, who had just returned to him after a prolonged sojourn in the Ḥawrân, asked to be shown the grave of his mother, and when Mḥammad took him there they found the dog lying upon it. The sand round about was much trampled, and scattered over it were the hairs of hyenas which the dog had driven away from the grave. The dog had quenched his thirst at a spring near by and had sustained himself on locusts and human and animal excrement at a deserted camp.

Through a stony pass we entered upon the southern highland of an-Nâṣfa and at 7.32 reached the vicinity of the well Ḳlejb al-Ḥelwât. North-northwest of it were situated the fresh wells of Abu T̲enijja, and westward were the salty Żelîb al-Mẓejjân and aṭ-Ṭajjârijje. Water was plentiful in al-Hûǧ and al-Ḥûl, but pastures were few. After we had encamped at 8.48 we fed our hungry camels with *soboṭ* straw, for not an annual was to be found.

Thursday, January 28, 1909. At 6.16 A. M. we proceeded through the same sandstone region farther to the south. East of aṭ-Ṭajjârijje there are several tabular hills called an-Nâṣfa; farther to the southwest rise the hills of aṭ-Ṭfâjḥa, west of them al-Ǧâjfa, and north of these to the southwest of Mlêḥ the long tabular hills of al-Ǧerânijjât. The district from Ǧaʿalat aš-Šhabaʾ in the north to the wells of al-ʿAssâfijje in the south, as well as the *šeʿîb* of Feǧr in the west and the sandy desert of the Nefûd in the east, consists of soft sandstone, which once formed high ranges that extended from west to east. Erosion has eliminated these ranges and has changed the mountainous region into a desolate level, al-Hûǧ. The channels where the rain water gathers have been eaten away more and more, the absorbent sandstone has been washed out and carried away by the wind until the channels have been worn into deep troughs and basins hedged in by precipitous walls. These basins, which are absolutely flat at the bottom but difficult of access, frequently measure many kilometers in circumference and are constantly enlarging as the steep bluffs cave in. Here and there isolated sandstone hillocks protrude from such basins, which seem to be high when viewed from below, although in reality they do not overlook the rocky upland. In due time even these hillocks will vanish. The upland itself is absolutely flat and is covered with coarse gravel. At the eastern brims of the basins the sand is piled in high drifts. The larger the basins and the higher and more precipitous the southern walls enclosing them, the higher and more compact the drifts deposited by the northwest and north winds.

Toward eight o'clock we perceived in the south light clouds of smoke, indicating the location of a camp of the Šarârât. According to information received from the Rwala who were watering their camels at Ḥdâğân, this camp belonged to the chief Eben Ḳrejṭân, who was a friend of the reigning family of Šaʿlân. Frejḥ planned to go directly to the camp, declaring that Prince an-Nûri had charged him with the delivery of an important message for the chief; but we had to keep our southerly course because of a narrow sandy strip consisting of high and almost impassable drifts that separated us from the camp. Having finally found a trodden path, we crossed the sand upon it and at 8.20 reached the stony level of al-Bwejbijje, glorified in a springtime splendor. It had been moistened by the *wasm* (Canopus, October) and *trajjâwi* (Pleiades, November) rains and hence was covered with fresh plants, annual and perennial, including *ẓamrân, ʿarfeğ, ğrajba, naṣi, žetâde, tarba, ḥamâṭ, brukân, ʿalḳa,* and *ḳṣîṣ*. The *tarba* and *žetâde* were already in bloom. Our camels, which had found no pasture the day before, eagerly nibbled the plants, and for their sake we should have liked much to stop; but it was inadvisable, for the Šarârât might have taken us for enemies and attacked us, whereas it was necessary to establish friendly relations with them.

Sighting their first camels, we rode toward them at a leisurely pace, looking for a herdsman. Suddenly a shot was heard on our left, followed instantly by the alarm cry of the Šarârât; in a few minutes another shot and alarm cry was heard ahead of us. Camel riders were rounding their scattered herds and escaping with them to the southwest: they had taken us for scouts (*sabr*) of a raiding party. Without stopping at the camp we rode slowly after the herdsmen, Masʿûd and Mḥammad Râʿi-s-Sabbâra calling without intermission: "O Šarârât, we are also Šarârât!"

Finally we were approached by an armed rider who, recognizing our fellow Mḥammad Râʿi-s-Sabbâra, cried out laughingly:

"Since ye are accompanied by Mḥammad Râʿi-s-Sabbâra,

ye are not enemies." We were soon surrounded with some twenty fighters armed with good rifles, who inquired about camps and accompanied us part of the way.

The Šarârât belong among the despised tribes of Arabia. They are divided into three groups: al-Ḫlese
Flêḥân
al-ʿAzzâm.

The head chief of all the Šarârât is Muḥammad eben Sejf al-Ḫlesi.

Al-Ḫlese consist of the following clans:

Ṣbejḥât	(chief: Ḥejrallâh eben Daʿêğe)
ar-Rešâjde	(„ Ḳrejṭân eben Râšed)
Âl Ǧwejnân	(„ Zejd eben Ǧwejni)
Âl ʿAmr	(„ Daḫîlallâh eben ʿAmr)
Âl Daffâf	(„ Ḥamdân walad Ḫaṣi)
ad-Dbâwîn	(„ Ḥâmed âl Homṭ)
aẓ-Ẓebâʿîn	(„ Mḥammad eben Ǧrajjed)

The Ḫlese have almost four hundred tents. Aẓ-Ẓebâʿîn do not belong to them but camp with them.

The Flêḥân consist of the following clans:

Âl Slejm	(chief: Čâseb âl Ḥâwi)
al-Ǧwâbre	(„ Mḥammad eben Dwêreğ)
Âl Ḏhejbân	

The Flêḥân have about five hundred tents. Their head chief is Fâleḥ eben Farwa. The head chief of the ʿAzzâm is Mesnad eben Ḫajjâl eben Ḳrejṭân.

From 9.20 to eleven o'clock our camels grazed in a small hollow. Behind us rose the irregular cones of Ḥelwât and Abu Ṯenijja, presenting a picture such as I had rarely seen before in the Orient. They looked like an enormous modern fort, oblong in form, pointing from west to east with circular pavilions projecting from the east and west ends. At the corners and in the center of the long southern side tall, round towers with flat roofs seemed to have been erected, while above the high southern fortification wall protruded a blunt tower like that of a church. The fortification walls, pavilions, and towers seemed to be equipped with several rows of loopholes for guns about two to three meters in diameter, apparently cut in solid sandstone strata, which were almost yellow in comparison with the soft ash-colored strata below. The solid strata in reality consisted of huge blocks fractured vertically, some of which protruded a little higher than those next to them, thus overshadowing them in such a way as to suggest gun holes. And this entire enormous fort was surrounded by high, light yellow earthworks — the sandy drifts.

Our eastern horizon was limited by the mysterious, reddish-yellow desert, the Nefûd; in the southeast there rose from the stony level innumerable, more or less high, isolated boulders and crags, the remains of sandstone hillocks. These are called al-Meẓâhîr, Moving families (Fig. 23), because from

FIG. 23—At al-Meẓâhîr.

a distance they resemble migrating Arabs with their riders, men on foot, camels with loads, herds of large and small camels, and so on. As we stood looking at these strange shapes I heard a shot, and a bullet whizzed over my head. I turned just in time to see at our right behind a large sandstone boulder several camel riders and the foremost one in the act of reloading his rifle, which was still smoking. He raised it to his cheek and took aim at me; for, since I rode at the head of my companions, both balls were of course meant for me. I saw the flash, the smoke. Would it hit me? Involuntarily I bent down. *Al-ḥamdu lillâh!* It whistled several centimeters above my head, but evidently the aim had been well taken. Instantly I seized my carbine, but at that moment the guide Mas'ûd rode between us, stretched out his mantle (*'aba'*), and called:

"O Šarârât, do not kill Šarârât!" Whereupon the assailants fell upon him and pulled him off his camel; but recognizing in him a Šarâri they apologized, declaring that Allâh had not willed that their bullet hit us. Not until the danger was over did a shiver run over me. It is a strange sensation to see a loaded weapon aimed at you and fired.

After the assailants had gone we were overtaken by Mḥammad Râ'i-s-Sabbâra and the chief of a smaller Šarârât family named Rḥajjet al-A'rağ who, with three escorts, wished to pay a visit to the Šarârât camping to the south. There were now twelve of us, enough to repulse any band of robbers. At 3.52 P. M. we reached the northern hill of the Rğûm an-Na'âm group, near which we stopped until 5.52.

Creeping upon my stomach, I made my way with Mas'ûd to a pile of stones at the top of the hill, behind which we concealed ourselves and scoured the vicinity through the binoculars.

To the south the horizon was enclosed by the high hills of al-Azwar, east of these by the Mšejṭât, and farther to the northeast by the crests of as-Senâm and the higher mountain of Ḥelwân al-Ḫunfa, in front of which were the hills of Abraḳ Zhejme half buried under piles of sand. Northeast of the last-named was the hilly range of ar-Rijâši, extending to the northeast as far as al-Luṛuf, a lowland that separates the rocky plain from the sandy desert. Within this lowland, almost due east from our point, glimmered the water of the rain pool Ḫabra umm aš-Šenîn, north of it the Ḫabra Šhajba, and west of this the Ḫabra 'Arûs, into which rain water is carried by the *še'îb* of al-'Assâfijje, or Nejjâl. On the right side of this *še'îb*, south of our position, stretched the desolate plain of al-Ğhara, to the southwest spread the undulating region of al-Mhejdijja, with the hills of Tlûl al-Banât, Baṛîṯ as-Samar, and Baṛîṯ al-Ḥamar.[39] Between Baṛîṯ al-Ḥamar and the Ḳûr aṭ-Ṭfâjḥa rose the hills of Zerbûṭ ar-Raḫama.

To the northwest showed the mesas of an-Nâṣfa and aṭ-Ṭfâjḥa and to the north gleamed as if in bluish phosphorescence the Cyclopean abodes of al-Hawğa and Ḥelwât (Fig. 24).

I could not turn my eyes away from the changing colors of this gorgeous picture. Sublime indeed are the works of the Creator! and yet even these superstructures will vanish. The wind and rain will crumble the soft sandstone and gnaw at

[39] Jâḳût, *Mu'ğam* (Wüstenfeld), Vol. 1, p. 676, mentions the white hills of Biṛâṯ, partly covered with sand, at the farthermost frontier of the Abu Bekr ibn Kilâb. — Since the encampments of the Beni Kilâb were in the region which we were traversing, we may identify Baṛîṯ al-Ḥamar and Baṛîṯ al-'Afar with the Biṛâṯ of Jâḳût.

the harder layers, and the wind will drive the sand into the bottomless desert of the Nefûd. In due time there will remain of the huge fort of Ḥelwât only a few piles of the harder limestone, just as has happened in al-Meẓâhîr; and even these will finally disappear.

FIG. 24—From the Rǧûm an-Naʿâm looking north.

"O Mûsa, what will not vanish in this world?" said the negro Frejḥ after I had explained to him the genesis of al-Meẓâhîr. "Everything will disappear, but the Creator will be forever the same." Since the crags al-Meẓâhîr provide a particularly suitable cover for bands of robbers, it was advisable to scan them frequently. Often I was deluded into thinking I saw camels or men, when the camels and men proved to be nothing but rocks and boulders.

Upon our return from the crest we ascertained the latitude and then had supper with our seven guests; and we were all hungry. In the evening we rode in the same direction through the stony region of al-Mhejdijje until eight o'clock, when we lay down in a dark, shallow swale.

AL-MEẒÂHÎR TO ḲULBÂN UBEJṬ

Friday, January 29, 1909. The district of al-Mhejdijja, which we traversed after 6.31 A. M., is covered with large blocks of sandstone and accordingly has but a sparse vegetation. At eight o'clock in a small hollow we found a clump of *ẓamrân* bushes, upon which our camels grazed until 9.20

(temperature at 8.10: 11.8° C); then we headed toward the wells of al-ʿAssâfijje at the *šeʿîb* of Nejjâl. Not being sure whether there were robbers near them, we remained vigilant and tried to keep within the hollows. At eleven o'clock we came upon the fresh tracks of two camels, which the chief Rḥajje followed, while another young Šarâri warrior ran cautiously to the wells. The tracks led into the *šeʿîb* of al-ʿAssâfijje east of the wells, so we rode after Rḥajje with our carbines loaded and kept close under the rocky walls enclosing the *šeʿîb*. Just then the warrior returned with the report that he had seen camel riders at the wells. At this we turned immediately into a side ravine and made our camels kneel, intending from the hillside to surround the riders resting at the wells. Suddenly we heard a voice and saw three women emerging from a little cave. The riders at the wells were not enemies after all but the belated members of a migrating clan of the Rwala, going from south to north in the hope of finding better pasturage.

When at 12.23 P. M. we reached the wells of al-ʿAssâfijje we found nobody there (temperature at 12.30: 20° C). These wells are about twelve meters deep and fill with rain water but slowly. The bottom of the valley is here only 150 meters wide and is enclosed by higher walls of sandstone. In the plain about the wells is a large cemetery (Fig. 25) with many of the graves surrounded by low round walls through which are narrow apertures. Before each grave stands a stone tablet about fifty centimeters high. My companions maintained that these graves are very old, dating from the time of the Awwalijje, or primeval inhabitants of Arabia.

Our camels had had so little water at Ḥdâǧân that they were very thirsty. Straightway, therefore, a young Šarâri undressed and descended into the well and we lowered the canvas bucket to him on a rope. As fast as he filled it with water we raised it and poured the contents into a deep vessel from which our thirsty animals could drink. After the Šarâri had drawn the contents of one well, he took hold of the rope, propped himself with his legs against the pole on which the bucket hung, and we pulled him out. Then he went down another well and the same process was repeated.

When we left the wells at 1.32, the Rwala and the Šarârât left us and went toward the southwest to the Ḫabra aš-Šubeka, where, according to hearsay, their relatives were camping; while we, accompanied by Masᶜûd, proceeded through the desolate plain of al-Ğhara. At three o'clock we reached the limestone hillocks of Abraḳ ar-Ruḫejma, where we paused from 3.32 until 6.15 to permit our camels to pasture (temperature at 4: 22.2° C).

The *šeᶜîb* of al-ᶜAssâfijje, or Nejjâl,[40] comes from the southwest out of the hills Ẓelᶜ al-Badda, al-Ṛorejra, and az-

FIG. 25—A grave at the wells of al-ᶜAssâfijje.

Ziblijjât and is joined on the left by the *šeᶜibân* of ᶜOḳejlat al-Fâṭer, al-Bikr, and al-Leḳijje. At the southeastern slopes of az-Ziblijjât are *ḫabâri* of the same name.

To the east of az-Ziblijjât stand the hills of al-Ṛurrab, to the south Ummahât Baḳar, and to the southwest the Tell al-Ğerîš. To the southeast of al-Ṛurrab glimmer the white surfaces of the rain pool Ḫabra al-Bwêẓa, which lies at the northern limit of the undulating district of al-Ṛmêrijje. Here

[40] The poet al-Kumejt mentions Nejjân and Ḏu Baḳar, and Ibn Mijjâde names the lowland of Nejjân and al-Ṛamr, all of which localities are sought by Jâḳût, *op. cit.*, Vol. 4, p. 854, in the environs of the oasis of Tejma. — Nejjân certainly is identical with our Nejjâl, Ḏu Baḳar with the Ummahât Baḳar, and al-Ṛamr I seek in the watering place of al-ᶜAssâfijje.

Jâḳût, *op. cit.*, Vol. 3, pp. 813 f., refers to a Ṛamr Beni Ğuḏejma between Ṯağr and the oasis of Tejma, two nights away from the latter toward Syria. It is a valley in which rain water remains underneath the surface deposits.

The poet al-Ḥuṭej'a mentions an al-Ṛamr in the territory of the Beni Ḏubjân (al-Bekri, *Muᶜğam* [Wüstenfeld], p. 696), which may be identical with the other, as the Beni Ḏubjân used to camp north of the oasis of Tejma. — From al-ᶜAssâfijje to Tejma is almost eighty kilometers. A loaded caravan must halt twice for the night before making this distance.

is interred the body of Zejdân eben Warde, renowned far and wide as a leader who never once returned from a raid without booty. All the robbers and raiders make pilgrimages to his grave to implore his assistance, and, if Masʿûd may be trusted, he always renders aid to his co-tribesmen, the Šarârât, who therefore kill a camel upon his grave, so that the blood will soak in, and daub the high tablet with the blood before cooking and eating the meat near the grave. If they have no camel to spare, they lay upon the grave a piece of *semḥ* bread or some gunpowder, or they pour upon it a few drops of water. Since Zejdân was himself a Šarâri he knows that the Šarârât are pitifully poor.

At 7.15 we came into the hills of al-Azwar and at eight o'clock crossed the rain pond of the same name and proceeded in a desolate, stony plain which forms part of the territory of al-Ḥûl and in which, here and there, rise rather low sand dunes. At 9.16 we encamped at one such dune near several large bushes of *ṛaẓa*. Scaling a hill in search of a better site, I scared five white antelopes that were grazing in a neighboring hole (*farše*). At night we were aroused several times by hyenas and wolves, which so frightened the camels that they roared and growled in low tones and could not be easily calmed. We did not want to fire upon the beasts for fear of betraying ourselves to any band of robbers that might be bound for the wells of al-ʿAssâfijje. Of the hyenas or wolves we had no fear, for they are too cowardly to attack anyone but a lone animal or a wounded man.

Saturday, January 30, 1909 (temperature at 6.25 A. M.: 4.2° C). At night and early in the morning I talked with my companions about our trip. I should have much liked to go to Tejma and explore the ancient burying ground of al-Meğenne (or al-Mğenne), about three kilometers southeast of the oasis and north of the black hill Ẓelʿ al-Ṛnejm. The Rwala and Šarârât told of castles built in the rocks there and of tombs hewn in the sandstone hills; so I hoped there might also be Nabataean inscriptions. On the other hand, Prince an-Nûri, as well as all the Rwala and Šarârât migrating from the north, talked of serious dissension that prevailed in the oasis of Tejma and the vicinity. The region belonged to the domain of Eben Rašîd, but for five months it had been in the grip of a civil war, with Eben Saʿûd in the south sequestering from Eben Rašîd one settlement after another, and an-Nûri eben Šaʿlân in the north preparing to seize the oasis of al-Ğowf. ʿAbdar-raḥmân eben Rašîd, residing with some slaves at Tejma, yearned to appropriate the district, but he lacked the power. Moreover, he was afraid that an-Nûri meant to attack not merely al-Ğowf but Tejma as well; hence should I, a friend of the Prince, go to Tejma, he would consider me an emissary sent to embroil the inhabitants in the strife against him. How would he receive me? Would he banish me, or would he detain me as a hostage? As long as the Rwala were camping in the vicinity of Tejma and watering their herds there at the wells of Haddâğ, I could have depended on them, and this I had intended to do. The Rwala, however, were migrating to the north, and only some families of the Nṣejr clan were left near Tejma. But would even they be there? If they too should leave for the north, the vicinity of the oasis would be occupied by the ʿAzzâm clan of the Šarârât, the Ṭwâl clan of the Weld Slejmân, and members of the Htejm and Beni ʿAṭijje tribes, all of whom are enemies of the Rwala. As long as Eben Rašîd had remained powerful, intent on the maintenance of order and security, caravans had safely visited Tejma; but now all the roads were occupied by robbers of various tribes, who not merely robbed the travelers but killed them. That is why the Rwala and Šarârât called all the roads leading to Tejma roads of death (*durûb al-mawt*). Trustworthy men assured me that not a single week passed in which a traveler was not killed near the oasis; and in many cases the settlers themselves advised the robbers as to the date and direction to be taken by parties leaving the oasis and were recompensed with a portion of the spoils. Should we elude these robbers? Would it be possible for me to reach the Nabataean burial ground of al-Mğenne and to remain there for any length of time? With the Rwala camping south of Tejma, I could work with facility in the oasis as well as in the vicinity, for I had numerous references to many of the settlers and to several members of Eben Rašîd's family, nay, even to Prince Saʿûd eben Rašîd himself. Saʿûd, however, had already been assassinated and his relatives slaughtered, banished, or held captive. Nevertheless, I held that my references to the settlers in Tejma had not lost their value since the settlers are dependent in many ways upon the citizens of Damascus who gave me the references. With the help of the settlers, therefore, and with the assistance of the Rwala camping near Tejma, I intended to carry out my work. But it was very desirable that the last of the Rwala should not leave before I got there.

Not wishing to reach these Rwala until after sunset in order to evade the robbers more easily, we did not set out until seven o'clock; then we proceeded in an arid region devoid

FIG. 26—From Ṣubîḥ looking west.

of plants except upon the sand dunes, on which here and there grew ʿaddâm, firs, ẓamrân, ḳorẓi, arṭa, ʿâḏer, and raẓa. New needles were already beginning to show on the raẓa. From 9.28 until twelve o'clock our camels grazed upon the eastern foot of the high sand hill of Ṣubîḥ (Fig. 26). Presently Tûmân, who was sitting on the top sketching a map, informed us that some Arabs were coming from the south (temperature at 9.38: 11.8° C). Immediately Masʿûd and I joined him and, lying on our stomachs, raised our heads above the sharp crest of the sand drift to scan the southern environs. Southwest of the hill we perceived camel riders, camels with tents and miscellaneous implements, herds of camels, and several horseback riders — apparently migrating Rwala.

We were so near Tejma that to the southwest the Tell abu Srejs already showed itself and southward the somber al-Ṛnejm, in front of which is the burial ground of al-Mǧenne where I intended to work! North of al-Ṛnejm and south of the Tell abu Srejs, in a deep lowland filled with tiers of quivering air, lay the oasis of Tejma. When should we reach it?

After a while we encountered two of the camel riders, who informed us that within the whole of Tejma there was not one Rwejli left. The chief of the Nṣejr clan, who came to me soon afterwards, advised me to leave all my baggage with him and to proceed to Tejma on light camels with only the negro Frejḥ and the guide Masʿûd. He considered it possible that we might reach the burial ground of al-Mǧenne

alive under the protection of Allâh and our weapons and by the speed of our camels.

"Like hyenas and wolves," he warned me, "the members of the Ṭwâl, Htejm, Šammar, and Šarârât are now prowling around Tejma, and ye belong to the Rwala."

Without my baggage and scientific instruments, however, I could not work effectively either in the burial ground or in Tejma; and besides, where was I afterwards to look for Mḥammad and Tûmân with the baggage? for the Rwala were migrating, and whether northward or northeastward or eastward who could tell? Yet I could not willingly decide to abandon my goal, and so we plodded silently on in the course we had planned. After the last of the migrating Rwala had disappeared from our view, Frejḥ sighed and said to me:

"O Sheikh Mûsa, we will follow thee wherever thou shalt go. If thou must go to Tejma, so must we, even though it may cost us our throats. Allâh will take care of our children."

Hearing that, I turned my camel to the northeast. It was 12.38 P. M. I had not originally intended to examine either Tejma or al-Mğenne anyway, as both were situated beyond the boundary of the territory I had planned to explore.

Turning to the east upon a road that passes through the range of aṭ-Ṭawîl to al-Ğowf, we hastened toward the wells of Ubejṭ to fill our water bags. At one o'clock we turned more to the northeast and rode through a hilly country where grew *ḥemḥem*, *ʿalḳa*, *ʿaḏḏâm*, *ḥaršaf*, *ṯḥama*, *slîḥ*, *meṣṣêʿ*, *ḥamâṭ*, *heğîne*, *šḥami*, *arṭa*, *metnân*, and *ʿâḏer*, promising good pasturage a few weeks later; after two o'clock we went through dry *ẖabâri* near which we saw many Jericho roses. At the wells of Ubejṭ we remained from four to 4.13 (temperature at 4.05: 16° C). These wells, situated in a wide depression, are about three meters deep and contain clear fresh water. All around them grow *ḥalfa* and low palmettos; the higher places had been converted into cemeteries. South of Ubejṭ and southeast of Ṣubîḥ are the sand hills of Ṭwejjel Saʿîd, aẓ-Ẓabʿ, Kḥejlân, and al-Wuḥajjed.

ḲULBÂN UBEJṬ TO AṬ-ṬAWÎL; THE NEFÛD

From the wells we went due north and at five o'clock came to the sandstone hills of aḏ-Ḏhejbât which form the western boundary of an undulating plain that slopes down to the east and southeast penetrating deep into the Nefûd, which here overlooks the plain by forty meters. In the western part of this nearly level stretch is the Ḫabra aš-Šubeka, south of it the rain well Mšâš aš-Šubeka, and in the eastern part the Mšâš ar-Rmêẓ, north of which tower the sandy pyramids Ṭuʿûs Ẓbâʿ. Our camels walked very slowly, for the ground was covered with irritating sandstone ribs ten to twenty centimeters thick, like plates standing on edge. From 5.52 to 7.40 we rested in a hollow (temperature at 6: 15° C) and at 8.23 encamped among some large sandstone boulders behind which our camels were entirely hidden from view.

Sunday, January 31, 1909. The night was cold but dry, with only a light dew. At seven o'clock we were again under way northward. The hills of aḏ-Ḏhejbât consist of steep, porous sandstone slopes, with flat crests topped here and there by low pinnacles resembling sugar loaves. The several hilly ranges point eastward and among them there are neither parallel nor intersecting valleys, but merely basin-like hollows which carry rain water into the *ḫabâri*. At our right rose the Tell al-Mrejžeb, north of which was the Želîb Mlêḥ; at the foot of the hills *ṯḥama, ẓamrân,* and *ʿarfeǧ* grow very sparsely. At 8.48 A. M. we ascended the broad upland of al-Ḳraje, which is covered with a coarse gravel, in color resembling black coffee. In the southern part of this upland are the rosy sand drifts of an-Naʿağa, extending to the north as far as the Ḳlejb as-Sâjle; in the west are the hills of Mšejṭât, north of which towers as-Senâm, and, still farther on, Ḥelwân al-Ḫunfa.

From 10.26 to 11.47 the camels grazed. Resuming our journey, we noted a little farther on, in the fine sand that covers the plain in places, the fresh tracks of camels. On examining them closely, my companions Frejḥ and Masʿûd concluded that they were imprinted by animals whose home was the Nefûd, for the hoofs of the camels of the Nefûd are cut by the sharp sand as if filed with a rasp; consequently their footprints are smooth or show a large number of minute corrugations. We judged that there were more than a hundred of them heading from the southeast to the northwest: hence the throng could be no other than the Bedouins of the chief Eben Raḫîṣ of the Šammar, who had been camping in the western part of the Nefûd and watering his camels at the wells situated at the border between the stony and the sandy regions. Because the Šammar were engaged in warfare with the Rwala, we surmised that Eben Rahîṣ had undertaken a raid upon one of the Rwala clans north of al-ʿAssâfijje. Should we not encounter these raiders?

We kept a sharp watch on the western hills. The hillock of as-Senâm is short and low but has several pinnacles on top. The Ḥelwân al-Ḫunfa is long and high and consists of five groups separated by deep gulches, of which the first and the third group, counting from the south, are lofty and dark, the others lower and reddish. At three o'clock we passed through the depression of al-Môʿada, which is favored by raiding parties because they are not visible in the deep hollow and yet, through their sentries stationed at Ḥelwân, they can be apprised of every movement of the enemy. In the east, at the base of the Nefûd, we could see the glimmering, yellowish surface of the Ḫabra al-Klejbijje and north of it the Ḫabra al-Musṭabra.

From 4.28 until 6.23 we were drawing a map of the neighborhood while our camels grazed. The sun set in a pageant of color. The western sky seemed to be covered with rough lava bathed in fresh blood. Out of the lava protruded a solitary volcano — a dark cloud — and into the blood-red volcanic region penetrated two light blue inlets of the heavenly ocean. The volcano appeared to grow, its shadow lengthened, the blood settled and darkened. The negro Frejḥ turned his face away from the western sky and implored Allâh to prevent the bloodshed (*ḏabḥa*) that the sunset seemed to foretell. At 8.20 we made ready to pass the night behind a sandstone ridge.

Monday, February 1, 1909. Setting out at 7.02 A. M., at 8.25 we reached, west of the Riǧm Msêʿîd, the foot of the low hills of Umm al-Ḳerš that converge with Ḥelwân. These consist not of horizontal layers but of strata that dip from north to south, and often it seems as if the outcrops of the harder layers were hung in the air. Thus far there was no trace of the raiding band of the Šammar. Perhaps it had not yet returned.

My companions were always eulogizing the late Prince Mḥammad eben Rašîd, during whose reign there was peace and affluence, for he had had a way of compelling all the tribes to order and obedience. In time so many tales will be wrought about Mḥammad that he will become a mythical personality.

In the west rose the Tlûl ar-Rijâši, running almost north and south. From 9.50 to 11.53 our camels grazed in the district of az-Zrejb, which reaches from Tlûl ar-Rijâši to the Nefûd.

FIG. 27—The ʿArejž an-Nefûd from the south.

At the western fringe of the latter we noted the rain pond Ḫabra umm aš-Šenîn and north of it the Ḫabra Šhajba, the vicinity of both appearing to be covered with huge stone tablets. In many of these tablets the wind and rain had etched cavities like large platters, which served as receptacles for rain water. The Šarârât name such hollows *ḳṣâʿ* and like to seek them out because they find fresh water in them. Masʿûd called our attention to Ḳṣâʿ al-Ksûrijjât in the south and to Ḳṣâʿ al-Moṛr northeast and Ḳṣâʿ aṭ-Ṭînijjât southeast of the Ḫabra umm aš-Šenîn. North of Ḳṣâʿ aṭ-Ṭînijjât, near the Nefûd, lay the rocky hole Ǧebw ad-Dḥejl which also holds rain water.

Farther on we proceeded through a boundless plain — the kind called *nijâṯ* — toward the rosy ʿArejž an-Nefûd (Fig. 27), a sandy projection which the Nefûd thrusts out against the wind toward the west, seeking, as the Šarârât declare, to destroy all their wells. The sand hills seemed to be close to us, yet we could not get near them. There were neither valleys nor channels in the plain but merely small hollows into which the rain water vanishes; here and there were low cones, cubes, and prisms — the remains of hills. In the fine sand we found many tracks of lizards, showing the sharp outlines of their feet on both sides of grooves made by their tails, and near many of the bushes we saw the deep spirals made by snakes, which lean upon their own bodies, especially when crawling upward. Several times we crossed the fresh tracks of antelopes, ostriches, hyenas, and wolves. Once we came upon the new grave of a Šarâri into which hyenas had penetrated; from within protruded the two shins of the dead, both gnawed off!

We hastened through the plain of Sḥûl ʿArûs toward the sandy hills beyond, but their distance from us did not seem to lessen. At 1.20 we noted at the left the Ḫabra ʿArûs, near which terminates the *šeʿîb* of al-ʿAssâfijje; the Ḫabra ummu Zwêr is to the northwest, within the Luṛuf. We urged our exhausted animals on, but the Nefûd seemed to retreat before us. I kept closing my eyes to convince myself after a few minutes that we had really made progress; but the plain was endless. The guide Masʿûd, riding beside me, had been singing the same short ditty, off the key, for over an hour. At last, however, the dark, solitary hill Tell Mčêḥîl, or Umm Kejḥîl, a landmark in the district of al-Ḫunfa, appeared on our right. It is a sign to travelers from the north that they will soon enter the stony desert, whereas to travelers from the south it heralds the proximity of the sandy waste.

Finally at 4.06 west of the Ḫabra aṭ-Ṭurûdi we reached the edge of the sandy desert and crossed over into the ʿArejž an-Nefûd, which rises gradually from the level plain to the north. Whoever views it from the south notices innumerable sand dunes ranging from west to east; some of these are six hundred, others only two hundred meters long, but all are of the same height and are separated by hollows twenty to thirty meters deep. Upon some of these dunes are cones, upon the others pyramids, and all are steep. The crests of the dunes are sharply pointed. Up to the height of about fifty meters above the level of their bases the dunes are overgrown with bushes of *ṛaẓa*, but the higher portions are bare, shifting sand. On the southern slopes grow *ḥaršaf*, *ʿalḳa*, *ʿâḏer*, *arṭa*, *mṣaʿ*, *ḥamâṭ*, and *ṛaẓa*.

Ṛaẓa is among the most beautiful plants of the desert. Frequently it develops into trees eight meters high and twenty centimeters in diameter (Fig. 28), but more often it grows in bushes (Fig. 29). The branches are long and elastic, the bark clear white, the needles freshly green. Camels eat the needles and young twigs with gusto. The wood is tough but easily broken, and when dry it is an ideal fuel, producing almost no smoke, burning with a white flame for a long time, and leaving only smoldering red coals and fine white ashes. No other fuel of the desert furnishes so much heat as the *ṛaẓa*, and its coals will smolder for over ten hours. What joy they give to a horseman or traveler shivering with cold, who dares not build a fire in the night although he yearns for warmth! Wherever the *ṛaẓa* grows in bushes it holds the sand by its roots, thus making a nucleus for the formation of small mounds of sand. A very sad spectacle is presented by bushes that have been uprooted by the wind. Their glistening, dry, white branches and trunks protrude from the sand so bent and broken that they seem like the bleached bones of men or camels covering a former battle ground. Indeed, the uprooted *ṛaẓa* does in reality lie scattered over a battle ground, but the battle has been fought not between men but between the frail plants and the indomitable, pitiless wind and its powerful ally, the treacherous sand. At the wind's bidding the sand forms a mound among and around the stems of the *ṛaẓa* into which it permits the plant's roots to sink; but hardly has the plant come to feel secure and safe when the sand obeys the wind again and the piteous *ṛaẓa* has to perish.

We found some of the sand dunes so steep that we could not climb them, hence we went round them to the west. On this detour we crossed fresh tracks of eight large and three small antelopes. From 5.04 to 7.25 our camels grazed; then we kept on until 8.05, when we made camp for the night in a secluded pit (*farše*).

Tuesday, February 2, 1909. We started out at 7.08 A. M. The ride was hard for us as well as for the animals, for we were already traversing the Nefûd proper.

The Nefûd is one of the most interesting and beautiful natural features of northern Arabia. The low, rosy dunes, with crests overgrown by *ṛaẓa* and other plants, gives it the appearance of a huge garden or a terrace-like cemetery planted with weeping willows and birches. The bare peaks and crests of the hills and dunes remind one of glaciers in high mountains, and the hollows among the dunes resemble green mountain valleys. There is no water, however, and the soil of this beautiful region consists of treacherous sand. Even the sea is not so dangerous as the shimmering, rose-colored sand which forms splendid, sleek plains. The eye lets itself be deceived; the rider takes it for granted that he may hasten ahead and urges his mount to a swifter pace. At places the sand is so solid that it does not even take foot prints, when suddenly the animal sinks up to the knees, and the rider must quickly

FIG. 28

FIG. 29

FIG. 28—*Ṛaẓa* tree in the ʿArejž an-Nefûd.
FIG. 29—*Ṛaẓa* bush in the ʿArejž an-Nefûd.

swerve his frightened mount if he is to avoid certain death. Often the camel has been going in long strides over the sandy level, when, on entering what looks like nothing but a small swell, he finds himself on the brink of a precipitous wall of sand: one more step and both animal and rider would lie, with shattered bones, in the deep pit (*farše*).

"In the Nefûd there are roads everywhere," mused our guide, "and yet in the Nefûd there are no roads. Whosoever does not know the Nefûd must not venture thither, and who loses his way in the Nefûd loses his life too."

Every migrating tribe and every raiding party provides itself with a guide who knows the Nefûd well, usually an ostrich or antelope hunter. Only he who is thoroughly acquainted with the passes among the various sand dunes (*flûḳ*) can travel through the Nefûd freely. These passes are usually near the funnel-shaped pits, or *farš*; at the edges of each *farše*, indeed, three or four horns of sand may be clearly noted, the lower portions of which run together (Fig. 30). The bottom of each *farše* is level and devoid of sand and is formed by the original rugged surface of the stony or rocky plain. Sometimes two or even three sides of the *farše* are so precipitous as to be almost perpendicular; to the east, however, the floor of the *farše* generally slopes up gradually to that of a larger elliptical hollow, or *ḳaʿara*, hedged in by dunes (*flûḳ*) and of which the *farše* is the deepest part. A pass usually may be found where the *farše* connects with the *ḳaʿara*. As a rule the *farš* yawn in the western part of the *ḳaʿar*, which trend from west to east. To the west above the *farš* the dunes are highest and the distance between them shortest. To the east they widen into sandy flats called *nawâzi*.

Besides numerous tracks of antelopes and ostriches, we noted in the sand the footprints of the rapacious *ẓarbûl* (pl. *ẓarâbîl*), which subsists on flesh and is said to attack lone camels and even sleeping travelers. From under an *arṭa* bush I scared out a yellow bird about as large as a domestic fowl and known as *tandara*. Its meat is reputed to be excellent. Flapping its wings heavily, it flew several hundred meters off and hid again in a thicket. I shot two dozing hares. The color of their fur was a blend of yellows and reds completely harmonizing with the sand, whereas the fur of the hares I had shot in the volcanic region was dark brown or black. Even the smaller birds I saw in the Nefûd were the color

FIG. 30

FIG. 31

FIG. 30—A *farše* in the Nefûd.
FIG. 31—In the Nefûd.

of the sand. The *umm sâlem,* as large as our sparrow, sings quietly and briefly but pleasantly.

From 10.52 to 12.42 P. M. our camels grazed (Figs. 31, 32). Later on we crossed several perilous slopes, so steep that we had to dig in the sand a succession of slanting steps down which we cautiously led our camels. A false step, a slip, and the animal would roll down the steep incline. The camels trembled, spread their legs, leaned upon their forefeet, and tested the ground before venturing ahead.

Often it seemed to me as if we were proceeding through vineyards; this was especially true where *arṭa* grew more abundantly, often developing stalks eight centimeters thick, twenty to thirty centimeters high, with a head sometimes as much as four meters in diameter. Its bare branches closely resemble the branches of vines and cover the mounds of sand just as the vine branches rest upon heaps of stone in many parts of northern Syria. The roots are thin and look like ropes and are sometimes as long as twenty meters. The narrow and long foliage, or needles, of *arṭa* is utilized by women in place of tan-bark in the tanning of hides.

To the northeast the level crest of the aṭ-Ṭawîl range was beginning to emerge, becoming clearer as we neared it. The southwestern portion of it, called al-Ḥeleme, looked almost black and appeared as if it were artificially hewn. South of this crest the Nefûd, wrapped in a violet veil, seemed nearly flat. From three to 3.32 our camels grazed, and at 5.08 we encamped on the eastern side of a *farše.* Since we were well concealed there, the camels tired, and the terrain arduous, I did not intend to proceed at night. We made a map of the environs, ascertained the latitude, and spent some time in changing the photographic plates. At night a wolf came prowling round the camp, *d̠îb al-ḫala,* or *waḥš,* as I called him, but Frejḥ immediately corrected my pronunciation to *wáḥaš.* The wolf took to his heels as soon as we made for him.

Wednesday, February 3, 1909. In the morning we built a cheery fire, heated our coffee, and set out at 7.02 A. M. The dunes in this part of the Nefûd run from northwest to southeast. Viewed from the top of these dunes the Nefûd looked like a level plateau, with nothing but solitary, red, bare mounds of sand perched upon it here and there. In reality, however, it is far from level, for it bristles with innumerable well-nigh impassable *ḳaʿar* and *farš*. Several days before, this district had been traversed by a large migrating throng of the Rwala: evidently hundreds, nay, thousands of camels had trodden the sand. We could see their tracks, however, only in the hollows (*ḳaʿar*); upon the higher flat areas of the Nawâzi ummahât an-Namel all the prints had been leveled even with the surface, which was again seamed by ripples shaped like ellipses with transverse axes running at right angles to the direction of the last wind. Only the camel dung indicated the direction that the migrating throng had followed. Far ahead of us we noted the aṭ-Ṭawîl range, which appeared to us actually lower than the Nefûd. Southeast of al-Ḥeleme rose the solitary group of black hills of Râf[41] near which, on the southeast, are the wells Ḳulbân al-Mrût and northeast of them the Ḳulbân aš-Šižîž (or aš-Šežîž).

From 10.02 to 11.44 we sketched a topographical map. We had come upon several antelope tracks, and the aṭ-Ṭawîl range is also the home of herds of long-horned ibexes. At 1.18 P. M. we crossed the road Darb al-Muʿaj, leading from the wells of aš-Šižîž through the defile Ṯenijjet al-Muʿaj to the pastures west of al-Bârde. The dry plants of the Nefûd are of various colors: dry *ḥamâṭ* is like silver, *naṣi* and *soboṭ* yellow like straw, *arṭa* is ashy, *ʿâḏer* dark green and almost black, *raẓa* brightly white, and its new young sprouts yellow with a greenish tinge.

Like the mountains of al-Ḥeleme, those of al-Bârde form several rocky groups, separated by the pass of al-Muʿaj from the narrow hill range of al-Klâḥ. The latter is connected on the north with the table mountains of al-Bawaʾ.[42]

Southeast of al-Bawaʾ the low hillocks of al-Bowlijjât extend up to the mountains of al-Ḥeleme. All the hills and mountains of the aṭ-Ṭawîl range form an embayment open toward the south, where the Nefûd enters it. The embayment where we were approaching it is not hedged by a steep wall, as it is farther west, but slopes gradually toward a basin that is enclosed on the north by the stony spurs of the range.

[41] According to Jâḳût, *Muʿǧam* (Wüstenfeld), Vol. 2, p. 734, Râf is the name of a sand desert. — Perhaps he had in mind the sand desert adjoining our hills of Râf, near which leads a transport route.

[42] Jâḳût, *op. cit.*, Vol. 1, p. 101, says that in Syria there is a place or a mountain of the name of Abawaʾ, a statement which he supports by citing verses of the poet an-Nâbiṛa, according to whom the vicinity of Abawaʾ had evidently belonged to the Ḏubjân tribe. — As the territory of the Ḏubjân reached as far as the range of aṭ-Ṭawîl, we may identify the table mountains of al-Bawaʾ with the Abawaʾ of old. In the dialect of the present day the *hamza*, with which the word begins, is omitted.

FIG. 32—Our caravan in the Nefûd.

We crossed this basin at 3.28. The Nefûd was now behind, while before us were the uplands of al-Bowlijjât and al-Ḳdêrijje, where we found freshly sprouting *ẓamrân* upon which our camels grazed from 5.58 until eight o'clock. The Rwala herdsmen whom we met told us that Fejṣal eben Rašîd, who had been residing in al-Ğowf as a vice-regent of his brother Prince Saʿûd eben Rašîd, had, after the assassination of the latter, ordered the wells of Ṣfân to be filled up, in order to deprive his enemies of the possibility of concealing themselves within aṭ-Ṭawîl with a view to attacking his people. This news was disappointing; for, as Ṣfân had always contained water even when all the other wells went dry, we had intended to water our camels there and to fill our bags. Besides, it seemed doubtful whether we should find water in the well of al-Mrût, for Eben Duṛmi, who was encamped near that well, was watering his herds at al-Ğowf. The only thing left for us to do, therefore, was to hasten on to the latter oasis.

AṬ-ṬAWÎL TO AL-ĞOWF

Leaving our camp at eight o'clock, we proceeded in an easterly direction toward the pass of al-Mustanda and at 9.43 descended through a deep gully into the eastern plain. Heading thence toward the north, we camped for the night, at 11.32, in a small hollow at the northern edge of the somber, desolate region of aš-Šaʿîra, which reaches south as far as the mountains of al-Mirteka.

Thursday, February 4, 1909. Starting at 6.09 A. M. we rode toward the north-northeast among the black and reddish knolls Burḳ aš-Šaʿîra, where, after the torrential *wasm* (Canopus, October) rains *semḥ* thrives abundantly. To the southwest the rays of the rising sun struck the aṭ-Ṭawîl range (Fig. 33), which we could view in its entire length.

The aṭ-Ṭawîl range begins to the south-southeast with the hills of Râf, mentioned above; north of these hills rise the mountains of al-Mirteka, al-Ḥṣân, Ḳalb al-Ğemal, and Ẓahrat umm Ruḳuba, which are separated by the pass of al-Mustanda from the precipitous walls of al-Ḥṭûl; north of these mountains gape the deep cuts formed by the *šeʿibân* of al-Ṛẓej and al-Muʿaj, and northwestward of these looms the crest of al-Fâğ. Still farther to the north appeared on the horizon the hills Umm Ḳlajʿa, al-Ğejb, and al-Ğedwa, which fall away to the east into the undulating plain of al-Lîṯejme. North of al-Ğedwa a dark, deep, and wide depression came into sight, beyond which, still farther north, rose the low, long ridge of al-Eẓâreʿ. The road from Majḳûʿ to al-Ǧowf runs at the southern foot of this mountain.

At seven o'clock, having found *ẓamrân* and *ṛaẓa* at the foot of a dune about half way between the dead wells of al-

FIG. 33—The range of aṭ-Ṭawîl from the northeast.

Žên to the west and the filled-up wells Ḳulbân Ṣfân to the east, we stopped and remained there until 8.54. Here and there this sandy level was adorned by the pink or white blossoms of *ʿasansal.* At 10.10 we entered the gulch of Ṛîrân al-Banât. It seemed as if the edges of the surrounding heights had been broken off, forming steep cliffs twenty-five meters high. In the gulch were innumerable small pyramids and cones — the remains of sandstone hillocks — presenting a curious spectacle with their horizontal layers of blue and ash color. Around them were growing *šnân, ʿaǧram,* and dwarf *ṛaẓa.*[43]

After 11.30 we heard a singular rumbling as if thousands

[43] Al-Bekri, *Muʿǧam* (Wüstenfeld), p. 163, says that Banât Ḳejn are familiar hills within the territory of the tribe of Kalb, where the latter were routed and pillaged by the Fezâra tribe. The chief of the Kalb tribe, Ḥumejd ibn Baḥdal, had exacted a tax from the Fezâra during the reign of ʿAbdalmalek and had annihilated many of the Fezâra at al-ʿÂh. ʿAbdalmalek made restitution to the Fezâra for all their losses on condition that they should abstain from revenge. With the money thus procured, however, they bought horses and weapons, allied themselves with clans of the Ḳejs tribe, and attacked and completely pillaged the camp of the Kalb at Banât Ḳejn. ʿAbdalmalek was so angry that upon his order the commander al-Ḥaǧǧâǧ marched upon the transgressors, captured two of their chiefs, and despatched them to the Caliph, who had them executed (Abu-l-Farağ, *Aṛâni* [Bûlâḳ, 1285 A. H.], Vol. 17, p. 115).

Jâḳût, *op. cit.*, Vol. 1, p. 738, writes that the spring water wells of Banât Ḳejn are situated within the desert of as-Samâwa of the Kalb tribe, and that they are thus named because al-Ḳejn ibn Ḳuḍâʿa camped there. In another place (*ibid.*, Vol. 4, p. 219) Jâḳût says that the water of Banât Ḳejn belongs to the Fezâra tribe, whereas Abu-l-Farağ (*loc. cit.*) distinctly asserts that the water of Banât Ḳejn is a possession of the Kalb tribe and that many of the clans of that tribe have camped there. —

Our wells of al-Žên, situated in a district called Ṛîrân al-Banât, have preserved both the names, Banât as well as Ḳejn. It is likely that the Fezâra, Kalb, and even the Ḳejn tribes have all camped there at different times; for their territories approach each other near these wells, and the frontier wells are usually appropriated by the neighbors. If they live in peace, all of them camp by the well; if in enmity, only the one of superior power ventures there, afterwards claiming ownership. Al-ʿÂh, where the Kalb tribe slew many men of the Fezâra tribe, is a pass leading from east to west through the range of al-Misma' south of the wells of al-Žên.

of riders were galloping behind us, and immediately we felt a violent blast of wind and were enveloped in a cloud of sand. This was the beginning of a sandstorm such as I had seldom experienced in the desert. The wind moaned and roared, driving clouds of sand in great drifts toward the northeast. Upon the level we had been crossing rose waves of sand two to five meters high, which surged toward the northeast, rising and falling as the violence of the wind fluctuated. Wherever the sand encountered an obstacle or a depression it swept away the obstacle or filled up the hole and rushed on over the leveled plain. What luck that the storm had not caught us within the Nefûd! We should certainly have perished. And what luck that the storm was blowing from the southwest to the northeast, thus pushing us ahead! At noon we met herds of the Rwala returning from the watering places at al-Ğowf. During the moments when the wind subsided somewhat we learned from the yelling herdsmen that Nawwâf had two days before entered al-Ğowf and proclaimed himself, in the name of his father, master of the oasis and its vicinity — news very pleasant to me, for I was certain of finding hospitality and protection with him. The poor herdsmen and their camels, bound toward the south, could hardly move a step ahead, and the animals were growling and wailing and at every particularly strong blast of wind turning their backs to it. While we were talking with the herdsmen, who had stopped for a while, the camels spread their hind legs and thrust their fore legs forward to gain support against the wind.

With the wind at our backs, we hastened to the northeast at a swift pace. Our mounts themselves, though exhausted and hungry, were eager to hurry on, but whenever they slowed or shortened their stride we urged them. The sand caused us acute pain, physical as well as mental. Our ears, mouths, nostrils, and especially our eyes were full of fine grains which irritated the sensitive membranes of those organs and caused great suffering. Moreover, the fine sand penetrated our garments and rubbed against the skin, thus exciting the nerves. And al-Ğowf was still so far away!

At last, at five o'clock, we sighted ahead of us a deep basin in the stony plain and within the basin the dark green heads of palm trees. It was the settlement of Dûmat al-Ğandalijje, or al-Ğowf, lying far below us. We made the descent through an opening in the rocky cliff and proceeded along the high adobe walls which enclose the palm orchards. Our camels took fright at every wall and palm tree and started to run when we had to pass a dead camel that lay in the road. Presently we were challenged by a soldier with a rifle

FIG. 34—Nawwâf's *kaṣr* at al-Ǧowf, outside.

in hand — a sentry, who inquired whither we were going. On learning that we sought Nawwâf eben Šaʿlân, he escorted us to a high rectangular tower and told us that Nawwâf lived within. Compelling our camels to kneel in front of the gate, we found ourselves immediately surrounded by the familiar negroes and warriors of the Rwala, who greeted me cordially.

SOJOURN AT AL-ǦOWF

The substantial building (*kaṣr*) in which Nawwâf resided was in the form of a square and was enclosed by a high wall reinforced at the southeastern corner by a low rectangular tower (Figs. 34, 35), and with another, but much higher, tower at the northwestern corner. East of the higher tower was a gate, the only entrance through which one gained access to a large court. On the eastern and western sides of the

FIG. 35—Nawwâf's *ḳaṣr* at al-Ğowf, inside.

court toward the fortification walls were smaller rooms. It was possible to climb to the flat roof of the western rooms by means of steps at the southwest corner; to the eastern roof, however, one could ascend only by scaling the trunk of a palm tree. Both roofs were overtopped by the fortification wall, the upper part of which was built of adobe. At the northwest corner of the court a wide door opened into the large rectangular tower, two stories high and reinforced in the center by a huge pillar. On the ground floor of this tower was a single dark room; against the southwestern corner of the room leaned the trunk of a palm tree up which one climbed into the first story, and a similar trunk connected this story with the second one. From the only room of the first story a narrow wicket opened upon the western roof.

Both towers, like the ground floor room, had loopholes but no windows. Nawwâf came to meet me and led me into the ground floor room, where, behind the pillar, flamed a great fire. We seated ourselves by it in such a position that we could not be seen from the door.

Nawwâf said he had come to al-Ǧowf with thirty-five soldiers, most of them young negroes, who never laid aside their loaded rifles. In the evening there came into the room about fifty armed men from al-Ǧowf, with their chiefs. The chiefs took seats at the fire opposite us, their escorts remaining in the yard. At the left, between us and the entrance, were stationed fifteen negroes with loaded rifles. Nawwâf did not trust the chiefs and, not meaning to be taken by surprise, he sat down with me in such a position that the pillar intervened between us and the door, thus protecting us from any shots that might be fired at us from the yard or from the small southwest tower. The chiefs were headed by Zeben eben Ḳaʿajjed, a man about forty years old, with features that reminded me strongly of the physiognomy of the ancient Babylonians. He was now the head chief in al-Ǧowf and as such came to invite Prince an-Nûri to take the reins of government within the oasis and its vicinity.

The oasis of al-Ǧowf, being situated on the southern border of northern Arabia, must of necessity maintain good relations with the tribe holding sway in that region, if its inhabitants are not to be at the mercy of every party of raiders and band of robbers. So long as the dominion of Eben Rašîd was strong and the Rwala friendly to it, Eben Rašîd's garrison was able to hold al-Ǧowf; but as soon as civil war began between the members of his family, both Fejṣal eben Rašîd, the last vice-regent of al-Ǧowf, and Eben Saʿûd invited Prince an-Nûri to take possession of the oasis. Having lost their master, the inhabitants of Dûmat al-Ǧandalijje and of the other settlements began to wage war among themselves. Immediately after the flight of the vice-regent Fejṣal, Eben Ḳaʿajjed, chief of the largest district, pronounced himself for Eben Šaʿlân and began banishing and robbing his own personal enemies, who took refuge in two of the strongest districts, Mâred and al-Ḫadne. But there still remained in al-Ḫadne about forty men of Eben Rašîd's garrison, and their commander Eben Naʿâme was desirous of capturing al-Ǧowf for himself. He and the chief of the above-named districts, therefore, with the many refugees, united in resistance to Nawwâf, who had joined Eben Ḳaʿajjed; whereupon the latter, well knowing the impregnability of the two districts occupied by the enemies, advised Nawwâf to destroy all the property of his opponents outside of Mâred and al-Ḫadne. Nawwâf was to disperse their animals, demolish their dwellings, cut down the palms, fill up the wells, and through starvation compel his enemies to capitulate.

I pleaded with Nawwâf to ignore this advice, because by obeying he would sacrifice the welfare of al-Ğowf for a score of years, and I advised him not to negotiate with Eben Naʿâme but with the chiefs of Mâred and al-Ḫadne (*râʿi-l-mâred wa râʿi-l-ḫadne*), as eventually these would have to concede that they could not count upon the aid of Eben Rašîd and hence would be unable to resist the Rwala. Nawwâf promised that he would conduct himself according to my advice. Before midnight I retired into one of the chambers at the western side of the court where I was to sleep, but the room was so full of people and of all kinds of small insects that rest was impossible. I was glad when the morning star rose above the eastern wall.

Friday, February 5, 1909. After sunrise (temperature at 7.30 : 14.3° C) I went out in front of the gate and surveyed the vicinity from a heap of ruins. Soon Nawwâf was beset by many of the inhabitants of al-Ğowf of all walks of life, who implored him to have me come to visit their sick and wounded. I was taken through several districts occupied by the friends and subjects of Nawwâf. Two of these sections were almost completely demolished, the houses deserted, the palms scorched, the garden walls undermined. I met men rolling before them young palms which they had dug up in the gardens of their defeated fellow citizens and purposed to plant in their own. The wounded were in a miserable plight, with their wounds full of filth and pus, their limbs swollen, and all suffering from fever. I learned that already over three hundred fighters had been killed and that shooting was still in progress. Some of the settlers informed me that at Sûḳ Mâred there was a stone with a strange writing on it imbedded in a wall, and of course I was eager to see it. No sooner, however, had I come out of the gardens into the free space between Mâred and the cliff that hedges in the basin on the west than I was greeted by two shots.

Upon my return I learned from Nawwâf that he had

sent a confidential messenger to the chief of Mâred. Presently the ambassador returned with the message that the inhabitants of Mâred desired either Nawwâf or ʿAbdallâh eben Ṭalâl, with the negro ʿÂmer, to come to them, saying that they would entertain them and would arrive at an agreement. Nawwâf and ʿAbdallâh feared some trickery, however, and so ʿÂmer went to Mâred alone. In the evening he reported to Nawwâf that the inhabitants of Mâred would recognize him as master upon condition that he return to them and to the refugees harbored with them all the property Eben Ḳaʿajjed had appropriated; but the latter objected to the proposal. Replies of like nature were received by Nawwâf from his adversaries in the other settlements of the basin of al-Ǧûba (or al-Ǧowf).

Eben Ḳaʿajjed urged Nawwâf that very night to attack the gardens of both the districts held by his adversaries and to undermine the walls and destroy the palms, which several mischievous youths were trying to do. We heard incessant shooting, battle cries, and lamentations (temperature at 12: 15° C; at 5: 16.5° C).

After ascertaining the latitude, I ordered Mḥammad to carry my blanket up to the western roof, but Nawwâf objected, warning me that I could easily be struck by a bullet. I was so exhausted, however, that I craved rest regardless of the danger; but I had barely lain down when the sentries about me began to shout an alarm and Nawwâf's warriors immediately occupied both the towers and the roofs, for Eben Naʿâme had undertaken an assault in the direction of our house. Being repulsed, he repeated the attempt twice more during the night. The shots rang in my ears incessantly and fighters were running all about me; several bullets even clicked upon the stone wall of the large tower. I could not sleep, and of course there could be no thought of attempting any quiet work. Therefore I arrived at the decision to return the following day to Prince an-Nûri. Nawwâf, who was anxious to have me close to himself, proposed that I visit the settlements of al-Ḳâra, aṭ-Ṭjêr, and Skâka; but, being aware that in those places there was a state of turmoil similar to that in Dûmat al-Ǧandalijje I postponed the visit until another time and prepared to depart. In making this decision I was influenced by the fact that there was no pasture for my camels in or near al-Ǧowf and it was not safe to let them graze alone fifteen to twenty kilometers away.

CHAPTER VI

AL-ǦOWF TO AL-HAWǦA

AL-ǦOWF TO MAJḲÛ'

Saturday, February 6, 1909. In the morning (temperature at 7: 15° C) several inhabitants of al-Ǧowf — or al-Jowf, as some pronounce it — came to ask me to visit the wounded men I had treated the night before. As my baggage was already loaded, however, and the wells of Majḳû', where Prince an-Nûri was camping, were a good two days distant, I referred them to Nawwâf, with whom I had left the proper medicines and bandages, and I set out at 8.28 A.M. My negro Frejḥ remained at al-Ǧowf, and we were escorted by a daring robber of the name of Mindîl al-Ḳaṭ'i. There was no perilous expedition in which he would not participate. He undertook raids into foreign territories and frequently was absent for months with two or three comrades, robbing travelers and cashing the booty. He had not saved anything, however, for he was as liberal as he was courageous. Nawwâf was sending him to his father, an-Nûri, to report on the eastern territories in which the man had been roaming for almost five weeks and from which he had returned but two days before. Besides other booty, he had brought three camels seized from the Ḳmuṣa group of the Sba'a tribe. He had attacked three robbers who were members of that tribe, had taken their camels from them, and had brought them upon their own mounts all the way to al-Ǧowf. The robbers complained to Nawwâf that the assault was unjustified because they were friends of the Rwala, but Nawwâf asserted that he would keep their camels until their co-tribesman, Blejhân, returned to me the camel he stole when he left me.

Ascending from the depression of al-Ǧowf to the highland of al-Mlajda on the west, we proceeded in a westerly direction past numerous holes that seemed like filled-up wells. The ground consisted of sandstone, its layers being convoluted and forming round, funnel-like cavities about five meters in diameter. The center of each cavity was usually half filled with sand, and thus the hole gave the appearance of an abandoned well. At nine o'clock the hill ʿAbd al-Ğowf was at our right. East from it rose the steep cones of Žîsân al-Ğowf, which are frowned down upon from the north by the high cliffs of the basin of al-ʿAžraba. Northeast of ʿAbd al-Ğowf protruded the spur of aẓ-Ẓullijje; to the west stretched the low, hilly range of ar-Rummâmîn, terminating in the southwest with the long hill of ar-Rammâm. South of the latter we noted the spur formed by the long ridge Ḥazm al-Eẓâreʿ; while far to the south rose from the pink sand the black cone of Râf, from which the precipitous eastern slope of the aṭ-Ṭawîl range runs in a half-circle as far as the Ḥazm al-Eẓâreʿ. At 11.30 we were in the flat channel Riğlet aš-Šejḫ, which has its origin north of ar-Rummâmîn within the broad height Ẓahrat al-Farğijje, as the eastern limit of the stony plain of Arẓ al-Ğrejmîs is called (temperature at 12.30: 18.5° C).

From 12.32 to 2.25 P. M. our starved camels grazed in the plain of al-Lîṯejme. Later we crossed the hilly range of al-Ğedwa, which is called al-Ğejb in its southern portion and forms the northern spur of the range of aṭ-Ṭawîl. From 5.10 to seven o'clock we were busy at the base of the high sand drift of ʿArejž ad-Desm sketching a geographical map of the environs, while the camels grazed upon the dry *naṣi* and the freshly-sprouting *soboṭ*. We then continued our journey over the slope Ẓahart al-ʿAḳâb and encamped at 9.10 in a small dip overgrown with *ẓamrân*. Unable to fall asleep, I thought about the many raiding parties and traders' caravans that throughout the ages have been treading the place at which we lodged that night. From the earliest periods transport routes have led thence to the oasis of Dûmat al-Ğandalijje in the east, to the depression of Sirḥân in the northwest, and to the oasis of Tejma in the south.

Sunday, February 7, 1909. Setting out at 6.53 (temperature at 6.30: 2.5° C), we proceeded in the undulating region of al-Ğedâjeb, south of the long, low scarp of Ḥazm al-Ḳṣâṣ, which forms the southern edge of the highland of al-Ğrejmîs. At 8.42 we swerved toward the west-northwest into a district where *ẓamrân* was growing. At 9.30 we sighted at the right of the road twenty-two vultures feasting on the carcass of a dead camel. The ground was becoming covered deeper and deeper with sand. At ten o'clock we had at our right two round, evenly shaped hills called an-Nhejdejn. In the vicinity we found growing *arṭa*, *ʿâḏer*, *mṣaʿ*, *ḳaṣbaʾ*, *ʿarfeǧ*, *metnân*, *ʿalḳa*, and *naṣi*, upon which the camels grazed from 10.16 until 12.15 (temperature at 11.30: 18.2° C).

Thence we rode on through the district of Ṛwêṭa Ǧerâd, upon which are scattered low sand hills. At 3.40 we had at the left the gray hills Tlûl az-Zâjed surrounding the wells of Majḳûʿ, toward which we turned in a southwesterly direction. The traveling was not very easy, for we had to go round many of the dunes and sand hills, and such delays prevented our arriving at the wells until five o'clock (temperature at 5.10: 20.3° C).

Sighting a large camp near the wells, we rejoiced in the assumption that it was the camp of Prince an-Nûri as well as in the anticipation of rest for ourselves and our animals. Our camels strode at a swift pace toward the camp, but the first herdsman we met disappointed us by saying: "An-Nûri migrated today toward Ḳulbân Mlêḥ." He had, then, left in the direction whence we had just come to al-Ǧowf, whereas I supposed that he was going east of the neighborhood of Skâka, as Nawwâf had assured me he would.

MAJḲÛʿ TO AL-HAWǦA

Watering our camels and filling our bags at the wells, which here are more than twenty meters deep, we set out at six o'clock southward after the Prince. For about an hour we trudged in a sandy region, but later, upon our entrance into the desolate, somber plain of al-Bsajṭa, we urged our camels to a quicker pace. The icy southwest wind hindered us, however, by blowing at full force into our faces. I wanted to stop, but nowhere was there a bush to be seen and hence no pasture for the camels or fuel for ourselves. It was not until 11.20 that we discovered a few dry bushes of *rimṯ*, which we decided to use for fuel in the morning; so we encamped by them.

Monday to Thursday, February 8 to 11, 1909. During Monday night we heard the barking of dogs and growling of camels: evidently the Prince's camp was close by. Leaving at 6.18 A. M. we sighted camels grazing upon the crest of al-Ḳnejfḏât, and at 6.58 we were at the Prince's tent. I was greeted on all sides and an-Nûri said:

"*Al-ḥamdu lillâh,* brother, that he hath directed thee hither alive and well! Thou undertakest raids the like of which even thy present companion Mindîl has not ventured upon."

After rendering the Prince a concise account of my journey and information about the pastures through which we had passed, I inquired his reason for marching into a region so unfriendly and unsafe and asked why he did not go east. He replied that even in the east it had not rained until recently and that he must wait until the local pastures were replenished. Moreover, the southern districts were not likely to be too inhospitable, for two Šarârât had assured him that he could find rich pasture north as well as south of the wells of al-Hawǧa and Mlêḥ and therefore he would encamp at Mlêḥ. When I repeated that I had found no pasture north of these wells and that our camels had not eaten fresh grass until we reached al-Bwejbijje, he replied that in that case we should encamp at al-Hawǧa, sending our herds thence to pasture at al-Bwejbijje under the care of Eben Ḳrejṭân, whose brother was accompanying us.

Nâṣer told me that our herdsman Mufaẓẓi had been shot by a Rwejli, but that the bullet hit merely the fleshy part of the calf of his leg.

After all the tents had been loaded, I remounted my camel at 7.47 and rode with the Prince at the head of the migrating tribe. I wondered at his youthful appearance: he had dyed black his eyelashes, beard, and hair and was dressed in a new garment. Later I learned that only two or three days previously he had divorced his wife, the mother of Saʿûd and al-Ḫafâǧi, and immediately afterward had married her sister who was sixteen years younger. Nobody except his nearest relatives and slaves knew of the marriage; he had not celebrated the event and there had been no feast. To the divorced wife and her son Saʿûd he gave a tent (up to that time the abode of Ḥmâr and his family), ordered it to be pitched close to his, and he visited the woman and his son just as he did the others. He told me that a courier had come with letters from Eben Saʿûd urging him to occupy al-Ǧowf and advising him that all the chiefs of the Šammar, except two, were asking for peace and promising to pay him tribute. At 2.47 we encamped in the dell Ḫabb al-Ǧemal, northwest of Obêrež aẓ-Ẓijân.

On Tuesday we set out at eight o'clock in the morning. I had been so busy chatting with the Prince at a small fire that we did not mount our animals until the camp was abandoned. A short distance from us two men were at work digging a grave for their brother, who had been sick a long time and had died while they were putting him upon a camel that morning. Their herd and the camels with the tent and other supplies were already gone, but his corpse was lying there upon the ground. Two camels carrying women's litters were kneeling by it, while two more were hitched by the reins to some stakes near by. Two women sat by the dead, his mother and his wife, both weeping quietly. When the grave was about forty centimeters deep the men lowered the body into it, covered it with sand, and over the sand strewed gunpowder, for the Rwala hold that the smell of gunpowder protects a corpse by frightening away hyenas that might molest it. On finishing the sad work, the men got upon their saddles and the women into the litters and rode swiftly after the migrating tribe without once turning back toward their dead. Except for them, no one had accompanied the dead brother to his resting place; yet he had been a brave warrior and a liberal host. The true Bedouin has an aversion for the dead, even though the deceased be his own father.

"What good has the tribe from the dead? That we all must die, we know; why then should we sadden our life by looking at the dead?" reasoned the Prince.

We encamped at 2.40 P.M. in the sand desert of al-ʿArejž. The next morning, Wednesday, we started at 7.20 A.M., but the laden camels advanced so slowly and we had to encircle drifts and pits so often that at 2.15 P.M. we pitched our tents while still in the sand. On Thursday we left at 7.32 A.M., at 9.10 reached the plain of al-Hûğ, and proceeded towards the wells of al-Hawğa, where we arrived at 3.35 P.M.

SOJOURN AT PRINCE AN-NÛRI'S CAMP, AL-HAWĞA

Within the basin of al-Hawğa water can be found by digging. It is not spring water, but underground rain water, which flows into the wells — slowly filling them to sixty centimeters at the most. Some of the wells are two meters deep, others as deep as fifteen meters. The deepest ones hold the most water, for the shallow ones soon become clogged and must be cleaned out every year. Early in the afternoon the Prince had sent two slaves ahead to seize the three best wells for him. The same was done by ʿAd̲ûb eben Meǧwel, whose father years ago had cleaned out the deepest filled-up well and who could therefore claim that it belonged to his family. The other Bedouins likewise hastened to the wells to seize this or that one and pitch their tents near it. A shallow rain water well which becomes clogged and is yearly cleaned and deepened is called *ʿaḳla*.

Soon after an-Nûri had designated the location for his tent there returned to him the slaves whom he had sent to seize for his tribe the other wells in the vicinity, in order that the camels of his men might be watered at Mšâš al-Mowt, Ḥdâǧân, and Mlêḥ. The Ḥlese clan of the Šarârât sent messengers to him with an offer to watch his camels upon their own pastures. The brother of the chief Eben Ḳrejṭân always rode behind the Prince and did not dare to sit near a fire by which he was sitting or to speak in his presence; yet Solejmân eben Ḳrejṭân was the richest and proudest warrior of his tribe. But he was only a raven, while an-Nûri was an eagle.

Friday to Monday, February 12 to 15, 1909. During these four days I barely left my round tent, for I was busy re-writing the account of my last expedition. The Prince came every day to see how I fared. Early Friday morning our camels were sent to pasture at al-Bwejbijje and did not return to be watered until Monday evening. Saturday there came to the Prince about thirty fighters, offering to accompany him upon the contemplated raid. He sent them back, however, postponing the day of the raid; whereat one of them exclaimed indignantly:

"Well, he cannot part from his young wife!" An-Nûri told me, however, that his summons had not yet reached all his clans.

On Friday and Saturday a torrid temperature prevailed (on Friday, temperature at 7.30: 6.2° C; at 2.45: 17.5° C; at 4.30: 18.3° C; on Saturday at 7.30: 10.8° C; at 1.30: 26.8° C; at 5.45: 20.2° C).

On Sunday we witnessed a terrific storm with a display of lightning in the east-northeast, whence came also the faint rumble of thunder. On Monday it turned considerably cooler (temperature at 7: 3° C; at 2: 18.5° C; at 5.30: 15° C).

On Saturday and Sunday morning the chiefs of the various Šarârât clans arrived to greet the Prince and offer their services. He dealt with them haughtily, hardly noticing them the entire afternoon but letting them sit alone in his tent while he entertained himself in my large tent with his head slave Ḥmâr and the scribe Ǧwâd. He would not enter my small tent for fear of its "evil smell," which had been caused by the overturn of my bottle of iodine while I was bandaging my herdsman's wound. Indeed, an-Nûri was so afraid of it that he even asked me quite seriously if the smell would not cause the wounds of his older fighters to reopen. Wounded and sick Bedouins fear nothing as much as an "evil smell." That is why they pull their kerchiefs up over their noses, stuff their nostrils, and even press them tight with their fingers when approached by a person whose scent is unfamiliar to them. I had taken with me into the desert several boxes of perfumed soaps for gifts to women. These were contained in a large bag, which emitted an odor so fragrant as we marched along that, in order to escape harm, the Bedouins used to dodge the camel that carried the bag. Still, everybody wanted a piece of that soap, and Nawwâf begged me to send several boxes of it to al-Ǧowf, that he might distribute it among the wives and the daughters of the settlers.

Tuesday and Wednesday, February 16 and 17, 1909. An-Nûri announced to me that on Thursday, February 18, he was going to undertake a raid, but he failed to tell me against what tribe. It was rumored that he was likely to attack the Htejm, but nobody knew anything for certain. He was, however, to pass by the settlement of Tejma; therefore he invited me to accompany him.

"Thou hast undertaken a raid against us with Âl Fâjez of the tribe Beni Ṣaḫr," he laughed, "hence I think thou shouldst accompany me against my enemies."

Thinking that I might be able to work at Tejma and explore the territory south of Ẓelʿ al-Ṛnejm, I readily promised to go along. The reports of the events in Tejma were contradictory. Solejmân eben Ḳrejṭân reported that a civil war prevailed there, whereas only last Sunday a Šarâri had arrived at our camp from the south, bringing the news that ʿAbdarraḥmân, the vice-regent of Eben Rašîd, had been driven out from Tejma and that Eben Rummân was now in control. As the latter was personally acquainted with an-Nûri, I could count with certainty upon being cordially received by him.

Wishing to make a geographical map of the district through which we were to pass on the raid, I summoned an older Kwêčbi who had been camping several years with the Weld Slejmân and Weld ʿAli and was acquainted with the local topography. The Kwâčbe camping with the Rwala had rebelled against Prince Fahad, who asked an-Nûri to discipline them. An-Nûri had subjugated them and as a punishment had dispossessed them of many herds of camels, whereupon most of them went over to the Dahâmše and ʿAmârât tribes. The Kwêčbi, my informer, had also moved to the region of the Euphrates at Kerbela and had come from there only a short time ago; therefore he was in a position to give me news about the districts between Ḫajbar and Tejma and even about the vicinity of the cities of Kerbela and an-Neǧef. He smoked incessantly an ill-smelling tobacco in a curious short pipe, called *bûz* — a combination of half an alum pipe and a piece of a hare's calf-bone. His original short pipe, *sebîl,* having broken at the bottom of the bowl where the nicotine settles, he had substituted for the broken part a piece of a hare's bone, sticking it into the break in the bowl and sewing round it a piece of hide to prevent it from shifting and to keep the smoke from escaping. He held the bone in his mouth and stuffed the rest of the pipe with tobacco (on Tuesday, temperature at 7.30: 8° C; at 1.20: 20° C; at 6: 13.2° C).

On Wednesday toward evening twelve fighters of the Weld Slejmân came to the Prince to settle various controversies that had arisen between their tribe and the Rwala. Evidently they were apprehensive lest the Prince meant to attack them. Late that evening Ǧwâd, the Prince's scribe, came to request me, in the Prince's name, to deposit in his tent all the rifles and revolvers that I did not intend to take along on the raid, because after the departure of the Prince upon the warlike excursion there would remain in the camp only two rifles, Nawwâf having carried with him many weapons and the remainder being needed for the raid. I informed the scribe that I should have only one rifle and one revolver to leave and that I should claim those whenever I needed them. The Prince having agreed to that condition, I handed the pieces over to him. An-Nûri desired to have my weapons and was always scheming to secure them under some pretense (temperature at 7.30: 9.5° C; at 1.30: 23.3° C; at 6: 17.2° C).

Thursday, February 18, 1909. We were all in readiness to depart upon the raid and merely awaited the Prince's command to mount the camels. An-Nûri, however, was in close negotiations with the Weld Slejmân and did not come out of his tent until ten o'clock, when he curtly commanded: "The mount camels to pasture." The raid was off! Inquiring the reason, I found that he had intended to attack the Htejm and upon his return the Weld Slejmân also, but that he had become reconciled with the latter and therefore had no reason for preying upon their herds. He said he had been unable to learn anything reliable about the whereabouts of the Htejm and the Arabs of Sirḥân abu Šâma. Some claimed that both were encamped south of al-ʿEla, others looked for them in the vicinity of Ḫajbar, and still others maintained that they were located in the upper portion of the valley of ar-Rmaʾ. In consideration of all this, the Weld Slejmân were requested to make inquiries as to their precise location and to advise him within eight days, at which time he would decide whether to march upon them or not.

One of the warriors of the Weld Slîmân — as the name of the Weld Slejmân is also pronounced — came into my tent to invite me to accompany him, saying that he would conduct me safely to al-Medîna, Ḫajbar, and Ḥâjel. When I asked him if he was friendly with all the clans of the Šarârât, Htejm, and Šammar, he replied that he was acquainted with most of them, living at peace with some and waging war with others.

"Then thou wouldst dread to lead me through the pastures of the clan with whom thou art at war," I answered, and went to the Prince to seek advice. An-Nûri said that it would doubtless be better for me to wait eight more days and accompany him on the raid than to forsake my men and my baggage and go forth into the unknown with a man who was incapable of bringing me where he promised. I decided to wait.

I was very anxious to leave immediately for the east, in order to explore that part of the desert and to finish my map of the country; but of course under the circumstances it was advisable to wait. As the district from the range of aṭ-Ṭawîl in the west as far as the wells of al-Ḥzûl and aṣ-Ṣammît in the east had recently been favored with abundant rains, and in the last two weeks, according to hearsay, it had rained there twice more, Prince an-Nûri wished to migrate thither with his clan as soon as his herds had exhausted the grazing in the district of al-Ḫunfa. After we were encamped at al-Ḥzûl I could undertake the trip north into the eastern half of the desert with greater facility and should be exposed to less danger than if I were to venture there alone with only a guide; for on my way from al-Ḫunfa to the east I should have to travel constantly along the boundaries of the various clans of the Šammar and approach the pastures of the aẓ-Ẓefîr tribe. All these were enemies of the Rwala and therefore of me also. Besides, it was entirely impossible for me to secure at al-Ḫunfa any guide who could protect me from all the clans of the Šammar.

FIG. 36—ʿAwde al-Kwêčbi.

Friday and Saturday, February 19 and 20, 1909. These two days I spent collecting information about the regions east and northeast of al-Ǧowf, working on the geographical sketch map, making corrections according to the accounts of various informants, and supplementing them whenever possible.

On Saturday six fighters brought home all the riding camels of Nawwâf's band and said that Nawwâf begged his father to encamp either in or near the oasis of al-Ǧowf and thus to augment Nawwâf's prestige by his presence. Nawwâf's difficulties in al-Ǧowf seemed to be increasing daily. ʿAwde al-Kwêčbi (Fig. 36), my old acquaintance and informant, who had just arrived from al-Ǧowf, told me that many of Nawwâf's adherents had gone over to his opponents, unable to withstand the arrogance and penuriousness of Eben Ḳaʿajjed any longer; that the enemy was making attacks on Nawwâf nightly, so that he could not leave his house and was suffering from lack of food; and finally that Nawwâf begged him to describe his misery to his father and move him to march to al-Ǧowf. But an-Nûri procrastinated. It seemed to me as if he mistrusted his son and was jealous of him. He pretended to me to be awaiting an answer from the Weld Slejmân and also the return of his messenger to Eben Saʿûd; but the negro preparing his coffee said:

"He does not attend to anything but his young wife and his fur coat, which he likes to lie on." (Temperature at 7: 4° C; at 1.30: 16.5° C; at 5.15: 14.6° C.)

Sunday to Friday, February 21 to 26, 1909. Sunday morning Mindîl al-Ḳaṭʿi arrived from al-Ğowf bringing to the Prince a written as well as a verbal plea from Nawwâf to send him food and money. An-Nûri had the written message read to him in my tent and he listened to the verbal account there; but he did nothing.

On Monday afternoon four couriers of the chief Âl ʿAwâği of the Weld Slejmân arrived, reporting that they had liberated (*fakkaw*) the camels of the Nṣejr clan. This clan had been attacked by the Šammar led by Eben Rmâl and had lost almost all their herds. On their return the victorious Šammar paid a visit to the camp of the chief Âl ʿAwâği, with whom they lived at peace. The chief, noticing upon the camels the brands of the Nṣejr clan, which is affiliated with the Rwala, with whom he had just negotiated a new peace, immediately requested Eben Rmâl to return the stolen herds or else the Rwala could accuse him (Âl ʿAwâği) of violation of the treaty for having rendered hospitality to their enemies, the Šammar. Eben Rmâl refused, whereupon a fight ensued in which he was routed. The Weld Slejmân accordingly returned the liberated herds to the Nṣejr clan, but Eben Rmâl declared war against them.

On Monday Ṭrâd eben Saṭṭâm came to me with a complaint about ʿAbdallâh eben Ṭalâl. The latter, he said, had taken unto himself as wife a daughter of an-Nûri, who complained of bad treatment at his hands and deserted him and now dwelt in the tent of her father, refusing to return to her husband. ʿAbdallâh was therefore seeking another wife. He had fallen in love with the sister of Ṭrâd and on Sunday came to him to ask for her hand, since Ṭrâd now stood to her in the place of her dead father. As the girl did not care for ʿAbdallâh, however, Ṭrâd refused to give his consent; whereupon ʿAbdallâh declared that he had reserved the girl for himself and would not permit her to marry anyone else, asserting that as her nearest relative he had the first right to her.

For several days an-Nûri's tent had also been occupied by another of his daughters, a slender girl about seventeen years of age, with diseased eyes. In her girlhood she had married Fâres, the son of Prince Fahad, but after the latter's assassination she escaped from her husband and established herself in the tent of her father. While we were camping at Ḍmejr she had married Mišref eben Kurdi, but she had deserted him only five days before and refused to return to him despite the pressure brought to bear by her father and the pleas of Mišref, who loved her dearly.

On Tuesday evening Eben Durmi, who had been camping east of the rain well Mšâš aš-Šubeče, came with a communication from the Weld Slejmân to the effect that the Arabs of Abu Šâma had departed toward the west into the volcanic district of al-ʿAwêreẓ, and that the Htejm were watering their herds at the wells in the valley of al-Ǧlâsi in Ḫajbar. Delivery of a more detailed and accurate report was promised within the next few days through some Sulejmâni (on Tuesday, temperature at 8: 17.2° C; at 12.30: 28.2° C; at 5.30: 22.8° C).

At noon on Wednesday another messenger from Nawwâf arrived. He said there was no doubt that Ḥmûd eben Subhân had perished by poison. He it was who saved the boy Saʿûd, a son of ʿAbdalʿazîz, and had escaped with Saʿûd and his mother, who was Ḥmûd's sister, to al-Medîna, whence he returned in the summer of 1908, killed Prince Saʿûd eben Rašîd, and proclaimed as prince his ward Saʿûd. It was he also who contrived to preserve the remnants of the former domain of Eben Rašîd, and from him salvation was expected by all the settlers. At the instigation of his ambitious brother Zâmel, he had been poisoned two months ago, it was said, but his death was kept secret and the report was spread that he was seriously ill. But now that at last the truth had become generally known, the people were the more inclined to join either Eben Saʿûd or Eben Šaʿlân. Nawwâf said that the chiefs of Mâred and al-Ḫadne at al-Ǧowf were again negotiating with him and that he had also received more favorable news from Skâka. Scheming to intimidate his opponents into submission, he again appealed to his father to march to al-Ǧowf and encamp for several days in the vicinity of the city. He commended the pasture south and southeast of the oasis, saying that the eastern boundary of the Nefûd, called al-Labbe, had been well moistened and promised abundant pasturage.

On Wednesday afternoon I made a trip to Šdâd umm Kûr, the eastern saddle of the tabular hill Ḳârt umm Kûr (Figs. 37, 38, 39), where the Rwala hunters wished to show me a large cave which I had not been able to find. I had, however, found several blossoming plants and a variety of minerals. The softer layers of the slopes abound in caves in which the Šarârât hide stores of which they are not in immediate need. For this concealed property of the Šarârât the Rwala, men and women, adults and children, daily searched, taking whatever they found. I had discovered several stones with crude images of camels, gazelles, and ibexes and even one of a lion; but I had hunted in vain for inscriptions. That afternoon one of my companions maintained that he had seen a herd of twelve ibexes; whereupon thirty men set out to hunt in the evening but returned Thursday afternoon worn out and empty-handed.

A strong west wind blew constantly during the night. Several times it turned into the northeast and damaged many of the tents. Those of the Prince, of Ḥmâr abu ʿAwwâd, and of several others were blown down, but their tenants nevertheless continued to sleep calmly under the upset roofs. Not until the gale blew such a mass of sand upon the roof that they could not breathe had the women crawled out, shaken off the sand, and disappeared again under the canvas.

VISIT OF ʿAWDE ABU TÂJEH

From morning till evening I was occupied with studies in folklore, in which I was assisted by Ḥmâr abu ʿAwwâd, Mindîl al-Ḳaṭʿi, and the Prince. The latter advised me Friday morning that we should not undertake a raid but that on Sunday we should march to the vicinity of al-Ǧowf. The same day about three o'clock six camel riders dismounted in front of his tent. They were ʿAwde abu Tâjeh, head chief of the tribe of al-Ḥwêṭât, and his retinue. Toward evening the Prince ordered a fat camel to be slaughtered for the guests. Although he had openly and explicitly forbidden anybody to dare take any of the flesh, nevertheless half of the camel was gone even before the animal was skinned. The meat was appropriated by the slaves and the *ṣunnâʿ* (blacksmiths).

Fig. 37

Fig. 38

Fig. 37—Ḳârt umm Kûr from an-Nûri's camp at al-Hawǧa.
Fig. 38—Looking northeast along the slopes of Ḳârt umm Kûr. (Continuation to right of Fig. 37.)

Saturday, February 27, 1909. The Prince's scribe came to me in the morning with the request that I examine the wounded arm of his guest, ʿAwde; so I went to the tent of the Prince where ʿAwde showed me his bandaged right arm. He had assaulted the Htejm and had robbed them of several

FIG. 39—Šdâd umm Kûr from the north.

herds of camels; but as he was returning he encountered near the range of al-Mismaʾ a Šammar raiding party whose commander Fâjed eben Ṛejfi shattered his right elbow in the battle that ensued. This incident had occurred fifty-two days before. The wound had drawn together on the surface, but the arm remained swollen and stiff, and in five places deep scars were visible where he had seared the limb with hot iron. These operations had been of no avail, however, and he complained that the arm was exceedingly painful, especially at night. I invited him into my tent, applied the proper remedy, bandaged the limb, and instructed him how to attend to it. Then I talked with him of my projected visit to the oasis of Tejma and the burial ground of al-Mğenne, questioning him as to the events in Tejma and about the Arabs camping in the neighborhood. As he wished me to stay with him for a longer period to treat his arm, he proposed that I accompany him first to his camp and thence with his men to Tejma, at which place, he said, I could arrive in two nights. As Prince an-Nûri agreed to the proposition, I decided to seize the opportunity and began to prepare the necessary instruments and supplies in order that we might depart early the next day.

Toward eleven o'clock the strong west wind began to blow again, carrying clouds of sand with it and overturning several tents. Even within my round tent, closed tightly on all sides and stuffed from within, the fine sand lay in places as much as three centimeters deep. The Prince paid me a visit and inquired how I liked the camel meat he had sent me. I thanked him for the bone, and asked his pardon for not being able to thank him for the meat, as I had received hardly half a *roṭol* (1.28 kilogram) of it. He declared that immediately after the fore part of the camel had been skinned he had sent me the entire front leg, and he could not understand, any more than I could, how all the meat had disappeared from the leg on the way from his tent to mine, the intervening distance being only thirty-four paces.

In the evening I again spoke with ʿAwde and learned that ʿAbdarraḥmân, Eben Rašîd's vice-regent, had once more penetrated with a troop of negroes into the oasis of Tejma and ousted Eben Rummân. This was unpleasant news to both an-Nûri and me, for we were in doubt as to how ʿAbdarraḥmân would treat me and my companions. ʿAwde was of the opinion that he would not be bold enough to repudiate me, but thought he might detain me in Tejma as a hostage. He was, for the present, absolute master of Tejma; but he was aware how untenable his position was and was seeking to secure himself. Had an-Nûri gone to Tejma with an array of raiders, or had he encamped near it, I could have depended with more certainty upon the continuity of my work. After the Rwala had left for the north, however, ʿAbdarraḥmân would be likely to utilize his immediate advantage.

These considerations prompted an-Nûri to try to dissuade me from taking the journey to Tejma. He was confident that a better opportunity would present itself later, perhaps after Nawwâf had captured the oasis and an-Nûri had appointed him as vice-regent over it. Reluctantly I had to agree with the arguments of an-Nûri and cancel my journey with ʿAwde. He alone could not protect me, nor could Eben Rašîd, because ʿAbdarraḥmân defied the present acting minister, Zâmel eben Subhân, and was plotting to usurp control over Tejma. ʿAwde said that the chief Âl Fežîr of the Weld ʿAli tribe intended to join the Rwala and march with them to al-Labbe and al-Ḥamâd because of lack of pasture in his territory southwest of Tejma, and the Prince likewise had been advised about this by the Weld ʿAli. Taking all this into consideration, they thought it probable that, after finishing my work in the eastern part of the desert, I would have an opportunity in the early summer to leave with Âl Fežîr for the southwest, visit Tejma and his territory, and perhaps return to Damascus from al-ʿElaʾ or Medâjen Ṣâleḥ. By that time, they said, Allâh would decide who the master of Tejma was to be (temperature at 6.45: 7.9° C; at 1: 25.2° C; at 5.30: 20.2° C).

Sunday to Tuesday, February 28 to March 2, 1909. An-Nûri announced that we should remain at the same camping ground several more days, because he could not leave his esteemed guest and ally ʿAwde abu Tâjeh, who had come to pay him a visit. As a matter of fact, ʿAwde had really come to demand that the Rwala should return to him several camels which they had taken from his wife and her escorts. He said that his wife, the daughter of Eben Rmâl, chief of one of the Šammar tribes, with which he had long been friendly, had set out with several slaves upon a visit to her mother and relatives among the Šammar. Upon her return she was accompanied by a few of her friends to the district of al-Hûǧ, where they encountered a raiding party of the Rwala, who were engaged in warfare with the Šammar, and who made an assault upon the retinue of ʿAwde's wife, robbed the Šammar of everything they had, and took away the best riding camels from two slaves.

On Monday afternoon the camp reverberated with the joyous shouts (*zarâṛît*) of the women; for Ḏlejjel eben Meǧwel, considered dead for some time, had returned. Thirty-two days before with thirty-eight companions he had undertaken a raid against the Aslam tribe of the Šammar camping at the south-eastern border of al-Labbe. They had surprised a smaller clan and captured four herds with numerous young ones. As the young ones could not hurry with the old camels, the party was compelled to go slowly. During the first and second nights they all kept watch with weapons in their hands, fearing an attack from the pursuing Šammar; but the third night, thinking themselves secure, they all lay down and the watches fell asleep. Before sunrise the Šammar overtook and surrounded them, leaving them no choice but to surrender without resistance. Only a few succeeded in escaping upon riding camels; the rest were captured and among them the leader (*ʿažîd*), Ḏlejjel. In the morning the Šammar divested them of all their garments and rode away with the booty, leaving them to their fate. Several perished of thirst; the rest wandered about in different directions until Ḏlejjel was discovered by two Ṣlejb and brought by them to the settlement of al-Ḳâra, where he found refuge in the house of the chief Ẓâher eben Selîm. He had known Ẓâher for several years and had fallen in love with his sister Ẓeba', but her father had refused to grant his consent to their marriage. Upon reaching al-Ḳâra with the Ṣlejb he learned that the father had died a short time before; whereupon he asked her brother for the hand of his beloved. Ẓâher consented and D̲lejjel immediately married the girl. Seven days later he set out to al-Ǧowf and thence with a camel trader to his tent in our camp. He was the only child of his widowed mother, who reveled in joy over his return; and his paternal uncle immediately slaughtered a camel, as he had promised Allâh he would, should D̲lejjel return alive and well.

On Tuesday I rode with Dawǧân, the son of Ḥmâr, upon the Prince's wounded horse to the southern rocks to search for blossoming plants. It was not an easy undertaking as the horse dropped every moment and we could not get very far from the camp lest we be robbed; besides, within a distance of five to ten kilometers south of the wells everything had been grazed off. In the almost inaccessible gulches, however, the plants *aḫḫejm, baḫatri, tarba, ǧrajba* (or *loṣṣejž*), *ǧamba, ḥazâr* (or *al-ḥmêra*), *ḥamma', ḫrîṭ, ḫzâma, ḫomṣân, drejhme, šiḳḳâra, ṣuffâra,* and *makr* were undisturbed; therefore we returned with a fair quantity of specimens.

CHAPTER VII

AL-HAWǦA TO ḪIŠT AṮ-ṮÔR

AL-HAWǦA TO BURḲ AŠ-ŠAʿÎRA

Wednesday to Tuesday, March 2 to 9, 1909 (temperature on Wednesday at 6.30 : 2°C). The rain wells of al-Hawǧa contained very little water and in most of them that little was salty and bitter; only two of them had fresh water. Since the Prince had announced on Saturday that we were to migrate, camels were constantly being brought to the wells to be watered and as we should not reach water again until six to nine days later, the Arabs were bringing their bags to fill. Thus, when our herdsman Mufaẓẓi returned with the camels on Tuesday evening, there was water left in only one of the wells and that was surrounded by the camels of the Prince. His herdsmen permitted my animals to come to the water upon his explicit order, and before the beasts had satisfied their thirst most of the Arabs were gone with their tents and baggage.

The Prince sat by me until all my property (*ḥelle*) was loaded. At ten o'clock we started northeastward. While still far off, we noticed that the pack camels of the Prince were prancing and stamping as if they were frightened, and we soon knew the reason why. Upon a steep path that led from the basin of al-Hawǧa to a height, one of them had been pulled down by his own load and had broken his left hind leg. Although the slaves had relieved him of the burden, they could not remove him from the narrow path, on the left of which rose a precipitous cliff while on the right gaped an abyss about thirty meters deep. They were unable to pull him upward and they had too much pity for the wounded beast, which was emitting heart-rending lamentations, to force him downward. There was no alternative but to end his misery on the spot, skin him, disjoint the carcass, and carry the chunks of meat up to where they could be loaded upon other animals. Unable to compel the rest of the camels to pass their crippled, groaning partner, the slaves sought another path and brought the camels up one by one. We went ahead of them and encamped at three o'clock north of Ḳârt al-Ḫonṣor, at the southern edge of the sandy salient al-ʿArejž.

On Thursday at 7.20 A. M. we started on our day's journey through the sandy desert, and at five o'clock in the afternoon

FIG. 40—A *ḳaʿara* in the Nefûd.

the Prince selected a camp site in a spacious hollow (*ḳaʿara*) (Fig. 40) (temperature at 6 A. M.: 3.8°C; at 4 P. M.: 19.8° C).

On Friday the migration began at 6.50 A. M. in a northeasterly direction between al-ʿArejž and the aṭ-Ṭawîl range, passing to the right of Obêrež aẓ-Ẓijân and Ẓelʿ al-Bârde. These mountains consist of bare rocks, dark gray and almost black, and through them extends the deep *šeʿîb* of al-Bârde within which are the small rain wells Ṯemâjel al-Bârde. Farther to the east we noted among the rocks of al-Bârde and al-Klâḥ the wide rift of Rîʿ al-Muʿaj. At two o'clock we had on our right the half-filled well Želîb Ḥedâǧân, and at 2.15 P. M. we encamped upon a prolonged, stony swell.

On Saturday we resumed our journey at six o'clock and at 8.20 reached the hills of al-Bawaʾ, which connect the aṭ-Ṭawîl range with the Nefûd. Being partly covered with sand, these hills glisten red and black in the rays of the rising sun. At this place we were joined by several men of the Durmân clan of the Rwala, who told us of having been attacked a few days before by a raiding band of the Šammar. They said their small camp (*ferîž*) was occupied by only four men, the

FIG. 41—Sandstone rocks of al-Ḳdêrijje.

rest having gone in quest of booty; hence the Šammar easily captured their herds. When, however, the enemy fell also upon the tents, intending to take them as well, all the women became belligerent. Arming themselves with tent poles, they defended their property and killed several of the Šammar. They were, of course, aided in the combat by the four men, who had hidden in the neighboring brush, from which they fired upon the assailants. The men described the fight to us in minute detail, showing us the bushes where they had lain, weapons in hand, and the spot where the women had beaten to death one of the aggressors. They did not show us his grave, for he remained unburied, a prey to rapacious animals and carnivorous birds. Only the gnawed-off skull was lying near by.

In course of time the entire eastern half of the hills of al-Bawa' will become the prey of the Nefûd. The sandstone rocks are already disappearing under the sands, with which the wind slowly though persistently covers their western, northern, and eastern sides and forms drifts, sand hills, and hollows (*ḳa'ar*) just as in the neighboring 'Arejž.

After eleven o'clock we left al-Bawa' and entered the hilly district of al-Bowlijjât and the range aṭ-Ṭawîl. From 11.38 until 12.20 the Prince and I scoured the vicinity through our binoculars, seeking grazing camels or a camp; for neither the Arabs nor even the Prince's relatives had any water and the Prince wished to obtain it from a camp, at least for use in his own tent. At length I sighted loaded camels and women's litters to the northwest upon the level crest of al-Ḥaršûfijjât and accordingly notified the Prince that a Rwala clan was moving there northwestward. The Prince gazed through his own binoculars in the same direction, but, seeing nothing, he would not believe me and asked me to lend him mine. In order to show in the presence of his slaves that he could get along without my assistance in setting the lenses of Zeiss binoculars, he adjusted them himself, but so badly that he could not see anything; whereupon he declared that such binoculars (*derbîl*) were worthless. Like any other Bedouin, the Prince despised a thing the utility of which he did not readily understand or which he did not know how to handle. Thus he had exchanged the first carbine I gave him for an old Turkish army rifle, and the second carbine he had had remodeled to hold only one charge. When, however, after firing several shots at a target with it, he was able to hit the mark every time, he informed everyone that he had never had a better rifle and immediately sent a slave for the exchanged carbine. But the report (*ḥess*) of the rifle was not to his fancy. It seemed too dull to him, for he believed that the louder the discharge the more powerful and fatal the shot.

In the afternoon we proceeded in a north-northeasterly direction, first among the sandstone rocks of al-Ḳdêrijje (Fig. 41), later through the southern spurs of the mountains of al-Ḥṯûl and the southern ones of Umm Ruḳuba, stopping at four o'clock upon the summit of al-Mustanda.

Toward the northeast and east we saw dense clouds, with funnels pointing from them down to the earth; the clouds spread over the entire region and seemed to touch the ground.

I thought that a storm was raging ahead of us, that a downpour was moistening the region whither we were bound, but it proved to be a sandstorm (*ʿağâğ*).

As the children and the mares of our Arabs were already suffering from lack of water, several of the men went north to the rocky crevice Žaltat an-Nağma, which is often filled with rain water, but they returned without finding a drop in the *žalta*. In a narrow gorge, impassable for the camels, I picked *ḏîl al-ḥoṣni, ḳafʿaʾ, barwaḳ, ḥasak, ḥoṣnijje, ḥalôla, ḥambâẓ, ḫâfûr, ruḳrûḳ, swajža, laḥjat at-tejs, nazaʿ, naʿîme, sufsûf, snejsle, raḳma,* and in the evening I determined the latitude. Meantime Mḥammad had gone with the Prince's slaves to al-Ğowf for water and Nâṣer was besieged at our tent by a stream of women who came to beg some of him. But all had to go back empty-handed, for Nâṣer assured them that we ourselves had none.

On Monday the migration began at 6.25 A. M. We descended from the aṭ-Ṭawîl ridge, crossed the head of the *šeʿîb* of al-ʿÂḏrijje, encircled the hills of Burḳ aš-Šaʿîra, which were covered with sand, and encamped at eleven o'clock among innumerable small hills each of which sloped off steeply to the east and among and upon which was a growth of *ṛaẓa, arṭa, ʿâḏer, orejnbe, barwaḳ, ṭarṯûṯ, ḥemḥem, hawaʾ, tarba, umm at-trâb, ḏaʿlûḳ al-mṭi,* and *ʿalḳa*.

MḤAMMAD'S THEFTS

Near by was a higher hill to which the Prince and I made a trip in order to look over the vicinity. On the way he asked me whom I had sent for water and, on learning that Mḥammad went, he said:

"Thou shouldst not have sent him, brother. He is a dog whom I do not trust."

Mḥammad's conduct had, indeed, been so impudent and almost arrogant of late that I had more than once rebuked him. It seemed as if he were unwilling to regard me as his master and were handling my property in the tent according to his own liking. This I could not tolerate, especially since I had reason to suspect that he was appropriating my property himself or disposing of it to others. Only two days before he had brought me a bowl, requesting me to fill it with sugar for the negro Ḥmâr. I said I was surprised at his coming to me with such a request, since he was aware that we all liked sweet tea and since he also knew how little sugar we had and how impossible it was to get any more at present. To this he retorted that if this were the case, he would fill the bowl with his own sugar which he had brought for himself from Dejr az-Zôr to Damascus, and he added that lately he had been sweetening his coffee with his own sugar anyway. This was too much.

"Thou camest to me in Damascus almost naked," I interrupted, "thou hadst not so much as a shirt; and yet thou broughtest with thee so much sugar that it has lasted thee seven months and even now thou canst fill such a bowl? Blest be he who would believe thee! Tomorrow thou mayst come and say that thou hast thine own coffee, rice, and the like, that all of this thou hast brought with thee from ad-Dejr! I will not endure it. My camels are to carry only my own property, except garments and smoking things for thee and thy companions."

He was so deeply offended at my words that he declared he would not drink our coffee or tea; whereupon he went out and did not return till night.

Saturday morning my people greeted me with the customary "*Ṣabbaḥk allâh bilḫejr,* Allâh grant that the morning be favorable to thee"; to which I replied as usual:

"*Allâh jeṣabbaḥk bilḫrejr,* Allâh grant also to thee that the morning be favorable." But Mḥammad did not greet me; paying no attention to me he began issuing orders to Nâṣer and Mufaẓẓi, assigning their work. When I asked him before we started:

"Why hast thou not greeted me yet?" he retorted, "I forgot," and walked away.

On the journey he complained to Tûmân that he could not bear such hardships and said he would leave us at al-Ǧowf. Sunday, as we rode along, I told the Prince about Mḥammad's conduct, whereupon he replied that it had occurred to him some time ago that Mḥammad was handling my property quite arbitrarily and said he would reprove him.

Before he started for al-Ǧowf after water I had entrusted to him 120 Maria Theresa dollars ($ 52) or, as the Arabs call them, *abu šûše,* with which to buy a camel that I had inspected there on my last visit, as well as to purchase salt and, if possible, dates also. On learning of this, the Prince remarked that I had been unwise, for Mḥammad could easily desert with either the money or the camel. The Prince also told me that he had talked with Mḥammad the night before and had urged him to fulfill his duties. None the less, he said, Mḥammad was an insolent man of unresponsive heart, who knew no gratitude to Allâh or to any man. His insolence had even led him to declare in the Prince's tent in the presence of the chiefs:

"I did not seek Mûsa and I do not seek him now."

"Thus speakest thou before me?" retorted the Prince. "Allâh has sent thee these earnings; never before hast thou fared so well; and now, after thou hast nurtured thyself somewhat, thou darest to speak to me thus? Dost thou not know, thou dog, that the Sheikh Mûsa has become one of us, that he belongs to my family, that he is my brother, and that I shall bend anyone who would defy him? Thou shalt serve him as well as he shall demand from thee for the money he pays thee, else I shall force thee. Were he to cut daily a slice of flesh from thy body, thou art not to murmur."

"Thus did I speak to him, brother," said the Prince. "But the scamp is too brazen because he has too much money. Dost thou not know of it, Mûsa?"

"I know that he hath two or three napoleons ($ 7.72 or $ 11.58)."

"Oh, no! Besides these he hath also other money, gold, and hath entrusted for safekeeping at least twenty gold pieces to a man I know."

These words instantly explained much that had been dark to me. Mḥammad had been hired for me by al-Ḥâǧǧ Dâûd as-Sâlem under the following conditions:

"He shall get four napoleons ($ 15.44) monthly, he shall sustain himself in Damascus from his wages, he shall likewise buy clothes with his own money. Shouldst thou, Mûsa, be satisfied with him throughout the journey, thou shalt reimburse him upon his return to Damascus for whatever he hath spent for clothing. He is not to take with him into the desert any money and shall not have any private property. Shouldst thou find with him, or with any other person, private money belonging to him, thou mayst drive him away as a dog without giving him his wage."

It was only upon these conditions that I accepted him; otherwise he could have cheated me in every transaction and have saved money for himself. When we came from Damascus into the camp of Prince an-Nûri in al-Rûṭa, he swore to me before Nawwâf that he had but fifteen piasters (67 cents), and again in Ḍmejr he swore he had no money. And now the Prince told me that he had deposited twenty napoleons ($ 77) with a man he knew and was carrying four or five napoleons in his pocket! Where had he obtained this money? The gold I had taken into the desert was hidden among photograph plates, medicines, and poisons, and none of my native escorts were aware of its presence. For the current small expenditures I usually took out a certain amount while changing photograph plates, and this money I carried secreted in my saddlebag upon which I slept and which lay in my round tent. Although this tent was never entered by anybody except the Prince, Nawwâf, Tûmân, and Mḥammad, I had noticed that the money in the bag was disappearing; but as I had caught no one I could suspect no one. Now I had found out who the thief was. Explaining matters to the Prince, I asked him to assist me in dealing with Mḥammad.

When the man returned on Tuesday from al-Ǧowf, I asked him before witnesses whether he had any private money. He replied that he did not own even a single *para* (0.11 cent), as all he had received for wages he had sent to his family or had used to buy clothing. At that I sent for the Prince and in his presence again asked Mḥammad whether he had any private money. He retorted insolently that he was not obliged to make explanations to another about his private property but that he had borrowed fifteen napoleons in Ḍmejr and had taken them with him into the desert and that in al-Mijâḏîn he had borrowed ten more, in order to be independent of me. At the Prince's order Nâṣer examined Mḥammad's saddlebag and found in it many things we had missed; whereupon the Prince declared that he should keep the gold which Mḥammad had deposited with a certain man until he proved where and how he had earned it. He then ordered Mḥammad to leave my tent instantly and never show himself near us again. Thus I lost the last servant whom my friends in Damascus, al-Ḥâǧǧ Jâsîn and al-Ḥâǧǧ Dâûd, had recommended. Gentlemen in Damascus do not know the desert, and neither do their own men; for it is one thing to sojourn a few days in Damascus expecting recompense and quite a different thing to stay in the desert buying and watching camels. Mḥammad was to remain in a tent on the edge of the camp until he had an opportunity to return to his homeland.

On Monday evening I was visited by Eben Ḥnejjân, chief of the al-Ḳaʿâžʿa clan, who had come to the Prince to arrange with him the course of the future migration; for on the boundary between the tribes of ad-Dahâmše and Šammar the Arabs dared not march or camp in isolated groups.

ʿAĞÂJEZ ṢFÂN TO AL-ḲÂRA

On Tuesday we started at eight o'clock in a northerly direction among the sand hills of ʿAğâjez Ṣfân, which were covered with bushes and small trees of *raẓa*. Nowhere in the Nefûd had I seen such strong bolls of *raẓa* as here; many of them were more than fifty centimeters in circumference. After approaching the clogged-up well of Ṣfân, we turned toward the east-northeast, and at eleven o'clock the Prince designated a new site for the camp. The Arabs were hungry and thirsty, but in many of the tents no baking or cooking could be done because water was lacking. They subsisted merely on camel's milk and even that was scarce. The Prince had not enough of it for two foals, and the mares were given no water for two days. We were all longing for the arrival of men sent to al-Ğowf for water.

Wednesday to Friday, March 10 to 12, 1909. On Wednesday morning the herdsmen drove the camels (which had not drunk since the preceding Wednesday) to al-Ğowf, each man taking along a handful of wheat or flour to give as a reward to the settlers of al-Ğowf for drawing the water. Our herdsman Mufaẓẓi also loaded on four water bags to be filled. Assisted by the scribe Ğwâd, I devoted myself to studies of folklore from the early morning until evening.

On Wednesday evening the Prince asked me to prepare a remedy for "the girl (*bint*)," meaning his young wife. She was feverish, he said, wanted to drink frequently, and rejected every lotion. I prepared a pleasant drink and sent it to her by the negro Ḥmâr. As we sat there together the Prince recited many ditties and poems to us, which Ğwâd and I jotted down. I was much interested in the manner in which he defended the originality of particular words and refused to concede that Ğwâd's version might be better; for the latter also knew many poems and songs but frequently differed with the Prince as to the position of the words in sentences and as to the phraseology.

"Even if that word does fit better there, still it does not belong there," the Prince would declare. "As I say it, thus I have learned it, and I do not wish that anything be changed." (Temperature at 6 A.M.: 5.6° C; at 6 P.M. : 20.8° C.)

On Thursday evening I visited an-Nûri's sick wife as she lay in the tent of her mother, her whole body and even her head covered with two fur coats. She would not even let me hold her hand to take her pulse, nor would she show her tongue, but kept complaining of thirst and of pain in her joints. At my question whether she had taken the drug I sent her yesterday, her mother informed me that the girl's sisters had taken it instead: tasting the medicine and finding it pleasant, they had swallowed it all before she could administer it to the sick one. Thereupon I put a salicylic powder into a lemonade and directed the mother to administer it to her daughter in my presence.

Toward evening the camels returned from the watering place. Mufaẓẓi had brought water, but such water! It was yellow and had the stench of putrefaction. And we were to drink it! Mufaẓẓi excused himself by saying that the *šujûẖ* (prince) would drink the same water, for his servants had filled their bags from the same pool.

Meantime the Prince was insisting that Nawwâf leave al-Ǧowf and return to him. By his order Nawwâf should have been with us the day before, but he had refused to come. Moreover, he persisted in asking his father for money, ammunition, and flour, while the latter, much incensed, kept despatching to al-Ǧowf one messenger after another. On Friday one of them returned from Nawwâf with a letter which I read, because in it he asked me to give him a watch. He begged to be allowed to remain in al-Ǧowf, to be supplied with food and ammunition, and asked to have his mother and his boy Sulṭân sent to him. I interceded for him, entreating the Prince to fulfil this wish of his good son; but it was a long time before he would promise to consider it and perhaps to do as Nawwâf wished.

Saturday to Wednesday, March 13 to 17, 1909. On Saturday morning I was awakened by the grumbling of camels, disgruntled because loads were being placed on their backs.

We were to migrate again in search of pasturage; we had not found an abundant grazing place in the last five months. Starting at 7.10 A. M. we moved in an east-northeasterly direction over sand drifts of varying height overgrown with thick old trees of *ṛaẓa*. Numerous swallows (*erḳêʿi*) accompanied us, flying about our camels and catching flies. I had seen the last swallow in 1908 about the middle of November and the first one in 1909 on February 27, the latter at al-Hawǧa. Those were altogether gray, whereas the ones that were now following us looked exactly like our European swallows. The Prince called my attention to a long, black snake with grayish speckles (*dâbb*).

In the north the horizon was obstructed by the hilly belt of aẓ-Ẓullijje; east of this rose the cliffs of al-ʿAžâreb and still farther east the ragged hills of al-Ḥamâmijât and al-Žîlijjât. In the west appeared the solemn walls of the aṭ-Ṭawîl range, in its western portion attracting my attention by the black mountains of Umm Ruḳuba, between which, through a deep gap, the cone Ḳalb al-Ǧemal was visible. Southeast of this stretched the high mountains of al-Mirteka, in front of which lay the Ḫabra Mlêḥ. Still farther to the southeast was the Ẓelʿ Râf, with the wells of al-Mrût, situated southwest of aš-Šižîž and said to be of early origin. These wells are in a long hollow (*ḳaʿara*) that slopes from the west toward the east. On the east aš-Šižîž adjoins the sandy plain of Šruft aš-Šižîž and on the west borders on aṣ-Ṣadje. Before us, upon the clear horizon, we observed the outlines of the sand hills of Ṭuʿejs al-Faḥâmi, and southeast of them we saw the Ṭuʿejs abu Râsên, along which there leads a road from al-Ǧowf across aš-Šižîž to Ḥâjel.

At twelve o'clock the Prince designated a camping site in a wide hollow (*ḳaʿara*) (temperature at 5.30 A. M.: 6° C; at 5.30 P. M.: 22.6° C).

On Sunday, before our departure, I heard two camels both whining for the same young one. At the Prince's order the negro Dâle had just slaughtered a young weak-boned camel which had been allowed to suck the udders of two mothers in order that both of them might yield milk. As the cruel Dâle had not driven the two camels away but had killed their suckling before their very eyes, they stood there over the young victim, writhing in its last agony, and wailed at the wrong the cruel man had perpetrated upon their beloved. The real mother would try to drive away the other one by biting her and then would return to her offspring, lick its legs, lift it by the back, and wail piteously when it fell back again to the ground. The foster mother would come back and wail with her, and as fast as they were driven away they would return by the shortest route. Finally Dâle pulled some skin off the young camel's back, buried the body in the sand, and rubbed the skin on the noses and heads of both camels; who then, being thus attracted by the scent of their child, followed the slayer willingly.

At 7.45 we began the march through the lowland of al-Lâjğa, which is more than three kilometers wide and twice as long and will soon be converted into hollows (*ḳaʿar*), for it is already hedged in by sand drifts. We came upon a growth of *ẓamrân*, but it was all dead, and the farther east we went the less pasture we found. The sand that covers this region is ash-gray. This variety, it is said, does not hold moisture long and so nothing will grow in it. Even the few bushes of *ṛaẓa* that we saw were undeveloped and half shriveled. To the east of us rose the level sand elevation Nâzjet al-ʿÂḏrijje, overgrown almost exclusively with *ʿâḏer* plants. To the north, northeast of al-Ḥamâmijât, the long crests of Ẓhejr Ḥmâr, al-Mṛejr, and al-Ḥmaʾ lifted themselves, hedging in the basin of al-Ğowf (or al-Ğûba) on the northwest. We encamped at two o'clock (temperature at 5.45 A. M.: 11.2° C; at 6 P. M.: 23.2° C).

On Monday, starting at seven o'clock, we rode northeastward toward the settlement of al-Ḳâra (temperature at 6: 14.2° C) and after 8.23 A. M. proceeded in a vast plain covered with coarse gravel. Far to the west and east the herds of camels surged on like waves, and between them were innumerable animals carrying tents, supplies, and litters. In the center of this far-flung though rather thin line, tossing to and fro upon the back of a bay camel, moved the litter called *abu-d-dhûr*, or *al-merkab*, which represents the sacred palladium of the entire tribe. All about it riders on camels were pressing ahead, while behind them, like huge butterflies, the women's varicolored litters (*žetab* and *ḳenn*) rose and fell in the heavy air. Young camels were bleating, old female ones were whining, the males grunting; children were crying and women were shouting to each other and to the camels carrying their belongings; herdsmen were attempting to lead on the animals in their care by singing a short melody, the last syllable of which they prolonged indefinitely; riders were galloping from one side to the other on horses or camels; and above the whole tumult the hot, almost impenetrable air hung in many horizontal strata.

At 10.40 we reached the rim of the basin of al-Ǧûba, which extends from al-Ǧowf in a northeasterly direction to the settlement of Skâka. On the north it is overlooked by the precipitous wall of a hilly district, whereas on the south it is connected with the level fringes of the Nefûd by a slope covered deep with sand. At the point where we descended into it the depression is about four kilometers wide and is penetrated by moderately long sand hills called al-Ḥeḳne, which extend from west to east.

North of al-Ḥeḳne, at the foot of the hills of al-Ḥamâmijât, is the forsaken settlement of the Ḳaṣr and Želîb al-Mwejsen, where a ghost is said to dwell. ʿAwde al-Kwêčbi, it seems, once rode with a friend from al-Ḳâra to al-Ǧowf. Beyond al-Mwejsen they met a kinsman bound in the opposite direction and, dismounting from their animals, they were eating dates together when suddenly a strange Arab approached them and asked for some of the dates. They gave him a handful, but he was not satisfied, and churlishly said:

"Either ye will give me enough to satiate my hunger, or else I will invoke al-Mwejsen upon ye."

"Invoke him, then," returned ʿAwde, who told me the story himself.

"O al-Mwejsen, I invoke thy protection!" called the stranger. Whereupon there was heard rumbling from within the rocks a thunderous voice:

"Here am I. From whom shall I protect thee?"

At this point ʿAwde and his companion swung upon their camels with the greatest possible haste and dashed off toward al-Ǧowf.

From 10.42 to 11.34 we rested, while the camels grazed upon blooming *arṭa* and the verdant branches of *raẓa*, *rimṯ*, *ʿalanda*, and *ʿalḳa*. At 12.05 P. M. we reached the basin at the rocks of al-ʿOḳde.[44] The rock forming this basin consists of sandstone, which rises toward the north in innumerable jagged cliffs. At 12.40 we paused for twenty minutes at the Khejf Haǧal (Fig. 42), the remains of a sandstone hill resembling an enormous mushroom, upon the stem and head of which we noted several inscriptions, which I jotted down. These inscriptions, carved centuries ago on the stem and under side

[44] On the authority of the poet al-Mutanabbi, Jâḳût, *Muʿǧam* (Wüstenfeld), Vol. 3, p. 694, refers to ʿOḳdet al-Ǧowf in the desert of as-Samâwa belonging to the Kalb tribe, between Syria and Irak. — Because our ʿOḳde is situated in the basin of al-Ǧowf, we may identify it with Jâḳût's ʿOḳde by way of which al-Mutanabbi fled from Egypt to Irak.

of the cap by nomadic merchants, had been chiseled by the sands for more than eighteen hundred years and yet to this day are quite legible. How many scores of thousands of years before that must the sand have been gnawing at the rock in order to shape it to the Boletus of the present!

FIG. 42—The Khejf Haǧal.

The Prince urged a speedy departure, for an oppressive, unbearable heat prevailed and we were all suffering from thirst. Here and there in the holes *šîḥ*, *ʿâḏer*, *ḥanẓal*, *šibriʿ*, and *ḳejṣûm* were blooming. At 2.40 P. M. we sighted beyond the edge of the northern range, almost due north, the palms of the settlement of al-Ḳâra, beside which the Prince at 3.50 designated a new camp site (Fig. 43) (temperature at 4: 29.8°C).

AL-ḲÂRA TO ŽALTAT AL-MḪARÛḲ

Al-Ḳâra is populated by the Durmân clan of the Rwala under the chief Ebḥejṯer eben Durmi, and by the Sirḥân, affiliated with the Šammar tribes, under the chief Ẓâher eben Selîm. These groups get along well together. Their settlement consists of eighty dwellings, with palm gardens extending from south to north and deriving their moisture from wells four to six meters deep. At both the western and the eastern end of the gardens is situated a tabular hill (*ḳâra*) upon which in the past a stronghold used to stand. Even the foundations of these are now gone, however, all the building material having been previously carried away and used in the erection of the present houses, all of which are equipped with towers two stories high. Outside, under the walls that enclose the settlement, are fields planted with wheat and barley. The grain was still low when we were there, yet it was already ripening. While we camped at al-Ḳâra, a woman at each of the fields was kept constantly busy chasing away the camels that invaded her crop. Alas, her efforts were not always effectual.[45]

As soon as I was off my camel a young Arab came up to show me his right wrist where he had been bitten by a snake (*dâbb*). He had been plucking green *šîḥ* and *ʿâḏer* for his ailing camel and had accidentally touched the snake, which bit him. Cutting his wound, I ordered him to suck out the blood; then I daubed the sore with sal ammoniac and later gave him a generous glass of cognac from my store. He shuddered, unable to stand the burning of this unaccustomed drink and had barely finished the glass when he lay down, fell asleep, and broke into a sweat. Thereupon his relatives, not having much faith in my manner of healing, summoned a sorcerer (*ḳarrâj*) who murmured unintelligible words over him for a long time and the next day claimed that he was the one who had cured him.

On Tuesday morning we determined the latitude (temperature at 5: 12.2° C) and at 7.50 A. M. resumed the march. The burning southeast wind was again blowing and filling the air with innumerable films of heat that made breathing difficult. On the left, where the basin al-Ǧûba bends to the north, we noted the settlement of aṭ-Ṭjêr and north of it the immense gardens of the settlement of Skâka. Northeast of the latter loomed several pointed cones, the highest of them called Tell al-Meǧâder. At 8.35 we left the basin — which it would be feasible to cultivate throughout — and began to ascend the sand drifts and hills of al-Liḳâjed.

From nine to 9.20 the camels grazed. At 9.52 we had on our left a black sandstone rock, northward from which ex-

[45] Jâḳût, *op. cit.*, Vol. 4, p. 12, informs us that Ḏu al-Ḳâra is the smallest of the settlements that are grouped with Dûma and Skâka. It is erected upon a hill and its fort is impregnable.

FIG. 43—Walls and palms of al-Ḳâra from the south.

At one o'clock we discerned to the north the precipitous scarp Ǧâl Amṛar, and west of it a group of small isolated hillocks, Tlêl as-Saḳḳâr, which indicated the position of the rain pools of ar-Raṣîf and al-Amṛar. Al-Amṛar is separated to the southeast by the rift of Ab-al-Ḳûr from the "nose" Ḫašm al-Mḫarûḳ, fronting which on the south are the tabular mountains of Ḳûr al-Aṣâbeʿ. At two o'clock the Prince designated a camp site near the rain well Žaltat al-Mḫarûḳ.

ILLNESS; COUNTRY TO THE NORTH

Thursday to Saturday, March 18 to 20, 1909. I had not taken any food or drink for two days, not even coffee or milk. I had chills, my head ached, and I felt sharp cutting pains in the bowels. The medicines I used gave me no relief; I could not sleep at night and I took no interest in my work, symptoms that caused me to fear a serious illness. Still, I resisted it and would not stay in bed. On Sunday morning, therefore, led by Tûmân and ʿAwde, I dragged myself to the southern crest of an oblong sandstone hill forming part of Amṛar to pick plants and to make a map of the vicinity. The slope rises almost one hundred meters high above its base.

Before us to the south spread an endless, desolate, rocky upland, with wide, deep gaps opening northeastward. Near by, to the east, we could see how precipitously this upland plunges toward the valley of Ab-al-Ḳûr. In the north-northwest there glistened upon the surface of the plain the Ḫabra al-Bedrijje, flanked on the northeast by dark strips marking the beginning of the Riǧlet al-Helâl, upon the left side of which extend far towards the northeast the tabular hills of Ḳârt ar-Raḫama. West of Ḫabra al-Bedrijje the great valley of ʿArʿar originates in the rain ponds Ḫabâri-l-Faskânât and the short ravines Riǧl at-Temrijjât. The latter, as well as Riǧl al-Ḫanẓalijjât and Riǧl ad-Dwêḫlât to the north, rise in the Ḫazm Zellûm, the northwestern extension of the steep escarpment Ǧâl Ṣwêr; Riǧl ad-Dwêḫlât converge with the Riǧlet al-Aḳraʿ, and then, north of the hill Tell al-Berṯen at the rain pool Ṛadîr aṭ-Ṭrejfâwi, merge with the valley of ʿArʿar on the left. On the right, west of the Tell al-Berṯen, the ʿArʿar valley is joined by the Riǧlet al-Bâʿaǧa, farther north by the Riǧlet al-Muʿajjele, at the Ṛadîr al-Ǧebâli by the outlet of the ravines of ar-Rûṯijjât, and at the rain pool Ṛadîr ab-ad-Defûf by Riǧlet Mḫêṭa. On the left side, southwest of the Riǧlet al-Muʿajjele at the Ṛadîr aṣ-Ṣafâwi, the ravine of al-ʿAwseǧi converges with the valley of ʿArʿar; south of the Ṛadîr al-ʿAwaǧ at the Ṛadîr al-Ǧebâli comes in the Riǧlet al-Ṛurâba;[49]

[49] Jâḳût, *Muʿǧam* (Wüstenfeld), Vol. 3, p. 795, seeks the valley of Ṛurejb, mentioned in connection with Ḍâḥi, in the territory of the Kalb tribe. — Our Riǧlet al-Ṛurâba winds through the former territory of the Kalb tribe, north of the sandy desert of aẓ-Ẓâḥi; therefore I identify it with Ṛurejb.

north of it, the Riǧlet al-Bdene; and still farther toward the north, at the Ṛadîr ab-ad-Defûf, enters the Riǧlet al-Lwejzijje.

The dry watercourses of ad-Dwêẖlât and al-Bdene extend from the southwest, from the wide, flat crest Ḥazm al-Ǧelâmîd that forms the boundary between the districts of al-Ḥamâd and al-Wudijân. On the southeastern part of this crest are the rain pools Ḫabra Mḥammala, aṭ-Ṭawsijjât, and Umm Ṣeda', and at the beginning of the Riǧlet al-Bdene are the rain pools Ḫaẓar al-Ma' and al-Maḥfûr.

In the lowland, at the western base of the steep scarp Ǧâl Amṛar, appeared the Ḫabra-r-Raṣîf and al-Amṛar, and northwest of them the low hillocks Tlêl as-Saḳḳâr. To the southeast were the tabular hills of Ḳûr al-Aṣâbe', and beyond them the horizon was limited by the gray slopes of ar-Rḥajja.

The map was not easy to make, for I had to force myself to work and was obliged to lie down several times to gain energy enough to finish it. When I returned to the tent I was so bathed in perspiration that I had to change my clothing; I then lay down shivering with cold.

Toward evening a storm came up. Dark clouds rose on the western and northern horizon, lightning flashed, and thunder rumbled over the desert; but it did not rain. Suddenly we were enveloped in a dense sand squall, which rushed on with a wild roar toward the east. Then the first large drops fell and with "Hail thee! hail thee!" the rain was joyfully welcomed from all sides. The first shower was not of long duration nor were the three more that fell during the night; for the main downpour centered to the northeast, where the sky blazed incessantly. I was awake most of the night with acute diarrhea.

On Friday it rained throughout the day at short intervals. Whenever the rain ceased the children ran out and waded about in the puddles, splashing each other and shouting in glee when any one fell down and got wet. The women dipped up the water and filled the bags with it. Water for the Prince was taken from the place where the camels rested and of course was full of dung. A few paces farther on there was enough pure water, but the slaves would not bother to carry the bags through the mire to get it.

On Saturday I was not able to sit up. My stomach refused even simple tea; it would retain nothing but a decoction made from dried apricots. The Prince came every hour to enquire after my health. We were to migrate that morning, but, fearing that I should not be able to endure the saddle — in fact, fearing I might die — he ordered the

Arabs, even after they had begun to strike the tents in the morning, to repitch them, saying we should stay there a while longer. Arabs kept coming to my large tent from all directions to ask Nâṣer how I fared.

Sunday to Thursday, March 21 to 25, 1909. Early Sunday morning I fell asleep for the first time after six successive sleepless nights; but as early as four o'clock I was awakened by the roaring of disgruntled camels that were being loaded with the Prince's effects by his slaves. As there was no pasturage anywhere in the vicinity, the Prince, hearing that I had slept somewhat during the night, decided that we must go on. When I came out of the tent the whole world seemed to whirl round and I had to sit down hurriedly to keep from falling. The air was clear and pure, birds were singing; but the blood pulsed in my temples, there was a film over my eyes, a buzzing in my ears, a cutting pain in my bowels, and I was tortured by an insatiable thirst.

ŽALTAT AL-MḪARÛḲ TO FÂĞ AṢ-ṢLUBI

At 8.40 A. M. we set out, at first in a northeasterly direction. The Prince was bent on finding a new camp site within the *šeʿîb* of aṭ-Ṭejri in the northeastern part of the upland of Amṛar; the camels were to graze in al-Wadʿa, Ṛâr al-Ṛaẓâri, and Ğufrat Naṣṣâr and to water in the Ḫabra al-Bedrijje. He had decided on this camping ground early that morning, relying upon the report of a Rwejli who had come from Ṛâr al-Ṛaẓâri and claimed to have found there an abundance of perennial plants which afford excellent pasturage. The Prince's relatives doubted the accuracy of the Rwejli's report, arguing that nobody else, whether Rwejli or Ṣlubi, had found any pasture in those regions, whereas the scouts had brought back information about the presence of water and pastures in al-Labbe. They believed they had prevailed upon him to go there, and even as late as the evening before he had apparently intended to do so. An-Nûri was obstinate, however, and reverted to the plan of going to Amṛar. As a result of this dispute, the chiefs and their clans as well as even his nearest relatives, left him, turning toward the southeast in the direction of al-Labbe. Our party was thus diminished to the Prince, his slaves, his son Saʿûd, and myself. About twenty minutes after the others had left we were overtaken by a young son-in-law of the Prince, Mišref eben Kurdi, who reproached his father in terse but vigorous words for braving great danger because of his obstinacy, and exhorted him to follow the others. The Prince accordingly swerved his camel toward the southeast, and we went whither the rest of the clan was bound, to al-Labbe.

At 9.28 we came to a rocky crevice that contained only a little rain water, and this was yellowish, resembling thin mortar. On our left stretched the long "nose" Ḫašm al-Mḫarûḳ. The district we were traversing was stony and almost bare, with no perennials except in the short valleys. From 10.27 to 11.25 we rested. Afterward the Prince rode ahead and, as early as twelve o'clock, designated a new camping ground at the western edge of the Ḫašm al-Mḫarûḳ, north of the tabular hills Ḳûr al-Aṣâbeʿ. During all this time I had not let go of the fore part of my saddle but grasped it tightly with both hands while Saʿûd steered my camel. As soon as she knelt I slid from the saddle and could not get up. When my round tent was up the men carried me into it and laid me down, but I could not fall asleep.

The next day we moved on again. I was still suffering from fever and diarrhea, my head felt oppressed, and I could hardly move my tongue. It was only by exerting all the strength I had left that I kept in the saddle. We set out at 7.30 in a southeasterly direction, going through a stony region. To the south we saw the level fringe of the elevation of ar-Rḥajja, extending from the southwest toward the north-northeast and approaching the Ḫašm al-Mḫarûḳ. South of the latter rose a small tabular hill, Riǧm umm Iḏen, at the western slope of which was the rain pool Kasr al-ʿAwaǧ. The word *kasr* denotes a pool that contains water only after torrential rains. At 9.40 we had on the right the seven peaks of al-Aṣâbeʿ. Nowhere had I seen any fresh annuals. The first downpour had moistened the region only two days before and would not benefit further either the annuals (*ʿešeb*) or the woody perennials (*šaǧar*). The grasses would wither in the rays of the hot sun, whereas the perennials would blossom forth only in the event of a heavy and protracted late spring rain (*aṣ-ṣejfi*).

Passing by the clans that had preceded us, we overtook a company of women, some sitting in cage-like litters examining their garments intently, others planted astride full water bags darning clothes and joking with the men who passed by.

The Prince was here joined by two Ṣlejb who were clad in long coats similar to shirts and made of gazelles' hides. They were our *ḳaṭṭâf* or *ʿassâs*, scouts or prospectors for our camp sites, whose duty it was to go ahead of us seeking pastures and water and to lead us where the pasturage was best. They recommended to the Prince the locations to which he might migrate in the future and were frequently upbraided by him when he was not satisfied with the locations they had determined.

From 10.50 to 11.35 we rested at the southern edge of the Ḫašm al-Mḫarûḳ. After one o'clock, traveling toward the northeast, we reached the district of al-Krajje,[50] where, in the depressions, our camels grazed upon various grasses, especially *ṣuffâra, ḳlejžlân, ribla, naṣi,* and *ḳafʿaʾ*. We had hardly stopped when the Prince jumped from his camel, swung upon the mare, and accompanied by a slave cantered towards the northeast to water his mount at a camp of the Ṣlejb lying in the lowland Fejẓat ummu Ṭlejḥa. Since he did not return soon, I myself at three o'clock designated the camp site, a plain at the southern foot of the Ḳârt ummu Ṭlejḥa. When the Prince returned about four o'clock he reproached me for having encamped so early and even then wanted to resume the march; but the Arabs — nay, even his own slaves — unwilling to reload, refused to obey. All I wanted was to rest.

On Tuesday we stayed at the same place (*mužîmîn*) and I slept the entire day. After my long illness I craved sleep; my headache had ceased and I was growing stronger. After ten days of fasting, I could eat soft cooked rice. In the evening we determined the latitude.

On Wednesday we migrated again, setting out at 7.42 in a northeasterly direction. On the left we had an oblong tabular hill and ahead of it the solitary irregular cones of Ḳârt and Ḫonṣor ummu Ṭlejḥa, so called after the wide-spreading *ṭalḥ* trees which grow in the plain adjoining them on the east. To the east of us rose the Ḳârt al-Ağlal and the two hills of ar-Raḥmân, with the two irregular cones of aḏ-Ḏrajjeʿât; west-northwest of ar-Raḥmân appeared the low range of

[50] Jâḳût, *op. cit.*, Vol. 2, p. 857; Vol. 4, p. 271, states that al-Karijje is a valley in the territory of the Kalb. — As our depression of al-Krajje is in the former territory of the Kalb tribe, I identify it with his.

al-Bwejtât. Within the latter are numerous remains of reservoirs and small dwellings of which only the foundation walls are left. On the northeast al-Bwejtât adjoins the wide, long crest Ḥazm aṯ-Ṯôr.

Ḫâled eben Saṭṭâm (Fig. 44) had returned to us that morning. From our camp at al-Hawǧa he had undertaken a raid against the Swejd clan of the Šammar and attacked them at a time when only a few men were left in the encampment, the majority being off on a war expedition. The Rwala had taken more than five hundred camels and had loaded even the tents on them. The fifth day, however, they were overtaken by the plundered Swejd, augmented by numerous fighters of Eben Rmâl. Ḫâled commanded only twenty-five camel riders and eighteen men on horseback, whereas the enemy numbered more than three hundred. As they had occupied all the wells in the neighborhood, they pressed Ḫâled and his party to such an extent that the latter had to surrender. The Swejd demanded as compensation all the horses and riding camels of the Rwala, but Eben Rmâl succeeded in persuading them to be contented with the restoration of their own plundered property, whereupon Ḫâled was free to depart. Coming to me, he was excusing his unsuccessful raid and trying to explain why he could

FIG. 44—Ḫâled eben Saṭṭâm.

not resist or evade the enemy, when I interrupted him with:

"*Al-ḥamdu lillâh* that all of ye have returned well. Allâh had predetermined the events."

The Prince was unpleasantly affected by my words and reproached Ḫâled for his imprudence.

"Woe to the Bedouin who depends upon Allâh," he declared. "Allâh would have no rest were he to straighten out all the trouble that an imprudent man causes. We alone shape our fate, Allâh granting us reason and time for it. Thou shouldst not have taken the tents too, for thou couldst then have got away faster with the booty. But if thou hadst wished to load also the tents and the supplies of the Swejd clan, then thou shouldst have altered the course upon thy return and thus deceived thy pursuers."

Ṭrâd, the half-brother of Ḫâled, departed for al-Ǧowf to join Nawwâf against the will of an-Nûri, whose wrath toward his son was constantly growing. Before his departure Ṭrâd asked me to prevail upon an-Nûri to support his son, else he would miserably perish in al-Ǧowf; but when I tried it the Prince retorted:

"Nawwâf went to al-Ǧowf against my will. Let him now do what he pleases."

To which I said: "That he may do what he pleases, send him money and ammunition;" whereupon the Prince smiled but remained silent.

From 10.30 to 11.15 we rested, and at twelve o'clock entered the stony dale of Fâǧ aṣ-Ṣlubi, encamping there at two o'clock. In the hollows our camels found *šîḥ, eǧdejjân, dabṛa, drejhme, umm iḏen, žirna* (or *raḳma*), *ḫrejme, ḫaššejna, erbijjân, riǧlet al-ṛurâb, ḫâfûr*, and *ṣuffâra*.

On Thursday I felt so much better that I resumed my topographical work and was able to enjoy some of the fresh butter and a piece of a young castrated kid which the Ṣlejb had brought to the Prince. In return for the treat, I gave an-Nûri a whole camel load of *burṛul* (peeled wheat), for I had noticed that his supplies were depleted. He was much pleased with the gift, declaring: "My tent is thy tent. Take what thou desirest."

TOPOGRAPHICAL WORK; TO ḪIŠT AṮ-ṮÔR

Friday to Sunday, March 26 to 28, 1909. On Friday I worked all day with the Ṣlubi Faraǧ, augmenting my geographical map of al-Labbe and al-Ḥeǧera. Having determined the cardinal points exactly, he proceeded to draw in the sand within my tent hills, valleys, and wells, piling up sand for the ranges and mesas, scooping it out for the valleys, and marking the individual wells by circular dips. He did not show the distances, but was precise in his designation of the respective directions. The map finished, I questioned him as to the distances between the various places. These he explained in terms of daily marches, estimating, for example, whether or not it would be possible for Arabs migrating from locality A to locality B to reach their destination the same day. At the same time, he took into account whether they were migrating in winter, when they can make at the utmost twenty kilometers, or in summer, when they make twenty-five kilometers if they travel from sunrise to sunset. The latter type of journey is called *marḥale ǧajjede.* Shorter distances are determined by the space traversed during a migration lasting from morning to noon, called *ẓuhrijje,* or from morning (when dew falls) to mid fore-noon (when dew dries), called *ẓaḥijje.* A day's march (*safar jowm*) is a distance that is ordinarily made on camelback (about 60 km.). When determining the distance to a particular watering place, one may arrive at the desired information more easily by asking whether the camels are driven from the camp A to the watering place B in the morning, watered, and taken back without making stops (20 km.); or whether they do not reach the watering place until afternoon, pass the night there, and return the next day (30 km.); or whether they pass the night some distance from the watering place, do not reach it until the next day, pass the second night beyond the watering place, and return to the camp the third day (45 km.). A more specific determination of distance or time is unknown to a Bedouin. During our calculations the Prince came in twice, always directing the Ṣlubi to answer all my questions accurately. He probed some of his statements and verified almost all as correct. When I dismissed Faraǧ that evening, my map contained much new topographical nomenclature, and my tent was full of yellow lice which he had left behind him.

Saturday was migrating day (*raḥîl*). We left at 7.30 A. M., all of us well armed because we expected an attack from the Šammar. We proceeded towards the south-southwest at the eastern base of the Ḳârat Nawmân, over Ḫ̮išt aṯ-Ṯôr and to the hill range of al-Bwejtât. The region we traversed was stony, with only a scanty growth. The *rûṯe* was dry but showed new sprouts.

From nine A. M. to 9.32 and from 11.05 to 11.42 we rested. At 12.50 P.M. the Prince designated a new camp site in a lowland north of the hills Tlûl ar-Raḥmân, but the camels with the loads did not arrive until after two o'clock. When my tent was pitched I invited ᶜAwde al-Kwêčbi to come in and help me name the plants I had picked during the past few days.

Sunday, assisted by Ǧwâd abu ᶜAli and Ḥmâr abu ᶜAwwâd, I continued taking notes on folklore. At noon the Prince came and notified me that we should not push forward in the direction of the watering places of al-Ḫzûl, as he wanted to be near his son Nawwâf in the vicinity of al-Ǧowf. I told him that I should immediately undertake a new expedition, but he was opposed to it and tried to dissuade me from it. He cited the perils that threatened me, but I answered that it was the will of Allâh that I should undertake this journey and that I must not resist. Therefore we sought a Dahmaši who would be able to protect me from his co-tribesmen, the enemies of the Rwala.

With the chief ᶜAdûb eben Meǧwel, a time-honored friend of mine, there were several families of the Dahâmše who, because of a blood feud, had left their own country, and visiting them was also a young Dahmaši who had returned with the camel traders (ᶜAḳejl) from Neǧd. The Prince directed Ḥmâr abu ᶜAwwâd to summon him. Ḥmâr did not obey, but, hiring a Ṣlubi for a Maria Theresa dollar (*abu šûše*: 44 cents), sent him to the distant camp of ᶜAdûb. An hour later the Ṣlubi came back with a certain ᶜAmâri who boasted that, whenever he gave the alarm, all the ᶜAmârât and Dahâmše would come to his help. The Prince did not know him and the ᶜAmâri could not name anybody in the camp who would vouch for him. Therefore I declined to accept him as a guide and Ḥmâr scolded the Ṣlubi for not obeying his order. He had to return the *abu šûše*, and another Ṣlubi was sent to ᶜAdûb.

After the second Ṣlubi's departure Ḥmâr abu ᶜAwwâd brought to me a Ṣlubi of the name of Mizᶜel abu Maṭar, who was called by the ᶜAmârât and the Rwala Aḫu Zaᶜêla, the brother of Zaᶜêla. He offered himself as a guide, but, since

I had already arranged with the Ṣlubi Sanad to accompany me as guide upon my next expedition, I declined his offer. Miz'el did not depart, however, but remained sitting in my tent and, when ordered by Ḥmâr and Ǧwâd to leave, crouched at my feet and begged me to accept him. His obtuseness and the malevolent expression of his face did not appeal to me.

Toward evening Ǧwâd asked me, on behalf of my discharged servant Mḥammad, to settle with the man in some way before my departure. After a conference with the Prince, in which he recommended that I indict Mḥammad before the Turkish Government, I decreed that I would let him have the gold he had stolen from me but would not pay him the three napoleons ($11.58) from his wages that he had not yet drawn. Thus, instead of being punished, he profited from the robbery to the extent of seventeen napoleons. He was satisfied and agreed that he had received all that he was entitled to. I reserved the right to prefer charges against him with the Turkish authorities should he provoke me. One of his families was in Bagdad, the other in ad-Dejr, while he himself often stayed in Damascus and other cities, where he could easily be arrested and imprisoned by the Government.

After Mḥammad's departure I began to prepare the supplies for the contemplated trip. Suddenly, as I was taking provisions out of a bag, I heard the hissing of a snake and a viper darted out from under it. Being barefooted, I leaped aside in a panic; but the snake, trying to crawl out of the tent, was killed by Nâṣer. It was twenty-eight centimeters long, as thick as one's finger, and on the head over the eyes it had two excrescences. This was the third viper that had come close to me on this journey.

Toward evening the Prince came again and repeatedly asked me to be careful and mindful of my safety.

"Had I known, my brother, that thou wouldst undertake such raids, I would not have allowed thee to pitch thy tent alongside mine," he protested. "I know not a single man amongst us who would be so daring as thou and, by Allâh, I speak the truth. Thou sayest that Allâh has prompted thee to undertake such raids. Well, what Allâh has ordained, let that be; but what should I say to thy friends in Damascus were I not to bring thee to them? I have promised them to protect thee, but how am I to protect thee when thou forsakest me and venturest into lands which I myself dare not enter without a convoy of at least a thousand fighters? There, in the place whither thou now wantest to go, lie in wait for thee a Šammari, a Muntefiži, a Ẓefîri, and besides these various robbers of the Dahâmše, ʿAmârât, Fedʿân, Sbaʿa, Šarârât, and Dlejm tribes. They may murder thee in the night without regard to thy Dahmaši. Still thou refusest to obey. I talk to thee, I try to restrain thee because I know those perils better than thou dost, but thou ignorest my words. Dost thou have no pity for thy relatives? thy family? Is there nobody amongst those living where thy relatives camp who loves thee, who would be grieved to lose thee? I know what thou wishest to reply — that I myself make raids. It is true, but I am accompanied by hundreds and hundreds of fighters. And who are thy escorts? Thy Tûmân, who knows not the country nor the people nor their language, and no one besides except two strange men, unknown to thee, who may betray thee at any moment or kill thee. For who knows what the *šejṭân* (devil) may tempt them to? And thou knowest the perils that the land itself is fraught with. This year Allâh hath not sent heavy rains into the territory of al-Wudijân and al-Ḥamâd. For days of marching thou shalt not find any water. Thou sayest thou wilt take water along; but what wilt thou do if the camels that carry thy full water bags should stumble or rub against a sharp rock and the bag be ripped and the water run out? Maybe thou couldst even kill thy camels and clean the water that their bellies contain and drink that; but what would then become of thee if thou hadst no animal to carry thee?" Thus he spoke, long and tenderly. The good an-Nûri was my friend and loved me sincerely; but since it was known throughout the desert that I moved before his face (*bi-waǧhah*) under his protection, he also feared that his prestige would be impaired if I should perish in the desert.

CHAPTER VIII

ḪIŠT AṮ-ṮÔR TO LÂHA

ḪIŠT AṮ-ṮÔR TO MOḲR AL-ŽETÂDI

Monday, March 29, 1909. In the morning (temperature at 5.30: 15° C) I was awakened by the grumbling of my own camels and was told by Nâṣer that we were again migrating (*raḥîl*). After a while the Prince came, barefooted and coatless, bringing me a bowlful of camel's milk, together with the tidings that the Ṣlubi had returned at midnight with the long-sought-for Dahmaši and that I might, therefore, begin my journey immediately.

Accompanied by the Prince, I went to the tent of the negro Ḥmâr, where I was to make an agreement with the Dahmaši and the guide Sanad. The Dahmaši, of the name of Ṭâreš eben Melfi, of the Mḥejne clan, did not appeal to me much. He limped, was blind in the left eye, and his upper incisors protruded from his mouth. According to the notion of the Bedouins, these attributes are not favorable omens. But he was a Mḥejni, a member of a foremost Dahâmše family, and I had no other choice. I made him an offer of half a *meǧîdijje* (45 cents) per day, this being as much as he had been paid by his last master, an ʿAḳejli. He declined, saying he preferred that I pay him a certain sum for the entire journey; whereupon I offered him ten *meǧîdijjât* ($ 9.00), to which the Prince added five more and promised him besides an extra compensation after our return. At this Ṭâreš signified his pleasure and consented to ride with me, not for the sake of the money but for the purpose of winning and securing the Prince's favor; and he promised to protect me against all the ʿAmârât and Dahâmše.

While I was bargaining with Ṭâreš, Sanad, whom I wanted to take along as a guide, had disappeared from the tent and now sent me word that he could not lead me, tidings that were confirmed by his brother Snejd and also by Farağ. This behavior of the Ṣlejb was strange indeed. Yesterday they had all besieged my tent, competing in pleadings to be hired, and now, when I was on the verge of departure, no one wanted to go. Ḥmâr reminded me of Aḫu Zaʿêla, who also sat in Ḥmâr's tent; but he likewise refused. It was evident that the Ṣlejb plotted to force me into paying them exorbitant wages. I was reluctant to bargain with Aḫu Zaʿêla; but the tents were already taken apart, a portion of my belongings loaded, the Arabs moving southward, and the Prince pressing me to a decision. Therefore I requested him to contract with Mizʿel for me. He offered him half a *meǧîdijje* a day, but the Ṣlubi, serving and working a whole week for a quarter of a *meǧîdijje*, demanded one *meǧîdijje* a day, besides asking eleven *meǧîdijjât* in advance payment. I was not inclined to agree to this, but the Prince pointed out that the Ṣlejb were evidently allied among themselves and that I should not find anyone who would lead me for less. Therefore I gave Mizʿel five *meǧîdijjât* in advance, and assured him that he would get one for every day he showed himself familiar with the country and actually led me. The Prince admonished him to serve me honestly, to respond to every gesture of mine, and to guard my camels.

Meantime all the Arabs had started southward; nothing was left on the old camp site except my men, my camels, and my baggage. The Prince and his guard, fifteen slaves, hurriedly helped us load, but in spite of the best intentions they bungled everything. What was intended for the expedition was crammed into the wrong bags and thrust on camels that were to remain with the Prince, and it was no easy task to find all the mislaid articles and reload them upon the camels that were to go with us. To my inquiry as to what kind of water bags we should need, the Ṣlubi replied that I had better take the two smallest, because he knew all the secret wells and would bring me to water every day.

"Why, are there wells even in al-Ḥamâd?"

"By Allâh, they are there but are known only to us, the Ṣlejb. I also know of them and will bring thee to them. Thou shalt refresh thyself and thy camels."

Finally, when I thought we had loaded all the necessary things, I mounted my camel and rode up to the Prince to thank him for everything and to ask him to watch over my tent and my property. He extended his right hand to me in silence, mounted the saddle, and rode off with his retinue toward the south, while I turned northward. It was then 7.15 A.M.

I took along only the most necessary articles, leaving the small round tent and the blankets behind with Nâṣer. We were lightly clothed, for the Prince had said:

"It is already hot; thou needst not fear cold or steady rain. Why shouldst thou add burdens to thy camels?" Of the four camels, Tûmân's and mine carried riding saddles, the third the water saddle (*mesâme*), and the fourth the pack saddle (*ḥedâǧe*). The third one also carried Ṭâreš, and the fourth Mizᶜel. Both men were talkative and repeatedly assured me that we did not have to fear anybody, as they had acquaintances among the Bedouins far and wide. Ṭâreš promised to protect me not merely from the Dahâmše and ᶜAmârât, but even from the Šammar, and added that he would render me accurate accounts of the clans and camps of these tribes. Mizᶜel swore that he knew the entire desert from Neǧd to Aleppo as thoroughly as he knew his palm, and was convinced that I ought to thank Allâh for having chosen him instead of Sanad, as there was no other man among the Ṣulbân (Ṣlejb) who could surpass him in knowledge of topography. To which I replied that I knew both men of words and men of action, and that I wished that he and Ṭâreš might belong among the latter and not among the former.

Until eight o'clock we rode in the district of al-Bwejtât; after that in Fâǧ aṣ-Ṣlubi. The first-named district consists of depressions and elevations. The depressions are covered with coarse white sand, and scattered in them are small swales (*rîẓân*). They are hedged in by steep slopes twenty to one hundred meters high. On ascending any of these through a defile (*ḫarîme*), the traveler finds himself upon a vast stony upland. At 8.40 we sighted to the west the extended lowland Fejẓat ummu Mâǧed, from which opens the Fâǧ aṣ-Ṣlubi. Ṭâreš told us that two years before twenty-eight of his co-tribesmen on camels had attacked here a camp of the Kwâčbe and captured numerous camels. The fighters of the Kwâčbe, however, occupied the four openings (*ḫarîme*) leading from the lowland and thus effected the capture (*hom wuḫeḏû*) of all the Dahâmše. Ṭâreš pronounced the consonants correctly.

By and by we were joined by the ᶜAmâri who had been brought to me by a Ṣlubi but whom the Prince had rejected. He was going to the wells of al-Barrît, where his clan was encamped. On the way he was so apprehensive of the Šammar that his fear prompted him to climb every hillock from which he could scan the vicinity and to keep urging us to move within the depressions and avoid elevations as much as possible. Miz'el ridiculed his fears and maintained that there was not a single Šammari who would venture to come into the region we were traversing (*riǧle minhom mâ tiǧi*). I agreed with the 'Amâri, however, and therefore aimed to proceed in the secluded depressions. Neither the Ṣlubi nor the Dahmaši was afraid of losing anything in case of an attack, for both rode my camels and were clad in their worst garments. The 'Amâri, however, sat upon his own animal.

While still in the camp I had found out that my guide Miz'el abu Za'êla was a roving poet, and on the journey he himself boasted that there was no eminent chief among the Bedouins or the Šwâja whom he had not visited and in whose honor he had not composed a poem. In a high-pitched voice he kept declaiming one poem after another, in a manner that reminded me vividly of our chanting of the psalms. He sang only the first and the last word of a verse, stretching out the latter and garnishing it with various trills; the other words he pronounced rapidly, laying stress upon the most prominent ones only. He would repeat the verses that appealed to his fancy five or ten times. His pronunciation was correct and intelligible, but different from that of the Rwala. Growing tired of his continuous declaiming, I told him to discontinue it as I had heard similar poems a good many times before. This offended him deeply. With great earnestness he tried to convince me that he had no equal among the living poets, while of the dead he considered greater and better no one but al-'Adwâni, because he composed long poems! (*kaṣâjed al-'adwâni ṭwâlâten!*) Al-'Adwâni is another name for the chief Nimr eben 'Adwân.

When Miz'el was not singing or declaiming, he was relating questionable stories. For instance, he said a certain Bedouin by the name of Meḥsen owned a black slave who was young and strong but of very ugly appearance. One day some of Meḥsen's guests made fun of this slave, declaring that no woman would ever want him. The slave disagreed with them, however, and assured them that there was no black or white woman who would repulse him. He challenged the guests to a bet. They accepted the challenge, and the slave wagered his camel that before the next morning he would bring them five leather belts (*berîma, ḳaḳw*) such as women wear upon their bare bodies. In the morning, after the guests had risen and were drinking coffee, the slave, who had returned, mounted the best camel belonging to the guests and, announcing that it was his, displayed before their astonished eyes seven women's belts. To his horror, Meḥsen recognized among them the one he had bought for his sister on the occasion of her marriage.

At 12.30 P.M. we came to sand hills that were about fifteen meters high and lay in a long row. They are called Tlejlât al-Ḥdâd and represent a boundary between two families of the Ṣlejb. The latter claim ownership (*mulk*) of some portions of the desert and know exactly to what family every valley and slope belongs. When a man wishes to marry off his son and seeks a wife for him, he does not pay for her (*mohr, sijâḳ*) but gives to her father or brother a portion of his property (*mulk*). From that time on only the father or brother of the girl is allowed to hunt in this portion of the property or to pasture his herds there, and he may eject any other hunter or herdsman. Among the hills of al-Ḥdâd, as well as in the whole vicinity, is found clear crystal salt. It is also found farther on. While we were camping on Fâǧ aṣ-Ṣlubi, a Ṣlubi left the tent of ʿEjâl Turkijje in the afternoon and before sunset returned with a fodder pouch full of crystalline salt.

Turkijje, the widow of Prince Saṭṭâm and mother of three married sons who had children of their own, nevertheless remained the most influential of the Rwala women. Whatever she decided must be done. The name of her eldest son, Ḫâled, was seldom mentioned, but hers was heard often. Guests were spoken of as quartered not by Ḫâled, the son of Saṭṭâm, to whom the tent belonged, but by his mother Turkijje. Even my versatile poet, Mizʿel aḫu Zaʿêla, had composed in her honor a poem (*ḳaṣṣad ʿalejha ḳaṣîde*) in which he eulogized her generosity. An-Nûri, Ḥmâr, and others had told me that Turkijje used to receive from her husband Saṭṭâm a hundred *meǧîdijjât* ($ 90) monthly, and that she required as much from her son; yet even the hundred *meǧîdijjât* were not sufficient for her. As Ḫâled's income by no means equaled that of his father, he begged his mother to be more economical.

"I have never learned to save and I never will as long as I live," replied Turkijje, and made a feint of leaving Ḫâled's tent and quartering herself in that of her slave. Ḫâled and the other sons — nay, even the Prince and the chiefs — had to go after her and entreat her for a long time before she would return, and then Ḫâled had no alternative but to guarantee to continue the payment of the hundred *meǧîdijjât* a month. As to where he was to get the money his mother did not concern herself. There was not a day, it is said, on which Turkijje did not entertain guests. In the partition reserved for women she served meals daily to at least fifteen women and she usually prepared the meals from the stores of her sons. Frequently she invited men also, and after supper would come into the compartment for men, choose the foremost seat, and monopolize the conversation. Nobody, not even the Prince himself, dared to argue with her.

My companions Mizʿel and Ṭâreš praised the Rwala chiefs. Ṭâreš said that an-Nûri distributed better mantles than Ǧezzâʿ eben Miǧlâd, head chief of the Dahâmše tribe. He spoke with especial warmth of the chief ʿAḏûb, who was very popular among the Dahâmše. Although the latter waged war with the Rwala, ʿAḏûb made frequent trips to them, he said, and, if any of the camels carrying his brand marks accidentally got among the captured herds, they were always returned to him.

At 2.39 P. M. we saw to the east the edge of the mesa Ḳârt al-Mṣâwri, at the northwestern base of which extends the Sâžît umm Ṭarfa'. In this channel are the rain wells Moḳr al-Mṣâwri, northeast of them Mḳejrât ad-Dekûk, and still farther north Ḥabra umm Ṭarfa'. On the left bank of the Sâžît umm Ṭarfa' rises the wide, level crest Ḥazm aẓ-Ẓbejṯ, upon which are four irregular cones. Southwest of the western cone are the wells of al-Barbak, and southwest of that the Moḳr an-Nḫejle, which at 3.10 was on our right. Southeast of Ḳârt al-Mṣâwri from south to north runs the "nose" Ḫašm Ṣennâr, in front of which gapes in the scarp Ǧâl ar-Raʿan the wide, dark opening of the valley Ab-ar-Rwâṯ. West of us at the head of the Riǧlet Slîmân, Mizʿel pointed out to me a small hill under which lies the rain pool Radîr al-ʿEšše.

MOḲR AL-ŽETÂDI TO ŠEʿÎB AB-AL-ḲÛR

At 3.32 we reached the rain well Moḳr al-Žetâdi, which was half filled with water from the last rain. We wanted to let the camels drink and to fill our bags to the top, but we searched in vain for the canvas bucket. Finally, as we were badly in need of water, I took the small bag of waterproof cloth in which I had wrapped my photographic plates. It was torn in two places, but I applied a round pebble to each hole, bound the cloth round it, and a bucket was provided. My native companions watched me skeptically and freely expressed their doubt of my success: they were certain the water would escape from my cloth pail. My only answer was to tie the bucket to a rope twelve meters long, insert in it a tin bowl, and direct Mizʿel to go down the well. Ṭâreš and the ʿAmâri held the rope while Mizʿel descended and with the bowl dipped up the water into the pail. When it was half full, they pulled it out and poured the water into a waterproof blanket that we had spread over a dip in the sand. The camels drank eagerly. After filling the water bags, we also filled the improvised bucket so as to have a supply for supper. Not a drop had leaked out; the bucket really was waterproof. My fellows wondered at it and admitted that even a leather bag was not always so tight.

As there was no pasture at the wells, we left at five o'clock. At 5.40 we came to a secluded depression southwest of the Ṛadîr aṭ-Ṭrejfâwi, where there were a few plants upon which our camels could graze. The ʿAmâri watched the camels, Ṭâreš grubbed dry bushes of *rûṯe,* Tûmân sketched a map of the environs and adjusted the watches and barometers, while Mizʿel and I prepared supper. By a lucky chance Tûmân had discovered our canvas bucket among the scientific instruments, where some obliging slave had tucked it. We were glad to see it; we needed for another purpose the improvised cloth bag in which we had carried the water: we had no other receptacle in which to mix the dough for bread! I had laid aside a large shallow pan, but our helpers must have mislaid it among the baggage that remained at the camp. Mizʿel declared that we could not bake bread, as we had nothing in which to prepare the dough. So I dug a small hole in the ground, laid the waterproof cloth over it, put upon it five handfuls of flour with some salt, placed the bowl of water near by, and ordered Mizʿel to mix the dough (*jeʿaǧǧen*). Without washing his dirty hands, he poured the water upon the flour and kneaded the dough. Meantime I picked up three stones all of equal size (*hawâdi*) and about six inches high, stood them up in the form of a triangle near the fire, poured water into the kettle, set it on the stones, and fed the fire. Mizʿel soon got tired of kneading the dough and asked Ṭâreš to go on with the work, saying that he would watch the camels instead. Ṭâreš knelt down by the bowl and with the words "In God's name (*bismi-llâh*)" resumed the kneading with his own dirty hands. Miz'el did not like to stay with the camels either, so he squatted by the fire and asked me to let him feed it (*ḫalli ʿannak*). After the water began to boil we threw into it four handfuls of *burrul* (peeled wheat) and let it cook over a slow fire. With some of the coals we built a bigger fire near by, putting on a considerable quantity of fuel. After it had burned out Mizʿel raked up the smouldering ashes and Ṭâreš brought the dough, tossing it up with his left hand and slapping it with his right to make it wider and thinner, until he had shaped it into a cake about thirty centimeters in diameter and three in thickness. Then he threw it skillfully on part of the ashes and with a stick raked the rest over it. The fire flamed all round the cake, upon which Ṭâreš kept raking fresh hot ashes. After a quarter of an hour he turned it over, and ten minutes later Mizʿel pulled it out of the ashes, tapped it with a stick, and threw it before me. The bread was baked. Out of a small leather bag Tûmân poured some butter on the *burrul*, and thus our supper was ready. My native companions ate with great relish, kneading large dumplings from the *burrul*, cramming them one after another into their mouths, and filling the free spaces with bread. It was only a few minutes before the bread as well as the *burrul* was gone. Then they licked their fingers and wiped their hands in the sand. Mizʿel eventually wanted to wash his hands, but I would not permit it (temperature at 6: 27.3° C).

At 7.10 we rode on. In a few minutes we had on our right in the river bed a large pool which, when filled with water, forms the Ṛadîr aṭ-Ṭrejfâwi. When it is full, herds of camels may be watered there for more than two months at a time. After 8.50 Mizʿel pointed out to me, in a rocky slope on the right, a large rift called Žaltat aš-Šefalleḥijje, into which rain water also flows. At 9.18, northeast of the Ṛadîr aṣ-Ṣlubi, we prepared to spend the night. We could not kindle a fire, but we let the camels graze, as an abundance of fresh grasses grew all about. Ṭâreš and Mizʿel were to watch the animals. The ʿAmâri went to bed without worrying about his camel. When I urged him to look after it, he answered that it would not stray but would return of itself. Ṭâreš wrapped himself in his cloak near the camels and in a little while was snoring. I walked about the camp before

I lay down; and when Miz'el saw that I had finally retired he drove the camels up to us, made them kneel, and tied their front legs. After midnight I was awakened by faint, despairing lamentations from the 'Amâri. Having been unable to find his camel, he begged my companions to assist him in searching for it. He wanted to mount mine in order to find his own sooner, but I refused to let him do so because I feared he might escape with it. I did not trust him; that is why I had advised Tûmân to tie his weapons to his body, which I likewise did, so that the 'Amâri could not steal them. He finally persuaded Miz'el to help him in the search and two hours later they returned with the missing camel.

Tuesday, March 30, 1909. Dawn had barely come when I was awakened by Ṭâreš (temperature at 5.30 A. M.: 11.6° C) who had planted himself near my head, coughed, yawned, and was singing off his morning prayer. I ordered him and Miz'el to release the camels for pasture; but Ṭâreš devoted himself to his prayer, while Miz'el absented himself because of necessity and was gone a long time. I freed the camels myself meantime. Tûmân kindled a fire and I poured water into the coffee kettle and ground the roasted coffee. When the kettle began to steam and the aroma of the coffee was perceptible, Ṭâreš finished his prayer and Miz'el his necessity. They wanted their breakfast. Afterwards, they were both so clumsy about the loading that Tûmân and I had to do all the work.

At six o'clock we got under way. To the southeast we noted the rosy elevation of aẓ-Ẓbejṭ, which adjoins a rain well (*moḳr*) of the same name. We were traversing a stony district where grow sparsely *rûṯe, ša'rân, ṣam', 'efejna, šîḥ, žetâde,* etc. From 7.50 until 8.52 our camels grazed, while we baked bread and ate it with melted apricot jelly (*ḳamareddîn*). When I beckoned to my companions to drive up the camels, Miz'el urged Ṭâreš to hurry, adding:

"Thou knowest that every traveler is ailing and the best remedy for him is to march (*aṭ-ṭurḳi 'alîl wa-l-masîr dawa'*)."

To the southeast, upon the level crest, showed the stone heap Riǧm Bajjûẓ. We were going in a northeasterly direction and at 10.10 saw on the right the rain well Moḳr al-Ḫfejse and east of it the Mḳejrât ar-Rḳejje. In the dips we found fresh *ǧirǧîr, mḥarût, ša'rân, ḳazḳâẓ,* and *roṛol.* The young sprouts of *ša'rân* and *ǧirǧîr* are edible, and the latter is also used in washing clothing. The root of *mḥarût* is baked like bread and is also edible.

After 12.15 P. M. we deviated more to the northward and sighted in front of us on the right the long hill of al-ʿEjr, and almost due north of it the white mesa of al-Ḫonṣor, at the base of which is a rain pool of the same name. East of the latter and northwest of the Ḫabâri al-Brejčât, is the well Mšâš (or ʿAḳlat) al-Ǧmejʿi. The region became more monotonous as we went on through vast lowlands, hedged in by precipitous sandstone walls dissected by numerous gullies leading down from the plateau surface, here covered by a coarse gravel in which few plants flourish. There are practically no valleys hereabouts. Rain water flows into the lowlands in shallow, almost level, swales and forms numerous *ḫabâri*. Upon the uplands are solitary irregular cones or domes, usually topped with heaps of stones. After the heavy rains, when the *ḫabâri* are full of water, as they were four years before, the lowlands swarm with camels, and behind every heap of stone there is a sentry; for in al-Ḥeǧera camp many clans of the ʿAmârât, Dahâmše, Rwala, Šarârât, and aẓ-Ẓefîr tribes, and even the Muntefiž are not likely to be very far away. What wonder that raids are so frequent! Since the year of al-Ašḳar — that is, since the defeat suffered by Saʿdûn al-Ašḳar, prince of the Muntefiž tribe, at the hands of the Rwala in 1905 — there has been insufficient rain in al-Ḥeǧera. For that reason the Bedouins had not gone there. Mizʿel explained to me how al-Ašḳar had attacked the Rwala. Seeking to flatter me, he addressed me only as "*aš-šejḫ* Mûse" (as he pronounced it). When he did not use this title, he saluted me thus: "O thou to whom Allâh grant a long life! (*jâ ṭawîl al-ʿomr!*)"

As we were riding along after one o'clock, my camel suddenly began to plunge and leap, frightened at a large lizard (*ẓabb*) that had run in front of her. The ʿAmâri jumped off his camel, pursued the lizard, threw over it his mantle (*ʿabaʾ*), and seizing it by its scaly tail brought it back to us. It was seventy-seven centimeters long and at its belly twenty centimeters wide; under the belly it was yellowish white and on its back grayish. Its spine and tail were scaly. Ṭâreš thrust it into the bag upon which we prepared our dough. It was destined to be roasted and eaten.

At 2.08 we sighted two gazelles. Mizʿel, who had boasted

that no gazelle could escape him, instantly seized his long flint musket and scurried after them. He returned a full half-hour later breathless and coughing — without the gazelles.

From 3.50 to 4.12 our camels grazed upon blooming *mḥarût,* of which we dug up three roots. These were of the thickness of a hand, forty to sixty centimeters long, and had

FIG. 45—Our camp near the Tell al-Ḫonṣor.

a black rind. Mizʿel discarded two of them, explaining that they were males and had a bitter taste; the third root, a female, we took along. At 4.49, finding southwest of the Tell al-Ḫonṣor a small meadow sixty meters long and twenty wide, verdant with *dhama, ruḳrûḳ, ummu rwejs, znejma, saʿʿêd, snejsle, šiḳḳâra, šilwa, ṣamʿ, ʿanṣalân, ḳafʿaʾ, ḳrêṭa, kamša, nefel, niḳd, wubêra,* and *rûṯe* (Fig. 45), we decided to cook our supper there. Ṭâreš baked bread and the ʿAmâri fed the fire under the kettle in which our *burrul* was to be cooked; Tûmân wound our five chronometers and determined the exact time by comparing them with the results of our observations of the meridian passages of some stars; I collected plants, while Mizʿel baked the lizard (Fig. 46) and the *mḥarût* root. He first cut the lizard's throat and built a large fire. When the fire was burning fairly well he raked the coals aside, dug a pit about ninety centimeters long by thirty wide near by, and scraped into it some of the coals and ashes. On these he laid the lizard, covered it with earth, and made a fire on top. He pushed the root near the fire, turned it over twice and the lizard thrice, and when the bread was baked and the *burrul* cooked he was ready to lay before me the root and the lizard. We broke the root into several pieces. Underneath the black rind was a white edible substance with a somewhat pungent taste and as dry as flour. Miz'el sliced the lizard and proffered me the best parts from the tail; he himself enjoyed the bowels. The meat I ate was composed of very many thin, tough skins superimposed one on another like sheets of paper and tasting somewhat like the meat of the crawfish. At first I had abhorred the sight of the lizard, but later, after the vision had left my mind, I indulged in the meat with relish. My native escorts ate the *'ejš* (cooked meal) and bread, and, while Tûmân and I ascertained the latitude, they finished the lizard (temperature at 5.30: 25.2° C).

FIG. 46—Miz'el and the lizard near the Tell al-Ḫonṣor.

Before we left an-Nûri's camp I had made it known that we should go to the wells of aṣ-Ṣammît on the right side of the valley of al-Ḫerr, and we actually did start in that direction. I acted thus for the purpose of deceiving the Ṣlejb and other strangers in our camp, for I feared they might communicate the direction and the goal of my journey to some robber band or raiding party. As a matter of fact, however, I had no intention of going to aṣ-Ṣammît, for the Šammar and Dahâmše were said to be encamped there, with Moṛâra and Ḥammâra *šwâja* (sheep- and goat-breeders) north of them, and I had no means of knowing how these clans would welcome me. Furthermore, near their tents I should have exposed myself to the danger of being attacked at any time by an enemy band. Had I continued westward, I should certainly have been followed by robbers, who could have leisurely murdered me and my escorts in the forsaken region devoid of camps. I also wished to keep clear of the Turkish authorities. Had I gone from aṣ-Ṣammît to al-Barrît, and farther by way of al-Aḫejẓer, to the settlement of Šeṯâṯa,

I should have approached settlements governed by the Turks, who would have greeted me affably but would have forbidden me to return into the desert, as they would have been held responsible for my safety. Therefore, I had made up my mind to proceed through the center of the territory of al-Wudijân and leave the above-mentioned localities on the right. I could reach them more easily later from Irak. My task was the exploration of the inner desert.

When I learned from Miz^cel that we might reach aṣ-Ṣammît within a day and a half, I asked him where the nearest water to the north was to be found. He replied that we were sure to find water in the Ḥesjân Ǧdejjedet ᶜArᶜar; whereupon I declared that we should proceed in the direction of those wells. Upon closer determination of the course we should follow, Mizᶜel advised me to place the pole star before the eyebrow of the right eye of my camel and, with the help of God, proceed in that direction; that is, toward the north-northwest.

The ᶜAmâri inquired whether I should go from the valley of ᶜArᶜar to the wells of al-Barrît; to which I replied that only Allâh knew.

"And I, what shall I do?" he faltered.

"I did not ask thee to ride with me. Pour out for thyself two bowls of water into thy small bag, take some bread, and, under the protection of Allâh, thou shalt come whither thou wouldst be. We have done but good to thee."

"By Allâh," interrupted Ṭâreš, "Mûsa is not lying (*wallâh mûsa mâ hu čâḏeb*)."

"Do thou good to us withal," I adjured the ᶜAmâri, "and make no mention of us before either enemy or friend."

He promised to do so and in the bright moonlit night took his departure from us toward the northeast, while we headed toward the north-northwest. Half an hour later we came into the wide, shallow *šeᶜîb* of Ab-al-Ḳûr, which extends toward the northeast through the immense lowland of Fejẓat al-Adjân and terminates in the Ḫabra an-Nâǧed at Ḫašm an-Nâǧed, the western edge of the undulating plain of Ḥmâr az-Zôr. Southeast of the Ḫašm an-Nâǧed rises the wall of al-Msâdde, and southwest of that al-Kaᶜabât, which encloses al-Adjân in the east. On the left side of the *šeᶜîb* of Ab-al-Ḳûr is the long, tabular hill of Ḳârt aẓ-Ẓabᶜ, in the caves of which hyenas are said to live. At 8.55 we encamped in a small, grassy meadow.

ŠE'ÎB OF AB-AL-ḲÛR TO WÂDI 'AR'AR; THE ṢLEJB

Wednesday, March 31, 1909. In the morning (temperature at 5.30 A. M.: 10° C) was reënacted exactly the same performance as the day before. Ṭâreš slept about thirty meters away from me, but as soon as it began to dawn he took a position at my head and started to pray. After he finished I asked him to pray at his own bed next time and thus gain forgiveness for the sins that he perchance might have committed on that spot. He could not comprehend why he was not to pray at my head. Had he but prayed! But during his prayer he coughed, blew his nose, examined his clothing, and threw at me all his lice. I had not slept much that night, for I had unluckily quartered myself upon a nest of large ants. The nest was in a crack in the ground and the ants entered my bed through a small opening which I had failed to notice. Toward midnight I was awakened by their attacks and I had to seek another place. This I could do in a short time, but it took much longer to rid myself of the ants that had invaded my clothing and my blankets. They were biting me so ferociously that I felt as if I had been rolling in nettles. I knelt for over two hours in the bright moonlight picking off the ants.

After we set out at six o'clock, Miz'el showed me on the northeastern horizon the long slope of the mesa of ad-Dabbûsa, an infallible indication of the proximity of the lowland of al-Adjân, which is to be seen even from the wells of al-Barrît. Whoever ascends this mesa perceives in the northeast, beyond the lowland, the white "nose" Ḫašm al-Ṛarra, between which and ar-Rwajje and al-Msâdde within a deep basin are the wells of al-Barrît. North-northwest of ad-Dabbûsa are the Ṛadîr and Ḫabâri 'Arejžât on the southwestern fringe of the lowland of al-Adjân.

A gray fox (*al-ḥoṣejni*), white under the belly, fled before us. My companions greeted it with joy, for it is regarded as a good omen to the traveler. We passed through many small, grassy meadows, an indication that the soil had been recently moistened by a timely rain (*arẓ wasmijje*). Our camels picked the grasses in big bunches and devoured them without stopping to chew them. Ṭâreš was of the opinion that, should such favorable weather and pasturage prevail during the rest of the journey, the animals would fatten and return broader than they were long (*baʿarînak jetaʿaddelen wa jarǧaʿen mur-*

FIG. 47—In the Riğlet al-Helâli.

abbaʿâten). In the lowest places I noted numerous Jericho roses (*ḳnêfde*).

A cold north wind was blowing. We were clad lightly, with our bare breasts exposed, and the wind penetrated to the bones. Vainly I enveloped myself in the only cloak I had taken with me, a light summer mantle that did not protect me from the cold wind. Only the summer sun could comfort us; but the sky was overcast, though narrow, horizontal beams of sunlight penetrated through the gray clouds near the horizon.

At 8.50 we reached the northern edge of Ṛâr al-Ṛazâri, upon which towers a high heap of stones that marks the rain well of the same name. At 9.28 we passed through the Riğlet al-Helâl (or al-Helâli) (Fig. 47) and remained beside it until 11.08. This originates in the southwest between the Ḳârt al-Wadʿa and the Ḳârt ar-Rahama, is joined on the left by the Riǧlet an-Neḳdijje, and merges with the valley of Ab-al-Ḳûr. In the channel *slajča* (also called *ḏerw*) grows abundantly. If pregnant asses eat it in quantity, they slink (*jaṭrahem*). At 12.45 P. M. we crossed the narrow channel of the Riǧlet aš-Šâẓi, which ends in the Ḫabâri ʿArejžât, and at one o'clock reached the northern fringe of the region that had been moistened by the current year's rain.

At 1.28 we rode into the Ḫabâri al-Mbowǧijjât. In the short, stony cross-gullies we noticed light green, thorny bushes covered with blue blossoms. It was the *šubrum*. Camels like it, and the Ṣlejb also eat the young sprouts and use them as a remedy for rheumatic pains.

The atmosphere had grown warm, almost sultry. The wind had ceased, and now there hung over the great, gray desert quiescent, horizontal, curtain-like layers of air, which caused in me a feeling of oppression that made me gasp for breath. Everything around us was ashen gray; in the distance, however, the surface of the desert appeared to be reddish. Above the level elevations hung exceedingly long strips of some subtile matter, while the depressions looked like lakes from which only the solitary higher crests seemed to protrude. Once in a while the delicately constructed matter was ruptured, and through the rift I could see innumerable dense, black monsters, large and small, rise and grow bigger above the earth. They swayed, tilted, swam upon the waves of the lakes, and then drifted freely into space. Often it seemed to us that we could see before us riders on camels. My fellows insisted that I look through the binoculars, but the riders always turned out to be low bushes barely sixty centimeters high, with which the *sarrâb* (mirage) was playing. I longed for something animated, for the verdant green of spring, but in vain I strained my eyes in search of spring flowers. The upland was absolutely desolate, dead, *majjete*, as the Bedouin is prone to say; while in the lower places appeared only the dry, lifeless bushes of *rûṯe, žetâde,* and *šîḥ*.

"*Al-ḥamdu lillâh!*" I cried out, when at 3.40 I spied the first green plant. We were again in a region that had been moistened by rain.

At 4.15 we crossed the shallow channel of the Riǧlet as-Swejf, which contributes to the Ḫabâri ʿArejžât. West-southwest of us Mizʿel called my attention to a hill, along the base of which, in the valley of ʿArʿar, are the Mḳûr al-

Ḫṣej. In the west we perceived the channel of Umm al-Ğeḏʿât, and northeast of it the dark strip of the Riğlet an-Nâṣfe, both of which converge on the left with ʿArʿar.

From 4.55 to 6.47 we rested in a lowland that afforded our camels rich pasture. Mizʿel told me that once, when his clan was celebrating the holiday of *ẓaḥijje* (remembrance of the dead) in this vicinity, two Bedouins came to them on foot (*zalamtên bedw ğâjîn ʿala riğlêhom*) saying they had had no water for two days. The Ṣlejb took pity on them and poured into their mouths first butter and then water. After they had recovered their strength sufficiently to talk, they said they belonged to the Ḳmuṣa group of the Sbaʿa tribe and that in a raid against the Šammar they had been repulsed, defeated, captured, and finally set at liberty, but without water or food. The Ṣlejb put them upon asses and took them to the oasis of al-Ḳâra, whence they returned to their own people. Mizʿel remembered with a thrill the quantity of meat they had that holiday. They had found in the desert four runaway camels, two of which they butchered and ate at the holiday feast, keeping the other two to use in scouring the wide desert for water and pasture (*ʿendahom rčâb jeʿassû ʿalejhen*). The man who is sent to find pasture or water and therefore a camping place also, is called *ʿassâs* by the Ṣlejb, *ḳaṭṭâf* by the Bedouins.

At 7.20 we left the rain-dampened soil of the Ẓahrat al-Bâjne. As early as eight o'clock, however, Mizʿel called my attention to the white color of the soil we were treading, this particular shade of whiteness being an indication of recent profuse rain (*al-ḳâʿa bêẓa tarâha marsûla*). According to him, the surface was white because it had been washed by the rain; otherwise, he added, it would be dark gray. He dismounted from his camel, loosened a handful of earth from the ground with his dagger, and asked me to feel it to convince myself of its dampness. To me, however, it seemed quite parched. Nowhere had we found a tract bearing annual or perennial growths. We passed on through long, wide plains where there was not a plant, and rejoiced when at 9.30 we saw before us a dark strip of withered *rûṯe* bushes, in which we encamped at 9.40 and lay down according to the four points of the compass with the camels in the center. We were lodging near the watering place of Ğdejjedet ʿArʿar; hence precaution was necessary.

Thursday, April 1, 1909 (temperature at 5.30 A. M.: 10.6°C). Setting out at 6.06 we passed in a north-northeasterly direction the wide, level highland Ẓahrat al-Bâjne, which extends on the right side of the valley of ᶜArᶜar. At our left we noted the Riğlet an-Nâṣfe converging with ᶜArᶜar; toward the northwest stone piles indicated the wells Ḥesjân al-Kaṭᶜijje, and still farther toward the north of it appeared the deep channel of Riğlet ᶜElebân. Ever since we left the camp of an-Nûri we had been accompanied by swallows. They circled round our camels in a way that reminded Tûmân and me of the swallows of our homeland. We had also started up several birds called *mrêᶜ*, similar to our quails but smaller. In the deep ravines we noticed bright green bushes of *lwejza*, used in the tanning of hides.

At 8.16 we spied in a bend in the Wâdi ᶜArᶜar two Ṣlejb tents. Dismounting from my camel, I scanned their neighborhood with my prism binoculars to see whether there were any camels kneeling; for that would prove that Bedouins were there. *Al-ḥamdu lillâh!* I perceived three black *ḥeḳâra* and eight white *šihâra* asses; at the wells farther east I saw more asses, black as well as white, and several Ṣlejb women. As we descended into the valley two girls ran to meet us, but as soon as we approached they hid in the channel. Mizᶜel coaxed them to come to us (*elḥaḳenna*) but they remained within their cover. The women were driving their asses away from the wells, fearing that we were Bedouins, their masters and extortioners. Upon the northern slope we saw several herds of goats and two asses carrying water bags and driven by a woman. At the wells of Ğdejjedet ᶜArᶜar I counted thirty-two asses, either the white thoroughbred animals (*šihri*, pl. *šihâra*), or the dark, common breed (*ḥeḳri*, pl. *ḥeḳâra*). Mizᶜel asserted that there must be a good many Ṣulbân (Ṣlejb) somewhere near, since there were so many asses (*haḏôl nâsen četîrîn ḥemârâten čṯâr*). Reaching the wells at nine o'clock, we found there only two young women, one man, one boy, and twelve asses, which the man was just preparing to water. Mizᶜel prevented him from doing so, however, as he would have used all the water and left none for us. The man was very angry. He took us for ᶜAḳejl camel traders, cursed me and my companions, and invoked upon us an attack by robbers to take everything we had, maledictions that might easily be realized, since we were on the shortest route that led from Bagdad by way of Šeṯâṯa to al-Ğowf and hence to Damascus or to Egypt.

The boy, purporting to be the son of Miz'el's brother, joined our party. The two women begged us for tobacco, and when Tûmân gave them some they kissed his hands and neck. They wished to do likewise unto me, but I declined. I do not smoke.

We unloaded our animals and watered them, the boy descending one well after another and pouring the water that had gathered there into the canvas bucket, which we would then pull up. These wells, which lie near the left bank of the channel (Fig. 48), are from four to eight meters deep and so wide that they cave in and fill up after every heavy rain. Such wells, called *'aḳl* or *ḥesjân,* are supplied only by the rain water which remains under the layer of sand and gravel that covers the rock below. An abundant rain had occurred in 'Ar'ar and the vicinity four years before. During the first and second year following it the wells were constantly half-full and the water could not be exhausted. The third year, however, it gathered but slowly, and the fourth year imperceptibly. After forty-eight hours the wells replenish only to the extent of a yield of five liters each or ten at the most, and even this small quantity will vanish unless a heavy rain occurs. We exhausted more than twenty wells, filling our bags only halfway at that, while our camels had barely laved their lips. To get even this small quantity of water we had examined over a hundred wells which the Ṣlejb had drained dry. On the edges of the channel and upon both its banks was a large growth of *lwejzijje* and *ḳorẓi.* The long, flexible, green sprouts of the former, entirely without foliage, were covered with fruit the size of almonds.

It was only the day before that Miz'el had assured us ceremoniously that we should find plenty of water in the channel of 'Ar'ar, since, according to news that had reached him, the 'Ar'ar channel was full of water and the entire dry watercourse was converted (*sâlat*) into a wild stream (*sejl*). These advices, however, and Miz'el's assurances proved to be mere fiction. I should have liked to head straight toward the wide crest of 'Enâza, but, as we lacked the necessary water and had not even watered the camels, we were obliged to proceed to the nearest watering place, al-Ğḥâjde in the valley of Tbel. Should we find water there? The boy told us that it had rained at al-Ğḥâjde fourteen days before. This intelligence had been brought back by an *ʿassâs* (scout) sent out by the Ṣlejb, but was it the truth? God knows! *Allâh jaʿlam!* While my companions were engaged in the search for water, I watched the camels and at the same time surveyed the valley to the east as well as the west. Suddenly a woman cried out:

"Figures of men in the east! (*zôl biš-šerž!*)" The dark human forms, enshrouded in the hot air as though veiled, were only, the boy assured us, Ṣlejb women coming to water their asses at the wells.

Awlâd Ṣalîbi, or Awlâd Ṛânem, is what these inhabitants of the inner desert call themselves. The Bedouins, who despise them, call them Ṣlejb, Ṣluba, or Ṣulbân, and contemptuously Ṣlubât; an individual they call a Ṣlubi.

The Ṣlejb are subdivided into clans (*bedîde*, pl. *bedâjed*) or, as they prefer it, *âl*, which means the same as *beni* with the Bedouins.

The Âl Mâǧed camp south of al-Kwejt. They count about one hundred and seventy tents. The chief's name is Ḥamad welad Šennûf.

The Âl Rwêʿi camp west of al-Kwejt. Sixty tents. Muḥammed welad Slejbîẖ.

The Beḏâḏle. South and east of as-Samâwa. Two hundred tents. Maṭar eben Brejč. To these belong the ʿAnâtre camping between aš-Šubejče and al-Mašhad (Mešhed ʿAli or an-Neǧef). Eighty tents.

The Âl Ǧemîl. In al-Kaṣîm, especially in the vicinity of ʿAjn eben Fhejd. One hundred and fifty tents. Ṛnejm eben Srejjeḥ.

The Âl Bennâḳ. In the wider environs of Ḥâjel. Fifty tents. Muṭejlež welad Ṭlejḥân.

The Âl Sijalân. South of Ǧaʿâra and Šennâfijje. Sixty tents. Muḥammed eben al-Ḥalêwi. The Âl Ḳabwân also camp with them.

The Âl ʿAraḳât. South of ar-Rhejmi and al-Ḥejjâẓijje. Thirty tents. Ṣâleḥ eben Frejǧ.

The Âl Ṭarfaʾ. From al-Ḥazel (or al-Ḥzûl) to al-Ǧowf and in al-Ḥamâd. Subdivided into Âl Wuḏîḥ and Âl Râẓi. One hundred tents. Ḥlejs ar-Ruḥejmi.

As-Saʿadât. In the vicinity of Tejma. Ninety tents. Smejjân eben Ǧerâd.

The Âl Msêlem. Between Bagdad and al-Kubejsa. Ninety tents. Mežbel eben Ḳuṭen.

The Âl Hazîm. In the territory of al-Wudijân. Subdivided into Âl ʿÎsa and Âl Mûsa. Eighty tents. ʿAbdân eben Dasmân and Ḥâbûr eben Ṛaẓab.

Az-Ẓbejbât. In al-Ǧezîre between the middle Euphrates and Tigris. Two hundred tents. Al-Mesâme belong to them.

Aṣ-Ṣbejḥât. In the territory of al-Manâẓer between al-Žerjitejn and Ḳebâžeb. One hundred tents. ʿAwejdât welad Fwejrân eben Mâleč. The family of Eben Mâleč is held in respect by all the Ṣlejb. Even the Ẓbejbât obey them.

Ḥamûle has the same meaning to a Ṣlubi that *ahl al-bejt* (mistress of the tent and her children) has to a Bedouin.

Ahl are all consanguinous relatives who are answerable for a murder (*illi jinṭaredû bid-damm*). *ʿAjle* includes the man, woman, and children who dwell in one tent.

Every Ṣlubi *ahl* pays to the Bedouins a stipulated sum for protection (*ḫûwa*), in consideration of which every large

FIG. 48—In the Wâdi ʿArʿar.

tribe appoints one or more brethren (*eḫwân*), whose duty it is to see that the Ṣlejb are compensated for anything that has been taken away from them by the members of that tribe. The mark for all camels belonging to the Ṣlejb is þ, called *mizbaʾ*, branded into the animals' temples. When a brother of the Ṣlejb hears that there is with his tribe a camel with this brand, he takes possession of it and sends word to the Ṣlejb to come and get it. The asses are marked by the Ṣlejb in all sorts of ways; the sheep and goats bear no marks at all, since they always stay with their owners.

The relatives of one *ahl*—that is, the relatives up to the fifth generation, inclusive—usually camp together. Their herds stay in the same place (*mrâḥ*) and for every such *mrâḥ* they pay one *meǧîdijje* (90 cents) yearly to each of the brethren. As there are about seventeen of such brethren, each *ahl* thus pays yearly for protection seventeen *meǧîdijjât* ($15.30), besides being obliged to feed hungry raiders, who frequently carry off their sheep and goats. What wonder that the Ṣlejb conceal themselves in the various ravines and flee at the sight of the Bedouins!

The following are the brethren (*eḫwân*) of the Ṣlejb in northern Arabia:
Eben Kwêčeb, the head chief of the Kwâčbe tribe.

Abu Ǧanfe of the Freǧe
Eben Ḥasan of the Durmân
Eben Badri of the Ešâǧeʿa
Eben Melḥâḳ of the Swâlme
al-Ḫorboṭli of the ʿAbdelle
Eben Šenn of the Weld ʿAli
Eben Mḥejne of the Dahâmše
Eben Ǧlâl of the Ṣḳûr
Eben Ṛubejn of the Fedʿân
Eben Dlejječ of the Ẓefîr
Abu Tâjeh of the Ḥwêṭât
Eben Ḥajjâl, chief of the ʿAzzâm clan of the Šarârât
Eben Sajjed of the Weld Slejmân
Ḥarb eben Muḥammad of the Beni ʿAṭijje
Eben Zeben of the Beni Ṣaḫr

It is interesting that the Ṣlejb consider al-Ḥasaʾ a territory from which many of their clans have emigrated. The people prepare their own gunpowder (*duwaʾ*). They mix brimstone (brought from al-Ḫalîže at the western boundary of al-Baṭn) with butter and heat it until the good sulphur separates from the brimstone; then they crush charcoal, add the good sulphur to it, grind it to powder, and the gunpowder is made.

At 10.20 we left Ǧdejjedet ʿArʿar and rode toward the two tents of the Ṣlejb. At 10.32 we reached the bend where they had been at nine o'clock, but did not find them. They had moved away. At a swift pace we followed the boy, who led the way, crossed the Riǧlet ar-Rûḥ, which joins Wâdi ʿArʿar on the left, and overtook two herds of goats driven by several women near the well al-Ḥesw in the valley of ʿArʿar. Mizʿel bought from them a *roṭol* (2.56 kilograms) of butter for one *meǧîdijje* and a small castrated buck (*ḫaṣw*) for two *meǧîdijjât* ($ 1.80). The women surrounded us, wanting us to kill the buck on the spot, cook it, and invite them to partake of the food. They begged that we would at least give them the head and all the intestines, but Mizʿel cut the buck's throat and fastened the carcase to his camel (temperature at 12: 26.3° C).

WÂDI ʿARʿAR TO RIǦLET AL-ṚWEJẒE

At 12.13 P. M. we finally left ʿArʿar,[51] which loses itself in the Ḫabra al-Ǧawsijje in the lowland of al-Adjân west of

[51] The valley of ʿArʿar is often mentioned in Arabic literature.
Al-Bekri, *Muʿǧam* (Wüstenfeld), p. 564, cites the poet Ḥakam al-Ḫuḍri, who speaks of ʿArʿar, al-Mushulân, Muwazzar, al-Baradân, al-Baṭaʾ al-Aʿfar.

Ḫabra an-Nâğed. We were bound in a northwesterly direction. Mizᶜel sympathized with his tribesmen, maintaining it was because of their hunger (*ǧûᶜânîn*) that they had to go to the wells of al-Barrît to beg the ᶜAmârât for food. At 1.40 we passed through the Riğlet umm al-Ṛîrân and sighted ahead of us toward the north-northeast a long, level upland overlooked by the oblong, tabular hills of Ḳârt al-ᶜEjš. This upland forms the eastern fringe of the undulating region in which we were traveling; east of the hills spreads a plain in which there are but few solitary hills. At 1.45 we crossed the route Darb al-Bârûde, used by raiding parties bound from Irak *via* Nḫejb, Ǧdejjedet Aḥâmer, Ǧdejjedet ᶜArᶜar, Ṛadîr ab-ad-Defûf, and Ḳulbân Ṣwêr to al-Ǧûba and al-Ǧowf. At 2.10 there lay before us the deep opening of the *šeᶜîb* of Aḥâmer, which is separated from ᶜArᶜar by the mesa Ḳârt an-Nâṣfe.

The *šeᶜîb* of Aḥâmer has its origin upon the Ḥazm al-Ǧelâmîd, and is joined on the right by the Riğlet al-Ḳerâri near Ṯaṛab al-Bowli and the Tell al-Bowli and, farther to the east, by the combined ravines Riğlet al-Lejle and al-Mḫaṭṭam. At 2.32 we descended into the depression of Aḥâmer, which is over four hundred meters wide and very deep. The channel, about sixty centimeters deep and six meters wide, is overgrown with *ḥambala*. On its left side is the dark Tell Wutejd, beside which is a *ṛadîr* of the same name.[52]

At 3.10, at the ravine of Ṛadîr abu Ṣafa, which merges at Ǧdejjedet Aḥâmer into the valley of Aḥâmer, we came to a wide swale (*rowẓ*) overgrown with fresh *rûṯe*, *šîḥ*, and dry

---

The poet Ibn Aḥmar mentions (*ibid.*, pp. 527 f.) a march from Ḳarḳîsija' by way of Furḍat an-Nuᶜm into the territory of ᶜArᶜar. — The city of Ḳarḳîsija' was situated on the left bank of the Euphrates at the mouth of the river al-Ḫâbûr. According to the poet, the throng marched from here along the left bank of the Euphrates to Furḍat an-Nuᶜm, as the city of ar-Raḥba (al-Mijâḏîn) was originally called. There they crossed the Euphrates and headed toward the south into the region which is penetrated by the valley of ᶜArᶜar, and which always abounds with verdant pasturage after heavy rains, in winter as well as in summer.

Jâḳût, *Muᶜǧam* (Wüstenfeld), Vol. 3, p. 645, citing the poet al-Musajjeb ibn ᶜAlas, reports that ᶜArᶜar is a valley where a famous battle was fought.

Al-Aḫṭal likewise mentions the valleys of Malṣ and ᶜArᶜar, between which there was a rich pasture (al-Bekri, *op. cit.*, p. 538). — Al-Aḫṭal was descended from the Taṛleb tribe, which possessed the entire area of our valley of ᶜArᶜar. I seek Malṣ in the valley of al-Mloṣi, where there is a watering place of the same name — probably identical with the Malṣ in question.

According to the poet Imrulḳajs (Jâḳût, *op. cit.*, Vol. 1, p. 666), the valley of Ẓabj lies in the vicinity of ᶜArᶜar.

The poet Abu Zubejd (al-Bekri, *op. cit.*, p. 286) mentions the camping grounds of Ḏu Ḥamâs and ᶜArᶜar.

[52] The poet al-Aḫṭal, *Dîwân* (Ṣalhani), pp. 87, 91, mentions the slope of Ḥâmer in connection with the sandy region of Ǧubba. —

Salhani absurdly identifies Ǧubba with the political district between Damascus and Baalbek, and Ḥâmer with the political district between Membiğ and ar-Raḳḳa (*ibid.*, notes d, f). I seek the sandy region of Ǧubba within the sandy area of the oasis of Ǧubba, situated in the center of the Nefûd, and Ḥâmer in our valley of Aḥâmer, which belonged to the tribe of Taṛleb.

naṣi, where we remained until 6.10 (temperature at 4: 27.1°C). Miz‘el skinned the buck, sliced the meat into small pieces, and cooked it, and we also prepared our usual dish, *‘ejš* of *burrul.* Miz‘el baked the buck's intestines in ashes and ate them with relish, without taking the trouble to clean them. Ṭâreš baked the bread. Tûmân and I wondered how much these two companions of ours could devour, though, to be sure, they had both boasted that they visited none but chiefs, at whose tents they could at intervals gorge themselves. At supper alone they emptied our kettle full of *‘ejš,* which on my other expeditions was sufficient for six or eight persons; and, in addition, each consumed at least half a kilogram of bread with apricot jelly or our sweet tea which they called *šâj.* We often had to cook *‘ejš* at noon lest they be hungry. On such occasions they poured the *šâj* upon the *burrul* and liked it. I thought they would get filled up after a few days, but they kept on consuming the same amount of food and merely grew more particular. They began to throw away the burned bread crusts and asked Tûmân to give them more sugar for their tea and more butter for their *‘ejš.* They urged him to mix the *burrul* with *ša‘arijje*—a floury meal resembling noodles and very popular in Irak; or at least to mix it with rice and other delicacies. The smell of the meat attracted several eagles and hawks. The latter could not be driven off. They would plunge at the pieces of meat which we were drying on a neighboring rock and, when pelted away by our stones, would fly barely fifty meters off and wait to see if there would be anything left for them.

Our journey beyond Abu Ṣafa led us across the Riǧl aṣ-Ṣafâwijjât, which approach from the Ḳârt al-Mu‘ajjeb and al-‘Ejš. When at noon I asked Miz‘el in which direction we should proceed to the water in the valley of Tbel, he said that we must put the pole star in line with the right nostrils of our camels, which meant that we were to go to the north-northwest. In the evening, however, I noticed that Miz‘el was

---

Al-Bekri, *op. cit.,* p. 285, writes that Ḥâmer is a locality near the Euphrates, between al-Kûfa and the territory of the Ṭajj, or else a valley that joins the Euphrates. He cites a verse of the poet Abu Zubejd ibn Ḥarmala ibn al-Mundir, a contemporary of the Caliph Othman, from which it is evident that the valley of Ḥâmer is to be sought close to Irak. — Our valley of Aḥâmer approaches from the southwest, from the territory of the former Ṭajj, and has its terminus in the district that belonged politically to Irak.

Jâḳût, *op. cit.,* Vol. 2, p. 187, seeks the valley of Ḥâmer within the region of as-Samâwa; he says the Beni Zuhejr ibn Ǧenâb (or Ǧannâb) of the Kalb and many others were wont to camp within it. In one of the verses of the poet an-Nâbiṛa Ḥâmer is mentioned in connection with Musḥulân, in another (*ibid.,* Vol. 4, p. 526) Musḥulân is connected with Ḥuṣajd and Tubel. — The valley of Tbel is about eighty kilometers north of Aḥâmer.

deviating now to the right and now to the left, and when I warned him to go in the given direction he replied:

"This is my native territory and I do not need the pole star here (*hâḏi dîratna mâ lana bil-ğedi ṛaraẓ*)." At 8.48 we encamped in the ravine of Ṛadîr al-Ǧandali, which the Ṣlejb call Telᶜet aš-Šubrumijje.

Friday, April 2, 1909. At 6.05 A.M. we headed in a north-northwesterly direction and at seven o'clock crossed aṣ-Ṣafâwijjet umm al-Ǧemᶜân. The northern sky was obscured by filmy clouds from which hung long shadows that almost touched the horizon. The march through the rocky region was difficult. Nowhere on the uplands had we seen any plants; in the wide watercourses grew *rûṯe, naṣi, šîḥ, niḳd, samne, baḫatri, sokub, selᶜ, šubrum, bzâr as-semen, taᶜmurra, ždejḥa, ṣfêra* or *ḥenwa, ᶜešbet al-ḥamâm, ğurb, ᶜešbet ar-râs, ğezar, ḥelleb, čaff al-čalb,* and *šidd al-ğemal,* but no grasses. Several flocks of birds as small as our goldfinch joined us; Mizᶜel called them *swêse.* They had yellow bellies, dark green heads, and light green backs, while the fringes of their wings were yellow with dark stripes. They were the first varicolored birds I had seen in northern Arabia.

At 8.05 we turned to the northwest, and at 8.31 entered the Riğlet aṣ-Ṣafâwijjet umm al-Aᶜwağ, which, southwest of the Ṛadîr al-Ḳdêḥât in the lowland Fejẓat ᶜAẓâmân, joins the valley of Aḥâmer. Farther to the northeast, in the channel of Aḥâmer, are the waters Ṛadîr al-Ḥejl, Žalta Ḫalîğe, Ḫubejra Ṛanam, and the large Ḫabra-š-Šenâna, in which the valley of Aḥâmer disappears. Southeast of this large rain pool, under the hill Ḥmâr az-Zôr, is the well Želîb al-Mačmi, or Mačmen, sixty *bâᶜ* (117 meters) deep. In places where the stony ground of the channel is somewhat covered with sand the iris (*ᶜeneṣlân* or *ᶜanṣalân*) grows abundantly. While looking for blossoms, I roused two snakes and many smaller specimens of lizards. From 10.05 to 11.35 our camels grazed; then we proceeded in a narrow path that had been recently trodden by migrating Ṣlejb.

Our omnivorous poet Mizᶜel aḫu Zaᶜêla was composing a a poem in my honor. Since a roving versifier must earn his living by his art, he apparently thought I would pay him well for a poem I liked. It was interesting to watch his procedure. He would ponder for several minutes and then recite two verses twenty or thirty times, substituting for some of the expressions new and better ones—*azjan*, as he called them. Then he would bid Ṭâreš pay attention and remember these verses. After Ṭâreš had learned them, Miz'el would be absorbed and silent again, and after a while would sing the first two verses and add the third to them. Having sung them to Ṭâreš innumerable times in his shrill voice, he would ask me to write them down while he composed the rest. When I found that he depicted me in his poem as sitting upon a *heǧîn* (mount camel) I demurred, saying that I rode a *ḏelûl*, that the Rwala do not say *heǧîn* but *ḏelûl*. The poet acknowledged this, but said he could not employ such a common word as *ḏelûl* in his poem, for in a poem one has to use the word that is more graceful even if less familiar.

At 12.30 P.M. we passed through the Riǧlet al-Ḥemâra, which is joined by the watercourses Šafalleḥi and al-Mezleḳa and merges into the Wâdi al-Obejjeẓ. It originates in the southwest, in Ḳûr al-Ṛalf. After one o'clock we crossed numerous paths trodden by camels, leading from the Ṛadîr al-A'waǧ in the valley of Tbel toward the east-northeast to the Ḫubejra Ṛanam. About a month before there had passed this way the herds of the chief Abu Bakr of the Ṣḳûr group affiliated with the tribe of the 'Amârât. Having drained the water of Ḫubejra Ṛanam, which was then full, they departed toward the north-northeast to the banks of the Euphrates. Miz'el and Ṭâreš said that they *ṛarrabow*, this being the Bedouin word to denote departure from the inner desert to the edge of the more populated region, no matter whether they go west or east, to Syria or to Mesopotamia and Irak. *Šarraḳow* they say when bound for the inner desert and here again they ignore the direction, whether it be north or south or west. *Ṛarb* denotes to the Bedouins an inhabited territory, whereas *šerḳ* means the inner desert, no matter whether their camp is in Syria or by the Euphrates.

We rode along the left of a forsaken Ṣlejb camping ground. For the fireplaces triangular pits had been dug, as the Ṣlejb, like the 'Aḳejl, stand the stones (*hawâdi*) one into each of the angles and set the kettle upon the stones for cooking. Around the tents they had made shallow furrows to conduct the water away; the Ṣlejb call them *nî'*, the Dahâmše *wuṭi*. At 2.28 there came into view to the southwest, at the eastern end of the Ḳûr al-Ṛalf, a high black, mound of stones marking the location of the Ṛadîr al-Ṛalf. In the depressions in which we were traveling our camels picked *ğezar,* which is used when dry as a remedy for *al-bağal* (hernia), or, as Ṭâreš called it, *al-balas.* The ailing people crush the *ğezar,* fill their pipes with it, and smoke it for forty days, one pipeful each morning.

The western sky was gradually becoming overshadowed by dark clouds. Miz'el was of the opinion that it was raining heavily to the west (*maṭaren ğajjed bil-ḥejl*). At 4.40 we turned toward the north and came into the *še'îb* of al-Meẓleḳa, which, though itself wide, has but a narrow floor entirely overgrown with *za'tar.* On both sides of the channel grow *roṛol, ruṛejla, ğirğîr, rûṯe, žetâde, ḏânûn, na'aẓ, ḫubbejza, 'ešbet ar-râs, 'ešbet al-ṛurâb, ta'murra, ḫâfûr, ḥafš, ḳwejṣîme, rubaḥla, ksejbre, ruḳejže, mu'assala, drejhme, dejdeḥân* or *ḥejmarân, zrejže,* and *ğa'ada,* while upon the upland is scattered *ḥamd,* which forms bushes similar to *rimṯ,* with which it is frequently confused. Upon the slopes prosper *ḳaẓḳâẓ* and *ṣam',* though rather sparsely. To the west loomed somber, rugged slopes, blocking on the left the ravine of al-Ṛejẓe. From 4.55 to 7.32 the camels grazed.

RECENT EVENTS IN THE FAMILY OF ŠA'LÂN

During the ride through the ravine of al-Ṛwejẓe, Miz'el related to me the recent events in the family of Ša'lân. After Prince Saṭṭâm died in the Riğlet al-Mḫaṭṭam and had been interred there, all the Rwala assumed that the most suitable successor to him was Fahad eben Hazzâ', a brother of an-Nûri. With the Ša'lân the dignity of princehood is as hereditary as it is with the other Bedouins and passes to the most capable member of the family: whoever the Bedouins concede to be most capable becomes prince. But Miš'al, the son of Prince Saṭṭâm, violated this custom. His mother was also the mother of Fahad and an-Nûri, for after Hazzâ''s death Saṭṭâm had married his widow, who later bore him Miš'al. At the time Saṭṭâm died Miš'al had a tent of his own, two wives, and several children. After his father's death he immediately carried into his own tent the ancient insignia (*abu-d-dhûr* or *al-markab*), around which all the Rwala rally, and proclaimed that he was going to rule as the successor of his father. Fahad and an-Nûri, who were older than he, reproached him and protested that by such a violation of the ancient custom he harmed the entire family of Ša'lân. But

Miš'al refused to acknowledge Fahad as prince and procured many adherents; whereupon Fahad and an-Nûri resolved to displace him by force. Presently, therefore, when in the course of a migration he came into a pass, an-Nûri occupied the exit with one part of his force and the entrance with another part, and demanded that he surrender *al-markab*. Instead of answering, Miš'al shot at him with his revolver, wounding Mḥammad, an-Nûri's own brother, in the forehead. Mḥammad fell off his horse. An-Nûri, thinking he was dead, aimed in anger at Miš'al and shot him through the heart, whereupon Miš'al's party surrendered. An-Nûri took the camel bearing *al-markab* into the tent of his elder brother Fahad, and thus Fahad became prince of all the Rwala.

But Fahad was not capable of ruling the tribe. In all important battles the command was in the hands of an-Nûri, while Fahad merely negotiated with the Government in matters of consequence. He cared only for the material welfare of his family. His eldest son, Fâres, was feared by all. Wherever he or his father saw any handsome mare, desirable camel, or good weapon, the son would come and take it either peaceably or forcibly — for his father, as he was wont to say. The taxes demanded by the Government were levied by Fahad threefold; two-thirds he kept for himself and turned over to the Government one-third. According to an old custom, he was to divide any such surplus money with the other members of the reigning family and even with the chiefs; but Fahad failed to do this. He kept it all, as he likewise kept the subsidy for sustenance (*ma'âše*), which the Government apportioned yearly to various clans.

The Rwala grumbled; but Fahad ignored them and depended upon the help of the Government and of 'Abdarraḥmân Pasha, the chief director of pilgrim expeditions (*emîr al-ḥâǧǧ*). The Government was satisfied with him because he turned in the taxes regularly; indeed, it was rather pleased that he was not liked by his tribe, for this left him all the more dependent upon Damascus. To all the charges and accusations against him the Government replied that it would not consent to his deposition and that it would revenge him should he be displaced. The chiefs of the Rwala therefore decided to show that they would not obey his orders. They had been camping south and east of Damascus, waiting for Fahad to receive the direction to levy taxes; but on the day the order was delivered to him they left their camps and retreated into the inner desert, leaving Fahad in al-Ǧowlân with only his slaves. The Government received no taxes that year.

The following year the Government invited the chiefs to a parley, at which they asked that Fahad's power be curtailed and proposed that taxes be collected by an-Nûri, who should, they said, be their *šejḫ al-bâb,* a chief who deals with the Government, while they would recognize Fahad as their war chief, *šejḫ aš-šdâd,* who might declare war and negotiate peace. They knew full well that Fahad had not proved himself a military commander, that he had avoided fights, and that he probably would continue to leave all dealings in the inner desert to an-Nûri. Fahad protested but finally had to be reconciled. An-Nûri gathered the taxes and divided the remaining money with the other chiefs, thus increasing his popularity. Fahad retaliated by refusing to recognize an-Nûri as *šejḫ al-bâb* and by stirring up hostility against him wherever he could, and his son Fâres ridiculed an-Nûri publicly. With the approval of Fahad, Ṭrâd al-ʿArâfa, who posed as Fahad's son but in reality was the son of Ḫalaf eben Iḏen, even forced one of an-Nûri's daughters into his tent intending to marry her. The girl jerked herself loose from him, however, and fled into the desert, where she was found by her brother Nawwâf, who, much incensed at the injury done to his sister, persuaded an-Nûri not to tolerate such a disgrace. An-Nûri went with three chiefs to Fahad to talk the matter over with him peaceably, and after a long conference it was agreed that Ṭrâd should not have an-Nûri's daughter for a wife and that an-Nûri should continue to collect taxes and deal with the Government as *šejḫ al-bâb.*

As a proof of amity, Fahad and an-Nûri afterwards camped together, but the peace did not last long. When they were camping in Syria and an-Nûri began gathering the taxes there, Fâres, Fahad's son, likewise went forth with his slaves and compelled certain clans to pay the taxes to him; whereupon the chiefs in a body aligned themselves on the side of an-Nûri and threatened Fâres with an uprising if he did not discontinue his insolence. Then the latter, conspiring with Ṭrâd al-ʿArâfa, persuaded his father Fahad to give his consent to the assassination of an-Nûri. A Šammari who was cooking coffee in Fahad's tent overheard the conversation. Feigning sleep and even snoring at intervals, he listened intently to their whispers and in the early morning informed an-Nûri, who would not believe the warning. Whereupon said the Šammari:

"Hear, O an-Nûri! Should Fahad come to thee today and ask thee to let thy daughter marry Ṭrâd and say that his son Fâres will take the mare thou hast received from Eben Meᶜǧel as a gift, know thou that death is menacing thee."

An-Nûri waited in suspense the entire day. The tent of Fahad was opposite his, but nobody came out of it. Washing was being done there. It was not until evening that Fahad emerged from the tent, paced in front of it a while, and then walked toward the tent of an-Nûri. He was naked, without even a shirt, merely enveloped in his mantle; but although several esteemed guests were sitting with an-Nûri, Fahad supped with them. After supper a shirt which had been drying was brought to him. He put it on and was conversing with the guests when suddenly he turned to an-Nûri with these words:

"Ṭrâd will shortly come for thy daughter; order her to go with him and let this brown mare" — pointing to the mare that had been presented to an-Nûri by Eben Meᶜǧel — "be taken by the slave ᶜÂmer to my son Fâres."

An-Nûri was startled; part of what the Šammari had predicted that morning had occurred. So he said:

"The girl is a sister of Nawwâf, and thou knowest he will not consent that she marry Ṭrâd. Talk with him."

"Where is he?"

"He sits in the tent of the slave ᶜÂmer."

Fahad arose and went with his slave to the tent of ᶜÂmer, about two hundred paces distant, where he seated himself at the fire opposite Nawwâf. A few minutes later an-Nûri with five slaves also came into the tent and said:

"Nawwâf, thy uncle demands thy sister and thy mare. What shall I do to him?"

"This," snapped Nawwâf, and thrust the butt of his carbine into Fahad's chest with such a force that it felled him, whereupon an-Nûri's slaves rushed at him immediately and with their swords cut him to pieces. Fahad's slave fired at them and was shot by an-Nûri. Straightway an-Nûri with Nawwâf started for Fahad's tent to get *al-markab*. The shots had been heard and one of the slaves said:

"These shots surely must be meant for our uncle," meaning Prince Fahad, for slaves refer to their masters by the term "uncle." The occupants of the tent strained their eyes into the darkness and sighted the white shirts of an-Nûri and his companions; whereupon Fâres and Ṭrâd fired several shots at them, which an-Nûri and his men returned. Realizing the futility of resistance, Fâres and Ṭrâd hastily mounted their mares and fled. Of an-Nûri's men one had been shot, while in Fahad's tent two guests lay dead, one a Kubejsi, or nomadic trader, the other a settler.

An-Nûri ordered that *al-markab* be immediately carried to his tent; he also appropriated Fahad's six herds of camels. Fâres placed himself under the protection of the chief Eben Smejr and demanded that an-Nûri return to him all the property of his father, but an-Nûri ceded to him only one hundred camels. Since that occurrence Fâres had been camping with his adherents — especially with the clan of Eben Ǧandal — among the enemies of the Rwala in the Ḥawrân, whence he made frequent raids into the territory where an-Nûri camped, seeking to avenge his father.

When, in July, 1908, I came to the tent of an-Nûri at al-Ǧâbija, I saw the women sewing up eight perforations in one of the tent-walls. The night before my arrival Fâres, with thirty raiders had appeared within shooting distance of the tent and had sought to kill his uncle an-Nûri and his cousin Nawwâf; but neither of them was in the tent at the time. Nawwâf pursued him with fifty-seven riders to a point east of the railroad station of aš-Šejẖ Miskîn, whence I then rode back with him to the camp.

Again, shortly before I went into the depression of Sirḥân, Fâres had attacked an-Nûri's camp twice in succession. It was because of this that, during our sojourn at al-Bîẓ and in the district to the southeast, an-Nûri's tent was surrounded by three chains of guards, placed at distances of 100, 300, and 500 meters from it. An-Nûri himself supervised these guards to see that they did not fall asleep, and he never slept in his own tent but always in that of one of his slaves, or even in mine.

Fâres yearned for peace, but presented conditions which an-Nûri could not accept. He demanded for himself an exclusive position among the chiefs, a threefold share of all moneys, the restoration of all the camels, and an-Nûri's daughter for Ṭrâd. When I once discussed these demands with an-Nûri, he said:

"Today is not yesterday. Once I should have granted him or his father almost anything, but now I cannot do so." How often, indeed, had an-Nûri sat pensive in my tent, seeing nothing, hearing nothing! Often he came three or even six times during the night to my tent or to my camels and stood there for a long time as if petrified, gazing steadily at the ground. What thoughts were passing in his mind? What was it that reappeared before his mental vision? What was depriving him of sleep? Was it his two brothers that he saw lying before him bathed in blood?

"Blood, especially the blood of a brother, cannot be wiped off," say the Bedouins.

RIĞLET AL-ṚWEJẒE TO ḤESJÂN AL-ĞḤÂJDE

Riğlet al-Ṛwejẓe,[53] in which we were traveling, forms a wide, shallow depression covered with a thick layer of white mold, which is washed out in numerous places. Such places, called *ḫerr*, must be encircled by the traveler.

Near the valley of al-Obejjeẓ we were unable to camp within the shallow *šeʿîb* of al-Ṛwejẓe, hence we hunted for a deep side ravine. We sighted one at ten o'clock, pushed on through it toward the west, and encamped at 10.18.

Saturday, April 3, 1909. The camels found no pasture in the morning, so we left at 5.50 A. M., crossed a low slope, and at 6.15 descended into the valley of al-Obejjeẓ. This depression is over three hundred meters wide and is enclosed by high, precipitous walls. The channel is from twenty to twenty-five meters wide and from sixty to one hundred and twenty centimeters deep and is covered with a coarse gravel in which grows *zaʿtar, slajča, naʿnaʿ*, and *ḳejṣûm*; the blossoms of the last are chewed for the relief of toothache. On the right, about one kilometer from our route, was Ḳlejjeb al-Wuʿêr, and about fifteen kilometers to the southwest the Ṯaṛab aṣ-Ṣahârîğ. This rocky rift, which fills with rain water, is situated in the Riğlet al-Ṛejẓe.

The valley of al-Obejjeẓ converges with the Wâdi Tbel. It originates, under the name of Riğlet al-Ḳlajje, in the northern end of the Ḥazm al-Ğelâmîd, east of the volcanic region of ʿAmûd by the rain pool of Mḥafûr ar-Rḥâli. The low tabular hills of Ḳûr al-Ṛalf separate it from

[53] The poet al-Aḫṭal mentions al-Ṛajḍ in connection with al-Bajḍatajn. Jâḳût, *Muʿǵam* (Wüstenfeld), Vol. 3, p. 828, seeks it between the city of al-Kûfa and Syria. Since our al-Ṛejẓe and al-Ṛwejẓe connect with the valley of al-Obejjeẓ — or al-Abjaḍ — I surmise that al-Aḫṭal had this region in mind.

the neighboring valley of Aḫâmer. In its central part it is joined on the right by the Riğl aṭ-Ṭarfât, al-Ṛejẓe, and al-Ṛwejẓe, and on the northwestern fringe of the lowland Fejẓat ʿAẓâmân by the Riğlet al-Ḥemâra, also called aṣ-Ṣafâwijjet umm al-Ṛalf. On its left it takes in, in the upper part, the Riğl al-Ḫanûṣ, aš-Šdejde, and al-Lejl, and north of the Ṛadîr Ḫudejde the Riğl aṣ-Ṣlâli and an-Naʿamâni. North of the lastnamed, in the valley of al-Obejjeẓ, are the small ruins of al-ʿEmâra or ʿEmârt al-Ḫnêfes, which, as Mizʿel explained to me, consist of innumerable small dwellings and large corrals. North of them the *riğlet* of aṣ-Ṣâlḥijje joins with al-Obejjeẓ. At the spot where the Riğl aṭ-Ṭarfât approach al-Obejjeẓ there are situated, in the channel of the latter, the wells of al-Fhede and Abu Ḳṭafa, both south of the Riğlet al-Ḫaṭṭ which merges with al-Obejjeẓ on its left side.

Ascending the upland on the left side of al-Obejjeẓ, we were struck by the icy north wind, which made us shiver. At 6.40 we reached the eastern edge of the Riğlet ar-Rowtijje, which merges into al-Obejjeẓ at the small well Ḳlejjeb al-Wuʿêr. At 8.18 we had passed through the Riğlet al-Ṛurâba.

On the left side of the Riğlet al-Ṛurâba rise, to the east, the mesas Ḳârt al-Mezwaʾ and Ḳârt al-Hezze, which terminate on their east side by the precipitous scarp of Ṛâr ab-al-Ṛurbân. Southeast of this scarp, within the valley of al-Obejjeẓ, are the wells of al-Mustağedda; northeast of it the wells of Nuḫba. Not far from the latter al-Obejjeẓ merges with the large Wâdi Tbel, which on the north is bounded by ʿEjârât as-Sleḳi and Ḳârat Rafḫa, and on the south by the immense slope of ʿAnz Nḫejb. At the eastern end of this slope the Riğlet az-Zôr rushes into Tbel, coming from the south out of Ḥmâr az-Zôr and Ḫašmet al-ʿEjâde and forming the eastern boundary of the lowland Fejẓat ʿAẓâmân. North of the Ḫabra-š-Šenâna and Ḫabra-n-Nḫala the valley of Tbel receives the Riğlet al-Ḥwejjer and the Riğlet al-Ḫafi. The latter contains, north of Ḫubejra Ṛanam, the well Mḳejr al-Ḫafi and west of Ḫabra-š-Šenâna the Moḳr Šenûf. In the upper part of the Riğlet al-Ḥwejjer, south of the Moḳr Nuḫba, is the Moḳr al-Ḳṭêwa. On the right side of the Riğlet az-Zôr, northeast of Ḳûr al-Ḫwejmer, protrude the irregular cones of al-Ğeṭûm and al-Ğaṭme, and north of them the mesas of ʿEjârât. East of the point where the valley of az-Zôr converges with Tbel are the wells of Ḏebâḏeb, and to the east of them stands the tree, Sidret Čenʿân; east of this lie the wells Ḥesw Fahad, Moḳr al-Wadʿi, Ḥesjân al-Mḥâṣât, Abu Marâğel, Žaltat al-Ḥefna, and Abu ʿAḳûla.

To the south of the central course of Tbel are the tabular hills Ḳârt al-Mezwaʾ and al-Hezze, from which the ravines al-Ḥsičijje, as-Sidarât, al-Ḳṭuwijje, Šefâwi al-Mdejsîs, Šefâwi abu Čahaf, and Šefâwi Šabwân, as the units comprising the Telʿât aẓ-Ẓlêʿijjât are called, approach the Wâdi Tbel.

To the west we noted the dark opening of the Šeʿîb al-Mraʾ (or al-Maraʾ), which comes from the slope Ṭâr an-Nedûf, as the northwestern spur of the Ḥazm al-Ğelâmîd is called. On the left there merge with it the Riğl al-Manḳûla, al-Bḫêra, al-Efâʿi, as-Sihlijje, al-Muʿtarẓe, and an-Nmâl, all of which originate in Ḥazm Šarâwa, the northern extension of the Ḥazm al-Ǧelâmîd. Farther east on the same side the shorter ravines of as-Sikke, Ramẓet al-Maʿzûle, Ramẓet al-ʿErž, and Ramẓet aḏ-Ḏubbân join with al-Mra'. On the right there unites with al-Mra' the Riǧlet Ǧwejjân, approaching from Ḫubejra Ǧwejfe on the southern slope of Ṭâr an-Nedûf; farther on there enter Riǧletên Ašbah, Riǧl al-Ḥašw and al-Ḳaʿûd, and finally Riǧlet aš-Šemrijje, all of which we had observed from the Ḳârt al-Mezwa to the southwest.

The vicinity of the central part of the valley of al-Obejjeẓ has a dismal aspect, with its dreary smooth swells bearing low, solitary, irregular cones or mesas, and everywhere masses of gray sandstone entirely devoid of vegetation. Mizʿel said it had not rained there for three years. Everything was parched. In the short ravines there were bunches of *niḳd,* from among the grayish-green prickly leaves of which peeped here and there grayish-yellow blossoms that looked as if they were dried. It seemed as if the entire region had been damned or bewitched: a dead, mortally wearisome desert.

At 9.20 we noted on the left, northwest of us, the solitary mesas of al-Ǧemîli, and before us the low, bright-colored hills Ḳûr al-Mḥejmât, in striking contrast with their somber environs. Beyond the latter to the north gaped the deep opening of the Riǧlet al-Ḥârdijje and south of it the Šeʿîb al-Mra', which merges with the valley of Tbel between ʿOḳêlt and Ḥesjân al-Bnejje. On our right the high slopes of al-Mezwa' and al-Hezze, in which originate the ravines of al-Ḥsičijje and aš-Šefâwijât, declined toward the north. The broad plain to the northeast seemed to vanish in the hot, hazy air. At ten o'clock we crossed the valley of al-Mra' and at 10.11 the ravine of Ramẓet al-Maʿzûle. Here we noted signs of the rain of March 20. The annuals had shot up, short and hair-like, but they were already withering. *Rûṯe* and *šîḥ* preserved more of the moisture and showed new sprouts.

From 11.42 to 1.28 P.M. we rested in the ravine of Ramẓet al-ʿErž. The heat was unbearable even though the sun was obscured (*mhadijje*) by gray clouds (*hadîha as-saḥâb*). All about us stretched great level swells covered with gray stones, monotonous and bare of vegetation. From them ran valleys with channels at first shallow but gradually deepening; yet we saw nothing in the depressions but dry *šîḥ, ḥawḏân, rûṯe, ḫomṣân,* and *slajča.* Above all hung the scorching, heavy air, which weighed upon us and, to me at least, caused moments of intense physical suffering. Our weary camels stumbled so frequently that we had to move carefully. Behind me rode Mizᶜel singing his poems in a high-pitched voice, composing new verses in my honor, and predicting that the finished poem would have at least forty verses.

At 3.18 we crossed the head of the ravine Ṛamẓet aḏ-Ḏubbân and drew near to the wide, deep Wâdi Tbel,[54] well known for its numerous rain wells.

This *wâdi* originates north of Ḥazm Šarâwa within the famous highlands of Lâha (or Ilâha) and terminates northeast of the settlement of Šeṯâṯa in the lowland Fejẓat Rezâza.

In the upper part, the Riğlet Habbîn converges with the Wâdi Tbel on the right at Ṛadîr al-Ṛâri; farther on the Wâdi Tbel receives al-Mẓella, al-Ferîs, as-Sehlijje, as-Shejlijje; as-Sella joins it at Moḳr an-Naᶜâm; al-Ḥârdijje is the next confluent on the right. On the left, west of the Moḳr an-Naᶜâm, comes in the Riğlet al-Mağna; at the Moḳr al-Ḳejṣûma, the Riğlet al-Fwêra; at ᶜOḳêlt an-Nâḳa, the Riğlet al-Aᶜwağ; at the Moḳr Ğôẖa and Moḳr al-Arẓumijje, the Riğl al-Fârât; at the Moḳr Ḳuᶜêd, the Riğlet Čalb abu Munṭâr; and finally Čalb al-Čaᶜači. East of the last-named ravine, in the channel of Tbel, are the wells of ᶜOḳêlt al-Čalb, al-ᶜOḳêle, ᶜOḳêlt abu Ẓlejf, Moḳr al-ᶜArîẓ, ᶜOḳêlt al-Bnejje, Ḥesjân al-Bnejje, ᶜAḳlat al-Mrêẖijje, ᶜAḳlat abu Nfejdejn, and finally Mḳûr abu Nufḳên, at which terminates the Riğlet Eḏêne approaching from the west-northwest. Farther to the east, near the Riğlet Šefâwi al-Mdejsîs, is the well Moḳr Ḳṭeri, and west of Šefâwi abu Čahaf the famous Ṛadîr al-Žerînên.[55]

North of the last-named watercourses extends an undulating plain which slopes toward the east and bears the mesas Ḳûr al-Habbârijjât. West of this plain rises Ḳârt al-Ḫerbân near which originates the Šeᶜîb al-Fâğ, which on the left is joined by the Riğl al-Wejzijje, ar-Rawṯijje, al-ᶜAwğe, and to the west of the solitary hill of ar-Rmâḥ, by the combined gullies of ar-Rmâḥ and Abu Sidr. On the right al-Fâğ is joined by the short valleys of Wudijât as-Sidr, which come from the mesa of Ḥezera, and the Riğlet Ḥzêrân abu Čahaf, in which are wells of the same name. East of the latter valley, in the channel of al-Erğâwi — as al-Fâğ is called in its lower part — are the rain wells Ḥesjân al-Faṣfâṣ.

Here and there we noted low, white sand drifts, which were especially numerous in the Telᶜet an-Nuẖejle, whither we had arrived at 4.39. This valley is short but wide. We found in it *ḥamâṭ*, *ḳorẓi*, *alḳa'*, and

[54] The valley of Tbel was known to the Arabic writers.

Al-Bekri, *Muᶜğam* (Wüstenfeld), p. 192, notes that Tubel is a valley in front of Ḥaṣîd (correctly Ḥuṣajd), because the poet al-Kumejt mentions it second in order, viz.: Ḥaṣîd, Tubel, Ḏu Ḥusum, al-Ḳuṭḳuṭâne, and ar-Riğal. — Ḥaṣîd certainly is identical with Ḥuṣajd, familiar from the history of Ḫâled ibn al-Walîd. I seek it on the right bank of the Euphrates to the southeast of al-Ambâr and north of the end of the Wâdi Tbel. Ḏu Ḥusum is nowadays called Ḏu Ḥeseb, or al-Ḥeseb; al-Ḳuṭḳuṭâne is the settlement of aṭ-Ṭuḳṭuḳâne.

According to Jâḳût, *Muᶜğam* (Wüstenfeld), Vol. 1, p. 824, Tubel is a valley several miles distant from al-Kûfa. Ḳaṣr beni Muḳâtel is situated below it, whereas the upper part of it reaches into the territory of as-Samâwa, which belongs to the Kalb. — Our valley of Tbel approaches from Ḳârat Lâha, which rises almost in the middle of as-Samâwa. The settlement Ḳaṣr beni Muḳâtel, which I identify with the modern Šeṯâṯa, is situated in the swamp into which the Wâdi Tbel disappears.

[55] Al-Ḥâzemi mentions a locality in the Syrian desert known as al-Ḳarînên (Jâḳût, *op. cit.*, Vol. 4, p. 80), which I identify with our al-Žerînên.

slajča with young sprouts, a proof that it had rained there during the last few weeks. In a bay in the side of the valley on the right we sighted a palmetto.

ḤESJÂN AL-ĞḤÂJDE TO MḲÛR AL-ČAʿAČEDI

At 5.05 we found ourselves in the valley of Tbel. The Ḥesjân al-Ğḥâjde there were full of water. *Al-ḥamdu lillâh!* We could not hold our camels back. They darted to the small, shallow wells in the channel, knelt, and drank in long draughts. Mizʿel had said we were sure to find some Ṣlejb there, but there was no trace of them. I wished to fill the water bags, but Mizʿel protested and even swore that there awaited us in Mḳûr al-Čaʿačedi so much water that to take any from here would be an unnecessary burden to our camels. He also asserted that we were certain to find many Ṣlejb there too, and might hire one of them with a small camel and four water bags to accompany us up to ʿEnâza. I asked him at least ten times whether he was absolutely sure we should find plenty of water at al-Čaʿačedi, and he answered every time in the affirmative and swore to it and finally reproached me for my distrust. Therefore we filled the bags only half full and at six o'clock set out, proceeding across the *šeʿîb* of al-Mesâjer and alongside the *šeʿîb* of Čalb al-Čaʿači until 8.32, when we encamped and determined the latitude. I was very tired and again felt the stinging pain in my bowels.

Sunday, April 4, 1909. Our camels were so hungry that as soon as it grew somewhat darker we untied them and let them go into the valley to seek young sprouts of *rûṯe*. Ṭâreš was to keep watch over them. He followed them until he was about three hundred meters away from us. I supposed he was watching the camels, but when it dawned and I failed to see either Ṭâreš or the animals, I ran out to look for them. The camels I found a long way off, and as I was driving them back I came upon their watchman, lying sound asleep, notwithstanding the fact that the Čalb al-Čaʿači lies in a very dangerous section, because the road from al-Ḳaʿara to the south leads through it.

Upon resuming the march at six o'clock we found in the yellow clay numerous prints of horses' hoofs. According to Mizʿel, my friend Metʿeb eben Haḏḏâl had passed there with a large raiding party, intending to attack the Šammar at al-Ḥzûl. He was observed too soon, however, and had to return without accomplishing his purpose. On his way back he watered his horses at al-Ǧhâjde, then at Mkûr umm aṣ-Ṣerîm in the valley of al-Radaf, then at the wells of al-Lmât in the valley of Ḥawrân, and finally at al-Ḳaʿara, whence he soon reached his folk, who were camping in the northeast.

In the *šeʿîb* of Čalb al-Čaʿači where we were traveling grew *šîḥ*, *rûṯe*, and *ḳejṣûm*, while on the slopes *ǧirǧîr* flourished; but everything was somewhat parched. At 6.38 we ascended to the upland. West of us rose several solitary pyramids about fifty meters high, and beyond them a wide, flat-topped ridge along which stretched the Riǧlet Čalb abu Munṭâr.

Ahead of us, toward the northwest, we noticed the tabular, gray rocks of Ḳârt al-Ḥabîle,[56] which form the watershed between Wâdi Tbel and Wâdi al-Radaf.

East of al-Ḥabîle extends a plain limited on the northwest by the Riǧlet Eḏena, which converges with Wâdi al-Radaf east of the wells of Umm aṣ-Ṣerîm. Also to the east of these wells beyond the Radîr al-Muǧejhîr on the left this valley is joined by the Riǧlet al-Ḥazîmi, by the Riǧlet al-ʿAšejše at the Radîr aš-Šubejče, east of the latter by the Riǧlet al-Erbijjâni, at the hills of Žaʿadân by the Riǧlet al-Muʿtadle, and still farther east by the Riǧlet al-Lwejzijje. All these ravines come from the tabular hills of Ḳârt al-ʿUmejra, aš-Šwâwîž, and al-ʿEmeše, which separate the valleys of al-Radaf, Ḥawrân, and ʿÂmež from each other. South of the oasis of aṯ-Ṯmejl and of the two solitary domes of Ṯadejjên the Ṯarab Ḳufrân is situated near the channel of al-Radaf, and farther to the east lie the rain wells Ḥesjân al-ʿAṣîbijje.

Upon the slopes of the Čalb al-Čaʿači — or al-Čaʿačedi, as the Slejb call it — dry *ḫâfûr* grew in abundance. At 9.58 we observed on the left a low, semicircular, artificial wall about forty meters long, enclosing a large mound of stones, while behind the wall, on the northern side, was a strip of ground about two meters wide and cleared of all stones. Mizʿel said that here Prince ʿAbdallâh eben Saʿûd al-Imâm prayed and relaxed when (about 1810) he was engaged in war with the Bedouins and was pursuing them to the settlement of al-Ḥumejra in aš-Šumbul, northwest of Palmyra. At 10.04 we passed some very old graves upon which were piled high cairns. From 10.15 to 11.26 our camels grazed. At 12.02 P.M. we perceived on the right the ravine of al-Ḥabîli, at 12.30 on the left the Telʿet al-Bnej, and at 1.25 the Telʿet al-Bnejje.

[56] According to al-Bekri, *op. cit.*, p. 264, Ḥâbilât is the name of the region west of the Euphrates near ʿArʿar. He corroborates his assertion by a verse of the Tarleb poet al-Ḳuṭâmi, who refers to Ḥâbilât in conjuction with Ḥamas. — Our mesa of Ḥabîle may be identical with the mountains of Ḥâbilât, because it rises upon both sides of the road that leads to the watering-places and pastures of ʿArʿar.

On the left side of the latter trough is a large corral for goats (*sîre*), hedged in by a wall about sixty centimeters high. It is said that a herdsman who drives his goats there may be sure no wolf will attack them, for no wolf would dare either to climb or leap over such a wall.

After 2.20 I ascended the rocky slope on the left and with my binoculars scanned the vicinity of the wells of al-Čaʿačedi. Failing to discover anything suspicious, I returned to my companions, and at 3.15 we arrived at the wells. We found no trace of the Ṣlejb nor any fresh plants, a sure sign that there was no water in the wells. Mizʿel went down fifteen of them, from four to seven meters deep, but he could collect barely ten liters of water. According to his estimate we should need water for six days; according to my calculation for ten days; hence there was nothing left for us to do but to return to al-Ǧhâjde in the Tbel valley and replenish our supply. Mizʿel had also assured me that we should certainly find the Ṣlejb in the upper part of the valley as-Saʿîd; it was evident, however, that he himself had not believed what he said. I directed that we return to al-Ǧhâjde the same way we had come, but Mizʿel promised to lead us by a shorter route.

RETURN TO AL-ǦḤÂJDE

Leaving the wells at 4.40 and the *šeʿîb* of Čalb al-Čaʿači at 4.55, we turned into the ravine of Telʿet as-Saʿîd toward the south. At 5.57 we came to the watershed between the Čalb al-Čaʿači and Čalb abu Munṭâr, and proceeded down the Telʿet aṣ-Ṣôr. Farther to the west the gullies of Telʿet ar-Rdûf, Telʿet aš-Šiṭêbât, and aḏ-Ḏembûḥ join the Čalb abu Munṭâr. At 7.32 Mizʿel asked me if we had been riding an hour and concluded that we should reach the water in another half-hour. After eight o'clock we rode down the ravine of Čalb abu Munṭâr toward the east. The sky was covered with dark clouds, in which to the north we saw flashes of lightning every once in a while. The night was very dark. Mizʿel paid no attention to the road; I myself had to seek the crossings in the channel — the sides of which were frequently pretty steep — while he issued from the rear advice and directions, especially when they were least needed. The half-hour of his calculation had passed long ago, and we had not yet reached the water. Riding eastward, we were exposed to a chilly wind that blew from that direction. I shivered with cold. The road was very poor, the channel washed out and full of turns separated by rocky spurs. Our camels were worn and starved, and there was no pasture anywhere. I thought we should find some plants in the vicinity of the Wâdi Tbel, where it had rained; but this valley continued always to be half an hour distant.

Unable to keep in the saddle or to endure the cold any longer, at 11.25 I swerved into a bay in the valley wall where we passed the night. After midnight the strong east wind carried away my blanket. Clad in only a long linen shirt and a caftan of the same material, I woke up cold, found the blanket, and this time weighed it down with stones. But the wind penetrated beneath the blanket, and no matter how I cowered or even hid my head under the covering to warm myself by my breath, I was shaken with chills and unable to sleep. The pains in my bowels tormented me even more during that sleepless night than upon my camel in the daytime. Ṭâreš got up and withdrew several paces northward, prompted by necessity. As he returned he was suddenly illuminated by the moon, which had appeared in a rift in the clouds. This vision frightened the camels, which sprang up and started to run on three feet toward the east. It took us some time to capture them all, calm them, and make them kneel. After that, we tied two of their legs.

AL-ǦḤÂJDE TO LÂHA

Monday, April 5, 1909. Without making a fire we rode away at 5.05 A. M., and at 5.45 (temperature: 7.3° C) reached the valley of Tbel at the Moḳr Ḳuʿêd. At 6.48 we dismounted in the valley at Ḥesjân al-Ǧḥâjde (Fig. 49). Unloading our baggage, we filled the water bags and prepared a receptacle for more water. The contents of our bags would last us for only three or four days at the most, whereas we needed water not for six days, as Mizʿel had said, but for ten, as I calculated, since there was no water all the way from al-Ǧḥâjde to ʿEnâza and from ʿEnâza to the settlement of Skâka. In what vessel were we to keep water for this long journey? I had taken along a large waterproof blanket, which I used to protect the photographic plates and the instruments and also to spread down in my tent when the ground was damp. On our scientific expeditions I covered the baggage with it to keep off humidity and frost. We gathered the ends together and tied them, thus procuring two large bags, which we filled with water and loaded upon the saddle provided for the transportation of water. Although two of us hoisted on each side, it required a considerable effort before we could lift it upon

FIG. 49—The Ḥesjân al-Ğḥâjde in the Wâdi Tbel.

the kneeling camel. Would not the water leak out? Would not the blanket rub open against the saddle? If it should rip or if the ropes should become loosened and the water run out, we were sure to be lost. We also filled the small bag in which we had carried water once before and which we were using for kneading dough. By this means we obtained a supply for one more day.

We left the wells at 8.32 and from 8.40 until 11.32 remained in the Telʻet al-Mesâjer, where there was pasture. I ordered enough bread to be baked to last for two days and *ʻejš* to be cooked for the day. I also forbade anybody to use a drop of the water without my permission. Whenever we stopped I examined the ground thoroughly for any thorns or sharp stones, before we ventured to lay our artificial water bag and the other bags down upon it. I myself dipped out the water and apportioned it for the preparation of food as well as for drinking purposes. At night I slept by the bags; for, since my native companions knew that I waked at the least sound, they would not dare untie the bags to get a drink.

In the *šeʿîb* of Čalb al-Čaʿači at 3.36 P. M. we passed the old graves we had seen before. At 3.55, as we found fresh pasture in a side ravine, we remained there until 4.20. At 6.20 we sought a covert in a bay in the wall of the *šeʿîb* while Mizʿel ran to the wells of al-Čaʿačedi to make sure that nobody was there and that the coast was clear for our further safe progress. He also drew the water that had gathered there since the day before. At 6.50 we were at the Mḳûr al-Čaʿačedi, where Mizʿel displayed before us a small bag containing about twelve liters of water, with which we prepared tea.

At 8.45 we were going in a westerly direction; at 8.53 we sighted the Telʿet al-Mismâs, and at 9.05 the Telʿet al-Frejǧe to the right. The soil here was of a yellowish and in places almost white clay in which plants prosper only after a heavy rain. As the rain that had filled the wells of al-Ǧḥâjde had fallen merely in an area of fifteen kilometers in diameter, we found the Telʿet as-Saʿîd and its vicinity entirely dead, covered with dry plants, the remains of an abundant pasture. At 10.50 we discovered a larger swale containing dry *ḫâfûr*, where we reposed. The camels ate this hay with relish. We clarified the water drawn at al-Čaʿačedi by making a pit in the clay, laying over it Tûmân's waterproof overcoat, and pouring into it the muddy water that it might settle and become clear. Then we tied the camels, gathered for each a heap of the dry *ḫâfûr*, and left it beside him. I examined the water bags again thoroughly before I retired, some time after midnight.

Tuesday, April 6, 1909. At 6.46 A. M. we were in the saddles again, riding in a west-southwesterly direction through the Telʿet as-Saʿîd (Fig. 50). Viewed from below, the slopes of all the valleys within the territory of al-Wudijân look as if they were artificially and evenly cut at an angle of 125°. They display horizontal layers of sandstone of uniform solidity and form the edges of immense, level plateaus. By the channel of Telʿet al-Mismâs we found much dry *jentûn,* which blacksmiths add to iron to make it softer; and we also saw dry *rûṯe, šubrum, šîḥ, slajča, šefallaḥ, ḳejṣûm, ǧeṯjâṯ, ḥaršaf, mšaʿ, čaff al-čalb, roṛejla, samna, erbijjân, riǧlet al-ṛurâb, žetâde,* etc.

At seven o'clock we had on our left the black rift of Ṯaṛab and the small pool Ṛadîr al-Mismâs.

Miz'el described to me the very different aspect of this region a year before, when there had been heavy rains here

FIG. 50—The Tel'et as-Sa'îd.

and everywhere flowed brooklets of water (*al-arẓ sâlat*), with abundant pasturage on all sides. He said the Rwala had camped near by; he pointed out to me the camps of the individual clans, even the locations of the individual tents, and related what had happened there. The Ṣḳûr, he said, attacked the Zejd clan of the Rwala, but were repulsed, surrounded, and lost one-third of their horses and almost one-half of their riding camels. According to Miz'el, the Rwala are invincible; theirs is the foremost place among all the tribes of northern Arabia. More than ten years previously the Fed'ân had also been powerful, but now all the 'Aneze and even the Šammar were somewhat dependent on the Rwala (*mâ lahom waǧh al-waǧh ṣâr lir-rwala*). When we came to the spot upon which the tent of Prince an-Nûri had been pitched, Miz'el recollected how he had baked truffles beside it and he even showed me the remains of the coals from the fire. According to him, truffles (*faḳaᶜ*) were abundant there a year earlier. He had gathered his mantle full of them one afternoon and in the evening presented them to an-Nûri, who gave one to each person present. Together they roasted them over the fire; even the Prince himself had fetched some butter, crumbled into it the baked truffles, and eaten them with relish. He said that gazelles dig the truffles from underneath the sand and enjoy eating them. Beside *faḳaᶜ*, according to Mizᶜel, mushrooms (*ṭaḳṭaḳ*) also grow under the sand. These are not edible but are used as a remedy for colds. Persons suffering with rheumatism dry them and smoke them in a pipe. Mizᶜel said he had left Prince an-Nûri's tent with two companions for the territory of the Muntefiž and after fifteen nights had arrived in the *aul* (blockhouse) of Ḳaṣr abu Ṛâr, which then was inhabited by Saᶜdûn al-Aškar. The few Ṣlejb (Ṣulbât) dwelling in Saᶜdûn's territory had killed a certain relative of Mizᶜel's, and he was on his way to get the blood price.

A strong, cold wind had arisen and the air again seemed to be swathed in innumerable veils of mist (*čitâm*). From 9.48 to 11.25 the camels grazed. At one o'clock we rode past the head of Čalb abu Munṭâr, north of the solitary, irregular cone of al-Munṭâr, and past many abandoned artificial reservoirs. These were about fifty meters long and twenty wide and were enclosed on three sides by high earthworks erected from the soil that had been dug out. In the past rain water used to gather in them, but now they are almost filled up with earth. The Bedouins of the present do not maintain the useful pools that were laboriously made by their predecessors. Both Ṭâreš and Mizᶜel asserted that all such artificial reservoirs were excavated by the Beni Taᶜâmer.

The rocky declivities we passed were gradually becoming lower, though they still appeared as if they were artificially shaped. North of us upon the upland we noted the Ḫabâri aṭ-Ṭuruḳ. The valley of al-Fâr abu-l-Aᶜwağ (or al-Aᶜwağ), in which we were riding, was getting wider and more shallow, and after three o'clock the ridges had dwindled into moderate swells within which originate the Riğl aṣ-Ṣâdjât, which converge in the Riğlet al-Fwêra. In the wide, shallow swales sand drifts were becoming more frequent: we had come to the ᶜÎṯa (pronounced ᶜEjṯe by the Ṣlejb), a tract which forms the boundary between al-Wudijân and al-Ḥamâd. The word *ᶜîṯa* means "covered with sand drifts." To the southwest there extended from south to north the long mesa of Ḳârat Lâha, at the northern end of which is a low dome. Under this is the Ḫabra Ḳrêʿat Maǧna, at which originates a *šeʿîb* of the same name. Towards the northwest extends a similar, still lower *ḳâra,* al-Metâha, from the northern slope of which comes Wâdi al-Ṛadaf, made by the uniting of the Šeʿibân al-Ṛdâf. On the right Wâdi al-Ṛadaf is joined by the Šeʿîb Awêseṭ abu Ḥamel, which extends from al-Metâha in a northerly direction along the western base of the Ḳârt al-Mahâd. At the northeastern base of al-Mahâd the Šeʿîb al-Ṛejde merges into al-Ṛadaf and east of it comes in the Šeʿîb al-Ṛwejde with the Riǧlet al-Muʿajjele. From 4.15 to 6.03 our camels grazed, and at 8.05 we encamped.

Wednesday, April 7, 1909 (temperature at 5: 9° C). As early as 5.03 A. M. we set out toward the west-southwest. On the left were several hills called Ḏembûḥ, where hunters look for ostriches. At the end of spring, when the Bedouins migrate to the fringe of the desert, the ostriches leave the Nefûd and the southern plains and revert to al-Ḥamâd and the western portion of al-Wudijân as far as the neighborhood of al-ʿElejjânijje and even as far as al-Ṛûṭa southeast of Damascus. While I was camping with an-Nûri south of ʿAḏra, his herdsman shot two ostriches there. In the fall (*ṣferi*) the ostriches return south again, where the Ṣlejb lie in wait for them. The Ṣlejb conceal themselves behind high piles of stone and upon sighting the ostriches endeavor to approach them against the wind.

From 8.55 to 10.45 we rested. To the southwest the horizon was obscured by the long, low Lâha, and to the west-northwest by the rose-hued Ḳârt al-Metâha, which the Ṣlejb call aš-Šîḥijje. At 11.45 we were crossing an upland covered with dark pebbles. The region is an enormous, undulating table-land with shallow valleys, moderate slopes, and vast levels covered with stones. These stretches are entirely barren except in the small swales and dips, where grow *ḳorẓi, rûṯe, žetâde, samna,* and *ḳerb* (or *ẖarrîṭ,* as the Ṣlejb call it). The highest point in Lâha[57] is the dome of

[57] Al-Bekri, *Muʿǧam* (Wüstenfeld), p. 97, writes that Ilâha is a table mountain in the desert of as-Samâwa of the Kalb tribe, situated on the boundary between the former territory of the Taṛleb tribe and Syria. — The term Lâha is paronymous with the classic Ilâha — or, as Jâḳût, *Muʿǧam* (Wüstenfeld), Vol. 1, p. 347, writes, al-Ulâha. It is of great importance that before the advent of Islâm the mountain is referred to as having formed the boundary between the territory of the Taṛleb tribe and Syria; from this it is evident that the territory of the Taṛleb reached as far as an-Neǧef and al-Ḥîra and also that Ilâha represented the farthermost boundary between the nomads who were subject to the Persians

al-Mešraf. The Ṣlejb say that the prophet Mohammed came as far as this and prayed at al-Mešraf. When the dome loomed out against an overcast sky, Miz'el greeted it thus:

"Allâh grant thee life, al-Mešraf! (*ḥajj al-mešraf, ḥajj, ḥajj, ḥajj!*)"

---

and those subject to the Romans. It marked the boundary between the Roman and the Persian empires.

Alfred von Kremer, *Gedichte des Labyd* (1881), p. 570, quotes a verse of an old commentary to the Koran: "We had come out of the desert Dahna' and made fast that Ilâha would approach us" (see Sprenger, *Moḥammed* [1869], Vol. 1, p. 289). — This "Ilâha" does not necessarily denote the sun; it may be an allusion to our upland of Lâha, toward which leads a road from ad-Dhana'. The Arabic *an ta'ûbâ* ("that . . . would approach us") recalls a custom of the Bedouins: upon perceiving from afar a range toward which they are heading, they cry out to it in supplication, beseeching it to extend its hand to them and to approach.

CHAPTER IX

LÂHA TO SKÂKA

LÂHA TO ʿENÂZA

Mizʿel was constantly ridiculing Ṭâreš, whom he called by no other name than the darling of beauties (*šowḳ az-zênât*), ironically inquiring why he had not married as yet. He boasted that he himself had been married sixteen times, although only thirty years of age. Eleven times he had married maidens (*banât*), and five times divorced women (*mâḫûḏât*). He enumerated these women to us by their names and in chronological order. Some of them had stayed with him only five to eight nights, then had left him without being divorced.

"It is not shame with us," he assured me, "if a woman leaves her spouse and marries another." For a longer time he kept with him a woman who bore him two boys and a girl; then, giving her twelve goats, he divorced her and married another, who bore him two girls and a boy. This boy was apparently a prodigy, and it was evident that Mizʿel loved him dearly; yet he said that he was going to divorce this woman also and take unto himself a younger one. He complained that during the last adverse years he had lost all his goats and so his family was without a source of livelihood and had not even milk. When I asked him how it could be that his family was in such a state when he was continually boasting of the valuable presents he had received from various chiefs for his poems — Saʿdûn al-Ašḳar having given him a mare a year ago and another chief a mount camel —, he replied that he had sold all these gifts to pay off his debts and had used the rest. Eight years ago, he said, one of the ʿAmârât chiefs had entrusted to his care twelve goats and twelve sheep, which he was to pasture. After three years the herd had multiplied to 132 head, which he delivered to the chief, receiving himself twenty-six of the animals for his work. Straightway, however, he was robbed of his animals by ʿAwde abu Tâjeh, chief of the Ḥwêṭât tribe, who was returning from an unsuccessful raid. He imprecated ʿAwde bitterly, saying that he who takes anything from a Ṣlubi commits the gravest injustice, for nobody from one heavenly horizon to the other has a right to appropriate any belongings of the Ṣlejb, who are themselves forbidden to steal anything from the Bedouins (*ʿalejna daʿwa an-neme min ṭâref as-seme elja ṭâref as-seme ḥelâlna ḥarâm ʿala-n-nâs wa ḥelâl an-nâs ḥarâm ʿalejna*). But all people are not alike (*an-nâs mâ hom wâḥed*), and all do not observe the precepts of Allâh.

Of all the chiefs he had ever met Mizʿel lauded most the deceased Ǧedʿân abu Ḳuṭne eben Mhejd, who, according to him, was very generous and prudent (*râʿi-l-karam wa-l-marǧale*). Of those still alive he praised most Fahad Bêč eben Haḏḏâl, head chief of the ʿAmârât and father of my friend Metʿeb. Fahad maintained three reservations for guests, one in the city of Kerbela, another in the settlement of Rezâza, and still another near his tenṭ. He served his guests every day with meat and always bestowed gifts upon them before their departure. In the opinion of Mizʿel, there was no ʿAneze chief who could equal him (*mâ bišjûḫ ʿaneze miṯleh alḥîn*).

Of the Rwala Mizʿel said that Šlâš ab-al-Hejjâl of the Zejd kindred was famous for his generosity. Once, when he was imprisoned by the Government in al-Mzêrîb, he ordered his men to encamp near and to send one camel daily to his guards. After twenty camels had been slaughtered in as many days, he was released. Once, when there was no water in the camp, there came to his father a certain Šarâri woman with a water bag, begging for a few mouthfuls. He referred her to his son Šlâš, who had her bag filled with butter and, after his slave had come with water, ordered him to fetch her immediately a whole bagful. Šlâš perished by a violent death. Becoming infatuated with the wife of a certain member of the Maʿabhel kindred, he sneaked after her into her tent, was caught in the act, and shot by the woman's spouse.

"Of the living Rwala the most generous is Fahad âl Mašhûr, but he has not the means (*ẓaʿîf*)," said Mizʿel.

At one o'clock we rode along the head of the *šeʿîb* of al-Maǧna, and at two o'clock passed the camel paths (*barârît* or *ǧwâd*) that lead to the Ḫabra Ḳrêʿat Maǧna.[58] In the

[58] Jâḳût, *Muʿǧam* (Wüstenfeld), Vol. 4, p. 432, mentions a station on the road from al-Kûfa to Syria of the name of Maḥna, — I read Maḥna as Maǧna and identify this station with our partially artificial rain pool of Maǧna. This is situated near the mesa of Lâha, and near it a road from Syria to al-Kûfa once led through the desert.

ground were numerous large holes, which Miz'el said were dug by an animal called *al-rorejri* in search of *ǧerbû'* and *ǧerdi* mice. From 3.44 to 6.08 the camels grazed. Afterwards we proceeded westward until 8.15, when we encamped in a large plain. I had no comfort even during the night for I could not get used to Miz'el's ash-colored lice. My garments were always full of the nits, and my skin was bitten until it bled.

Thursday, April 8, 1909 (temperature at 5: 7.2°C). Starting at 5.56 A.M. we headed toward the west until 6.43, when we let the camels graze till 7.20 in a shallow dip containing fresh plants of *ḳerb*. Ḳârat Lâha still remained in view to the southeast, apparently very desolate. At 7.45 we turned toward the northwest and crossed the head of the Še'ibân al-Ṛdâf, which trended toward the northeast, converging with the Awêseṭ abu Ḥamel.[59] On the right and toward the northeast, the plain ascends toward the wide upland of al-Metâha, which extends from west to east.

From ten to twelve o'clock we rested and then proceeded northwestward in a monotonous region whence rain water flows into Ḫabâri al-Ḥuwwa. Before us to the northwest a rosy, seemingly translucent belt formed by the mighty level crest of 'Enâza appeared to vibrate in the air. To the southwest we observed a huge dark blue lake containing clear transparent water, its shores lined with sprouting bushes. There were small bluish islands in the lake and beyond it what appeared to be a high mountain range. The outlines of the range, of the level shores, and of the islands were reflected distinctly in the water; but this entire enchanting panorama looked as if it were veiled, and it kept changing and vanishing. It was merely an optical illusion, teasing our nerves and inciting within us a longing for the verdant plains of our native land.

This part of al-Ḥamâd constitutes an immense, almost absolutely level plateau, strewn with flints and other calcareous concretions left from the erosion of overlying strata. These concretions rest upon a thin but very hard calcareous crust which is impervious to water. In places there are shallow, irregularly shaped pans or depressions, also filled with cal-

[59] Al-Aḫṭal, *Dîwân* (Salhani), pp. 41, 216, mentions Wâseṭ. In his comment (note b) Salhani asserts that Wâseṭ was a settlement west of the Euphrates opposite the city of ar-Raḳḳa near Ḳarḳîsija' and formerly was possessed by the Taṛleb tribe. — But the vicinity of ar-Raḳḳa is well known, and nowhere is there any mention of a settlement of the name of Wâseṭ. Possibly Wâseṭ denotes a camping ground of the Taṛleb tribe which may be identical with this valley.

careous concretions, which the run-off has covered with fine deposits of silt. Through chemical action these deposits have been cemented and now present smooth, somewhat slippery surfaces about half a meter below the general level of the surrounding plateau. Water, which accumulates in the depressions, is blown across them by the prevailing westerly winds, and in dry times the winds pile up accumulations of fine dust along the eastern edges. Hence it is on the eastern sides of the pans that the finest deposits of silt accumulate and the soil retains moisture the longest. Here annual and perennial plants take root forming meadows (*rijâẓ* or *rîẓân*). The tangled matting of roots catches the water seeping through the soil and for a while stimulates the growth of the *rijâẓ*, but as each *rowẓe* (sing. of *rijâẓ*) widens less and less water reaches its eastern margin. As a result the plants there dry up, wither, and revert to dust; and the soil, deprived of the support of the roots, is blown away by the wind or washed away by the run-off. Thus a *rowẓe* for a time grows on the western side and disappears on the eastern. Most of the *rijâẓ* are longer from north to south than from east to west, some of them being over 300 meters long by 200 meters wide.

After one o'clock we rode past many artificial reservoirs (*maḥâfîr*) and by 3.03 P. M. were passing through the Ḫabâri al-Ḥuwwa.[60]

At four o'clock we turned toward the north-northwest and from 5.35 until 7.10 we rested. When we started again my camel was unable to go on. She breathed with difficulty and kept stopping to rest. For fear she might collapse and be unable to get up any more, we had to encamp again at 8.22.

Friday, April 9, 1909. Because of the clouded sky on this day and the preceding day we were unable to ascertain the latitude. We were all cold, the water bags were frozen, and we had no winter underwear or good coverings with us. Besides, I was fearful about my camel. When we set out at 5.45 A. M. she was hardly able to rise and tottered long before she had sufficient strength to stand firmly on her legs. At 6.20, when we reached the base of the mesa of ʿEnâza, we had to stop, for she knelt down and would not get up again (temperature at 6.45: 6.2° C). Ṭâreš seared her with a piece of heated iron above the tail and between the front legs. He said that she was suffering from consti-

[60] Jâḳût, *op. cit.*, Vol. 2, p. 371, refers to an al-Ḥuwwa in the territory of the Kalb, which I identify with these rain pools.

pation and that searing was the best remedy. After it grew a little warmer we gave the camel ten liters of water, which helped. A few minutes later she began to graze.

ʿENÂZA TO ḪABRA ʿARÛS

Tûmân and I ascended the crest of ʿEnâza, seated ourselves behind a heap of stones that was piled upon the highest point, and sketched a map of the entire vicinity. ʿEnâza[61] extends from the south toward the north, rising some twenty to thirty-five meters higher than the surrounding country.

To the north rose the wide, hilly belt of an-Neẓâjem, to the east loomed the two domes of Nhejdejn, and on the northeast the upland was enclosed by the Ḳârt al-Ṛidf. Farther to the north a boundless, undulating plain stretched from west to east. On the southeast the horizon was obscured by the table-shaped belt of Lâha, while to the southwest, peering like a hideous monster between the low clouds beyond the white Ḳwêrât al-ʿEnûz, glowered the black volcano Umm Wuʿâl and south of it the lower Ktejft al-Ḥanǧar, which mark the northeastern boundary of the volcanic region. Below us, starting from the shallow channels upon the eastern slope of ʿEnâza, Wâdi Ḥawrân trended northeastward, receiving on the left al-Ḫalli, which approaches it from the Ḫabra al-Mčêmen and Ḫabâri Zênât al-Maʾ, which in turn originate at the Ḳârt an-Neẓâjem. Farther to the east, at the boulder of Ruẓumat ar-Rwejje, which is worshiped by the Ṣlejb, the Šeʿibân aṭ-Ṭarfât converge with Wâdi Ḥawrân. In the lower portion of aṭ-Ṭarfât the watering place Ḳulbân al-Ǧidd,[62] with the wells al-Ḳaṣîr, aṭ-Ṭawîl, and aš-Šellâle, is situated near the valley of aṭ-Ṭrêfâwi, which originates in the Ḫabâri aṭ-Ṭabʿât.

In the ravine Riǧlet ar-Rwêḥel, which joins Wâdi Ḥawrân on the left, coming from the Ḫabra Ḳṭajje, there also are wells, aṣ-Ṣbejḥât; these, however, lose their water when it does not rain for a long period. When they contain water, they are among the most dangerous spots in the desert; for all the raiding and robbing parties take the route near them. The channels of al-Ṛadfet ummu Nhejdejn, Awdijet al-ʿAlâwijje, and ar-Raḳḳâṣi, which rise in the Ḳârt al-Ṛidf and wind by the western slope of the Ḳârt ar-Raḳḳâṣi, converge and join the Wâdi Ḥawrân on the right. In the Šeʿîb ar-Raḳḳâṣi is a small pool, Barčet aṭ-Ṭrejfâwi. The Riǧlet al-Jenṯûlijje winds along the eastern base of the Ḳârt ar-Raḳḳâṣi and merges with Wâdi Ḥawrân on the right.

[61] Al-Aḫṭal, *op. cit.*, p. 170, mentions the grazing ground in the vicinity of ʿUnâza. Al-Bekri, *Muʿǧam* (Wüstenfeld), p. 671, holds that it is located in the territory of the Taṛleb tribe. — The classic ʿUnâza is pronounced in the dialect as ʿEnâza. It is situated in the former territory of the tribe of Taṛleb, of which, with the belt of Ilâha, it apparently marked the western frontier.

[62] Jâḳût, *op. cit.*, Vol. 2, p. 39, says that al-Ǧudd is a water in Mesopotamia mentioned by al-Aḫṭal, who tells us (*Dîwân* [Salhani], pp. 52, 81, 247) that the Taṛleb liked to camp there in the early summer. — Arabic writers call al-Ǧezîre (Mesopotamia) not only the region between the middle Euphrates and Tigris, but also the eastern half of north Arabia west of the Euphrates. As our watering place is situated in that territory, which formerly belonged to the Taṛleb, I identify it with Aḫṭal's al-Ǧudd.

From the Ḳûr ʿEjârât the ravine ar-Raṭba, which joins Wâdi Ḥawrân in the plain of an-Nâẓra at the wells of the same name, runs toward the north. As noted above (p. 75), northeastward in the Ḳârt an-Neẓâjem originates the *šeʿîb* of al-Waleǧ, later called aṣ-Ṣwâb, which, like Wâdi Ḥawrân, makes its way down to the Euphrates. West of the crest of ʿEnâza the run-off flows through the valleys of ar-Rwêšdât into the lowland of Manḳaʿ ar-Raḥba on the edge of the Ḥawrân territory. Therefore ʿEnâza marks the most important divide of Arabia Deserta.

At 8.52 we resumed the march southward, homeward toward the camp of an-Nûri. Our hurriedly improvised emergency water bag stood the test well. The water stayed clear, was free from odor, and did not evaporate as rapidly as that in the two leather bags. The cover resisted all friction and even seemed to grow tougher and more rigid. At 11.30 we reached the spur of Ḥmâr ʿEnâza, where Ṭâreš, following Mizʿel's example, likewise began to sing. He knew we were bound for the camp of an-Nûri where he would get his wages and perhaps even a reward; that is why he felt like singing. But Mizʿel was not pleased. He wanted us to listen to him alone; for he was a real poet, while Ṭâreš could do nothing but sing the songs or repeat the verses of others. Therefore he began to ridicule him:

"There is no singer like thee, O Ṭâreš, and there is not as handsome a man among all the Dahâmše as thou art. Any beautiful woman would be proud of thee. Thy voice reminds me of the squeaking of the water wheels by the Euphrates and in thy dainty face any toothless old woman may see herself."

From 11.48 to 1.35 P.M. we rested. At 5.10 we were overtaken west of the Ḫabâri aš-Šrûzijje by a snow flurry with rain. *Al-ḥamdu lillâh* that it lasted only a short while, but during the night the thermometer dropped below zero (Centigrade).

Saturday, April 10, 1909. In the morning (temperature at 6.30 A. M.: 2.1° C) we set up the theodolite as best we could with our stiff hands and determined the latitude. My small water bag was frozen so hard that we had to warm it by the fire in order not to break it. Setting out at 6.46 we noted to the northwest the low hills Ḳwêrât al-ʿEnûz, on the southwestern fringes of which is situated the Ḫabra ʿAnḳa, while on the eastern side extends a valley within which are the rain pools Ṛadîr aš-Šejḫ and Ṛadîr al-Ḫejl. This hilly district is bordered on the south by the hollow al-Ḫôr (or al-

Ḫawr). At the southern base of ʿEnâza is situated the Ḫabra an-Nûḳ, and west of it in al-Ḫôr are the Ḫabâri Bardwîl. To the east, about midway between us and the mesa of Lâha, glistened the yellow-white surfaces of the Maḥâfîr and Ḫabâri aẓ-Ẓuhejrijjât. At 8.16 we rode by the rain pools of Umm Ṭarfaʾ. After ten o'clock we crossed trodden paths leading westward toward the Ḫabra al-Bḳara in al-Ḫôr.

From 11.04 until one o'clock our camels grazed in the region of the Ḫabâri al-Haǧm. The sky became completely overcast and a strong wind blew the clouds; here and there strips of rain were noticeable. The high humidity made the cold the more unbearable. I had not suffered so much from cold on any of my previous expeditions as I did on this one; and yet the Prince had encouraged me by saying it would be hot! The cold and the icy wind lasted throughout the day and night. Our camels were shivering as much as we were and were losing flesh perceptibly. Water and a warmer region were still far to the south, many days distant, and only Allâh knew whether our animals would hold out so long. If they should collapse, we too should have to perish. When the day was misty and the night dark, Mizʿel could not determine the direction and hence the leading was left to me — as it had been ever since we left al-Čaʿačedi. It was a weary task, for I had to be constantly on the alert, scanning the ground before us to discover any minute objects lying in our path — not so easy a thing to do in the level, monotonous plain.

At two o'clock we reached the wide crest of al-Ḳaʿasa; at 2.36 P. M. we crossed the western spur of the mighty crest of Šarâwa and passed nine artificial reservoirs. These were surrounded by dams over five meters high and thus were protected comparatively well from wind; therefore the water in them could be preserved for several months and might last until summer. Now all of these *maḥâfîr* (artificial reservoirs) are filled with earth, but they could easily be cleaned. The Prince had asked me to look out for wells in the Ḥamâd; these artificial reservoirs, if cleaned out, would serve him for wells. But an-Nûri was a Bedouin and as such had no comprehension of the benefit of work of this sort.

From four to 5.45 we prepared and had our supper and then rode until 7.50. In the homeland the bells were ringing, everything was jubilant over the resurrection of the Savior; and here were we, alone, forsaken! Forsaken? Allâh was with us and we were traveling under His protection. *Hallelûjâh!*

Sunday, April 11, 1909. We nearly froze throughout the night; it was impossible to get warm. We could not build a fire that was not likely to be seen by enemies or robbers, and we had no clothes or coverings to keep out the cold (temperature at 5.30 A. M.: 5.8° C). At 6.05 we plodded south-southeastward. On the left there extended from north to south the wide crest of Šarâwa, near which are situated the Ḫabâri al-Brejčât and az-Zhejrijje. West of us loomed the mighty slope of as-Saddja, while between it and ourselves rose the still higher hills of al-Ḳaʿasa. At 6.50, discerning to the east the Ḫabra al-Barḳ, we turned toward the south-southeast, or, as Mizʿel expressed it, turned toward the Southern Nose from the left side.

Both the Bedouins and the Ṣlejb think that at each of the earth's four corners there is, far beyond the horizon, a high mountain, half of which rests upon the land while the other half is immersed in the sea. These mountains slope precipitously toward the sea, while toward the land they project in sharp spurs, each called a nose (*ḫašm*). Upon these four principal world mountains rests the sky. During the rainy season the spirits — nay, even Allâh — like to dwell near the southern mountain — which is called *aš-šerḳ* — because it is located in the inner desert; in summer they move to the northern mountain (*jeṛarrebow*).

At 8.10 we had at our left five artificial reservoirs, Maḥâfîr al-Ḳaʿasi; from 8.35 until 10.32 we rested at the eastern edge of the slope of al-Ḳaʿasa. At eleven o'clock we were east of the Ḫabra ʿAṣda and for the first time saw to the southwest the whole of the mighty giant ʿAmûd. First we sighted one pinnacle of it, then a second, then a third, until finally we had in view the entire extinct volcano. From 11.10 to 11.25 we stopped for the purpose of determining the exact direction in which it lay. Mizʿel persistently deviated toward the east; but I refused to follow him, adhering to my belief that the settlement of Skâḳa was located where we had determined it to be. I held that to be sure of reaching it without deviation we must keep the direction somewhat to the left of south.

"What do we care for the door (*bâb*) or direction (*ṣowb*)? Whoever would get anywhere must watch the landmarks

(*ʿalâmât*), for every region has its more frequented routes (*kill arẓ laha mamša*)." Mizʿel was loath to follow me and tried to coax Ṭâreš not to expose himself to certain peril.

At twelve o'clock there appeared to the northeast rosy mounds hedging in the artificial pools of Brejčât al-Mraʾ and Brejčet ummu Ḥsejje. The gravel that covered the plains was becoming coarser and coarser and began to be mixed with lava and basalt, a proof that the volcanic region reached deep into the Ḥamâd. It had not completely overwhelmed this region, but like an army of occupation it had thoroughly fortified the subjugated district. On the right, from the northwest toward the southeast and thence toward the southwest, we saw rows of black lava colossi situated at regular intervals and thus resembling the battlements of a fort. Farthest to the north loomed Ktejft al-Ḫôr and Ktejft al-Ḥanǧar and, south of them, Zellâḳa, the dark, somber ʿAmûd, and the group of ar-Rḥaʾ. Each is connected with the other by a wall of black lava fifteen to twenty meters high, with precipitous slopes, trenches, and wide earthworks. This volcanic formation was enshrouded in heat waves which made it look as if it were swimming in a sea. Tell ʿAmûd forms the southeastern corner of the volcanic region (*ḥarra*), but one of its salients reaches much farther east into al-Ḥamâd. This, however, is nothing more than a lava flow from ʿAmûd, merely a black claw imbedded forever in the yellow clay.

From 3.28 P. M. until 5.05 the camels grazed east of the Ḫabra al-Bowbehi. It seemed to us that the yellow clay at the Tell ʿAmûd reached almost to the base of the volcano; but, as a matter of fact, to the northwest and southwest the first lava flow had formed a low, wide platform in front of the wall of lava built up by subsequent outpourings. At 6.15 we reached the Ḫabra ʿArûs and at 7.10 made camp for the night. As the sky had partly cleared, we were able to determine the latitude.

ḪABRA ʿARÛS TO RIǦLET AL-BDENE

Monday, April 12, 1909. When we set out at 5.27 A. M. the entire western sky was overhung with dark grayish clouds which touched the summit of the as-Šhami volcano, while in the east an enormous dark circle was formed by the wide, level crest of an-Nedûf. Later in the day the strong west wind drove before it clouds of dust and sand (*ʿaǧâǧ*) which obstructed the view and caused some small birds to press themselves to the ground in fear. So like the sand were they that they could not be distinguished from their background. Where the gravel is black or brown, the birds likewise are dark-colored, almost black; whereas in the yellow Ḥamâd they are yellowish-gray. Even the hares of the Ḥamâd have a light brown, almost yellow, fur, whereas the fur of those in the volcanic region is dark brown. Above us circled several eagles and a hawk. Were they waiting for us? Would they feast upon our flesh? *Sitrak jâ rabb!*

At 7.20 we reached the spur of lava that extends from ʿAmûd toward the east, looming about fifty meters above the surrounding country. The march in the lava was very hard for our camels; hence I endeavored to use the narrow camel paths (*mutribe*) as often as they led in our direction. Mizʿel and Ṭâreš did not like the paths and continued to drive their burdened animals through the all-but-impassable lava. Again and again I warned them to keep in the path and when I realized that they deviated from it intentionally, I threatened to force him who would not obey to dismount his camel and walk.

"Thou shalt not do that," retorted Ṭâreš rudely.

"And who is there to prevent me?" I asked, turning toward him with a loaded revolver in my hand. My native companions had been worrying me ever since we left ʿEnâza. They had evidently agreed between themselves to do everything they knew would exasperate or hinder me. Tûmân and I had to watch them day and night to see that they did not run away with the supplies and the camels. They would not help us with any of the work, they stole from our provisions anything that was edible, they hid articles of our clothing in their saddles, and they tormented the animals whenever they could find the slightest pretext. The real instigator was the Ṣlubi Mizʿel, who was angry with me because I did not let him have his own way unreservedly and because I had proved that he did not know the Ḥamâd. He was at home in the district of al-Wudijân where he had dwelt most of his life, but in the Ḥamâd he was a stranger. As I had explored the western and northern part of the Ḥamâd and had drawn a map of the eastern fringe of the region according to the testimony of various reliable men, I was in a position to judge whether he was right or wrong and could prove his error immediately whenever any of his statements were wrong. He asked very frequently:

"Why askest thou me, since thou knowest?"

"Before the Prince thou hast claimed to me that thou knowest the Ḥamâd like the palm of thy hand; the same thou hast repeated in al-Wudijân, and for this thy knowledge thou hast demanded one *meǧîdijje* (90 cents) a day. Am I to believe thy fabrications without being permitted to make inquiries of thee? What will the Prince say? What will the Arabs say after they hear how Aḫu Zaʿêla has conducted himself on this journey?"

At 8.55 it began to rain and we halted to protect our baggage. The eagles and the hawk were still circling above us. I shot down the latter. Mizʿel called it *hdejje* and suggested that I throw it away because its beak was curved. A bird with such a beak should not be eaten by anybody, he sneered.

"Thou mayest eat a lizard, though?" I retorted, taking the dead hawk. During our noon rest Tûmân and I baked it in ashes and ate it. Ṭâreš would have liked a piece, but Mizʿel would not let him touch it. As the rain soon ceased and our camels were in need of pasture, we resumed the journey at 9.30. We crossed the edge of the lava spur, in which were several small depressions and small rain pools (*ḫabâri*), and from 10.16 to 12.02 P. M. we stayed between the Ḫabâri al-Arnabijjât and Ummu Ǧdejr, west of the head of the valley of al-Obejjeẓ.

It was drizzling and the storm (*ʿaǧâǧ*) was not abating. Gradually the rain became heavier, until finally it poured. Mizʿel wanted us to halt and camp. It was impossible to consent to the suggestion, however, as we were within a lowland in which the water flowing on the surface of the ground would have soaked our baggage through, whereas the baggage could be saved from the surface run-off as long as it remained loaded on the camels. It was not until 1.48, when we had come to a small rise, that I made my animal kneel. As soon as I had jumped off the saddle, the camel rose and ran to the nearest puddle where she drank long draughts.

When Mizʿel and Ṭâreš, who had deliberately been lingering far behind, came up, they immediately unloaded all the baggage and wanted to proceed with preparations for the night. The rain soon ceased, however, and the sun appeared; therefore, as soon as the camels had finished drinking, I ordered the baggage to be loaded again and at 2.10 we proceeded. Before our departure Tûmân and I had ladled water from the puddles to replenish our supply. Miz^cel sneered, declaring we should find plenty of water in the *ḫabâri* and that we surely should reach Skâka early tomorrow morning. According to his earlier statements, we were to be in that settlement Monday before noon; now he declared that it would be Tuesday morning and tried to persuade Ṭâreš not to help me any more, since Skâka was so near.

At three o'clock, as we found a considerable quantity of *mḥarût* and some *rûṯe, šefallaḥ, ʿalanda, ǧaʿada, čḥejl an-naʿâm,* and *ḳejṣûm* we halted until 4.45. Tûmân and I prepared supper for ourselves. Mizʿel and Ṭâreš would not do any work for us; but Mizʿel had built for himself out of wood — mainly *rûṯe* — a high wall behind which he proposed to find protection from the wind and perhaps from rain. When he noticed that we were eating, he asked for his supper.

"Here is flour, peeled wheat (*burṛul*), butter, and tea," I answered. "If thou wouldst have supper, bake thine own bread, cook thy *burṛul,* and thou shalt get also the tea and butter; but make haste, for we shall proceed on with the evening (*nasri*)."

When he was convinced that we would not give him any of our supper, he set to work, assisted by Ṭâreš, while I watched the camels. After he had the *burṛul* cooked, Tûmân poured plenty of butter upon it for him, and Mizʿel took the spoon, as usual, to stir the butter in; but I noticed, as I had noticed for ten consecutive days before, that he left the butter on one side and later put it all upon his own plate with his portion of *burṛul.* After he had prepared both plates and was about to begin eating, I told him he must wait until Ṭâreš had made the camels kneel, and when the latter came up I handed him the plate upon which Mizʿel had put his own supper. Mizʿel understood my motive and refused even to touch the *burṛul.* Ṭâreš, on the contrary, praised it, saying that he never had had such a good supper. When he learned the reason for the good taste of that particular supper, he was very angry with Mizʿel, attacked him, and yelled that he would rip his abdomen open because he had deprived him for so many days of his fat. Thus I estranged the conspirators and secured Ṭâreš for myself.

We were going along the western spurs of Ḥazm al-Ǧelâmîd, overlooking the sources of the Riǧlet al-Bdene, which joins Wâdi ʻArʻar. West of us extended a large plain, Shîl ʻÂmer, bordered on the north by the volcanic district of ar-Rḥaʼ and Mečâmen ar-Rḥaʼ and on the west by the hills of al-Ṛarâjes, the isolated volcanic groups of aṯ-Ṯâjât, and the hills of al-Mefrežijje. East of the Ḫašm al-Ṛarâjes in the plain of Shîl ʻÂmer are situated the Ḫabâri Masḥa, east of which are the Ḫabâri al-Mḥâṣ, and east of the latter the Ḫabra Ṛaraḳa. At 5.25 Ṭâreš pointed out to me the battle ground where his chief Eben Meǧlâd was defeated by the Ḳaʻâžʻa clan two years before. He had made a raid against them, was repulsed and surrounded, and had lost all his riding camels. At six o'clock we passed the head of the Riǧlet al-Bdene and at 7.20 camped for the night in a small depression to the east of it.

RIǦLET AL-BDENE TO SKÂKA

Tuesday, April 13, 1909. Ṭâreš now helped us willingly with the loading; Mizʻel was left to himself. At 5.35 (temperature at 5.30 A. M.: 4.2° C) we broke camp and from 6.38 until 7.02 remained in a *rowẓe*[63] overgrown with grasses, upon which our camels fed with eagerness. From 8.20 until 10.20 we rested east of the Ḫabâri Masḥa.

Going southeast, we crossed the fresh tracks of eleven asses belonging to Ṣlejb bound from the south-southeast to the northwest to ar-Rwêšdât. Mizʻel praised the asses raised by his kinsmen, who breed both thoroughbred and common beasts. The former are tall animals of white color, more rapid and of more endurance on the road than the best mare, and are called *šihri* (pl. *šihâra*). The common asses are dark and are called *ḥeḳri* (pl. *ḥeḳâra*), a yearling of this breed being known as *ḥawli* (pl. *ḥawâli*). The general name for asses is *ǧeḥaš* (pl. *aǧḥâš*) or *ḥemâr* (pl. *ḥamîr* or *ḥamârât* and *ḥemrân*). In summer an ass can go two days without water. The Ṣlejb sell them at Bagdad and Damascus, but the asses do not last long in the city, for they miss their accustomed fodder and the pure air of the desert. I have heard that as

[63] See above, pp. 259—260.

late as a hundred years ago there were wild asses roaming in aš-Šâma near the depression of Sirḥân, where they had an abundance of water and, in the volcanic district, good pasture and still better hiding places. It is said that the last wild ass was shot at the wells of al-Ṛamr, southeast of the lake of al-Azraḳ. Old Ḥmâr told stories of his grandfather's hunts for wild asses near the depression of Sirḥân; but since firearms have come to be used by the Bedouins wild asses have become less and less numerous. They are still to be found in al-Ğezîre, between the middle Euphrates and Tigris, whence the Ṣlejb often bring asses for breeding purposes.

The ground we were treading consisted of reddish clay mixed with dark stones. Rain water carries the soil to the *rijâẓ*, but the stones remain lying where they were, covering the levels and thus giving the landscape a dreary aspect. In the east the horizon was obscured by the long, flat crest of the Ḥazm al-Ğelâmîd (Fig. 51), to the west of which the undulating plain is called al-Ḥamâd, and to the east the plateau furrowed by deep valleys and ravines is named al-Wudijân.[64]

At two o'clock we had on the left the Ḥabra ŭmm Ṣeda' and were passing through the Riğl ad-Dwêẖlât, which extend between the Ḥazm al-Ğelâmîd and the Ḥazm Zellûm to the Riğlet al-Aḳraʿ and then, joining the latter, reach Wâdi ʿArʿar. Through the opening of al-Aḳraʿ we had a glimpse to the southeast of an endless, gray, undulating region that falls away toward the west in a fifty-meter slope called Ḥazm Zellûm. To the west protruded from the plain the black group of at-Ṯâjât volcanoes, south of which originates the *šeʿîb* of al-Ḳutb, winding in the stony plain Siḥle Ẓalma toward the southwest into the depression of Sirḥân.

At 3.21, between the Ḥabâri aṭ-Ṭawsijjât and the Ḥabra Ṛaraḳa, we again found a considerable quantity of *mḥarût* and hence we remained there until 5.02. The leaves of this plant are a greenish vermilion in color and look as if they were covered with a white veil; the blossoms grow in yellow clusters, the root is long, black, and as thick as one's hand. The new plant emits a peculiar odor, which also emanates

[64] An-Naṣr (Jâḳût, *Muʿğam* [Wüstenfeld], Vol. 1, p. 398; Abu-l-Faḍâ'il, *Marâṣid* [Juynboll], Vol. 1, pp. 100 f.) refers to al-Awda' as the region intersected by many valleys between al-Kûfa and Syria. Others give the name Awdât al-Kalb to the numerous valleys extending from the lengthy ridge of al-Malḥa eastward, while the valleys trending westward are called al-Bijâḍ. — The last-named region is identical with the present district of al-Bijâẓ north of the oasis of Dûmat al-Ğandalijje. Al-Malḥa is to be sought in the Ḥazm al-Ğelâmîd. Al-Awda' and al-Awdât are different forms of the word *wâdi* in the plural, just as is *wudijân*.

from camels after they have grazed long upon it. The Bedouins drive milch camels away from it as it would also give their milk the unpleasant smell. At first camels enjoy the *mḥarût* but soon they seek *rûṯe* or *šîḥ*. The night was bright and

FIG. 51—The Ḥazm al-Ǧelâmîd from the east.

warm. I should have liked to ride on, but the animals were worn out; therefore at 7.25 we stopped for the night at the head of the valley of aš-Šwejḥeṭ.

Wednesday, April 13, 1909 (temperature at 5.15 A. M.: 4.1° C). We were on the road at 5.31. The landscape was ever the same: level swells, wide valleys that were shallow at first and deepened gradually toward the southeast, coarse gravel and long, narrow, grassy strips (*rijâẓ*). We followed the right side of the wide valley of aš-Šwejḥeṭ, with the precipitous slope of the Ḥazm Zellûm rising over one hundred meters high on the left. To the southeast, east of Ḳwêrât ar-Rijetên, we noted the relatively high mountain of aẓ-Ẓabʿ. From 6.43 to 7.15 the camels grazed on fresh annuals, which were to be found in ever-increasing quantities in the *rijâẓ*. From eight to 9.27 we again halted in a depression where there was a luxuriant growth of *baḫatri, ḥenwa, ḫomṣân, šiḳḳâra, mḥarût,* and *rûṯe*. The clay in this depression is not yellow or reddish as farther north, but white and it is intermingled with large white stones; therefore the territory is called al-Bijâẕ (white lands).[65]

At 11.40 we discerned far ahead and below us the mesas Ḳûr al-Žijâl. The plain of the Ḥamâd ceases abruptly, falling almost perpendicularly more than fifty meters into a basin in which are numerous large and small hills of all conceivable shapes. The eye may perceive low and high pyramids, domes, cones, tarbooshes, etc. I was most attracted by a mighty cupola resembling a huge rotunda; to the west there extends from west to east a hill, the top of which appears to have been trimmed off horizontally with an irregular cone resting on the east side of it. None of these hills are higher than the neighboring plateau. Southeast of the irregular cone runs a line of hills called Umm al-Mežâber, within which there is said to be an old cemetery, which may, according to a description given to me at the settlement of Skâka, be a Nabataean burial ground. The sepulchers are reported to be in groups connected by subterranean passages, through which one may walk some distance under the ground among the rocks. I was told that there were still a few remains of old structures in this ancient burial ground, but I found it impossible to visit it. On my way to Skâka I was unaware of its existence and from Skâka it was altogether inaccessible.

At twelve o'clock we reached the edge of the rolling upland of al-Bijâẕ (Fig. 52). To our left, barely five hundred meters distant across a gully, stood two gazelles, staring at us curiously. Perhaps they knew there was no danger, since a deep ravine yawned between them and us. Leading our camels and running with them by leaps, in twelve minutes we were down in the valley that winds among al-Žijâl.[66]

We stayed in al-Žijâl until 12.33 P.M. (temperature at 12: 26.3°C); then we began to follow the valley which gradually

[65] Al-Hamdâni, *Ṣifa* (Müller), p. 131, writes that there is a road from Tejma northward through the territory of the D̲ubjân tribe to the district of al-Bijâḍ and to the Ḥawrân. The Kalb are said to have camped with the D̲ubjân in the district of ʿUrâʿir. Whoever goes through the territory of the Kalb to the east of the Ḥawrân, first through the desert of as-Samâwa and later through ad-Dahna, will come to the palm orchards by the Euphrates without having met any other tribesmen except the Kalb. —

Al-Bijâḍ is identical with our al-Bijâẕ, a district extending to the northwest as far as the southern projections of the Ḥawrân. I seek ʿUrâʿir within the district of al-ʿArejʿerijje, which formed the western frontier of the Kalb's territory in the earlier days. Whoever goes from the Ḥawrân southeastward will cross the entire former district of as-Samâwa and the northwestern corner of the sand desert of ad-Dhana and will see between al-Kûfa and al-Baṣra the palm orchards of Irak.

[66] Al-Bekri, *Muʿǧam* (Wüstenfeld), p. 757, and Jâḳût, *Muʿǧam* (Wüstenfeld), Vol. 4, p. 26, refer to a Ḳijâl near Dûmat al-Ǧandal. Abu-l-Fatḥ ʿOt̲mân ibn Ǧinni (Jâḳût, *loc. cit.*), who died in the year 392 A.H. (1001—1002 A.D.), also places Ḳijâl in this same vicinity. — Our al-Žijâl is certainly identical with this Ḳijâl.

widened and terminated in a large *ḥabra*. After two o'clock we rode south-southwestward through a rocky district covered with sand, the hills consisting of two layers of sandstone, one bluish, the other crimson, and the soil around them composed of rosy or white sand in which stood the gray-green shrubs

FIG. 52—Plain of al-Bijâẓ from the south.

of *ḳorẓi* and the bright green *ṣollejân*. The sun sent down its scorching rays, tinging everything with a singular hue that would have gladdened the heart of a painter. But I could not remain to wonder long at these charms of nature, for I had to seek the most easily passable places for my camels in a region made difficult to traverse by reason of innumerable jagged crags. From 2.22 to 2.52 we were forced to pause to let the camels rest; then we rode on until 5.50, when we encamped east of the basin of Nejsûba (temperature at 6: 20° C). A storm was approaching, and the night was so utterly dark that it was impracticable to think of going ahead. We had consumed our last drop of water that morning!

Thursday to Sunday, April 15 to 18, 1909. Distressed with thirst, we left our camp at 4.25 and rode south-southeastward, later southeastward in many dry *ḥabâri* hedged by red sandstone crags. A multitude of camel paths led to them and I followed one that ran in our direction. Miz'el did not care whether he kept the route or rode over the crags and thus he wore out his camel, which could go no farther. My admonitions were of no avail and were even met with derision. Finally I said to him.

"Get off and walk."

"Render me my wages and I will get off." He stopped his animal and I was preparing to pay him, when Ṭâreš warned me:

"Not now, O Sheikh; wait till the sun rises."

As soon as the sun appeared Mizʿel was paid off. At first he would not accept his wages, explaining that the Prince had hired him "from his tent to his tent." Finally he took the money, but he mounted the camel again, and thus we rode on.

ARRIVAL AND SOJOURN AT SKÂKA

At seven o'clock the palms of the oasis of Skâka came into view, to our inexpressible joy. We had not strayed, and here before us were water, food, rest, and security. Our jubilation did not last long, however. A shot snapped forth, then another, and I perceived several men from the settlement running toward us. As they approached, I saw that they carried rifles. What was going on? Were not the inhabitants of Skâka friends of the Rwala? The Prince had told me to visit Skâka upon our return and inquire there for the location of his camp. Ahead of the men five youths were running. When they came within thirty meters of us, they put their rifles to their shoulders, took aim, and then walked leisurely toward us. Mizʿel greeted them but received no reply. Their leader, a man about twenty-five years old with a sympathetic face, which, however, bore a trace of cruelty, asked roughly:

"Who are you?"

Ṭâreš and Mizʿel informed him shortly. Scornfully looking at Mizʿel, the leader decided:

"Thou art a Ṣlubi. The Ṣlejb are our enemies, and I know not the Bedouin (meaning Ṭâreš) and do not believe that ye speak truth. If ye would save your necks, surrender and follow me; if not, we will shoot ye."

Meanwhile the others had surrounded us and now they led us in their midst into the settlement. In front of the house of the chief Raǧaʾ eben Mwejsil — for this was the name of the youthful leader — we were compelled to stop and force our camels to kneel. I wanted to drive immediately to water, but they pulled me off the saddle. The chief ordered his men to bring all our baggage into his house immediately. When I protested and begged that he would first listen while I explained, he smiled kindly, hit me in the chest, and seized my carbine; whereupon two of his men seized me from the back, and an old woman — later I learned that she was his mother — jeered at me and spat in my face. I had to look on while they carried away my baggage, unsaddled the camels, and drove them through a narrow gate into a long passage. Then they dragged me into the square yard, where they shoved me into a large room, which soon filled with men. They pressed upon me and showered me with questions, but I made no answer. Just then Mizʿel leaped into the room.

"Who are ye?" one of those present asked him.

"Who are we?" Mizʿel repeated the question. "Hear ye, men of Skâka, hear ye my answer;" and he began to recite a poem which described how he had come to Prince an-Nûri and asked his permission to accompany me and told by what routes we had come to Skâka.

"All that is a lie. He is a poet and a poet always lies," said the men in reply to his efforts.

Sometime after, Raǧaʾ, the chief, came in and invited Tûmân and me to follow him. He led us to a room on the first floor of the house, which was built of adobe, and began to question us. Indignant at such treatment, I warned him to beware the wrath of Prince an-Nûri and of Nawwâf, his son, the master of Skâka. He replied that his men might have shot me and that I should thank Allâh for being safe, for having fallen into his hands; for had I been seen by the Ḳreše — the inhabitants of the northern part of Skâka, who were at war with the Rwala — they surely would have killed me. I laughed at his words scornfully and maintained that I had no fear of the Ḳreše clan or of his own men, as powerful avengers stood behind me. My haughtiness surprised him and he inquired calmly whether I was really the Sheikh Mûsa who marched with an-Nûri.

"Why dost thou ask me, O Raǧaʾ? Thou knowest well who I am. There were standing in front of thy house eight or ten men, of whom some had seen me in al-Ǧowlân, others in al-Ṛûṭa, in the depression of Sirḥân, in al-Ǧowf, and also in al-Ḳâra. I am sure they recognized me and told thee that

I had lived for eight months with Prince an-Nûri, and I know that thou hast ordered them to keep silence."

"I?"

"Aye, thou, O Raǧa'."

"Well, I do not believe them."

"Neither believest thou me because thou wilt not believe."

"Aye, I must convince myself. I shall send a letter to an-Nûri that he may verify by his seal that thou art the Sheikh Mûsa."

"I can now show thee a letter with the seal of Prince an-Nûri affixed."

"No, no, he must write me."

He summoned his scribe and dictated to him a letter for Prince an-Nûri, which Miz'el was to deliver. Raǧa' said that an-Nûri was watering his camels at al-Ḳâra and that Miz'el could reach him that very day. Miz'el was reluctant, but Raǧa' took away from him the wages I had paid him and declared that he should not have his money until he returned with an-Nûri's reply.

Meantime, down below, the men who had captured us (*ahadûna*) were arguing about the division of the spoils. Each one wished to take his share home with him at once. Raǧa' listened. After a while he said, his eyes glittering like those of a leopard:

"Hear thou, shall I give thee over to them? Open thy door lest I do so. What wilt thou give me? Give me thy revolver."

"I will give it to thee if thou wilt permit me to load my camels at once and march onward."

"Thou shalt see but good from me (*'ajjen al-hejr*). The revolver belongs to me, then. What else wilt thou give me? Garments, money, I want; money, gold, I want."

"Take it all. Here are my garments," and I began to divest myself of them. "And my gold thou mayest find for thyself."

He searched my garments. Then I had to accompany him into a dark room where our baggage was deposited. He scrutinized piece after piece but found nothing to his fancy.

"How much gold wilt thou send me from an-Nûri?"

"I shall consult the Prince about that. If thou wilt treat me honorably, my bounty will surely repay thee for thy magnanimity. May I then proceed with the saddling of my camels and the loading at once?"

"Aye, by Allâh, thou mayest." Whereupon I called to Ṭâreš and Tûmân to saddle and load.

Hearing this, the four men who in company with Raǧa' had captured us instantly darted from their room into the yard, yelled in alarm, and with their relatives filled the yard, the passageway, and the anteroom of Raǧa's house. I said to Raǧa':

"Thou, O chief, hast pledged me thy word. Thou hast the first voice in the settlement of Skâka. Prove that thou hast also the power to fulfill thy word."

Thereupon Raǧa' seized his Martini rifle and ran out. A wild howl issued from his mouth, a multitude of like howls answered him, daggers and sabers flashed, rifles were put to shoulders.

Raǧa' came back to me. "Wait, Mûsa; this would result in bloodshed."

"And the blood would stain thee, O Raǧa'."

A relative of Raǧa' by the name of Marrân grabbed me and whispered in my ear:

"They want to afflict thee. Flee!" He pulled me away, with Tûmân running after us. We leaped from a side yard into a garden, ran through it, and crossed two or three more before we reached the house of Marrân. He opened the gate, immediately closed it behind us, and stationed beside it his adult son armed with a Martini rifle, giving him orders to admit no one. We stayed with him several hours. Finally Raǧa' came, accompanied by his brother and two negroes, and announced that we might return. He explained that Miz'el had betrayed us to the Ḳreše, who had thereupon occupied the road leading to the settlement of aṭ-Ṭwêr. He informed us further that, according to the latest news, an-Nûri had left that morning for the wells of Ṣfân and therefore Raǧa' had sent the letter by a swift messenger to Nawwâf in al-Ǧowf.

In Raǧa''s house we were again surrounded by a crowd of wildly howling, gesticulating men. A tall chap grabbed me and dragged me into a corner, vociferously demanding my gold; Miz'el had told him I had a bagful.

"Hast thou given it all to Raǧa'? Aye, he has had his, but we are still hungry." Barely had I freed myself from his grasp when I was held by three or four others. Then two slaves of Raǧa' took me between them and led me out into the garden, whence we escaped into the house of an ʿAḳejli who was a protégé of Prince an-Nûri. There we remained until sunset. As we were returning, a young man shouted after me:

"Damned strangers! All ye present, let us slay them and we will tear the bowels out of their bellies!"

Turning his way, I asked: "Why dost thou speak thus, son? Have I harmed thee?"

"Allâh damn thee!" was his retort.

The following day Mizʿel told me that he had sent a report to Nawwâf in my name and had promised the messenger three *meǧîdijjât* ($2.70).

"Why didst thou not ask me first?" I inquired. "Whatever thou hast done without my consent is no concern of mine."

Meantime my camels were starving. The first day I had bought for them about twelve kilograms of *sobot̤* straw for one and a half *meǧîdijjât,* and on Friday and Saturday I procured some dry *šîḥ* and *rûṯe* for two *meǧîdijjât.*

On Friday Raǧaʾ came with new demands. According to him, Mizʿel had told all over the settlement that I had given him, Raǧaʾ, ten pounds, and now his four companions also wanted ten pounds apiece.

In the afternoon the lucky star began to twinkle for me. I learned that Ḥmâr abu ʿAwwâd, an-Nûri's chief negro, had arrived in Skâka, and I found him in the house of the ʿAḳejli. Hearing of the treatment I had received, he was very angry and immediately took me under his protection: that is, he offered me his services. The Skâka settlers, well aware of his influence with an-Nûri, awarded him first place and waited on him as if he were a big chief. They were not a little surprised, therefore, when they saw the mighty slave Ḥmâr leave his rug, forsake his room, and come half-way to greet me and then himself prepare me a seat, pour coffee for me, and serve me. From that moment I was master. I should have been glad to leave Skâka that very day, but I had to wait for Ḥmâr, who wished to marry the white daughter of a blacksmith and take her back to the camp.

On Friday and Saturday many people with sore eyes came to me and begged me for medicines. Among them was the youth who would have torn the bowels out of the strangers' abdomens. Said I to him:

"See, my son! Yesterday thou wouldst have ripped me and today thou comest and askest of me, the 'damned stranger', medicine for thy ailing mother. What am I to do about thee?"

But I gave him the medicine, visited his mother, and told him how to take care of her.

As already noted, the northern portion of the Skâka settlement is inhabited by the Ḳreše clan, the southern by the Maʿâžle. The Ḳreše consist of the families Âl ʿAli, Âl Ẓwêḥi, and Âl Maṭar and occupy about two hundred dwellings; their chief is ʿAssâf eben Lḥejjed. The Maʿâžle are divided into Âl Ǧḥejš, Âl Nṣejr, and Âl Šelhûb and own about three hundred dwellings. Therefore the settlement has about three thousand inhabitants. They grow palms, vegetables, and a little barley. As the palms must be watered frequently, much work on the part of the inhabitants is required, since the wells are from twenty-five to thirty meters deep. More than a third of the settlers migrate yearly with the Rwala to Syria. There they work for farmers, for the money thus earned purchase clothing and wheat and barley, and by the end of summer return with the Rwala back to their settlement. Thus to maintain good relations with the Rwala is the primary condition of their existence. When the dissolution of Eben Rašîd's domain began, civil war also flared up in the settlement of Skâka. The Ḳreše, wishing to appropriate some of the gardens of the Maʿâžle, attacked them but were repulsed with the loss of ninety-seven men in one night. Ever since October, 1908, the fighting had been raging in Skâka,[67] the number of fallen on both sides amounting to over two hundred men. We could hear the shots day and night.

On Friday a young man stole into the Ḳreše district and lay in ambush for a man who had killed his father. When his victim finally emerged from his house, the youth aimed at him and shattered his skull. Saturday he came to me to ask me to examine his rifle, as the lock had not seemed to function well since the day before.

When Nawwâf entered al-Ǧowf, the Maʿâžle proclaimed themselves for him, the Ḳreše against him. Whereupon the Rwala launched repeated raids against the latter, captured their herds, and killed more than forty men. It was his

[67] Literature has preserved very few records of this settlement. Jâḳût, *Muʿǧam* (Wüstenfeld), Vol. 3, p. 106, writes that as-Skâka is a settlement in the oasis wherein is also situated Dûmat al-Ǧandal, but that this is not fortified as strongly as Dûma, in which there is more activity. Ḥaǧǧi Ḫalfa, *Ǧihân numa'* (Constantinople, 1145 A.H.), p. 531, records that the fort of Skâka is a day's travel from the fort of Ḳâra, which is built of adobe upon a hill.

knowledge of these facts that had prompted Rağa᾿ to say I ought to thank Allâh that I had not fallen into the hands of the Ḳreše. That I should have fared badly at their hands was beyond the shadow of a doubt, for they feared no one. They were secure in their solidly built houses, were well armed, and in their high-walled gardens were in a position to resist for years the attacks of the Bedouins. Nawwâf, who had now been occupying al-Ǧowf for over two months, had the support of many Rwala but was still unable to bring the inhabitants of Mâred and al-Ḫadne to subjugation. Since the Maʿâẑle, friends of the Rwala, treated us thus, what would their enemies have done to us? The same, or perhaps even worse, should we have fared in Tejma.

Rağa᾿ and the elders of the Maʿâẑle clan did not rely much upon the protection of an-Nûri.

"He will soon leave with his Rwala for the territory of the settlers and will forsake us here to our fate. We must then help ourselves," said Rağa᾿.

On Saturday afternoon the messenger returned from Nawwâf with one letter for Rağa᾿ and another for me. Nawwâf wrote that he had reproved Rağa᾿ for capturing and robbing us and had demanded him to restore all that had been taken away from me and to escort me wherever I wanted to go. He reassured me of his friendship and begged me to forgive Rağa᾿ his affront, as he had not acted thus intentionally, but merely because of ignorance.

CHAPTER X

WITH AN-NÛRI IN THE NEFÛD; SOJOURN AT AL-ḲÂRA

SKÂKA TO AN-NÛRI'S CAMP

On Saturday evening we ascertained the latitude and on Sunday morning at seven o'clock left the settlement of Skâka. As my camel was unable to rise after I had mounted her, I had to get off, allow her to rise, and then swing myself upon her over her neck. We were accompanied by thirty-four warriors, who were to defend us in case of an attack by the Ḳreše. As we had not yet passed out of the gardens when my camel began to show an inclination to kneel again, there was nothing for me to do but get off and walk. Every one of us had a loaded rifle. Raǧa' and Ḥmâr advised me to watch carefully the sand drifts to the south for any Ḳreše who might be hidden in them, but I did not detect any. At 8.25 we reached the settlement of aṭ-Ṭjêr, as the Rwala call it, consisting of about fifty dwellings with three hundred inhabitants, all of them blacksmiths (*ṣunnâ*ᶜ). Our armed escorts were to wait there until we reached al-Ḳâra; nevertheless, there were still eighteen men and six women, most of them relatives of the young wife of the negro Ḥmâr, who went on with us. The bride sat upon my camel. Mizᶜel, whom I had discharged, walked.

At 9.06 we had at our right, upon a small rock, the remains of a fortress called Ḳaṣr eben Ḳdêr, and to the northeast the wells of the settlement of al-Ḳwêra. It is said that almost anywhere in the basin al-Ǧûba, especially between the settlements of Skâka and al-Ḳâra, one may dig down to the ruins of ancient stone and adobe walls and the remains of caved-in wells, a proof that the region was formerly inhabited and cultivated.

We stayed from 9.19 until 9.40 in the settlement of al-Ḳâra, where we filled our water bags and then started on in a south-southwesterly direction. At 10.06 we reached sand drifts, where we met camel riders who had been sent by Eben Mašhûr for water and who told us that an-Nûri was camping in al-ʿÂdrijjet umm Arṭa. The ascent to the southern upland proved exhausting for my wearied camel, who paused every fifty paces and panted. As we had eaten nothing that day, we halted from 12.13 to 1.12 P. M., the camels grazing meantime upon blossoming *ʿarfeǧ, soboṭ, ʿalḳaʾ, ḳlejžlân, žirna, ḳaṣbaʾ,* and *ḳafʿaʾ*.

WITH PRINCE AN-NÛRI; POLITICAL RELATIONS WITH EBEN RAŠÎD

At three o'clock we approached the Prince's camp. Ḥmâr gestured to his young wife to dismount, saying that he would send her a woman. We were being actively discussed in the camp, for at noon a man from aṭ-Ṭjêr had brought the news of what had happened to us in the settlement of Skâka and the Prince was planning to come to our help with riders if we did not arrive before evening. When I entered his tent, he rose, the chiefs and all others present following his example; then he rushed to meet me, grasped my right hand and pressed it warmly, while my other hand was shaken by one chief after another and by other Rwala. The Prince then turned to the men who had come from Skâka:

"Know ye not, ye men of Skâka, that Mûsa belongs among the foremost of chiefs? If ye have deprived him of so much as one hair, I shall have ye all chained in irons. Speak thou, O Sheikh Mûsa! Hast thou missed anything? Ye slaves, take the rifles from the men of Skâka and do not give them back to them until they have restored to Mûsa all they have taken from him."

I narrated in detail what had occurred at Skâka and briefly described my expedition, the Prince frequently interrupting me with manifestations of indignation at the behavior of the Ṣlubi Mizʿel. The latter listened to my report; but he could not deny its truthfulness, since Ṭâreš and the men from Skâka verified all I told.

During my absence the Prince had repulsed an attack of the Šammar while he was camping at Ǧaw Moṛejra. One night just before midnight the alarm cry "O riders! O riders!" was heard, and it was found that about seventy Šammar had assaulted a detachment of the Kwâčbe tribe and had driven off its herds. The Prince pursued them with his slaves, overtook them, and regained the herds, besides capturing thirty-four riding camels and twenty-eight rifles. Of the Šammar four men fell and two more were wounded. Of the Rwala the only one wounded was Ṣâdda, brother of the negro ʿAbdallâh, who had accompanied me to ar-Reṣâfa; he was shot in the breast. Two mares belonging to the Prince were killed and two wounded, a calamity which annoyed him exceedingly.

Soon after my departure a courier had come from Prince Saʿûd eben Rašîd with letters suing for peace. An-Nûri's slaves, as well as the majority of the Rwala, were for war and intended to join with Eben Saʿûd against Eben Rašîd. They wanted to help Nawwâf; hence, being well aware of the disaffection between the Prince and his son and anticipating that the former might feel inclined to renew peace with Eben Rašîd, they turned upon the poor courier who had brought, with gifts, the offer of peace to an-Nûri, submitted him to humiliations, and menaced him with threats that he should not escape their hands alive. An-Nûri reprimanded them for this conduct and punished two of the slaves. Two days later he released the courier with several letters.

Presently a slave of Zâmel eben Subhân, the minister of Eben Rašîd, came, accompanied by three men, all of them dressed in silken clothes. The Prince received them in a very friendly manner and during their stay of eight days had two wethers slaughtered for them. He renewed peace with Eben Rašîd, but only so far as he himself was concerned and under several conditions. Then Eben Subhân's slave went to al-Ǧowf to negotiate with Nawwâf, who would not agree to the peace ratified by his father, but the following nights attacked the adherents of Eben Rašîd, demolished two of their houses, and ordered the palms in two gardens to be cut down. The Prince said to me:

"Nawwâf and the chiefs are free. Let them do as they please."

That evening I was visited by Marrân (with whom I had taken refuge in the settlement of Skâka), who came to ask gifts for himself and for Raǧaʾ eben Mwejsil, the chief of the Maʿâžle clan. I directed Nâṣer to give him my half-worn silk caftan (*zebûn*) and my shirt. A little while after, Marrân returned to thank me for the gift, but he was very dejected about it. When I tried to cheer him by telling him how well my silk *zebûn* would fit him, he smiled sourly and replied that every gift came from Allâh, but that Allâh had been parsimonious in this instance. I was surprised at his words and asked him to let me see the *zebûn* I had given him. Then I found out that Nâṣer had deceived him, that instead of giving him my silk *zebûn* and my shirt he had palmed off on him whatever of his own clothes he himself could not use. He fulfilled my first order only upon my vigorous admonition.

Ṭâreš received his promised wages of fifteen *meǧîdijjât* ($ 13.50) and five *meǧîdijjât* ($ 4.50) more as a gift, as the Prince had promised. He was so well satisfied that he declared he would remain in my service; but the Prince answered in my name:

"Thou hast received thy money; leave then my camp immediately and go to thy protectors!"

"They camp far, by aš-Šežîž."

"Let me not behold thee in the camp tomorrow morning!"

Monday to Wednesday, April 19 to 21, 1909. Monday morning I observed several camel riders dismounting in front of the Prince's tent. They were ʿAḳejl (camel traders) who came to join the Rwala in order to go along with them to Damascus. The herds of camels they had bought in the desert were with a band that had already moved in a northwesterly direction; they themselves had come to the Prince to pay him their respects and to secure his protection. I immediately sent a message to the Prince asking him to delay the ʿAḳejl, as I wished to entrust them with some letters. After five months this was the first opportunity that had presented itself to me to send information about myself to Damascus. The Prince sent back word that I must make haste, and ten minutes later his slave stood at my tent inquiring whether I was ready.

I spent the entire day sketching a topographical map of the regions through which I had traveled. Toward evening the Prince came, eager to tell me what had taken place in my absence. He said that Mamdûḥ eben Saṭṭâm was married (*ʿarras ʿala binet*), and I asked him when his son Saʿûd would marry.

"That, O Mûsa, depends on Allâh. He loves the sister of his mother, who also is the sister of my present wife, and she loves him; still he cannot marry her until ʿAbdallâh eben Ṭalâl grants his consent."

"What does the girl care about ʿAbdallâh?"

"Much, indeed. True, he is not as closely related to her as Saʿûd is, but he has reserved her for himself. A few days after her birth he said before witnesses to her mother, Turkijje, that he reserved the girl for himself. Ever since then she has belonged to him, and no one may marry her without his consent. We could compel him to release her, but we do not wish to alienate him."

"And what say the brothers of the girl?"

"They say that they will not permit the marriage of their sister with ʿAbdallâh, but they will give her to Saʿûd, who is the son of their elder sister."

On Tuesday and Wednesday I continued my cartographical work. One by one I read aloud to ʿAwde al-Kwêčbi and other trustworthy men all the names in my record, writing down each name in Latin characters, while Ǧwâd wrote it at the same time in Arabic. My informants frequently argued over the situation of the individual localities, but in general they conceded the accuracy of my notes.

As the Prince sat by me on Tuesday, a Bedouin entered exclaiming:

"Rejoice, O an-Nûri, in the glad tidings! Four hundred riders on camels, besides sixty-five camels burdened with loads, are coming from Eben Saʿûd to the assistance of Nawwâf. Today they camp at Ǧaw Moṛejra."

"Hast thou seen them?"

"Nay. I heard it from the settlers from al-Ḳâra."

"Depart thou quickly!"

On Wednesday the Prince received a letter from Nawwâf notifying him that a force of eight hundred riders upon camels dispatched by Eben Saʿûd was coming to his assistance. Ṭrâd eben Saṭṭâm, who delivered the message, informed me that Nawwâf was on the verge of despair because his father did not send him weapons, money, or provisions, nor would even allow his mother to come to him with his boy Sulṭân. He begged me in the name of Nawwâf to persuade an-Nûri to abandon his obduracy.

Thursday to Tuesday, April 22 to 27, 1909. On Thursday we migrated (temperature at 5.30: 14.8° C). Starting at 7.15 A.M. in a southwesterly direction, we stopped as early as 9.38, the Prince having chosen a new camping ground (Fig. 53). As soon as my pack camels arrived, I pitched my circular tent and began writing my topographical account, which occupied me all day Friday also, from sunrise to sunset (temperature at 5: 23.5° C).

Toward evening I heard the sound of several shots and a loud, monotonous chanting, and upon stepping out of the tent I saw a long line of armed men from Skâka dancing along on their way toward the Prince's tent. Preceding them

FIG. 53—Camping ground in plain of al-ʿÂḏrijjet umm Arṭa.

was an old man, who was swaying a sword above his head and going through the same antics as the men behind. These would hop twice forward and then waggle first on their right and then on the left legs, tilting their trunks in the same way. Back of them followed about forty camels with luggage, the property of firearms merchants from ʿAnejza in al-Ḳaṣîm, bringing rifles and ammunition that had been purchased in the port of al-Kwejt. The men stopped in front of the tent and formed themselves into an ellipsoid, whereupon the man who had been their leader in the dance now kindled a fire in the center of the open side, stood between it and his companions, and began to dance again. His companions, who were so crowded that they almost touched shoulders, grasped one another's arms and danced as before until they were exhausted.

In the evening the scribe Ǧwâd came in, bringing letters from the Imâm Eben Saʿûd and from Fejṣal, brother of the assassinated prince Saʿûd eben Rašîd, who had fled to ar-

Rijâḍ. Both of these letters were brought by the messenger who had been sent by an-Nûri to Eben Saʿûd at the beginning of February from Majḳûʿ.

On Saturday we migrated again (temperature at 6.30: 17.8° C). Departing at 7.18 A. M. in a west-northwesterly direction, we proceeded along the northern fringe of the plain of al-Lâjǧa, which is covered with innumerable sand hillocks sixty to one hundred and twenty centimeters high held together by the roots of the *arṭa*. Among them grow *ʿalḳaʾ* and *ʿâḏer*. At 8.40 we came to higher drifts, upon which flourish *ʿâḏer, ṛaẓaʾ, meṣṣêʿ, ḳaṣbaʾ, sobot, iḏen al-ḥmâr, ʿasansal, burrejd, čḥejl, ḥamṣîṣ, ʿaẓîd, saʿdân, marrâr, metnân, mrâr, karrâṯ, ʿešbet al-ǧerw*, and *ṣollejân*. In the stony ground grows *ʿarfeǧ*, which forms bushes covered with yellow blossoms that look as if they had been dried. In the north was visible the abruptly ending, sharp edge of the al-ʿAžraba upland. From 11.40 to 12.10 P.M. we rested and at 12.37 dismounted at a new camping ground.

In the afternoon I had a long chat with the Prince. I had been requested by many chiefs, among them Fahad eben Mašhûr, the next most powerful after an-Nûri, to use my influence in moving him to proclaim himself a friend of Eben Saʿûd and to announce that he would go to al-Ǧowf to assist Nawwâf with all his might. I hesitated long, being averse to interfering between father and son; but, hearing the remark that Nawwâf would throw off his father's yoke, I feared an open war and therefore talked to an-Nûri more plainly than I ever had before. The conversation lasted over two hours. At the end of it the Prince rose and left in silence. What would he do?

On Sunday morning I saw many horseback riders and camel riders arriving at the Prince's tent. Soon he came out and mounted his riding camel, stopping beside me merely long enough to say: "To al-Ǧowf"; to which I answered, "*Al-ḥamdu lillâh!* Allâh be praised!" He was accompanied by over two hundred riders, took money along, and upon two camels he had loaded rifles and ammunition for Nawwâf. My intercession had not been amiss, then. He returned that evening.

On Monday we migrated again. The Prince mounted his camel at seven o'clock, and at the same moment the camel that carried the symbol of his power, the ornate litter *abu-d-dhûr* also started out.

FIG. 54

FIG. 55

FIG. 54—Camels eating *ṛaẓa*.
FIG. 55—Mežḥem in a *ṛaẓa* bush.

"Nawwâf greets thee, O Sheikh Mûsa," he said to me as he passed. "If Allâh wills, that which thou hast recommended shall be. I know I have no truer friend than thou."

On Saturday the Ṣlubi Sanad had been sent out, charged with the task of discovering water and a camp site in the

FIG. 56—Camels eating *raẓa*.

vicinity of the aṭ-Ṭawîl range. He did not return until early Monday morning, when he reported that he had found good pasture, fresh perennial growths especially, in the vicinity of the Ḫabra Mlêḥ, in al-Ḥaršûfijjât, and in Ṛwêṭa Ğerâd. There were no annuals anywhere, he said, but the grasses that are called *šetîl* might yet come up if a sufficient rain should fall.

"Hast thou seen any raiding bands?" asked the Prince.

"Nay. Only the traces of about forty riders have I seen."

The western sky was overcast with dark clouds, in which there were flashes of lightning. Portions of the clouds were being driven over our heads by the west wind and rain from them sprinkled us five times; but we pulled our cloaks over our heads and went on. At ten o'clock the Prince cantered ahead to find a good site. He came back in half an hour, turned to the south-southeast, and at eleven o'clock we encamped in a sandy hollow (*ḳaʿara*).

On Tuesday the folding of the tents was begun before dawn and at 6.30 A. M. the clan started on the march in a southeasterly direction. At nine o'clock we came to several sand drifts bearing green bushes of *raẓa* (Figs. 54, 55, 56) and the Prince resolved to camp there. He jumped off his camel and pointed out to me the spot where I should pitch my tent. An hour later the pinkish drifts with their green *ṛaẓa* bushes were dotted with hundreds upon hundreds of large and small black tents. The clear, bright blue sky looked as if it had been washed and the black eastern edge of the aṭ-Ṭawîl range was bathed in gold.

Meantime a messenger had come from Nawwâf with the report that in the night between Sunday and Monday he was attacked by the warriors of Eben Rašîd, who were, however, repulsed and later routed. Their commander sought to protect himself in the fleeing throng, but was shot and with him also fell two women, while four other women were wounded. Five warriors of Eben Rašîd were captured and immediately killed. After this news, on Monday and Tuesday small bands mounted on camels kept leaving us to harass the Šammar clans. Thus did Prince an-Nûri open war upon the subjects of Eben Rašîd.

Wednesday to Friday, April 28 to 30, 1909. I occupied myself Wednesday with my ethnographical notes. Toward the evening I heard cheering cries that signified victory: the raiding band of Duṛmân was returning with 150 head of sheep and goats which they had captured from the Ḳreše clan. Nawwâf had sent Rašrâš, the son of ʿAdûb, for rifles and ammunition, and he returned the same evening with forty camels carrying 11,000 cartridges and forty rifles. The Prince had bought them from the merchants from al-Ḳaṣîm. An-Nûri wrote to the slave of Eben Subhân, who was still in the stronghold district of al-Ḫadne, asking him to come and negotiate with him as to the manner in which he would surrender al-Ḫadne and Mâred, as he desired to secure for himself the entire basin al-Ǧowf with all of its settlements, either through mediation or by force. Should the emissary fail to present himself, an-Nûri would consider this as a sign of enmity and a signal for war.

An-Nûri was completely transformed. He was despatching daily small raiding bands against the Šammar and stronger ones against the opponents of Nawwâf in the settlement of al-Ǧowf. The Rwala were pleased with him and hopeful of crushing the power of Eben Rašîd, whose abuses they had endured for so many years.

Thursday was *raḥîl* (migration, moving) again. We advanced in a northeasterly direction from 6.43 A.M. to 8.40.

Friday, starting at 6.27 A. M., we continued in the same direction. At eight o'clock we were overtaken by two Ṣlejb, who told the Prince they had seen the tracks of about twenty camel riders trending from the northwest to the southeast. The Prince remarked that it was probably the emissary of

FIG. 57—Camping ground in plain of al-Lâjǧa.

Eben Rašîd with his retinue and that he must not fail to capture him and especially the letters he carried. From 8.50 to 9.25 we paused. Meantime eighty-two riders had supplied themselves with water and the necessary provisions and had hurriedly ridden after the emissary in the direction indicated. We trudged slowly along until twelve o'clock, when the Prince designated a new camp site (Fig. 57).

Saturday to Sunday, May 1 to 9, 1909. On Saturday I was busy supplementing my notes on the habits and customs of the Rwala. My informant Ḥmâr abu ʿAwwâd, who, it will be remembered, had recently remarried, was very drowsy and wished to lie down in my tent and sleep. Like all Bedouins, he was accustomed to take to bed during the hot season sometime between seven and ten o'clock. Such repose is called *ẓaḥa*. At this time the entire camp is lifeless. The men retire into the rooms for women, the entrances are covered to prevent anyone from looking inside, and everybody slumbers except the small boys and girls, who romp about. The women usually rise about noon, the men lie until two or three o'clock. Ḥmâr had pestered me for several days by begging for a tonic that would restore his waning vigor; he was convinced that among my many drugs I must have something that could rejuvenate him. He was then about eighty years old and had a youthful wife. He would not believe that I could not help him and kept maintaining that I did not want to do so. Accordingly he went to the Prince and begged him to intercede with me in his behalf. Presently he came back with the Prince and said:

"Shouldst thou not, O Mûsa, give me any of that medicine, I shall have to return to my wife with my face blackened. I have promised her surely to bring from thee this very necessary medicine and thou — may Allâh prolong thy life! — wouldst thou now blacken my face? My honor heretofore has been white. If thou likest me, do not blacken me in my old age."

On Sunday we changed our camp to another place (*raḥîl),* starting out at 6.50 A. M. toward the northeast. Soon we were joined by ʿAḏûb, Mamdûḥ, Ṭrâd, and others, who had pursued the emissary and his Šammar and had returned during the night. ʿAḏûb said they overtook the party on Friday night far southeast from the wells of aš-Šežîž. At first the Šammar merely put the question:

"Who are ye riders upon camels? (*wuš entom jâ hla-l-ğejš?*)" but, instantly recognizing the Rwala, they fired upon them and turned to flee. The Rwala pursued, striving to encircle them. Realizing the impossibility of escape, some of the Šammar jumped off their saddles and hid among the *ṛaẓa* bushes, while others surrendered their weapons. Four of them were shot to death, one was mortally wounded. One of them, named Raʿjân, would have been able to escape, as he had a swift camel; but ʿAḏûb wanted the camel. He therefore called to the Šammari to surrender, promising to spare his life and to give him another animal. Concluding that ʿAḏûb, who likewise was riding an excellent mount, might overtake him or shoot him down, Raʿjân heeded the challenge, surrendered, and received for his fine runner an old worn-out camel. Not another camel was left to any of the Šammar and the Rwala took not only their animals but their weapons and even their provisions and water. Dreading thirst in the center of the sandy Nefûd, the Šammar begged their enemies to shoot them on the spot, but this the Rwala declined to do, saying that by killing the defenseless they would blacken their own faces. As I later learned, not one of them ever returned to his clan. The Prince, with whom I discussed the episode, said carelessly:

"The sandy desert of the Nefûd wants her sacrifices, therefore we must render them unto her."

From 8.36 to 8.57 our camels grazed. I shot down a *ṭarše* bird. Later we rode in a level plain covered with coarse gravel; all the plants were grazed off. Thence we descended into the basin al-Ǧûba and at 12.02 P. M. reached the settlement of al-Ḳâra, where we encamped at the same spot as before, on the southern edge of the village. On our arrival the settlers hastened to reap their last wheat: they did not trust the camels of their friends the Rwala. The air was charged with dust and sand, the heat unbearable. The camels with loads did not reach us until three o'clock.

AT AL-ḲÂRA

On Monday I invited the Ṣlubi Sanad to come to my tent that I might discuss with him the customs and habits of his kinsmen. I labored with him for two hours, but to no purpose. He kept contradicting himself, asking for food and tobacco, and leisurely exploring his shirt, throwing about him what he found in it. Accordingly I sent for another Ṣlubi, Farağ. This man responded with intelligent statements at first; but Sanad, who was loitering about the tent outside, called to him:

"Why dost thou teach him? He will be paid for every word in gold, but what wilt thou get?" Thereupon Farağ became silent and I had to stop my work. When I complained to the Prince about it, he said:

"Dost thou not know, Mûsa, that the Ṣlejb are the worst scoundrels in the desert? Cursed be their ancestors for a progeny of such dogs!"

In the afternoon I continued making notes of the songs and verses of the Rwala and kept on with this occupation for several days from sunrise to sunset. The scribe Ǧwâd was constantly bringing me new informants, whom the Prince exhorted to be attentive and thoughtful. This kind of work was very strenuous for the nerves, especially since the temperature in the tent and, therefore, in the shade, stood all day long at over 40° centigrade. The west breeze, always so refreshing, could not reach us, for the settlement of al-Ḳâra was situated in a basin and it was also behind a cliff extending from north to south and thus completely blocking the passage through which the wind might otherwise have penetrated. In addition to this, regularly toward evening we had a sandstorm, which tore down many of the tents and filled our eyes and all our pores with sand.

The tent of the Prince was full of warriors, men from Skâka who kept coming to ask him for rifles and ammunition. On an average, he entertained fifty persons every day and yet he himself was hungry most of the time. As host he was not allowed to eat with his guests and there was nobody to serve him in the women's compartment, for his young wife preferred to stay with her relatives and the servant and slave women cared most for their children and husbands; the Prince was not related to them; he was a stranger. Yet there were women relatives in his tent. Staying with him were his two daughters who had run away from their husbands; but they were she-dogs (*člâbât*), as the Prince was wont to call them, not fit for anything. They would usually sit in the tent drinking coffee, smoking their long pipes, and listening to the talk of their numerous visitors. Even while the tent was being folded or repitched they would repose in the shade of their litters and wait until the slaves tied the litters on the camels; then they would put in their fluffy blankets, seat themselves upon them, and watch the men and women passing by. They were not at all scrupulous about dirt. Only once did I see one of them, Ṣâlḥa, whose mother was a Šammarijje, wash her white kerchief. Although her younger sister and an-Nûri's young wife were sitting by her at the time, chatting with her and scratching their heads repeatedly, it did not occur to them to wash their own dirty kerchiefs or, for that matter, their hands and their hair. The scribe Ǧwâd, whose attention I called to it, said:

"Ṣâlḥa was not reared in the tent of the Prince; she was raised by the relatives of her mother, whom the Prince had divorced, where there were not so many slave women as there are in the tent of the Prince or in the tent of Turkijje, whence his young wife comes. The women are accustomed to change their clothes only when the slave woman brings them new ones."

It appeared to me that Prince an-Nûri also changed and cleaned his clothing only when compelled by someone to do so. Often I heard the scribe reproach him about his looks and urge him to put on new garments. He could not do so

in his tent, however, for that was always full of people; and at night he had to hide under his head the clothes he took off, for, should any slave or servant see one of the Prince's garments lying about, he would immediately appropriate it.

"The pocket of the Prince is deep and wide; the Prince will not be walking about naked," say the slaves and servants. In his relations with me he saw that I demanded cleanliness in everything; hence he washed and changed his clothing more frequently, doing so always in my tent. His own tent was full of women, but it was next to impossible for him to find one who would do his washing. He asked me frequently to let my servant Nâṣer wash his shirt, but I persistently refused to agree to it, always remarking that this kind of work was better suited to a woman.

"By Allâh, do not believe it, O Mûsa! If I entrust any of the slave women with my shirt, she returns it to me more soiled than it was when she took it." The scribe was later charged with the task of finding a woman in some of the settlements who would wash for Prince an-Nûri eben Šaʿlân, King of Northern Arabia, as he was called. Poor king, indeed!

The raiding bands of the Rwala were pressing hard upon the Šammar of Eben Rmâl and Eben Raẖîṣ and were returning with much booty; but, according to news brought by a Ṣlubi to Nawwâf, who hastened to notify his father, Zâmel eben Subhân, minister of the youthful Saʿûd eben Rašîd, had just sent ammunition and provisions to the garrison in Mâred and in al-Ḫadne. The Prince immediately despatched a large detail of camel riders to occupy the neighborhood of the wells of aš-Šežîž and the pass of al-Mustanda in the aṭ-Ṭawîl range; and on Thursday evening the riders returned with the prize. They had concealed themselves in the hollows (*ḳaʿar*) of the Nefûd and in the ravines of the aṭ-Ṭawîl range, stationed sentries upon the highest sand hills, and waited until these should espy the camels carrying the supplies to al-Ǧowf. They did not have to wait long, for the caravan (*ḥadra*) was sighted on Wednesday before noon. Surrounding it, they waited until its members retired and at dawn, when the Bedouins sleep soundest, they captured it (*maʾẖûḏa*). I did not learn what became of the men accompanying the camels — the Rwala failed to mention that. As none of them ever reached al-Ǧowf or al-Ḳâra, however, it was evident that they all perished, but whether by the weapons of the Rwala or by thirst and hunger, only Allâh and the Rwala knew.

On Wednesday a Ṣlubi came bringing word to the Prince that eight camels carrying weapons and goods for clothing had arrived from al-Mašhad — that is, from Kerbela — at the camp of the Ṣlejb in al-Bwejtât. The camels and the loads were the property of merchants hailing from al-Mašhad and residing in the settlement of Skâka with the Ḳreše, enemies of the Rwala. These Mašâhde were in a difficult position. As merchants they wished to sell not only to the Ḳreše and the Šammar clans, but to the Maʿâžle and the Rwala as well, and hence they were desirous of peace; but, since they resided with the Ḳreše and sold them weapons and ammunition, they thereby alienated the Maʿâžle and the Rwala. They had sent many messages and gifts to an-Nûri, appealing to him for peace and trying to excuse their dealings.

"Should we not sell arms to the Ḳreše, how would they treat us?" they pleaded. "They would demolish our houses and rob us of our property; and whether they would spare our necks Allâh only knows."

"Ye supply our enemies with arms and ammunition; therefore ye are to blame for their defiance, and I do not want to mediate with ye," responded an-Nûri curtly. When, therefore, the caravan of the Mašâhde was detected, fifteen young men immediately saddled their mares and rode out to meet it, but they returned empty-handed; for as soon as the Ṣlejb, who sided with both the Rwala and the Šammar, perceived the cavalcade, they hid the camels of the Mašâhde in a small basin. The ground being stony, the Rwala could not find any tracks, and, not having taken along any water for their horses, were obliged to return. Nevertheless, they stationed sentries at the wells of Ṣwêr and Ǧaw Moṛejra and also watched the vicinity nearest the settlement of Skâka. There and at al-Ǧowf fighting was the order of the day. Both sides did their utmost to wreck the greatest possible number of garden walls and to cut down the most palms.

On Sunday our camels returned from pasture and were watered.

Monday to Sunday, May 10 to 16, 1909. On Monday morning I was awakened by the grumbling of camels that were being loaded with supplies by the Prince's slaves in front of his tent. Thus we were moving again, although the

Prince had told me we should remain at al-Ḳâra for at least seven days. I had been well pleased at the prospect of continuing my scientific work without interruption, but instead there was *raḥîl*! Shortly before sunrise the Prince came to ask whether I was going with him.

"I shall leave the women, the tents, and the stores in al-Ḳâra," he said, "and go east with only the herds and mares, and I shall return in the next five or six days. It is because the Ṣlejb advised me during the night that they have found a good pasture in the vicinity of al-Wadʿa and al-Mẖarûḳ, hence I should like to stay there until the end of this month."

When I found the Prince was going to approximately the same camping grounds that I had visited already, I immediately responded that I should prefer to remain in al-Ḳâra and work; whereupon he recommended that I move my tents into the garden of the chief Ẓâher eben Selîm, where they would be better protected than on the present camp site. His scribe wished to remain behind with me. Thus we moved into the gardens adjoining the house of Ẓâher and pitched our tents under the palms, the Prince sending word to Ẓâher by the slave ʿÂmer to permit nobody to enter my tent and to watch over us day and night. After seeing my luggage safely housed, I went over to the Prince to bid him good-bye and to commend my camels to his care.

"This is not necessary, brother Mûsa," he answered. "Thy belongings are deeper within me than my own, and, by Allâh, I speak the truth."

I ordered my herdsman Mufaẓẓi always to stay with my camels among the other herds and never to pass the night in any other place than where the Prince and his party lodged. Presently an-Nûri departed with most of the men, leaving the women and children in the settlement. Ǧwâd and I returned to my notes on folklore and I did not leave the tent until after sundown.

The nights were not restful. Thirty paces from my tent there had been pitched the tent of a Šammari whose daughter was seriously ill. The poor girl moaned, coughed, and lamented day and night, until finally on Sunday death liberated her. They shrouded her in her own shirt and buried her before dawn.

Every night after midnight four laborers with three camels came into the garden to draw water from a well about forty paces from my tent and to water the palms. They accompanied their work with singing and with yells at the camels intended to urge them to steadiness and speed; if the camels failed to respond promptly, the drivers emphasized their persuasions with louder yells and blows. The workmen gave particular attention to the palms that were in bloom, pushing away the foliage nearest to the blossoms and freeing the leaves of thorns. They shook the pollen from the male blossoms upon the female ones and inserted a branch with male blooms on it into the midst of branches bearing female blossoms, tying the two into a cluster. Because male blossoms are slow in showing themselves, the crown of each of the palms was examined every second or third day. Each tree had to be watered every fifth day. The water was first drawn into a large reservoir, from which it flowed in shallow ditches to the individual trees, where it was caught and held in a sort of bowl from one and a half to two meters in diameter hollowed out in the soil around the base of each tree.

On Tuesday we learned that at the wells of Ṣwêr the chief Zeben al-Kwêčbi had subdued a band of the Šammar who were seeking the Rwala in the depression of Sirḥân and that beyond the settlement of Čâf they had captured camels of the Sirḥân which carried salt. Returning with the booty over ʿAmûd and the head of the valley of aš-Šwejḥeṭ, they succeeded in reaching Ṣwêr, where they considered themselves out of danger because they thought that some of their clans were camping at al-Bwejtât. But they were not destined to return to these relatives. A certain Kwêčbi, prowling about in search of *naṣi* for his mare, sighted them just as they were relaxing during the heat of noon and summoned his fellow tribesmen. The Šammar lost all their booty and all their camels besides. To the Rwala had also fallen two camels carrying goods of the Mašâhde to Skâka. They had, it seemed, promised a camel to a certain Ṣlubi, who, to make sure of it, betrayed his own fellow tribesmen to the Rwala by pointing out the route by which they could capture the booty.

On Thursday there came to the settlement of al-Ḳâra several families of the Nṣejr clan, who had been camping with the Šammar in the district of al-Ḥzûl but had migrated immediately after the declaration of war between the Šammar and the Rwala. Their chief asked me where Prince an-Nûri's camp was and told me that the men of Eben Saʿûd had approached the city of Ḥâjel, the residence of Eben Rašîd. According to him, Zâmel eben Subhân was encamped with his fighters at the fortress of at-Truba, and Eben Saʿûd had sent against him a small detachment with orders to attack the enemy and then flee. This was done. Eben Subhân gave pursuit and in his absence Eben Saʿûd and his men attacked his camp, assaulted him from the rear, and captured all the white tents of Eben Rašîd's slaves as well as their horses and camels. Only thirty riders succeeded in fleeing upon horseback to Ḥâjel. The soldiery of Eben Saʿûd, the man said, was now in the vicinity of Baḳʿa (or Ṭajjebt Ism) where it menaced all the roads converging on Ḥâjel.

On Sunday there came to us a Ṣlubi from al-Ǧowf bringing news that the Duṛmân had routed a raiding band of the Tûmân, who are affiliated with the Šammar, and had captured fifty-eight riding camels. Nawwâf, he said, was building a strong tower northwest of Mâred, whence he intended to fire upon his enemies.

Monday to Friday, May 17 to 21, 1909. On Monday morning I heard in front of my tent the grumbling of a camel that was being forced to kneel. Peering out, I saw the Prince, who rushed up to me with a hearty greeting, sweat streaming down his face. His people were migrating to al-Ḳâra and he had hastened ahead upon his fine animal that he might see me as soon as possible, he said. I readily believed that he had hastened to me, though less for my sake than in anticipation of the full meal and the rest that he knew awaited him in my tent. He had been moving about every day for the last eight days, passing not a single night inside a tent. He complained of not having found abundant pasture anywhere nor a sufficient quantity of water, and twice they had had to keep riding all night because of the appearance of enemy raiders. When I asked him about my camels, he replied that my two best riding animals had been stolen. My herdsman Mufaẓẓi did not lodge near his animals, he said, but went to his relatives on the outskirts of the camp, and in his absence two Šammar who served with the Rwala had taken my two fine animals and escaped upon them. They had stolen provisions, water bags, and firearms from their masters and camels from me. The Prince said he had demanded compensation from the masters for my animals and would assist me to my right, otherwise his face would remain blackened.

"Thou, Prince, art in duty bound to do so," I said. "According to your customs a host or a master is responsible for the acts of his guest or his servant. This is known to everybody and is conceded by all. Shouldst thou not compel the masters of these thieves to make retribution, it would be plain that thou dost not concern thyself with the property of thy friend and neighbor. The Prince an-Nûri eben Šaʿlân surely will not let this come to pass."

"*Wallâh* (by Allâh), I shall not let it pass; I know thou boughtest both of the stolen animals for 158 *meǧîdijjât* ($142.20), but this year camels are lank and do not fetch the price they sold for last year. I appraised thy animals at one hundred *meǧîdijjât* ($90). If thou agreest, the masters shall pay thee this amount." I agreed and asked the Prince to expedite the settlement of the matter.

In the night the scribe Ǧwâd brought me word from the Prince that we were to remain in al-Ḳâra until Saturday. This pleased me, for I expected to finish by that day the greater portion of my notes on folklore. The Prince came to see me every day; but, if he saw that I was very busy, he would keep quiet or else help me by sending away anyone who was bent on paying me a visit.

Many of the chiefs, the young ones especially, were desirous of procuring various articles from me, but they did not dare ask me for them. It was generally known that the Prince was my close friend; but I did not allow any of the chiefs to become too intimate. My deportment toward them all was kindly and courteous, but it was reserved whenever any of them sought to treat me as his equal. In such a case I pretended not to hear what was said, or else I replied curtly in the negative, immediately afterwards engaging the man in a pleasant conversation as though nothing had happened. I never permitted myself to accept an invitation to supper from any of the younger chiefs and I never visited any of them. It was very seldom that I entered the tent of the Prince and when I did I stayed but a little while. My round tent was always open to him, but it was closed to the other chiefs. They were permitted to seat themselves in my large tent, whence I would invite one or another to my presence.

I never greeted the younger chiefs first, but as soon as one of them saluted me I returned the greeting and inquired in a friendly manner as to this or that. If anyone failed to greet me, I rode by as though I neither saw nor heard him.

My raids, as they called my scientific expeditions, were known to all, and no one had any doubt about my courage. Once, when the youthful chief Mamdûḥ eben Saṭṭâm, who was famous for his bravery, sought to quiz me by asking whether I had no fears while thus rambling alone in the unknown desert, I answered him in the presence of the other chiefs:

"What is fear, O Mamdûḥ? What is the unknown desert? I was roaming through it on a camel's back while thou wast being carried through it in a saddlebag." Mamdûḥ's face flushed and he retreated. In the bags that are tied to camel saddles the slaves on marches put the young sons of their masters who are too young to know how to ride.

It was through such demeanor that I had so won the respect of the Prince's family that none of the young chiefs dared to prejudice anyone against me; and it was only for the sake of preserving this steadfast position to the limit that I demanded reimbursement for my stolen animals. It was to be proved whether the Prince would or would not actually demonstrate his friendship for me.

On Thursday afternoon I finished most of my notes, thus carrying out an important part of my scientific work. Toward evening I went with Ẓâher to visit a tent where on the morrow several boys were to be circumcised. In front of it a company of girls were dancing. In the gardens I plucked *ḫâfûr, siğîl, ʿešbet al-ʿaḳrab, ḫubbejza, rešâd, snejsle, ḳtejṭ, hewâbeka, nkejda, abu nešr,* and *lubbêna.* On the way back we stopped to examine the rock of al-Mešrefe, where there was once a small fortress. On the rock, which was artificially hewn, I discovered a brief Nabataean inscription to which I decided to return on the morrow, as I could not make it out very well in the fading light.

On Friday I felt very tired. I had been drinking a good deal of black coffee during the last weeks in order to sustain the activity of my mind in the prevailing heat, and now I suffered a relapse. I could scarcely get off the bed. The blood throbbed in my head until everything about me seemed to go round in a circle. Nâṣer helped me from my small tent into the larger one, where I sat a while. About noon there broke over us a violent sandstorm, which tore down both our tents and forced us to seek protection behind a garden wall. The storm did not subside until after sunset, when it was too late to visit the rock of al-Mešrefe. In the evening Ǧwâd brought me seventeen Turkish pounds ($76.50) as reimbursement for my stolen camels and, better still, the tidings that on the morrow we were to start on our march to the populated regions. The Prince had kept his word. This fact, together with my joy at the prospect of finally leaving the inner desert, served to raise my spirits.

CHAPTER XI

AL-ḲÂRA TO DAMASCUS THROUGH THE WÂDI SIRḤÂN

AL-ḲÂRA TO ḲULBÂN AN-NBÂǦ

Saturday to Friday, May 22 to 28, 1909. On Saturday we had a great deal of trouble in loading the camels (Fig 58). They were so frightened by the palms that at every breath of wind which made the leaves rustle they would get up — in spite of the fact that their front legs were tied together — and throw off their loads. Finally we had to carry our belongings out of the garden and load them in the open space. Nobody could help us, for all were having the same difficulties. While my servants brought out the baggage, I watched the camels. No sooner was the task of loading accomplished than a servant came from the Prince with the request that I visit him at once. I found him southeast of the settlement in the midst of a group of fighters, dividing cartridges among them. He begged me to give some medicine to two settlers from Skâka, one of whom had his left hand shot through while the other suffered from the reopening of an old stab wound in the right ankle. Before I had cleaned and dressed their wounds the whole throng was on the march and the Prince was impatiently urging me to hurry, so as to overtake them in time. Thus I again missed the Nabataean inscription.

At 6.20 A. M. we left al-Ḳâra and rode through the basin al-Ǧûba toward the southwest. As soon as we passed the southern corner of the cliff that encloses this basin, we felt the cool current of the west wind for which we had longed so at al-Ḳâra. From 8.10 until 8.32 we rested, and at 11.40 encamped at the southern base of al-Ḥamâmijât. I saw the Prince, mounted on his camel, driving before him about twenty men and beating them with his bent stick. They were some youths from Skâka who wished to go to Syria with us. The Prince would not permit it, however, because he feared that the number of his adherents in Skâka would be so much lessened.

On Sunday we started on our way at 5.24 A. M. and at 6.47 reached the Ḳaṣr al-Mwejsen,[68] a forsaken fortress built upon a solitary rock. South of it were several dilapidated houses and half-buried wells.

FIG. 58—Departure from al-Ḳâra.

In the vicinity of al-Mwejsen there are a great many boulders of multiform shapes which make one think of herds of resting cows. The basin is hedged in by a precipitous rocky cliff against which, in the southern part, masses of sand have drifted and formed rising terraces, called al-Ḥeḳne. West of the Ḳaṣr al-Mwejsen, between these drifts and the bare, rocky cliff on the north, is a free space about fifty meters wide where *ʿâd̠er* and *ṛaẓa* grow. Halting from 7.10 until 7.25, we reached at 8.38 a rain pool filled with water. It is situated

[68] Al-Bekri, *Muʿǧam* (Wüstenfeld), p. 564, records that the Beni Ṭarîf ibn Mâlek of the tribe of the Ṭajj own a place with a little water, Muwejsel.

Jâḳût, *Muʿǧam* (Wüstenfeld), Vol. 4, pp. 691 f., writes that a certain member of the Ṭajj tribe warmed some sour milk and added to it water from the spring of Muwejsel in the hope of curing himself of some malady. Another Bedouin praised the wholesome air between Muwejsel and Ǧâwa. —

Ǧâwa is situated eight kilometers south-southwest of our Mwejsen; it is therefore apparent that we may identify it with the Muwejsel of al-Bekri and Jâḳût, because the *l* and *n* are often interchanged.

north of the western end of the drifts of al-Ḥeḳne, near which is the settlement of Ǧâwa. We watered our animals from the pool. The camels that were not burdened by any load waded to the middle of the water, where they drank and excreted at the same time that the women were filling their water bags with this liquid!

At 9.10 we deviated somewhat to the northwest to encircle al-Ǧowf. True, the chief ʿAd̲ûb had asked an-Nûri to encamp at al-Ǧowf, but the Prince feared lest some of the women perish during the fighting; hence we rode through the stony district of Ǧîsân al-Ǧowf. The short ravines of this region are narrow and deep, with sides that are almost impassably steep. Nowhere was any green bush to be seen — everywhere merely the bare, gray, waste rocks. At one o'clock we descended into the extensive lowland Fejẓat al-Ǧarba, where we found dry *ẓamrân*, a fact which influenced the Prince to encamp there at 1.32 P. M.

Rašrâš, the son of ʿAd̲ûb, joined us here. He had come from Nawwâf and had brought letters and greetings for me, together with the news that Nawwâf had married a girl from al-Ǧowf a few days before. She was his sixth wife; he had divorced four, and a like fate threatened the fifth one. The latest reports of the victorious advance of Eben Saʿûd had improved Nawwâf's weakened position, and because he now was sure of his father's approbation he was filled with the hope of ultimate victory.

On Monday we were in the saddle by 5.39 A. M., circling in a southwesterly direction the hilly stretch in which we had failed to find pasture. The Arabs were hungry. Since most of the camels had ceased to yield milk because of insufficient food, the majority of the natives had lost their only sustenance. During our migration, while I was riding somewhat apart from the Prince, a woman who was sitting upon her loaded tent asked me why we had not encamped at al-Ǧowf, and sighingly said:

"We are looking for bread, but the country where there is no bread is not sweet (*ḥenna nudawwer ʿala ṛarîf, ad-dîra alli mâ biha ṛarîf mâ hi zêna*)."

At 7.10 we had on our left the hill of ʿAbd al-Ǧowf and on our right the wall of aẓ-Ẓullijje; then we turned somewhat westward and from nine until 9.25 rested (Fig. 59). At noon we took a course through the channel of the Riǧlet aš-Šejḫ toward the southwest, as we had been told there was a good pasture at the southeastern edge of the Ḥašm al-Eẓâreʿ. At 1.20 P. M. the Prince made his camel kneel, a signal that the camp site had been chosen. It was amidst sand drifts, from which the strong west wind blew clouds of sand toward us.

FIG. 59—Near hill of ʿAbd al-Ǧowf.

The next day many of the chiefs went to al-Ǧowf, and a number of the Arabs brought water from there. I occupied myself with notes on the poems and songs of the Rwala. Toward evening there was heard an alarm cry — the herdsmen had perceived an enemy band. Straightway the fighters, headed by the Prince, set out to the south, but failing to find the enemy they returned near midnight all worn out.

On Wednesday morning the alarm cry was heard again. The Prince was just preparing to have a drink of coffee with me; he did not finish the drink, but set the cup down on the floor, leaped upon his mare, and galloped toward the east. He returned half an hour later, saying he had seen the enemy fleeing south, but they were too far off for him to follow. At 5.25 we set out toward the west-northwest. On the way the camel that was carrying the tent of the Prince threw off the burden, and the slave women were not strong enough to reload it. They lamented and cursed the men because they would not help.

At 9.25 the Prince stopped in the sandy strip of ʿArejž ad-Desm and under a bush of *raẓa* kindled a small fire upon which we warmed our unfinished coffee. The chief ʿAḏûb had hunted down a hare, which he threw upon the fire and when it was baked divided among us. We ate the whole of that hare, even to the intestines. From 9.57 to 11.47 we were in the saddle and then rested until 12.23 P. M.

To the north the steep slope al-Ķṣâṣ, part of the uplands of al-Ǧrejmîs and al-Bijâẓ, was in sight; to the south the spurs of the aṭ-Ṭawîl range; and to the west a desolate, stony plain in which merge several valleys. The riding was not hard, but it was wearisomely monotonous. The sun was scorching and the wind drove sand into our eyes. On the right we could see a uniformly white, rocky precipice of the al-Bijâẓ region, on the left tiresome brown and reddish swells, while ahead of us the endless plain shimmered in a grayish haze. The camels were hungry and ran from one shrub to another seeking to graze. They grazed from 2.08 until 2.50 but were not relieved of riders and loads until, southeast of the wells of al-Baķķâr,[69] we reached the sandy hillocks Ķaṣîmt ar-Ruḫejme, which were overgrown with green *raẓa*. The tents were left folded, for we intended to resume the journey early next morning.

As early as a little after one o'clock my slumbers were interrupted by the grumbling of the camels, displeased because they were being loaded. At three we were under way. The west wind was damp, cold, and very unpleasant. The young camels had lost their mothers in the darkness and growled and wailed, while their mothers emitted a peculiar guttural sound called *ḥenn*, resembling the distant rumbling of thunder. Many a camel who could not wait until her youngster appeared, but started back on a run to find it, threw off her load and had to be caught and compelled to kneel by force. She would growl, beat her head, and otherwise act as if she were desperate. At 5.35 A. M. the Prince dismounted from his

[69] According to Jâķût, *op. cit.*, Vol. 1, pp. 698 f., Baķķâr is a locality in the sand desert of ʿÂleǧ near the two Ṭajj mountain ranges. — Our watering place of al-Baķķâr is situated on the northwestern border of the Nefûd — the ʿÂleǧ desert of old — but far from the ranges of Aǧa' and Salma' (i. e., the Ṭajj ranges). Near this Baķķâr, on the frontier of the territory of the Ṭajj, al-Bekri (*op. cit.*, p. 579) records a place called an-Nâṭilijje. Accordingly Baķķâr is to be sought on the frontier of the territory of the Ṭajj, a statement which fully conforms with the location of our Baķķâr.

camel near several bushes of *raẓa*, and until 5.54 we warmed ourselves by a fire. On the right we passed by the wells of Sbâjḥa and at ten o'clock reached the wells of Šrâr, where our thirsty camels were to be watered. Alas, only one of the wells had water in it; the rest of them were either half or wholly filled with earth. The individual families each gathered around a different well, which they proceeded to dig out and clean. The Prince also ordered a well to be dug and when the slaves shirked the work he drove them to it with a stick and curses. He then invited me to water my camels at his well. It took over four hours of hard work to water sixteen camels! There was very little water in the well anyway and, with four groups watering there, only each fifth bucket could be poured out for my camels. At the bottom of the well, which was about four meters deep, two men ladled out the water with rather flat bowls and poured it into the bucket. The men who pulled up the filled bucket and poured the water out for the camels kept up their spirits by singing short ditties (*ḥdaꞌ*).

The vicinity of the wells of Šrâr[70] is abundantly overgrown with *mṣaꞌ* bushes (Fig. 60), which were covered with berries, either still green or already red and of somewhat salty taste. Both adults and children picked and ate them. The soil consists of sand interpenetrated with salt and grows *ꞌačreš*.

Toward evening the Prince tied in front of my tent a yearling wether that had long, fluffy, black wool and a white head. It was a gift to him from a sheep merchant, who had bought in Neǧd about one hundred head of sheep which he was driving with us to Damascus. When I asked him why he did not kill the wether in his own tent, he answered:

"With thee, brother, I may eat to my content at least

[70] In the desert of as-Samâwa, belonging to the Kalb tribe and near Irak, there was situated, according to Jâḳût, *op. cit.*, Vol. 3, pp. 303 f., a place called Šaṛûr. He quotes the Arabs as saying:

"Whoever has used the water from Šaṛûr has approached Irak." According to the same authority, there was a similar saying concerning Ḥaḍn in connection with Neǧd. — The poet al-Mutanabbi (*ibid.*, Vol. 3, p. 304) mentions the watering places of Ṣwar, aṣ-Ṣubâḥ, Šaṛûr, and Ḍuḥaj. According to him we should seek Šaṛûr northeast of Šwêr, which is the same as his Ṣwar. If it is true that al-Mutanabbi failed to preserve the geographical order of the individual watering places, we may identify his Šaṛûr with our Šrâr. Whoever had watered his camel at Šrâr did not reach another water until he was in the settlement of Dûmat al-Ǧandal, which belonged to the administrative district of Irak and whence even today it imports its goods.

The *mṣaꞌ* bushes were also observed by Pietro della Valle, who tells (*Viaggi* [Venice, 1664], Vol. 4, p. 608) of his travels through a place overgrown with thistle thickets, the heart-shaped leaves of which were barely as large as the smallest nail of the human hand. The bushes bore round fruit resembling large corals, of sweet taste though somewhat salt, and having small seeds.

twice a day, but in my tent I might not perhaps even taste the meat."

On Friday we stayed at Šṛâr because the pack camels were too tired to go on. The Prince came to me early in the morning and worked with me until evening. There was

FIG. 60—*Mṣaʿ* bushes near wells of Šṛâr.

a shortage of food in his own tent, but he kept sending flour for bread to the tent of the orphans of his brother Mḥammad.

Saturday to Saturday, May 29 to June 5, 1909. On Saturday we resumed the march at 6.14 A. M. No sooner had we left the camp site than we were overtaken by a camel rider who brought the message that ʿAdûb, who was then camping at the Ḳulbân ʿArfeǧa,[71] was going to ride with his

[71] The wells of ʿArfeǧa are situated on the old route from Syria to the oasis of Tejma. They are mentioned by al-Muḳaddasi, *Aḥsan* (De Goeje), p. 253, who writes that in the depression of Sirḥân, in a pleasant, wholesome neighborhood, are situated two rain pools, ʿArfaǧa.

people along the western fringe of the depression of Sirḥân, as he had been informed that a fairly good pasture (*ṭwejbe*) was to be found there. The Prince declined to follow him, however, preferring to go direct to the wells of an-Nbâǧ because his people were already suffering from hunger.

At seven o'clock we were riding past the wells of Šṛajjer. To the east we sighted the *šeʿîb* of al-Ḳutb, which comes from the hills of al-Mefrežijje. The hills of al-ʿArâjef, which form the western border of the upland of Siḥle Ẓalma to the east of Wâdi Sirḥân, are neither so high nor so precipitous as those of al-Ḳṣâṣ. From 8.56 until 9.40 our animals grazed on *ʿaḳûl*. Then we rode west of the Ḳulbân al-Ǧerâwi[72] until noon, when the Prince designated another camping ground in the plain of ar-Raṭṭâj, amid bushes of *arṭa*.

In al-Ǧerâwi I was able to complete the southern portion of my map, for in the tent of the Prince I found a man from al-Ḳaṣîm who was familiar with the places southeast of Ḥâjel. In the evening I learned from the scribe Ǧwâd that Saʿûd, the younger son of the Prince, who lived with his mother in a tent of his own, had not had any bread or *ʿejš* (cooked meal) for four days. So I looked over my provisions, laid aside enough food to last my household from ten to twenty days, and sent the rest of the flour and *burṛul* to Saʿûd and his mother. When the Prince learned of it, he said to me:

"The Arabs can and must accustom themselves to suffer from want, but thou, brother, and thy men, ye must have enough to eat."

On Sunday we began to move at 5.16 A. M. At seven o'clock we noted on the right the Želîb Ḥlejžîm, east of it low, yellow hills in which is the abandoned settlement of an-Nabk abu Ḳaṣr, and still farther to the east the wide openings of the *šeʿibân* of Ṛarâjes, which approach from the at-Ṯâjât volcanoes. From 8.02 until nine o'clock the camels grazed on *roṛol* (Fig. 61). Later we were overtaken by a chief of the Kwâčbe tribe who was going from Skâka to the volcano of ʿAmûd and thence to Sḥîl ʿÂmer. He informed the Prince that in our vicinity there was lurking a raiding party of

[72] Jâḳût, *op. cit.*, Vol. 2, p. 46, writes that al-Ǧurâwi refers either to the waters in the territory of al-Ḳejn or to the wells adjoining the route of the Ṭajj tribe to Syria; according to him a watering place of the Ṭajj in the two ranges has the same name. — Our well of al-Ǧerâwi is situated in the former territory of al-Ḳejn, on the road of al-Mneḳḳa which leads through the depression of Sirḥân from Damascus to Ḥâjel near the Aǧa' range, where the Ṭajj tribe had their center.

350 men, which had attacked the encampment of the clan of al-Ḳaʿâžʿa at Mečâmen ar-Rḥaʾ; whereupon the Prince sent his slaves to urge the belated members of his family to make haste and be more alert, or they might easily be cut off

FIG. 61—Camels eating *roṛol.*

and robbed. We waited from 10.52 to 11.43 for the throng to gather. Meantime a messenger of Fahad âl Mašhûr arrived with the report that he was camping at an-Nbâǧ and that there was no pasture at the wells of Šâjba. The Prince accordingly changed his intention of camping at these wells and deviated westward. At two o'clock we dismounted at the Ḳulbân an-Nbâǧ, where we had camped once before (see above, p. 119).

ḲULBÂN AN-NBÂǦ TO ŠŽEJŽ AḎ-ḎÎB

I stopped in front of the chief Fahad's tent and immediately took my camel to water, but the Prince entered the tent at once. After watering the animal, I brought her likewise to the tent, where she knelt. The Prince greeted me:

"Long live the rider upon this camel! (*ḥajj râʿi haḏ-ḏelûl!*)"

To which I replied:

"Allâh preserve the life of thy children! (*allâh jeḥajji nabâk!*)"

All present rose except the young chief Ḫâled, the eldest son of the deceased Prince Saṭṭâm, who could not do so without difficulty; but he rose half-way. Fahad pointed me to a place opposite the Prince, whereupon the Prince asked me to take a seat beside him. But that seat was occupied by the chief Ḫâled, who was leaning upon the same saddle as the Prince. I complied with the Prince's request and Ḫâled had but to make room. Greeting everyone present, I inquired pleasantly of Ḫâled at what time he had arrived. Fahad served me with tea and dates. I invited only the Prince to join me at the meal. After my *maẓhûr* (the camels with the baggage) had arrived I left the tent to assist at the unloading. The water in the wells of an-Nbâğ is fresh, clear, and plentiful.

On Monday morning nobody seemed to know whether we should stay or migrate. The Prince was sleeping and no one ventured to wake him. At last he presented himself and directed us to make ready for the march. At 6.28 A. M. we set out, heading north-northwest through the marsh of Nowdân, which is covered for miles with a salty white crust that glitters in many places like smooth ice. We avoided such places, fearing that our camels might slip (*jezlaḳen*) upon them. Arriving east of the Ḳulbân al-Mejseri, we turned northward. Far to the east we could see the dark lava hills of Obêržât aẓ-Ẓbâʿ, half covered with sand. It is in these hills that the *šeʿibân* of al-Maʿâreč, ar-Ršâjde, and as-Sendela originate, thence extending down into the depression of Sirḥân. North of as-Sendela the edge of the upland north of Wâdi Sirḥân bends far back toward the east. Within this giant bend the Šeʿibân abu Slêlijjât terminate. Northwest of these rises the solitary cone Tell al-Žalta, around the northwestern base of which winds the *šeʿîb* of al-ʿAjli. The Tell al-Žalta and east of it the volcanoes of Lejla and ar-Rḥaʾ mark the southern boundary of the volcanic region. From 8.40 until nine o'clock our camels grazed upon a sandy slope where *ʿaḳûl, ḳaṭaf, mṣaʿ*, and *šnân* grew. At 10.38 we were forced to go around a large, brilliantly white expanse of salt. In the west and north we saw various mirages (*âl*). It appeared to us that the marsh of Nowdân bordered on a silvery lake wreathed in verdant trees and foliage. The shore, especially to the northwest where the sun was glowing most fiercely, appeared all overgrown with a vegetation that was reflected in the lake.

At eleven o'clock we reached a watered district (*marabb*) within which many short channels disappear. Its growth consists of *ḳaṣba, ḥalfa,* and *ʿačreš.* The Prince requested me to lead the tribe, and he himself trotted ahead to seek a snug location for the camp. The *salaf,* or armed convoy of the migrating tribe, now rode behind me. Beyond the *marabb* we crossed the edge of the marsh of Nowdân and from 11.50 until 12.22 P. M. waited at another *marabb* for the pack camels to overtake us. At one o'clock we came to a large *marabb,* where the Prince awaited us, and at 1.22 we encamped. The heat was intense. The Prince had made a shady arbor under a *ṭarfa* bush and invited me to sit with him. I had to carry thither my bag and my saddle to save them from the hundreds and thousands of camels that were passing by. As I started to lift the bag there sprang from under it a snake about sixty centimeters long, a finger thick, gray and speckled. Ǧwâd, the scribe, killed it.

On Tuesday the migration began at 5.07 A. M. First to start out was the camel that carried the *markab* or *abu-d-dhûr* litter. Then the Prince swung into the saddle and we followed his example. The camel with the *markab,* escorted by slaves and slave women, remained at the head of the pack camels (*meẓâhîr*) while the Prince and I rode in front. As soon as the *abu-d-dhûr* fell out of sight we stopped to await its approach. In this marshy lowland of al-Ḫ̮aššâbijje the camels of burden had to proceed very slowly and carefully to avoid slipping. Even more caution was required on the fringe of the Sabḫa Ḥaẓawẓa (or Ḥaẓowẓa), an arm of which we crossed in the center.

The Sabḫa Ḥaẓawẓa is a salty swamp extending from al-Ḫ̮aššâbijje to the al-Misma' range and from the volcano of ʿAbd al-Maʿâṣer in the east as far as Šeʿîb al-ʿAbed in the west. Almost from the very center rises a black hill. The Bedouins say that the hill contains a cave which is full of gold, but that it is impossible to get to it. No one can swim or wade across the swamp and whoever would ride into the Ḥaẓawẓa upon a camel would disappear with his mount before he could take ten steps. The Ḥaẓawẓa would gape open to swallow in a trice the struggling camel and rider, shrieking in vain for help. His companions, who might perhaps be standing only a few paces off upon solid ground, would have to gaze upon his mortal fight, unable to help him. It seemed to me as if a somber veil hung above this sultry marsh.[73]

To the north beyond the marsh the blue range of al-Misma' appeared, with its saddle peak Šdâd al-Misma' overtopping the horizon. Still farther north we perceived the outlines of the sharp tooth Sinn al-Misma'. In front of the range, at the eastern fringe of the depression of Sirḥân, is situated the somber hill of 'Abd al-Ma'âṣer. East of the range the ridges of al-Esêḥmât and al-Metâha extend toward the northeast and beyond, still farther toward the southeast but closer to the depression of Sirḥân, runs the higher belt of Lejla.[74]

Southeast of Lejla two almost blue cones belonging to the group of Mečâmen ar-Rḥa' appeared upon the horizon. West-northwest of us and west of the Ḥaẓawẓa, the deep mouth of the al-Esejd valley gaped in the northern edge of the lava. Near its termination the spring 'Ajn al-Mâbijje gushes forth.

At 7.40 we sighted on the right a palm tree and under it the well Želîb al-Mu'êṣer. At eight o'clock we arrived at the shallow wells Ḳulbân al-Ma'âṣer, where we pitched our tents. Here a messenger of the chief of the settlement of Čâf met the Prince and imparted to him the news that some of the Rwala clans were camping at al-Ġowlân and had been there for almost a month. According to the same informant, Eben Smejr had engaged in a fight with the Circassians and had lost thirty-five men, the Rwala killing two Turkish soldiers. He said that the Druses were again fighting the Government and had occupied the city of Boṣra'. These advices moved the Prince to head straight for al-Ġowlân, where he hoped to assist his people and Eben Smejr.

---

[73] Possibly the hill in the marsh of Ḥaẓawẓa is identical with the mountain of Ḥadawḍa of the Arabic writers.

Jâḳût, Mu'ǧam (Wüstenfeld), Vol. 2, p. 289, writes that Ḥadawḍa is a mountain in the west, whither, before the advent of Mohammed, the Arabs banished their exiles.

According to az-Zabîdi, Tâǧ al-'arûs (Bûlâḳ, 1307—1308 A. H.), Vol. 5, p. 20, Ḥadawḍa is a mountain or an island in the sea, whither the Arabs banished their exiles. —

Our hill of Ḥaẓawẓa rises almost on the western border of Arabia proper, from salty swamps which after heavy rains become transformed into a single lake. At such times the black hill of Ḥaẓawẓa becomes an island. It is very difficult to reach this mysterious mountain during floods and quite impossible at other times.

[74] Jâḳût, op. cit., Vol. 1, p. 554; Vol. 2, p. 859; Vol. 4, p. 374, writes that Lajla is either a solitary small cone or a table mountain. He asserts that a certain member of the Kalb tribe mentions two heights of Lajla in connection with the lowland Rawḍat al-Mamâleḥ, while a member of the Fezâra tribe speaks of Lajla and Barad. —

Lajla, mentioned by the member of the Kalb tribe, is certainly identical with the western spurs of our Lejla, whence rain water flows into the depression of Sirḥân, into the salty swamps of Ḥaẓawẓa, which may be correctly designated as Rawḍat al-Mamâleḥ. The member of the Fezâra tribe had in mind the volcanic region of Lajla, wherein he was camping. Through the northern arm of this volcanic region, called Ḥarra Tenân, there leads a route to the mountain of Bird. This mountain is identical with Barad.

As soon as my tents were pitched I began rewriting the topographical names and I added several brief songs to my notes.

On Wednesday we migrated at 5.02 A. M. in a southwesterly direction, which led us through the marsh of Nowdân (or Nawdân), and at seven o'clock reached the fringe of an arm that the Sabẖa Ḥaẓawẓa thrusts out to the southeast. We had to cross this arm by a few paths only thirty centimeters wide. Our camels would not enter them without much coaxing. They walked slowly, cautiously, one after another. Right and left of the paths lay white crusts of salt which concealed a quaggy morass. It seemed to me that I was walking on a frozen lake. Here and there even the paths bore a thick crust of salt, which seemed to thaw and vanish under the camels' feet. Frequently a path was broken by soft mud. In such places the utmost caution was necessary. Many of the animals slipped and were unable to rise. Several pack camels broke their legs and had to be left lying in the mire beside the paths, the men and women carrying the baggage to more solid ground, where they added it to the load of other camels in spite of the animals' protests. By eight o'clock all the paths had disappeared. The southwestern part of the arm of the Ḥaẓawẓa marsh consists of a rigid salty crust that forms innumerable cakes which pile one against the other, with edges so sharp and hard that the crossing was misery for the camels.

At 8.42 we halted at the Želîb al-Ḳdejjer, which is situated about a kilometer west of the arm of the Ḥaẓawẓa marsh. I anxiously sought out my own *maẓhûr,* or pack camels, to see if any of them had fallen. At last I found them and counted them: not one was missing. *Al-ḥamdu lillâh!* At 9.20 we proceeded farther to the west-northwest through a sandy region where *ʿačreš* (Fig. 62), *ʿerž* (Fig. 63), *šwaḥwaḥ, ʿâḏer,* and *mṣaʿ* were growing, with here and there even *mṭi, ḳaṭaf, ḳorẓi, ḳaṣba,* and *ṯḥama.* From 10.30 until 11.08 our camels grazed. At 12.17 P. M. we pitched another camp.

Shortly after the arrival of the camels carrying the Prince's property I saw him beating his young wife with a camel stick. She lay on the ground, retarding the blows with her hands but uttering no sound whatever. I heard no moans, no sighs, yet she was getting a thrashing in full measure. Later, when the Prince came to see me, he inquired whether men of my tribe beat their wives. He complained of his young wife's supineness and her care-free way of giving everything into the hands of slaves and slave women who pilfered his stores so thoroughly that nothing whatever was left of them. If he wanted a drink of sour milk he had to solicit it in a stranger's tent, even though he owned two hundred female camels. Before we left al-Ḳâra there were delivered to him from Skâka two loads of dates (about 340 kilograms), and when six days later we encamped at the wells of Šṛâr he had not a date left, although he himself had not eaten a single one.

As we thus sat engaged in conversation, the alarm cry rang out. The Prince leaped to his feet, darted into his tent, threw crosswise over his shoulders two belts with 120 Mannlicher cartridges, seized the carbine, and barefooted, with nothing on but a shirt, swung into the light saddle of his white mare and galloped off to the west. One by one the other riders hurried after him, with no mantles or kerchiefs and their long plaits flying in the air. About twenty minutes later we heard reports of firearms, first singly, then in volleys. Then the alarm cry was renewed. Even the mares that nursed foals had to be saddled and when these proved insufficient mount camels were gathered, an indication that the enemy were very numerous. To secure our camp from a sudden attack, we occupied the next oblong tabular hill and thoroughly surveyed the vicinity northeast of the well of al-Ḳdejjer; but we could discover nothing, nor could we hear more shots. Our fighters returned near midnight.

The Prince had deemed his small band of thirty-six, on mares, sufficient to attack an enemy of sixty-five rifles on camels. Perceiving the Prince with his cavalcade, the enemy had dismounted and forced their camels to kneel in a sheltered hollow, while they themselves advanced to take shelter among the thickets that crowned a slight ridge. The Prince, not proposing to risk his horses and fighters in the open, had commanded his men to dismount, tie the horses, and open fire. He himself aimed at the hollow where the camels of the enemy had been secluded.

"I could not see the camels," he explained to me, "but I remembered their general direction and adjusted my carbine to see if it would carry as far as thou hast claimed. I fired thrice without knowing whether the bullets had reached the

Fig. 62

Fig. 63

Fig. 62—*ʿAčreš* bush.
Fig. 63—*ʿErž* bush.

mark. After the fourth shot I heard an outcry. I kept the range and fired three or four times more; and, behold, now I saw the camels running out, frightened, and leaping on three legs. I had aimed well and the bullets had carried. The enemy were unprepared for an attack upon their mounts. When they heard the alarm of the guards and saw the camels running wild, they quickly left their position, recaptured the camels, and fled. We pursued them, but our mares' hoofs kept sinking into the swamps and the enemy escaped. I did not permit the camel riders to take up the pursuit after they came to our assistance. Night had set in and they would have had to go round the arm of the Ḥaẓawẓa marsh, and how were they to find the enemy when their tracks were mingled with those of our own camels? Two of their animals were found dead, and many bloody streaks bore witness to the wounds suffered by either the fighters or the animals. The enemy have had a taste of their own blood and certainly will not hinder us any more."

On Thursday we set out at 5.47 A. M. From 6.45 until 7.14 we waited west of Ǧwej al-Ṛanam for the *abu-d-dhûr* litter and at nine o'clock entered the lava spur that penetrates fifteen kilometers into the depression of Sirḥân, with a width of seven kilometers. The march among the sharp stones was so hard for the camels that by ten o'clock we had only reached the Ḳulbân al-Amṛar, which are situated at the western end of the lava. These wells, from two to four meters deep and in the shade of three high palms and a few bushes, contain salty and bitter water. In the vicinity grow *mṣaʿ*, *ḥawwaʾ*, *bwêẓa*, *ǧamba*, *ṣâbûn al-ṛurâb*, *ṭarfa*, *ṭḥama*, *ẓaram*, *ʿerž*, *ʿešbet umm sâlem*, *ḥaršaf*, *ḥrejẓa*, *ẓorrêṭ an-naʿâm*, *ʿaḳûl*, *ʿačreš*, and *neǧîl*. We left the wells at 11.45 and proceeded close to the base of the *ḥarra* toward the north-northwest, reaching at 12.42 P. M. the wells of Šžejž aḏ-Ḏîb, where the Prince pointed out a camp site. These wells, which have been excavated in rocky ground, are only two meters deep and barely sixty centimeters wide, but they have plenty of water, which flows continuously. As all the plants in the depression of Sirḥân are of a salty taste and are covered with salt, we had to water the camels every second day.

About midnight there was a partial eclipse of the moon. Two-thirds of the moon's face was obscured by a reddish veil; only the right or western edge remained bright. The Prince came to ask me what the phenomenon signified.

ŠŽEJŽ AḎ-ḎÎB TO ṚOṬṬI

At 5.06 A. M. we left Šžejž and proceeded over the wide spur of the *ḥarra*. The ground was covered with fragments of lava, among which the camels proceeded cautiously, but here and there were larger or smaller basins in which there was no lava. Because the western upland also sends out a "nose" toward the east, Ḫašm aẓ-Ẓwâjen, the depression of Sirḥân narrows here until it almost disappears.

Two men who had a dispute to settle came to the Prince for assistance. One was a Rwejli, the other a Šarâri. Several days before they had exchanged riding camels. The Rwejli gave to the Šarâri his camel, adding a shirt and two kerchiefs, and in return received the camel which heretofore had been ridden by the Šarâri. On Wednesday the Rwejli mounted the exchanged camel to pursue the enemy upon it. On Thursday the beast was not able to rise, and, when she finally did get up, she was limping perceptibly upon her right front leg. Because of this defect the Rwejli accused the Šarâri of withholding from him the fact that the camel might become lame after a fast ride and sought to return the animal to the former owner. It was interesting to listen to the presentation of their cases and to their different dialects. The Prince heard them silently. After they had finished, he addressed the Šarâri:

"Thou wilt bring me witnesses to testify that thy old camel never limped before."

To the Rwejli he said: "Thou wilt bring me witnesses to testify that thy new camel did not go lame because of careless riding across the lava and the swamp."

From seven until 7.18 we rested. Presently the Šarâri brought his witnesses, but the Rwejli was unable to procure any.

"How wouldst thou judge them, O Sheikh Mûsa?" asked the Prince.

"I would not judge them; they have judged themselves."

"*Wallâh* (by Allâh), that is true!" said the Prince, leaping into the saddle of his kneeling camel and leaving without saying a word to the disputants.

At 8.35 we had on the left the Ḳulbân umm al-Fanâǧîl and at 9.04 stopped at the Ḳulbân al-Mḫejẓer, which are situated in a gap between two ridges of lava. At 9.29 we began to follow the road Darb al-Mneḳḳa[75] in a northwesterly direction. This road has been artificially restored in places. The lava stones have been gathered and piled up to form two inclosures between which runs the roadbed — a proof that it was once frequented by large mercantile caravans, for the Bedouins would hardly have labored thus of their own initiative.

At noon we again reached the depression of Sirḥân, where our camels grazed until 12.39 P. M. At 1.23 we encamped in the marsh of ᶜUjûn ᶜEḏwânât. The Arabs did not intend to pitch the tents, but toward three o'clock the southwestern sky became overcast with dark clouds and it began to lighten and thunder. In the brief shower which followed all that was not under cover was drenched. The boggy ground became still softer, causing many camels to fall with their loads and break their legs. Many of the Arabs had gone with their camels to the wells of al-Ǧarbûᶜijje and now could not return until the ground dried.

Toward evening the Prince told me that he was going to send Ḥmâr abu ᶜAwwâd to the Ḥawrân to secure reliable information about the political situation in Damascus and its vicinity. Ḥmâr was already approaching eighty, but he was so sagacious and keen-witted that the Prince could depend on him for anything.

On Saturday morning many of the Arabs had their belongings already loaded when the Prince's servant proclaimed that we were not going to migrate. ᶜEjâl Turkijje's camel, it appeared, had fallen at the wells of al-Ǧarbûᶜijje and could not rise. She was the best camel of the Saṭṭâm herd and Turkijje was very fond of her. For this reason Turkijje had asked the Prince not to migrate until the ground was firmer and the camel more rested. Since the camel could not get up, she had been guarded all night where she fell. The other camels were grazing on *ḥalfa*, which was also being gathered by the slaves who attended the horses (Figs. 64, 65, 66).

I was perusing the third volume of *Arabia Petraea* and busying myself with inquiries as to certain matters that

[75] Jâḳût, *Muᶜǧam* (Wüstenfeld), Vol. 4, p. 669, mentions a nomad road to Syria called al-Munaḳḳa, which we may identify with our road of al-Mneḳḳa.

had not been clearly explained to me at the time I wrote it, when toward evening the Prince visited me to tell the news that the chief of the settlement of Eṯra had sent him. The Government, he was informed, had expelled all the Rwala from al-Ǧowlân, and they were now camping north and northwest of al-Azraḳ. Before Beirut twenty-three English warships were anchored, and from Constantinople forty-one regiments of the army were marching to Syria. In Damascus ninety-one dignitaries had been imprisoned, many more having escaped to the Druses for protection from the Government. These tidings were brought to the settlement of Eṯra by the people of the Ḥawrân, who had come for salt. Consequently the Prince had decided to advance toward al-Azraḳ slowly and await the return of Ḥmâr. There was no means of telling when he would return, as we were not sure whether he could even succeed in reaching the station of Ḏerʿât (or Eḏraʿât). It was the opinion of the Prince that he should be at al-Azraḳ on Saturday and at Ḏerʿât on Monday morning. But the Rwala were waging war both with the Ahâli al-Ǧebel and with the Sirḥân, and both of these tribes were camping near the road that led to Ḏerʿât; it was therefore quite possible that they might capture Ḥmâr. He was to leave his camel in Ḏerʿât with the local confidant of the Prince and proceed to Damascus by rail, deliver the letters, return with the answer by rail to Ḏerʿât, and thence upon camel to us. He could be expected Sunday or Monday, after a journey of nine or ten days.

ʿEjâl Turkijje's camel was at last pulled from the mire, but she collapsed after a few paces and had to be brought to the camp on blankets by twelve men. Her improvement was anxiously awaited. An-Nûri declared that she was worth fifteen ordinary camels.

Sunday to Monday, June 6 to 21, 1909. On Sunday morning we marched from 5.38 A. M. until nine o'clock through the marsh that extends from the south as far as the wells Ḳulbân al-Ǧfêrât and encamped near the Ḳulbân al-Bîẓ. After my tents were pitched I began examining the plants that were picked on the way from al-Ḳâra, recording the Arabic names; I also photographed the environs of our camp. Several armed men walked to the Ḳulbân al-Ǧfêrât to cut meat from the sick camel, which had been killed. The men had carried her as far as there but, realizing the hopelessness of her condition, had been obliged to kill her.

FIG. 64

FIG. 65

FIG. 64—Camels eating *ḥalfa.*
FIG. 65—A camel with a load of *ḥalfa.*

On Monday we migrated at 5.45 A. M. We were still going through marshes. At 6.35 we had on the northeast the two solitary pyramidal hills of al-Ḫṣejjên, about two kilometers from which is situated a third similar hill, Abu Ḥsejje, and

FIG. 66—*Ḥalfa* being brought for horses.

southeast of it the Ḳlejjeb umm al-ʿEbi. About two kilometers west of al-Ḫṣejjên dark thickets of *ṭarfa* bushes cast their shadows upon the Želîb aṭ-Ṭrejfâwi. Between the hills of al-Ḫṣejjên the crest of al-Maḳl towers above the flat top of aš-Šâma.

We left the marsh (*sabḫa*) at nine o'clock and now rode upon limestone ground on which grew *firs, mṭi, šîḥ, ḳaṭaf, ṭarfa,* and scattered *mṣaʿ*. On the right, to the northeast, the white surface of the depression of Sirḥân reaches up to the black hills far away at Farʿat al-Ḳrênijje. The western slopes of the range to the east are almost perpendicular, the summits flat, the intersecting ravines deep and fairly wide. The depression of Sirḥân penetrates them in many places, and in such spots are located various settlements. The settlements of Roṭṭi, Ḳlejjeb Ṭalâl, al-Wašwaš, and Etra could be discerned to the northward; west and northwest of these lay al-ʿAḳejla, Ḳarḳar, Minwa, and Čâf. Date palms were visible also at al-Ḳṣejba and Ḳlejbât al-Wurejč. All these settlements, including the largest of them, Čâf, are called Ḳerâja al-Meleḥ (Salt Settlements), because of their situation amid wide marshes and because of the fact that their inhabitants gather and trade salt.

Between al-Wurejč and al-Wašwaš is seen the large, dark, isolated volcanic tract of al-Ḳaʿejdât. Southwest of us extended a yellowish, limestone region through which many shallow valleys converge toward the depression of Sirḥân.

From 9.40 to 10.10 our camels grazed west of the wells of al-Ḳṣejba near the valley of Bâjer, which begins in ar-Rḥaʾ at the watershed between the depressions of Sirḥân and of al-Ǧafar and is formed by the combined *šeʿibân* of aṭ-Ṭrejfi, Aḫejẓer ad-Dwejmi, Aḫejẓer as-Saṭîḥ, and Aḫejẓer al-Metâha. In this valley, thirty-five kilometers southwest of Roṭṭi, are the wells Ḳulbân Bâjer and the ruins of a large khan[76] of the same name.

Not far from the wells the *šeʿibân* of al-ʿAwseği join the valley of Bâjer on the right, and on the left the Šeʿibân al-Ḫejbrât.

[76] ʿAmr ibn al-Ḥâreṯ, the Ghassanian king, marched one spring (about 620 A. D.) against the Beni Murra, who had defied him. He wended his way through the volcanic region Ḥarrat Râǧel, past Ubajr and al-Kawâṯel. The Beni Murra were camping in the Rowḏet Nuʿmi and the Dât al-Aǧâwul and also on both sides of Arîḳ and ʿÂḳel between al-Ǧenâb and ʿÂleğ (an-Nâbiṛa, *Dîwân* [Derenbourg], pp. 97—99). — ʿAmr took the old transport road from the Ḫân at-Trâb to the depression of Sirḥân, which runs between the eastern boundary of the Ḥawrân and the Ḥarrat Râǧel. Crossing the depression of Sirḥân, he came upon the transport road which runs from ʿAmmân and Boṣra' to the oasis of Tejma and passes by our wells of Bâjer. Therefore I identify these wells with his Ubajr.

Ḥâtem aṭ-Ṭâ'i, *Dîwân* (Schulthess), p. 43, records a camp in the Ḥawrân and one at Abâ'ir. — In the dialect Abâ'ir sounds like Bâjer.

Ḥamza al-Iṣfahâni, *Ta'rîḫ* (Gottwaldt), Vol. 1, p. 117, writes that Ḥâreṯ ibn Ǧabala had built a castle between Daʿǧân, Ḳaṣr Ubajr, and Maʿân. — Daʿǧân is the Daʿǧânijje of today; the settlement of Maʿân still preserves its original name; Ḳaṣr Ubajr must be identical with our Ḳaṣr Bâjer.

Al-Bekri, *Muʿǧam* (Wüstenfeld), p. 63, says that Ubajr is a mountain in the territory of the Ḏubjân tribe. He gets his authority from a verse of the poet an-Nâbiṛa in which the latter describes the approach of the troops that had been despatched against the tribe of the Ḏubjân by the Ghassanian prince ʿAmr ibn al-Ḥâreṯ. — These implications do not mean that this army had already reached the territory of the Ḏubjân, but merely show that the army was headed for this territory over the heights of Ubajr and al-Kawâṯel. The Ghassanian army, marching from the north southward into the territory of the Ḏubjân tribe, could — nay, must — have passed by our Ḳaṣr Bâjer, which is located in the territory of the tribe of al-Ḳejn. Al-Kawâṯel, or al-Kawâtel (Ahlwardt, *Divans* [1870], p. 22), is to be sought south of Bâjer.

Ar-Rammâḥ ibn Abrad ibn Mijjâde relates (Abu-l-Farağ, *Aṛâni* [Bûlâḳ, 1285 A. H.], Vol. 2, p. 108) that the Caliph al-Walîd ibn Jazîd ibn ʿAbdalmalek sojourned during the spring season in Ubâjer. — Al-Walîd II liked to resort to the desert south of Palmyra and east of the ancient Moab. He dwelt most often at the water of al-Radaf in the district of al-Azraḳ, where the vast ruins of the Ḳaṣr aṭ-Ṭûba are still preserved. Thence he could

ṚOṬṬI TO AL-ḤADÎṮA

At 10.44 we had the small settlement of Ṛoṭṭi to the north-northeast. It consists of two peels, or blockhouses (*ḳaṣrên*), surrounded by large palm gardens. To the northwest the numerous palms of the settlement of Čâf came into view, situated at the base of the solitary, almost round hill aṣ-Ṣaʿîdi which still bears the ruins of old buildings.

North of Čâf in the depression of Sirḥân terminates the *šeʿîb* of al-Wudej, which runs out from the southern borders of the Tlejlât al-Bṛejṯât through the lava region of al-Ṛurejfa. West of the Tlejlât al-Bṛejṯât spreads the brown plain Ḳâʿ ad-Dâfne, bounded on the north by the volcanic region of al-Awtejdât and on the west by the volcanoes Tlûl as-Sûd and Tlejlât al-Fraʾ. South of Ḳâʿ ad-Dâfne the hills of al-Ṛurejfa, as-Samraʾ, and Ḥzêm Saʿîd slope to the depression of Sirḥân. The plain of Ḳâʿ ad-Dâfne is penetrated by the *šeʿîb* of ar-Ratâmi, which comes from the Tlûl al-Awtejdât, and farther west by the *šeʿibân* of al-Hazîm, al-Ṛamr, and al-Ḳaṭṭâmi. The latter begins between the Tlûl al-Ğeṯûm and the Tell Mismâr, takes in on the right at the Ṛadîr al-Wusâd the *šeʿîb* of Ab-ar-Rmam, and forms the border between the regions of aš-Šâma and the Ḥarrat aš-Šhaba.

Toward eleven o'clock we were overtaken by the settlers of Čâf. Although the Prince had summoned them, he hardly glanced at them. He responded to their greetings briefly and in a faint voice and rode on in silence.

"O thou whose life may Allâh prolong! (*jâ ṭawîl ʿomr!*)"

---

easily visit Ubâjer, our Ḳaṣr Bâjer, which is barely seventy kilometers to the southeast. Abu-l-Farağ records the name as Ubâjer. In the dialect, where the initial *hamza* is frequently omitted, Ubâjer is converted into Bâjer. In the work cited, Vol. 11, p. 87, where the place is also mentioned, it is referred to as Ubajr. That it is the same place is supported by the fact that it belonged to the Beni al-Ḳejn, who were camping between the ancient Moab and the depression of Sirḥân, therefore just where the Ḳaṣr Bâjer is situated.

Al-Muḳaddasi, *Aḥsan* (De Goeje), p. 253, reports that Wubajr is the name of some fresh-water wells situated in a delightful and extensive plain. — This Wubajr is represented by a station on the route from ʿAmmân to the oasis of Tejma, and its location fully conforms with that of our Ḳaṣr Bâjer. The spelling Wubajr is not correct. The *W* should not be joined to Bajr; it is a conjunction that goes before this word, just as it would precede any other local name. Therefore it should be written "wa Bajr" or "wa Ubajr." The form Bajr is probably the classic Ubajr in the popular dialect.

Naṣr al-Iskandari (Jâḳût, *op. cit.*, Vol. 1, p. 109) refers to Ubajr. It is a watering place of the Beni al-Ḳejn ibn Ğasr. — As mentioned above, the Beni al-Ḳejn used to camp in the eastern part of al-Belḳaʾ and in the steppe as far as the depression of Sirḥân. Hence they occupied the district of our Ḳaṣr Bâjer.

Jâḳût, *op. cit.*, Vol. 1, p. 415, also records a watering place of the name of Ubâjer (wrongly printed Ujâjer), which he seeks in Syria, north of the Ḥawrân. He takes his authority from the poet ar-Rammâḥ ibn Mijjâde, who there visited the Caliph al-Walîd ibn Jazîd. — Jâḳût does not tell where he got the information about Ubâjer's being north of the Ḥawrân, but this location is incorrect. Al-Walîd II resided during most of his reign in the steppe south of the Ḥawrân at al-Azraḳ and al-Ṛadaf, and it is impossible that he would have retired in the spring season to the settlements north of the Ḥawrân. The watering place of Ubâjer is never mentioned in connection with that region, whereas south of the Ḥawrân this watering place is known by the name of Ubajr. Either the form Ubâjer was used by the poet for the sake of the verse or it was a colloquialism. The Rwala prolong the first vowel of a diphthong even to this day, especially in proper nouns. Thus, they say Tâjma instead of Tejma, ʿÂjed instead of ʿAjd, al-Âjde instead of al-Ajde.

the settlers addressed him, greeting him also in the name of their neighbors who had remained behind in Čâf.

"Thy protection I beseech, O Lord! (*sitrak jâ rabb!*)" responded the Prince and then kept silent.

At 12.15 we reached another fortified farm, al-ʿAḳejla, where we encamped among *mṣaʿ* bushes near several wells, which were two meters deep and contained nothing but salty and bitter water. The Prince continued to ignore the Čâf delegation. Divesting himself of his garments, he plunged into one of the wells and proceeded to wash himself, recommending that I do likewise. Toward evening several camel loads of tribute were brought by the inhabitants of Eṯra and Čâf to the chiefs of the Šaʿlân, whereas for the Prince there was but a single load of flour and one of barley. Eṯra belongs to ʿAbdallâh, whose father, Prince Ṭalâl, had annexed it. Most of the gardens in Čâf are the property of the sons of Saṭṭâm.

On Tuesday we remained in camp (*mžîmîn*) because the Prince had many disputes to judge and the Arabs wanted to procure salt. Whoever had the money could purchase wheat and barley. The Prince nominated ʿAwwâd, the son of Ḥmâr, as his vicegerent at Čâf.

The settlement of Čâf has over sixty dwellings, which represent three districts (*ḳṣûr*). The first, Ḳaṣr aš-Šerḳi, is subject to the chief Muṭâweʿ eben Ḥ̮zejr; the second, Ḳaṣr al-Ṛarbi, is subject to the chief Mufaẓẓi eben Ḥ̮amîs, while the third and smallest one, Ḳaṣr al-Wasṭâni, belongs to the vicegerent of the Prince and his associates. The vicegerent contributes to the Prince five hundred *meǧîdijjât* ($ 450) yearly in taxes and receives no salary from him. The inhabitants of all the settlements in the region of Čâf are engaged in the salt trade, the commodity being procured at many places through evaporation, especially at the settlement of Eṯra. They sell to Syria yearly five or six thousand camel loads. One load, or sixteen *midd* (288 liters), of salt is worth one *meǧîdijje* (90 cents), half of which goes to the vicegerent, who in addition collects a duty, or rather a levy, for the protection of animals and loads. A merchant carrying money pays eight *meǧîdijjât*; if transporting a load of stuffs, six *meǧîdijjât*; if tobacco or butter, three *meǧîdijjât*. Should he be robbed of anything in the district of Čâf, to which the entire depression of Sirḥân belongs, he demands compensation from the vicegerent. If he is attacked and robbed by a kinsman of the Ẓana Muslim or the Šarârât, the vicegerent sends a messenger to the clan of the malefactor and demands in the name of an-Nûri either the stolen article or a double indemnity. If the malefactor was of the Beni Ṣaḫr, or of the Ḥwêṭât, or of any other tribe, the vicegerent endeavors to capture a kinsman of the tribe, puts him in irons if he gets him, and sends word to his kin that he will be released upon the delivery of the stolen things. Most of the settlers of Čâf and the other villages come from al-Ǧowf, where they have relatives; hence the Prince had decreed that nobody was to shelter any of his opponents from al-Ǧowf on pain of forfeiting his property, if not his life. There was so little wheat and barley in Čâf that the Arabs were obliged to pay two *meǧîdijjât* for one *midd* (18 liters) of wheat and thirty piasters ($ 1.45) for one *midd* of barley.

I was busy supplementing my topographical account the entire day, except for the diversion that Ǧwâd brought me in the shape of two numbers of an Arabic newspaper. It was the first newspaper I had read in ten months. I learned from it that the Turks had another ruler. Toward evening the Prince conversed with me on political topics, in which he showed a considerable interest. According to the news brought by the settlers of Čâf, the Turkish Government had decided to compel all the Bedouins to surrender their weapons. Accordingly, the governor of Bagdad had notified all the chiefs of the ʿAmârât and Dahâmše tribes that within a month they should give up all their rifles and revolvers; to which they replied:

"An-Nûri eben Šaʿlân is the king of north Arabia. Should he deliver his arms, we will do likewise. Should he not, neither can we, for he could then treat us like women."

This reply the governor had sent to Constantinople. The Prince did not trust the Turkish Government, not having dealt with it personally since he became prince, and he was apprehensive lest the Government deceive him and surround him with its army. When he left me he said:

"How shall I, brother, ever be able to part with thee? We have all become so used to thee! I love thee so — and, by Allâh, I speak the truth — and now thou wouldst leave us."

On Wednesday we started on the march at 6.38 A. M., as the Prince could not finish his council with the settlers of Čâf any sooner. At 7.08 we noted to the east the precipitous, dark slopes of Farʿat al-Ḳrênijje and al-Ṛurejfa. The latter merges into the undulating plain Ḳâʿ ad-Dâfne, which in places is covered with sand drifts. We proceeded through a marsh thickly overgrown with *ṭarfa*. At 7.49 we crossed the valley of Ḥṣâjdet al-Faṣja; this valley, together with two other valleys called Ḥṣâjde, begins at Waḳf aṣ-Ṣawwân among the hills of aṯ-Ṯlejtwât. North of it, in the depression of Sirḥân, are the hills of aẓ-Ẓerwa, which form the southern boundary of the lowland Fejẓat ar-Rašrâšijje. North of the latter the Tlejl ʿArejfân lifts its head, and still farther north rise the still higher tabular hills Ḳârt ammu Ḫšejš and as-Samraʾ, which mark the northern boundary of the depression. East of Ḳârt ammu Ḫšejš the mouth of the *šeʿîb* of ar-Ratâmi was visible, and southeast of it, below the slope, the wells Mḳejrât al-Ṛurejfa and ar-Rukubân appeared.

At 9.10 the Prince designated a new camping ground at the Ḳulbân an-Nabč al-Ṛarbi, where the camels could graze upon fresh *ʿačreš* in the neighboring Fejẓat ar-Rašrâšijje. West of the wells, which are from two to three meters deep, were three palms.[77] I occupied myself until evening with topographical work.

On Thursday we set out at 5.24 A. M. and at 6.14 ascended the edge of the western upland. This trends south-southeast and consists of porous limestone which easily yields to the ravages of wind and rain. At 6.43 we were passing through the deep glen Ḥṣâjdet umm Ṯemâjel, in which grow *šîḥ, firs, širšîr, frejṯa, ṣrêra, ʿaddês, ʿaranṭa, ʿaẓîd,* and *žetâde*. Several days before, a rain had fallen in the region of aṣ-Ṣawwân and consequently water was flowing in all the *šeʿibân*. All the perennials had put forth new sprouts and the camels grazed upon them from 7.50 until 8.07.

At 8.46 we were in the deep ravine of Ḥṣâjdet umm Ṛurubât, through which at 9.12 we reached the large rain pools of the same name (Fig. 67). The Prince jumped down from his camel, threw off his clothes, and plunged into the water, and the rest of his men followed his example. I went to collect plants: *ḫoṭmi, rešâd, rûṯe, ruʿejṣa, halajṭa, roṛol, brukân, ṭummejr, rḳêṭa, ždejḥa, ḫubbejza, ḥenwa, ǧurrejs, ḥumbejẓ, ḥasak, ḥlêwa,* and *ḥambâẓ*. At 9.32 we resumed the march, but encamped as early as 9.40. The right bank of the channel of Ḥṣâjdet umm Ṛurubât is steep, about ten meters

[77] Al-Muḳaddasi, *Aḥsan* (De Goeje), p. 253, gives the name an-Nabk to two pools of rain water, one containing fresher water than the other. The Pilgrim Road by way of Nuḫejlât leads between them. — This water of an-Nabk is identical with our an-Nabk al-Ṛarbi, by which a pilgrim road used to run. Nuḫejlât is to be sought in the palm orchards of Ṛoṭṭi.

high, and consists of soft limestone. The deep channel contains many pools, the largest of which is about ten meters wide and sixty meters long and at places attains a depth of three meters. It is enclosed in a circle of diminutive poplars (*ṛurab*) (Figs. 68, 69, 70). All these pools (*ṛudr*) were full of rain water: the Arabs had a chance to bathe! Groups of men and children congregated at each of the pools to utilize the long-deferred opportunity to take a bath. Toward evening the water was entered by women and girls.

Friday, June 11, 1909. The tents were loaded at 5.04 A. M. I rode alongside the Prince in the last line of march, as an enemy detachment had been reported somewhere to the south and an-Nûri wished to prevent any attack upon his clan or any robbery of the belated. Here and there where the tents had been pitched small fires were burning out, at every one of which were to be seen the three black hearthstones (*hawâdi*). Already, however, the tents and their tenants were gone. Only a few dogs were left running about from fire to fire, sniffing and howling, hunting for their lost mistresses. Several *sulḳân* (hounds) followed us for a considerable time, but presently they stopped, howling and barking pitifully, unable to recover the scent of their masters. The sense of smell is undeveloped in all Arabian dogs, especially in the hounds. They readily attach themselves to strangers and follow them until driven off.

At seven o'clock we crossed the first *šeʿîb* of Umm Rukubân and turned northwest. At 8.14, learning from the Prince that the ruins of al-Ḥadîṯa, which I wanted to visit, were quite out of our way on the right, I turned eastward and cantered away, the Prince calling after me to beware of the enemy band, exhorting me to return, and finally sending ʿAwde al-Kwêčbi to accompany me. We reached the depression of Sirḥân at 9.10, after passing through a rolling plain covered with small pebbles, and at 9.25 arrived at the ruins of al-Ḥadîṯa (Fig. 71). There we found a garden 903 and 474 meters long by 469 meters wide on the south side and 482 meters on the north, enclosed by a low, crumbling wall which at the southeastern corner was reinforced on both sides by pillars. In the northwestern corner was an aqueduct, dug in the ground and provided at intervals of eighteen meters with rectangular structural openings through which it had once been possible to enter and clean the conduit. The aqueduct is said to come

Fig. 67

Fig. 68

Fig. 67—A *ṛadîr* (rain pool) in the Ḥṣâjdet umm Ṛurubât.
Fig. 68—Ṛadîr umm Ṛurubât.

FIG. 69

FIG. 70

FIG. 69—From Ḥṣâjdet umm Ṛurubât looking south.
FIG. 70—Rwala boys at Ṛadîr umm Ṛurubât.

from al-Azraḳ. Northwest of the garden are supposed to be the ruins of a building, but we failed to find them.[78]

AL-ḤADÎṮA TO ḲAṢR AL-AZRAḲ

The heat was intense, and we had failed to take along a supply of water. At 12.15 P. M. I finished my work in the ruins, leaped to the saddle, and galloped northwest toward the camp. The vicinity abounded in low mounds of sand, while larger drifts were visible upon the plain Ḳâᶜ ad-Dâfne to the north. Only the southwestern edge of as-Samraʾ is dark brown, almost black, and covered by lava. West of it are situated the Ḳulbân al-Hazîm and southwest of these, in an embayment of the lowland, the Ḳulbân al-Ṛamr. In the vicinity of the al-Ḥadîṯa ruins and the adjoining Fejẓat aẓ-Ẓâḥčijje[79] the ground is arable.

Passing through the Šeᶜibân umm Rukubân, at 1.43 we reached the *šeᶜîb* of al-Mḥarûḳ, in the upper part of which is the Ṛadîr aḏ-Ḏîb. Northeast of aḏ-Ḏîb is the Ḫabra al-Ǧaᶜağa. North of Wâdi Sirḥân, beyond the Tlejlât al-Fraʾ, appeared the wide Ḥazm Flûḳ Dalma, extending from the southwest toward the northeast. West of the Ḥazm Flûḳ Dalma rise the long hill of Aṣejḫem and the groups of the volcanoes of as-Sbâra, al-Menâsef, Tell al-Aṣfar, and ar-Rjetên. All these hills and volcanoes are landmarks that show from afar the location of the ruins and the ponds of al-Azraḳ.

Shortly after my return the Prince came to me to inquire about the ruins. Upon being told of the abundance of water that had been and perhaps still was to be found there, he said that he would build a blockhouse at the ruins and settle it with husbandmen from the Ḥawrân.

That evening we were worried about Tûmân, who had left the tent at sunset and had been gone two hours. I asked Nâṣer, ᶜAwde, and the scribe Ǧwâd to call him by name throughout the camp, but he did not respond to their shouts. We were afraid something had befallen him, and our fears were the

[78] Al-Muḳaddasi, *op. cit.*, pp. 26, 253, notes that al-Muḥdaṯa is a station in the desert, from which the oasis of Tejma may be reached. There is an aqueduct there built of black stones. — Al-Muḥdaṯa was situated on the transport road from Syria through the depression of as-Sirr (Sirḥân) to the oasis of Tejma. Therefore it is identical with our al-Ḥadîṯa, where there is an aqueduct of black stones.

[79] Ibn as-Sikkît (Jâḳût, *Muᶜǧam* [Wüstenfeld], Vol. 3, p. 459) mentions the water of Ḍâḥek as being in the depression of as-Sirr belonging to the tribe of the Balḳejn. — Ḍâḥek is to be sought in the numerous wells of our plain of aẓ-Ẓâḥčijje, as the depression of as-Sirr is identical with the depression of Sirḥân of today. Aẓ-Ẓâḥčijje is situated within the former territory of the Balḳejn tribe.

more justified because the herdsmen had found in the afternoon tracks left by several robbers. The Prince thought them to be those of the Ḥeǧâja and consequently issued an order that the camp and all the herds be watched closely. It might have

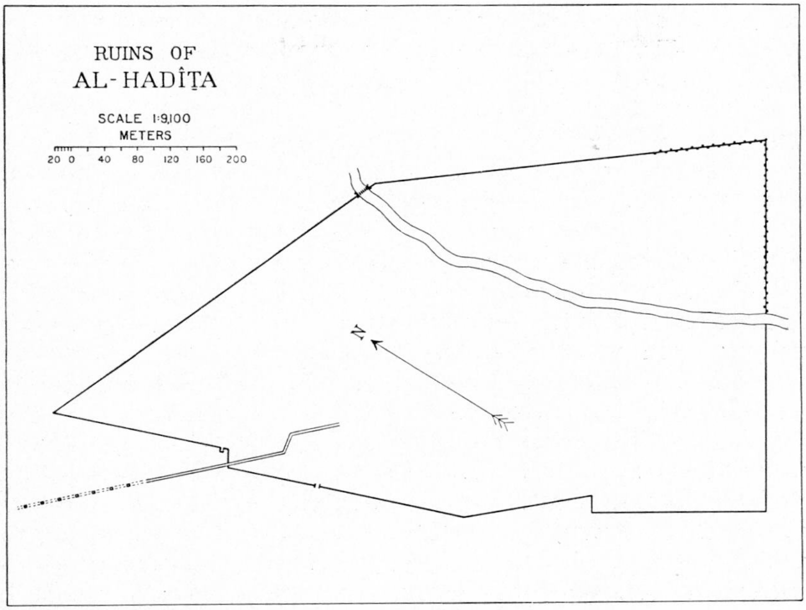

FIG. 71—Ground plan of ruins of al-Ḥadîṯa.

happened that one of the sentries had perceived Tûmân in the darkness and called to him and receiving no reply — for Tûmân did not know Arabic — had stabbed or shot him. Hence the Prince sent out several men to seek for him in the neighborhood. He was finally found about two hundred paces from the tent, lying in a small ditch sound asleep. He was shivering with cold when brought into the tent; the malaria, which had been troubling him for several days, had become acute.

On Saturday we again got under way. Following the course of the easternmost of the *šeʿibân* of al-Žeššâš in a southwesterly direction, we came at 6.23 A. M. upon several pools filled with rain water (*ṛudur*), where we stayed until seven o'clock. Then we rode toward the northwest through barren plains covered with flints (*ṣawwân*) and bearing no vegetation whatever. Only in the wide, shallow valleys of al-Žeššâš was a scant pasturage found for the camels. It had not rained there the preceding winter. The Šeʿibân al-Žeššâš end in the vicinity of the Ḳulbân al-ʿEmeri in the lowland Fejẓa Čâbde. North of al-ʿEmeri the Riğlet Slejmân enters the depression of Sirḥân, and east of Slejmân, at the southern base of the mighty height of the Tlejlât al-Fraʾ, looms the solitary cone Tell al-Ḳarma. To the north the three hills of ar-Rjetên, which mark the southern boundary of the Ḥawrân, were slowly appearing through a veil of thin clouds. At noon we pitched a new camp.

On Sunday, starting at 5.24 A. M., we traveled through shallow valleys in which grew *mwâṣala, šnân, šîḥ, ruḳejže, lwejza, nedd, nkejda, zaʿtar, lisân al-ṛurâb, selʿ, šağarat al-ğerâd, šağarat al-ḥarâḏîn, šağarat al-ẖanejzîr, šağarat an-naḥel, kalša, čḥejl, brukân, rûṯe, roṛol, niḳd,* and *ḥaršaf*. The landscape was wearisomely monotonous — nothing but a gray rolling plain with wide, shallow hollows. At six o'clock we entered the valley of al-Ṛadaf, in which is the ruined castle of Ṭûbt al-Ṛadaf, or, as the Beni Ṣaẖr call it, aṭ-Ṭûba.[80]

To the southwest rose the low, wide crest of aẓ-Ẓabʿ; to the northwest of it towered the mighty slope of al-Ḥâfra; and north of that ran the ridge of aṣ-Ṣafraʾ, trending toward the east. The sun, just rising, flooded their yellow slopes with its rays and made them appear as if they were sprinkled with gold. Before them to the northwest showed the ruin of al-Ḫawrâna (or al-Ḫarâni, as called by the Beni Ṣaẖr), resembling a fabulous castle. From all its sides and corners sparks seemed to blaze forth, surrounding the entire structure with rosy light, which caused it to contrast sharply with the blue of the sky. Suddenly the apparition faded away and a cloud enveloped the castle, for the spirit who inhabited it would not brook the gaze of the sons of Adam.

On the eastern threshold of the slope of aṣ-Ṣafraʾ gaped the deep depression of al-Buṭum, where we beheld another grotesque structure. It was the famous Ḳuṣejr ʿAmra, inhabited by an evil spirit (*ṛôla*). Veiled in thin vapors, it appeared and reappeared as the breeze rent and rejoined the shifting

[80] Al-Walîd ibn Jazîd with his men left the residence of the Caliph Hišâm in the city of ar-Reṣâfa and settled at al-Azraḳ, between the territory of the Balḳejn and that of the Fezâra, at the water of al-Aṛdaf (Abu-l-Farağ, *Aṛâni* [Bûlâḳ, 1285 A.H.], Vol. 6, p. 104). —

Al-Azraḳ denotes here the district at the center of which the fort of al-Azraḳ was located. Al-Aṛdaf, or al-Ṛadaf — as the word sounds in the dialect — is identical with our wells of al-Ṛadaf at the castle of aṭ-Ṭûba, which is situated between the former territory of the Balḳejn tribe and that of the Ḍubjân clan of the Fezâra tribe.

mists. But how melancholy the castle looked from a distance! Standing deep in the lowland enclosed on all sides by high, gray, desolate slopes, it appeared to be a part of the hillside. Between it and the sky were vaporous exhalations from the earth, which prevented the sunbeams from penetrating to it. The castle stood as gloomy as if it were forsaken by heaven itself. No wonder the Arabs attribute such a place to none but the ghoul (*rôla*).

From 7.55 until 8.28 our camels grazed about the valley of al-Bsâs. East-northeast, the region of Ḍrejlat Ḥarbi was visible, with its ragged hillocks and with the deep Wâdi Râğel separating it into two uneven parts. Wâdi Râğel approaches from the Ḥawrân, extends southward through the plain Ḳâʿ aš-Šubejče, and in the stony plain of aṣ-Ṣafâwijjât on the right takes in the *šeʿîb* of aṣ-Ṣafâwi, which begins at the Tlûl al-Baʿâjeṯ. In the channel of Râğel are the Ṛadîr al-Fhedâwi, al-Mellâḥ, and Abu-ṣ-Ṣjar. South of these rain pools Râğel is joined on the left by the Šeʿîb Selâḥîb, coming from the volcano of an-Neẓâjem in the Ḥarrat aš-Šhabaʾ. On the southern base of the Ḥazm Flûḳ Dalma the Wudej al-Maʿâši joins Wâdi Râğel on the left; the Wudej al-Maʿâši separates Flûḳ Dalma from the lava hills of as-Sûd and al-Fraʾ. North of Ḍrejlat Ḥarbi and west of Wâdi Râğel there extends toward the north-northwest a hilly belt in which the black groups of Aṣejḫem, as-Sbâra, al-Aṣfar, and ar-Rjetên are prominent. West of these the cones of al-Menâsef may be seen. Wâdi Râğel winds through the volcanic desert of ar-Rağla and terminates in the depression of Sirḥân. The latter I identify with the classical depression of Syrmaion and the Baṭn as-Sirr[81] of the early Arabic writers.

[81] Stephen of Byzantium, *Ethnica* (Meineke), Vol. 1, p. 593, says that the plain of Syrmaion is situated between the nomads and the Nabataeans. — The depression of Sirḥân formed and still forms a boundary between the settlers, or breeders of goats and sheep, and the nomads proper, or Bedouins, who are breeders of camels.

Al-Hamdâni, *Ṣifa* (Müller), p. 206, writes that the territory between the sand desert of ʿÂleğ and the volcanic region of ar-Rağlaʾ in Palmyrena belonged to the Kalb tribe in the eighth century. — Indeed, Ḥarrat ar-Rağlaʾ sends arms clear into Palmyrena proper. It is bordered on the west by the depression of Sirḥân and reaches almost as far south as the Nefûd desert, which formerly was known as ʿÂleğ.

Al-Bekri, *Muʿğam* (Wüstenfeld), pp. 274, 399, says that Râğel denotes a volcanic region, but he is not sure whether it is identical with the volcanic district of ar-Rağlaʾ, which he seeks in the territory of the Ğuḏâm tribe. — Neither the Arabic poets nor the Arabic geographers were cognizant of any Ḥarrat ar-Rağlaʾ in the territory of the Ğuḏâm, all agreeing that it was in the territory of the Kalb.

Jâḳût, *Muʿğam* (Wüstenfeld), Vol. 2, pp. 728 f., refers to the valley of Râğel in Neğd and also to the volcanic region between as-Sirr and the frontier settlements in which the valley of Râğel has its head, ending in the depression of as-Sirr. Az-Zamaḫšari (*ibid.*, p. 248) seeks the volcanic district of Râğel between as-Sabbaʾ and the frontier settlements in the Ḥawrân. The poet an-Nâbiṛa (*ibid.*) mentions the Ḥarrat Rağlaʾ. — No other Arabic writer mentions the local name as-Sabbaʾ near the Ḥawrân. I am of the opinion that, as used by Jâḳût, it is an erroneous transcription of Sirr. The final *r* might easily have been transformed into a final *i*, while the *b* might have originated from the junction of the *s* with the *r*, especially if it were not provided with the diacritical dot. Our valley of Râğel

Through a desolate gravel-covered plain we came at 9.10 to the valley of aš-Šômeri and encamped there at 9.40 (Figs. 72, 73). Here the Prince was visited by four chiefs who came to report on their skirmishes with the Turkish soldiers in the

FIG. 72—Our camp, valley of aš-Šômeri.

Ḥawrân. Also several camel riders who had been sent out to find pasture and water (*ḳallâṭ*) returned one after another in the evening. One of them reported that all the *ṛudur* (holes in a dry watercourse) in the channel of al-Ḥarṯ were full of water, but that the pasture was much less abundant, though better than in the vicinity of al-Azraḳ; whereupon the Prince

---

rises in the volcanic region east of the Ḥawrân and terminates in the depression of Sirḥân, which is called Baṭn as-Sirr.

Abu Manṣûr (Jâḳût, *op. cit.*, p. 755) says that the Ḥarrat Rağla' is a plain littered with coarse stones. Abu-l-Hajṯam (*ibid.*, p. 755) holds that it is a region impossible to cross on horseback or by camel. The volcanic region of Rağla' is in the territory of the Beni al-Ḳejn between al-Medîna and Syria. A certain poet (*ibid.*, p. 248) mentions al-Ḥarrat ar-Rağla' in connection with al-Ḥadâla and the lowland of Luğğân, or Lağğân. —

The Beni al-Ḳejn camped northeast of the Ğuḏâm tribe and west of the Kalb tribe, hence about north of the present oasis of Tejma and west of the depression of Sirḥân, the Ḥarrat ar-Rağla' thus forming a frontier between them and the Kalb tribe. This is corroborated by the poet al-Aḫnas ibn Šihâb (Jâḳût, *op. cit.*, p. 248), who also places the Ḥarrat ar-Rağla' almost at the frontier of the Kalb tribe. Al-Ḥadâla is the al-Ḥadâla of the present. Lağğân I seek in the lowland of al-Leğğâl, as *n* is frequently replaced by *l*.

Near the Ḥarrat ar-Rağla', between al-Medîna and Syria, Jâḳût, *op. cit.*, Vol. 2, p. 187, refers to the watering place of al-Ḥâla, belonging to the Balḳejn tribe. As the territory of the Balḳejn tribe extended in the east as far as the Baṭn as-Sirr (the present depression of Sirḥân), the watering place of al-Ḫâla is to be sought in the northern part of the depression of Sirḥân, which is bounded on the east by the volcanic region of ar-Rağla'.

Al-Bekri, *op. cit.*, p. 790, quotes a verse of the poet an-Nâbiṛa mentioning the watering places of Ḫâla (or Ḥâla), aḏ-Ḏunâba, and Suwa'. All these belonged to the Kalb tribe and were situated in the region of al-Manâẓer. — Al-Manâẓer is called the eastern boundary of Syria from al-Belḳa' up to al-Ḥawwârîn. If we are to seek the water of Ḥâla in the northern part of the depression of Sirḥân, and Suwa' in Sab' Bijâr, we must look for aḏ-Ḏunâba between them. The watering place of al-Ğwejf, which is situated at the end of the valley of aḏ-Ḏenâba, would seem to correspond with this location.

Another watering place of al-Ḥâla (al-Ḫâla) — see Jâḳût, *op. cit.*, Vol. 2, p. 391 — was known also in the eastern half of north Arabia: I seek it in the basin of al-Ḳa'ara.

According to Jâḳût, *op. cit.*, Vol. 1, p. 491, in the Baṭn as-Sirr there was also the water of al-Batîle.

decided that we should march into the valley of al-Ḥarṯ, leaving al-Azraḳ on the right. Upon hearing this I resolved to ride immediately to al-Azraḳ. For this purpose I sent Nâṣer after my riding camel, but he could not find her.

FIG. 73—Our camp, valley of aš-Šômeri; my tents.

I rode out to the fort of al-Azraḳ on Monday, starting at 2.08 in the morning in company with ʿAwde al-Kwêčbi. The direction was indicated by a large fire ignited by one of the Rwala clans in the dry reeds south of al-Azraḳ in order that a better pasture might be obtained the following year. At 3.18 we crossed the channel of al-Buṭum and at 4.24 entered the marsh that extends to the Ḥarrat al-ʿWejned.[82]

At 4.28 we had on the right, two hundred meters ahead of us, the ʿAjn al-Asad, where, it is claimed, the last lion had been shot. Ahead of us loomed the spur al-Mežâber extending from the northwest to the southeast; here we stopped at 5.24 because I wanted to draw a map of the environs. Upon finishing this work, we started again at 6.08 and cantered toward the north-northeast to the ruins of al-Azraḳ. Crossing the channel of ar-Ratam, we reached the southern edge of the *ḥarra* and proceeded on between it and the marsh. Since we were not sure whether robbers might not be lurking in the ruins, we loaded our carbines and started ahead at a gallop; but no bullet greeted us and nowhere did we see fresh tracks. Feeling secure, therefore, we allowed our camels to kneel down

[82] Al-Muḳaddasi, *Aḥsan* (De Goeje), p. 253, says that the station of al-ʿAwnîd is situated in the sand desert and that it includes two rain pools containing clear water. — From the description of the road which al-ʿAwnîd adjoins it is evident that this station is identical with al-ʿWejned, and yet there is no sand desert in the vicinity. The Arabic spelling of ʿAwnîd should be ʿUwajnid; the written word is easily mispronounced.

FIG. 74

FIG. 75

FIG. 74—Al-Azraḳ from the south.
FIG. 75—Al-Azraḳ.

leisurely at 6.57 near the southern end of the ruins. ʿAwde stayed with the camels, while I went in.[83]

Ḳaṣr al-Azraḳ (Figs. 74, 75, 76) is situated on the edge of the volcanic spur that extends from al-Menâsef southward and

FIG. 76—From Al-Azraḳ looking southwest.

ends about one kilometer farther to the southeast. To the east, about two kilometers from al-Azraḳ, begins the depression of Sirḥân which here forms a deep embayment to the north towards the *šeʿîb* of al-ʿEnḳijje, which comes from al-Menâsef and disappears between the spring ʿAjn al-Bêẓa to the south and the low volcano of Tlejl al-Ḫanejzîr to the northeast. South of the latter a large *ḫabra* penetrates wedge-like into the depression as far as the *šeʿîb* of Aṣejḫem; while south of

[83] Al-Muḳaddasi, *op. cit.*, p. 248, refers to no other city in the Arabian desert except Tejma and to no other lake or river except al-Azraḳ.

Jâḳût, *op. cit.*, Vol. 1, p. 232, writes that al-Azraḳ is a valley in the Ḥeǧâz and a watering place in the region of Mecca upon the Pilgrim Road that leads to Syria, on this side of the oasis of Tejma. — The pilgrims from Syria frequently went from Damascus by way of al-Azraḳ and the oasis of Tejma to al-Medîna. Hence the watering place of al-Azraḳ was situated upon the Syrian Pilgrim Road.

According to a note of Abu-l-Feda', *Taḳwîm* (Reinaud and de Slane), p. 229, Azraḳ is a castle which was built by order of al-Malek al-Muʿaẓẓam on the edge of the desert. Through the desert, on the right, a road leads to Tebûk and al-ʿEla, and on the left one leads to the oases of Tejma and Ḫajbar. Boṣra' is situated north of al-Azraḳ. — Al-Malek al-Muʿaẓẓam (1196—1218 A. D.) built various stations on the western edge of the desert. The roads mentioned by Abu-l-Feda' are described by al-Muḳaddasi.

al-Azraḳ spreads the boggy, impassable al-Žijâši, a lowland overgrown with high reeds and thickets, which sends a swampy arm far to the southeast. ʿAwde urged me to hurry through my work, for he was fearful of an attack by the Ahâli al-Ğebel.

ḲAṢR AL-AZRAḲ TO ḲUṢEJR ʿAMRA

Therefore, at 7.25 I mounted my camel and we returned westward over the route by which we had come. From 8.07 until 9.13 we paused in the channel of ar-Ratam by a small *radîr*, about two hundred paces from which I discovered the foundation walls of a solitary building. At 9.38 we ascended al-Mežâber, whence I sketched a map of the district to the west and south. The spur of al-Mežâber runs northward parallel with the hilly belt Umm al-Ḫazne.

At 10.18 we headed toward the pools of al-Žijâši (Figs. 77, 78, 79), dismounting by them at 10.38. These large ponds are so choked with reeds that they are difficult to reach. The southwestern one, which is enclosed by a wall sixty centimeters to one meter wide, is hexagonal in form, its eastern side being 270 meters long, with an outlet a meter and a half wide at about the center. Both ends of the hexagon are rounded out into extensions almost seven meters wide, and the southwestern wall is reinforced on both sides by round pillars. The ponds abound in a great variety of fish and crabs. We saw large flocks of birds fly over from one pond to another, apparently so unconcerned at our presence that I could approach within ten to fifteen paces of them. Finishing my work, I shot down twenty-two birds with but five charges. On our return we held high feast upon them in my tent.

At 12.15 P.M. we headed toward our camp. The heat was excessive. It seemed as if the ground were seething under my feet. So stifling was the atmosphere that it was difficult to breathe; every inhalation seemed to burn the mouth and throat. And the heat became even more unbearable when, at 1.32, we entered the small volcanic area Ḥarrat al-ʿWejned. Here the camels could proceed but very slowly through the black lava, and the air over it was intensely hot.

At 2.25 we stopped and I ascended a lava mound to verify from it the direction of al-Mežâber and the Ḳuṣejr ʿAmra. The mound was barely 150 meters from the spot where I left my camel, yet it took me over a quarter of an hour to get to the top of it. I had to climb over large fragments of lava, the angles of which were sharp and the flat sides smooth, presenting no foothold. Most of the boulders reclined one against another, with openings one or two meters deep gap-

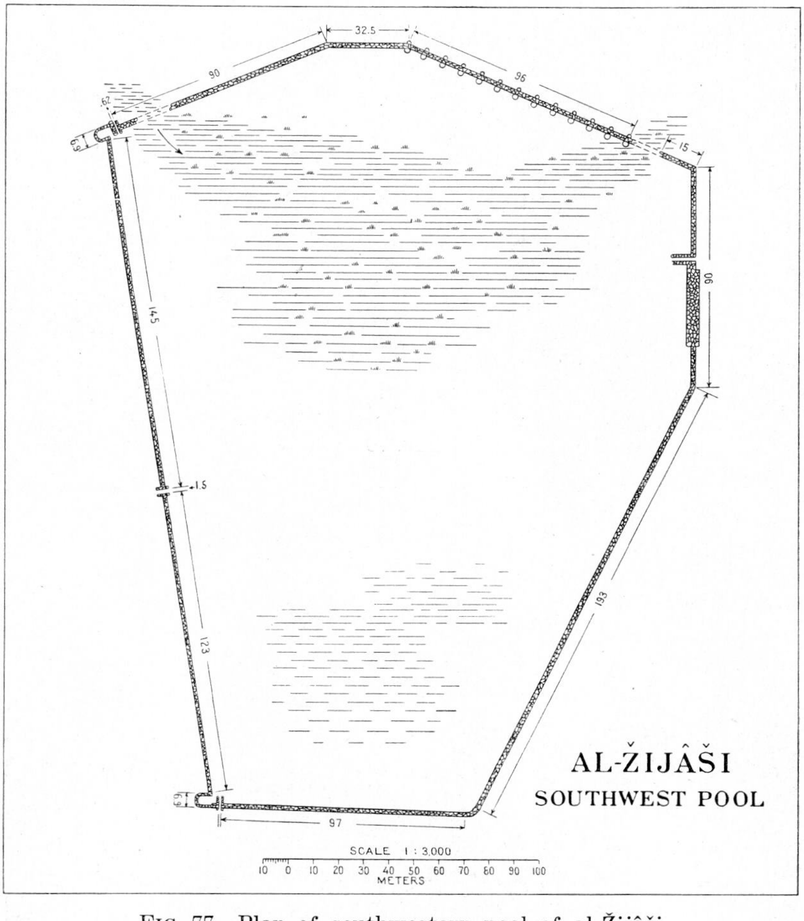

FIG. 77—Plan of southwestern pool of al-Žijâši.

ing between them. Carrying a plane-table upon my back and its tripod in my hands, I slipped several times into these holes and bruised my hands and feet. After finishing the work, I discovered upon one of the boulders a brief Ṣafaʾ inscription, which I copied. Then we resumed our ride at 3.20 and reached

Fig. 78

Fig. 79

Fig. 78—One of the pools of al-Žijâši.
Fig. 79—View west from al-Žijâši.

at 3.27 the western end of the *ḥarra*, thence continuing onward through the wide valley of al-Buṭum, where grew *nbejṭa, nečîʿ, ḳaṭaf, šnân, šîḥ, ʿaẓw, ratam, firs, ṯḥama, nefel, šaʿrân,* and the curious *ṛaṭṛafân*, with its large leaves lying flat on the ground.

At 5.47 my camel knelt in front of the castle of ʿAmra (Fig. 80) and after eight years I reëntered the familiar rooms. I yearned to copy the principal inscription, for it was possible that we might move onward the following day, but ʿAwde would not wait. We did not know where the Prince's camp was, but we were well aware that there were no Rwala in our rear, a fact which increased the possibility of our being attacked by robbers. Therefore I stopped my work at 6.14 and we rode along the valley of al-Buṭum and later along that of al-Ḥarṯ, until at 7.17 we found the camp of Prince an-Nûri. Tûmân was complaining of fatigue and general lethargy; he wanted nothing but sleep and food.

Tuesday, June 15, 1909. We did not migrate, for the Prince was still awaiting the return of Ḥmâr; therefore, taking along the dispirited Tûmân and Nâṣer, I went back to ʿAmra to photograph the important inscription. The neighborhood had changed very much since I first saw it (Figs. 81, 82). Four years before, rain had fallen so plentifully that the Sirḥân, who were camping near the castle on both the right and the left bank of the Wudej al-Buṭum, cut out and burned all the bushes. Since, however, the rain had been insufficient in the next two years and almost absent during the year just past, not even annuals had grown, while perennials had either been grazed off or rooted out and burned. Consequently the vicinity now resembled an arid desert. Even the younger terebinth trees had disappeared, only the oldest ones remaining (Fig. 83). These stood south of the castle, at the channel above the artificial *ṛadîr*. The latter had been filled with water about a fortnight before. Hundreds, perhaps thousands, of camels had drunk and left their excrement in it. The dung was lying many centimeters deep at the edges of and even in the water, which was of a dark brown color and had the putrid stench of a stagnant puddle. And yet Nâṣer filled our canvas bucket with this water, cooked coffee for us with it, and we drank the coffee—nay, when later it became very hot, the very water itself! I could smell the stench of the dung water on my hands for the next three days.

Fig. 80

Fig. 81

Fig. 80—Ḳuṣejr ʿAmra from the north.
Fig. 81—Ḳuṣejr ʿAmra from the southeast.

FIG. 82

FIG. 83

FIG. 82—Ḳuṣejr ʿAmra from the southwest.
FIG. 83—The largest terebinth tree at Ḳuṣejr ʿAmra.

The ʿAmra paintings had suffered great damage. In the year 1901 we had to remove the patina, clean the paintings, and wash and daub them with various chemicals. Through this process the colors had been temporarily refreshed, but the particles of paint were falling off and the pictures were vanishing. The painting opposite the one we had taken from the wall[84] had disappeared. Intending to take that with us too, we had plastered canvas over it, cut the canvas in sections, and by rapping the plaster had tried to get the picture off the stone of the wall. Unable to separate it, however, as our escorts urged us to hurry along, we had to leave the work unfinished, with the canvas still over the picture. The unusual sight of the surface plastered over with canvas puzzled the Bedouin herdsmen, who poked off the canvas with their daggers and lances and thus destroyed the entire painting. I should now have liked to study the Arabic and Greek inscriptions under the pictures of the individual rulers,[85] but the most important parts had crumbled and fallen. The principal inscription[86] suffered a good deal from the washing of 1901 and yet I wanted to photograph it. But I found this no easy task. The arch containing it was over three meters above the ground in a recess that had no window, and, since the room itself was very dark, the inscription could not be photographed from the ground. Hence we piled stones into a heap about two meters high, upon which I placed the camera and photographed the inscription in parts. Because the letters were small and because I photographed from a distance of a meter and a half, I had to keep shifting the camera and to focus very accurately — no easy business upon a base of sliding stones! Alas, this laborious and even dangerous work came to nought, for not even one of the twelve photographs proved good. I made one more exact copy of the inscription.

Tûmân still complained of the weakness that had attacked him. He had no pains and his fever had subsided, yet he said that his stamina was gone, his will flaccid, and his only desire to lie and sleep.

In the afternoon a slave of the Prince came after me with the request that I come back immediately, as Ḥmâr had returned and he wanted to consult me on matters of importance.

[84] See Alois Musil, *Ḳuṣejr ʿAmra,* Vol. 1, p. 98.
[85] *ibid.,* p. 220.
[86] *ibid.,* p. 214.

For some time the Druses and the miscellaneous malcontents from Damascus who had taken refuge in the Ǧebel ad-Drûz had been urging an-Nûri to ally himself with them and attack the Turkish garrisons, but I had counseled the Prince not to act hastily and to be mindful only of the welfare of his tribe. Now the governor of Damascus had sent him a friendly message requesting that he and his tribes enter Syria and preserve order in the territory around his encampments.

ḲUṢEJR ʿAMRA TO DAMASCUS

On Wednesday we set forth at 6.20 A. M., going up the valley of al-Ḥart̲. I rode beside the Prince as usual. At eight o'clock we were joined by a Bedouin about fifty years of age. He saluted the Prince and the latter inquired:

"How dost thou fare?" "*Al-ḥamdu lillâh,* well." "Where do ye camp?" "At the Tell al-Adʿam." "Have ye not been attacked?" "Eight camels were stolen from me." "Have ye not pursued the robbers?" "Aye, my son pursued them." "Has he overtaken them?" "Aye." "Who were they?" "I wish I knew; likely the Ḥeǧâja." "Why, has not thy son recognized them?" "I know not." "Has he not told thee?" "Nay." "Hast thou not asked him?" "Nay; I could not speak with him." "How is that? Has he not returned?" "Nay." "And thou hast not searched for him, then?" "Aye, I rode after him." "Hast thou found him?" "Aye, I did." "Hast thou spoken with him?" "Nay." "Why?" "I found his body at the Ḫabra al-Ḳlejžlân, with the head shot off. The vultures and the hyenas had already visited him. I buried my son and returned." "When didst thou come back?" "Yesterday." "What sort of pasture is there here?" "Poor, but there is no pasture at all at ar-Rukubân. Have thy tent pitched here." "Where thou wilt?" "I seek the slayers of my son."

At 7.40 we observed to the east on the western base of the Zemlet umm al-Ḫazne a group of terebinth trees called Šaǧarât al-Muḥejlât. At nine o'clock we encamped. I collected plants and arranged my botanical collections. Tûmân continued to complain of his illness.

On Thursday morning we started out at 4.40 A. M. in a northwesterly direction. At 5.29 we passed the ruins of the village of al-Ḥart̲, where we paused until 5.46. At six o'clock we crossed the divide between the depression of Sirḥân and the

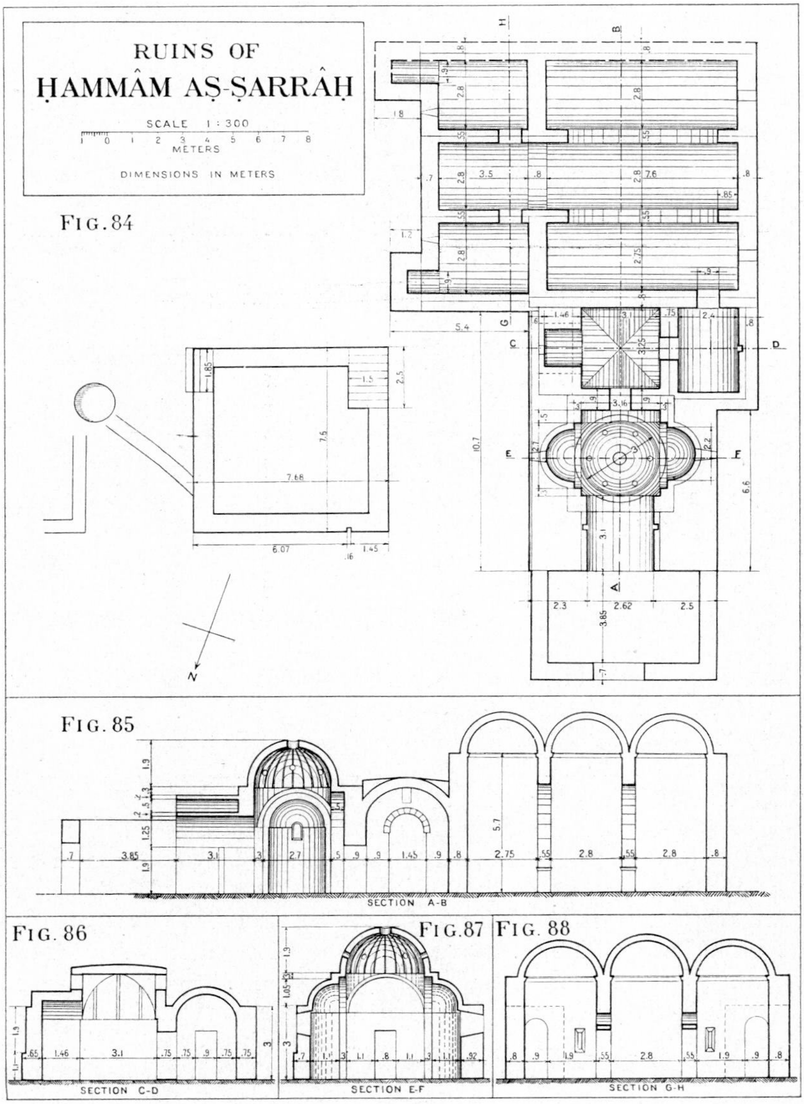

FIGS. 84-88—Ḥammâm aṣ-Ṣarrâḥ. Scale: 1:300.

FIG. 84—Ground plan. FIG. 85—Section A-B. FIG. 86—Section C-D. FIG. 87—Section E-F. FIG. 88—Section G-H.

Fig. 89

Fig. 90

Fig. 89—Ḥammâm aṣ-Ṣarrâḥ from the northwest.
Fig. 90—Ḥammâm aṣ-Ṣarrâḥ; the dome.

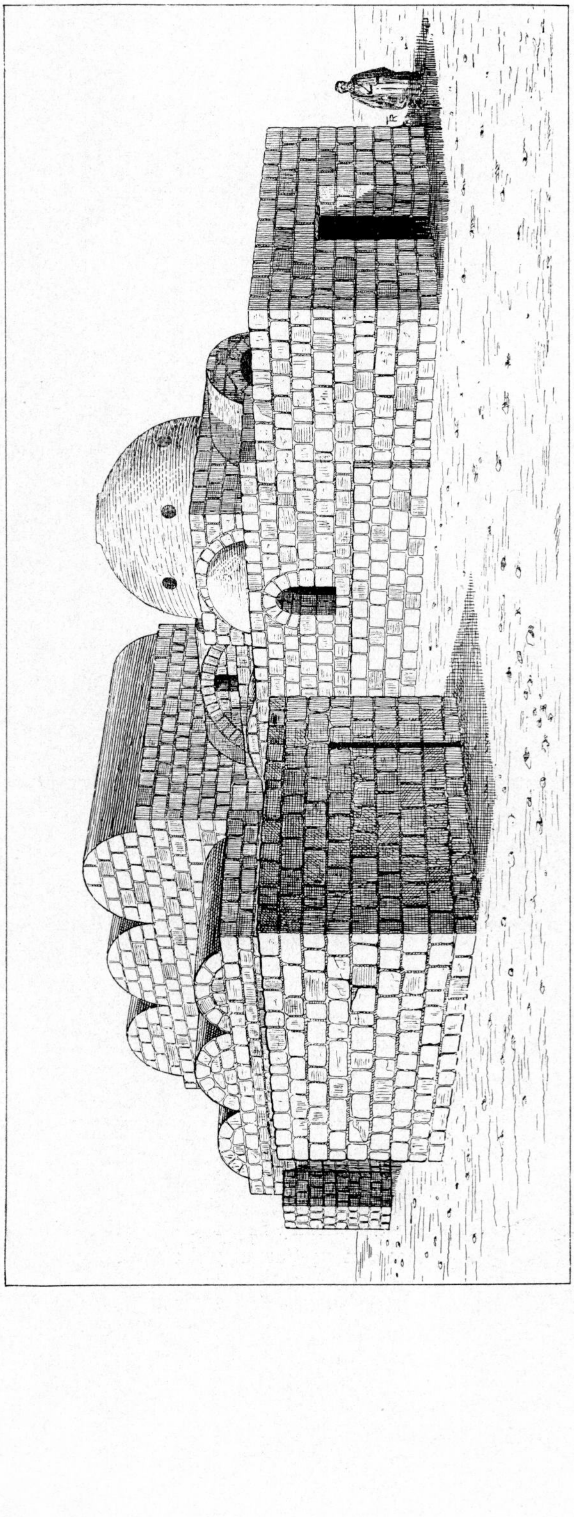

Fig. 91—Ḥammâm aṣ-Ṣarrâḥ; reconstruction.

brook az-Zerḳaʾ, following from here the *šeʿîb* of Abu Ṣawwâne, which runs into the valley of ar-Rukubân. At 6.20 we had on the right the Ṛadîr abu Ṣawwâne and at seven dismounted at the ruins of Ḥammâm aṣ-Ṣarrâḥ, situated in a large basin at the point where the valley of ar-Rukubân merges with the valley of aẓ-Ẓlejjel, which comes from the east.

Ḥammâm aṣ-Ṣarrâḥ (Figs. 84, 85, 86, 87, 88, 89, 90, 91) resembles the Ḳuṣejr ʿAmra very closely. Its southern side is formed by a large room that is divided into three vaulted apartments. The middle apartment has an arched extension which is adjoined on the right and left sides by vaulted chambers. From the left apartment a door opens into an oblong room and thence into a rectangular chamber with a cross arch. This chamber joins on the left side a quadrangular room that has a dome resting on pendentives and extended by two conchae facing each other. An oblong arched hall connects this room with a court which might formerly have had a flat roof and which is entered through a wide gate in the middle of its long side. Near the northern corner of the large room is a large rectangular cistern with a well beside it. There is another well farther toward the north and a third one on the south-southeastern side in a large court which is enclosed by a stone wall. The southern wall of the large room is entirely ruined. On all the unimpaired walls are remains of paintings, and it is evident that all the rooms were once painted.[87]

At 9.15, in company with ʿAwde al-Kwêčbi, I left the Ḥammâm aṣ-Ṣarrâḥ and sped west toward the ruins of the Ḳaṣr al-Ḥallâbât, reaching there at ten o'clock (Figs. 92, 93, 94). At 11.10 we again sat upon the camels, watering them at 1.15 P. M. at the Ṛudur az-Zaʿatri. After 1.32 we rode through an undulating plain bare of pasture. To the east we saw the mountains of the Ḥawrân; to the west, beyond the Pilgrim Road, peered the crest of al-Maʿḳûf; and far to the north the snow-covered summit of Ṭwîl al-Felǧ, as Hermon is called by the Rwala, beckoned us on. At 4.20 we encamped west of Umm al-Ǧemal, but we pitched no tents.

On Friday we set out at 4.30 in a northwesterly direction. At 4.45 we crossed the first Roman highway (*ar-raṣîf*) and at six o'clock the second. From seven until 7.32 and from 9.40

[87] Ḥamzat al-Iṣfahâni, *Taʾrîḫ* (Gottwaldt), p. 117, relates that the Ghassanian king Taʿlaba ibn ʿAmr built residences in ʿAḳa and Ṣarrâḥ al-Ṛadîr on the boundary of the Ḥawrân and al-Belḳaʾ. He determined according to this *ṛadîr* the location of the buildings of Ḥarba and Zerḳa which are ascribed to the Ghassanian king al-Mundir ibn al-Ḥâreṯ. — Az-Zerḳa is situated barely thirty kilometers west-southwest from the Ṛadîr abu Ṣawwâne.

Fig. 92

Fig. 93

Fig. 92—Ruins of Ḳaṣr al-Ḥallâbât.
Fig. 93—A Moslem building at Ḳaṣr al-Ḥallâbât.

until 10.20 our camels grazed, this time upon fields which had already been harvested. At eleven o'clock we arrived at the railroad track.

Prince an-Nûri eben Ša'lân had entered the territory of the settlers (*daḫal ad-dîra*). The camp was no sooner pitched

FIG. 94—Ḳaṣr al-Ḥallâbât; an ornament.

upon the fields of the Naṣîb settlement than it was visited by the elders of the various adjacent villages, who came to pay fealty to the Prince and to invite him to dine with them. In the afternoon streams of camels, donkeys, and asses kept arriving laden with gifts of wheat, barley, and flour for the Prince and the other chiefs. It was the tribute (*ḫuwa*) by means of which the settlers purchased protection and safety from the Arabs.

The Prince sat by me until late in the night talking about our imminent parting. We had become true friends; he had often declared openly that I was dearer to him than his first-born son, Nawwâf.

On Saturday, June 19, 1909, with all my companions and camels, I left the camp of the Prince and marched to Damascus, where I arrived Monday, June 21, 1909, in the afternoon.

PART II

1912

CHAPTER XII

AR-RUMÂDI TO AN-NEǦEF (MEŠHED ʿALI)

In March, 1912, I undertook an exploring expedition with Prince Sixtus of Bourbon through Palmyrena to the middle Euphrates and southern Mesopotamia.[88] We were accompanied by Rudolf Thomasberger, of the Military Geographical Institute of Vienna, and by two servants, Nâṣer al-Marlûḳ and Muḥammad al-Ḥamûṭe from al-Žerjitejn. We rode camels. At ar-Rumâdi we left the Euphrates, returning to it again at an-Neǧef, or Mešhed ʿAli.

AR-RUMÂDI TO ʿAJN AT-TAMR

Monday, April 22, 1912. At 11.30 A. M. we left ar-Rumâdi and at 11.47 arrived at the bridge Ḳanṭarat al-ʿAzîzijje, where we remained drawing water until noon. In the neighborhood of the bridge are gardens where various kinds of vegetables are raised, as well as pomegranates and palms. Adjoining the gardens are huts and warehouses belonging to members of the tribe of Dlejm. Beyond the Nahr aṭ-Ṭâšš the low crest of al-Ḥamra' rises to the east, and to the southwest are the hills of al-Ḫarfaše and as-Serîm. At 12.05 P. M. we crossed the shallow channel of the valley of Čerijjân, which runs through an absolutely bare and sterile stony plain. To the southeast appeared the broad blue surface of Lake al-Ḥabbânja, which receives the overflow from the canal of aṭ-Ṭâšš. Whenever the water of the Euphrates rises, the water of al-Ḥabbânja rises likewise, and when the river recedes the lake reverts to mere swamps.[89]

At 1.40 we sighted on the west side of Lake al-Ḥabbânja the shrine Ḳabr Saʿad al-ʿÂṣi; at 2.14 we were riding through

[88] The portion of this journey which lay through Palmyrena is described in the author's *Palmyrena*; that along the Euphrates and in southern Mesopotamia in the author's *The Middle Euphrates*. Both of these volumes are to be published in the series of which the present volume forms No. 2.

[89] Jâḳût, *Muʿǧam* (Wüstenfeld), Vol. 2, p. 193, writes that Ḥabbânijje belongs to the political district of al-Kûfa, the inhabitants of which were defeated there by a horde of the Kharijites in the time of Zijâd ibn Abîh (therefore in the latter half of the seventh century of our era).

the salty everglades of al-Ḫaẓar. To the northeast the rosy peaks of al-Ḥamra' could be seen and east of them al-Mšêhed with the old sanctuary of al-Imâm ʿAli. East of the shrine, upon the tabular hill of ar-Raʿjân, is the large mound formed by the Tell ar-Raḥâja ruins, and northeast of us, upon the height of al-Ḥejtân, was the shrine of aš-Šejḫ Masʿûd. The low salient of al-Ḥamra' penetrates deep into Lake al-Ḥabbânja and forms the peninsula of al-Munsarbe, which in its rosy hue contrasts sharply with the blue expanse of water. Upon the shores tents were visible as dark specks. After three o'clock we rode again upon the stony ground of al-Mehedd. To the west rose the peaks of al-Ḳurʿ, while before us unfolded the wide *šeʿîb* of al-Eḳêreʿ, which originates west of the oasis of aṯ-Ṯmejl in two branches, aṯ-Ṯmejli ab-al-Ḥnej and aṯ-Ṯmejli al-Wasîṭ. Into the first branch converges a ravine coming from ʿAjn ab-al-Žîr; into the other the Riǧlet umm Deḫân. The vicinity of aṯ-Ṯmejl has such an abundance of water that the various clans of the Dlejm tribe sow grain there and raise vegetables, but not a single palm, it is said. The inhabitants live in tents and dwellings made of branches and straw. In Ab-al-Žîr bitumen exudes from the ground. The local springs moisten the fields, which are tilled by the family of al-Bu Člêb.

At 4.20 we camped in the *šeʿîb* of al-Eḳêreʿ, here overgrown with all sorts of fresh grasses and woody plants. Under almost every bush was hidden a nest of the *ḳaṭa'* (sand grouse) — a mere dimple dug in the sand, without any feather lining and containing three eggs each the size of a large hazelnut and of a brown tinge with dark specks. In some of the nests the bare young ones were already piping. The feathered birds were running about like chickens and were easy to catch. They supplied us with delicious soup. A drizzle fell during the night and a southerly wind came up.

Tuesday, April 23, 1912. We set out at 5.32 A. M., riding in a region of low tabular heights that rose higher toward the west. The ground was rocky, with vegetation in the hollows only. This district is called Ab-al-Frûḫ, because the entire region is the domicile of the *ḳaṭa'* birds. Their young ones (*frûḫ*) were everywhere; in almost no time we gathered enough for dinner and supper. Many birds of prey flew about us in quest of the *ḳaṭa'*.[90]

[90] Al-Aḫṭal, *Dîwân* (Salhani), p. 10, mentions a depression of al-Ḳaṭa', which, perhaps, is identical with that of the present day, as it also belonged to the tribe of the Taġleb.

At 7.35 we reached the depression of Ab-al-Frûẖ and from 8.10 until 8.25 were drawing water from the wells of that name. In the vicinity grow *rimṯ* and *šafallaḥ*. From 9.45 until 10.45 we rested southeast of the spring of al-Aʿwaǧ in the hollow of an-Naẖla, which is bounded on the west by the hills of Bradân. The watering place of Bradân is situated in the valley of al-Ṛadaf west of an-Naẖla.[91]

At 11.40 we were in the broad lowland of ar-Rôẓa, where the valley of al-Ṛadaf terminates. The lowland is in cultivation and belongs to the head chief Fahad eben Drejm eben Haḏḏâl of the ʿAmârât tribe. His fortified farm, al-Ḳṣejr, is at the southeast edge of the fields and he maintains a small house at the spring al-ʿEṣêle. The low and rugged hillocks to the west are called Abu Musrân and al-ʿAṣîbijje. At 1.20 P. M. we had to the west the spring and low hillocks of al-ʿAṣîbijje and to the east isolated mounds of disintegrating limestone.

At 2.10 we came into the basin of Čerd al-Alwâni, where also there are tilled fields, and remained there from 2.32 until 3.30 to give our camels a chance to graze. At 3.50 we crossed the valley of al-Mâleḥ. Toward noon the south wind calmed down, but at 3.58 the wind rose again from the west and brought thick clouds of sand. The sky became overcast with an opaque, yellowish veil which even the sunbeams could not penetrate. At 4.40 we passed through the shallow valley of Ṯaʿejleb, in the eastern part of which flows a stream of the same name. East of the stream spreads the swampy lowland of al-Bḥêra and al-ʿEneb, containing the isle of al-Mešrefe.

At 5.05 we were in the lowland of al-Ḥesjâs, in which *ṭarfa* grows, and at 5.30 we had on the left the stone tower of al-Manṭar. Similar towers could be seen to the south and southeast around the large palm gardens of the settlement of ar-Raḥḥâlijje, which was gradually revealing itself to our eyes. These towers serve as a protection and stronghold for the husbandmen against the attacking Bedouins. To the southeast rose the hill Ḳalʿat Jenḳ. West of it and south of the tower of al-Manṭar was the green grove of Ubêra, where four

[91] Jâḳût, *op. cit.*, Vol. 1, p. 552, states that al-Baradân is the name of a water in the district of as-Samâwa, between al-Ğenâb and al-Ḥeni toward Irak. Ibn al-Kalbi records the death there of Wabara ibn Romanos, the contemporary of King an-Noʿmân ibn al-Munḏir (580—602 A. D.), who was on the way to Syri aand was interred at al-Baradân. —

Jâḳût designates the location of al-Baradân from the city of Ḥama', guiding himself by a tradition preserved by Sejf ibn ʿOmar. But neither Jâḳût nor Abu-l-Faḍâ'il knew the situation of al-Baradân correctly, whereas Ibn al-Kalbi was well aware that it is situated on the road from al-Kûfa to Syria. Al-Ḥeni is identical with al-Ḥnej. Al-Ğenâb is to be sought between Bradân and ʿAjn at-Tamr.

springs bubble up and unite in a rivulet. In its water we saw fish, crawfish, and snakes. To the west rose the tabular crest of al-ʿAẓâẓ and to the southeast spread a forest of palms and *ṭarfa*. From 5.35 until 6.07 we drew the bitterish water and the gendarmes watered their horses. The wind had become a sand storm. At times the sand would envelop us so that we could not see each other; but presently we were sheltered by the palms, among which we were entering and which were themselves bowing low before the fury of the storm, their leaves whining like infants. It was after seven o'clock when we reached the small dwellings of the village of ar-Raḥḥâlijje, and at 7.30 we encamped behind a high wall at the southwestern end of the village. Almost simultaneously the storm ceased with several large drops of rain and the stars began to twinkle above the horizon. Our starved camels dispersed through the gardens so excitedly that they broke two saddles in prancing among the trees.

Wednesday, April 24, 1912 (at 5.30 A. M., temperature: 19° C). We departed at six o'clock in a southerly direction. The palm gardens spread east and southeast of the settlement, which is situated upon a low spur of the crest of al-ʿAẓâẓ. East and south of the village extend swamps of various names. To the east is the swamp Hôr aš-Šummâne, with its spring ʿAjn Šerrâd; south of this is the Rôẓat Ajjûb, with the springs aš-Šeʿejb, al-Hwêr, and Ammu-n-Nemel; still farther to the south is al-ʿUwêne, with the springs Abu Ṣaḫr, aṣ-Ṣfejḥa, and Ummu Ṣfejje. Near the settlement itself spouts the spring az-Zerḳaʾ, which contains the best water.

The settlement of ar-Raḥḥâlijje is inhabited by about fifty families living in the fortified enclosures: Ḳaṣr al-Bêčât, Ḳaṣr al-ʿUwêne, and Ḳaṣr al-Bu Slîmân, which is the largest. The people till fields in ar-Rôẓa which are the property of the family of Eben Haḏḏâl of the ʿAmârât tribe. The chief at this time was Žijâd eben Muḥammad âl Bandar. At ar-Raḥḥâlijje the Turkish Government had established a gendarme station and had appointed a *mudîr* (governor of a small district).

At 6.20 we crossed the valley of Abu Sidr, where we found a growth of *sidr* and *ṭarfa*. At 6.40 we rode through the wide valley of al-Erǧâwi, upon the left side of which looms a white dome that had been built about 1880 by the chief of ar-Raḥḥâlijje for his wife Môẓaʾ. Al-Erǧâwi disappears in the meadows Rôẓat Ajjûb. At 6.47, at the shallow spring Ammu

Swejse, we turned to the southwest. To the southeast we perceived upon a high cone a tower called Ḳaṣr Bardawîl, and next to it, at ʿAjn al-Eṯle and ʿAjn ʿAlijje, a clump of large trees. Ahead of us was visible the white sanctuary of aš-Šejẖ Aḥmed eben Hâšem, with the residence of a dervish adjoining it. The sanctuary was built by Ṣâdeḳ Čelebi of Kerbela, who maintains the dervish. Everywhere lay the remains of walls, from which the husbandmen from ar-Raḥḥâlijje select material for their dwellings.

At 7.40 we entered the ruins of ʿAjn at-Tamr[92] and from eight until 8.47 remained in concealment behind the walls of the devastated fort, since our guide feared a possible attack

[92] Ğuḏejma al-Waḍḍâḥ ruled the territory between al-Ḥîra, al-Anbâr, Baḳḳa, Hît, ʿAjn at-Tamr, and the edge of the desert as far as al-Ṛumejr and al-Ḳuṭḳuṭâne (Jâḳût, *op. cit.*, Vol. 2, pp. 378 ff.).

About the year 600 A.D. the Persian governor of the region from ʿAjn at-Tamr as far as al-Ḥîra, a district embracing thirty settlements, was Ijâs ibn Ḳabîṣa of the tribe of Ṭajj (Abu-l-Farağ, *Aṛâni* [Bûlâḳ, 1285 A.H.], Vol. 20, p. 134).

At the beginning of 634 many Moslems fell at ʿAjn at-Tamr and were buried, men who had been under the command of Ḫâled ibn al-Walîd. According to some reports, the defenders of the fort of ʿAjn at-Tamr contracted a peace with Ḫâled (al-Belâḏori, *Futûḥ* [De Goeje], p. 248). According to others they fought the Moslems bravely, but, upon the realization of the futility of resistance, sued for peace, which was refused them, and Ḫâled took possession of the fort by force, capturing an assemblage of youths that he found in a certain sanctuary. It has been alleged, however, that these youths were captured in another settlement (*ibid.*, p. 246 f.). Al-ʿAbderi says that Ḫâled captured youths, who were learning to write, in the settlement of an-Nuḳejra not far from ʿAjn at-Tamr (Jâḳût, *op. cit.*, Vol. 4, pp. 807 f.). —

An-Nuḳejra probably was a cloister near ʿAjn at-Tamr. Bearing in mind the conservatism of the Orient, we may identify this Christian cloister with the present Shiite cloister of aš-Šejẖ Aḥmad eben Hâšem, about four kilometers northeast of ʿAjn at-Tamr.

At the end of the year 633 and at the beginning of 634 A.D. the Moslems were making hostile incursions into the vicinity of the cities of Kaskar, Ğusûr, Miṯḳab, ʿAjn at-Tamr, and the districts of al-Falâlîğ and al-ʿÂl (aṭ-Ṭabari, *Taʾrîẖ* [De Goeje], Ser. 1, p. 2203). The district of al-ʿÂl was situated on the left bank of the Euphrates (*ibid.*, p. 2077; Jâḳût, *op. cit.*, Vol. 3, p. 592).

In the year 659—660 A.D. the master of the settlement of ʿAjn at-Tamr was the Caliph ʿAli, who had his garrison there. The garrison was attacked by the army despatched by Moawiyah, against which it defended itself outside of the settlement (aṭ-Ṭabari, *op. cit.*, p. 3444).

In the year 687—688 A.D. a battle was fought at ʿAjn at-Tamr between the adherents of the Caliph ʿAbdalmalek and those of Ibn az-Zubejr (*ibid.*, Ser. 2, p. 773).

Aṭ-Ṭabari, *op. cit.*, Ser. 2, p. 922, mentions the settlement of Neğrân in the year 695—696 A.D. in the vicinity of ʿAjn at-Tamr, which was also called Neğrân al-Kûfa.

In the year 701—702 A.D. al-Ḥağğâğ, vicegerent of the Caliph ʿAbdalmalek, hastened from al-Baṣra through the desert. He had arrived somewhere between al-ʿOḏejb and al-Ḳâdesijje (where he intended to encamp), when the rebels from Irak harassed him. As he was retreating before them, he reached Wâdi as-Sibâʿ; whereupon he turned to the left and encamped in Dejr Ḳurra, while his opponents took their quarters in Dejr al-Ğemâğem. Al-Ḥağğâğ longed to reach the settlement of Hît at the earliest possible moment, that he might be closer to Syria and Mesopotamia, whence he expected reinforcements. Dejr Ḳurra was situated in the vicinity of al-Falâlîğ and ʿAjn at-Tamr, and al-Ḥağğâğ encircled his camp there with trenches (*ibid.*, Ser. 2, p. 1072).

In the year 718—719 A.D. the Caliph ʿOmar issued an order that his deposed vicegerent of Irak, Jazîd ibn al-Muhalleb, be confined at ʿAjn at-Tamr (*ibid.*, p. 1352).

In the year 744—745 or 746—747 A.D. Ibn Hubejra, the commander of the Caliph Merwân II., marched from the canal of Saʿîd and encamped by the farm of Ṛazza (ʿAzza) at ʿAjn at-Tamr, where he defeated the rebels and advanced to al-Kûfa (*ibid.*, pp. 1914, 1945). — The Nahr Saʿîd turned away from the right bank of the Euphrates about thirteen kilometers northwest of Ḳarḳîṣija'. Aḍ-Ḍaḥḥâk, an adherent of the sect of Kharijites in Irak, had rebelled against the Caliph Merwân, and Ibn Hubejra was to subjugate him.

In the year 748 A.D. the poet Abu-l-ʿAtâhija is alleged to have been born in ʿAjn at-Tamr (Abu-l-Farağ, *op. cit.*, Vol. 3, p. 127).

Ibn Ḫordâḏbeh, *Masâlik* (De Goeje), p. 8, and Ḳodâma, *Ḫarâğ* (De Goeje), p. 236, were acquainted with the administrative district of ʿAjn at-Tamr.

from raiders. The fort is eighty paces long by sixty wide, with a gate in the center of its eastern wall (Fig. 95). Along its eastern and northern sides are scattered heaps of adobe and small stones, and about a kilometer west seven springs called the Râs al-ʿAjn gush out in the valley of aš-Šrejš. Our guide explained that the city of ʿAjn at-Tamr was built by Bardwîl eben Râšed, one of whose sons had outraged his own sister. She fled south in grief and bathed herself in the spring of al-Mšejžîž, the water of which has been red ever since.

To the west protruded the yellowish mesas of al-Čahâf, beyond them the Ḳârt umm Ḳaṭaf, and south of the latter the Ḳârat Masʿûd, Ṭwêr al-Ḥammâm, and aṣ-Ṣafâḥa. To the

In the year 899 A.D. the Caliph Muʿtaḍed had despatched an army from the city of ar-Raḳḳa against the tribe of Beni Šejbân. The army marched toward the settlement of Hît. As soon as the Bedouins learned of its approach, they forsook the cultivated fields around the city of al-Anbâr, fled to ʿAjn at-Tamr and al-Kûfa, and hence into the desert, some going to the Pilgrim Road leading to Mecca, others to Syria (aṭ-Ṭabari, *op. cit.*, Ser. 3, pp. 2189 f.).

In the year 927 A.D. the Carmathians came to ʿAjn at-Tamr, wishing to cross the Euphrates near al-Anbâr, but the residents of that city had untied the boats which formed a bridge across the river. The Carmathians encamped on the right bank, captured the boats at al-Ḥadîṯa, and upon them crossed the Euphrates at al-Anbâr (Ibn al-Aṯîr, *Kâmil* [Tornberg], Vol. 8, p. 125).

In the year 928 A.D. in ʿAjn at-Tamr and the vicinity there were very many Carmathians, whose leader ʿÎsa ibn Mûsa attacked al-Kûfa (*ibid.*, Vol. 8, p. 136).

Ibn Serapion, *ʿAǧâʾib* (Le Strange), p. 13, mentions a brook that flowed through the district of ʿAjn at-Tamr, thence through the desert, and thence into the Euphrates below the town of Hît. — Perhaps this refers to a swampy depression through which a brook flows only after protracted rains and which runs into the Euphrates only after it has first flooded the entire lowland of al-Ḥabbânja, the superfluous water then flowing over into the Euphrates at the present settlement of ar-Rumâdi. This occurs only when the river is not swollen.

In the year 974—975 A.D. ʿAjn at-Tamr was inhabited by the members of the tribe of Asad, whose incursions into the vicinity of Bagdad prevented the import of grain. In 978—979 an army was sent against them from Bagdad; whereupon the leader fled, leaving his property and his family behind, and the army occupied and pillaged the settlement in retaliation for the spoliation its residents had perpetrated at Mešhed al-Ḥusejn, or Kerbela (Ibn al-Aṯîr, *op. cit.*, Vol. 8, pp. 476, 522).

Al-Muḳaddasi, *Aḥsan* (De Goeje), pp. 114, 117, was familiar with the fortress of ʿAjn at-Tamr, the inhabitants of which were very greedy. It belonged, together with al-Ḳâdesijje, an-Nîl, Sûra, al-Ǧâmiʿân, and Ḥammân ibn ʿOmar, to the political district of al-Kûfa. — The northern boundary of this district was therefore the Euphrates and the Nahr Sûra.

At the end of the year 1055 through the efforts of Maḥmûd of the tribe of al-Ḫafâǧe, the Fatimide al-Mustanṣer was nominated caliph in the settlements of al-Kûfa, al-Ḥilla, ʿAjn at-Tamr, Šefâṯa, and Sûra (Quatremère, *Mémoires*, Vol. 2, p. 323; Ibn al-Aṯîr, *op. cit.*, Vol. 9, p. 423).

According to Jâḳût, *op. cit.*, Vol. 3, p. 759, ʿAjn at-Tamr is an old provincial city situated on the edge of the desert not far from al-Anbâr, west of al-Kûfa. Many varieties of dates were exported from there, as well as from the neighboring settlement of Šefâṯa, which was famous for its palm orchards. — Šeṯâṯa, or the Šefâṯa of Jâḳût's time, is about twelve kilometers distant from ʿAjn at-Tamr. In the past the lowland at ʿAjn at-Tamr was planted with palm trees stretching almost thirty kilometers from north to south in a strip fifteen kilometers wide. Thousands and thousands of these palms are still growing. Those that are not under cultivation bear fruit that is small, yellow, and hard, but the cultivated trees still yield excellent fruit. In October and November, when the palms are being stripped of their dates, the Bedouins and the raisers of goats and sheep from Palmyrena and the eastern half of northern Arabia flock to Šeṯâṯa for the fruit. At that time a load of about 150 kilograms sells for the equivalent of from two to four dollars.

Abu-l-Faḍâʾil, *Marâṣid* (Juynboll), Vol. 2, p. 294, records that the provincial city of ʿAjn at-Tamr, which commonly is called al-ʿAjn, is situated west of the Euphrates on the fringe of the desert amid various settlements, one of which is called Šefâṯa. The local palms are not generally cultivated, hence the fruit which is exported is small and hard, though sweet. — Of the settlements in the vicinity of ʿAjn at-Tamr, ar-Raḥḥâlijje and Šeṯâṯa are still inhabited; of the others there are almost no traces.

northeast was visible the long, yellowish island of al-Mešrefe, and to the southeast glimmered the white, rugged, tabular hills of al-Bûb, near which salt is obtained.

ʿAJN AT-TAMR TO AṬ-ṬUKṬUKÂNE

South and southeast of al-Bûb appeared the green of the gardens of the settlement of Šeṯâṯa, toward which we started from ʿAjn at-Tamr in a southeasterly direction. We crossed the wide, salty valley of aš-Šrejš and rode on through the ruins of Kasrûnijje, where we noted many long walls. On the left we had the ragged rocks of Čahaf Aḥmed eben Hâšem. After 9.12 we were passing through demolished gardens. Our guide said that these gardens had belonged to the inhabitants of Kasrûnijje, who, having removed to ar-Raḥḥâlijje, had transplanted the younger palms and cut down and burned the old ones. At 9.40 we noted to the south, quite near at hand, the spring of Umm al-Hašîš, with *meṣṣêʿ, rimṯ, ʿarâd, ṯḥama, ʿerž,* and *ṭarfa* growing all about it. At 9.50 we ascended a rocky ridge extending from the northeast toward the southwest. At 10.20 we were riding among the hills of Ẓhejrât al-ʿEžêd, near which spouts the spring ʿAjn Saddaẖ, and at 10.40 we approached the rugged hills of al-Bûb, in which is the spring of Ammu-n-Nemel, with the moderate slopes of as-Saddâẖijjât rising on the right. At 11.04 we rode by the spring ʿAjn abu-Ṣaẖr. A cool west wind had arisen. Far to the south-southwest were glimmering two jagged irregular cones of the range of al-ʿErğ. At 12.08 we perceived amid the fields the gushing spring of al-Brake and presently entered the palm orchard of the oasis of Šeṯâṯa. As the soil itself is marshy, there is no necessity for irrigation here.

The settlement of Šeṯâṯa contains several dilapidated old structures. The present residents number about six hundred families and dwell in strongholds: Ḳaṣr al-ʿAjn; Ṯâmer, belonging to Âl Rumejjed; al-Bu Hawa; al-Mâleḥ; al-Ḥasâwijjîn; al-Bu Ṭrejmîš; al-Bu Ğarbûʿ; al-Bu Ṯadjân; as-Semnijje; Darâwše; al-Isâli; al-Bu Ḥassân; al-Hwêdi; Ummu-r-Rmejle; al-Bu Ḥardân; and al-Ğenûn. Each of the buildings has a chief of its own, Meḥsen âl ʿAbbâs of the Ḳaṣr al-ʿAjn being the most powerful by reason of the greater number of inhabitants in his precinct. The Government had appointed Fejṣal al-Ḥasâwi as mayor of Šeṯâṯa. The Ḥasâwijjîn hail from al-Ḥasa, the native land of the Carmathians, and possibly are the descendants of Carmathian garrisons. The climate of Šeṯâṯa is very unhealthy. It is fatal to foreigners, who die there of recurrent malaria; and even the *mudîr* and the gendarmes cannot endure it a year.[93]

In the vicinity of ar-Raḥḥâlijje and Šeṯâṯa are over ten thousand palms and there is enough space for one hundred thousand more. The best dates are borne by the *al-azraḳi* and *al-ḥastâwi* varieties. One *wazne,* or seventy-two *oke* (87 kilograms), of these costs from three to five *meǧîdijjât* ($ 2.70 to $ 4.50), whereas one *wazne* of the *az-zahdi* variety sells for two to two and a half *meǧîdijjât* ($ 1.80 to $ 2.25) and even as low as one *meǧîdijje* (90 cents) when the crop is large.

[93] The name of Šeṯâṯa is first mentioned in 1055 A.D., when the Fatimide al-Mustanṣer was proclaimed Caliph there (Ibn al-Aṯîr, *op. cit.*, Vol. 9, p. 423; Quatremère, *op. cit.*, Vol. 2, p. 323). The fact that it is not mentioned early is noteworthy, especially since we have many records of its vicinity and since the place which Šeṯâṯa occupies certainly must have been populated long before. Therefore I think that the present settlement of Šeṯâṯa had a different name and I associate with it Ḳaṣr beni Muḳâtel, of which there is no mention in the literature of the period since the ninth century.

In the year 636 A.D. an-Noʿmân ibn Ḳabîṣa, son of the mayor of the city of al-Ḥîra and a member of the Ṭajj tribe, commanded the Persian garrison in Ḳaṣr beni Muḳâtel (aṭ-Ṭabari, *op. cit.*, Ser. 1, p. 2350).

Early in October, 680 A.D., al-Ḥusejn marched to the Persian fort Ḳaṣr beni Muḳâtel, presided over at the time by ʿObejdallâh ibn al-Ḥurr al-Ǧuʿfi. Finding a profusion of water there, al-Ḥusejn commanded his retinue to supply themselves with it, whereupon he marched to al-Ḳâḏerijje at Kerbela (*ibid.*, Ser. 2, pp. 305 f.). — No fort could have been situated at al-Aḫejẓer, where there were no fields nor gardens. The record specifies clearly that there was a profusion of water in Ḳaṣr beni Muḳâtel. There was plenty of it also in Šeṯâṯa. But the same was not true in al-Aḫejẓer, where the underground rain water evaporates whenever a protracted rain fails for two consecutive years in the valley of Tbel. From Šeṯâṯa to al-Ḳâẓerijje, as the northwestern gardens of Kerbela are still called, is a distance of fifty kilometers; hence a day's march.

In September, 739 A.D., the deposed governor Ḫâled al-Ḳasri retired from the city of al-Kûfa into the fort of his brother Ismâʿîl at Dûrân, beyond the boat bridge at al-Kûfa. Ḫâled's son Jazîd hastened through the territory of the Ṭajj tribe to Damascus, and Ḫâled with several of his friends intended to take the same route. They were to supply themselves with all their necessities at Ḳaṣr beni Muḳâtel, but the new governor had learned of their intention and had dispatched to Ḳaṣr beni Muḳâtel a cavalcade which had seized all the supplies. When Ḫâled and his friends arrived there and found that everything had been requisitioned, they took the route past Hît to ar-Reṣâfa (*ibid.*, Ser. 2, p. 1813). — Ḳaṣr beni Muḳâtel, like Šeṯâṯa today, was the starting point of the road through Dûmat al-Ǧandal to Syria.

In the year 786 A.D., shortly before he ascended the throne, Harun ar-Rashid sojourned for forty days at Ḳaṣr Muḳâtel, hunting in the vicinity (*ibid.*, Ser. 3, p. 575).

Jâḳût, *op. cit.*, Vol. 4, p. 121, did not know the exact location of Ḳaṣr beni Muḳâtel, as he fixes it somewhere between ʿAjn at-Tamr and Syria. As-Sakûni (*ibid.*) sought it near al-Ḳuṭḳuṭâne, Sulâm, and al-Ḳurejjât. ʿÎsa ibn ʿAli ibn ʿAbdallâh, it is asserted, demolished this stronghold, but later re-erected and appropriated it. — Al-Ḳuṭḳuṭâne is the aṭ-Ṭuḳṭuḳâne of today; Sulâm is the water that nowadays is called al-Aslâm, or as-Slâm; and al-Ḳurejjât is a different name for the settlements situated within the oasis of Dûmat al-Ǧandal. This shows that neither as-Sakûni nor Jâḳût knew the exact situation of Ḳaṣr beni Muḳâtel and that in their time this settlement was either in ruins or had a different name. The latter is probably nearer the truth; for, when it was rebuilt and appropriated in the early part of the ninth century by ʿÎsa ibn ʿAli ibn ʿAbdallâh, it was probably renamed by him.

Jâḳût, *op. cit.*, Vol. 1, p. 824, places Ḳaṣr beni Muḳâtel in the lower part of the valley of Tbel, which conforms to the location of Šeṯâṯa.

Abu-l-Faḍâ'il, *op. cit.*, Vol. 2, p. 423, states that Ḳaṣr beni Muḳâtel was situated between ʿAjn at-Tamr and Syria, close to al-Ḳuṭḳuṭâne. — Syria is northwest of ʿAjn at-Tamr, al-Ḳuṭḳuṭâne southeast of ʿAjn at-Tamr; hence it is apparent that Abu-l-Faḍâ'il did not know the location of Ḳaṣr beni Muḳâtel, connecting the name with the starting points of the roads which lead through the desert to Syria.

Near Ḳaṣr beni Muḳâtel is to be sought the location of Zawra ibn Abi Awfa, which is frequently mentioned in connection with it.

From 12.32 to 2.40 we rested at the ʿAjn al-Ğbejl at the northwestern end of the gardens (temperature at 12.50: 28.5°C). The pool of stagnant water there was animated by various aquatic creatures. A very interesting study of the aquatic fauna of the vicinity of Šeṯâṯa could be made. The local ponds

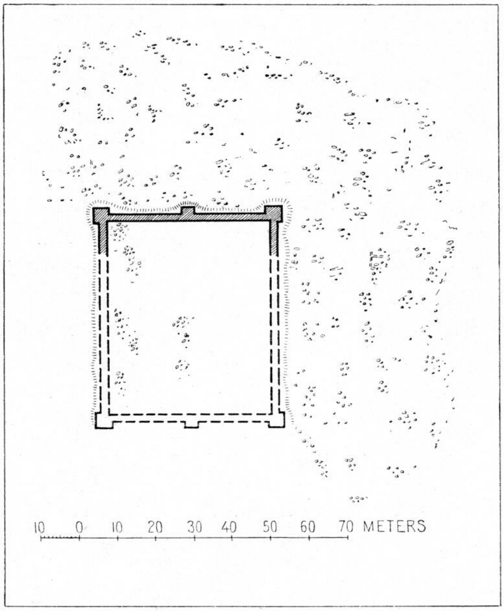

FIG. 95—Ground plan of ruins of ʿAjn at-Tamr.

and rivulets were formerly connected with the Euphrates, but today they are over seventy kilometers away.

Exchanging the gendarmes and procuring the necessary barley, we set out with a new guide toward the south. At three o'clock we crossed the *šeʿîb* of Fwâd, which comes from the ruins al-Ḫarâb, and wended our way afoot through the salt marshes as-Sabḫa. At 3.48 we had on the right, at the salient of al-ʿErğ,[94] the spring of aẓ-Ẓlejf.

To the east we perceived two tabular hills, Âbže and Bnejjetha. At 4.10 we abandoned the marshy ground and

[94] Al-Bekri, *Muʿğam* (Wüstenfeld), p. 653, mentions the water of al-ʿUrejğ belonging to the Kalb tribe and alludes to a verse in which the poet Ğarîr speaks of the camping ground of al-ʿUrejğ. — In the vicinity of our ʿErğ the Kalb tribe used to camp during the eighth century. The water, which the poet al-Ğarîr does not mention, is to be sought in the spring of aẓ-Ẓlejf.

entered upon a stony hillside where the ʿAjn ummu Ṣfejje gushes out. The marshes as-Sabẖa extend quite far to the southeast, forming a basin, al-Mšarraẖ, the end of which we reached at 4.50. Beyond that we traveled southeast in a plain covered with coarse gravel. The eastern part of this rocky level, which is about forty meters above the Sabẖa, is penetrated by the valley of al-Obejjeẓ, which, turning toward the northeast, terminates in the salt marsh of al-ʿEneb northeast of Šeṯâṯa. At 5.47 we sighted to the southwest the pretentious castle of al-Aẖejẓer and at 6.50 encamped on the right bank of the Wâdi al-Obejjeẓ.

Upon the low bank have been dug several wide wells (*ʿaḳûla*) two meters deep, in which fresh rain water gathers. The government officials residing in Šeṯâṯa do not drink the local water but send for their supply to the wells of al-Obejjeẓ, as there is no wholesome water in the vicinity of ar-Raẖẖâlijje and Šeṯâṯa. A foreigner who drinks the local water will die within a year, it is alleged. But the supply of water in the al-Obejjeẓ wells is not constant. It gathers very slowly in the autumn, and the lack of sufficient rain for as short a period as one or two years causes it to vanish altogether. It is not spring water but rain water, which is conserved upon the rocky beds beneath the layer of clay. We ascertained the latitude (temperature at 7: 23.2° C).

Thursday, April 25, 1912. We set out at 5.30 A. M. and from 5.48 until 6.07 remained in the castle of al-Aẖejẓer. I did not see in the vicinity the ruins of any large settlement or even the remains of gardens or vineyards.[95]

[95] I hold that al-Aẖejẓer is identical with the Dâr al-Heǧra of the Carmathians. Aṭ-Ṭabari, *Ta'rîẖ* (De Goeje), Ser. 3, p. 2124, records that Hamdân al-Ḳarmaṭ, the founder of the Carmathian sect, lived in the district of an-Nahrejn, which, according to Ibn Ḫordâḏbeh (*Masâlik* [De Goeje], p. 8) and Ḳodâma (*Ḫarâǧ* [De Goeje], p. 236) belonged, together with ʿAjn at-Tamr, to the district of Bihḳubâḏ al-Aʿla.

According to Aẖu Muḥsin (as recorded by an-Nuwajri, *Nihâja* [De Sacy], Vol. 1, pp. 192 f.), the Carmathians built a central stronghold and refuge in which to gather and conceal themselves. They selected for the purpose the district called Bihḳubâḏ (not Méhimabad, as read by De Sacy) situated within the fertile confines of al-Kûfa and pertaining to the district that adjoined the Euphrates and formed that portion of the Sultan's estates which was called Kâẓemijjât. They conveyed thither large stones and soon constructed a strong wall, within which they erected a roomy building in which many men and women from various districts could take refuge. This structure they called Dâr al-Heǧra, "house of emigration." After the year 890—891 A.D., in which these events took place the whole world feared them, but, having become more powerful than ever, they had no fears.

Al-Masʿûdi, *Tanbîh* (De Goeje), p. 381, states that after the year 922 A.D. the districts between Mecca in the west, al-Baṣra in the east, and ar-Raḳḳa in the north were ruled by Abu Ṭâher Slîmân ibn al-Ḥasan ibn Behrâm al-Ǧannâbi, the lord of al-Aḥsa (al-Baḥrejn). He intrusted the government of the vicinity of al-Kûfa to a chief hailing from al-Jemâma. This chief was Ismâʿîl ibn Jûsef ibn Muḥammad ibn Jûsef, commonly called al-Uẖajḍer.

Ibn Ḫaldûn, *ʿIbar* (Bûlâḳ, 1284 A.H.), Vol. 4, p. 98, writes about the family of al-Uẖajḍer.

Snouck Hurgronje, *Mekka* (1888), Vol. 1, p. 37, records that the Beni Uẖajḍer, descendants of Ḥasan, migrated into the territory of al-Jemâma, where they became chiefs.

We turned in a south-southeasterly direction toward the stronghold of al-Ḫẓêra, traversing a rocky plain and crossing the *šeʿibân* of al-Mšejžîž and ar-Raḳḳâši. Beyond ar-Raḳḳâši several head of sheep and cows were at pasture. As soon as the herdsman perceived us, he called an alarm and fled with his herd to al-Ḫẓêra, from which five men came running out and hid behind the *ṭarfa* bushes. Dismounting, we called to them and then sent to them our guide from the oasis of Šeṯâṯa. In a little while Ẓâher, chief of the al-Moṛara clan, who owns al-Ḫẓêra, came out and welcomed us. We stayed from 7.35 until 8.25. Ẓâher escorted us upon his mare. In al-Ḫẓêra a spring of bitter water spouts forth, moistening a small field that was sown with barley. Ẓâher said that sometimes he found in his spring chunks of bitumen (*žîr*), with which he had scoured the roof of his house. He owned a stick (*maḳwar*)

Ibn al-Aṯîr, *Kâmil* (Tornberg), Vol. 8, p. 136, mentions that in the year 928—929 A.D., there congregated in the fertile region of Wâseṭ over ten thousand Carmathians with their chief Ḥarîṯ ibn Masʿûd, while many more of them were in ʿAjn at-Tamr and the vicinity under the chief ʿÎsa ibn Mûsa. They exhorted the inhabitants of the surrounding districts to believe in al-Mahdi. ʿÎsa settled in the neighborhood (*biḍâher*) of al-Kûfa and collected land taxes, at the same time repelling the government collectors. Ḥarîṯ ibn Masʿûd went to the canal of al-Muwaffeḳi, where he erected a stronghold which he called Dâr al-Heğra (see also: Ibn Ḫaldûn, *op. cit.*, Vol. 3, p. 378). —

According to this report also, the Carmathians had their center between al-Kûfa and ʿAjn at-Tamr. The fact that Ibn al-Aṯîr mentions only the building of Dâr al-Heğra for Ḥarîṯ's horde gives rise to the supposition that the horde of ʿÎsa already had a "house of emigration" (*dâr al-heğra*) in which he was residing. The Arabic *biḍâher*, or outskirts of a city, sometimes include territory extending to a great distance.

The old negro Ḥmâr advised me to say Ḳaṣr eben Aḫejẓer or Ḳaṣr âl Aḫejẓer instead of Ḳaṣr al-Aḫejẓer, because the castle had formerly belonged to Eben Aḫejẓer, just as it now belongs to Eben Haḏḏâl. The idea was prevalent among the Rwala that Âl Aḫejẓer denoted the former owner. After Âl Aḫejẓer the castle became the property of the chief of the Ḫafâğe tribe; hence the Rwala continue to call it Ḳaṣr al-Ḫafâği. Several Arabic historians establish the fact of the government of the Ḫafâğe tribe in the vicinity of al-Kûfa (Ibn Ḫaldûn, *op. cit.*, Vol. 4, pp. 257—259; Ibn Ḥawkal, *Masâlik* [De Goeje], pp. 160 f., note o).

Massignon, *Mission en Mésopotamie* (1907—1908), p. 6, writes: "The first and doubtless the only European that had beheld al-Oḫajḏer — without mentioning its name — before our advent there in the year 1908, is a certain Englishman of whom Niebuhr merely says that he was traveling from Aleppo to Baṣra." Nevertheless, we have several older descriptions of this castle by Europeans who visited it in the seventeenth century.

Thus, for instance, writes Pietro della Valle (*Viaggi* [Venice, 1664], Vol. 4, p. 599): "On June 29, 1625, we started our march in the early morning and two or three hours before noon stopped at a certain water not far from the ruins of a large old structure built of bricks. The structure forms a quadrangle and on each side has thirteen pillars or round towers and many other spacious arched rooms, while inside there is a number of courts and chambers with openings in the roof and also a rather small courtyard — if, indeed, it was a courtyard and was not spanned by a roof. The Arabs call this structure Cafr Chaider (Ḳaṣr Ḫajḏar). I could not ascertain whether it used to be a castle, a church or a fort, but it would seem more likely to have been a castle rather than anything else. When the day's march was half over, we had on the right Mesched Hussein (Mešhed Ḥusejn)."

On April 21, 1801, the castle of al-Aḫejẓer was visited again by a prince of al-Jemâma, whence Eben Aḫejẓer had come. This was Saʿûd eben ʿAbdalʿazîz, who, with his Wahhâbites, on the preceding day had attacked Mešhed Ḥusejn or Kerbela and pillaged the sanctuary of al-Ḥusejn, and who counted and divided the booty at the castle of al-Aḫejẓer (Rousseau, *Pachalik de Bagdad* [1809], p. 156; Mengin, *Égypte sous Mohammed Aly* [1823], Vol. 2, p. 524; Musil, *Zeitgeschichte* [1918], p. 50).

Massignon, *op. cit.*, p. 1, writes that the vicinity of al-Oḫajḏer was formerly irrigated from the canal of Pallakopas, built by the Greeks from the city of Hît on the Euphrates to the city of Obolla on the Persian Gulf. — According to Greek authors, however, the canal of Pallacotas diverged from the Euphrates southeast of Babylon and hence over 250 kilometers from Hît. In the vicinity of the castle of al-Aḫejẓer there is no trace of a canal emerging from the Euphrates.

about seventy centimeters long, the head of which he himself had kneaded from the pitch. Al-Ḫẓêra is situated on the left bank of a valley of the same name.

At 9.30 we arrived at the bitter spring ʿAjn Ṛûne. On the right were visible the hills of al-ʿOwejn and Ẓubejʿe, while on the left, to the east-northeast upon the precipitous slopes of the Ṭâr as-Sejhed, could be seen a green meadow with the well of as-Sbêʿi. From there a road leads toward the east over the Ḫirbet al-Mûžde to Ḫân ʿAṭšân. From 11.10 until 12.30 we rested. At 1.07 we passed through the *šeʿîb* of aṭ-Ṭrejfâwi and ascended the Ṭâr al-Aslâm, as the southwestern projection of the Ṭâr as-Sejhed is called. On the right upon the slope could be seen at 2.40 the well ʿAḳlat al-Aslâm.[96]

At 3.14 al-Aḫejẓer could again be seen behind us. We stopped southwest of the Ḳarʿa Muḳardeš and until 3.50 were busy sketching a map of the environs.

Aṭ-Ṭrejfâwi comes from the tabular mountains Ḳûr al-Ḫwejmer and their eastern spurs Ḫašmet al-ʿEjâde and al-Ṛarra, trends north-northeast, and, northeast of the ʿAjn Ṛûne at the base of the slope of as-Sejhed, forms the marsh Ǧufr al-Mâleḥ. Here terminate the *šeʿibân* of al-Ḫẓêra, ar-Raḳḳâši, and al-Mšejžîž. Beyond al-Mšejžîž the Ǧufr al-Mâleḥ narrows into the channel of al-Bizzeḥ, which, west of the tabular hills of al-Ḳaṭṭâr, merges with al-Obejjeẓ and sends a branch east into the Fejẓat umm Slîmâne. The slope of as-Sejhed extends from the Fejẓat umm Slîmâne southward to the ʿAḳlat al-Aslâm; in the east the Ṭâr as-Sejhed gradually merges into the bare plain about al-Kûfa. In its southern part the Ṭâr as-Sejhed is also known as al-Lisân.[97]

Ẓâher told us that in January, 1911, much snow had fallen on the Ṭâr as-Sejhed and to the west of it, the snow lying twenty centimeters deep and remaining for seven days and seven nights (*arbaʿatʿaš waḳet*) causing many head of sheep to perish but stimulating a prodigious growth of grass.

At 4.20 we sighted some horsemen toward the south, upon the crest of al-Lisân. Not having encountered any camp or herds, we surmised that this was a band of raiders, the members of some half-*fellâḥîn* tribe which in summer and

[96] Naṣr al-Iskandari (1164—1165 A. D.) (Jâḳût, *op. cit.*, Vol. 3, p. 113) says that Sulâm is a locality near Ḳaṣr beni Muḳâtel between ʿAjn at-Tamr and Syria. According to others cited by Jâḳût, as-Sulâm is a station west of Ḳaṣr beni Muḳâtel upon the route to the desert of as-Samâwa. — The first statement is very indefinite, for from ʿAjn at-Tamr to Syria three roads led in different directions: toward the northwest by way of ʿOrḏ (aṭ-Ṭajjibe), toward the west by way of Ḳurâḳir, and toward the southwest through Dûmat al-Ǧandal. Our well of al-Aslâm, or as-Slâm, is situated at the branch of the last-named road. The second statement also points to this road, as al-Aslâm is situated about fifty kilometers south of the settlement of Šeṭâṭa, in which I seek the former Ḳaṣr beni Muḳâtel.

[97] It is stated by Ibn an-Naǧǧâr (Jâḳût, *op. cit.*, Vol. 4, p. 633) that the desolate side of al-Kûfa is called al-Lisân, while the side that is moistened by the Euphrates is called al-Mulṭâṭ.

autumn inhabit the banks of the Euphrates and in winter and spring migrate into the adjacent desert. All the tribes of the ʿAneze were camping in the north, and the Ẓefîr, whose pastures lay far to the south, would not have dared a distant raid upon horses. The half-*fellâḥîn* of the Euphrates are notorious for their cruelty, and our gendarmes feared them as their principal enemies.

Accordingly, we turned at once into a neighboring hollow, unloaded the stores, tied the camels, took all the cartridges and water bags, and crawled to the summit of a small hill where we lay down and observed the raiders. They had sighted us also and rode toward us at a gallop. There were thirty-five of them. When they had approached to a distance of three kilometers we each fired three shots. They stopped — evidently not expecting that our arms could carry so far —, swerved around, and disappeared in a hollow. About twenty minutes later they reappeared and charged us at a gallop. We fired five shots each: we could see horses and riders fall. They hastily took these riders up on the unharmed horses and disappeared still farther toward the west but soon emerged and dashed through the plain toward the sun, evidently intending to attack us directly from the west, hoping the glare of the setting sun would partly blind us. We fired between them and the sun several times, lest they reach their vantage point. They retreated and, stopping somewhat farther off, began to confer. After a while a solitary rider from their midst approached us waving his white sleeve. We sent our guide Ẓâher to meet him and began running to and fro to create the impression that we were a large body of men.

On his return Ẓâher told us that the enemies were of the Ḫazâʿel half-*fellâḥîn*, who had set out to attack the herds of the ʿAmârât tribe camping west of the oasis of Šeṯâṯa. Their casualties were five horses and three riders wounded. When their leader was told by Ẓâher that we belonged to the Government and that we still had two loads of ammunition, he swore not to repeat his attack. He knew that he could defeat us, yet he reasoned that the booty would not balance the casualties which he might suffer; besides, he feared the Government, the half-*fellâḥîn* being more subordinated to it than the Bedouins were. We watched the riders until it was pitch dark. They continued to ride toward the north.

As soon as darkness had fallen we mounted the camels

and cantered toward the southeast. At first we rode in a plain, but at 7.16 we entered the rugged rocks of al-ʿArâjes, among which our camels could walk but very slowly. While we were in the plain, we had fears of the enemy's overtaking us, but in the rocks we were sheltered. At 8.20 we crossed the wide channel of al-Ḫerr, which is enclosed between high banks of clay, and at 9.09 encamped at the fortified farm of al-ʿAṭijje, situated at the spring ʿAjn al-Ḥejjâẓijje. Such a fortified farm, called *ḳaṣr*, resembles a quadrangular fortress, enclosed by high walls that are strengthened at every corner by a tower. The gate ordinarily is either in the corner by the tower or else it is fortified by a smaller tower of its own. It opens into a large yard flanked with small, flat-roofed dwellings. When an enemy attacks, the husbandmen drive their herds into the yard, close the gate, get upon the roofs, and shoot through small loopholes provided for that purpose in the higher fortification wall. We should have liked to ascertain the latitude, but the sky was overcast by clouds, the presence of which compelled us to abandon our attempt after two futile endeavors.

Friday, April 26, 1912 (temperature at 5: 15° C). We left at 5.30 A. M. On the southwestern side of the stronghold were fields bearing very good wheat but barley of a poorer quality. Alongside the fields runs a small brooklet; another larger creek, al-Ḥejjâẓijje, rises to the southeast. The stronghold belonged to al-ʿAṭijje, who hailed from aṭ-Ṭuḳṭuḳâne. From here we headed first southeastward toward the settlement of aṭ-Ṭuḳṭuḳâne. At 5.50 we crossed the valley of aš-Šaʿajjeb, in the southwestern part of which rises a spring of the same name. To the southwest loomed up the mesa of az-Zaḳla, in which the valley of Ḳeṭêḳeṭ, which passes by aṭ-Ṭuḳṭuḳâne, has its origin. To the north the rays of the rising sun were reflected from the sharp edges of the crumbling rocks of al-ʿArâjes, whence the ravine Telʿet al-Ḥesjân leads to al-Ḫerr. This ravine contains rain wells.

At 6.10 far to the east flashed the golden, gleaming dome of the sanctuary in the city of an-Neǧef, or al-Mašhad, while just before us in the depression of Ḳeṭêḳeṭ lay the settlement of aṭ-Ṭuḳṭuḳâne (or aṭ-Ṭuḳṭuḳâna). A palm orchard extending from the southwest to the northeast hid the dwellings from view, but about in the middle, amid a pile of ruins, we could see a quadrangular fortress with walls narrower at the top than at the bottom. As soon as the inhabitants perceived us, they began to beat on boards and run in alarm toward the fortress. Since we were barely two kilometers distant we could see the entire oasis as it lay beneath us. Although we scanned with our binoculars the settlement as well as the whole neighborhood, we discovered no old houses nor larger ruins.[98]

AṬ-ṬUḲṬUḲÂNE TO AN-NEĞEF

Not wishing to waste time in negotiations with the alarmed residents of aṭ-Ṭuḳṭuḳâne we turned at 6.35 toward the east, where the golden dome in an-Neğef could be seen on a high ridge, pointing the way as if it were a lighthouse. We were hastening to get out of the desert, so as to escape nocturnal attack by the incensed fighting men of the Ḫazâʿel. At 7.22 we were riding upon soft ground covered with a salty crust. On the left was the ʿAjn aṣ-Ṣejjâḥ; farther to the north were clearly visible the white banks of the channel of al-Ḫerr; on the right stood low knolls of salt.

From 8.15 until nine o'clock we rested between hills of sand in the shade of a *ṛaẓa* bush. At 9.20 at about two and a half kilometers to our left was the Ḳaṣr ar-Ruhbân, a rectangular structure with solid walls that were somewhat demolished. Inside could be seen heaps of old building material and a full rivulet running through an aqueduct into a capacious walled cistern. East of the *ḳaṣr* spread the saline swamps of al-Mâleḥ, from which the residents of Irak get salt. The valley of al-Ḫerr widens and disappears. At 9.50 we rode past the salty spring ʿAjn al-Msajjer. To the north, near the slope above al-Mâleḥ, are situated the rocks of as-Sṭêḥ; and

[98] The present aṭ-Ṭuḳṭuḳâne is the ancient al-Ḳuṭḳuṭâne. Ǧuḏejma al-Waḍḍâḥ, also called Ǧuḏejma al-Abraš, was the first man to create a kingdom on the borders of Irak. He was joined by the Arabs, with whom he made raids. He camped among the settlements of al-Ḥîra, al-Anbâr, Baḳḳa, Hît, and ʿAjn at-Tamr, and also along the edge of the desert as far as al-Ḳumejr, al-Ḳuṭḳuṭâne, and Ḫafijje (aṭ-Ṭabari, *op. cit.*, Ser. 1, p. 750).

Shortly before the battle of Ḏu Ḳâr the Persian king notified the commanders of the frontier guards at al-Ḳuṭḳuṭâne and Bâreḳ and at other settlements near Ṭaff Safawân, summoning them hastily to his assistance (*ibid.*, pp. 1030 f.).

In the year 635—636 A.D. al-Muṯanna marched out with his fighters and stationed them between Ḳuḍej and al-Ḳuṭḳuṭâne for the purpose of guarding the frontiers (*ibid.*, p. 2215). Ḳuḍej is situated near al-Baṣra (*ibid.*, p. 2223).

Al-Jaʿḳûbi, *Taʾrîḫ* (Houtsma), Vol. 2, p. 229, relates that aḍ-Ḍaḥḥâk ibn Ḳejs undertook an attack upon al-Ḳuṭḳuṭâne, which remained loyal to the Caliph ʿAli.

While al-Ḥusejn was drawing towards al-Kûfa from Mecca in the year 679—680 A.D., his enemies occupied the entire boundary between Ḫaffân, al-Ḳâdesijje, al-Ḳuṭḳuṭâne, and Laʿlaʿ (or al-Ḳalʿ) (aṭ-Ṭabari, *op. cit.*, Ser. 2, p. 288). — Al-Ḳalʿ may be an erroneous transcription of al-ʿÂʿ, which is the name of a well at Šerâf, to the south of al-Ḳâdesijje.

Al-Bekri, *Muʿǧam* (Wüstenfeld), p. 150, quotes a verse of the poet Aws ibn Ḥağar which mentions Maʾfiḳa, al-Ḳuṭḳuṭâne, and al-Burʿûm.

between them, in a ravine of the same name, is the water of Maʾ al-Ṛarab. To the south the horizon is cut off by the tabular range of as-Swejǧa. At 10.20 we were wending our way among the hills of al-Eṯele, where there are numerous huts called al-Mekâjîl, belonging to the workmen who are engaged in extracting salt. To the north the line of the horizon is cut short by the high, yellowish slope of as-Sejhed, beside which winds the channel of al-Ḫerr.

From eleven until 12.45 P. M. the camels grazed at the spring ʿAjn as-Saffâr. To the west of this spring issues the ʿAjn umm Ḳûs, to the south the ʿAjn Ḥajjâč, and to the east the ʿAjn al-ʿEbâdi. A violent east wind had sprung up. At 1.10 we had on the left the ʿAjn ʿEbejd and at 1.25 the water of al-Waššâšât (which is called also al-Ḥakkân), with the village of ar-Rhejme to the south. In order to get out upon the rocky ground of the slope of Abu Lele we turned toward the northeast. The channel of al-Ḫerr, which we crossed opposite the ʿAjn ʿEjjâd, forms a barren, level belt about two kilometers wide, so encrusted with salt that it was hard for the camels to walk on it. To the east it widens into a lowland which is usually filled with water and hence is named al-Baḥr (the lake). This lowland forms the fringe of the cultivated region of aṭ-Ṭaff.

At two o'clock we were upon dry ground. From 3.55 until 4.36 we rested under the rock Abu Lele aṣ-Ṣarîre. To the northwest, upon a height, we saw a heap of ruins, Umm al-Ṛarâf. The depression of al-Baḥr was full of water which had flowed into it through the channel of al-Ḫerr from the southwest, where heavy summer rains (*aṣ-ṣejfijjât*) had fallen. By 5.30 we had reached the rock of Abu Lele al-Čebîre, at the end of al-Baḥr. Between it and the road that leads along the base of the slope of Umm Ǧûʿâne there are perched two large, partially disintegrated rocks known as Bâb al-Hawa. We had intended to encamp beyond them near the gardens, but at 5.48 a violent sandstorm compelled us to saddle the camels, reload them, and seek refuge in the city. At 6.45 we entered the southwestern suburbs of aṯ-Ṯelma, passing among the storehouses of Ḥawwâš and ʿAṭijje abu Koḥle and the cemeteries of al-Mahdi and al-Mefâṯîl, near the western city wall. We found a lodging in a khan beside the northern gate. Since all the rooms adjoining the enclosing wall of this khan had already been rented, the innkeeper offered us three dark chambers used as a morgue for the corpses of Shiites brought from Persia to be buried in the shade of ʿAli's sepulcher; but the chambers were pervaded by so foul a smell that we preferred to lie down in an open niche on the eastern side of the yard of the khan. As long as the wind blew from the southeast we fared well enough; but toward midnight, when it swerved to the west and blew up a sandstorm, we soon found ourselves covered with a layer of sand and dry manure almost ten centimeters deep, although we were lying in a yard that was sheltered by high walls. Under the circumstances sleep was impossible. When the storm subsided toward morning we set about cleaning our bags and coverings.[99]

[99] The continuation of this expedition to Kerbela and thence into Mesopotamia is narrated in the author's forthcoming volume, *The Middle Euphrates* (see above, p. 357, note 88).

PART III

1914—1915

CHAPTER XIII

DAMASCUS TO AZ-ZEBÎBIJJÂT

In the middle of November, 1914, I arrived at Damascus, where I was visited by Prince an-Nûri eben Ša'lân, who begged me to vouch for him and secure him a permit whereby he could leave with his tribe for the inner desert. All his clans were already camping there, but he and his slaves were still held at Ḍmejr by the Government. On the very day after I obtained the permit for him he notified me that he was going to flee from the cage at Ḍmejr. I asked him to wait for me, or at least to leave a dependable companion for me at Ḍmejr; but he replied smilingly that he did not trust the good will of the Government and that therefore he must leave immediately. He said he was unable to provide me with a dependable companion, but his people as well as the tribes allied with him knew me, he said, and would protect me. He had with him no reliable members of enemy clans able to escort me. Upon my insistence, however, he promised for eight to ten days to stay to the east or southeast of Ḍmejr on the borders of Tlûl al-'Ijâṯ, provided no disquieting news about the Government or about his clans in the desert reached him; but he advised me to hurry.

I was, however, unable to leave Damascus as speedily as I wished to; for at first I could not obtain the necessary camels, and by the end of November there came a heavy rain lasting several days. In this expedition all the scientific instruments were to be under the supervision of Karl Waldmann of the Military Geographical Institute at Vienna, who was commissioned to assist me in drawing maps; and I was to be accompanied by three servants, Nâṣer and Manṣûr al-Maṛlûḳ of al-Žerjitejn, brothers, who were hired for the entire trip, and Nâṣer eben Muḥammad al-Ḥsejnâwi, who was engaged for part of the trip. I took along my old tents, supplies for eight or ten months, and ten camels.

DAMASCUS TO ḌMEJR

Thursday, December 3, 1914. In the morning all my baggage was transferred in a wagon to the sanctuary of aš-Šejḫ Ruslân by way of the Bâb Tûma and there loaded upon camels. Accompanied by a few friends, we set out at 10.20 A.M., going by the highway leading to Ḥomṣ through the gardens of the suburbs of az-Zejnebijje, Mezd al-Ḳaṣab, aš-Šejḫ Ǧâber, Ǧisr Ṯôra, and al-Ḳâbûn. As the camels took fright at every wagon, pressed themselves against the walls of the gardens, and frequently slipped upon the muddy ground, we did not get ahead very fast. In the gardens we passed among olive trees the fruit of which was being picked, or rather, together with many of the branches, being mercilessly beaten down with poles. At 11.52 we arrived at the flourishing settlement of Ḥarasta and at 12.33 P.M. passed by the side road that leads to the town of Dûma, the residence of a *ḳâjmaḳâm*. In Dûma the houses are picturesquely built in large gardens about the base of the mountain range of Ḳalamûn. The main highway we were traversing had been recently repaired and provided with stones marking the kilometers.

At 1.25, not far beyond the fourteenth kilometer, we had on our left the pool Birket ar-Rîḥân,[100] and a little while later we were riding along beside the left wall of the old fort Ḫân al-Ḳṣejr,[101] which is built on the left side of the brook Nahr as-Sikke. We crossed this stream by a bridge.

In the north, upon the slope of Ab-al-ʿAfaʾ, forming a part of the Ḳalamûn range, Nâṣer showed me an old bridge over which led the original road from Damascus and Dûma to Ḍmejr and which is even now resorted to whenever the highway we were traversing becomes impassable or too slippery. We forsook this highway at 2.15, for it turns toward the northeast and at the Ḫân ʿAjjâš and the sanctuary Ḳubbt al-ʿAṣâfîr, or Ḳubbt an-Naṣr, rises to the pass which separates the Ab-al-ʿAfaʾ slope from the range of Hwaʾ to the east. We

[100] Abu-l-Baḳa aṣ-Ṣaffûri (died 1626 A.D.) derived income from the settlement of ar-Rajḥân near Ḥarasta (Wüstenfeld, *Fachr ed-dîn* [1886], p. 149).

[101] In the year 529 A.H. (1134—1135 A.D.), Saladin accompanied the Atabeg Zenki to the settlement of al-Ḳṭejfe. The Damascan soldiers set fire to some straw at the settlement of ʿAḏra' and fled when Saladin approached. The latter encamped at Ḫân al-Ḳuṣejr, where the bridge had been broken and disconnected (Ibn Munḳiḏ, *Iʿtibâr* [Derenbourg], Vol. 2, p. 111).

Jâḳût, *Muʿǧam* (Wüstenfeld), Vol. 4, p. 126, names the stronghold of al-Ḳuṣejr as the first station on the road from Damascus to Ḥomṣ.

Thevenot (*Voyages* [Paris, 1689], Vol. 2, p. 85) left Damascus in the spring of 1664 through the gate Bab-Thoma and arrived at Essaïr, a village by a small river which separates it from a khan with two strongholds. — Essaïr is al-Ḳuṣejr, for the *ḳ* (resembling *hamza*) is hardly audible in the dialect of Damascus.

proceeded eastward in a depression where clay preponderated, following the left side of the brook of as-Sikke which trends toward the village of ʿAḏraʾ. On the right, south of the brook, we noted a large farm (*ḥowš*) called al-Fâra, built amid fields

FIG. 96—ʿAḏraʾ; farm of Dâûd an-Nebki.

planted with cotton. At 2.38 we rode among old ruins containing large hewn stones and innumerable fragments of pillars.

At 3.02 we were in the village of ʿAḏraʾ and quartered ourselves in the farm of Dâûd an-Nebki (Fig. 96), who had bought most of the marshy meadows in the vicinity of ʿAḏraʾ. These he had drained and prepared for cotton culture. They were being tilled by renters, whom he had provided with efficient European implements and who received half of the net profits. South of the farm he had planted a section of the grounds with fruit-bearing trees, which thrive well. Several residents of ʿAḏraʾ who had guided themselves by his example also had fields that were yielding them a generous profit. The old marshes had disappeared and fertile fields were penetrating farther and farther to the south and east. Everywhere in the village and around it we saw old foundation walls, hewn boulders, and fragments of pillars and capitals — evidence of an ʿAḏraʾ that used to be much larger and more imposing. The sanctuary Ǧâmeᶜ as-Sâdât at the western end of the village is partly erected on original ancient walls. West of the Ǧâmeᶜ as-Sâdât were the sepulchral sanctuaries of the Sheikhs ᶜAwde and ᶜOtmân, also built from the stones of older structures. The present village of ᶜAdraʾ[102] numbered about 120 huts, inside which were to be found more fragments of pillars and their capitals. The residents wreck the old structures and sell the building stone thus procured in Dûma, Ḥarasta, and Damascus.

North of ᶜAdraʾ rises the bare, rocky Ḳalamûn range, the northeastern part of which is called Ab-al-ᶜAfaʾ. Beyond it the snowy slopes of al-ᶜArᶜûrijje lift themselves. East of the gorge, through which a highway leads to Ḥomṣ, the range is known as Hwaʾ. It is asserted that this portion contains many caves and long subterranean passages. To the east, upon the southern spur of the Ab-al-Ḳôs range, is the settlement of Ḍmejr, the white fort of which, al-Ḳalᶜa, once an old pagan temple, now dominates the huts. South of Ḍmejr is a passage that is hedged in on the north by the brown Ab-al-Ḳôs range and on the south by the black volcanoes Tlûl al-ᶜIjâṯ. This narrow passage connects the fertile fields of Damascus with the wastes of Arabia and is the most convenient gate for the migrating Bedouins, whose camels thus avoid the steep rocks of the northern range and the sharp edges of the lava which is piled high in Tlûl al-ᶜIjâṯ. Each of the extinct volcanoes, from aš-Šâmât in the north to the much eroded crater of Dekwa, which looms on the southwestern boundary of the *ḥarra*, may be clearly distinguished from ᶜAdraʾ. West of this volcanic region spreads the fertile depression of al-Ṛûṭa, now

[102] Ibn al-Ḳalânisi, *Ḏajl* (Amedroz), p. 247, writes that in the spring of 1135 A. D. Zenki encamped with his army between ᶜAdraʾ and al-Ḳuṣejr. Elsewhere he asserts (*ibid.*, p. 272) that Zenki camped at ᶜAdraʾ again in the year 1140 A. D. and burned down many villages, among them Ḥarasta at-Tîn.

On April 29, 1151 A. D., the vanguards under the command of Nûraddîn encamped in the vicinity of ᶜAdraʾ and the following day encamped at as-Sahm and an-Najrab, intending to attack the Damascan army from the mountains. This army learned of their plans in advance, however, and retreated to Damascus. Nûraddîn then encamped with his entire army at the springs of Fâserijja between ᶜAdraʾ and Dûma and a little later in the vicinity of al-Ḥaǧîra and Râwijja, which is also called Ḳabr as-Sitt. Thence the army advanced to Mesǧed al-Ḳadam and Mesǧed al-Ǧedîd, or Maḳbarat al-Muᶜtamed, between Mesǧed al-Ḳadam and Mesǧed al-Felûs. On June 1 Nûraddîn was camping in the settlements of Faḏâja, Ḥalfablatân, and al-Ḥâmisân, in close proximity to Damascus (Abu Šâma, *Rawḍatejn* [Cairo, 1277—1278 A. H.], Vol. 1, pp. 79 f.; Barbier de Meynard's edition, *Recueil*, Vol. 4, p. 69).

Jâḳût, *op. cit.*, Vol 3, p. 625, says that the familiar settlement of ᶜAdraʾ, belonging to the administrative district of Ḥawlân, is situated on the edge of the al-Ṛûṭa lowland near Damascus. Whoever descends through the pass of al-ᶜOḳâb and casts his eyes over al-Ṛûṭa perceives on the left side closest to the range the settlement of ᶜAdraʾ with its high tower. Ḥuǧr ibn ᶜAli al-Kindi was killed and buried at ᶜAdraʾ. Some relate that it was he who occupied it for the Moslems. Not far from the settlement lie the meadows of Râheṭ, where the adherents of Ibn az-Zubejr engaged in fight with those of Merwân.

sodden with mud, in which trees of the village of Mêdaʿaʾ[103] appear southwest of ʿAḏraʾ.

We passed the night in the farmyard of Dâûd an-Nebki among the baggage and among the camels, which were very shy.

Friday, December 4, 1914. We resumed our journey at 6.20 A.M., following the road that led east through the fields. Right and left of us were puddles of water. The sky was overcast with gray, heavy clouds, and the air laden with dense vapors which obscured the view. About eight o'clock the mists and clouds lifted and mild, humid breezes blew up from the east. At 8.20 we noted to the north at the base of Hwaʾ, south of the ancient road on the Ḳalamûn slope, the ruins of ar-Rumâdi and east of them the Ḫân al-Maʿêṣre. The depression in which we were traveling is called as-Sill; on its southern fringe the small grove Šağarât Ṛejṯ appeared as a blur, and west of the latter the knolls of Rumejdîn. Crossing a hollow we scared out nine wild swine. The nearer we drew to Ḍmejr, the more efficient was the cultivation of the lowland; the higher fields were being plowed.

At nine we reached the gardens of Ḍmejr, at 9.40 the settlement, and at ten o'clock the wrecked barracks al-Ḳalʿa above the ruins of al-Maksûra, where we camped (temperature at 12.30: 13°C). The barracks here, like those at al-Žerjitejn (al-Ḳerjitejn), Arak, as-Suḫne, and Râwa, were built in the late seventies of the last century by order of the governor, Midḥat Pasha. Midḥat had also sought to prevent the mounted guards from imposing upon the residents by inducing them to stay outside the settlement; and he tried to inspire them to carry out their duties, which included the prevention of Bedouin encampments near the settlements. After his recall the fortresses were deserted and the guards moved back into the settlement. The *ḳalʿa* (barracks) at Ḍmejr is built of old materials. It forms a rectangle with only one gate. On the ground floor are accommodations for horses, on the first floor quarters for men, and from the flat roof, which is enclosed by a parapet it is possible to shoot through loopholes. Southeast, below the fortress, is an old pool into which empties an aqueduct that is laid from the north. The water flowing from this pool used to irrigate vast gardens to the south and

[103] Jâḳût, *op. cit.*, Vol. 4, p. 713, records that one of the descendants of the Omayyads resided in the settlement of Mêdaʿaʾ, in the administrative district of Ḫawlân, which had been the property of his ancestor, the Caliph Moawiyah.

southeast, which were planted at the order of Midḥat Pasha and of which there now remain but a few fig trees.

ḌMEJR TO AL-BUṬMIJJÂT

The Nuʿêr family of the al-Riȷ̣âṯ clan keep their flocks of goats and sheep in the *ḳalʿa* of Ḍmejr. The chief Ḳâsem eben Nuʿêr, his brother Raẓbân, and five other members of the ruling family had preserved order since 1912. Prior to that they had been fighting with the Government since 1898. In 1910 and 1911 Eben Nuʿêr stood at the head of the insurgents who were making constant incursions from the nearly impassable ravines of the volcanic region into the fertile Damascan lands, attacking caravans, charging smaller military detachments, driving off herds of cattle, and jeering at the Government for its inability to pursue them into the volcanic tract. Seeking to subordinate the insurgents, the Government engaged in negotiations and bribery. Ḳâsem eben Nuʿêr was won over with various gifts and was appointed commander of the frontier guard at a salary of 250 piasters ($ 11.75) per month. Ḳâsem, the former chief of robbers, since 1912 had guarded the eastern boundary of the Damascan lands, but he was not contented. It annoyed him to see that the gendarmes stationed in Ḍmejr were getting more than he was, besides having an opportunity to extort gifts from the settlers.

Ḳâsem was not at home; he had been in Damascus for several days. His brother Raẓbân told me that Prince an-Nûri had left Ḍmejr ten days before, going in a southerly direction toward the volcano of Sejs and beyond into the region of ar-Rwêšdât. Besides this I learned that east of Ḍmejr, in the region of al-Buṭmijjât, were camped Sulṭân âl Ṭajjâr and Saʿûd eben Melḥem, who, though not subordinated to Prince an-Nûri, associated and marched with him. Knowing that an-Nûri wished to reach al-Ǧowf in the shortest time, I should have preferred to follow him immediately by forced marches, but between him and myself there were no camps of the ʿAneze tribes, my friends. Instead, there roved in that direction numerous robber bands of the clans of al-Riȷ̣âṯ, al-Ḥasan, al-Mesâʿîd, al-ʿAẓâmât, and aš-Šrufât, and also raiding parties of the Druses.

As all these clans were engaged in warfare with the ʿAneze, I, being a friend of the ʿAneze, needed a protector.

Hence I inquired among the Nuʿêr family whether there was not camping with them or staying in Ḍmejr some member of one of these clans. No one could be found except a member of the clan of the ʿAẓâmât, ʿAǧâǧ eben Šamlân by name, and he was a man of little influence. He could, indeed, as our companion, protect us from the ʿAẓâmât (*jerfeḳna ʿan al-ʿaẓâmât*), but he could not protect us from the rest of the clans, because his kin (*ahl*) were powerless. Ṛaẓbân, the brother of Ḳâsem, could protect us from the Ṛijâṯ, but he had spilled the blood of the Ḥasan clan and was not respected by the clans of al-Mesâʿîd, al-ʿAẓâmât, and aš-Šrufât—or, as these three clans are called, the Wasamt al-Bâhel. The Ḥasan are notorious robbers, who abuse the sacred right of companionship. The Ṛijâṯ and my companions told me that the Ḥasan had looted caravans that were accompanied by their own kindred, with whom they even divided the spoils. Having had experience enough with such wretches, I was disinclined to expose myself to needless danger.

Toward evening there came to me from Ḍmejr a gendarme sergeant, with the Turkish official (*mudîr*) and several neighbors, and offered me five mounted gendarmes (*ẖajjâle*) who would escort me to the main body of the Ṛijâṯ camping in the valley of aš-Šâm. Thence, they believed, I could proceed after Prince an-Nûri and under his protection. I declined this offer, knowing very well that the gendarmes would leave me with the Ṛijâṯ and that the latter would jump upon me as upon prey sent by Allâh. The escort by gendarmes and my sojourn in the valley of aš-Šâm would have drawn to me the attention of all the robber bands and only a miracle could have led to my escape from the volcanic region. The sergeant flouted at my objections and appealed to the attestation of the *mudîr* and the neighbors from Ḍmejr that the Ṛijâṯ would fulfill every wish of mine; he assured me that the gendarmes would not leave the camp of the Ṛijâṯ until the chief returned with my letter announcing that I had reached an-Nûri safely. Intending to test the offer of the sergeant, I finally consented to ride with the gendarmes to the Ṛijâṯ and gave him money to purchase forage for the horses and food for the men. ʿAǧâǧ eben Šamlân was to accompany us and carry the forage and provisions upon his camel. Thereupon the sergeant departed to make the arrangements, but in an hour he returned with the news that the gendarmes had refused to comply and that none of them were willing to ride to the Rijâṯ. He advised me to wait until he could get to Dûma or to Damascus, bring new orders, and enforce the obedience of the gendarmes. Being familiar with this game of the frontier guards, I thanked the sergeant for his proffered protection and declared that I would protect myself. The gendarme came again at midnight with another offer, or order (*amr*) as he called it, but I would not even listen to him and directed him instantly to return because it was about to rain.

Saturday, December 5, 1914. After midnight it began to rain and continued until ten o'clock in the morning (temperature at 8: 9.8°C). Reconsidering the situation, I decided to go east to the Beni Wahab of the ʿAneze, who were camping with the chiefs Sulṭân âl Ṭajjâr and Saʿûd eben Melḥem at al-Buṭmijjât, and thence to go farther after Prince an-Nûri. I was to be accompanied by Raẓbân eben Nuʿêr, his kinsman Ḥasan al-Maẓlûm, and ʿAǧâǧ eben Šamlân. With these our party counted eight well-armed men able to fight a band of even twenty robbers, whose firearms and ammunition are usually poor (temperature at 5: 10.5°C). It began to rain again toward evening, but about ten o'clock the sky cleared and we hoped that we could start at last. I did not place much trust in the sergeant from Ḍmejr, fearing that the *ḳâjmaḳâm* (governor of a *ḳaẓa*, district) himself might come from Dûma and bother me with his proposals.

Sunday, December 6, 1914. We started at 6.40 A.M. and proceeded eastward past the crumbling Roman camp of Ḍmejr al-ʿAtîže. The plain was full of puddles of rain water and the ground so boggy in places that at first we had to lead our animals. Dense, gray vapors half shrouded the Ab-al-Ḳôs range, but at 8.40 an east wind came up, dispersed the mist, and allowed the sun to shine. At 10.05 we had at about a kilometer and a half to our right the ancient Roman fortress of aš-Šâmât. We did not follow the road Darb as-Sâʿi but rode along the base of Ab-al-Ḳôs in order to survey the plain better toward the south, where rose the extinct volcanoes of Karawišât, Ab-al-ʿAjš, Ammu-r-Rḳejbe, Umm al-Maʿʿâze, and the numerous somber volcanic spurs of al-Mkejmen, thrusting their fingers out into the eastern plain. North of al-Mkejmen glistened the surface of the immense rain water pool of Sejḳal, while to the east the horizon was blocked by the mighty height of al-Buṭmijjât, upon which we noted through the binoculars at eleven o'clock a vast Bedouin camp of our friends of the Beni Wahab. We did not head straight for them but preserved our original course. The camels could find better going where we were, and our position allowed us to survey the depression to the south through which wind the robber trails.

From 11.30 until 12.20 our camels grazed while we dined (temperature at 12: 11.2° C). At 11.30 we saw the ancient Roman fortress Ḥân at-Trâb about three kilometers to the north beside a deep gorge called Šaḳḳ (or Mešaḳḳ) Semri, which separates the higher western part of the az-Zbejdi range from the lower eastern part. Through this gorge leads the only passable road from the south northward. Because the range from Ḍmejr as far as Šaḳḳ Semri plunges precipitously into the southern plain, there is no passage for caravans. The road through the gorge of Šaḳḳ Semri runs thence through the pass Ṯenijjet al-Jabârde to the wells of Abu Ḥjâja. East of this road there are the wells Ǧebb az-Zbejdi and al-Fâᶜi; the road reaches the ruins of al-Maǧrûne and ascends the Šeᶜeb al-Lôz range through the pass of al-Ḥaǧûle. Thence it runs into the valley of az-Zammarâne, follows this up to its end, and at the village of Ersâl descends into the valley of the same name, through which it reaches the settlement of al-Ḳâᶜ between the Lebanon and Antilebanon.

At two o'clock Ḥasan al-Mazlûm cantered ahead of us into the camp to notify the young chief Sulṭân âl Ṭajjâr of our arrival. We likewise turned southeastward, going through the shallow valleys of al-Buṭmijjât. At five o'clock, when the sun was already low, we perceived upon a small rocky hillock in front of us three riders, and a little farther away two more, all coming toward us at a gallop. In another moment small groups of riders had emerged upon several of the eastern heights. Knowing not whether they were friends or foes, we seized our weapons and awaited the first shot. The riders were waving their arms, but they kept silent. The first three approached to a kilometer away without either firing or shouting their greetings. As we were surrounded on all sides, we could not fight. The first three riders rode up to us and the first one, a swarthy youth of about twenty years, jumped off his brown mare, thrust his hand out to me, and cried: "Welcome among us, Mûsa." I recognized in him the chief Sulṭân âl Ṭajjâr, my young friend whom I had not seen since the year 1908. We were overjoyed at so unexpected a meeting. The other riders reached us in groups, expressing their wonder that they had met a friend when they had ridden out to meet an enemy. Many were not satisfied, and Sallûm, a small man holding a long spear, swore like a trooper when he realized that he could not partake of the things loaded upon my camels. Sulṭân then explained to me the reason why his men gave me so strange a welcome. When he had learned from Ḥasan al-Maẓlûm of our arrival, he feared that we might fall into the hands of robbers that had been circling about the camp after sunset in quest of booty, strayed camels, or abandoned sheep. He wanted to ride toward us, but he had in his tent only two slaves, the rest of the men being engaged in rounding up the returning flocks. He did not hesitate long, however, but, firing three shots from his revolver, shouted in alarm, "O riders! (*jâ hla-l-ḫejl!*)" and waved his rifle toward the northwest as he darted from the camp in that direction. His alarm cry was repeated by all who heard it; everybody turned to the northwest, and soon groups of riders hastened after their chief to rout the supposed enemy. Thus we were joined by about fifty riders, who laughed heartily when they learned of the clever manner in which Sulṭân had summoned them. They all greeted and accompanied me to the camp, which we reached at 6.20.

I encamped southeast of the tent of Sulṭân. He ordered a fat wether to be slaughtered for me, and I sat in his tent until almost midnight. He assured me that he would march southward as quickly as possible in order that I might join Prince an-Nûri the sooner. His grandfather on his mother's side, Saʿûd eben Melḥem, would do likewise, he said, since a week ago the latter had received an order from General Zeki to hasten to Prince an-Nûri. Camping with the Beni Wahab there were also many clans of the Fwâʿre tribe, all of them fleeing with their herds from the neighborhood of Damascus and Ḥomṣ to save them from the greed of the Turkish Government. They did not take any interest in the European war. They discussed the fighting of the Turkish Government with the English on the Egyptian boundary, at al-Kwejt, and at al-Baṣra, of which they had learned in Ḥomṣ, as they would discuss a fight of two strange tribes which did not concern them. Many wished for the defeat of the Turkish Government, while others feared that in that event the English would occupy the cultivated regions with guards so strong that it would be impossible to steal anything from the settlers.

Monday, December 7, 1914 (temperature at 7.25 A. M.: 7.5° C). Saʿûd eben Melḥem the head chief of the Ḥsene, a group of the Beni Wahab, came with his sons Fendi, Turki, and Muḥammad, to pay homage to me and to show me the order of Zeki Pasha instructing him immediately to join Prince an-Nûri. He said that he was determined to sacrifice even himself, his children, and his tribe at the behest of the Turkish Government and the Sultan in Constantinople, to whom Allâh would certainly grant victory. Upon being told that I had brought new directions, he admonished those present to listen respectfully to the words of the supreme Government which my servant Manṣûr was to read. The large tent of Sulṭân was filled with visitors, and in front and back of it a curious crowd was also pressing, eager to hear the desires of the Government and the news of what had occurred after their departure from the cultivated region. When Manṣûr had finished, many shouted: "Allâh grant victory to the Government and the Sultan!" but the majority remained silent. Several minutes later all kinds of topics were discussed, but there was no further mention of the Government or the war.

Saʿûd eben Melḥem was much pleased to discover in my guide ʿAǧâǧ eben Šamlân a member of the ʿAẓâmât clan, which was camping with the Ḥasan, whose chief, ʿEjṯ eben Žeʿer, had stolen from him several camels. He asked Manṣûr to write for him a letter minutely describing the booty and the marks of the camels and then requested ʿAǧâǧ to deliver the missive to ʿEjṯ, promising him in return five *meǧîdijjât* ($ 4.50) for every camel that should be restored. Sulṭân âl Ṭajjâr also wished to send by ʿAǧâǧ two letters to the clan of the Mesâʿîd. He had entered into a truce (*ʿaṭwa*) with them that had been solemnly sworn to by twenty members of the Mesâʿîd, who had appointed a special procurator (*čefîl al-ʿaṭwa*). Nevertheless, the clan had robbed him of a mare and ten camels, and Sulṭân's letters demanded of the procurator that the stolen beasts be returned to him if the procurator's face were to remain unblackened (*čefîl abjaẓ*). He promised ʿAǧâǧ fifty *meǧîdijjât* ($ 45.00) for the return of the mare and five *meǧîdijjât* for each restored camel. But he did not cherish any great hope of ever beholding the stolen animals again, since the group of clans known as Wasamt al-Bâhel, to whom the ʿAẓâmât belong, are notorious for their duplicity. A certain member of the ʿAẓâmât had been camping with Sulṭân for two years as his neighbor (*ḳaṣîr*) and Sulṭân had protected the man's herds from his kinsmen; hence he felt sure that the ʿAẓâmât would respect his property. Nevertheless, the very brother of this neighbor had stolen from him several camels, while the neighbor himself had run away with his brother to the ʿAẓâmât and had never returned the stolen beasts.

At Sulṭân's request, Manṣûr wrote a lengthy letter to the Emîr Nawwâf at al-Ǧowf, setting forth that Saṭṭâm, Sulṭân's father, had in the year 1898 bought a house with a large adjoining palm garden (*ḥawṭa*) at Čâf, a settlement in the depression of Sirḥân. Ḫalaf, an old slave of Sulṭân, had kept the purchase agreement, which had been attested by ten witnesses, and Sulṭân requested of Nawwâf, the lord of Čâf, that he acknowledge his right to the house and the garden (temperature at 12.30 P. M.: 10.8° C).

About noon two slaves brought a large copper platter filled with *burrul* (peeled wheat, moistened and dried), on top of which was a covering of rice and on top of all a small heap of mutton. Saʿûd and his sons ate with me. We had barely begun our meal when an alarm cry was heard. The younger men threw off their coats, seized their arms, leaped upon mares that stood ready, and darted out toward the north, whence the alarm was sounded. They returned a quarter of an hour later reporting that there was no enemy. There merely had been a fight between two shepherds, one of whom sounded the alarm, which was taken up by other herdsmen unaware of its source and repeated until it reached the camp.

After dinner I invited Sulṭân and Saʿûd with their sons to my tent, wishing to discuss with them the political events and the war. Saʿûd eben Melḥem was about sixty-five years old. Rather small of stature, plump, with a large, curled lower lip and small, shifty eyes, he resembled a calm settler more than a wandering son of the desert. He owned a house in Ḥomṣ and others in the villages of al-Bwêr and aš-Šejḫ Ḥmêd north of al-Forḳlos. His wife, who hailed from Ǧerûd and was a good cook, preferred living at Ḥomṣ, which was also Saʿûd's favorite residence because he could procure all manner of delicacies. He had not entered the inner desert (*mâ šarraḳ*) since he was a young man. During the rainy season he lived in his stone house at Ḥomṣ or in huts at al-Bwêr and aš-Šejḫ Ḥmêd, while in the dry season he tented in the open air between Ḥomṣ and those villages. After the outbreak of the war he betook himself to the inner desert, not for the purpose of serving the Government, but to protect his property from the avaricious officials.

"Thou knowest, Mûsa," he said, "that I have a house at Ḥomṣ and huts in two villages east of Ḥomṣ. I cannot take these with me into the inner desert, hence I must proceed cautiously (*sijâse*). In the settled territory as well as here in the desert there are many ears that keep for the Government all they hear. Thou knowest the Government. It takes everything but gives nothing. I do not want it to confiscate all I have among the settlers, so I often must speak otherwise than I am thinking. It is *sijâse* (diplomacy). I am troubled with gout and I cannot ride; still I have forsaken my house and taken to the inner desert. They have levied a war tax (*eʿâne ḥarbijje*) upon us and leased it to all kinds of collectors. Whoever pays it will be ruined and whoever does not pay it and remains in the tilled region will likewise be ruined. They take away from my husbandmen pack camels, donkeys, flocks of goats and sheep, and they have emptied my grain barns. That I might save some of my property, the past month I sent my camels, goats, and sheep into the desert while I myself only waited until I could get from Zeki Pasha the assurance that my house would not be confiscated. He ordered me to join an-Nûri. I want to go to him, but the gout torments me."

To my question whether he would stand by the Government or would plunder the settlements from the fastnesses of the inner desert, he answered evasively that it lay with an-Nûri to decide. He begged me to write to the Fedʿân and Sbaʿa tribes, exhorting them to make peace with the Beni Wahab, adding:

"As long as those of my own affiliation press upon me, I cannot care for strangers."

AL-BUṬMIJJÂT TO TLÂʿ AS-SIRRI

Tuesday, December 8, 1914. The camp was moved southeast. We left the old site at seven o'clock in the morning and rode with Sulṭân âl Ṭajjâr through the undulating region of al-Buṭmijjât. Sulṭân (Fig. 97) was rather small of stature, broad-shouldered, with large thick lips, black sincere eyes, and so swarthy a complexion that I could not help surmising that his blood was infused with the blood of some negro. His father, Saṭṭâm, the son of Ṣâleḥ, had vainly yearned for children. Eventually he married Ḫazna, the daughter of Saʿûd eben Melḥem, who bore him Muḥammad and Sulṭân. Muḥammad was sent by the Government to a school established in Constantinople by Abdul-Hamid for the sons of chiefs. He returned in the year 1901, at the time when his father was killed by the Druses, and died shortly after his return. Of the reigning family of Ṭajjâr only Sulṭân was left, who at that time was six years old. His mother had married Muḥammad, the son of Dûḫi of the family of Eben Smejr, and the little Sulṭân was left to the care of the old slave Ḫalaf, who camped with him for three years at ʿAdraʾ. When twelve years old, he was married by Ḫalaf to Ḳuṭna, and two years later to Rafʿa, who was older than he and who bore him two girls, ʿEǧâzi and Sakra. He divorced Ḳuṭna, but he loved Rafʿa dearly, never engaging in any undertaking without consulting her. His only regret was that she had heretofore failed to bear him a son. His father Saṭṭâm, the chief of the Mašṭa clan and commander of the Weld ʿAli group of the Beni Wahab, had been most affluent, possessing several villages near Ḥomṣ and innumerable flocks of goats and sheep. After his death, however, several citizens of Ḥomṣ by bribing the officials had had his villages transferred to their names; the flocks of goats and sheep had diminished, and soon very little was left to Sulṭân. Sulṭân was being paid by the Government 280 Turkish pounds ($ 1260) yearly for the protection of pilgrims, but he had to pay yearly 320 pounds ($ 1430) in taxes (*wudi*) for his Mašṭa clan. His family is much respected throughout the desert as the foremost and the most bountiful

FIG. 97—Sulṭân âl (or eben) Ṭajjâr.

of all the families of the Âjde subdivision of the Weld ʿAli, to which al-Mašṭa belong. The fireplace (Fig. 98) in the main compartment of his tent was always made large and round and upon old camp sites its traces could be seen even after many years.

The members of the Âjde, subjects of Eben Ṭajjâr, and the Ḥsene, subjects of Eben Melḥem, now engage principally in the raising of goats and sheep; hence they are not Bedouins, but *šwâja* (goat and sheep raisers). Far and wide in the land I saw scattered flocks of goats and sheep. The chiefs were joined on their way to the inner desert (*mušarreḳîn*) by many settlers from the vicinity of Ḥomṣ and Ḥama, whose flocks either swelled their ranks or were entrusted to their own shepherds. The shepherds managed the flocks very badly. Toward evening they would offer fat wethers for sale in the tents and the next day would ride throughout the camp proclaiming that the animals had strayed and begging to be informed if anybody should see them. Every shepherd was attached to one of the chiefs who was to protect the flocks from robbers. In return for this service the chief could select one from every ten young, either a ram (*ḫarûf*) or a ewe (*faṭîma*). The shepherd's compensation is either monetary or *ʿadâjel* (use and profit) derived from a stipulated number of head of sheep between the first and the third year. If paid in money, he receives 500 to 1200 piasters ($ 22.50 to $ 54.00) per year, according to the size of the flock. If participating in profits, he is consigned yearling ewes (*ḳerâḳer*), which he milks and shears for the next two years for his sole benefit; after that the animals are returned to their owner. Their young ones do not belong to the herdsman but to the owner proper.

There were flocks of goats and sheep drinking from the rain water pool of aṭ-Ṭarfâwi, which we noted at 9.20 about three kilometers to the right. The region is overlain by blocks of basalt which is massed southwest of aṭ-Ṭarfâwi in immense deposits connected with the crater of Ab-al-ʿAjš. Towards eleven o'clock a southwest wind arose. We were riding at the base of a wide highland that extends from north to south and is known as al-ʿEjṯa, or al-ʿÎṯa. We encamped at its southern slope.

Wednesday, December 9, 1914 (temperature at 6: 6° C). We did not advance because Saʿûd eben Melḥem wished to extend to me his full hospitality. In the forenoon I made an excursion to a hill near by, from which I wished to jot down accurately the individual craters of the volcanic region of Tlûl al-ʿIjâṯ. The members of the al-Âjde and al-Ḥsene clans were familiar with the table-shaped volcano of Sejs and the group of al-Bowzelijjât north thereof, also with the saddle-shaped volcano of Ab-al-ʿAjš; yet they often contradicted themselves in naming the other hills.

East of the volcanoes of Ab-al-ʿAjš, al-Bowzelijjât, and Sejs winds the shallow valley of at-Tejs, east of the head of which we were encamped. West of the basin of al-Ǧwejf it fills the rain water pools (*ḫabâri*) Drejhmât and Umm ar-Rmam and receives on the left the small *šeʿîb* of Ǧlêṛem, which begins north of the basalt rocks of al-Mḫarûṯa and ends in the depression of ar-Raḥba, as the Âjde pronounced it. East of the mighty undulating highland of al-ʿEjṯa extends the valley of Sabʿ Bijâr, which, after being joined by the *šeʿibân* of al-Mdejsîsât and al-Ḫrejṯât, forms the valley called al-Hejl or aḏ-Ḏenâba and terminates in the basin of al-Ǧwejf.

At noon I was visited by Mišḫaṣ, the daughter of the assassinated Prince Fahad eben Šaʿlân. She was the first wife of the Emir Nawwâf, to whom she had borne a son Sulṭân, and had afterwards married Fendi, the son of Saʿûd eben Melḥem. She begged me to carry her regards to her son Sulṭân and to Nawwâf. She would gladly have returned to them but disliked an-Nûri, upon whose hands she saw her father's blood (temperature at 2 : 16.5° C).

Toward two o'clock Sulṭân âl Ṭajjâr came to conduct me to the tent of Saʿûd. About a hundred persons were gathered there in the form of a rectangle and at my entrance all arose. I was assigned a place of honor at the wall separating the space for men from that for women. Muḥammad, the son of Saʿûd, came to meet me, conducted me to the seat of honor, and seated himself in the center of the long western side of the tent. After the customary greetings, a slave poured several drops of water on the fingers of my right hand, and six negroes brought in a huge platter heaped with *burṛul* and mutton, which they set down in the middle of the rectangle. Muḥammad invited me and five other men to eat. On my right was squatting Sulṭân âl Ṭajjâr and on my left Turki, the son of Saʿûd; and both selected the choicest pieces of meat to lay before me. Behind every one of us stood a negro with a dish of water. We had not eaten more than four minutes when we arose and resumed our former places and Muḥammad invited ten other guests to partake. After these the feast was for fifteen persons, then for eighteen, and finally for twenty. Not until these had finished did Muḥammad himself take his seat with three small children by the platter to pick at the bones. The meat was gone, but enough of the *burṛul* was left for a satisfying meal. Upon his command the negroes carried away to the women the platter with the bones and what was left of the *burṛul*, regardless of those present who had had no access whatever

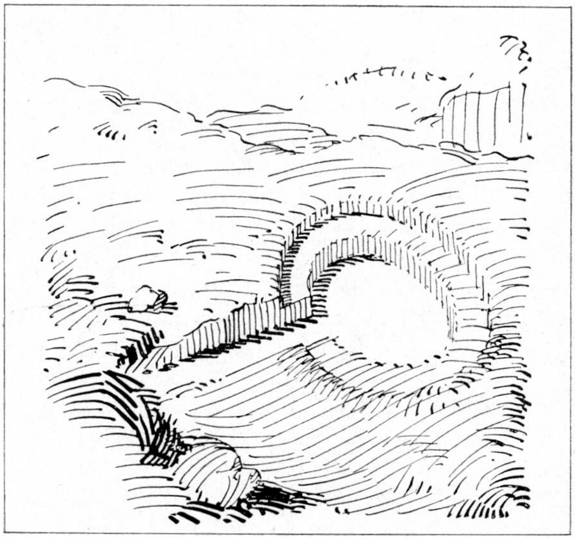

FIG. 98—A fireplace of Sulṭân âl (or eben) Ṭajjâr.

to the meal. The aged chief Saʿûd was in a corner picking at a wether's head.

After the feast an unrestrained conversation ensued. The war, however, was not mentioned. We talked about the grazing lands, the need of an abundant rain, the maladies of the goats and sheep, the thieving in the camp, and the threatened raid of the Fedʿân. None but Saʿûd, tormented by gout, bestowed a thought upon the Government or the British. He expressed a wish for an early termination of the war in order that he might return to his home in Ḥomṣ (temperature at 5: 13° C).

On Thursday, December 10, 1914, we migrated again. Departing at 8.20 A. M. we noted on the right the white walls of the basin of al-Ǧwejf, southwest of them the dark volcano of Aḳren, southeast of it the volcano Umm Iḏen, and northeast of both the enormous crater of Ṛurâb al-Ḥadâli. We reached the new camp site north of the wide depression of aḏ-Ḏenâba, about fifteen kilometers from al-Ǧwejf, at 1.35 P. M. Before the tents were pitched we drew a map of the vicinity from the top of a neighboring hill. There had been thick mists resting upon the range of ar-Rawâḳ to the north for several days, but the volcanic region Tlûl al-ʿIjâṯ was wholly clear. In the evening we ascertained the latitude.

Friday, December 11, 1914. I looked over my notes and ministered to the sick. Among others there came with her mother and her aunt a weak girl about twelve years old. Her name was Faẓẓa, and she was the daughter of al-Hubejli of the Sirḥân clan, who was camping with Saʿûd eben Melḥem. She was suffering from a neglected cold which had developed into a fever. She had barely gone when Sulṭân âl Ṭajjâr inquired as to the state of her health and explained that he had married her ten days before. He said that he did not intend to have any intercourse with her until after their return from the inner desert. I advised him to leave the girl for at least five years with her relatives and to be satisfied with his wife Rafʿa, who was fully developed and hence fit to bear him a much stronger boy than the fragile Faẓẓa could. He spoke of Rafʿa as a woman beneath his foot (*ḥurma illi taḥt riǧli*). Sulṭân did not worry about the rearing of his little daughters ʿEǧâzi and Sakra, who were cared for by the slaves and taught the most vulgar of abusive words. I had heard a slave teaching ʿEǧâzi to call her father and mother foul names. When the child repeated them, her father and the slaves present were convulsed with laughter.

The standard of morality among the Mašṭa and the Ḥsene does not appear to be very high. Never among the Rwala did I hear the implications of unrestrained lechery which were frequent among these people, nor the jests about intimacies of young men with slave women, or even of young slaves with high-bred daughters. From such intimacies, perhaps, come the negro characteristics of many high-bred sons.

With Saʿûd and even more with Sulṭân the slaves presume to a great degree of power, doing what they please and caring not for their masters, or "uncles," as they call them. They did not venture within my tent, but they were always hanging about my servants, demanding one thing or another for themselves and their "uncles." Sulṭân himself was greedy of many things he saw. He did not ask me himself but prevailed upon my servant Nâṣer al-Ḥsejnâwi to solicit this or that for him. Nâṣer promised him everything, while advising me to give him nothing, and then would complain to Sulṭân that I was a miser who was unwilling to give a single gift.

Every day Nâṣer al-Ḥsejnâwi was causing me greater trouble by stirring and exhorting the slaves against me and complaining of my alleged severity. He pretended to have come from the sacred city of the Shiites, Kerbela, or Mešhed Ḥusejn as they say in Arabia; hence his name al-Ḥsejnâwi. He had served several years as a mercenary (*sḳorṭi*) under Muḥammad eben Rašîd and also under his successors ʿAbdal-ʿazîz and Sulṭân. He left the latter — or, as others had it, was driven away by him because of a theft — and then settled in the oasis of al-Ǧowf, where he joined Nawwâf eben Šaʿlân. But Nawwâf disposed of him shortly, whereupon he went to the tribe of the Sardijje in the Ḥawrân, remaining there until the fall of 1912, when Nawwâf sent Nâṣer's brother Ḥabîb as his governor to Čâf in the depression of Sirḥân. Ḥabîb took Nâṣer along and used him in Syria for carrying messages from Nawwâf. Thus in the latter part of November, 1914, he had brought a letter from Nawwâf to the governor at Damascus and called upon aṣ-Ṣafadi, a representative of Nawwâf, to beg for money and various necessities for his wife (*ahali jaʿni an-niswân*). There he was met by Ǧwâd al-ʿÂni, the scribe of an-Nûri, who knew his past well and warned aṣ-Ṣafadi not to give him anything. Nâṣer bewailed his misery, came to me begging for help, and offered himself as a servant. Since I was in need of a servant and since Nâṣer assured me of his familiarity with inner Arabia from al-Aflâǧ to ar-Raḥba and from Kerbela to al-ʿElaʾ, professing to know the country like the palm of his hand, I promised to take him with me to Prince an-Nûri, where I could make a further decision. Should the Prince or one of the chiefs vouch for him, I would hire him as a servant; otherwise he would have to stay at home.

My other servant, also named Nâṣer, who hailed from al-Žerjitejn, assured me that he would watch closely so that al-Ḥsejnâwi could not steal from us. Before we left the city I had bought the latter stuff for his garments and presents for his wife. He was very obliging in Damascus and Ḍmejr, but as soon as we came to the Mašṭa of the Âjde he grew unruly and began to proclaim himself as my guide and protector, asserting that it was only his love for me that had led him to forsake Čâf with his local palace and the immense wealth which it would have been possible for him to amass there in no time. He professed that more than five hundred camels were awaiting him at Boṣra and that he was expected to lead them to Čâf and protect them from the Ẓana Muslim and the Šarârât, his compensation being a quarter of a *meǧîdijje* (23 cents) for each camel. Only his love for me had led him to relinquish this stupendous profit. He stated that for six days he had guided the English traveler, Miss Gertrude Lowthian Bell, from al-Azraḳ, receiving from her six English gold sovereigns and a ten-shot pistol. He enjoyed imitating the manner of speech of the Englishwoman (*al-marat al-inklîzijje*), despite my prohibition of such ridicule on several instances. I regretted taking him along and would have gladly rid myself of him; but that was an impossibility, as nobody wanted to shelter him.

In the evening we ascertained the latitude.

Saturday, December 12, 1914. We migrated again, starting at 8.15 A. M., with the white cliffs of al-Ǧwejf glimmering on our right. At 8.35 we saw the black volcano of Ṛurâb al-Ḥadâli looming to the west. Farther in the same direction rose the crater Umm Iḏen, which tapers off toward the east and to the northwest of which appeared the riven crater of Aḳren. Near al-Ṛurâb emerged the mighty black rocks of al-Mḥarûṯa, in which Ṣâleḥ, the grandfather of Sulṭân, is interred. He fell in a fight with the Druses. South of al-Mḥarûṯa the somber wall of the *ḥarra* on the west contrasted with the adjoining yellowish plain. There was no view to the east; in that direction the valley of al-Hejl was bounded by a massive elevation. There was hardly any pasture in the valley, notwithstanding the fact that the ground had been moistened by the *as-shejlâwi* (Canopus, October) rain in the past three years. Unless, however, *as-shejlâwi* is supplemented by abundant *aṯ-ṯrajjâwi* (Pleiades, November) and *al-ǧowzâwi* (Gemini, December) rains, there is no hope for pasture and the land is not good (*ṭajjiba*) for the flocks.

At 11.25 the chief Saʿûd eben Melḥem pitched camp, Sulṭân following suit a few minutes later. The slaves gossiped that Saʿûd was marching slowly on purpose to miss an-Nûri; but

Saʿûd himself often openly expressed his regret at being troubled and delayed by his gout, which prevented him from executing the wish of the supreme Government as expeditiously as he desired. He spoke thus in order to defend himself before the informers, who were numerous among the settlers that moved with him. My assistant Waldmann and I busied ourselves sketching a map of the vicinity and in the midafternoon making preparations for the exact determination of time. Toward evening, however, the sky became overcast with dark clouds which made observation of the stars impossible.

TLÂʿ AS-SIRRI TO RÎŠT AD-DWÊḤLE

Sunday, December 13, 1914. We set out at 7.50 A. M. and marched through the Tlâʿ as-Sirri district, which slopes toward the valley of al-Hejl. We saw to the southwest the rain pool Ḫabra-l-Časb (Booty Pool). This pool was named thus by the Weld ʿAli because it had saved the life of the warriors who were returning with their chiefs Saṭṭâm eben Ṭajjâr and Muḥammad eben Dûḫi, the father of the chief Ršêd eben Smejr, from a victorious expedition in distant lands. They had no water, the land was arid, and many a mare could no longer move forward. They slaughtered several camels and refreshed themselves somewhat with the stale water contained in the animals' entrails; but there was very little of it, because the camels also suffered from thirst. Just then they noticed on the left a rain pool — a boon sent by Allâh! It saved not only their lives but their booty (*časb*).

At 9.14 we had the half-buried well of as-Sirri about 150 meters to the right. At ten o'clock from a height we noted almost due west of us the blunt cone of the volcano of Sejs and to the west-southwest the volcano of Ṛurâb al-Ḥadâli, from which a mighty spur projects toward the southeast. South of this volcano was the dark, conical al-Ḥadala. To the southeast we saw in an extensive lowland numerous artificial reservoirs, now dry. Nowhere was there any rain water except to the south of us in the Ḫabra Merfijje, by which Saʿûd encamped at eleven o'clock. Sulṭân went ahead of us, and by 11.15 we had in front of us the lowland of al-Bwejb, in which there were also many reservoirs bordered with mounds of yellow clay. Sulṭân, who always camped near Saʿûd because he feared the Ahâli al-Ǧebel, wished to ride on and at nine o'clock sent ahead a camel rider to find a good camp site amid verdant pastures. Such a rider is called *ḳallâṭ*. Our *ḳallâṭ* returned at one o'clock, reporting that he had found no pasture, as many Arabs had been camping in the region ten days before and their herds had grazed over the entire neighborhood. Upon hearing this report, Sulṭân's slaves jumped off their camels, stopped his animal, and proceeded to untie the saddle while it was still occupied by their master. They pretended that a storm was impending and that the sun had set, whereas the rain cloud was only a narrow one that sent down but a few drops; the sun was still high in the sky, as it was only one o'clock. Nevertheless, the slaves would go no farther, and Sulṭân pitched the camp west of the Ḫabâri al-Bwejb in a region where there was no pasturage except *šaʿrân* and dry *šîḥ*.

The deeper we penetrated into the heart of Arabia, the more Saʿûd and Sulṭân feared an attack by the Fedʿân and Sbaʿa tribes. I had persuaded Prince an-Nûri as early as 1909 to offer peace to the Fedʿân and their allies, the ʿEbede. I had also been negotiating with the head chiefs of the ʿEbede and the Fedʿân to effect a peace between the Ẓana Muslim and the Ẓana Bišr; but after the Government had treacherously captured Prince an-Nûri in August, 1910, and the Rwala had attacked the Turkish garrisons and pillaged the frontier settlements, the Government again stirred the Fedʿân and the ʿEbede against them. I had remonstrated with the Governor for these tactics in 1912, when I succeeded in liberating Prince an-Nûri from jail, and had asked him to renew the peace; but the Rwala resented the treachery of the Fedʿân tribe and were attacking them whenever they could. In vain the Government proposed peace to the chiefs of the warring tribes. The Fedʿân, who were also provided with arms by the officials, were revengeful, sparing not even the lives of children.

In November, 1914, Zeki Pasha and the governor of Damascus asked me to induce the Fedʿân to make peace or at least an eight-month armistice, for they estimated that the war would be ended within eight months. At that time I wrote to my friend Barǧas eben Hdejb, chief of the ʿEbede, to influence the Fedʿân toward peace, but I failed to receive an answer. Hence I repeated my persuasion from Sulṭân's camp and promised to do the same from the camp of an-Nûri. A civil war was raging among the members of the Ḳmuṣa tribe. My good friend, the head chief Ṛatwân eben Meršed, had for years been living at peace with the surrounding ʿAneze tribes, but his brother Bišîr, who in 1910 had married a certain eccentric European (*franǧijje*), had defied him and was pillaging camps of the Arabs as well as settlements of the *fellâḥîn*. Arbitration with Bišîr and his adherents, for whom the Sbaʿa had no respect, was out of the question: they must be subdued by sheer force.

Therefore I parleyed with Saʿûd and Sulṭân, proposing that together with an-Nûri they assail him, an expedition in which all of them displayed more interest than in the Turkish Government and England. They saw in the Government merely a bureaucracy of tormentors who were of no benefit to the Arabs in general or the Bedouins in particular but, on the contrary, injured their interests whenever possible. They did not know much about Islâm, and Islâm had no ties by which to link them with the Government. Had the Turkish Government guaranteed them a large booty from the war, they would have risen against the British; on the other hand, if the British had promised them that they would be permitted to loot the settlements subject to the Turkish rule, they would have risen against the Turks. It is only the desire for booty that inspires the inhabitants of the desert to great deeds; they have no conception of love for one's country or for one's religion. They could not expect that the Turkish Government would let them pillage without restraint, especially since the Government had exploited them from the very beginning. Universal peace in the inner desert was their goal only in order that they might fall upon those settlements that were left without any protection, regardless whether such settlements were under Turkish or British rule. This was the motive which prompted them to ask me to effect a peace with the Sbaʿa and the Fedʿân.

Monday, December 14, 1914. We remained on our camp site. Sulṭân asserted that we were going to march on; but Saʿûd was tormented by gout and so decided to camp by us and decreed that we were not to move until his pains abated. I busied myself all day long with my notes and maps. In the evening we determined the latitude.

Before midnight two scouts (*ṭallâʿên ṯentên*), who had scoured the region to the south returned, with the report that they had found no pastures within a day's march. They further reported that there were better pastures in the district of al-Ḥrejṯât to the east, but that even this region had already been visited by numerous herds. They had brought back a camel with stab wounds and the marking of the Weld ʿAli, probably one which had run away from enemy raiders. A certain falconer (*saḳḳâr*), who had made a hunting trip to the volcano of Ṛurâb al-Ḥadâli, brought word that he had sighted an enemy detachment, and that very night Saʿûd sent about forty riders toward Ṛurâb.

Tuesday, December 15, 1914. We marched from eight until nine in the morning, encamping on the boundary of the region alleged to be devoid of pastures. The riders despatched to Ṛurâb having failed to return, we awaited them here. Meantime we had no news of an-Nûri. We had encountered no traveler (*ṭâreš*) who might have brought information about him. I wanted to seek him myself, but Sulṭân resented such a suggestion and persuaded me to patience. The Shaytan, he said, presses men to impetuous action, whereas a deliberate decision is the gift of the Most Merciful (*al-ʿağala min aš-šejṭân wa-r-râẓa min ar-raḥmân*). I myself realized that I could not leave the camp while an enemy band was lurking near. Although it is always dangerous to venture into the unknown desert without a companion and without protection, it is much more dangerous to adventure there when enemies are near. Waiting and still more waiting ever tries one's patience in the inner desert. In the evening we determined the hour. The riders returned late in the night, reporting that they had found neither an enemy band nor any traces of one.

Wednesday, December 16, 1914. We left the camp at 7.40 A. M., riding on the rugged upland Ṭaraḳ aḏ-Ḏîb. With us rode many wives of the settlers, mounted on donkeys. The slaves poked fun at them, saying they looked like the daughters of Eben Mâleč, as they named the Ṣlejb who camp along the eastern boundary of the Ḥawrân. At 8.33 we came to a large mound of clay and ashes by which a fireplace of a peculiar shape had been dug. Sulṭân instantly recognized it as one that had been made by Ršêd eben Smejr (Fig. 99), the head chief of the Weld ʿAli, who had camped there years before. After resting for twenty minutes we rode on; at 9.05 we passed a dry rain pool on the right and again rested from 9.33 until 9.48. At 10.30 we had on the left a large rain pool and perceived in the hollows freshly grown grasses and among them several mushrooms with white stems and heads.

The Bedouins call these *fejlaẓân*; the *fellâḥîn*, *melles*. They tasted sweet, and many ate them raw. From 10.30 until 11.48 we made hardly three kilometers, as our camels grazed on the way. Hence we encamped.

In the afternoon we finished our preparations for leaving our friends and came to an understanding with several men

FIG. 99—A fireplace of Ršêd eben Smejr.

who wanted to join us in order that they might more conveniently get back to their relatives who had gone into the inner desert early in September and October.

Thursday, December 17, 1914. We loaded our tents and supplies and at 7.40 A. M. departed from Sulṭân's camp. For over an hour Sulṭân, with a single slave, accompanied us. After a time eight other men caught up, one of whom, Swêlem eben Meḥlef, rode a mare, while the rest were mounted on camels. They all went along with us. At eight o'clock we sighted upon a small hillock to the left four large eagles (*nsûr*), who were watching our approach with curiosity — a good omen, according to Sulṭân. At 8.40 the two rocks of al-Ḥadala were about sixteen kilometers away. Beyond and southwest of them the bluish, extinct volcanoes of the eastern border of the Ḥawrân became ever more distinct. Sulṭân parted with me, his eyes moistened with tears, and earnestly declared that he would remain my true friend (*ṣiddîž*) forever.

From 9.07 until 9.17 our camels grazed; then we rode until 10.32 in a plain that was covered by numerous flints (*ṣawwân*); here we rested and dined until 11.13. We passed through an abandoned camp site, which my companions scrutinized very closely. At such places the nature of the tracks and excrement indicates whether there has been a camp of Bedouins or of the breeders of goats and sheep (*šwâja*), and likewise whether the camp has been abandoned for a short time, for a month, or even for years. The size of the space where camels rested through the night and the tracks of horses mark the place where the chief himself camped, and the size and form of the fireplace tell his name and dignity. As soon as the visitors at such an abandoned camp site have decided on the chief's name, they know also who camped with him and then seek the tents of individual families. Being familiar with the approximate number of camels owned by the individual tenants, they inspect the particular spots for the camels (*bejt wa ʿendah mrâḥen zên*), look for stones upon which women put their kettles and which everyone fastens in the ground in her own peculiar fashion, measure the dimensions of the compartment reserved for men, observe the depth of the fireplace in which coffee is cooked, and distinguish the owner. Then come reminiscences of the tenants, of rendezvous and raids. It takes a long time to exhaust all the material for talk which such an abandoned camp furnishes.

Our route led us over low hillocks and wide, shallow swales into the region of ar-Rijâši, where, in the valley of Rîšt ad-Dwêḫle, our camels grazed upon fresh grass from 1.30 P. M. to 1.50. After two o'clock my companions showed me, about six kilometers to the southwest, a speck in the gray of the desert. It was a rugged rock called al-Ḫarbe. Some of them said there was a wall of an old structure, while others asserted that no walls had ever been erected there, but that there was a soft rock used by the Arabs in making their short smoking pipes (*sublân*).[104] At 3.20 we encamped at a rain pool in the channel of a wide *šeʿîb*.

[104] Abu-l-Farağ, *Aṛâni* (Bûlâḳ, 1285 A. H.), Vol. 10, p. 28, and al-Bekri, *Muʿğam* (Wüstenfeld), p. 308, write that al-Ḫarba is a region in the territory of the Ghassanians, in a valley of which al-Ḥâreṯ ibn Ẓâlem once killed a camel that belonged to the Ghassanian king Jazîd ibn ʿAmr and was executed for it.—The neighborhood of our al-Ḫarbe is a very suitable camp site and formerly belonged to the powerful Ghassanian tribe; hence I seek in it the ancient region of al-Ḫarba.

RÎŠT AD-DWÊḤLE TO ḪABRA DEBÂDEB

Friday, December 18, 1914. We mounted the camels as early as 6.10 A. M. but dismounted soon afterwards and walked, for white hoar frost was forming and the damp cold penetrated to our bones. At 8.30 we had the Ḫabra umm Sâhlijje about three kilometers to the southeast. The region we were traversing was overgrown by a large variety of fresh perennials. It had been moistened in the season of *aṣ-ṣejf* (middle of April to middle of June) and again by the *at-trajjâwi* (Pleiades, November) and *al-ǧowzâwi* (Gemini, December) rains and hence was an *arẓ maṣjûfa wa murabbaʿa* (a land of plenty) where camels would find pasture for the entire ensuing year. At 10.40 we had on the left an upland with a cairn and adjoining it the large rain pool Ḫabra ummu Rǧejm. From 10.11 until noon we rested about five kilometers west of the high mound of stones Riǧm al-Mezâjen.

East of the undulating slope of al-Mezâjen is the Ḫabra aṭ-Ṭrêfâwi. A short distance to the south of it are situated the Ḫabâri al-Ḫâmel and al-Menâǧi, which are filled from the short valley of al-Atna that comes in from the south. On the southeastern edge of al-Mezâjen is the beginning of the long valley of Rwêšed abu-ṭ-Ṭarâfi, the northern branch of which is called aš-Šḥami, the northeastern al-Ḳarʿa, the eastern ad-Dwêḥle, and the southeastern an-Neẓâjem. Between aš-Šḥami and al-Ḳarʿa the Ḫabâri al-Edênijje and al-Meǧles are located; between ad-Dwêḥle and an-Neẓâjem is the Ḫabra aṭ-Ṭrejbîl. South of the latter rises the table mountain Ḳârt an-Neẓâjem.

These rain pools are situated on the watershed between the Euphrates and the Manḳaʿ ar-Raḥba. In their vicinity there is pasturage throughout the year. Everywhere we saw cairns piled up by Bedouins that they might orient themselves in the otherwise featureless plain.

Going in a southeasterly direction in the undulating plain of ar-Rijâši we came upon a large camp site that had been abandoned but recently and within its area saw the site of a large tent containing numerous hoofprints of horses (*mrâḥ ʿalêh bejten čebîr w marabb al-ḫejl*). Suddenly one of my escorts picked up from the site of the large tent a piece of ostrich feather like those with which the Rwala embellish their national emblem, *abu-d-dhûr*. This led us to surmise with a fair degree of certainty that this place had been camped upon by Prince an-Nûri, in whose tent *abu-d-dhûr* is kept. We could not determine his route, however; for the entire region was a maze of tracks, and the late rains had obscured even the most recent prints. Most of the tracks, especially those of flocks of goats and sheep, converged toward the northeast, while the footprints of camels pointed toward the south. As no breeders of goats or sheep were migrating with Prince an-Nûri, we agreed upon seeking him to the southward.

At two o'clock we crossed the tracks of galloping horses and soon reached a spot where a battle must have been fought not many days before, for the ground was cut up by hoof-prints and the picked skeletons of two horses lay not far away. As we later learned, a band of warriors of the Ḳmuṣa and ʿEbede tribes, commanded by Bišîr eben Meršed, had attacked there a small detachment of the Ḥsene under the chief Sfûḳ eben Melḥem, had taken for booty several herds of camels, and had also seized five tents of the small encampment of the Ahl ʿÎsa clan. A band of reinforcements (*fazʿ*) of the Ḥsene had been repulsed by Bišîr's riders, and the raiders fled. They left the flocks of goats and sheep, doubtless fearing that they would be overtaken by bands from other camps should they drive the goats and sheep slowly before them.

Toward three o'clock we noted in the shallow valley of az-Ẓelʿijje a herd of at least a hundred gazelles, which fled instantly upon getting our scent. At 3.10 P. M. we found an abundant pasture in the valley and decided to stay there overnight. The men who had joined us wished to leave us on the morrow and seek their relatives in the neighborhood of aṭ-Ṭrejbîl and al-Basâtîn. Since they had no provisions whatever, we gave them two days' supply of flour. Their departure left us alone again except for the presence of ʿAwad, a youth of about twenty years and a member of the Freǧe clan belonging to the Rwala, who accompanied us as a herdsman.

Saturday, December 19, 1914. We left at 5.55 A. M. in a southerly direction, riding through a region of reddish loam strewn with innumerable fragments of stone. By the action of wind and rain the soil in such places is carried away and the stones remain. They cover the ground to a depth of five centimeters, protect it from more rapid disintegration, but at the same time thwart the growth of annuals and even of perennials. The undulating highlands and their slopes are barren; *šîḥ*, *rûṯe*, and *šaʿrân*, much enjoyed by camels, grow only in the low places, where top soil accumulates. At 8.15 we descended into the deep valley of Rwêšed abu-ṭ-Ṭarâfi, where the camels grazed until 8.32. The numerous holes in the channel were filled with clear, fresh water, and everywhere green grasses were sprouting. South of Rwêšed abu-ṭ-Ṭarâfi the slopes of the individual heights are steeper and the intersecting ravines more numerous as well as more fertile. We walked most of the time.

I walked with my new herdsman ᶜAwad, who had traversed almost two-thirds of Arabia in his young life. His father had died of heart failure, leaving his mother a widow, with but one camel with which to support four girls and three boys. The relatives were likewise poor. Desiring to help his mother, ᶜAwad, the eldest boy, hired out to the ᶜAḳejl (camel traders) as a herdsman. He traveled with them as far as the border of ᶜOmân, crossed the entire territories of Eben Saᶜûd and Eben Rašîd, and was twice in Egypt. Returning from Egypt for the second time in August, 1914, he tended for a time five hundred camels which Prince an-Nûri had conveyed to the Government as a tax, and then went to the camp of Fâres eben Šaᶜlân at the ruins of al-Baṣîri. With Fâres and Eben Ǧandal he had participated in a raid against the Fedᶜân tribe at al-Bišri. West of the settlement of as-Suḫne, at the base of al-Ḳlêlât, Fâres had met the Selḳa clan, which, being at peace with the Fedᶜân as well as with the Rwala, was obliged to warn the former. Fâres feared that he would be encircled by the Fedᶜân, therefore he turned westward. At as-Sûḥa he found the camp of the division of the Ḥadedijjîn headed by Eben Sirḥân, with whom the Rwala lived at peace; but the warriors of Eben Ǧandal maintained that a Ḥadîdi had once stolen a camel from one of their number, hence they descended upon the herds and drove off several as booty. Fâres forbade his fighters to participate in such villainy.

ᶜAwad, who, as a Freǧi, was subject to Eben Šaᶜlân, had not received any of the booty. Being loath to return empty-handed, he set forth in company with two men in search of loot (*ḥanšal*) to the camp of the Ḥadedijjîn division of the chief Eben Turki near the settlement of as-Suḫne. Not even then, however, did Allâh deign to bestow any booty upon him. East of ar-Raka (Arak) they encountered five robbers of the ᶜAḳêdât tribe, whom they joined at their fire. The ᶜAḳêdât inquired whether they belonged to the tribes camping north or south of Tudmor. Upon being told they were Rwala, the robbers instantly seized their rifles, and ᶜAwad and his two companions, who had only old revolvers, fled to the rocks. Unfortunately, a herdsman, who was pasturing a flock of goats near by, shot at them and hit one of ᶜAwad's men in his shin. ᶜAwad and his uninjured companion begged the herdsman for mercy and protection from the ᶜAḳêdât, handing over to him their revolvers and cloaks as an inducement; whereupon the shepherd, from a point of vantage in a ravine, defended them against the attacking ᶜAḳêdât and gave an alarm cry, at which the robbers instantly fled. The herdsman was a Ḥadîdi from the very camp that ᶜAwad was going to rob. They tied two tent poles to the injured leg of their companion, put him upon a camel, and took him to Tudmor, where they left him with a family related to him. ᶜAwad returned without a weapon and without clothes to Fâres, who was camping at al-Bẖara, south of Tudmor, and who gave him an old fur coat, in which he set out for Damascus to earn some money. In the camp of Saᶜûd eben Melḥem he learned about the war, the constant conscriptions, and the compulsory labor; hence he decided to return home to his mother and therefore joined me. He was a composed, prudent youth, whom I could consult. Whatever he knew, he told; if he did not know anything he did not chatter and make misrepresentations, as al-Ḥsejnâwi did. He was not a guide and he did not know the country; but he took good care of my camels and obeyed without hesitation or objection. Al-Ḥsejnâwi lamented from morning till night for fear we should go astray and perish. He yearned for his "castle" in Čâf and cursed the day when charity had moved him to accompany and protect me. Oftentimes my hand itched to strike him, but I had to be patient.

At 9.25 we had on the left two small rain pools. At 10.30 we descended into the valley of Rwêšed as-Saṭîḥ, which rises in the height of ᶜEnâza to the south of the Ḳârt an-Neẓâjem. In the Rwêšed as-Saṭîḥ is the Ṛadîr al-Ḳaṭab. From eleven o'clock to 11.40 we rested in the *šeᶜîb* of al-Ḳerârijje. Shortly after noon there appeared southwest of us, between Rwêšed al-Ğeẓîᶜa and Dmejṯet ummu Ḳṣejr, the mesa of al-Ḫarğa, and at three o'clock we came into a wide basin that could be overlooked from the northeast, east, and southeast.

At 4.10 P. M. we encamped near a small hill in a deep dry watercourse. East and west of us glimmered rain pools; plenty of pasturage and an abundance of dry perennials lay about us; our camp fire was concealed under a steep, high bank; our baggage was hidden among boulders in the channel, in the soft sands of which we made our beds. It was a camp such as the traveler will seldom find in the desert. But woe to us if a heavy rain should occur in the east on the Ḳwêrât al-ʿEnûz! Our channel would be filled with a rushing torrent. Everything would be swept away that could not be saved by a quick escape. We observed the sky carefully. It was partly overcast in the southeast but not in the east. After midnight several large drops of rain fell, but otherwise the night passed uneventfully. Toward morning, however, a strong southeast wind sprang up, the herald of imminent rain.

Sunday, December 20, 1914. The sky became clouded in the east at five o'clock, while in the southeast bolts of lightning zigzagged constantly. A light rain began to fall. We set out at 6.10 A.M. One could not see even five meters ahead, but there were rifts in the clouds to the southeast which gave us hope that the rain would not last long. ʿAwad and I walked in front of the camels, going in a southerly direction. The rain ceased for a while, but presently the sky became entirely overcast and we had such a downpour that at 7.50 we had to stop. To the left and also ahead of us glimmered the pool of Debâdeb, which the rain water was forming, while on the right rose a steep slope on which the camels slipped in the sodden ground. During the downpour we pitched the larger tent and got the baggage under cover before it was drenched through, but we ourselves were soaking wet up to our knees. With difficulty we kindled a fire and dried our clothing and footwear. The fire scorched my shoes. The rain lasted throughout the day and evening, but since our tent was visible from a distance of at least fifty kilometers to the east—from the top of ʿEnâza—we dared not risk having any fire or light after dark.

Monday, December 21, 1914. As the rain had not ceased, we remained where we were. Toward noon the wind began to blow from the west and dispersed the clouds, but the rain continued at intervals until evening and it was not until during the night that the sky cleared.

ḪABRA DEBÂDEB TO AZ-ZEBÎBIJJÂT

Tuesday, December 22, 1914. The sun appeared at eight o'clock, and at 8.40 A. M. we set out toward the south, circling the western edge of the Ḫabra Debâdeb, a rain pool at least fifteen kilometers long from north to south and four kilometers wide from west to east. From 9.25 to 9.42 we filled our water bags from a fine *radîr*, or hole filled with rain water. The camels were so satiated that they took no notice (*mâ hen âčelât*) of the exuberant sprouts of *rûṯe* as we rode through them. We reached the southwestern end of the Ḫabra Debâdeb at about 10.30.

This shallow depression narrows toward the west and forms the head of the valley of al-Ğeẓîʿa. The Rwêšed al-Ğeẓîʿa merges with the Rwêšed as-Saṭîḥ and forms the Rwêšed abu Ḥefna, so called after the pool in the river channel. On the left side of al-Ğeẓîʿa, north of the Ḳârt al-Ḫarğa, is the rain pool of Sûfa and southwest of it ad-Dwâra. East of Debâdeb rise the low, tabular hillocks Ḳwêrât al-ʿEnûz and southwest of them appears the wide, furrowed slope Ḥazm ʿAnḳa. Between Ḥazm ʿAnḳa and the Ḳwêrât al-ʿEnûz is the rain pool Ḫabra ʿAnḳa and east of the latter the Ṛadîr aš-Šejḫ.

Crossing a wide, rocky upland, at 11.35 we came into the region of ad-Dmejṯât, where we rested until 12.05. This region forms a rolling, stone-covered plain overgrown with solitary bushes of *firs* about half a meter high, on which camels like to graze. In the depressions *šaʿrân, rûṯe,* and *šîḥ* flourish. Camels munch these perennials with relish, but they do not fatten on them, because of the laxative action of the plants. That is why the Rwala never remain long on ad-Dmejṯât. The best winter pasturage (*mašta*ʾ, never *mšatta*; plural, *mašâti*) is to be found in the vicinity of al-Ḫôr, Ḫabra ʿAnḳa, and Lâha. If one asks a Rwejli "Where have ye grazed this winter? (*wên šattejtu has-sene*?)," one is likely to receive for answer: "Our winter pasturage was al-Ḫôr (*maštâna bel-ḫôr*)." In the spring they prefer grazing (*marbaʿ*; plural, *marâbiʿ*) in the depression al-Ğûba ("we passed the spring in al-Ğûba, *rabbaʿna bel-ğûba*") and on the northern edges of the Nefûd. In the country of al-Bijâẓ between al-Ğûba, Tell ʿAmûd, and the volcanic country one can find pasturage in the season of *aṣ-ṣejf* (from about the middle of April until the middle of June; *maṣjaf*); whereas from the end of June until the end of August they pasture (*maḳîẓ*) in the region of an-Nuḳra south of Damascus. In the autumn they like best to sojourn in the vicinity of the depression of Sirḥân; there is the *maṣfar* (autumn pasturage). If it does not rain in the Ḥamâd and in the Wudijân, they migrate to the vicinity of Tejma or to the eastern boundary of the Nefûd, where rains are more regular.

At 2.50 P.M. we reached the shallow valley of Dmejtet ummu Ḳṣejr and found there the tracks of two riding camels and a female hound (*sleḳa*). ʿAwad was of the opinion that the riders were falconers and therefore that there was an Arab camp somewhere near. At 3.10 we made camp.

I noted a high mound of stone upon a solitary hill south of our encampment and directed my steps toward it; for fear that an enemy band might discover our tracks and attack us in the night I wished to survey the northern environs thoroughly through the binoculars. The region was open toward the north to a distance of at least fifteen kilometers; but there was nothing to arrest my attention, although the slanting rays of the sun, already sinking low in the west, so illuminated the entire region southward that every bush stood out distinctly. Then I turned my eyes toward the west and again toward the south, gazing at the solitary volcanoes that loomed south of the castle of Burḳuʿ. The most conspicuous among them were the rugged crater of al-Heber, the abruptly-ending Eḳren, the imposing an-Naʿejǧ, and, far to the south, the Ktejft aṭ-Ṭrejf, which resembles a horse saddle. Turning the glass somewhat more to the left, I suddenly beheld upon a high, sunny slope a row of camels. Some of them were grazing, others moving about. It occurred to me that they might belong to a band of resting raiders; but, upon scrutinizing the individual animals more closely, I did not observe saddles on any of them but noted numerous young camels among them, a certain proof that it was a herd returning home after grazing during the day. Without ascertaining the exact direction, I hastened to our encampment to call ʿAwad, who, it developed, was guarding camels some distance away. Al-Ḥsejnâwi ran for him immediately, but before ʿAwad could get there and climb the hill a dark cloud had obscured the sun and he could see nothing. We were watchful during the night, but nobody approached us.

Wednesday, December 23, 1914. We left our encampment at six o'clock and walked in a southwesterly direction, as ʿAwad was of the opinion that the camels I had seen were in a camp somewhere by the Dmejtet ummu Mḥafûr. The sky was overcast with dense clouds, portions of which were separating and drifting to the ground. ʿAwad expected a heavy fog (*jaǧîna kubs, ṭall*); and indeed, at seven o'clock there descended upon us a mist so dense that we could not see ten meters ahead.

We hastened forward with compass in hand, at the same time examining the ground in order not to lose sight of eventual tracks of camels and horses. At eight o'clock we climbed a height that my companions thought was the one upon which I had seen the camels, but I disagreed with them, for I had estimated the distance to be at least thirty kilometers. From eight to 8.20 our camels grazed, after which we continued in the same direction for over an hour without finding the least indication of Arabs. After nine o'clock the fog began to lift and the sun appeared and shone across the broad plain to the west. We looked eagerly for traces of smoke but in vain. ʿAwad thought the Arabs might be camping at the western base of the hillocks we had left; therefore at 9.30 we turned toward the northwest, but nowhere were any herds to be seen.

Shortly after ten o'clock we spied to the northwest two camel riders and one man afoot. As we had not detected any herds of camels, my companions maintained that those I had seen yesterday were a band of raiders and that these three men were spies (*ʿujûn*). In vain I argued that none of the animals had saddles, that there were young camels among them, and that they were at least thirty kilometers distant; I could not convince my companions, who were intimidated by the constant lamentations of al-Ḥsejnâwi. We hid our camels in a shallow *šeʿîb*, crawled forward, and lay in the path of the unknown men. When they were within about one hundred paces of us, ʿAwad called to them to continue on their way if they were of the Ẕana Muslim, but to flee if they were enemies. Al-Ḥsejnâwi leaped up and began to imitate the motions of horseback riders who trot about their chief as a manifestation of their pledge of loyalty (*ʿarâẓa*). The same thing is done in the desert by camel or horseback riders when they want to assure a band they may encounter that they have no hostile motives. But the unknown riders did not trust the words of ʿAwad or the motions of al-Ḥsejnâwi. They swerved their mounts, the one afoot leaped behind one of the riders, and they galloped away toward the northeast. Al-Ḥsejnâwi ran after them, shouting and waving the tail of his mantle, but all in vain: they shortly disappeared in the hills. Their panicky flight and the bulging bags upon their saddles proved conclusively that they were peaceful travelers. Hoping they would summon to their assistance (*lajta faza'aw 'alejna*) Arabs who might be camping in the vicinity, we waited until 12.45 P. M.; but no rider appeared.

From 12.45 to 1.20 we rode in an easterly direction, then to the southeast. At 2.40 we came into the extensive plain of Dmejṯet ummu Mḥafûr and proceeded southward until four o'clock, when we encamped beyond a rise near the artificial rain pool of al-Mḥafûr.

There is not a single spring in the plains of the Ḥamâd and almost no wells of spring water. The Arabs draw their water from natural basins or depressions in which rain water gathers and forms larger or smaller pools. Where there are no such natural pools, many artificial reservoirs are to be seen, frequently measuring thousands of square meters in area and as many as three meters deep. The excavated clay forms wide banks in which are left large openings through which rain water flows into the pools. The chiefs who directed these gigantic feats of engineering displayed great ingenuity in thus securing for their herds the water which was so indispensable to them in these regions, where otherwise they could not camp at the end of spring. Moreover, camping here, they saved the pasturage adjoining the natural waters for the times when the water in the artificial pools evaporated. Many thousands of diligent hands were necessary to excavate these basins. I am inclined to believe that the work was not done by the Bedouins, or camel raisers, but by the *šwâja*, who raise goats and sheep. Perhaps they were helped by the inhabitants of the settlements south of Damascus, who drove their herds in late autumn to the eastern desert in order to save their crops. They could find pasture in the desert from the first rains in November until May, provided they supplied themselves with the water necessary for their sheep and goats; and hence they may have excavated the artificial rain pools for this purpose. At the end of May or the beginning of June, when the last of the water had evaporated, they would return to their settlements, where meantime the harvesting had begun and their herds could thus graze in the stubble fields. The same method could — nay, ought — to be employed even now by a powerful government which has the welfare of the settlers at heart.

We were vigilant throughout the night, for we might have been attacked if the unknown riders had hastened to Arabs and incited them to pursue us. We were of the opinion that they were friends who were camping in the vicinity, but during the night even a friend is dangerous if he is unaware that it is another friend he meets. The night was cold and misty and in the morning hoar frost glittered upon our covers.

Thursday, December 24, 1914. We set out at 6.05 A. M. in a southerly direction, reaching, at 6.48, a height from which I recognized, several kilometers ahead of us, the saddle-like crest I had seen two days before in the rays of the setting sun. I immediately called my companions, telling them that that was the crest on which I had seen the camels going from pasture and that we certainly should find fresh tracks there. We stopped and surveyed the landscape in all directions. We were in the region of short valleys, Šeʿibân al-Ğerânijjât, which carry the water flowing from the east into the large pool of Dowḳara. The region is bounded on the south by a huge elevation which slopes from the east toward the west and along which extends westward the *šeʿîb* of aṭ-Ṭrejf with numerous holes in the channel (*ṛudrân*). Near aṭ-Ṭrejf could be seen the cleft crater of Ktejft aṭ-Ṭrejf, south of it the al-Ḫaṭîmi and ʿÂžer groups, and west of the latter the imposing volcano of Liss. Almost due southwest of us rose the sharply-pointed Eḳren and southeast of it the dome of al-Ḥenw; but we saw no Arabs or herds. An hour later we reached the base of the crest where, as I firmly believed, I had seen camels two days before, and, indeed, there we found the first fresh tracks.

Pausing, we waited from 7.45 until 8.14 for ʿAwad, who was to look for the herds from the crest through my binoculars. We had arranged with him that we were to ride southward should he disappear to the south beyond the ridge (which stretched from southwest to northeast), but should he follow the crest eastward we were to go southeast. At 8.14 we noted that he turned eastward; hence we headed in the same direction over an undulating slope which rose to the south and was covered with coarse basalt gravel. In a few minutes we perceived near ʿAwad some riders and two men on foot, who shortly disappeared. ʿAwad signaled us with his mantle to come quickly and then he ran toward us. Reaching us, he said that strange Arabs had taken away from him the binoculars, his carbine, and his cartridge belt and had sounded an alarm.

We knew that they would pounce upon us shortly; hence we hastened as fast as possible to the crest, in order to observe the camp. We had barely made the ascent when we perceived numerous groups of riders, who, on seeing that we awaited them calmly, came to a halt. But there was another group approaching us through a ravine like a pack of hungry wolves. They were beating their mares with their heels and rifles, and the mares were virtually flying. They did not see us from the ravine. The reason they hurried so fast was for fear the other fighters might outstrip them and get the best share of the booty. About fifty paces from us they darted up the slope and for the first time perceived us, as well as the other band, which still stood about a hundred paces away. Thereupon they emitted yells like those of ferocious beasts, beat their mares, and made one last leap toward the prey. The manes and tails of the horses and the long braids and sleeves of the riders fluttered in the air. Horse and rider seemed to be one, a winged, flying monster, its trunk black and half-naked, its left hand swinging a rifle and its right curved like a hungry talon, while its white teeth appeared as though lusting for warm, bloody flesh.

We heard a commanding voice from among the ranks of the first band, and suddenly there stood before me a young rider proffering me his hand and saying: "Mûsa, thy brother Mšâš welcomes thee!" He was the commander of the first group that had reached me at a gallop. I stood several paces in advance of my companions. The other riders of the first group tried to stop the second group but they did not succeed, for the rascal al-Ḥsejnâwi had driven two camels toward the second group and invited them to loot them. They made the camels kneel and were beginning to snatch the things that were loaded upon them. With a few leaps my camel was among them. I beat them with the butt of my rifle and shouted that they should pay me a hundredfold for everything they damaged. The rider who had greeted me and others who had reached us by this time came to my assistance and thus the robbers were repulsed. They returned piecemeal everything they had taken.

The rider who had greeted me introduced himself as Mšâš eben ʿAli. He was the brother of Ḥadîṯe, chief of the Ḫreše clan, who joined us a while later with ʿEnâd eben Mâdi, chief of the Ahl ʿÎsa, who were camping near by. In 1909 Ḥadîṯe and his brother Mšâš had met me and talked with me in the camp of Prince an-Nûri in the depression of Sirḥân. They told me they had visited an-Nûri only a few days before, when he was camping by the volcano Umm Wuᶜâl. ᶜEnâd eben Mâdi had attacked me in the spring of 1901 at Ḳuṣejr ᶜAmra, where I was staying with Hâjel, a brother of Prince Ṭalâl eben Fâjez of the Beni Ṣaẖr; but he had returned our stolen camels and I had given him a nickel-plated eight-shot revolver. Both men also greeted me in the name of Prince an-Nûri.

We all thanked Allâh that he had guided us to friends. Surrounded by thirty riders we proceeded in all glory to the camp, where every woman and girl gazed curiously at this extraordinary procession. Within the camp the riders staged a mock battle, attacking, pursuing, and shooting at one another, until both chiefs gestured them to stop. At 10.40 I entered the tent of Ḥadîṯe, where I was served with coffee, tea, and rice. He inquired about the war and complained that ᶜAbdarraḥmân Pasha Jûsef was hiring camels for the Government from the tribes that were camping by the Pilgrim Road to Mecca, but was failing to pay the charges and at the same time was maintaining his soldiers with the stores and herds of the Arabs. My tent was pitched alongside the tent of Ḥadîṯe, who visited me in the afternoon with his eight-year-old son, ᶜAli. I discussed with him my journey to an-Nûri, which I proposed to resume on the morrow. In the evening we determined the latitude. I sat in front of the tent until late into the night, absorbed in reminiscences of my homeland and my dear ones. It was Christmas Eve!

CHAPTER XIV

AZ-ZEBÎBIJJÂT TO AL-ĞOWF

AZ-ZEBÎBIJJÂT TO AN-NÛRI'S CAMP NEAR ḪABRA AL-HAĞM

Friday, December 25, 1914. At 6.20 A. M. we marched eastward in the direction of Prince an-Nûri's encampment, accompanied by Zejdân eben Ṯamed, the elder brother of the chief Ḥadîṯe and his servant Ḥamed.

At 6.50 we sighted the mighty volcano of Umm Wuʿâl, which extends from northwest to southeast. Somewhat to the west of southwest the sharp-edged Eḳren hovered above the low mists, with the dome of al-Ḥenw southeast of it; southwest of us and almost east of al-Ḥenw were visible the two summits of Ktejft aṭ-Ṭrejf; south of them several dark pinnacles of the group of al-Ḫaṭîmi; and farther south beyond them the protuberant summit of ʿÂžer, with the cone of Liss west of it. Still farther westward al-Ufejḥem rose like an isle among the gray mists, while south of Liss the black northern edge of the volcanic region trended northeastward. Perched upon it rose the volcanoes of al-Mačmen, with Zellâḳa northeast of them and, north of Zellâḳa, Ktejft al-Ḥanğar, ar-Rdêʿânijje, and Ktejft al-Ḫôr.

Before us the extensive volcano of Umm Wuʿâl was enveloped in a transparent veil of vapor, and far to the east and northeast a wide, violet crest loomed above the horizon, trending from the north toward the south. The undulating slope of az-Zebîbijjât which we were traversing rises eastward and has a surface of basalt and lava gravel. In the dales grow *firs, šaʿrân,* and *rûṯe.* The entire region is of a dark color, the depressions forming isles of yellowish green in a sea of black. At 8.14 a cold east-southeast wind began to blow and everything was covered with glittering hoar frost. At 8.44 we found abundant pasture and remained there until 9.03. Our new companions had disappeared with al-Ḥsejnâwi into a neighboring tent and did not overtake us until past ten o'clock.

Meanwhile we were joined by a chief of a lesser clan of the Weld ʿAli, whose members were migrating eastward. He rode a young camel, behind his saddle sat his falcon, and beside the camel scampered a female hound (*sleḳa*). The chief recognized me instantly and we greeted each other. He told

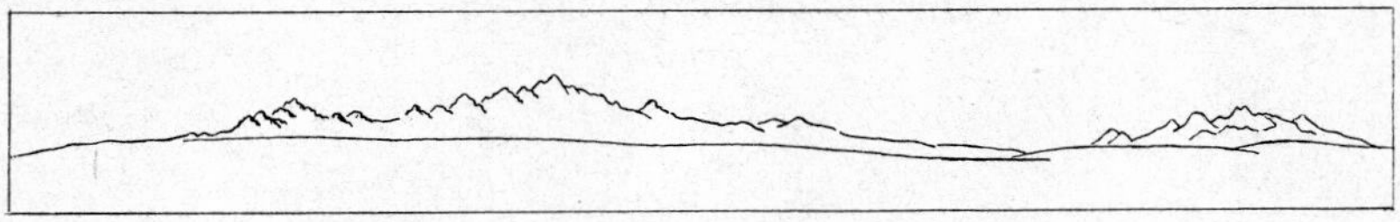

FIG. 100—Umm Wuʿâl and Wuʿejla from the west.

me that Emir Nawwâf had arrived the night before from al-Ǧowf to visit his father an-Nûri, and that they were expecting ʿAwde abu Tâjeh. He surmised that they would all be pleased at my arrival and that many a fat camel (*ǧezûr*) would be slaughtered. This prospect of feasting captivated his fancy to such a degree that he resolved to accompany me to an-Nûri, who, he said, was camping at al-Ḫôr. He summoned the negro leading his mare, entrusted to him his falcon and his *sleḳa*, and ordered his clan to encamp close by the volcano of Umm Wuʿâl; then he drew up alongside and began to inspect my weapons eagerly.

The volcano of Umm Wuʿâl has two hollow craters: one in the center; the other, much smaller, at the northwestern edge. From the central crater a stream of lava about four meters deep runs toward the southeast and terminates at the lower, but prominent, volcano of Wuʿejla. South of the latter a rather deep ravine which conducts rain water into the natural pool Ḫabra Ṣfajje winds from the southwest toward the east in the depression of al-Ḫôr. From 10.43 until 11.25 we rested. At noon we found in the ravine a deep *ṛadîr* full of clear water, by which we remained for ten minutes drawing water. At two o'clock we met a camel rider who was headed westward. Zejdân and the chief of the Weld ʿAli engaged him in conversation. About half an hour later Zejdân caught up with us and informed us that we could not reach an-Nûri that night, as he had migrated; whereupon the chief of the Weld ʿAli returned with the rider to his people, as he did not enjoy the prospect of passing the night under the open sky, especially since it was not certain when and where we should find an-Nûri. We surmised that an-Nûri would not stop very soon; therefore I directed that we also move onward after supper until the moon set.

We rode past Umm Wuʿâl and Wuʿejla (Fig. 100).

The group of Umm Wuʿâl consists of two horizontal strata, the lower one light gray, the upper dark red, whereas in the case of Wuʿejla the lower layer is gray and the upper one black with a bluish tinge.[105]

Beyond Umm Wuʿâl gapes a huge depression which trends from the north southward and in the east is bounded by a violet slope with numerous wide gullies. It is called al-Ḫôr and contains many large and small rain pools. On the west it is bounded by the Ḥazm ʿAnḳa, az-Zebîbijjât, and the volcanic region. On the east, above the central part of the depression, the plateaus of as-Saddja and al-Ḳaʿasa gradually rise like great stairs, whereas to the northeast and southeast no such features are apparent. The depression of al-Ḫôr extends north as far as the Ḳwêrât al-ʿEnûz and south to the volcano of as-Shami—nay, almost to ʿAmûd. In its northern part is situated the rain pool of Bardwîl. Ahead of where we were, in the central part of al-Ḫôr, lies the Ḫabra Ṣfajje; farther south, to the east of Ktejft al-Ḫôr, is the reservoir of al-Ktejfe; south of Ktejft al-Ḥanğar is the Ḫabra Šdejjed; and east of the volcano; of Zellâḳa is the Ḫabra Mḳannaʿ, near which ends the Wudej ʿAmr. On the southeastern side of al-Ḫôr are the rain pools of al-Lwejzijje, al-Bowbehi, and, at the southern end of the steppe of al-Ḳaʿasa, the Ḫabra ʿAṣda. On the northeastern side are the Ḫubejra (dim. of *ḫabra*) ad-Daḥal, al-Bḳara, and an-Nûḳ.

At 3.15 we stopped in the ravine southeast of Wuʿejla. The camels grazed while we drew a map of the region to the east from the top of a neighboring height. Below in al-Ḫôr we noted the long rain pond Ḫabra Ṣfajje, about five kilometers wide, from which emerged various isles. Upon the eastern slope of the depression, especially in the wide valleys, clustered groups of tents, the black color of which contrasted sharply with the lighter tones of the ground. Somewhat to the south of east we noticed, in about the middle of the slope, a large, solitary tent and, because it lay in the direction we were going, we decided to pass the night near it, especially since we were likely to obtain there definite news of the Prince. At 5.45 we began our march through the ravine into al-Ḫôr. In the depression we turned first northward, then southeast-

[105] Jâḳût, *Muʿğam* (Wüstenfeld), Vol. 4, p. 933, says that Wuʿâl is a mountain in the district of as-Samâwa, belonging to the Kalb, between al-Kûfa and Syria. He cites the verses of the poets an-Nâbiṛa and al-Aḫṭal. An-Nâbiṛa names Wuʿâl after Ḥubej. Al-Aḫṭal, *Dîwân* (Salhani), p. 156, mentions the camp sites: Ḥâjel, Wuʿâl, ʿÂleğ, Zubâla, al-Keṯîb, al-Adḥâl, al-Basîṭa, aš-Šaḳîḳ, aḍ-Ḍawğ, Ruwajje, and Ẓiḥâl. —

Ḥâjel is identical with the valley of the same name in the Ṭajj territory, east of the Ağa' range; Wuʿâl with our Umm Wuʿâl; ʿÂleğ with the Nefûḏ desert; Zubâla with a station of the same name on the Pilgrim Road from al-Kûfa; aš-Šaḳîḳ with the watering place of aš-Šižîž. The local names al-Keṯîb and ad-Adḥâl are common appellations, hence they are hard to define. Aḍ-Ḍawğ, Ruwajje, and Ẓiḥâl are yet to be ascertained.

ward, and finally southward, circling the pools and walking most of the time. At eight o'clock we finally headed toward the northeast and at 8.32 reached the valley in which we had seen the large tent. Zejdân eben Ṯamed and al-Ḥsejnâwi, who sat behind his saddle, were grumbling over the necessity of traveling in such cold (it was only 8° C), and Zejdân tried to convince me that we had already left the tent behind. I retorted that he might immediately return to the camp of the Ḫreše clan, which also was behind us. At 8.43 I jumped off my camel, made her kneel, tied her by the left leg, and lay down by her. The others followed my example.

Saturday, December 26, 1914. We were shivering with cold in the morning. The temperature at 6.30 A. M. stood at 2° centigrade. The camels, the baggage, the blankets — everything was covered with thick hoar frost. Starting at seven o'clock, we rode in the valley eastward and after a full hour reached the tent we were seeking, where we learned from a herdsman that Prince an-Nûri was migrating to a destination somewhere east of the Ḫabra al-Hağm or Ḫubejra ad-Daḥal. Turning toward the southeast, we ascended after nine o'clock to the top of the mesa which borders al-Ḫôr. About four kilometers northeast of us glimmered the surface of the Ḫubejra ad-Daḥal. To the south rose the flat range of the Ḥazm al-Ḳaʿasa and still farther east the slope of the Ḥazm Šarâwa, these two heights forming the western termination of the wide plateaus which spread from north to south. Whoever here ascends such a *ḥazm* (flat-topped ridge) from the west, on reaching the top will behold before him an undulating plateau rising somewhat toward the east and bounded on the eastern horizon by a slope like the one up which he has just climbed. The largest of these rolling plateaus is the Ḳârat Lâha. These plateaus are like colossal stairs and form the watershed between al-Ḥamâd and al-Wudijân, as the western and eastern halves of northern Arabia are called.

The Rwala hold that during the Deluge the Ḥazm Lâha protruded from the waters like an island. They believe that the heavenly water with which Allâh flooded the world imbued stones with the power to emit sparks when struck — only those upon the Ḥazm Lâha, which was not touched by the water, produce no such sparks.

There are almost no channels in the plateaus mentioned above. At the base of the slopes, however, which verge stair-like toward the west, the run-off gathers in numerous pools.

This entire broad region swarmed with grazing camels. Huge herds of them were straggling toward the east and southeast, and to the northeast were many tents. A herdsman told us that Ršêd eben Smejr, head chief of the Weld ʿAli, was camping there. From 10.50 to 11.30 we dined. Upon resuming the march we met larger and smaller bodies of migrating Bedouins, who informed us that Prince an-Nûri was going to encamp east of the Ḫabra al-Haǧm. At noon there flew over us more than a hundred large birds with roseate breast feathers, black-edged wings, white necks, and dull, yellow bills. ʿAwad called them *rahaʾ*. At 2.30 P.M. we reached the Ḫabra al-Haǧm (Figs. 101, 102), where we filled one water bag in ten minutes. This pool has been artificially enlarged, but the part thus excavated is so clogged with earth that it fills with water only in years of abnormal rain.

ARRIVAL AT AN-NÛRI'S CAMP. MOVE TO THE EAST

From the east could be heard shots fired at short intervals, indicating that the sons of the reigning family were shooting at a target. An-Nûri's tent was pitched in a small pit, so that we were unable to see it until 3.10. No sooner did we make our appearance than the shooting ceased and all present pushed up to the front of the tent, surveying us curiously. Suddenly the slave ʿAli shrieked: "The Sheikh Mûsa!" He ran to meet us and led my camel to the left side of the tent. I had not yet dismounted when the Prince stood before me and pulled me into his embrace, hugging and kissing me as if I were his brother. Behind him stood the Emir Nawwâf (Fig. 103), extending both his hands to me; then followed a long line of my old, loyal friends, all of whom I embraced and kissed before entering the tent. Nawwâf seated me between himself and his father, and from all sides there poured upon me greetings and inquiries after my health. I felt so much at liberty among these good people that I considered myself at home, among brothers.

I looked the gathering over, searching among them for my three good friends, ʿAdûb eben Meǧwel, Mamdûḥ eben Saṭṭâm, and Saʿûd, the son of Prince an-Nûri. Not seeing them, I asked where they were.

"They are gone (*râḥaw*)," said the Prince. "ʿAdûb was

Fig. 101

Fig. 102

Figs. 101, 102—Ḫabra al-Hağm.

robbed of several camel herds by the Šammar at the watering place of al-Ḳejṣûma. He intercepted the raiders, recovered the animals, but was hit by a bullet and fell dead on the spot. His mare returned with the saddle empty and spattered with blood."

"And where did Mamdûḥ perish?"

"He had undertaken a raid against the Šammar. He circled the Nefûd on the west and south sides and found the Šammar and the Weld Slejmân at the wells of Bêẓa Neṯîl. He took as booty twelve herds of camels and was fleeing with them westward when the enemy, who had occupied the gorges of al-Misma', attacked him, and Mamdûḥ fell in the pass of al-ʿÂh. The survivors of the raid reached us while we were camping at ʿAmûd."

"And where hast thou lost Saʿûd?"

"He fell through treachery. He was killed by the dogs, over whom barks Eben Ğâzi, at the approach of the valley of Nâʿem into the depression of Sirḥân north of the settlement of Ḳarḳar. There he was watching herds of camels with six riders, when ten riders mounted on camels approached and greeted them, explaining that they were under the command of ʿAwde abu Tâjeh, our friend. As the garb of his part of the Ḥwêṭât is the same as that of the Ḥwêṭât of Eben Ğâzi and the camels of the newcomers had the brand of Abu Tâjeh, Saʿûd readily believed them and invited them to join him at his fire. The riders unsaddled their camels and carried the saddles to a neighboring rock, where they pretended to kindle a fire. Suddenly without warning they seized their rifles and fired upon Saʿûd and his companions, and soon Saʿûd and four others lay dead. The other two saved themselves in the high *ratam* thicket and hastened for help. The Ḥwêṭât tried to escape, but the Šaʿlân horse riders soon overtook them. Seeing they could not get away, they jumped off their camels and hid in the dense underbrush in the middle of the depression of Sirḥân. The pursuers surrounded the underbrush, kindled numerous camp fires, and watched the men throughout the night. The following morning the Ḥwêṭât begged for mercy, but the riders tied them, took them to the spot stained by Saʿûd's blood, and killed them one after another with their heads turned southward, which is the manner in which sheep are killed. They deserved it for their treachery."

The Prince's voice did not falter in the least while he

described the death of his friend ʿAdûb, his brother-in-law Mamdûḥ, and his own son Saʿûd.

"What wouldst thou, brother, against the will of Allâh? Two-thirds of us men depart this life through violence (*raṣ-*

FIG. 103—The Emir Nawwâf.

ban). There is not a single one of the remaining third who does not carry his wounds and scars. Thus it was, Mûsa, before us, so it shall be after us. O Allâh! O Merciful!"

Toward evening I went into my tent, whither the Prince sent me supper of *burṛul* with pieces of mutton on top of it.

Sunday, December 27, 1914. We were intending to migrate, but the Bedouins were disinclined to leave their tents. A thick fog obscured the sky, penetrated the tents, and contributed to the drop in temperature to 1.7° C at 7.45 A. M. Inside the tents fires were burning and the Bedouins crouched beside them. The cold pierced to the marrow of our bones. It is said that nowhere in inner Arabia is it so cold as upon the plateau between ʿEnâza and Lâha. After nine o'clock there came to us Mâneʿ eben Ḫadâʿ, the chief of that family of the Freǧe clan to which our herdsman ʿAwad eben Šubejčân belonged, to vouch for ʿAwad's dependableness and loyalty.

After ten o'clock the Prince came to ask me to mount my camel, as the migration was about to begin. I rode with him and we were presently joined by Nawwâf and several of his escorts, by various chiefs, and by slaves (Figs. 104, 105). The camels carried us by quick strides out of the moving throng, until we rode at its head. The Bedouins sat on their camels with their heads entirely shielded; from under their chins they pulled up their kerchiefs so that only their eyes could be seen. Their bodies were clad in a diversity of garments — as many of them as would go on under their short, loose fur coats with sleeves half a meter longer than their arms. Over their fur coats and kerchiefs were wrapped cloaks, which they clutched tightly to their breasts with their left hands. On their feet they wore either sandals or crude, low shoes, but some wore red riding boots (*ǧazme*). Their calves and knees were entirely bare, for the wind kept flapping open the bottoms of their shirts and mantles, letting the damp cold penetrate to their waists. Many eyed me pityingly because I had no fur coat, and Ṭrâd eben Saṭṭâm was preparing to divest himself of his own lest I freeze, when the Prince chuckled:

"O Ṭrâd, not Mûsa but thou sufferest from the cold. Seest thou not his footwear? Thy knees are bare; his are covered with leather boots. Most likely his chest is protected as well. And why should Mûsa buy a fur coat when soon he will reach a land where he will sweat day and night?"

Nawwâf had donned in my honor thin, half-silk stockings and low shoes of patent leather with rubber soles; his hands were encased in white transparent gloves, which he proffered to me the moment he noted my bare hands. These pieces of finery were the gifts of various merchants trading in the settlements of the oasis of al-Ǧowf. He had ruled there but five years and yet had already acquired the manners of the settlers. From his saddle hung a sword with a remarkable hilt, the blade bearing a Dutch inscription dating back to 1672. The hilt had been adorned with precious stones and gold and silver ornaments by his young servant.

The good-hearted, though vacillating, youth that Nawwâf had been in 1908 and 1909 had grown into a severe and determined man. His face showed traces of the hardships he had experienced; it bore the aspect of an unconquerable will that does not flinch even from cruelty. In his merry eyes was a jovial smile, but to me the smile looked like the leer of a gratified, rapacious animal. Two warriors comprising his personal guard constantly rode about ten paces behind him. He had come to visit his father, accompanied by several hundred warriors mounted on camels and carrying at the head of the line a peculiar banner (*bêraḳ*). To a long spear embellished with ostrich feathers was fastened a strip of black material upon which was sewed the form of a sword cut out of white cloth and embroidered crosswise with the words: "There is no god but God, and Mohammed is his prophet (*lâ ilâh ill-allâh wa muḥammad rasûl allâh*)." The fighters of Nawwâf always camped together in large white tents grouped about the round one reserved for him. They were mercenaries serving for their wage and maintenance, and even their equipment belonged to Nawwâf. The least insubordination was punished severely, the transgressor being tied to a heavy tent pole which he had to drag along during the march. Greater transgressions were punished by execution.

The money and food that Nawwâf needed for his soldiers he succeeded in providing from the sale of loot captured from defiant enemy tribes. He had come to an-Nûri for the purpose of consolidating with his Bedouins and making joint raids against the Šammar, Fedʿân, and Druse tribes. The young chiefs and slaves were pleased at the prospect of these raids and they seemed to look forward to fights no less than they did to the prospective booty. A Bedouin yearns for booty day and night, not so much to enrich himself with it as for the thrill of capturing it; and the greater the danger the more alluring the adventure. As soon as the booty is safe in his hands, it ceases to please him: he gives away what he had captured and plans whither to go after fresh loot. It has always seemed to me that the Bedouins consider fighting as sport.

FIG. 104

FIG. 105

FIGS. 104, 105—Our retinue.

THE RWALA'S OPINIONS OF THE WORLD WAR

From 10.40 until 11.20 we warmed ourselves at a large fire which had been built by the slaves at the order of the Prince. Marfûd, an old chief, asked me whether I would participate in the raid against the Fedʿân. Desiring to learn what this plain son of the desert thought of the holy war of which so much has been said in Europe, I replied:

"Dost thou not know, O Marfûd, that the Caliph hath declared holy war against the unbelievers and hath forbidden the believers to war among themselves?"

"What doth the Caliph know? What do we care for the Caliph? The Fedʿân are unbelievers to us, hence we fight them."

"Why, the Fedʿân belong to the ʿAneze just like thy Rwala, hence they are thy co-tribesmen and they are of thy faith."

"I know that they are related to us through their blood and faith, but they have deceived us, hence they are worse than all the foreigners and Christians and we are in holy war against them. And the Šammar of Eben Rašîd and the Druses of the Turkish Government are just as bad. What do we care about the Caliph's holy war?"

Prince an-Nûri and Nawwâf had announced their loyalty to the Caliph in Constantinople and yet Marfûd declared:

"Ye obey whomsoever ye want to. We guide ourselves by the law of the desert; is it not so, comrades?"

Echoing from all sides was heard the avowing chorus: "Thou hast spoken the truth, thou hast spoken the truth."

Marfûd interpreted public opinion, while the Prince and Nawwâf subscribed to a political policy which they did not feel in their hearts. Religion, nationality, unity: these are conceptions incomprehensible to the average Bedouin. His religion is diametrically opposed to the religion of the Christians or of the Moslems. By his very nationality he differs from all his neighbors, even though they speak Arabic just as he does, and his unity ceases with his kinship. But even if the various tribes form alliances among themselves for the sake of more effectual defense, it never happens that a Bedouin allies himself permanently with a settler. There is no unity between the free tribes of the inner desert and the subjugated settlers of the tilled regions; therefore it is incorrect to include inner Arabia among such Arabian countries as Egypt, Syria, or Irak. Inner Arabia is a peculiar world of its own and one that is difficult to understand.

I was surprised to find that so many of the Rwala had been converted to Islâm since the year 1909. In 1908 and 1909 I had not seen a single Rwejli pray, but in the year 1914 it was different. I think that it was the result of Nawwâf's activity, for, having captured al-Ǧowf and other settlements, he was obliged to recite prayers with the fanatical settlers. His soldiers, hailing from the villages by the middle Euphrates and from al-Ḳaṣîm, were accustomed to prayer and many of them could recite an entire chapter from the Koran, teaching others and exhorting them to the observance of religious precepts. The soldiers from al-Ḳaṣîm, like the settlers from al-Ǧowf, were pervaded with the ideas of the Wahhâbites; hence Nawwâf had no alternative but to join them and uphold, outwardly at least, the Wahhâbite teachings. Therefore *al-ḫaṭîb* (the conductor of prayers) loudly ordered his soldiers to the recitation of the prescribed prayers and prayed with them. Prayers were said near an-Nûri's tent also, but invariably in the evening. Nobody prayed in the morning, as the Bedouins slept long after sunrise; but they occasionally prayed in the afternoon. Many a Bedouin followed the example of the chiefs and prayed also. He would imitate all their motions but did not repeat the prayers, for he did not know them. This I learned by asking many men in vain to repeat the prayers.

What amazed me most in the Rwala was their increasing hatred of the Christians (*naṣâra*) in general and the Inklîz (English) in particular. This had resulted from the wars of the Turkish Government with Italy and the Balkan States. Not that the Bedouins cared in the least about the Government's loss of large territories in the Balkans and in Tripolis; on the contrary, they wished to see it defeated and weakened. But they did resent deeply its action in requisitioning from the ʿAḳejl for military purposes the camels they had bought from the Bedouins. Naturally the ʿAḳejl were indisposed to buy camels now, since they could never hope to get as much for them from the Government as they would have received in Egypt; consequently the Bedouins, unable to sell their camels, were suffering from want. Moreover, when at the end of June they entered the tilled region where the Government was stronger than they were, they were dispossessed by troops who commandeered their horses and camels for the Sultan in Constantinople.

Since the year 1910 the Bedouins had fared badly. Strange to say, however, they did not blame the Government as much as they did the Christians and the Inklîz. Had not the Christians, they said, provoked the Government, the Government would have let the Bedouins alone; and when the Christians did attack the Government, the Inklîz should have repulsed them. The Inklîz, they said, had promised to protect the Sultan in Constantinople from the Mosḳûb (Russians) and therefore they were bound to protect him from the other Christians as well. Since they failed to fulfill their promise, they were regarded by the Bedouins as guilty of treason (*bowḳ*) and at the same time as instrumental in bringing about their own plight. For the Bedouins knew that the fewer pastures the Sultan had in the vicinity of Constantinople, the more he would strive for the appropriation of those belonging to themselves, and that, should he be defeated in the great war of 1914, he would oppress them so much the more. Moreover, since the grazing lands of the Inklîz were not sufficient even for themselves, it was rumored that they were bent on seizing the territories belonging to the Muntefiž and Eben Ṣabbâḥ Arabs and that this was their motive for despatching soldiers to al-Kwejt and al-Baṣra. For these reasons the Bedouins were imperiled by them also. Thus commented the Rwala who were riding with me; but the Prince and Nawwâf kept silent.

We were traveling through a monotonous, undulating region covered with dark, fine gravel. Only in the swales there grew long, narrow strips of various plants, among which *rûṯe* predominated. There were no valleys. The *šeʿîb* of Arḳaṭ, where we encamped at 3.20, is a lowland which slopes toward the southeast. In the upper part is situated the Ṛadîr Ḳabr Bṭejjen and north of it Ḫafâje Lâha. Bṭejjen, whose sepulcher is near the *ṛadîr* which bears his name, was the father of Ṛaṯwân eben Meršed. He was head chief of the Ḳmuṣa tribe and was renowned far and wide for his hospitality and for his fondness for coffee. His slaves had thrust into his grave a high tent pole as if to commemorate the tent in which nourishment and protection had been found by so many travelers. Whenever the Ḳmuṣa pass by his grave, they lay upon it a small cup containing a few drops of coffee, the drink he had liked so much. The Rwala ridicule this custom, but the Ḳmuṣa, who camp most of the time in Palmyrena, where graves are held in reverence, persist in imitating the local settlers in this respect.

NORTH ARABIAN POLITICS

Monday, December 28, 1914. The thermometer registered only 0.1° centigrade at seven o'clock. We remained in the camp, where I occupied myself by rewriting my notes. Before noon an-Nûri and Nawwâf came to me to discuss the political situation and the sentiment of the Bedouins. An-Nûri advised me to believe neither his propaganda nor what he wrote to the Government.

"Thou knowest my heart, brother," he said. "Thou knowest that I do not trust the Government and it does not trust me. Were it not for thee, I should still be sitting in al-Ḳûṭa as an honorable prisoner of the Government. My clans were already far in the desert and I could obtain release neither from the *mušîr* (brigadier general) nor from the governor. They pretended to need me in the war against the Inklîz. Said I: 'Of what good shall I alone be to ye? Send me into the desert and I will bring ye thousands of warriors and we shall slay the Inklîz'; but they kept postponing the date of my departure from day to day. I was apprehensive lest they imprison me again. Finally Allâh sent me thee. Thou hast vouched for me that I will not attack the Government, and the Government hath released me. The Government believed thee when it would not believe me. They fear I might fight them. Truly, I should like to do so, but I cannot. They instigated against me the chiefs Ḥâčem eben Mhejd and Eben Rašîd. Ḥâčem is attacking from the north, Eben Rašîd from the south. Help me to make peace with both.

"Why should we, sons of Arabia, massacre one another in the interests of a foreign government? They incite us against each other and we respond. We are lacking in reason. If we lived in a peaceful alliance, the Government would tremble before us; now, however, they deride us. They want me to assist them, me, an-Nûri, whom that same cursed Government sought to hang four years ago! me, an-Nûri, who languished for two years in their cage! me, an-Nûri, whom thou hast saved from the gallows, whom thou alone, Mûsa, hast delivered from prison! Now I am to help the Government and march against the Inklîz! In that cage I learned to conceal even matters that were consuming my heart.

"The Government can do damage to me and to mine. We are in need of clothing, of grain for ourselves and our horses, of arms and ammunition. Arms and ammunition are brought to us by the ʿAḳejl from al-Kwejt and al-ʿAžejr, but they cannot supply us from there with clothing and grain. It is too far away. We are dependent upon the settlers from Syria and Irak, and they are still in the power of the Government. They will sell us nothing without the sanction of the Government, and we cannot take anything from them by force. Our fighters are impotent in the gardens and among the stone dwellings and an easy aim for the rifles of the Government soldiers. The settlers hate the Government as much as we do, but they are united with it against us.

"What are we to do but to wait patiently and prepare for fighting? I have promised the Government all they have asked of me and shall continue to promise both verbally and in writing. I pay the taxes as they come due, contribute to the expense of the war, give the Government camels as well as mares, feed it with gold, and — curse it. Accursed be they who devour my gold! Sâmi Pasha (commanding general in Syria in 1910) had eaten several *roṭols* (1 *roṭol* = 2.56 kg.) of gold and when I reproached him he had me sentenced to the gallows. Since then I remonstrate not. The present governor hath not required gold from me. He asks that I remain loyal during the war and promises after the war to help me against Eben Rašîd. Whether he speaketh the truth or a lie, I know not."

"He lies, father," interrupted Nawwâf. "How could he speak the truth when he knows that Enver Pasha considers Eben Rašîd his most loyal ally and sends him arms, ammunition, and money? At the beginning of this year he sent him by rail to al-Ḥeǧr fifteen thousand Mauser rifles, four hundred thousand cartridges, field guns, and so much gold that ten camels could hardly carry it. Zâmel eben Subhân transported the arms to Ḥâjel and distributed them among the Šammar and even the Ṣlejb. Before that the Šammar had barely five hundred good rifles; now they have so many that they sell Mauser rifles in Ḥâjel for two Turkish pounds ($ 9.00) apiece. And what did Enver send these rifles to Eben Rašîd for?

That he might the more easily defeat Eben Saʿûd, who eighteen months before had driven the Turkish soldiers out of the province of al-Ḥasa.

"The same Enver Pasha had appointed Eben Saʿûd the governor and commandant of the whole of Neğd, had assured him of the Sultan's grace and his own favor; yet he gave to Eben Rašîd the arms with which to wage war against him. Who, then, would trust Enver Pasha? And the governor of Damascus does not know of this? Eben Rašîd has broken, at the order of the Government, the peace he made four years ago with Eben Saʿûd and also the armistice between him and my father and myself which was agreed upon a year ago and which was to last for two years. Today the guns sent him by Enver are battering at the settlements of Eben Saʿûd in al-Ḳaṣîm, and the troops, armed with Enver's Mauser rifles, are annihilating the bands of my father and myself.

"My father pays the Government over four thousand Turkish pounds ($ 18,000) annually in taxes, buys from his own means the arms and ammunition necessary for the protection of the lives and belongings of his people, and yet is supposed to protect also the interests of the settlers and the Government; while Eben Rašîd is being paid by the Government two hundred and thirty Turkish pounds ($ 1035) monthly, is overwhelmed with arms and ammunition, and is being incited to steal our herds and kill our men.

"Tell me, brother Mûsa, dost thou understand our Government? And this Government wants us to help it against the Inklîz. They have ordered my father so and have written likewise to me. Why do they not write thus to their friend, Eben Rašîd? His deputy, that traitor Rešîd Pasha, is feasting in Damascus and in Constantinople. He telleth the Sultan of the power of Eben Rašîd, and all that he speaketh is a lie. Where is Eben Rašîd? Great was his power in the days of Muḥammad and ʿAbdalʿazîz! Today there is nothing left of that power but the name and that is a mere shadow without a sun. Zâmel eben Subhân, the minister of the impotent Prince Saʿûd, the son of ʿAbdalʿazîz, was killed this spring by his relative Saʿûd, the son of Ṣâleḥ eben Subhân, who some time ago had nineteen of the foremost men in Ḥâjel put to death. Many of the members of the reigning family took refuge with Eben Saʿûd and under the command of Fejṣal eben Rašîd made ready for a fight against the minister Saʿûd. In Ḥâjel and among the Šammar are many men who are averse to obeying the members of the family of Eben Subhân, whose forefather was a slave. They have appealed to me for aid; and, had it not been for the arms and gold supplied him by Enver, there would today be no trace left of the name of Eben Rašîd.

"Is Enver blind that he doth not see the wiles of Eben Rašîd's minister Saʿûd and his Constantinople representative Rešîd? The latter negotiated with the consul of the Franǧ in Damascus and promised aid to him as well as to the Franǧ *sefîr* (ambassador) in Constantinople, provided they will convey their soldiers to Syria on vessels. He divided the gold with the minister Saʿûd. My men captured a messenger carrying Rešîd's dispatches to Ḥâjel; thus I got the information. Some time ago there was in Ḥâjel a consul of the Inklîz from al-Kwejt and a certain lady. Why were they there? The consul from al-Kwejt also came from Ḥâjel to me at al-Ǧowf. I was not at home at the time. He sought to gain my substitute, the negro ʿÂmer, for the Inklîz and then rode from al-Ǧowf to Egypt. No doubt he had made a treaty against the Government with Saʿûd eben Subhân, and the Government and Enver have no favorite except Eben Rašîd. Shame upon such a Government! Whoever would believe that they will support us after the war is an artless child."

"And what dost thou, son Nawwâf, propose to do? Art thou strong enough today to destroy Eben Rašîd?"

"I am, father. If allied with thy fighters, we shall have at least five thousand rifles."

"What is that against fifteen thousand, or, say, against only ten thousand or five thousand rifles belonging to Eben Rašîd, who has plenty of good ammunition, while we must be sparing of bad ammunition? Thou mightst overpower Saʿûd eben Subhân, perhaps thou couldst take from him a large booty, but never couldst thou drive him out of the settlements. He would gather strength and attack thee again. Nay, sonny, we must not march against Eben Rašîd. We must obey the Government and wait."

"How long?" asked Nawwâf.

"Until the great war between the Government and the Inklîz ends. This time the Government wants peace among us. We, the Rwala, need peace also. Two years have I been in prison and two years the Rwala have been fighting among themselves and against the Government. It was only five years ago that thou didst wring from Eben Rašîd al-Ğowf, which our forefathers had lost. Against me agitates my relative Fâres, the son of Fahad eben Ša'lân, and against thee Eben Der', whom thou hast banished from al-Ğowf. If the Government will not support these, our opponents, we shall easily rid ourselves of them. If we strengthen ourselves at home, we shall be that much stronger on the outside. Why should we disobey and refuse peace? The aim of the Government is different, but we both may use the same means. Let us complain in Damascus and Constantinople that the Fed'ân and Eben Rašîd do not want peace. Thou knowest very well that Enver has already sent three messages to Sa'ûd eben Subhân asking him to make peace with us. They wrote and telegraphed to Ḥâčem from both Damascus and Aleppo asking him to guarantee the preservation of peace. Neither Eben Subhân nor Ḥâčem eben Mhejd obeyed. Dost thou not see that the Government will resent it? Their disobedience may be useful to me and to thee."

"Of what avail will a government which is constantly changing be to us? We have received nothing and we shall receive nothing. Will they defend us from the Fed'ân and Eben Rašîd? Will they send an army against them?"

THE AUTHOR PROPOSES MEDIATION WITH EBEN RAŠÎD

"I believe thy father is right, Nawwâf," I said. "Ye do not know what awaits ye, hence ye must not weaken yourselves. Try to strengthen yourselves at home and ye will be feared by Eben Rašîd as well as by the Government. In so far as I know, the Fed'ân and 'Ebede tribes will make peace with ye if ye ask them."

"What! dost thou mean that we should ask Eben Hdejb and Eben Mhejd for peace?" exclaimed both an-Nûri and Nawwâf.

"I am of the opinion that ye both should ask Eben Rašîd for peace as well."

"O Mûsa, dost thou think that Eben Ša'lân will ever write to the son of a slave?"

"O brother an-Nûri, thou shalt not write to the son of a slave, that is, to Eben Subhân, but to Sa'ûd eben Rašîd."

"But then the Fed'ân as well as Eben Rašîd would boast

of our fear of them,'' exclaimed Nawwâf, "and thou seest that we are making ready for a raid."

"O Nawwâf, who advised thee to take al-Ǧowf? Who persuaded thy father to give his consent? Who aided thee with advice as well as deed? Thou knowest who he was. Since I now advise thee to offer peace to Eben Rašîd and urge thy father to offer it too, so am I willing also to aid with deeds. Thou hast waged war for five years. For five years thy settlers and Bedouins have suffered. I know them well. I am sure they will be glad of the peace for which they are yearning. Give it to them regardless of contemptuous jeers. Thou knowest thine own strength best; others cannot add to or subtract from it. Offer peace. Thus shalt thou prove to the people of al-Ǧowf thy good will and they will cling to thee. And thou, brother an-Nûri, offer peace not only to Eben Rašîd but to the head chiefs of the Fedʿân and ʿEbede tribes as well. The head chief of the latter, Barǧas eben Hdejb, is a friend of mine. I know that he esteemeth thee and that he will persuade Ḥâčem, the head chief of the Fedʿân, to subscribe to the peace. Prove to thy Rwala and to the Fedʿân that thy reason is more provident, that thou canst see more clearly into the future than others. They will esteem thee so much the more. Why dost thou waver? Thou alone in battle defendest thy weary and wounded fellows; protect them now also. Conquer thy pride for a while and thou shalt conquer both Ḥâčem and Eben Rašîd. Why cannot an-Nûri be also a victor in politics?"

"By Allâh, Mûsa, it seems to me that thou art right. I will write to both Ḥâčem and Eben Rašîd and thou shalt take the message with thee."

"Thou wilt have the messages written and wilt send them thyself. One of thy slaves will go to Ḥâčem, another to Eben Rašîd."

"But then everybody will know that I am suing for peace."

"Why shouldst thou conceal it? Thy message might be lost, or Ḥâčem as well as Eben Rašîd might deny it; but thy slave will not get lost."

"What if Ḥâčem or Eben Rašîd should reject my offer? It would be an insult to me."

"Ḥâčem will not refuse," I replied. "My friend Barǧas eben Hdejb will take care of that; I myself will see that Eben Rašîd does not refuse. Thy slave shall go with me. He shall render thy message and Nawwâf's in my presence and I will act. He shall not come back until peace be effected, which shall be affirmed to thee by a special letter from Eben Rašîd signed also by me. Thou wilt have the message written and wilt send it by a special slave."

"I will."

"And thou, Nawwâf?"

"I will do as my father does."

"Wilt thou promise it?"

"I will, but my heart bleeds. What booty we could have taken! Who will compensate us for that?"

"Allâh, and that soon, I believe."

Then I inquired about Fâres, the son of the murdered Prince Fahad, who had been camping with Bišîr, the brother of Ṛaṯwân eben Meršed. With them also dwelt Eben Ǧandal with his clan, the Swêlmât. After the arrest of an-Nûri in the autumn of 1910 the Turkish Government had proclaimed Fâres prince of all the Rwala, but nobody except Eben Ǧandal joined him. I persuaded both an-Nûri and Nawwâf to do everything possible toward effecting a reconciliation with Fâres, a cousin of Nawwâf, the son of an-Nûri's brother, and thus toward winning over Eben Ǧandal also. They were of the opinion that they might gain the latter more easily before reconciling the other, as Fâres was very capricious and conceited.

Tuesday, December 29, 1914. We remained at the same camp and I made notes of my conversation with an-Nûri and Nawwâf. Toward noon I was visited by ʿAwde abu Tâjeh, head chief of the Ḥwêṭât who were camping with the Rwala. The chiefs of the Ḥwêṭât, to whom belongs the neighborhood of Maʿân on the Ḥeǧâz railway, were defending their freedom against the Government, which had been steadily gaining ground in Maʿân since the beginning of the century. Resolved to weaken the Ḥwêṭât, the Government had announced in the year 1900, after the death of the head chief ʿArʿar eben Ǧâzi, that it would recognize as chief only Ḥarb or, rather, his son ʿAwde abu Tâjeh, and that it would deal only with him. ʿAwde, the most daring but also the most cruel man known to me in Arabia, had soon swept with him almost all the Ḥwêṭât. He kept making invasions into the adjacent and distant regions and always returned with booty, which won for him the hearts of the Ḥwêṭât. ʿAbṭân eben Ǧâzi, the son of ʿArʿar, took refuge with his relatives in Egypt and later with Abu Šâma, chief of the al-Mwâhîb clan, camping in the volcanic region of al-ʿAwêreẓ northwest of al-Ḥeğr. ʿAwde collected taxes and transmitted them promptly to the Government; he pursued

FIG. 106—From pools of al-Arnabijjât looking east (see p. 456).

the vandals who damaged the railway, protected the settlers from robbers, and thus won fame as the best chief along the Ḥeğâz Railway. In the summer of 1908, however, the Government grew afraid of his popularity, made terms with ʿAbṭân, corrupted the other chiefs with bribes, accused ʿAwde of various crimes, and issued a warrant against him.

ʿAwde and his clan retreated to the inner desert and engaged in an unrelenting campaign of revenge against the Government and its adherents. At first ʿAbṭân had the support of the soldiers guarding the Ḥeğâz Railway, but in 1912 at the order of Enver he allied with Eben Rašîd and made incursions against the Rwala and the Ḥwêṭât clans that camped with them. In June, 1914, he attacked the settlers of al-Ğowf who were gathering *semḥ* (*sammâḥ*) in the region of al-Bsajṭa, robbed them of more than sixty camels, and killed one of their men. After the outbreak of the World War the Government directed ʿAbṭân to effect a reconciliation with both Nawwâf and ʿAwde. ʿAwde also had instructions to become reconciled with ʿAbṭân and to come to the Ḥeğâz Railway, as all of his transgressions were pardoned; but he laughed at this graciousness:

"Does the Government think that I don't understand? It exhorts all of us to peace. It thinks that we will bring thousands of fighters to its aid. It doth not trust the Christians in Syria, it doth not trust the Druses in the Ḥawrân, and it needs camels for the march to Egypt. It knoweth that so long as there is no peace amongst us we shall shirk by pointing to the others — I to ʿAbṭân, an-Nûri to the Fedʿân, Nawwâf to Eben Rašîd, and they to us, and thus we shall all stay at home. Hence comes the unrelenting effort of our Government to help us all to peace. We want peace and need it, but for ourselves, not for the Government. This thou mightest do, Mûsa: write to the Government that thou hast found among us all the willingness to help our just Government, but only after it has helped us and has forced all our opponents, whom it has been inciting against us for so many years, to become reconciled with us. Thou knowest us, thou knowest the Government. We remain the same always, but how many governments, how many officials, have changed since the year 1909 when I first met thee!"

"Well, ʿAwde, wouldst thou really march to the aid of the Government against Egypt?"

"So long as there is no peace, I shall not move from the desert. If I become reconciled with ʿAbṭân and Eben Rašîd, and my affiliated Ḥwêṭât camping in Egypt call to me for help, then I will march there. The Government promises me arms and also gold at some station of the Ḥeğâz Railway. I need both. I shall take both arms and gold but I shall fight him whom my affiliated Ḥwêṭât fight. If they arise against the Inklîz, I shall combat the Inklîz; if they rise against the Government, I shall massacre the government troops. I shall not separate myself from my fellow tribesmen."

Nawwâf asked me if it was true that the Inklîz fight only in the middle of the sea, where no rider upon camel or horse can overtake them. Both an-Nûri and Nawwâf believed that the Inklîz had occupied Egypt as late as August or September, 1914. Up to that time, they thought, it had belonged to the Turkish Government and to the Sultan. When I told them that the English had ruled Egypt since the year 1882, they believed me but shook their heads seriously; for, since the English had been the masters of Egypt so long, why was it that not until three months before had they forbidden the ʿAḳejl to transport to Egypt camels from territory belonging to the Sultan and the Government.

Often the Rwala asked me if it was true that the Inklîz had exiled all the Arabs and Moslems from Egypt, settling the land with foreigners and Christians. I wondered who it was that used this manner of inciting the Arabs against the foreigners and Christians. An-Nûri and Nawwâf declared that they would not march into Egypt for any cause whatever. It was too far, they asserted, and one must go through and across seas in which are fish that devour Bedouins as well as camels. They would not believe that Egypt could be reached from the depression of Sirḥân in ten nights, that it is not necessary to wade through the sea, that the "sea" (Suez canal) might be crossed by a bridge just as the Euphrates is crossed at al-Fellûǧe or al-Msajjeb. ʿAwde, who had visited his Egyptian relatives several times, marked in the sand with his camel stick the route from the watering place of Majḳûʿ to al-Ḳanṭara in Egypt, designating wells and naming tribes whose territories must be traversed; but an-Nûri invoked the intervention of Allâh against every request that he march beyond the confines of Arabia.

"Let the Government promise me whatever it will, I will not march beyond the Dead Sea. Why, death menaces whoever ventures there and everything there is dead. Why should I go there? I have no relatives there. From Ḥaleb (Aleppo) as far as ʿOmân camp the ʿAneze; here I am at home. In this territory I can march even a hundred days from north to south, but ten days west of Majḳûʿ I have not a relative and I will not go there. Why should I go to bring death to myself?"

ʿAwde laughed at an-Nûri, but Nawwâf agreed with him.

"Thou, ʿAwde, art at home in the ravines by the Dead and the Red Seas. Thy relatives sit there. They will help thee, but who there would help us?"

"Allâh."

"Allâh? Allâh does not want us to make raids in the west. Had he wished so, he would have settled some of our relatives there. But he hath left all the ʿAneze in Arabia."

"Against whom wouldst thou like best to march?" I asked an-Nûri.

"Against the Druses, Mûsa."

"Why? Because they are friends of the Inklîz and would help them if they invaded Syria or Palestine?"

"What do we care that the Druses are friends of the Inklîz? The Inklîz are strangers as much as the Government is. The Government protects the Druses and they rob us. They are our bitterest enemy. I may become reconciled with all the Bedouins, nay, even with settlers and Christians, but never with the Druses and the inhabitants of the volcanic region of the Ḥawrân, the Ahâli al-Ǧebel. Like sly hyenas they crawl out of their dens, creep in the night toward our camp, steal our mares and camels, drive off the flocks of goats and sheep under our protection, and take them into their lava lairs whither we cannot pursue them either on horse or on camel. Whatever they steal, they sell cheaply to the Druses in the range of aš-Šejẖ (Hermon), to the Čerkes (Circassians), and Turkish officials. When, in July and August, we camp west of the Ḥawrân, we frequently meet our mares and camels that have been stolen from us by the Ḥawrân vultures. We prove by trustworthy witnesses that the animals are ours, but the Government never concedes our right to them, insisting that we apprehend and bring the robbers before them. Go and look for a robber who has attacked thee in the blackness of the night! Go and seek him in the volcanic ravines whither even infantry will not venture! We rage, and the Circassians, Druses, and Turks snigger. If prudence deserts us and we punish the Druses or the Circassians with arms, in will rush an army of the Government to surround our camp and threaten to open fire from their field guns upon our wives and children unless we compensate the Druses and the Circassians for all their losses. Thou knowest, Mûsa, for thou didst negotiate with the Government four years ago in a like case. Oh, that the Government would permit us to watch the Circassians and the Druses! We would repay them all they have loaned us for years past. It would not be only I,

FIG. 107—The volcano, Tell ʿAmûd, from the east (see p. 457).

an-Nûri, who would march against them, but all the tribes from Ḥaleb to Tejma as well. Have I not spoken the truth, ʿAwde?"

"Thou hast, an-Nûri. We all shall march against the Druses and the Ahâli al-Ǧebel, even the Fedʿân, the ʿEbede, the Fwâʿre, and the Beni Ṣaẖr. Woe to them, woe to the Circassians and to the Turkish officials, who have protected them heretofore! We shall settle there with our herds. We shall destroy and graze off their fields and gardens, and shall shut them in their settlements until they perish of hunger. If the robbers from the volcanic region have nobody to whom to sell horses and camels, they will not go robbing. O Allâh, render us this gratification! Let us write to the Government that we want to watch the Druses closely that they may not ally themselves with foreigners."

"Let us write," mockingly consented an-Nûri and Nawwâf.

ʿAwde likewise acknowledged the necessity of peace among the tribes and promised to offer peace to ʿAbṭân and to recognize him as the head chief, provided the majority of the

Ḥwêṭât approved. Nawwâf declared that he himself could not write to such a herdsman of goats and sheep, but asked ʿAwde to add that both an-Nûri and Nawwâf would recognize a peace closed by him and would not take any action to oppose it. We summoned my servant Manṣûr, who wrote the missives to the chiefs Barǧas eben Hdejb, Ḥâčem eben Mhejd, Saʿûd eben Rašîd, ʿAbṭân eben Ǧâzi, Fâres eben Šaʿlân, and to the Government at Constantinople and at Damascus. An-Nûri, Nawwâf, and ʿAwde, who could not write, affixed their seals at the bottom of the messages by means of their seal rings daubed with ink. The notes to the Government were to be delivered by Zejdân eben Ṯamed to Ḥadîṯe, who was to forward them to Ḥabîb al-Ḥsejnâwi at Čâf. Thence they were to be taken by some salt merchant to Boṣra, where he was to hand them to a Turkish official. Whether the letters reached their destination, I do not know; but it matters little whether they did not, as they contained words which obscured the beliefs of their authors. It was politics (*sijâse*), as an-Nûri said.

Wednesday, December 30, 1914. The thermometer registered 9° C at seven o'clock in the morning. A moderate northwest wind was blowing and it rained almost all day. I wrote down my conversations of the day before. A little past ten o'clock the Prince came out and, with a camel stick, drew for me a map of the volcanic region south of the volcano of al-Heber and one of the neighboring settlements of Eṯra and Ḳarḳar, where his son Saʿûd had fallen.

OPINIONS OF THE RWALA ON WORLD POLITICS

In the afternoon I went to an-Nûri's tent to greet the three chiefs of the ʿAmârât, ʿÂjed eben Bakr, Râẓi eben Dejdem, and Tabʿân eben Ḥẓêri, who had come to settle various discords. The ʿAmârât had been camping in August and September between al-Fellûǧe and Bagdad and later at Kerbela and already knew of the occupation of al-Baṣra by the English. They were much more interested in the World War than the Rwala were and were eager to know the grouping of the various governments. They had considerable difficulty with the terms Fransa and Franǧ. Both the Rwala and the ʿAmârât had believed that all Europe was Fransa and that all the inhabitants of the continent were called Franǧ or Franž (Frank); now they were learning that Fransa was merely a part of

Europe and Franğ the name of the tribe camping in that part. Why, then, were all the Europeans called Franğ, even though they did not all belong to the tribe of the Franğ? This is how the Prince explained it:

"Franğ is the family still reigning over all Europe. As Eben Sa'ûd rules a large territory and various tribes, so the Franğ have held under their sway many tribes like the Almân (Germans), Namsa (Austrians), Ṭaljân (Italians), Inklîz (English), Rûsija (Russians), Mosḳûb (Muscovites), Serbja (Serbians), Rûm, and others. Very many years ago the Rûm (Greeks) threw off their yoke, and this is the reason why they are called Rûm and not Franğ. The Inklîz also have won a good deal of independence and are guided according to their own counsel and will; but by some they are still counted among the Franğ, while others hold that they are a free country. Now, the Almân and Namsa tribes have revolted against the Franğ, although the Serbja, Rûsija, Mosḳûb, and Inklîz still support them. The enmity is bitterest between the Inklîz and the Almân, about as it is between the Drûz (Druses) and the Rwala, or between the Akrâd (Kurds) and the 'Amârât or the Fed'ân. The Inklîz have many islands in the sea, upon which live many peoples whom they send against the Almân. The latter are the most proficient in the manufacture of arms; the best rifles, revolvers, and pistols come from them or from the Namsa. But of what avail are arms when men to use them are lacking? The Almân and the Namsa are very clever, but they have a small army. Hence the Government and the Sultan in Constantinople decided to send their soldiers against the Franğ and especially against the Inklîz. These three governments — those of the Almân, Namsa, and Atrâk (Turks) — have made an alliance (*helf*) not so much against the Franğ as against the Inklîz (*taḥâlafaw 'ala-l-inklîz*); for the Franğ have not taken anything belonging to the Sultan, but several months ago the Inklîz dispossessed him of Egypt and it is their intention to take al-Baṣra and the whole of Irak away from him also."

One of the company remarked that the Mosḳûb were very numerous too and that they wanted to drive the Sultan from Constantinople. Said an-Nûri:

"The Mosḳûb are very numerous, but the tribe Rûsija exceeds them greatly. Many kingdoms belong to the Rûsija and they are feared by even the Persians; yet they have not liberated all of their own blood. Even the tribe of my brother

Mûsa forms a part of the Rûsija as we do of the ʿAneze; yet his tribe must obey the Namsa. The Rûsija are very numerous, but they are not brave. I have heard that they have been routed from their own territory by the small tribe of Jâbân (Japanese). The most terrible of all the warring tribes are the Inklîz. They are very rich, yet they are covetous for new countries. Ye shall see that they will be victorious even at al-Baṣra, not through arms but through politics (*sijâse*). ʿAḳejl that have come from the territory of the Hend (India) have told me that nobody keeps as good order as the Inklîz. But what credit is that to them when they take away freedom? Who of ye wants to be a *mamlûk* (serf)? We can resist the Government, but can we resist the Inklîz when they come to offer gold for our freedom?"

The aged chief Râẓi said:

"Fear not, an-Nûri; our forefathers have been free and the Inklîz shall not snatch from us our inherited freedom either with weapons or gold!" And all present agreed with him.

I asked the chiefs of the ʿAmârât whether they would enter the holy war against the Inklîz.

"Our holy war is to protect our tents and herds. Should the Inklîz try to touch them, woe to them! As long as they fight the Government in the territory of the settlers, let the Government send its soldiers and its settlers against them. Up to now the Inklîz are neither our friends nor our enemies. What they will become to us, only Allâh knows."

"Thou hast spoken the truth, brother," said an-Nûri, "but we must obey the Government. May Allâh grant it victory!"

When he was accompanying me back to my tent, he said: "O Mûsa, how mindful I must be of politics that nobody may blacken me with the Government! The Government orders us to wage *ğihâd* (holy war) against the unbelievers, against the Inklîz. Of what have the unbelievers or the Inklîz robbed me? But the Government, of what has it already deprived us! They wanted to hang me arbitrarily. Dost thou know against whom I should like best to march? Dost thou know against whom I bear a hatred much greater than I do against all the Inklîz and unbelievers combined?"

Thursday, December 31, 1914. The temperature dropped at 7.00 A. M. to 3° C and the entire region was covered with a hard hoar frost. I finished my notes. Prince an-Nûri, to whom, as well as to Nawwâf, I had brought a fine army rifle (provided with a telescope sight) and a hundred cartridges, would have liked very much to see what other weapons I had and he went away considerably disgruntled when told that I should not unpack them.

In the afternoon ʿAwde abu Tâjeh, in company with an-Nûri and Nawwâf, came to bid me good-bye. We discussed the results of our mutual conferences. They all promised that they would not undertake any large raid against either the Arabs or the settlers without my knowledge; and they resolved to offer the protection of the desert to all the refugees from regions subject to the Government. So long as it remained impossible for them to buy the grain and clothing indispensable for maintaining life anywhere except in Syria and Irak, they were obliged to abide in peace with the Government, for they could not exist without grain and clothing. They might perhaps have supplied themselves with the necessities for several months through the use of sheer force, but in the end they would have had to submit to the Government. If they attacked the tilled region, the settlers would only draw the closer to the Turkish soldiers. An-Nûri and Nawwâf would not even hear of an auxiliary expedition to Egypt. ʿAwde abu Tâjeh was willing to march to Egypt only upon the summons of his affiliated Egyptian Ḥwêṭât and was ready to fight either against the Government or the English, according to the decision of his clansmen.

The English army at al-Baṣra was far beyond the scope of the Rwala of Prince an-Nûri. Nawwâf asked me whether the Inklîz camping at al-Kwejt and al-Baṣra were of a different clan from those who some time ago had occupied Egypt.

"Why, Mûsa, there are as many Inklîz clans as there are clans of the ʿAneze. With some of them we live at peace, others we fight. My relatives Eben Ṣabbâḥ and Eben Saʿûd live at peace with the Inklîz at al-Kwejt, while my relative Âl Ašḳar is at war with them. Thou knowest that Eben Ṣabbâḥ, the master of al-Kwejt, and Eben Saʿûd, the Prince of ar-Rijâẓ, belong to the ʿAneze the same as my father and I do. Âl Ašḳar, chief of the Muntefiž tribe, also descends from the ʿAneze, but he fights me and he fights the Inklîz. I am related to Eben Ṣabbâḥ and Eben Saʿûd and I will not undertake anything against their friends the Inklîz; but, if the Inklîz should seek to deprive me of al-Ǧowf or Eben Saʿûd of ar-Rijâẓ, we should march against them together. If they are now occupying the territory of the Government, let the Government defend itself. It did not aid me either against Eben Rašîd or Âl Aškar; on the contrary it supported them both against me. Am I not acting wisely in guiding myself by its example?"

PLANS FOR JOURNEY TO EBEN RAŠÎD

Both an-Nûri and Nawwâf, and ʿAwde as well, feared for my life in the territory of Eben Rašîd and pleaded with me not to venture there.

"Look, Mûsa," said Nawwâf, "the minister Saʿûd is a traitor and a traitor knoweth neither Allâh nor honor. He knoweth that thou art my friend, that thou hast aided me in the conquest of al-Ğowf. He will be incited to action against thee by the very men I expelled from al-Ğowf. Who will protect thee? May Allâh preserve thy life, but I fear I shall behold thee no more. He will not kill thee in the open, but his slaves will attack thee in the night or will poison thee."

"Do not fear, brother! Allâh will help me and I shall help myself. Not all the Šammar are traitors like Saʿûd. I shall not go to him until I find among the Šammar a powerful protector. I know many a chief of the tribes of the Sinğâra and ʿAbde. The Sinğâra detest Saʿûd, the descendant of a slave, and they are more powerful than he."

"But how wilt thou reach the Sinğâra?"

At this juncture ʿAwde said: "My brother Muḥammad found at ʿAmûd a Šammari who had been starved and was near death. He took him into his tent, dripped butter into his throat, and revived him. As I was departing I overheard that his name was Nâzel and that he was descended from the family of Eben Ṯnejjân. I will go back today and send him over to thee. He is sick and thou, Mûsa, hast the medicines; thou mayst cure him." Nawwâf and an-Nûri both assured me that the family of Eben Ṯnejjân belongs among the foremost Šammar families. Thus I could obtain in Nâzel the best escort, provided, of course, that ʿAwde had told the truth. I begged him to send the Šammari to me immediately, which he promised and departed.

Friday, January 1, 1915. An-Nûri brought me an elderly man of the name of Unejs eben Bnejje, who for years had been a neighbor of Eben Rmâl, a powerful chief of the Šammar, to whom he wished to return with several camels. He wanted to join me. Unejs, believing that Eben Rmâl was camping somewhere in the vicinity of Ǧubba, tried to persuade me to go to Eben Rašîd by the al-Ḫall route leading from al-Ǧowf through the watering places of aš-Šižîž and Ǧubba to the town of Ḥâjel. Nawwâf likewise was in favor of this route; but it did not appeal to me, for it was too well known. I should have preferred to go through either the eastern or the western part of the Nefûd. I had intended to question Unejs about the vicinity of Ǧubba, but I found that he was wholly unqualified for giving topographical descriptions.

Nawwâf complained that his people were dissatisfied because the raid could not materialize. When an-Nûri asked his slaves which of them wanted to go with me to Eben Rašîd, ʿAbdallâh volunteered. He was the one who had accompanied me on my journey from Ḍmejr to ar-Reṣâfa in 1908, and, knowing him to be a reliable man though lacking in foresight and energy, I accepted him.

Saturday, January 2, 1915. We migrated, departing at 10.10 A. M. in an east-northeasterly direction. Nawwâf soon overtook me and, from afar, greeted me thus:

"Mayst thou be strong, Mûsa! (*ḳaww jâ mûsa!*)"

To which I replied: "Welcome! May strong himself be the man who wishes me strength!"

I talked with him about the proposed mediation with Eben Rašîd. We agreed that Nawwâf would march with his clans to the boundary of the Nefûd, where he would await word from me. Should the minister Saʿûd refuse reconciliation, I was to turn to the Sinǧâra and try to persuade them to join Nawwâf; whereupon he was to come with his own fighters and an-Nûri's, join with the Sinǧâra, and strike at Saʿûd from the north, while Eben Saʿûd was to press him from the south. I well knew the danger the plan involved. I was aware that Enver Pasha and the Turkish Government trusted Saʿûd, the minister of Eben Rašîd, as their most loyal friend, and that they would accuse me of agitation in the interests of the English. I was also familiar with the fact that Saʿûd possessed more effective arms than ours and that we should be unable to drive him out of Ḥâjel if he once fortified it. I regretted my contribution toward a new civil war among the Šammar, who had spilt so much of their own blood during the last fourteen years, but I reasoned that, should we fail in curtailing Saʿûd and his party, they would cause more harm than we ever could.

From 10.50 until 11.20 we warmed ourselves at the fire. Later Nawwâf returned to his warriors, while I rode with an-Nûri at the head of about two hundred camel riders. An-Nûri implored me not to go to Eben Rašîd.

"Go, Mûsa, to Eben Saʿûd. He is my brother and friend, a man honorable and loyal, but Eben Rašîd is a weakling and his minister is a traitor."

"I shall go to Eben Saʿûd also, but it will be from the territory of Eben Rašîd. I know that Saʿûd, the son of ʿAbdalʿazîz eben Rašîd, the prince of the Šammar, is a weakling; likewise I know that his minister Saʿûd is a traitor. I am forewarned; he shall not take me by surprise. Allâh willeth me to go, therefore I shall go. How many times hast thou, brother, cautioned me not to go hither and thither where Allâh had willed that I go! But I went and I returned — and I am sure I shall return from Eben Rašîd also. Should I not come back, however, only think of the many before me who have camped in this region and have gone, never to return."

At 12.25 P. M. the Prince pointed out to me the spot on which to pitch my tent; then he jumped off his camel and the tribe began to build a new camp. In the evening we ascertained the time and the latitude.

Sunday, January 3, 1915. (Temperature at 7.00 A. M.: −2° C.) At eight o'clock, as I was sitting writing on the ground in my tent, in came Nawwâf, bringing along a short, pale, lean man of about thirty years, who wore a ragged shirt and an old mantle. Shivering with cold, he fell to the ground in front of me and implored my protection. He was the Šammari, Nâzel eben Dûḫi eben Ṯnejjân, of whom ʿAwde abu Tâjeh had told me. Nawwâf introduced him thus:

"Behold, Mûsa, this is Nâzel eben Ṯnejjân, the most renowned commander of the Šammar raiding forces."

I smiled. Could it be possible that this little man was a celebrated leader? However, there was a peculiar twinkle in Nâzel's eyes which immediately changed my estimation of him. In this slender body I discerned a powerful spirit. Nawwâf rejoined:

"Brother, I know Nâzel and vouch for him. Talk with him and trust in whatever he may promise. I must say farewell to thee. I depart now and thou wilt depart in four days.

Come back to me. Thou knowest that thou hast a brother in al-Ǧowf."

We embraced and Nawwâf departed. Thirty riders were waiting in front of my tent to accompany him on his round of tax-collecting among all the tribes and clans subject to him and his father. He needed money and supplies for his standing army and when raids were scarce he sought the aid of his tribes. He intended to return to al-Ǧowf in about twenty days and await my advices. Meantime he gave me a letter to his regent in al-Ǧowf, the negro ʿÂmer, directing him to welcome me in holiday dress and to obey me as he would obey Nawwâf himself. Indeed, he even went so far as to inform him that during my sojourn in al-Ǧowf he had transferred all power from him, ʿÂmer, to me; and he proclaimed to the inhabitants of al-Ǧowf that I went to arbitrate a peace with Eben Rašîd.

After Nawwâf's departure I had Nâzel lie down in the large tent to warm up and sent my servant Nâṣer to the peddler (*kubejsi*) to purchase whatever the man needed.

Meanwhile I received a visit from Muḥammad abu Tâjeh, brother of ʿAwde, who told me of Nâzel's sufferings. It seemed that Nâzel eben Ṯnejjân was entrusted with the delivery to Nawwâf of important letters from his cousin Fahad and other Sinǧâra chiefs, who wished to ally themselves with Nawwâf. Two men, a Freǧi and a Šarâri, accompanied him from his tent. Nâzel and the Freǧi rode camels, while the Šarâri walked. At the northern base of aṭ-Ṭawîl they learned from herdsmen that Nawwâf had gone to al-Misma' at the depression of Sirḥân; so they turned that way. During the night Nâzel's companions disappeared with his camel, his rifle, and all the supplies; and yet Nâzel had protected them in the territory of the Šammar and they had promised to protect him in the territory of the Rwala, to which the Freǧe clan belongs and with whom the Šarârât were camping. Thus they betrayed him — may Allâh betray them likewise! For three days and two nights the deserted and betrayed Nâzel trudged toward the northeast. He obtained drink from various puddles but found nothing to eat, as fresh grasses had not yet sprung up. Finally he collapsed from exhaustion. Muḥammad, who was out hunting with a *selḳi* hound and a falcon, found him, took him into his tent, and revived him. For five days Nâzel was not able to stand. An-Nûri, who investigated the occurrence, thought that the Freği in the case might be identical with Ḫalîfa eben Ṛaṯjân. He directed the relatives of the man to compensate Nâzel for the injury, but they objected that it had not been proved that one of their blood had committed so contemptible a deed. They agreed, however, to interrogate Ḫalîfa themselves and compel him to make restitution should he be convicted. Nawwâf promised to look for the Šarâri, upon whom the Freğe were heaping the guilt. Of the three chiefs of the ʿAmârât tribe dwelling as guests in an-Nûri's tent, Nâzel was recognized by ʿÂjed and Tabʿân, who sympathized with him. An-Nûri offered him a good camel and a saddle.

Toward evening Nâzel came to me and begged me to let him stay in my tent, as he feared the revenge of the Duṛmân clan, six of whom he had killed in a fight on the Pilgrim Road from al-Kûfa. An-Nûri announced from his tent that Nâzel was my guest and that whoever harmed him would fare badly. The Duṛmân, who had learned of his presence, sneaked about my tent like hungry wolves, but none of them offended Nâzel by word or deed.

Monday, January 4, 1915. I talked with Nâzel about the route we were to follow. Many persons who had come with Nawwâf wanted to accompany us to al-Ğowf, and an-Nûri advised that from al-Ğowf I go over the al-Ḫall route. Nâzel pointed out, however, that she would not find pasture there. He said that, as it had not rained between aš-Šiżîż and Ğubba for three years, the region was a waste (*maḥal*) and south of Ğubba everything had been grazed off by the herds of the ʿAbde tribe. Furthermore, neither the Prince nor his minister was in Ḥâjel, but both were camping south of the valley of ar-Rmaʾ, somewhere near Ḏbejb, while Eben Saʿûd was encamped in al-Aṣjâḥ. Accordingly, if I wanted to reach the Prince in person, he said, it would be better to go along the edge of the Nefûd to the fortress of al-Ḥajjânijje, where we might learn of Eben Rašîd's camp. An-Nûri objected, saying that we were sure to encounter raiding bands on the borders of the Nefûd. At this juncture Nâzel smiled lightly and said:

"May Allâh prolong thy life! It is said that I am the best chief of raiding bands, hence I surely know how to protect myself from them and elude them."

I immediately decided to travel along the eastern borders, where vast scientific work was beckoning me. We were to fulfill an-Nûri's wish that we stop in al-Ǧowf to ascertain from ʿÂmer whether it had rained in the eastern part of the Nefûd, and then we were to take the route that Allâh had destined for us.

FIG. 108—Head of valley of al-Bdene (see p. 458).

Wishing to test the extent of Nâzel's ability in determining the directions of individual localities, I questioned him about regions with which I was familiar. I asked him to designate with two pebbles on the ground inside my tent the position of the pole star and of the south and tested his representations with the compass. The horizon was overcast by a thick fog; the sun was entirely obscured. Nâzel glanced at the upper part of the tent, took the pebbles in his right hand, stretched out his hand, and scratched a long, straight line in the sand. Then he placed the larger pebble at one end of the line and the smaller pebble at the other and, pointing to the larger, said:

"This, O Chief, is the polar side (*al-ǧedi*) and this is south (*ǧenûb*)."

I glanced at the point of the compass needle and saw that he had deviated but five degrees. I was much pleased with his accuracy, for I knew it would facilitate my work.

He then took a handful of pebbles, spread them before him, and, using them as a medium, designated the location of various watering places and other cardinal points in the regions known to me. He fashioned the mountains from sand and cut

FIG. 109—From our camp south of al-Bdene, looking south (see p. 460).

the valleys between them. Watching him, I became convinced that he was familiar with the country and that I should get along well with him after we had become acquainted.

Tuesday, January 5, 1915. The herdsman, ʿAwad, notified me that his foot ached and that he was unable to take care of my camels; I suspected, however, that this was a subterfuge prompted by his dread of the journey to Eben Rašîd. Our camels were driven to pasture by Šwardi eben Farwân. An-Nûri took a trip to a neighboring camp of the Kwâčbe tribe where some discord had arisen.

I worked all day with Nâzel, who drew for me the Pilgrim Road from Ḥâjel to al-Kûfa, the wells and valleys between al-Kûfa, Abu Ṛâr, and al-Baṣra, and the vicinity of the valley of al-Ḥeseb. I endeavored to test his statements by a medley of questions to find out whether they were contradictory, but I was unable to trip him up. I became convinced, therefore, that he was not only a renowned military commander but a formidable leader of robbing bands as well. One so familiar with the vast desert may easily take and keep the booty.

But my lengthy conversations with Nâzel were exasperating to my younger friends among the Rwala, the sons of Nawwâf. The eldest of them, Sulṭân, who was about eleven years old and a son of Mišẖaṣ, had learned how to write in al-Ǧowf and boasted that he had sent his first letter to his mother, who was now wedded to Fendi eben Melḥem. He questioned me eagerly about her, wanting to know how she looked and when she would come to him. Fawwâz, the son of Mišâʿel, did not know how to write, but he said he could hold his seat upon a galloping, unsaddled mare, whereas Sulṭân would fall off. The youngest of them, the nine-year-old Nawwâš, son of Shejla, usually kept quiet but would examine closely everything he saw in my tent. Several times the slaves had also brought to me Nawwâf's younger sons. Mišâʿel had borne him two boys, Fâjez and Anwar, and Fhêde had borne him ʿÂfeṭ. Mišâʿel had been suffering with cataracts on both eyes in 1909 and had now lost her sight entirely. Of the chiefs, I was visited several times by H̱âled and Ṭrâd, the sons of the late Prince Saṭṭâm, by my former helper Mežḥem, the son of an-Nûri's murdered brother Mḥammad, and by an-Nûri's son al-H̱afâǧi. Besides these, my old acquaintance ʿAwde al-Kwêčbi had come from a distant camp to greet me. None of these visits were of long duration, however, for I was loath to waste time.

Wednesday, January 6, 1915. The Prince entered just as we were at breakfast. He showed surprise at the large quantity of milk we had, asserting that he had not had any milk for over a week, that of all his camels only two had been yielding, and that now even these had ceased to give any.

"Nay, brother, thy camels have not ceased giving milk."

"How dost thou know?"

"This milk is their milk."

"The milk of my camels? And, pray, who fetches it for thee?"

"Thy herdsman Fhejd. I promised him a quarter of a *meǧîdijje* daily if he would bring me milk for breakfast, which he does."

"O that rascal!" exclaimed the Prince. "He carries it to thee for a quarter of a *meǧîdijje* and then he tells me he has not milked any."

"Do not be angry, brother. Tomorrow I depart and thy camels will give milk for thee only."

"May the milk of my camels give thee health, Mûsa!"

The breeding period for camels is from December 11 to January 21 and during this period their milk dries up. Camels that have cast young need their milk for them and yield very little until there is an abundance of fresh annuals and perennials.

We made preparations for departure and apportioned the loads. A strong camel is capable of carrying as much as one and a half *ḳunṭâr* (almost 300 kg.) but a camel thus loaded cannot go more than three kilometers an hour. Our camels were to make on the average four and a half kilometers per hour, therefore we could not load them heavier than sixty-five to seventy-five *roṭols* (about 150 kg.). Many of them were very emaciated and lank, but Nâzel gladdened me with his prediction that they would soon fatten in the territory of the Šammar, where they would find profuse pasture. We bought one additional camel for fourteen Turkish pounds ($ 63) because we did not want to burden the other camels with too much luggage. We did not intend to take along a herdsman, as Nâzel had promised to procure me a Šammari.

FROM EAST OF AL-HAĞM TO NEAR BWEJB AL-ṚAZWÂN

Thursday, January 7, 1915. Loading all the tents and supplies upon the camels, we left an-Nûri's camp. When I went to the Prince's tent to bid him farewell, he commended me to the protection of Allâh. Mežḥem and al-Ḫafâği accompanied me part of the way and Nâzel rode alongside me.

We set out at 7.35 A. M. in a southerly direction. An-Nûri had warned me of the proximity of the Šammar, who had attacked the camp of the Beni Ṣaḫr only two days before at the Ḫabra as-Shami but had been repulsed by Nawwâf, who went with assistance. From 8.50 until 9.10 the camels grazed. One by one we were joined by twelve men who were returning to Skâka and al-Ğowf. The sky had darkened and a cold southeasterly wind was blowing. After ten o'clock we had in sight on the southwest the undulating highland of Šarâwa and on the right the wide and shallow depression of Arḳaṭ. At 12.10 P. M. we came upon a verdant pasture, where we remained until 12.45. About one o'clock we reached the watershed between al-Wudijân and al-Ḥamâd. The view here was boundless but monotonous. There was no natural prominence visible; nothing but undulating heights and wide depressions unrolled before our eyes. Toward the east and southeast rose the heights of az-Zhejrijje, and beyond them lay the head of the valley of al-Mara᾿ (or al-Mra᾿), which conducts rain water to the Euphrates. In the west the extensive height of Šarâwa stretched from the north southward, while in the south were the low domes of an-Nedûf. At 1.40 we rode between the Brejčât al-Mra᾿, which are partly natural and partly artificial reservoirs. Southeast of us, in a wide depression, was a camp of the Kwâčbe, toward which we headed, as our escorts feared rain and were averse to passing the night in the open.

At 2.18, south of the Kwâčbe, we pitched our large tent so as to protect our luggage from rain. Mafrûd eben Wḥejf, the chief of the camp, called on me and invited me to visit him. I thanked him and stayed at home, where Nâzel told me many things about the tribes and clans of the Šammar. Late that night Mafrûd came again, to beseech that I would persuade an-Nûri to reduce his taxes, which he had not paid for five years. He and his clan had deserted an-Nûri five years before to join the ʿAmârât; but after the outbreak of the World War he returned to an-Nûri because he thought he would be safer in the inner desert under his protection than with the foreign ʿAmârât on the banks of the Euphrates. An-Nûri welcomed him heartily, but told him he must pay all the assessments levied during the last five years. Against this decision Mafrûd protested that he had made payments to the head chief of the ʿAmârât; but an-Nûri disregarded his plea.

Friday, January 8, 1915. It rained until nearly five o'clock. We set out at 6.24 A.M. toward the south. In the depressions hung a thick fog, out of which the black tents of the Kwâčbe protruded like great boulders of lava. At 6.40 we had an-Nedûf to the south-southeast. Nâzel told me that fifty days before there had been a heavy rain north and east of Ḳna᾿ in the Nefûd and that consequently there was plenty of water everywhere. He said the Šammar were camping contentedly among perennials that offered abundant pasture for camels (*mukajjefîn biwasṭ haš-šağar*). In the region in which we were traveling rain had also fallen about two months before (*biṣ-ṣferi*) and hence the camels found good pasturage.

Our way led through the midst of innumerable herds of grazing camels, which came toward us from all directions and, forming into two long lines, stood eyeing us curiously, swaying their long necks and, with dropped lower lips, growling quietly.

FIG. 110—At-Tâjât volcanoes from the east (see p. 463).

The weaned foals would lick our camels, romp about them, and run after them. Their mothers had ceased to give them any attention; for the breeding period had begun, when the parent no longer cares about the young she has been nursing for twelve months. Here and there could be seen a female camel with a foal but a few days old. The movements of the baby camels were clumsy, and when one of them stumbled its mother would lick it and lament over it pitifully. Occasionally a male would come charging toward us from a distance, the thick foam dripping from his nostrils, and herdsmen would have to chase him away. Whenever we viewed them from an elevation, the herds looked to us as if they were swimming in a sea, an illusion caused by the fog which covered the depressions to a height of a meter and a half and enveloped the camels up to their humps and heads. Since the movements of their feet were not visible, the fog as it shifted appeared to carry the whole herd along with it and whenever it lifted

FIG. 111—Ḫabra al-Mezâreʿ from the north (see p. 467).

somewhat the herd would vanish as if it had fallen into the sea, only to reappear a while later much farther off.

Turning at 7.38 somewhat more toward the south-southeast, we arrived at 7.43 at a small rain pool, filled our bags with water, and went on at 8.10. In the dark clouds to the westward were serpent-like flashes of lightning followed by the roll of thunder. At ten o'clock a mild south-southwest wind arose. Our camels walked with long strides toward the south. It seemed as if the individual heights were approaching us instead of our approaching them. Said Nâzel: "O Chief, all that lieth before the camel rider is near; and all that lieth behind him is far."

From 11.42 until 12.17 P.M. we ate our dinner in the *šeʿîb* of al-Mraʾ. At one o'clock there appeared to the southwest the dark volcano of ʿAmûd, while to the south-southeast glimmered the many rain pools of al-Arnabijjât (Fig. 106, p. 436). At 2.32 we entered a region covered with basalt and lava gravel. At 3.10 through the binoculars I discerned to the southeast two camel riders standing upon a height scanning the region. Not being certain that they were not scouts of a robbing band, we sent our companions with the camels through a depression while Nâzel and I kept watch on the riders. In a few minutes they disappeared toward the southwest. We continued our journey until 4.43, when we made up for the night in a small hollow in which we had found a growth of perennials. We neither built a fire nor pitched the tent.

Saturday, January 9, 1915. At 1.10 A.M. a squall came up from the west and snatched away everything that had not been fastened down. Soon large drops of rain began to fall, flashes of lightning crossed and recrossed, and in the west thunder rumbled. Fearing our supplies would be drenched, we began to pitch the tent, but it took a long time to tighten the ropes sufficiently for the tent to withstand the impact of the wind. There was no thought of sleep, for every little while a peg would be pulled out and the tent poles would collapse, making it necessary for us to prop the tent and secure it anew. At 2.20 both wind and rain ceased and here and there in the sky stars appeared. We started on at 6.12.

At 7.41 a mild wind sprang up from the south-southwest. Far to the southeast we saw dark tents and ahead of us about sixty gazelles and numerous brown vultures. At 8.40 the volcano of ʿAmûd (Fig. 107, p. 440) was almost due west of us, while about six kilometers to the northeast glimmered the Ḫabra Ašbah. To the southwest the black Tell al-Ğdejr glowered upon the horizon, beyond which were visible the Ḫabâri Masḥaʾ and before them three yellowish causeways girdling the artificial rain pools Maḥâfîr al-Ğdejr. We rode upon low, smooth swells called *ğelîbe,* in the region of al-Arnabijjât. At 9.10 Nâzel fainted and would have fallen off his camel if I had not caught him. We laid him on the ground and rubbed him until he regained consciousness, but he was very weak. I had tea brewed for him and tried to find out the cause of his collapse. He told me that he was subject to cramps in the stomach and swooned easily. What should I do if he were taken sick or if he died? I wondered. When he first came to me he was very feeble, but he had regained much of his strength since then. I gave him medicine and made up my mind to shorten the day's march that he might have a good sleep that night.

In the south numerous tents began to appear and at 9.52 we started toward them. On the way two men and a woman of the despised al-Ḥawâzem tribe joined us. The Ḥawâzem camp over almost the whole of Arabia with different Bedouin tribes; they are met even in an-Nuḳra south of Damascus and in al-Ğezîre between the Euphrates and the Tigris. These Ḥawâzem were of the clan camping with Eben Ḥrejmîs of the Fedʿân tribe and were visiting kinsmen who were camping with the Arabs of Abu Tâjeh. At 10.40 the artificial pools Maḥâfîr al-Ğdejr lay west of us, with the volcanic region reaching to them and bounding the yellow plain of al-Ḥamâd

FIG. 112—The Mâred tower, al-Ğowf, from the south (see p. 467).

like a high, black wall. At 10.51 we crossed the head of the valley of al-Bdene (Fig. 108, p. 450) which merges with Wâdi ʿArʿar. We traveled over a plain coated with a yellow, clayish soil and dotted with numerous large and small rain pools. From 11.20 to 11.32 we drew water and at 12.32 P.M. encamped upon a low height amid pools in which many camels of the migrating Ḥwêṭât were wading. I laid Nâzel in my tent where he soon fell asleep and woke up toward evening refreshed.

That evening ʿAwde abu Tâjeh came to visit me, but he did not stay long, for the herdsmen discovered in the southeast an enemy band, supposedly of the Šammar, who had to be scared away.

Sunday, January 10, 1915. Our neighbor brought me a little milk in a wooden trough. After drinking some myself I handed the vessel to Nâzel, who exclaimed: "*ʿIšt*, long life to thee!" When I wished the same to him, he said: "That ye say 'long life to thee' is dearer to me than if ye should say 'mayest thou fall' (*ḳawlekom ʿišt ašwaʾ min ḳawlekom taḥt*)." At six o'clock we set out. At 8.25 A. M. a cool wind rose from the west. From 9.05 to 9.18 we drew water and from 9.35 to ten o'clock we rested. From riders returning out of the southeast we learned that the enemy band which had been seen the day before by the herdsmen consisted of fifteen Šammar who had escaped toward the southeast. At 10.22 several volcanoes appeared deep below us to the west and southwest, all of them table-shaped with sharply defined outlines. At 10.30 the wind dropped altogether; after eleven o'clock the sun shone, the temperature gradually rose, and at 11.42 when we stopped for dinner in the plain of al-Bijâẓ the thermometer registered 17.5° C. We set out again at 12.18 P. M.

The young man from al-Ğowf who used to prepare coffee for Prince an-Nûri and now was returning home in our company, walked the first day. The second day Nâzel took pity on him and let him ride on his camel, the cook settling himself comfortably behind the saddle. The third day he seated himself nonchalantly in the saddle and told Nâzel either to walk or to climb upon one of my camels. After Nâzel was taken sick, we laid him upon a camel between two knapsacks. When he recovered, however, he wanted to ride his own camel again, but the cook informed him insolently that when he was with the Prince he used to ride this camel and that he should ride it to al-Ğowf. His relatives, who detested the Šammar tribe, joined him in treating Nâzel's camel as if it were theirs. I did not want to mix myself up in the controversy but when the negro ʿAbdallâh began to spread the untruth that the camel belonged to the cook and not to Nâzel, I rode into the midst of the arguing men, made the cook get off the saddle, and warned him and his companions that if they offended Nâzel again by word or glance I would not give them a gulp of water or a mouthful of food and would throw all their baggage off my camels. I made it clear to ʿAbdallâh that I was his "uncle" during his stay with me and he my slave; that if he kept this in mind, well and good; but if he

FIG. 113—The southern part of Dûmat al-Ǧandalijje.

forgot the fact I would impress it upon him painfully. From that moment ʿAbdallâh kept near us and followed me like a faithful puppy. Nâzel thanked me for having saved his honor with the settlers of al-Ǧowf.

On the way we frightened out several foxes. Nâzel said that Allâh must like foxes since the fox is the only creature to which he sends prey no matter whether it is awake or asleep or buried in the ground. Once upon a time the foxes wanted to find out whether Allâh would send them something to eat if they buried themselves. So they selected one of their number for the trial and dug a small grave in the yellow clay; one of them lay down in it and the others covered him up. Only the whiskers of the buried fox protruded above the ground. Then the other foxes ran away and waited at a distance to see what would happen. And behold! A hare came out in search of food. He saw the protruding whiskers of the buried fox and, thinking they were dry stalks of grass, came nearer and nearer and began to sniff at the whiskers and pull them. At that the buried fox stirred and bit the poor hare to death.

At 3.44 we stopped (Fig. 109, p. 451) and let the camels graze while we prepared our supper. From 5.30 until 8.05 we rode over a clayey plain and then lay down beside our camels. The night was very damp.

Monday, January 11, 1915. We were on the march at six o'clock. The air was very still. At first we walked over a rolling plain covered with fine gravel and in places with sand

FIG. 114—The northern part of Dûmat al-Ǧandalijje.

dunes. Unejs eben Bnejje wanted to know if I was going with him to Ǧubba to Eben Rmâl and invited me into his tent. When I asked him why he camped with strangers, he replied:

"It is my fate, Mûsa. My forefathers once owned yonder the entire northern and eastern boundary of the Nefûd. Dost thou know aš-Šižîž? Well, ask thou to whom belong the wells of az-Zhejri and ar-Rarîfi and ask to whom belong the different watering places east of the Nefûd and thou wilt be told that they belong to Eben Bnejje. In bygone days my forefathers were more powerful than either an-Nûri or Nawwâf is today, but Allâh has taken away from us our power and our property and has given them to others. I, Unejs, had as neighbor a Sulejmâni, of the tribe of the Weld Slejmân. He had been camping with me for years. Seven years ago our tents were at as-Sfer in an-Nuḳra below Damascus. What was to come about between us happened—I killed my neighbor. Then with my relatives I fled from the avenger to the inner desert (*ila-š-šerḳ*) to find refuge with Eben Rmâl in the center of the Nefûd. On the way we were attacked by the Ẓefîr and robbed of all our camels, so that we came to Eben Rmâl without tents, without herds, without provisions. He gave us shelter and food. I should have liked to return

FIG. 115—A yard in the gardens, al-Ğowf (Dûmat al-Ğandalijje).

to my own country, but the avenger demanded as recompense for the spilled blood fifty camels, a mare, and equipment. Whence was I to get them? But Allâh moved the hearts of an-Nûri and my co-tribesmen and they promised aid to me. I returned to an-Nûri two months ago. He gave me twenty-five camels; from other Rwala I have solicited twenty-five more, a mare, and equipment. I have satisfied *zajjantah* (the avenger). Now I ride with a few camels to fetch my relatives (*ahli*)."

From 6.55 to 7.15 the camels grazed. To the northwest the volcanic region loomed over the horizon, appearing from afar like a lofty, dark blue wall, while in front of it, nearer us, were the single black groups of the aṯ-Ṯâjât volcanoes (Fig. 110, p. 455). At 8.10 the heights and the Ḥabâri ʿAğrûmijjât could be seen in the east. After 9.18 we had a cool south wind. At 10.30 we stopped to dine, continuing on our way at 11.12. By 11.55 the south wind had become very blustering.

We were going through the region of al-Bijâẓ, which is favored by Šammar when they travel to Syria. Watering their camels at Želîb Ṣwêr, they circle al-Ğowf to the north, drink at an-Nabk abu Ḳaṣr and then at al-Azraḳ, and finally may rob the settlers at Boṣra and on the western edges of the Ḥawrân. We noted tracks of two raiding bands. Nâzel prayed: "O Allâh, cast a veil upon them and cast it upon us too! (*allâh jester ʿalejhom wa ʿalejna!*)"

The volcanoes of aṯ-Ṯâjât were enveloped in thin vapor which made them seem immensely huge and mobile. Said Nâzel: "A mirage (*sarâb*) beguileth us." At 1.25 P. M. the scenery of the desert changed. Far to the south in what appeared once to have been a high escarpment there gaped innumerable rifts, caves, clefts, and gorges, dividing the escarpment into larger and smaller pillars, cones, pyramids, boulders, and domes. In front of the escarpment two domes seemed to stand, with a mound of black stone upon each of them; the space between them looked like a gate. Nâzel called this Bwejb al-Ḳazwân (Little Gate of Raiders) and declared that he had passed through it at least a hundred times at the head of troops. Northwest of the gate extends the valley of as-Sîž, coming from the volcanoes of aṯ-Ṯâjât and terminating in the basin of Nejsûba. West of the gate and south of the valley the rugged wall is called ar-Rijetên.

BWEJB AL-ṚAZWÂN TO AL-ǦOWF

From 3.05 until 5.35 our camels grazed and we ate supper near Bwejb al-Ṛazwân. Ascending a rock dome with a fairly large *riǧm* (pile of stones) upon it, I lay down flat on my stomach and through my binoculars scanned the landscape for smoke or raiders. After supper we loaded the camels and rode until seven o'clock, when we made ready for the night near two solitary pillars called ar-Rijetên, a name which has also been given to the whole vicinity. Nobody was permitted to talk or to smoke on the way for fear the sound, the odor of smoke, or the glow of a burning pipe or cigarette might draw attention to us. We hid the camels and the baggage between boulders so effectually that we could not be seen from a distance of ten meters and we all prayed that Allâh would envelop us in his veil.

Tuesday, January 12, 1915. We started at 5.40 A. M. toward the south. Nâzel said that *semḥ* grew in abundance on the right bank of the valley of as-Sîž. There are two kinds of *semḥ*: the taller variety, of a reddish tint, is called *al-ḥorr* or *ḥamr wâžef*; the shorter, with seeds that are dark but much more palatable, is called *daʿâʿ*. The plant shoots out as late as March but only after the soil has been thoroughly soaked by the *aṯ-ṯrajjâwi* (Pleiades, November) rain.[106]

From seven until 7.35 the camels grazed and we ate breakfast. During the meal ʿAbdallâh told us how ʿAbdallâh eben Menfes, wanting to entertain an-Nûri, had said to him:

"I seek to entertain thee as my guest. What shall I slaughter for thee? A sheep? Thou deservest something more valuable. A camel? It is not worthy of thy greatness. What then? Behold, I have a son. I will kill him for thee and yet even this will not equal thy highness."

At 9.30 we arrived on the fringe of the basin al-Ǧûba. To the right and behind us we saw a boundless plain with scattered boulders, large and small, gnawed by erosion; while ahead of us rose thousands of higher or lower solitary tabular hills bathed in a rosy, flickering light, the darker spots a glowing violet. From all the angles upon which the sunbeams

[106] I brought home a specimen of *semḥ*, which Professor Velenovský classifies as *Mesembryanthemum Forskahlei*, Hochst. It is identical with *faṯṯ*.

Al-Muḳaddasi, *Aḥsan* (De Goeje), p. 252, writes that in the Arabian desert grows a plant known as *al-faṯṯ*, which resembles *ḫardal* (mustard seed). It casts its own seeds. After it has ripened, it is taken to pools of rain water and soaked, an operation which makes the seeds fall out. The seeds are then ground and made into a bread that is the chief sustenance of the natives.

broke sparks seemed to spurt, so that the whole vicinity seethed with the hot redness of molten iron. I could have gazed at it a long time, but the camels would not wait. The road was very steep, running through a series of defiles. Many a camel

FIG. 116—A draw well, al-Ğowf.

lost its load and upon many another the load had come sliding down sidewise. We ran leaping to help the beasts and to calm the panic-stricken. At 10.25 we reached the lowland of al-ʿAžraba, which slopes southward, and immediately began to take the loads off the camels in order to strap them on more securely. Nowhere was there a single green bush or blade of grass except the dry *ḳorẓi,* which grows there in profusion and which at the time had young sprouts. *Ḳejṣûm* and *šîḥ* were not yet awakened to new life.

FIG. 117—A draw well, al-Ğowf.

All the solitary tabular hills consist of horizontal strata of unequal degrees of hardness. The harder ones resist wind, sand, rain, and frost, and so outwear the softer layers. The topmost stratum is, as a rule, always harder than those below, which crumble away, while the upper one rests solidly; hence it is impossible to scale such hills. Scattered over the plain are thousands of boulders of all sizes — the fragments of the harder layers which have collapsed as their supports have given way.

At 11.25 we started on over the plain among solitary tabular hills (*ḳûr*) and fallen boulders. At noon we were proceeding across the wide, dry, rain pool Ḫabra al-Mezâreʿ (Fig. 111, p. 456), from which rise several rocky, table-shaped hills. Their sides have many crevices that hold rain water. Such crevices are called *žalta* (pl. *žlât*). At about one o'clock we entered the gorge of Bâb al-Faw, which is fifteen meters wide and more than two hundred meters deep.

At 1.28 P. M. we sighted al-Ǧowf, or Dûmat al-Ǧandalijje, as this settlement is rightly called. Far off beyond the arid, gray plain, almost on the southern border of the basin, appeared the dark green of plentiful date palms, in welcome contrast with the bare rosy slopes over which we were toiling. Among the palms the high yellow walls and towers of the settlement gleamed in the sunshine. Looming above the walls and palms was the main tower of the Mâred (Fig. 112), surmounted by four smaller but substantial towers; to the right of the Mâred on the top of a slope rose the quadrangular tower of al-Farḥa and north of it the smaller al-Frejḥa.

At 1.42 we stepped from the gorge into the plain of Ṣafaʾ Ṛadîr Marzûḳ, in the western part of which there is a depression where rain water remains for a long time. The surface of this plain is light gray, rocky, and eroded by wind-blown sand. To the west appeared the solitary dome of al-ʿAbd; southeast of it the tabular hill of aš-Šajba; south of it and southeast from us, on the very brim of the cliff, lay the ruins of al-Ḥasjaʾ; and east of these stood the old fortification of al-Birǧ. Far to the southwest the basin of al-Ǧowf is bounded by the height of al-Ǧedîlijje. To the east, above the palms of al-Bḥejrât, we noted the high, black Riǧm Nûra and beneath it numerous rocky clefts, Žlât al-Bḥejrât, alongside which rose the precipitous wall of the Ab-al-Ḳows ridge.

At 2.12 we were riding in the hollow of Ṛadîr Marzûḳ. About two hundred meters eastward we noted two cup-like heights, Subbt al-Wâdi, in which gypsum (*šîd*) was being dug for use in plastering and whitewashing houses. At 2.40 we came to the dilapidated habitations of Âl Ḥsejn and Âl

FIG. 118—Gardens, al-Ğowf.

FIG. 119—Gardens, al-Ğowf.

Ḥasan. At the beginning of 1909 these were sturdy, fortified buildings with vast gardens abounding in tall palms and spreading vines; but in 1915 the buildings were destroyed, the garden walls demolished, the palms cut down — sacrifices to the relentless fights of the period from January, 1909, to July, 1910. At the strange sight of crumbling walls and blackened palms our camels took fright and hence we led them along the western edges of the gardens up to the Mâred fort. The wide wooden gate swung open before us; we drove the camels into the space enclosed on the north, east, and south by high buildings and on the west by a high wall; and here we were at last in the courtyard of the Mâred!

SOJOURN AT AL-ǦOWF

I hastened to look for ʿÂmer, Nawwâf's regent, and finally found him in a large room that had no windows, sipping his coffee by the western wall, near a corner in which he could not be shot from the door. After greeting me, he seated himself in the foremost place and awaited my interrogations. I handed him the message from Nawwâf and then directed him to show me all the inscriptions there were in al-Ǧowf in languages that the people did not understand. He answered that while deepening the well in the Mâred tower they had found a number of marble slabs bearing strange inscriptions, but that nobody seemed to know what had become of them. He also told me that in a street near the Mâred there was set in the wall a stone with strange writing. I told him that I was going to look at the stone and that meanwhile he must see to it that those marble slabs were found. On squeeze paper, with a brush and water, I made an impression of the Nabataean inscriptions on the stone in the wall and then, as there was no wind in the narrow street, I let the paper dry on the stone and returned to the courtyard. ʿÂmer sat there on the high steps laboriously reading Nawwâf's orders to about two hundred listeners.

As soon as the inhabitants of al-Ǧowf who were present perceived me, they began to cheer me and to wish me success in the negotiations with Eben Rašîd. They all longed for peace.

"O Chief," they pleaded, "deliver us from this prison! We have not dared to show ourselves beyond our fortification walls for five years. Our enemies prowl after us day and night. Our herds have died, our trade has ceased, we live only on dates and on those grains of cereal that we ourselves raise in the gardens."

They brought me but two fragments of legible Nabataean writings. Although I had promised a Turkish pound ($ 4.50) for every complete inscription they could find, I had secured only these two. Either they had taken the other writings to Syria or they had walled them up in the Mâred, the flanking towers of which had been undergoing repairs.

Meantime ʿÂmer had donned his best holiday clothes and with the elders of al-Ǧowf was ready to welcome me formally in the name of his master, Nawwâf. Toward evening I went with him to the al-Farḥa tower and questioned him about the route I should take. He recommended that I go along the eastern fringes of the Nefûd, where it had rained amply twelve days before and where, therefore, I should find water in every rocky crevice. Learning from Nâzel that two Šammar were imprisoned in al-Ǧowf, I asked ʿÂmer to release them. He did so immediately upon our return, taking them before me and directing them to thank me for their liberation. As they were clad only in ragged shirts, I bought them new shirts, kerchiefs, and mantles and asked them to bear greetings from me to their chiefs. One of them belonged to the Nebhân clan, the other to the Zmejl. Unejs eben Bnejje wanted to know when and in which direction I was going; but I gave him no definite reply in order that any probable ambush by robbers might be thwarted by their lack of information. In the evening we determined the latitude. I slept in my tent inside the courtyard.

Wednesday, January 13, 1915. We rose early. The courtyard was crowded with sick and wounded in need of advice and medicines. After getting through with them I went with ʿÂmer into the main Mâred tower. It is round in shape and narrows toward the top, to which a crude spiral staircase leads from Nawwâf's apartment, which is in about the center of the structure. The tower is entered through a narrow aperture closed by a heavy door sheathed with iron. A still smaller aperture leads into a meager hallway whence one may enter Nawwâf's apartment, in which were stored enough arms, ammunition, and provisions to enable him to withstand a long siege. Keys to open the door leading to the hallway were kept only by ʿÂmer and by Nawwâf's mother, who was his caretaker. He did not trust his wife, a native of al-Ǧowf. The mother greeted me cordially, led me through the house, displayed the two goats that lived with her in the tower, and showed me how she could draw water straight from a well of fresh spring water lined with stones and dug under the tower. From Nawwâf's room, which was stuffy and damp because the old, thick stone walls constantly perspired, we went up the spiral staircase to the top of the tower, which was enclosed by a low wall perforated on all sides with loopholes for guns. The fortress had suffered much in the last combats. The four smaller flanking towers had been re-erected by Nawwâf, but were made of adobe, while the original walls are of hard stones.

In the courtyard ʿÂmer's guards showed me a young antelope which had been brought by the Šarârât from the Nefûd. Later we climbed up the towers of al-Frejḥa and al-Farḥa to sketch a map of al-Ǧowf from the top.

The settlements of al-Ǧowf (the basin, the cavity) are situated, as the name itself implies, in a basin extending from the west northeastward. This basin is about one hundred kilometers long, about ten kilometers wide, and forty to fifty meters deep. The run-off flows down the surrounding heights into it and remains throughout the year on the underlying rocks under a layer of coarse sand and gravel, emerging at many places in the form of springs and elsewhere filling wells from four to twenty meters deep. In the deepest wells the water is quite tepid and somewhat salty. It is, of course, the abundance of water that accounts for the presence of men and settlements at al-Ǧowf. The largest settlement is called by the inhabitants Dûmat al-Ǧandalijje, while the appellations al-Ǧowf and al-Ǧûba refer to the entire basin with the remainder of the settlements.

Dûmat al-Ǧandalijje (Figs. 113, 114) comprises about four hundred dwellings and is subdivided into ten precincts: on the west, Sûḳ al-Ṛarb, Sûḳ as-Sḥara, Sûḳ al-Wâdi, Sûḳ aš-Šâjbe, Sûḳ Mâred; north of these, Sûḳ Sarrâḥ, Sûḳ ar-Rḥejbijjîn, and Sûḳ ʿAlâǧ; south of the Mâred, Sûḳ al-Ḫadne, and finally, Sûḳ an-Nžejb. In the neighborhood of the town are small gardens: an-Nwêḳîṭ, al-Wusîʿa, Ǧâwa, al-Ḳnejje, ʿUjûn Kibre, ʿAjn aš-Šejḫ, ar-Ršejde, etc. Ar-Rḥejbijjîn, it is alleged, are the descendants of merchants who immigrated from ar-Raḥba beside the Euphrates or from ar-Rḥejbe in Syria. According to the natives, the inscription on the stone in the Sûḳ al-Ṛarb reads thus:

"Elf bil-Ğowf račijje	"A thousand are the draw wells in al-Ğowf,
w elf ʿejn ğarijje	A thousand are the flowing springs —
wa min ḥass sbaḳat al-ʿobejje	And who has heard that the ʿObejje mare won the race
wa hije ṯenijje."	Though but five years old?"

Except in the case of the Sûḳ Mâred, every precinct has palm gardens, in the midst of which are the houses. The gardens are surrounded by high walls. Through a substantial gate one enters a narrow street between two inner garden walls and, following it, comes to a small yard shaped like a cross (Fig. 115), from which four solid gates open into four houses. At the place where the four gardens meet there usually is a well (Figs. 116, 117) from which camels and cows draw water for the irrigation of the gardens (Figs. 118, 119).

Of the dates grown at al-Ğowf, *al-msejḥijje* ripens earliest. It is a bit smaller than a walnut, yellow, and somewhat sour. The most palatable variety is *ḥelwa,* black and almost as long as a finger, but thicker. *Ḥelwet al-ḥsejn,* which is yellow, is also large and delicious. *Ḥamr šûṭ* can be preserved the longest and it has the best flavor when the new crop of *al-msejḥijje* is nearly ripe. Dates are measured by *ṣâʿ* (1 *ṣâʿ* = 9 liters).

The dates are prepared in various ways. When they are good but unripe they are mixed with cut *ʿâḏer* and cooked over a moderate fire until all the juice evaporates; then they are divided in the middle to dry, strung on twine, and preserved as food for travelers. Another method is to roast *semḥ,* grind it, and mix it with ripe, black dates. The *semḥ* will absorb all the juice and the mixture will last over a year without spoiling. This is called *bečîl.*

In the gardens figs, oranges, lemons, apricots, grapes, and various vegetables also grow luxuriantly. Beside the walls are usually planted slender *eṯel* trees, which resemble *ṭarfa.* The wood of these trees is used in the making of flat roofs. Immediately outside the gardens and sometimes inside them are small fields planted with wheat or barley. The civil war in 1909–1910 caused the destruction of many houses and gardens.

It is apparent that the Nabataeans founded a large colony in Dûmat al-Ǧandal and, therefore, had a burial ground. I discovered no trace of it, however. It is alleged that in aṣ-Ṣwêneʿijje, near the Mâred, old caves were unearthed, but that nothing was found in them and they were immediately covered up again.[107]

[107] The continuation of this expedition into northern Neǧd and thence into Mesopotamia is narrated in the author's forthcoming *Northern Neǧd* and *The Middle Euphrates*, both of which will form parts of the present series.

APPENDIXES

APPENDIX I

NORTHERN ARABIA IN THE ASSYRIAN PERIOD

The North Arabian Tribes

The ancient Assyrian records mention Arabia and the Arabs as early as the ninth century before Christ. In the year 854, Gindibu with a thousand camel riders from the Aribi land aided the king of Damascus against Salmanasar III at Ḳarḳar (Monolith Inscription [Rawlinson, *Cuneiform Inscriptions* (1861—1884), Vol. 3, pl. 8], col. 2, l. 94; Peiser in: Schrader, *Keilinschriftliche Bibliothek* [1889—1900], Vol. 1, p. 172). — According to this report Gindibu brought only riders upon camels; hence we must look for the site of his camp somewhere southeast of Damascus.

Tiglath Pileser IV (746—727 B. C.) endeavored to insure the trade highways which pass through Syria and converge on the Mediterranean. To this end he subjugated the independent principalities of Syria and established Assyrian provinces, persuading the more distant kings and chiefs to recognize his dominion. The *Annals* of Tiglath Pileser IV (Rost, *Keilschrifttexte* [1893], Vol. 2, pl. 16; Layard, *Inscriptions* [1851], pll. 50 b, 67 a), l. 154 (see also Rost, *op. cit.*, Vol. 1, p. 26), record that in the year 738 Zabibi, the queen of the Aribi land, sent him tribute. — Where Zabibi resided and what tribes she ruled we do not know; probably she ruled the oasis of Adumu and was high priestess of that Ḳedar tribe to which this oasis paid tribute.

In 732 B. C. Tiglath Pileser IV engaged in war with Samsi, another queen of Aribi, who had broken a great oath sworn by the god Šamaš. He conquered two of her cities and laid siege to her camp, so that she humbled herself before him and sent a tribute of camels, male and female. Her subjugation being complete, Tiglath Pileser appointed a resident (*ḳêpu*) for her court (*Annals* [Rost, *op. cit.*, Vol. 2, pl. 23; Layard, *op. cit.*, pl. 66], ll. 210—217; see also Rost, *op. cit.*, Vol. 1, p. 36). Perhaps Samsi had incurred his wrath by aiding the hard-pressed king of Damascus. The cities which the Assyrian monarch conquered after the fall of Damascus lie along the southeastern boundary of that city's domain, possibly on the caravan road in the southern Ḥawrân. These cities, like all the settlements on the line between the tilled fields and the desert, had been tributary to Queen Samsi. Tiglath Pileser's resident, living in one of these cities, was to transmit to Syria complete reports upon the conduct of the queen and her tribes.

These tribes were likewise forced to recognize Assyrian dominion. The annals record that in the year of Samsi's fall the Mas'a tribe, the city of Têma, and the tribes of Saba', Ḫajappa, Badana, Ḫatti, and Idiba'il, inhabiting the distant western section of the country, had sent in tribute gold, silver, camels, and spices of all kinds. The identity of these tribes has already been discussed by me in some detail in my book, *The Northern Ḥeǧâz*, pp. 288—291, where it was shown that they may be identified with the Madianites and associated tribes of the Bible. Without repeating what was there discussed, we may add here a few observations more particularly on the Mas'a and Idiba'il tribes.

The Mas'a

In *The Northern Ḥeǧâz*, p. 288, it was explained that the Mas'a tribe was probably identical with the Biblical tribe of Massa (Gen. 25: 13 f.) and that it had its encampments east or southeast of Moab. Here the camp sites of the other tribes allied with the Mas'a may have been situated, and here the Assyrian record which makes mention of the Mas'a places this tribe.

Dhorme, *Les pays bibliques* (1910), p. 196, seeks the tribe of Mas'a among the inhabitants of the south Arabian port of Muza. This identification, however, seems utterly untenable.

Delitzsch, *Wo lag das Paradies?* (1881), p. 302, quotes a report of the Assyrian resident to an unnamed king: "After thy departure from the Niba'âti tribe, Malik-Kamaru, the son of Ammê'uta' of the Mas'a tribe, slew and robbed the members of the (Niba'âti) tribe. One of them, who had saved himself by escaping, came to the city of the king" (Rawlinson, *Cuneiform Inscriptions* [1861—1884], Vol. 4, pl. 54, no. 1). — The resident refers to an expedition conducted by the unnamed king into the territory of the Niba'âti tribe and alleges that this tribe had been attacked from the north or northwest by the chief of the Mas'a tribe. The Niba'âti or Nabaitai tribe, the Biblical Nebajôt (Nabataeans), according to other Assyrian records had their camping grounds in the southern half of the depression of Sirḥân. Therefore we must seek the territory of the Mas'a tribe north or northwest of them in close proximity to the southern border of the Damascan territory and the western bounds of the Aribi, for the context of the Assyrian records also mentions Mas'a in immediate connection with the territory of Queen Samsi.

The Idiba'il and Other Tribes

Readers of *The Northern Ḥeǧâz*, p. 291, will also remember that a certain *ḳêpu* Idibi'il of the land of Arubu was appointed by Tiglath Pileser IV as his representative and informant on the Egyptian frontier and that to this Idibi'il were apportioned fifteen settlements of the Askalon district. The tribe of Idiba'il and the *ḳêpu* Idibi'il certainly bore the same name, the name, perhaps, of a reigning family, precisely as now the name Eben Rašîd is occasionally applied to the Šammar tribe as a whole. Because Idibi'il was appointed a *ḳêpu* of lands lying near Egypt and was given settlements belonging to the city of Askalon, it would seem to follow that the camping grounds of his tribe must have been in the Sinai peninsula and that his influence must have extended north even beyond Gaza. The fact that he was said to have been of the land of Arubu would go to prove that the Sinai peninsula, as well as the regions on the frontiers of the Damascan settlements and the oasis of Adumu, was regarded as belonging to the Aribi.

This seems to be confirmed by Esarhaddon's annals, which place the kings of the Aribi in the same region (Rogers, *Esarhaddon*, obverse,

l. 20; Rawlinson, *op. cit.*, Vol. 3, pl. 35, no. 4, reverse, l. 2). In short, we should take the "Aribi" and "Arubu" of the Assyrians to refer to the nomads and nomads' lands not only of Arabia proper but also of the districts south of Palestine and east of Egypt. It is inconceivable that the Aribi domain should have been any one single region of limited area.

The Assyrian Idiba'il is surely identical with the Biblical tribe of Adbeêl which, according to Genesis 25: 13, was descended from Ishmael. East of the tribes of Adbeêl and Ḫatti, southeast and east of Beersheba, there used to encamp two other lineages, the Mibsam and the Mišmaʿ, who according to Genesis, *loc. cit.*, were also sons of Ishmael. According to 1 Chronicles 4: 25—27 the Mišmaʿ belonged among the Mibsam clans, who, being the strongest of the tribe of Simeon, had founded numerous settlements. The situation is clear. The Ishmaelite clans of Mibsam and Mišmaʿ, whose encampments lay south of Palestine, through intermarriages became linked with the Simeonites and gradually settled in various Simeonite villages where they became a majority. Thus we see that we may locate the habitations of Ishmaelite tribes on the Sinai peninsula. This cannot be done in the case of the Madianite tribes.

The tribes of Têma, Saba', Ḫajappa, and Badana, wishing to preserve their trade connections, had sent gifts to Tiglath Pileser IV and were under the sole political influence of the Assyrians. The real political power of the Assyrians extended during that time no farther south than the northern end of the Gulf of ʿAḳaba and in the desert to the east no farther south than the northern end of the depression of Sirḥân.

Sargon II relates in the year 715 B. C. (Cylinder inscription [Rawlinson, *op. cit.*, Vol. 1, pl. 36; Lyon, *Keilschrifttexte Sargon's* (1883), p. 4; Winckler, *Keilschrifttexte Sargons* (1889), Vol. 2, pl. 2, no. 1], line 20; see also Peiser in: Schrader, *Keilinschriftliche Bibliothek* (1889—1900), Vol. 2, p. 42) that he defeated the tribes of Tamudi, Ibadidi, Marsimani, and Ḫajappa, and established the survivors in Samaria. The identity of these tribes also is fully discussed in *The Northern Ḥeǧâz*, pp. 289, 291—292.

Assyrian Campaigns in Arabia Deserta

Campaigns of Sargon II and Sennacherib

The army of Sargon II undertook an expedition into the southern part of Edom and beyond, where the tribes named above had their camping grounds and whence they were in the habit of harassing the inhabitants of the regions subject to Assyria. Sargon marched over the transport road which runs from Syria to southwestern Arabia, successfully attacked the camps of the marauders, and drove his captives north to settle them in Samaria. At the time of this victory even the Sabaean chief It'amara was obliged to send gifts and tribute to Sargon (Great Inscription of Khorsabad [Botta and Flandin, *Monument de Ninive* (1846—1850), Vol. 4, pl. 145_2, l. 3; Winckler, *op. cit.*, Vol. 2, pl. 65], line 27; see also Peiser in: Schrader, *op. cit.*, Vol. 2, p. 54). — Sargon does not refer to It'amara as "king"; perhaps the latter was merely governor of the northern Sabaean settlements with his residence in Dajdân or the Biblical Dedan.

In the same year the annals of the king Sargon also mention the tribute of Queen Samsi of Aribi (Great Inscription of Khorsabad, *loc. cit.*; Peiser in: Schrader, *loc. cit.*). — The tribute consisted of white female camels which the chiefs of the individual clans surrendered to the Assyrians in the name of their queen. Winckler (*op. cit.*, Vol. 2, pl. 62, and *Geschichte des alten Arabiens* [1897], p. 465) published an Arabian inscription which names four chiefs who, in the name of Queen Samsi, brought to the Great King 164 camels, specifically designated as "white." — White camels, called *maṛâtîr*, are today the pride of the whole clan.

In the year 703 Jati'e, the queen of Aribi, sent her brother Basḳanu with troops to help the Babylonian King Marduk-apal-iddina against Sennacherib, king of Assyria. In February, 702, Basḳanu, together with his troops, was taken prisoner by the Assyrians (British Museum Cylinder 113, 203 [Smith, *First Campaign of Sennacherib* (1921), p. 62], l. 28).

About the year 688 B. C. Sennacherib undertook an expedition against Telḫunu, the queen of the Arabs, defeated her in the desert (*madbari*), and captured many camels. The queen, forsaking her tents, fled with Ḫazâel into the fort of Adumat, situated in the center of an arid desert waste (Ungnad in *Vorderasiatische Schriftdenkmäler*, Vol. 1, no. 77 reverse, ll. 22—27; Scheil, *La campagne de Sennachérib* [1904], cols. 69 f.).

According to the inscriptions of Esarhaddon (681—668 B. C.) and Asurbanipal (668—626 B. C.) Queen Telḫunu went over to the Assyrians. Because of her disaffection Sennacherib possessed himself of Adumu, the fort of Aribi, and took to Nineveh all the local gods and the queen herself (who was the priestess of the godess Dilbat), together with the princess Tabûa (British Museum Tablets K 3087 and K 3405; Smith, *History of Sennacherib* [1878], p. 138; Winckler, *Textbuch*, pp. 48 n.; Streck, *Die Inschriften Assurbanipals* [1916], Vol. 2, pp. 217 f., 223; Prism S [Scheil, *Le prisme S d'Assaraddon* (1914), pl. 4], col. 4, ll. 2—6; Scheil, *op. cit.*, p. 18).—

Adumu, the fortress of the Aribi land, denotes the oasis of Dûmat al-Ǧandal. According to Genesis 25: 13 ff. the inhabitants of the Dûma oasis belonged among the Ishmaelites. The Assyrian annals do not divulge whether Sennacherib marched to Adumu from the east or the west, but I believe that he set out from Babylonia, which lies to the east. If the oasis of Adumu was a central point for the tribes camping in northern Arabia, the influence of Queen Telḫunu must have extended up to the Babylonian frontier, since it was from Babylonia that trade caravans brought grain, cloths, and other articles necessary to the dwellers in the city of Adumu. The tribes of Queen Telḫunu, pressed on the west by the Assyrian legions, were the more willing to join the Babylonians, who up to that time had still preserved a certain degree of independence. Hence it is comprehensible that her tribes engaged in every rebellion of the Babylonians against the Assyrians, giving their aid in return for the Babylonian alliance and commerce. During the battles of Sennacherib with Babylonia Queen Telḫunu probably camped with her tribes upon the Babylonian frontier, supporting from this strategic position the Babylonian legions, while some of her troops plundered the Assyrian provinces in Syria. Until the Babylonians were subjugated,

Sennacherib was not in a position to undertake a more extensive expedition against Queen Telḫunu. Having taken Babylon in 689 B. C., he sought to insure his territories against further plundering and attempted to destroy the desert allies of his enemy. He attacked the camps of the clans subject to the queen, and routed and pursued them into the inner desert around Fort Adumu.

Ḫazâel, who fled with Telḫunu to Adumu, was the chief of the Ḳedar tribe, which then held sway over northern Arabia as the ʿAneze of today or the Kalb of the Middle Ages. The individual clans of the Ḳedar and of the tribes dependent upon them were camping in Palmyrena, in the volcanic district east and southeast of Damascus, and in the desert as far as the Nefûd and Babylonia. The settlers of the large oasis of Adumu (Dûmat al-Ǧandal) were dependent upon the Ḳedar, because without the patronage of the latter trade caravans could not penetrate the desert. The Ḳedar had in Adumu their own sanctuaries, their own deities, and their own priestess of the foremost deity, who was at the same time mistress of the dwellers in the oasis. If she excelled all rivals, she was acclaimed by the nomads also as their queen. The oasis of Dûma even today belongs to the ʿAneze, and its inhabitants are tributary to them. The ʿAneze have in the oasis their warehouses in which they keep part of their provisions and implements during their sojourns in the desert. If the master of such an oasis is a surpassing ruler, he may easily become the head of all the neighboring tribes, like the master of the oasis of Ḥâjel, who has been acknowledged prince of all the Šammar. As today it is not necessary for the prince to be at the same time commander-in-chief of his warriors, so the priestess queen Telḫunu could have employed another to command her forces. I think that her lieutenant was Ḫazâel, the king of Aribi. They both had fled before Sennacherib to their fortified oasis of Adumu. Around the fort spread the settlers' gardens and orchards, which Sennacherib must certainly have demolished, had there been a protracted siege. Since by so wanton an act he would have destroyed the welfare of the settlers for several score years, their mistress and priestess submitted. Ḫazâel and his warriors opposed surrender, for they would not have suffered any loss by the destruction of the gardens. Thereupon a dispute developed between Telḫunu and Ḫazâel; as the Assyrian chronicle records: "Telḫunu, who had become angry at Ḫazâel, the king of Aribi... and had brought about his defeat" (British Museum Tablets K 3087 and K 3405; Streck, *loc. cit.*).

As Sennacherib could not surround the entire oasis, Ḫazâel and his nomads were able to save themselves by fleeing into the inner desert. After Sennacherib's death Ḫazâel went with many gifts to Nineveh, where Esarhaddon received him graciously. Ḫazâel and his tribes had been very dangerous adversaries, because they could ride upon marauding expeditions in all directions and thus do harm to the Assyrian subjects themselves as well as to their trade caravans and to the settlers under their rule. Ḫazâel brought from Nineveh the idols Diblat, Daia, Nuḫaia, Ebirillu, and Atar Ḳurumaia, captured in Adumu (Prism S [Scheil, *op. cit.*, pl. 4], col. 4, ll. 10 f.; see also Scheil, *op. cit.*, p. 18).

Having been merciful to Ḫazâel, Esarhaddon sought to gain also the Adumu settlers. For this reason he appointed as their priestess and mistress Princess Tabûa, who had resided in his palace for many years. Though she remained loyal to the Assyrians, her loyalty cost her the favor of her new subjects in Arabia.

Campaigns of Esarhaddon

Esarhaddon recognized Ḫazâel as the head chief of all the Ḳedar and increased the tribute which he was to pay by sixty-five camels. Ḫazâel died in about 675 B. C. and left a son Uaite' (also written Ja'lu, Jata') whom Esarhaddon (Prisms A and C [Rawlinson, *Cuneiform Inscriptions* (1861—1884), Vol. 1, pll. 45—47], col. 3, l. 20; see also Abel in: Schrader, *Keilinschriftliche Bibliothek* [1889—1900], Vol. 2, p. 130; Prism S, col. 4, l. 18; Scheil, *loc. cit.*) placed upon his father's throne (Ungnad in *Vorderasiatische Schriftdenkmäler*, Vol. 1, no. 83, col. 1, ll. 3—19; Streck, *op. cit.*, p. 377), forcing him to promise to pay annually a thousand *minae* of gold, a thousand precious stones, fifty camels, and a thousand measures of spices more than his father had had to pay.

A rebellion broke out against King Uaite'. It was fostered by Uabu, who, having seduced the Aruba, schemed to usurp the kingdom. The Aruba endured the Assyrian supremacy reluctantly and were perhaps incited to revolt by both the Egyptians and the Babylonians. But Esarhaddon sent against Uabu an army which defeated and captured him and led him prisoner to Nineveh (Prism S, col. 4, ll. 9 ff.; Scheil, *op. cit.*, pp. 18f.). Nevertheless, the resistance against the Assyrians did not cease with the defeat of Uabu. Uaite' placed himself at the head of his tribes. "He hath forgotten the treaty, he hath forgotten the good deeds shown him." He plundered with his tribes the Assyrian provinces which adjoined the desert. The Assyrian armies again displayed their efficiency, attacking his camp, capturing his gods, and precipitating his flight into distant lands (Ungnad in *Vorderasiatische Schriftdenkmäler*, *loc. cit.*; Streck, *loc. cit.*). From the chronicles it is not certain that Esarhaddon himself came to Arabia on this occasion. It would appear that the Assyrian army did not enter Adumu (Dûmat al-Ǧandal), for Tabûa, its mistress, remained faithful.

Dhorme, *Les pays bibliques* (1911), p. 208, surmises without reason that Princess Tabûa was Ḫazâel's wife. On page 207 he relates how Esarhaddon marched with a large army into the inner desert to Adumu and even farther to Egypt. Such a march conducted with a large army through the inner desert from Babylonia to Egypt would have been a miracle of which there is no parallel in history.

After suppressing the rebellion of Uaite', the Assyrian king made another expedition against the Arabian tribes encamped in the region of Bâzu and Ḫazû (Prisms A and C [Rawlinson, *loc. cit.*], col. 3, ll. 25—52; Abel in: Schrader, *op. cit.*, Vol. 2, pp. 130, 132; Broken Prism [Rawlinson, *op. cit.*, Vol. 3, pll. 15, 16], col. 4, ll. 10—26; Winckler in: Schrader, *op. cit.*, Vol. 2, pp. 131 f., 146 f.; Delitzsch, *Wo lag das Paradies?* [1881], pp. 306 f.). According to Prisms A and C and to the Broken Prism, Esarhaddon undertook a punitive expedition against (Arabian) kings. Having made 140 or 150 miles, he continued over sandy, arid roads, and through salt marshes to the distant region of Bâzu. Thence he marched twenty miles through thickets and over *pî ṣabîti* stones in which reptiles swarmed like locusts, pushed even farther to the mountain range of Ḫazû, passed around a mountain of *šaggilmud* stones, and hastened into regions never before explored by any king. He killed eight kings of these districts and carried off to Assyria their gods, their chattels, and their people. He subjugated Kîsu of Ḫaldili; Akbaru of Na(?)-pi-a-te (or Il-pi-a-ti [Winckler in: Schrader, *op. cit.*, Vol. 2, pp. 146 ff.]); Mansaku of Magalani; Japa', the queen of Diḫrani (Diḫtani); Ḫabisu of Ḳadaba'; Niḫaru of Ga'pânu; Bailu, the queen of Iḫilu; and Ḫabanamru of Buda' (Puṭa'). King Laili of Jadi' saved himself by flight but later went to Nineveh and begged for mercy. Esarhaddon gave him back his gods and named him the tributary king of the Bâzu district. —

According to the Assyrian report Esarhaddon marched through marshes and swamps by a route which must have been long and tedious, because the scribe especially mentions the salt marshes along it. Salt marshes lie between the middle Euphrates and the Tigris, in northern Palmyrena (at the base of the Šbêṯ and al-Ḥaṣṣ range), in the districts west and south of Palmyra, and in the depression of Sirḥân.

Dhorme seeks these salt marshes (*Le pays de Job* [1911], p. 104) in the neighborhood of al-Ǧowf, where it is alleged that salt is almost at the surface of the ground and spoils the water of the wells; he also seeks them (*ibid.*, p. 201) in the regions southwest of al-Ǧowf. He manifests his lack of familiarity with the neighborhood of the oasis of al-Ǧowf and the regions spreading southwest of it.

There can be no consideration of the salt marshes between the Euphrates and the Tigris and in northern Palmyrena. The marshes near Palmyra and to the west are small. There are left only the salt marshes in the depression of Sirḥân, which extend for two hundred kilometers with a width at some places of twenty kilometers. These cannot be marched around, because the ground is broken on the west by steep-walled ravines which enter the depression and because of the tracts of lava — always difficult to cross — which enclose the depression on the east.

Supposing that Esarhaddon marched from Nineveh over the ordinary military road to Damascus, we gather from the Assyrian chronicle that it was thence 140 or 150 miles to the depression of Sirḥân by way of the trade road leading southeast to the oasis of Dûma. This great trade road connected the commercial center of Dilmun (al-Baḥrejn) on the Persian Gulf with inner Arabia and the oasis of Dûma as well as with the western provinces of the Assyrian domain. Caravans could use this road without regard for the political situation in Babylonia. Esarhaddon insured the oasis of Dûma for himself by appointing as mistress there the Princess Tabûa, who had been tutored at his court. Therefore it must have been his ambition likewise to acquire the long depression of Sirḥân which the trade road penetrated. The depression of Sirḥân is tillable. There are even now several settlements there, and we may presume that it was also inhabited in the time of Esarhaddon and that it was then of much greater importance to the world's commerce than it is today. The danger to caravans, however, is much greater in the proximity of fortified settlements than in the open desert where only nomads camp. Caravans may march many days under the protection of a single nomad chief, while the protection of the master of a settlement generally extends but to the gardens of his neighbor, a situation which forces the merchant to make a separate pact with the master of every settlement. When the "kings" of these individual settlements revolted against their Assyrian lord, they were in a position to impose their will upon the caravans.

The name Bâzu may be compared with the name of the important watering place Ḳulbân al-Bîẓ, and the name Ḫazû reminds us of the name of the district Ḥaẓawẓa in the depression of Sirḥân. Since the spoken ẓ of the Rwala sounds almost like ḏ, it would be possible to write these names Bîḏ and Ḥaḏawḏa. This tendency is seen in the faulty pronunciations of *maẓrûb* instead of *maḏrûb*. The Ḫazû range would then signify the mountainous district of aš-Šâma which closes the depression of Sirḥân on the east. Bâzu and Ḫazû, however, are identical with the Biblical Bûz and Ḫazô. According to Genesis 22: 21 Bûz and Ḫazô were brothers of ʿÛṣ. Job lived in the territory of ʿÛṣ, which we seek in the vicinity of Ḫirbet ʿÎṣ near the settlement of aṭ-Ṭafîle. His friend Elihu was from Bûz (Job 32: 2). Other Biblical accounts also would seem to confirm our placing of Bâzu (or Bûz) and of Ḫazû (or Ḫazô) in the northern half of the depression of Sirḥân. Jeremiah 25: 23 connects Bûz with Dedan and Têma, which are situated on important trade roads.

The Assyrian description of the districts of Bâzu and Ḫazû conforms well with the physiographic features of the depression of Sirḥân. I have already mentioned the salt marshes. The *pî ṣabîti* stones, literally gazelles' mouths, can be nothing else than the small rounded pieces of quartz that cover the western edges of the depression. They are even today called cats' heads. In the depression itself trees and bushes, which in course of time form impenetrable thickets, grow everywhere. Snakes and lizards infest the region, although they do not abound like locusts; the description of an Assyrian march was always exaggerated.

It would seem that Esarhaddon started from Ḫazû (Ḥaẓawẓa or Ḥaẓowẓa) in a northerly direction, taking the trade road which leads from the depression of Sirḥân east of the Ḥawrân past the Ṛadîr al-Wusâd, Burḳuʿ, and Ḫân at-Trâb to Jabrûd. The range of *šaggilmud* stones should then be sought in the volcanic region, here overlain with basalt and lava. The eight "kings" defeated by Esarhaddon dwelt in the depression of Sirḥân, along the eastern boundary of the Ḥawrân, and in the lowland of ar-Raḥba. Ḳaṭaba answers to the valley of al-Ḳaṭṭâmi. Jadiʾ, the residence of the king Laili, is perhaps identical with Čâf, now the largest settlement within the depression of Sirḥân. At Čâf the "little valley", or al-Wudej, terminates, the name of which suggests Jadiʾ with the *j* changed to *w*, a change which might easily have occurred. The name Di-iḫ-ra-ani recalls the Dacharenoi (Stephen of Byzantium, *Ethnica* [Meineke], Vol. 1, p. 223), who were Nabataeans. Even this comparison brings us back to the depression of Sirḥân, which, under the name of Syrmaion Pedion (*ibid.*, p. 593), once formed the eastern frontier of the Nabataean dominion. The Diḫrani (Dacharenoi) were identical with the Ṣaḥar, from whom the merchants of Damascus purchased their best wool (Ezek. 27: 18). The value of the Hebrew ṣ is equivalent to the Arabic ḍ. These Diḫrani were therefore a clan of the Biblical Nebajôt (Nabataeans), who were affiliated with the Ḳedar and were famous for their flocks of goats and sheep.

To summarize, we see that according to these reports the Assyrian army punished the oases situated in the northern half of Bâzu (Sirḥân) and also some of the clans camping east and north of the Sirḥân depression in the mountainous desert of Ḫazû. The army returned by the trade road which leads along the eastern base of the Ḥawrân to Damascus.

Upon this campaign the Assyrian army pierced the boundary of the Nabaitai tribe (Nabataeans). It was therefore in this period that the Assyrian resident must have made his report (quoted above, p. 478) that the Niba'âti (Nabaitai) had been attacked by the chief Malik-Kamaru, son of Ammê'uta' of the Mas'a tribe.

After Esarhaddon's death in 668 B. C. Uaite', the son of Ḫazâel, sought to effect a reconciliation with Asurbanipal. He soon succeeded, for Asurbanipal at first discarded the aggressive policies of his father. Uaite' was pardoned and his idol Atarsamain was returned to him (Cylinder B [Rawlinson, *op. cit.*, Vol. 3, pll. 33 f.], col. 7, ll. 87—92; Streck, *Die Inschriften Assurbanipals* [1916], Vol. 2, pp. 130 f.).

Campaigns of Asurbanipal

As long as Asurbanipal lived at peace with the king of Babylon the tribes of northern Arabia were likewise tranquil. As soon as Šamaššumukin revolted against him, however, hostilities recommenced in this region. The tribes were far more friendly to Babylonia than to Assyria and Šamaššumukin's offensive gave them an opportunity to plunder the rich provinces of Assyria. Uaite', son of Ḫazâel, king of the Ḳedar Arabs, plundered with his clans the western borders of the desert from Edom in the south to Ḥama' in the north. He also dispatched reinforcements to Šamaššumukin in Babylonia under the command of Abijate and Aiammu, the sons of Te'ri.

Upon Asurbanipal's order, the Syrian garrisons marched out to oppose Uaite', driving him back into the desert. Various encounters took place in the vicinity of Azarilu, Ḫiratâḳaṣai, Udume, in the pass of Jabrudu, in Bît Ammâni, in the districts of Ḫaurîna, Mu'aba, Sa'arri, Ḫargê, and Ṣubiti.

Udume is identical with Edom, Mu'aba with Moab, and Ṣubiti with Ṣôba' (an Aramean kingdom mentioned in the Bible), all of which are to be sought on the outskirts of the desert. The pass of Jabrudu is identical with Ṯenijjet al-Jabârde. It is situated about seventy kilometers east-northeast of Damascus on the old road that connects Ḥomṣ with the Sirḥân depression. I seek to locate the district of Ḫaurîna in the vicinity of the settlement of al-Ḥawwârîn, and Ḫargê in the ruins of the settlement of Ḫarîḳa (al-Ḫarîža), about sixty kilometers east-northeast of Ḥomṣ.

The Ḳedar under King Uaite' were therefore unable to hold a position in the territory of the settlers and found themselves forced to return to their desert. In the retreat they must have suffered heavy casualties. It is possible that many were discontented and perhaps even threatened Uaite'. That he might save himself and at the same time procure aid for his tribes, he took refuge with Natnu, king of the Nabaitai (Rassam Cylinder [Rawlinson, *op. cit.*, Vol. 5, Part 1, pl. 9], col. 7, ll. 82—123; Cylinder B [Rawlinson, *op. cit.*, Vol. 3, pll. 33 f.], col. 7, ll. 93—100; col. 8, ll. 1—22; Streck, *op. cit.*, pp. 64 ff., 132 f.). After Uaite''s flight the Ḳedar acknowledged Ammuladi as their king and chief, and Uaite''s wife placed herself under his protection. But while Ammuladi was making fresh incursions into Moab, he was captured, together with Queen Adija', by Kamasẖalta', the king of Moab, and both were sent to Nineveh (Cylinder B [Rawlinson, *op. cit.*, Vol. 3, pl. 34], col. 8, ll. 31—44; British Museum Tablet K 2802 [Rawlinson, *op. cit.*, pll. 35—36], col. 5, ll. 15—30; British Museum Tablet K 3096 [Rawlinson, *op. cit.*, pl. 36, no. 5], reverse ll. 4—9; Streck, *op. cit.*, pp. 134, 202, 332, 334).

Abijate, the son of Te'ri, chief of the Ḳedar reinforcements in Babylonia, also came to Nineveh. Having been defeated, he had first betaken himself with all his warriors to Babylon. When later the Babylonian garrison began to suffer hunger, he cut his way through the besieging Assyrian army and regained his freedom with the loss of most of his soldiers. With the remainder he appeared at Nineveh and appealed for mercy. Asurbanipal pardoned him and, after the defeat and flight of Uaite', son of Ḫazâel, appointed him king of the Ḳedar under the condition that he should duly render tribute in gold, precious stones, eyebrow dyes, camels, and donkeys (Rassam Cylinder [Rawlinson, *op. cit.*, Vol. 5, Part 1, pll. 9 f.], col. 8, ll. 30—47; Cylinder B [Rawlinson, *op. cit.*, Vol. 3, pl. 34], col. 8, ll. 24—30; British Museum Tablet K 2802 [Rawlinson, *op. cit.*, Vol. 3, pll. 35—36], col. 5, ll. 6—14; Streck, *op. cit.*, pp. 68 f., 134, 202).

In this manner Asurbanipal secured himself in northern Arabia. When, in 648 B. C., Babylon also fell, Natnu, the Nabaitai king, decided likewise to acknowledge Asurbanipal's supremacy. His tribe camped far away and none of his forefathers had sent envoys to the court at Nineveh; yet Natnu did not trust the resourceful Asurbanipal and sought to secure his favor. For this reason he delivered into the hands of the Assyrians Uaite', the Ḳedar king, who had sought refuge with him (Rassam Cylinder [*loc. cit.*], col. 8, ll. 1—14; Cylinder B [*loc. cit.*], col. 8, ll. 45—57; Cylinder C [Rawlinson, *op. cit.*, Vol. 3, pl. 34], col. 9, ll. 34—49; British Museum Tablet K 2802 [*loc. cit.*], col. 5, ll. 31—42; Clay Tablet Fragment, Berliner Museum, Vorderasiatische Abteilung, 5600 [Ungnad in *Vorderasiatische Schriftdenkmäler*, Vol. 1, no. 83], col. 3, ll. 4—16; Streck, *op. cit.*, pp. 66, 134 f., 144, 202 f., 378).—

Because the Ḳedar clans and the tribes dependent upon them camped on the southeastern boundary of Arabia Deserta, in Palmyrena, and east of the Ḥawrân, and because all were either directly or indirectly tributary to the Assyrians, we must seek the Nabaitai in the southwestern part of Arabia Deserta, west of Adumu (Dûma), because here only the Assyrian influence had not previously penetrated.

The tranquillity of Arabia was of no long duration. Abijate, the Ḳedar king appointed by Asurbanipal, had perhaps not yet returned to the camps of his tribes when these acknowledged as their head chief Uaite', son of Bir-Dadda and nephew of the earlier King Uaite', son of Ḫazâel. Abijate had but one recourse. He made terms with Uaite' and planned with him another rising against the Assyrian power. The Ḳedar and the tribes dependent upon them again plundered the neighboring provinces of Assyria. Their temerity provoked in Asurbanipal the firm resolve to undertake a mighty expedition which would crush and suppress them forever. The Ḳedar sought aid of the Nabaitai and, as the latter's king, Natnu, was fearful for his own independence, he allied himself with the Ḳedar and sent a detail of his troops against the approaching Assyrian army (Rassam Cylinder [*loc. cit.*], col. 8, ll. 65—124; Streck, *op. cit.*, pp. 70, 72). Besides the Nabaitai, the Ḳedar under Uaite', the Isamme', and the Atarsamain tribes participated in the hostilities (Rassam Cylinder [*loc. cit.*], col. 9, ll. 1—26; Streck, *op. cit.*, pp. 72, 74).

From the Assyrian accounts of Asurbanipal's ninth campaign (about 640—638 B. C.), we learn the places where the Assyrian army was awaited by these tribes. The Assyrians advanced over a hundred miles before meeting the enemy. Their army must have marched from Nineveh over the ordinary military road and first entered the desert on the right bank of the Euphrates near the settlement of Ḫadatta, for this plan of campaign conforms with the one hundred miles mentioned. The accounts allege that the Assyrians, before approaching the Arabs, scaled high ridges overgrown with forests and, forcing their way among the tall trees, cut a path through thistles and underbrush to march into a land of thirst where neither gazelles nor wild asses graze. —

It is noteworthy that the Assyrian accounts mention mountains overgrown with forests and a march among tall trees. It is just this information which helps us determine the road over which they proceeded. Mountains with forests and slopes with tall trees are not to be found in the northern Arabian desert except in Palmyrena, in the range of al-Bišri, and in the mountains of Abu Riǧmên and ar-Rawâḳ. South of Palmyra spreads an undulating upland where trees have never grown. The thistles mentioned in the Assyrian account are the *širšîr* plants (*Tribulus terrestris*, L.), which thrive especially in the wide depressions south and southwest of Palmyra. When these plants become dry, their thistles harden into spines that injure the bare foot.

The mention of mountains overgrown with forests leads us into the Palmyrene mountains, and it is there that we must seek the places recorded in this first section of the account of the ninth expedition. The Assyrian army marching from Nineveh, after covering eighty-four miles, reached the ford of the Euphrates below Carchemish. After another sixteen miles it had reached the vicinity of Bâlis on the right bank of the Euphrates, where the name of the ruins of al-Ǧdejde recalls the Aramaic word Ḫadatta. At this spot the Assyrians turned into the inner desert. Bâlis and al-Ǧdejde are situated on the border between the desert, or steppe, and the tilled region. It seems that the Ḳedar under the chief Uaite' and the Nabaitai (Nabataeans) led by Abijate were camping between Ḫadatta (al-Ǧdejde) and the Abu Riǧmên range and that they retreated before the army which bore down upon them. In Laribda, an inclosed place with numerous spring wells, the Assyrians supplied themselves with water and proceeded on through the land of thirst to Ḫurarîna. The Isamme', the Atarsamain, and the Nabaitai were defeated in the desert between Jarki and Azalla. Men, donkeys, camels, and goats were captured in multitudes. The Assyrian army pursued the enemy for eight miles and returned to Azalla, where it found plenty of water. From Azalla it marched six miles in a waterless land and at Ḳuraṣiti surrounded the position taken by the Atarsamain and the Ḳedar. Uaite''s gods, his mother, his sister, his wife, numerous Ḳedar, and innumerable donkeys, camels, and sheep became the booty of the Assyrians, before whom they were driven to Damascus.

I seek the watering place of Laribda either at the wells Ǧebb al-Ḳdejm situated on the spurs of the al-Lâbde range, or at ʿOrḍ, the present aṭ-Ṭajjibe. Many springs issue at aṭ-Ṭajjibe, and the place must have been walled in ancient times to afford security to the trade caravans which passed through it from the south. At Laribda the Assyrian army turned toward Ḫurarîna, which is identical with the ruins Ḳalʿat al-Ḥurri situated in the Palmyrene range northwest of Arak. The name Ḫurarîna suggests that of the Ishmaelite tribe, Ḥarar, which was affiliated with the Ḳedar. In Genesis 25: 13 f. it is written Ḥadad, yet the Hebrew *r* might have been interchanged with the *d*. The army marched from Laribda through the wooded range of Abu Riǧmên, where the Arabs were seeking cover for themselves and for their herds. Upon arriving at Ḫurarîna (Ḳalʿat al-Ḥurri), the Assyrians missed the enemy, for the Isamme' tribe and the warriors of the Nabaitai had pitched their camp in the plain between Jarki and Azalla, where ample pasturage and water were available for herds. I am inclined to identify Jarki with the settlement of Arak and Azalla with the watering place of al-ʿElejjânijje, where the valley of ʿAzzâle terminates. The Arabs still like to camp between Arak and al-ʿElejjânijje because the many wells here furnish water for their donkeys and sheep. These animals can endure but a day without drink. Abundant pasture lies upon the slopes of the northern range and in the southern plain. The Assyrian army, however, dispersed the camps of the Isamme' and Nabaitai between Jarki and Azalla, captured their herds, and pursued the defeated enemy eight miles beyond Azalla. The Assyrian army had to return to the watering place, however, because the arid desert promised death by thirst. The fighters of the Isamme' and Nabaitai fled upon camels through the desert into the volcanic region northeast of the Ḥawrân.

The news of the defeat of the Isamme' and Nabaitai soon reached the camps of the Ḳedar and Atarsamain tribes, scattered over the vales southwest of Palmyra. Both of these tribes likewise hastened into the difficult volcanic region north of the Ḥawrân, but they were delayed by their herds and especially by the sheep, which made it possible for the Assyrian army to dash upon them after a march of six miles from Azalla. It surrounded the throngs of the Atarsamain and Ḳedar led by Uaite', son of Bir-Dadda, at Ḳuraṣiti. Uaite' saved himself with his fighters by fleeing, but his gods, his mother, his wife, his family, his donkeys, his camels, and his sheep were captured by the victorious Assyrians and taken to Damascus. The location of Ḳuraṣiti I fix at the head of the valley of al-Baṣîri. The name Ḳuraṣiti perhaps is a derivative of the Arabic *ḳurrêṣ* (a bean-like annual) which denotes *Trigonella hamosa*, L. *Ḳurrêṣ* grows everywhere in the vicinity of al-Baṣîri. The Arabs like to camp by the wells of al-Baṣîri (Ḳuraṣiti) because they are situated at the intersection of two important roads. After the Assyrian soldiers had occupied the hills and slopes about these wells, the Ḳedar and Atarsamain had no choice but surrender.

The last resort of the dispersed Isamme', Atarsamain, Ḳedar, and Nabaitai was the range of Ḫukruna, before which the Assyrian army arrived in a single night's march from Damascus. The range of Ḫukruna must be identical with the volcanic region of Tlûl al-ʿIjâṯ, north of the

Ḥawrân and east of al-Leğa. From afar this looks like a high range with numerous towering peaks. Mere passage through this volcanic region is extremely difficult; and it must have been still more difficult to seek or to dislodge hidden nomads among its rocks and fastnesses. The innumerable basins bounded by high walls of lava offer sufficient room for camps and herds, while people as well as animals may hide in the craters of extinct volcanoes. Defense is simple because the aggressor who rides upon a camel or a horse must wind his way between masses of lava by narrow paths which the defender may easily block by dislodging boulders from the heights. The region was in antiquity and still is today the resort of breeders of goats and sheep and even of the husbandmen of the neighboring settlements whenever they are menaced by the Government or by the Bedouins, the breeders of camels. Neither regular army nor camelry have ever even tried to dislodge nomads from these lairs. Since they know that such an attempt would merely invite casualties, they usually seize upon all the wells outside the region and wait until hunger and thirst compel the fugitives to sue for mercy. Not a single spring or well is to be found in the entire region of Tlûl al-ʿIjâṯ. Rain water kept in a few natural and artificial receptacles must fail but the sooner the more men and animals depend upon it. The Assyrian accounts of the range of Ḫukruna thus harmonize with the peculiarities of the volcanic region of Tlûl al-ʿIjâṯ. Perhaps even the name Ḫukruna may be recognized in the names of the volcanoes ʿÂḳer and Aḳren. The second is a landmark for the entire region.

At Ḫulḫuliti on the boundary of this region Abijate camped with the camel riders dispatched as reinforcement by the Nabaitai. Delitzsch, *Wo lag das Paradies?* (1881), p. 299, identifies Ḫulḫuliti with the settlement of Ḫulḫula situated southeast of Damascus, in full conformity with our supposition that Ḫukruna is identical with Tlûl al-ʿIjâṯ.

The camels of the riders headed by Abijate were not accustomed to the volcanic region, having come from deserts of sand. Abijate was therefore forced to remain on the borders where he could perhaps defend important watering places. His legions, however, were routed and he and his brother Aiammu captured. The Assyrian army did not venture into the volcanic region of Ḫukruna (Tlûl al-ʿIjâṯ), having satisfied itself by seizing upon all of the watering places at its edge. The fugitives among the rocks were tortured by thirst. They opened the camels' paunches and drank the liquid they found within. Many died and the survivers surrendered. The soldiers drove the men, women, donkeys, camels, cows, and sheep in great numbers to Assyria (Rassam Cylinder [*loc. cit.*], col. 9, ll. 27—89; British Museum Tablet K 2802 [*loc. cit.*], col 3, ll. 1—23; Streck, *op. cit.*, pp. 74—78, 198—200).

Uaite', the king of the Ḳedar, who did not seek covert in the Ḫukruna range, remaining with his fighters in the desert, had been threatened by his own men after the rout and, as it seems, delivered into the hands of Asurbanipal. At the order of Asurbanipal a rope was pulled through his lower jawbone, and by it he was tied to the gate of the city of Nineveh. Later he was granted pardon, but he did not return into his desert homeland (Rassam Cylinder [*loc. cit.*], col. 9, ll. 90—114; Streck, *op. cit.*, pp. 71ff., 199, 205).

The Ishmaelite Tribes

The Ḳedar

The accounts of the Assyrian expeditions against the Ḳedar make it easy for us to ascertain the territories in which camped the tribes of Ḳedar, Ḫarar, and Nabaitai or the Nabataeans (whom the Bible calls Nebajôt). According to Genesis 25: 13 the Ḳedar, Ḫarar, and Nebajôt belonged to the Ishmaelites. Most frequent mention is made of the Ḳedar. According to Isaiah 21: 16 f. they were a powerful tribe with many archers, yet their power was broken within a single year, and those of their archers that survived were negligible. According to Isaiah 42: 11 the desert and its settlements and the camps in which the Ḳedar dwelt were to resound with cries of mirth, while the inhabitants of the rocks were to rejoice and give vent to their exultation upon the mountain tops. —

The words of Isaiah mean that the Ḳedar dwelt in the desert, in settlements, in camps, among rocks, and upon high mountains. This is confirmed by the fact that their dwellings were in Palmyrena and south-east of Damascus. The Bible calls their dwellings *ḥaṣôr* (pl. *ḥaṣerîm*), which implies strong, permanent buildings as well as movable camps. The Aramaic word *ḥêrtâ* (Arabic *ḥîra*) conveys the same meaning. It may designate a strongly built camp or a movable camp of tents. According to the majority of reports the Ḳedar were breeders of goats and sheep and were also engaged partly in tillage, to which end they raised cattle and asses. They inhabited strong settlements. Whenever threatened by danger they sought covert with their flocks and chattels among the rocks in the mountains of their territory. They posted guards upon the highest peaks, who exultantly informed them when the peril had passed.

Jeremiah 49: 28—33 also mentions the danger threatening the Ḳedar and all the kingdoms of the *ḥaṣôr* dwellings from Nebuchadnezzar, the king of Babylon. It would therefore appear that the Ḳedar and the rest of the nomads (Arabs) actively participated in the rebellion against Nebuchadnezzar (604—561 B. C.).

The Prophet warns the Ḳedar and the Bene Ḳedem, predicting that they will be subdued and their tents, sheep, implements, and camels captured. He exhorts the *ḥaṣôr* dwellers to flee and to conceal themselves in the basins, for the *ḥaṣôr* camps themselves would become but the home of jackals. —

The kingdoms of the *ḥaṣôr* were the territories of Arabian chiefs dwelling in camps composed of tents. In Aramaic they are called the kings of *ḥêrtâ* and in Greek the kings of *paremboles* (encampments). Because the raisers of sheep and goats camp annually at the same place, the wild animals quit such a neighborhood. If jackals appear in a once habitable location, their presence indicates that the nomads have either been annihilated or dislodged. The admonition to conceal themselves in the basins refers to the habits of nomads camping at the edge of a volcanic region. When they are endangered, they seek with their herds basins enclosed in high masses of lava; here they block off all passes giving access to their line of retreat and from the lava walls easily repel attack; for the assailants, especially if they come from the settled region or from the sand desert, cannot advance across the lava.

The Bene Ḳedem, the inhabitants of the east, were either raisers of camels or the Ḳedma who, according to Genesis 25: 15, were Ishmaelites and therefore were related to the Ḳedar. These Ḳedma (Arabic Šerḳijje) are perhaps identical with the classic Saracens. According to Stephen of Byzantium, *Ethnica* (Meineke), Vol. 1, p. 556, the Sarakenoi camped east of the Nabataeans; hence we must seek their territory south of the Ḥawrân, east of the northern part of the depression of Sirḥân, which, under the name Syrmaion Pedion (*ibid.*, p. 593), formed the eastern Nabataean frontier. Thus we arrive within the closest proximity of the territory of the Ḳedar.

According to Isaiah 60: 7 the Ḳedar and the Nebajôt possessed large flocks of goats and sheep. According to Ezekiel 27: 21 all the Ḳedar chiefs who engaged in the trade of rams, wethers, and bucks were dependent upon traders from Tyre. Jeremiah 2: 10 f. pleads with the Israelites, telling them to pass over the shore of Kittîm and to send unto Ḳedar in order to see whether any nation can change its gods. — The phrasing of this passage is intended to suggest an antithesis. Because the shore of Kittîm was situated west of the Israelites, we must seek the Ḳedar east of the Israelites. This agrees fully with the actual geography, as the Ḳedar and the tribes affiliated with them were the nearest neighbors of the Israelites on the east.

The Hagar

Of the other Ishmaelite tribes neighbors of Israel on the east, we know of the Hagar, Jeṭûr, Nafîš, and Nôdab as well as the Ḳedar.

The Hagar tribe is mentioned in the latest books of the Old Testament. It is not possible exactly to determine whether they were a separate tribe or whether the name is merely another appellation for the nomads or Ishmaelites. 1 Chronicles 27: 30 f. relates that the herds of David's camels were watched by the Ishmaelite Obil and the herds of goats and sheep by the Hagarite Jazîz. Here some distinction between Ishmael and Hagar would seem to have been drawn. However, the Ishmaelites comprised various tribes and, according to the Bible, all of these tribes derived their origin from Hagar, Abraham's concubine. It seems probable that the Hagarites were those Ishmaelite tribes which camped near the settled regions and which were engaged in the raising of goats and sheep, while the Ishmaelites proper were raisers of camels and dwelt in the inner desert for many months of the year.

This distinction is supported by 1 Chronicles 5: 10, where it is said that in Saul's time Reuben waged war with Hagar and seized his camps along the entire eastern boundary of Gilead. In the eighteenth and nineteenth verses an account is given of the tribes of Reuben and Gad, allied with half of the Manases tribe, which was warring with the tribes of Hagar, Jeṭûr, Nafîš, and Nôdab. But immediately following, the twentieth and the subsequent verses mention only the Hagar, telling that they were attacked and lost 50,000 camels, 250,000 head of sheep, 2000 donkeys, and 100,000 men and that they lived in camps until the time of their capture. From the context it may be surmised that Hagar was the general name of the tribes of Jeṭûr, Nafîš, and Nôdab. Jeṭûr is one of the names of the Ishmaelite tribes. There is no mention elsewhere of the Nafîš and

Nôdab, though it is probable that they were lesser Ishmaelite tribes or clans, for the entire eastern border of Israel had been inhabited by Ishmael's descendants. These Hagar engaged chiefly in the raising of sheep and expelled those tribes of Israel which had settled east of Jordan. Psalms 83 : 7 f. decries the alliance against Israel of the tents of Edom, Ishmael, Moab, Hagar, Gebal, Ammon, and Amalek. According to other accounts (1 Chron. 4 : 43) the Amalekites were annihilated in the time of the Judaic king Hezekiah (727—699 B. C.), many hundred years before the term "Gebal" was first applied (as in the centuries just before and long after Christ) to the tribes and clans dwelling in northern Edom and in most of Moab. The composer of this psalm names tribes old and new without regard to chronological or topographical order. Therefore we cannot infer even from this authority that the Ishmaelites differed from the Hagar. We seek the camp sites of the Nafîš and the Nôdab in the southwestern part of the Ḥawrân, while the territory of the Jeṭûr tribe (Iturea) we know to have been in the northwestern Ḥawrân.

The Nabaitai

All accounts indicate that the Assyrian Nabaitai were identical with the Biblical Nebajôt. The latter also issued from Ishmael and were the strongest of his tribes (Gen. 25: 13). According to Genesis 28 : 9; 36 : 2 f. Esau took to wife a daughter of Ishmael and a sister of Nebajôt. This relates the Nebajôt to the Edomites (descendants of Esau). As they are also related to the Ḳedar and aided the Ḳedar, we must follow up the hint by looking for their habitations between the Edomite and the Ḳedar territory. Assyrian accounts place the Nabaitai tribe in the southern part of the depression of Sirḥân and in the desert which spreads to the south. This situation fully confirms the Biblical accounts, according to which their territory spread east of Edom, upon which it bordered, and south of the pastures of the Ḳedar which reached to Adumu (Dûmat al-Ǧandal). Pliny, *Nat. hist.*, V, 65, sought the Nabatei in the neighborhood of the Cedrei, our Ḳedar. Because they camped away from the roads over which the Assyrian armies used to march, they could uphold their independence longer than their allies. As yet we lack a single Assyrian account to testify that the Assyrian army marched from Adumu westward to Edom, or that it entered the desert from Edom and thus got into the territory of the Nabaitai.

The territory of the Nebajôt was pierced by three important trade roads: one led from the Persian Gulf by way of Adumu northwest to Damascus; one led to the west in the direction of Gaza and Egypt; one led northwest from the oasis of Tejma. Thus the Nebajôt were in constant connection with trade caravans, probably leasing camels to them. They were also engaged in trade upon their own account and pressed over the transport roads in the east toward the Persian Gulf and in the west toward Edom, which they bordered on and were gradually subjugating.

Situation of the Ishmaelite Tribes

The extent of the region in which the Ishmael tribes camped may be determined by reference to the Assyrian accounts. The borderland between Egypt and Palestine belonged to the Abdeêl (Idiba'il) tribe.

In the plains enclosing northwestern Babylonia the inhabitants of the oasis of Dûma (Adumu) held sway. The southern boundary of the land of Ishmael's descendants was formed by the oasis of Adumu, while the northern boundary was formed by the mountain range which extends northwest of Palmyra and which was the habitation of the tribe of Ḫarar (Ḫurarîna). The Ishmaelites therefore held sway over the Šûr district along the Egyptian border. They controlled the roads leading across northern and northwestern Palmyrena. They bordered in the south and southeast on the districts of Ḥawîla (Gen. 25: 18). Ḥawîla included the Nefûd desert and the plains northeastward of this desert as far as the Euphrates near Babylon and was identical with a part of the Arabia Felix referred to in the classics.

The original camps of the Ishmaelites were, according to Genesis 21: 21, in the steppe of Pârân, i. e. in the rift valley of al-ʿAraba and the adjacent Sinai peninsula. This central location of Pârân, which formed the eastern confines of Egyptian influence, fully agrees with the later expansion of the Ishmaelites eastward as well as westward.

In the west, between Palestine and Egypt — hence in the Šûr district — camped the Abdeêl; east and southeast of Beersheba the Mibsam and the Mišmaʿ; south of the Ḥawrân and east of Moab, the Massaʾ. South of the Massaʾ and east of Edom the pastures of the Nebajôt extended to the oasis of Dûma. The inhabitants of this oasis controlled the trade roads leading north-northeast to Babylon. North of Dûma and east of the depression of Sirḥân camped the Ḳedma Bedouins, or Bene Ḳedem, whose pastures extended to the Euphrates west of Babylon. The southwestern fringe of the Ḥawrân belonged to the Nafîš. The Jeṭûr probably camped and dwelt northwest of the Ḥawrân. The Ḥarar (not Ḥadad) had their center in northeastern Palmyrena, while the Ḳedar tribe held the volcanic region east and northeast of the Ḥawrân and the steppes of southern Palmyrena as far as the Euphrates.

According to the Hebrew text of Genesis 25: 15 the Têma also were descended from Ishmael; the Greek text, however, substituted for the Têma the Taiman tribe, which, according to other Biblical records, inhabited the eastern part of northern Edom. To me it seems that the Greek has preserved the original spelling both in the enumeration of Ishmael's descendants and in that of the sons of Abraham by Ketura. Between Saba and Daidan the Greek text places Taiman (in the accusative), whereas in the Hebrew version Têma is missing. The position of the oases and the camps of the Saba and the Daidan would lead us to expect that the inhabitants of the oasis of Tejma ought to belong among them; that is, among the descendants of Abraham by Ketura and not among the sons of Ishmael. In consideration of this relationship, therefore, Genesis 25: 15 should be read Têman, according to the Greek, and not Têma. Because Têman dwelt and camped with the Edomites, reference is made to him in Genesis 36: 11 as the descendant of Edom, just as the Mibsam and the Mišmaʿ for similar reasons, are classified among the descendants of both Ishmael and Simeon.

The descendants of Ishmael surrounded their relatives of Israel on the south, east, and northeast; as Genesis 16: 12 expresses it, they have sat upon their nape; they plundered in the settled region and scampered into the desert like wild asses.

APPENDIX II

THE BENE ḲEDEM

The Bible never identifies the Arabs with the Bene Ḳedem. In modern Arabia the term Arab denotes all who live under tents of black goat hair, therefore all nomads regardless of the location of their camps or of their occupation. Those Arabs who raise camels and dwell either constantly or at least half a year in the inner desert are called Bedw or Šerḳijje. The latter word is derived from *šerḳ*, the term applied to the inner desert in central Arabia. Whoever marches through this region, whether he goes west, or east, or south, is referred to as *šarraḳ, tašrîž* (going into the inner desert).

From the word *šerḳ* in the sense of the inner desert is derived the classical name Sarakenoi, or Saraceni, just as the Biblical Bene Ḳedem is derived from *ḳedem*. The Hebrew *ḳedem* refers to exactly the same region as does the Arabic *šerḳ*. "Bene Ḳedem" is therefore identical with "aš-Šerḳijje" or, as modern usage has it, "al-Bedw." This primitive significance of *ḳedem*, or Bene Ḳedem, is evident in many Biblical records.

Genesis 29: 1 tells how Jacob came on his way from Betel to the land of the Bene Ḳedem and thence to Harran. As the situation of Betel and Harran is known to us it follows that we must look for the land of the Bene Ḳedem in the southern half of the ancient Palmyrena.

To this location we are also led by the statement in Numbers 23: 7 that Balak, a Moabite king, brought the seer Bileam from Aram out of the Ḳedem mountains. On his way from his homeland to Moab it is to be expected that Bileam would have taken the shortest route, or that which lay through Palmyrena, and would have crossed the mountain range stretching from Damascus northeast to the Euphrates. The Bible does not state that the mountain range of Seʿîr, which belonged to the Edomites, was at any time called the range of Ḳedem. We cannot therefore assume that Bileam came from Edom and not from Aram.

The Bene Ḳedem are known also to have been east of Jordan. In Judges 6: 3 we read that the Bene Ḳedem, together with the Madianites and the Amalekites, were accustomed to enter Palestine by crossing the Jordan. According to Judges 6: 33 they encamped in the plain of Jezreel; they had many camels (*ibid.*, 7: 12) and after they were routed by Gideon fled from Palestine across the Jordan and did not encamp until they reached Ḳarḳor (*ibid.*, 8: 10).

These Bene Ḳedem were various Ishmaelite tribes or clans camping in the desert east of Moab and Ammon. They were allied with the Madianites, who used to transport to Phoenicia and Syria upon their own camels the merchandise of south Arabian traders. The route of the Madianites lay along the boundaries of the Bene Ḳedem, from whom they might have leased camels and whose protection they sought. Ḳarḳor, where the defeated Bene Ḳedem encamped for an extended period, I identify with the important watering places of Ḳarḳar or Ḳerâḳer (Ḳerâžer) situated in the depression of Sirḥân 180 kilometers southeast of ʿAmmân, at the intersection of two important transport roads (see my *The Northern Ḥeǧâz*, p. 284).

The Bene Ḳedem did not foresee that Gideon would pursue them so far beyond the Israelite frontiers, hence they did not station watches and laid themselves open to surprise and rout. Should the identification of Ḳarḳor with Ḳarḳar or Ḳerâḳer be correct, it is obvious that the Bene Ḳedem in reality must have been Bedouins.

Jeremiah 49: 29—33 also mentions the Bene Ḳedem east of Jordan, in the vicinity of the Ḥawrân, where there had been a center of the Ḳedar. He denounces the Ḳedar and the kingdoms of the *ḥaṣôr* camps and exhorts the army of Nebuchadnezzar, king of Babylon, to march out against the Ḳedar, to defeat the Bene Ḳedem, to take their tents, their sheep, their camels, and all their implements, and to pronounce unto them: "Let there be terror on every side!" He advises the Ḳedar and the Bene Ḳedem to flee, to run fast, and warns the inhabitants of the *ḥaṣôr* camps to conceal themselves, for Nebuchadnezzar, king of Babylon, had decided to take them by storm. The seer demands that the soldiers of Nebuchadnezzar march out against a tranquil people, a people who live in safety, who live in seclusion, who have neither doors nor bolts. He warns that their camels shall be a booty, that their many herds shall be a prey, that Jehovah shall disperse them in all directions, and that upon those whose heads are partly shaved he shall heap destruction from all sides so that none but jackals shall dwell in the *ḥaṣôr* camps.—

This admonition of Jeremiah concerns on the one hand the Ḳedar and on the other the kingdoms of the *ḥaṣôr* camps, which it does not distinguish from the Bene Ḳedem. We may therefore distinguish between the Ḳedar and the Bene Ḳedem and surmise that the latter were identical with the inhabitants of the *ḥaṣôr* dwellings. As we know from the Assyrian accounts, the Ḳedar dwelt in settlements and engaged mainly in the raising of sheep and goats. The Bene Ḳedem in this instance likewise were probably raisers of camels, Bedw or Bedouins. *Ḥaṣôr* does not seem to have been a surname, as there is no mention of the word in that sense in the Hebrew; nor did the Greek read it as a surname. We have already seen (see above, p. 490) that *ḥaṣôr* is the equivalent of the later Aramaic *ḥêrtâ* and Arabic *ḥîra*, either a permanent or a movable Bedouin camp; this is supported by the thirty-first verse, according to which the inhabitants of the *ḥaṣôr* are said to have had neither doors nor bolts and to have lived in seclusion. This must have meant in a camp on the steppe. The booty of Nebuchadnezzar, consisting of sheep, camels, tent covers, and various implements, likewise indicates that their habitations were nomads' dwellings. According to the thirtieth verse they are warned to flee and conceal themselves in basins. In the Ḥawrân and its vicinity there are deep basins (*mačmen*, pl. *mečâmen*; hiding place) bounded on all sides by high cliffs of basalt and lava. The local dwellers take refuge in such basins even today and have certainly found refuge in them for thousands of years. By blocking the laboriously constructed entrances they are absolutely safe and can repulse an enemy with little difficulty.

Southeast of the Ḥawrân probably camped the Bene Ḳedem who, according to Ezekiel 25: 4, were to erect in the devastated land of

Ammon their enclosed stables and their dwellings, *ṭîrôtêhem* and *miškenêhem*. The word *ṭîrôt* is not identical with *miškenîm*. *Ṭâr* or *ṭejrân* in Arabic of the inner desert denotes a moderately high slope rising to a flat crest and likewise a small wall enclosing the place where herds sleep at night. The same meaning is conveyed by the Hebrew *ṭîrôt*, which I translate "enclosed stables."

Ezekiel 46: 23 relates that in each corner of the large temple in Jerusalem there was a small yard, around which was a *ṭîrôt* or *ṭûr* — a low wall with a fireplace built into it. It is evident that *ṭîrôt* or *ṭûr* signifies a low wall enclosing a vacant space or yard. That the walls were not high is indicated by the fact that they contained fireplaces for the cooks to prepare meals. These *ṭîrôtêhem* were not higher than 120 centimeters. When nomads enclosed vacant spaces by such walls they did it merely to afford protection to their herds of goats, sheep, and camels. When the entrance was closed the goats, the sheep, and the young camels could not run out, while the old camels, which in stable always have both legs or at least one front leg tied, could not step over. Likewise jackals and wolves, the common beasts of prey, avoid such walls for fear that in leaping over they might fall into a hole or trap.

The Israelites burned all the Madianite *ʿarêhem* and *ṭîrôtâm* (Num. 31: 10). It is explicitly said of *ʿarêhem* that the Madianites lived by them; while *ṭîrôtâm* denotes merely stables guarded by herdsmen and erected far from settlements, as is the case today whenever a herd does not pass the night within a camp, but alone, in *manda* (camp far from water).

In Psalms 69: 26 the poet also distinguishes between stables and tents, praying that empty might be the stables (*ṭîrôtâm*), of his adversaries and that none might dwell in their tents (*oholêhem*). 1 Chronicles 6: 39 records the descendants of Aaron according to their residences and their stables, that is, according to their pastures (*môšebôtâm le-ṭîrôtâm*).

In the Song of Solomon 8: 9 the brothers wish to shield their sister from a barbarous bridegroom and declare that were she a wall they would build around her a breastwork (*ṭîrat*) of silver, and that were she an opening (an open door) they would close her in with boards of cedar. Even here *ṭîrat* (correctly *ṭîrôt*) can signify nothing but a low stone wall which could prevent the youth from having access to the girl, just as cedar boards could prevent his entrance by an open door or opening.

Such walls enclosing the camp site of herds, and thus forming stables, the Bene Ḳedem were to erect in the devastated land of Ammon and perhaps also in Moab, which, according to Ezekiel 25: 10, had also fallen to them.

Job (1: 3) is alleged to have been the most powerful of all the Bene Ḳedem, although, as a matter of fact, he did not belong to them, being a settler (see *The Northern Ḥeǧâz*, p. 248). He owned many settlements and large herds, which proves that many clans were dependent upon him and testifies to the respect the Bene Ḳedem bore him, just as today the ʿAneze or Šammar Bedouins respect the settler Eben Saʿûd. Job's herdsmen camped with the Bene Ḳedem. As we seek Job's homeland, the district of ʿÛṣ, southeast of the Dead Sea, the Bene Ḳedem, whom Job excelled, must likewise have camped southeast of the Dead Sea and east of Edom.

The theory that the Bene Ḳedem also dwelt in the eastern half of the Sinai peninsula can be supported only by Isaiah 11: 14 f., where the Jews, having become reconciled with God, are to smite the Philistines, to plunder the Bene Ḳedem, and to subjugate the Edomites and the Moabites. The Bene Ḳedem are named here between the Philistines and the Edomites. As the regions of the Philistines and the Edomites are known to us, we might seek the Bene Ḳedem between them. However, these Bene Ḳedem might easily have been the allies of the Philistines or the Edomites camping either in the south or east of Edom. From various Biblical accounts it is known that the nomads whose habitations we seek south of Edom, southeast of the port of Elath, were aiding the Philistines and the Edomites as well (see *The Northern Ḥeǧâz*, p. 274).

In Genesis 25: 6 there is no mention of the Bene Ḳedem on the Sinai peninsula, where it is asserted that the sons of Abraham born not in wedlock emigrated during his lifetime into the land of Ḳedem. Abraham, with his sons by Keturah and his descendants by Hagar, camped first in the eastern half of the Sinai peninsula, the Hagarites especially in Pârân. The sons by Keturah must all have left the Sinai peninsula, for from the Biblical and Assyrian accounts we cannot prove that any one of them had remained there. On the other hand, some Ishmaelite (Hagarite) clans did remain there. However, bearing in mind that a great majority of the descendants of Abraham by his concubines emigrated from the Sinai peninsula to the territories south, east, and northeast of Edom, we must likewise seek the land of Ḳedem in those regions.

According to Genesis 10: 30 the sons of Joḳtan (among them Ḥawîla) inhabited the region from Mešâʾ up to the range of Ḳedem on the road to Sefar. — We cannot determine exactly the situation of this Ḳedem range, for Sefar is not mentioned elsewhere in the Holy Writ.

The Bene Ḳedem were famous for their wisdom. Only the knowledge of Solomon towered above theirs (1 Kings 5: 10). — Therefore the homeland of the Wise Men who followed the star to Jerusalem (Matthew 2: 1 f.) may be sought in the Biblical East, in Ḳedem, or in the Arabian desert among the wise Bene Ḳedem.

APPENDIX III

ARABIA DESERTA ACCORDING TO THE CLASSICAL AUTHORS

Various Classical Accounts

Many Greek writers occupied themselves intensively with Arabia. This is quite comprehensible, for Arabia was of the utmost importance to the commercial city of Alexandria. The Alexandrians recorded information about its shores and inland districts. In the very earliest accounts Arabia was divided into several main divisions, of which the most prominent were Arabia Deserta (or Arabia Eremos, in Greek) and Arabia Felix (or Arabia Eudaimon, in Greek). (For the sake of uniformity the

Latin terms Arabia Deserta and Arabia Felix only are used in the following pages. Classical place names are also given in the Latin rather than transliterated from the Greek forms.)

Northern, Western, and Southern Boundaries

Eratosthenes (Strabo, *Geography*, XVI, 4: 2) states that the distance from Heroöpolis at the end of the Arabian Gulf to Babylon by way of the city of Petra was 5600 stades. This line runs east into the summer sunrise, penetrating the territories of three Arabian nations: the Nabataei, the Chaulotaei, and the Agraei. South of these Arabia Felix extends for 12,000 stades to the Atlantic Ocean. The inhabitants of Arabia are neighbors of the Syrians and the Jews and engage in similar tilling of the soil. Within the boundary stretches a sandy region of but little fertility, supporting a sparse growth of palms, acacias, and tamarisks. Wells are met infrequently, as in Gedrosia. The region is the possession of the Scenitae, Arabs whose occupation is the breeding of camels.—

Eratosthenes' account of the northern boundary of Arabia Felix is but general, yet it is of the utmost importance. The boundary is represented as a line leading from Heroöpolis (near the present Suez), east-northeast to Babylonia. Just as the city of Petra did not actually stand on the boundary of Arabia Felix, so this boundary did not extend to Babylon itself. Since the Nabataeans living at Petra, their capital, ruled the western part of the domain enclosed by this boundary, the tribe of Chaulotaei is to be sought to the east of them and the Agraei east of the Chaulotaei.

The Agraei might have been masters of the mercantile centers either at Hagra or Gerrha. The classic Hagra (the present al-Ḥeǧr) is situated south-southeast of Petra. Gerrha (the Arabic Ǧerʿa) was situated near the medieval city of Haǧar in the vicinity of the oasis of al-Hufhûf. Since, in conformity with the context, the Agraei of Eratosthenes lived to the east of the Nabataeans, they are to be recognized as the masters of this center and to be identified with the inhabitants of the city of Gerrha. Having control over the trade roads converging from the southeast and west on Babylonia, they must also have ruled the entire western bank of the Euphrates, and their influence must have extended to Babylon, beyond the confines of Arabia Felix proper. The masters of the oasis of Haǧar exercised in the Middle Ages and still possess a certain dominion over all the tribes camping west of the Euphrates between al-Kûfa and the Persian Gulf.

The tribe of Chaulotaei had its camps between the Agraei on the east and the Nabataeans on the west. Its center might have been the oasis of Dûmat al-Ǧandal, and it possessed the great desert of the Nefûd with, perhaps, the oases near the Eǧa' and Salma' ranges.

The Arabian inhabitants who engaged in tillage dwelt, according to Eratosthenes, east of the cities of Chalcis and Emessa, therefore in Palmyrena and in the narrow zone between Damascus and the port of Aela. This zone formed the center of the Nabataean domain and of the later Roman provinces of Arabia and of Palaestina Tertia. South of Palmyrena and east of the Nabataean domain dwelt nomads whose names Eratosthenes does not enumerate, calling them collectively Scenitae.

Diodorus, *Bibl. hist.*, II, 54, calls Arabia Felix that part of Arabia which trends southward. In the interior of Arabia dwell nomadic Arabs who pastured large herds on the limitless plains. Between this land and Arabia Felix spreads the waterless desert (*eremos*). The western part of Arabia consists of boundless sandy plains where travelers guide themselves solely by the pole star. In that part of Arabia which borders Syria live husbandmen and merchants who furnish by their useful barter the necessities of both countries. —

It is evident that Diodorus had in mind Palmyrene Arabia in the northeast and Nabataean Arabia stretching along the borders of Syria from Damascus in the north to the port of Aela in the south. In both of these main divisions husbandmen and merchants flourished. South of Palmyrena and east of the land of the Nabataeans spreads, according to Diodorus, Arabia Deserta and south of it Arabia Felix. Arabs with herds roam in the interior of the latter.

Strabo, *Geography*, XVI, 2: 2, writes that Syria is bounded on the east by the Euphrates and by the Scenitan Arabs and on the south by Arabia Felix and Egypt. Syria extends from the Euphrates as far as Palmyrena, south of which it borders the desert, across which wander Arabs who dwell in tents. Along the Gulf of Aela Syria borders on Arabia Felix, west of which lies Egypt.

In another place (Strabo, *op. cit.*, XVI, 3: 1) it is recorded that the part of Arabia which spreads between Coele-Syria and Mesopotamia near the Euphrates belongs to the Scenitan Arabs, who have founded small principalities there. They live in unfruitful lands, sterile because unwatered. Hence they seldom engage in tillage, owning, instead, herds of domestic animals, especially camels. Beyond them lie many deserts. The country stretching still farther to the south belongs to the inhabitants of Arabia Felix. The northern side of Arabia is, therefore, formed by the desert (*eremos*), the eastern by the Persian Gulf, the western by the Arabian Gulf, and the southern by the Great Sea which, rolling between both the gulfs, is known as the Red Sea. —

The small Arabian principalities should be sought in the corner known to us as Palmyrena, between the present cities of Aleppo on the north, Ḥama and Ḥomṣ on the west, and the Euphrates on the east. South and southeast of these principalities spreads, according to Strabo, Arabia Deserta, beyond which to the south lies Arabia Felix, bounded on the south by the Red Sea (Indian Ocean), on the west by the Arabian Sea (Red Sea), and on the east by the Persian Gulf.

Pliny, *Nat. hist.*, VI, 142 f., states that Arabia begins at the Amanus range and assumes the form of a peninsula spreading between two seas, the Red and the Persian. It is alleged to be widest in the north between the cities of Heroum and Charax. Also according to Pliny (*op. cit.*, V, 65) Arabia stretches beyond the Pelusiac branch of the Nile to the Red Sea and to Beata, where spices and scents abound. —

Pliny thus includes as Arabian the entire northern part of Syria up to the Amanus mountains north of Antioch, and also the entire Sinai peninsula as far west as the Pelusiac branch of the Nile.

The anonymous *Geographiae expositio compendiaria* (Müller), p. 499, asserts that beyond Judea as far as the end of the Arabian Gulf spreads Arabia Petraea. The territory between the nations of Arabia Petraea and the western shore of the Persian Gulf is termed Deserta and is inhabited by Arabian tribes. The country converging with Arabia Deserta and Arabia Petraea to the south and spreading between the Persian Gulf and the Arabian Gulf of the Red Sea is called Arabia Felix.

Eastern and Northeastern Boundaries

All of these accounts are so general, that not even the boundary of Arabia Deserta with the Persian Gulf need be taken literally.

According to Ptolemy, *Geography*, V, 19, the country northwest of Babylonia and west of the Euphrates is called Auranitis. South of Auranitis Arabia Deserta borders the Chaldean territory, within which were the cities of Barsipa and Orchoë (see also Strabo, *Geography*, XVI, 1: 6).

Auranitis is the vicinity of the Wâdi Ḥawrân which joins the Euphrates about 250 kilometers northwest of Babylon. Barsipa is identical with al-Biris of today. Hence it may be surmised that according to Ptolemy Arabia Deserta did not reach the Persian Gulf proper, but merely to the northern fringe of the Chaldean swamps, at the settlement of Orchoë (now Warka; lat. 31° 15′ N.; long. 45° 40′ E.). The Chaldean swamps, called Amardocaea by Ptolemy, begin south of Warka.

Marcianus of Heraclea, *Periplus* (Müller), p. 526, writes that Arabia Felix is bounded by Arabia Petraea, Arabia Deserta, the Persian Gulf, and the mouth of the river Tigris.

The boundary lines between Arabia Deserta and Arabia Felix are not defined accurately. Eratosthenes seeks the boundary on the line from Suez east-northeast through the ruins of the city of Petra toward Babylon. Strabo, *Geography*, XVI, 4: 1, points in the same direction, arguing that Arabia begins in the district of Maecena. Beyond Maecena lies on the one side the desert (*eremos*) of the Arabs, on the other the Chaldean swamps which are swelled by the overflow of the Euphrates and beyond which lies the Persian Sea. Although the climate of the latter country is detrimental to health, fogs and rain are frequent and the heat is intense, fruits and even vines grow in the swamps if planted in baskets woven of rushes and filled with sufficient earth. The baskets are frequently displaced by the water and it then becomes necessary to push them back into place with oars.—

Strabo includes the Maecena region in Arabia. According to the context his Maecena spreads along the Persian Gulf in Babylonia near the mouths of the rivers Euphrates and Tigris. "Maikene" is an erroneous transcription of "Maisene." The classical Maesena is situated just where Strabo places his Maecena. According to Strabo, the Arabian country of Maecena was bounded on the northwest by the Arabian desert (Arabia Deserta) and on the southwest by the Chaldean swamps. As the latter begin about sixty kilometers south or southwest of Babylon, Arabia Deserta must have reached only to the former city of al-Ḥîra and present an-Neǧef. Hence the Chaldean swamps spreading to the southeast were regarded as a part of Arabia Felix. This division is supported by Aristobulus (Strabo, *op. cit.*, XVI, 1: 11) and Arrian (*Anabasis*, VII, 21), who relate that Alexander covered eight hundred stades from Babylon down the Euphrates and advanced through the Pallacotas canal into the splendid lands of the Arabs. This Pallacotas canal conducted water from the Euphrates into the swamps. — The splendid country mentioned must have formed a part of Arabia Felix, which Alexander sought to conquer.

Pliny, *Nat. hist.*, VI, 138, records that the district of Characene is named after the Arabian city of Charax on the inner Persian Gulf, at which Arabia Felix begins. —

Pliny regards Characene as a part of Arabia Felix. It is evident that the latter extended not only as far as the northern end of the Persian Gulf but much farther.

Chronicles of the exploits of Emperor Septimius Severus (193—211 A. D.) attest that the northeastern boundaries of Arabia Felix were fixed by classical authors in the vicinity of Babylon.

Zosimus, *Historia nova*, I, 8, relates that the Emperor Septimius Severus attacked the Scenitan Arabs and subjugated the whole of Arabia. Herodian, *Ab excessu Divi Marci*, III, 9, writes that Septimius Severus in 195 and 199 A. D. marched through the regions between the Euphrates and the Tigris and the territory of Adiabene and undertook an expedition into Arabia Felix, whence there was an export trade in various fragrant spices and other scents. Having conquered numerous settlements, it is alleged that he invaded the territory of the Atreni. Cassius Dio, *Historiae*, LXXV, 2 f. and 9, says that Septimius Severus crossed the Euphrates to enter Arabia Deserta. Severus, having ordered ships to be built on the Euphrates (198 A. D.), embarked a part of his army in them, while the other part marched along the bank and soon occupied the cities of Seleucia and Babylon. His ships had been swiftly and solidly constructed, for the forests along the Euphrates yielded him plenty of lumber. Having plundered Ctesiphon, he penetrated no farther but returned along the Tigris. —

These accounts are of much interest, because they show that the classical writers sought Arabia Felix in the vicinity of Babylon. Septimius Severus did not penetrate to the Persian Gulf, yet he is said to have invaded Arabia Felix. It is certain that he plundered Babylon, Seleucia, and Ctesiphon. Therefore it is to be expected that he made a short incursion upon the right bank of the Euphrates where there was a great transport road over which the merchants of Gerrha (Ǧerʿa) and Palmyra exported precious incense and spices to Syria and Italy. Septimius Severus perhaps plundered the commercial depots. His biographers record that he penetrated into Arabia Felix, whereas in reality he approached no farther than the district south or southwest of the present city of an-Neǧef. Having turned into the territory of the Atreni, who were masters of the commercial city of Hatra (al-Ḥaẓr) on the river aṯ-Ṯarṯâr, he humbled the Arabs dwelling in tents, the Scenitae, between the middle Euphrates and the Tigris. The forest along the Euphrates is mentioned also by the Arabic writers. Today it is called *az-zôr*. It comprises for the most part tamarisk trees and Babylonian poplars.

It is evident from these classical accounts that Arabia Deserta was inhabited by various tribes. Some writers record their proper names; others call them commonly Nomades, Scenitae, or Saraceni.

According to Strabo, *op. cit.*, XVI, 1 : 28, the Euphrates formed the boundary of Arabia Deserta. The left bank was held by the Parthians and the right bank down as far as Babylonia by the Romans and the Arabian phylarchs. Some phylarchs joined the Parthians, others the

Romans, of whom they were neighbors. The Arabs who dwelt in tents near the river Euphrates, where they engaged in the breeding of cattle, were less inclined to favor the Romans than were those who camped nearer Arabia Felix. —

The phylarchs of the Arabian tribes camping along the Euphrates derived a greater profit from the Parthians than from the Romans, for the commercial centers from which incense and aromatic spices were exported to the whole Roman world lay within the Parthian domain. The transport roads led either along the Euphrates or across the desert on either side. These routes ran through the territory of Arabian tribes which leased their camels to the traders and guaranteed their safety. The Arabs dwelling nearer Arabia Felix were, according to Strabo, the Nabataeans and the tribes dependent upon them. Neighbors of the Romans and engaging the Roman cities of the interior in commerce, they were as much devoted to them as the Arabian phylarchs were to the Parthians. Strabo did not value the Arabs highly. He writes (*op. cit.*, XVI, 4: 23; XVII, 1: 54) that they were not efficient soldiers on the land and were far worse upon the sea.

Pliny, *Nat. hist.*, VI, 125, states that by the city of Charax camps the Arabian tribe of Attala, while to the northwest camp the Scenitae and along the Euphrates as far as the wastes of Syria and Palmyrena the Nomades. Elsewhere (*ibid.*, VI, 142—145), he states that the Nomades and Scenitae live near the Chaldeans in tents made of skins. The territory of these nomads dwelling in tents extends from the Chaldean swamps toward Palmyrena in the northwest and toward the city of Petra in the west, where it adjoins the Nabataean territory. — Here, as elsewhere, Pliny uses the words "Nomades" and "Scenitae" in a way which makes it appear as if he were designating different Arabian tribes, whereas they really are general appellations denoting all nomads dwelling under tents. At places it seems that his "Scenitae" must denote the Bedouins, or Saraceni, dwelling in the inner desert. Ammianus Marcellinus, *Rerum gestarum*, XXIII, 6: 13, writes that the Scenitan Arabs were later given the name Saraceni. — It is evident that Scenitan and Saracen Arabs are general terms. Nevertheless, Ammianus is mistaken if he thinks that both are the same. All the Saraceni are Scenitae, but not all the Scenitae are Saraceni.

Marcianus of Heraclea, *Periplus* (Müller), p. 526, holds that the territory of Arabia Felix bordering with Arabia Petraea and Arabia Deserta is inhabited by Saraceni, who have various names and who possess the distant deserts. — This report is of much interest because it implies that Saraceni is a general term denoting the nomads of the inner Arabian desert. Marcianus does not give their tribal names.

Diodorus, *Bibl. hist.*, II, 50, records that carnivorous beasts, lions and panthers, are numerous in Arabia near the Syrian border. Ostriches are also found.

The Boundaries of Arabia Deserta According to Ptolemy

Ptolemy's dissertation upon Arabia Deserta is more minute (*Geography*, V, 14: 5 and 19; V, 18). According to him the northern border extends to the southwest from Alamatha — or rather from the Ford (*tifsaḥ*), Thapsacus, on the right bank of the Euphrates — toward the range of Asalmanus (or Alsalmanus; the present Ḥawrân) as far as longitude 71° 33′ E. At the eastern spurs of this range the boundary turns to the south-southwest and (here separating Arabia Deserta from Arabia Petraea) reaches (at lat. 30° 30′ N., long. 70° E.) a point where it meets the boundary separating Arabia Petraea on the north from Arabia Felix on the south. The latter boundary leaves the shore of the Red Sea at a point somewhat to the south of the port of Aela (lat. 29° N., long. 66° E.) and runs to the northeast. From the point where this boundary meets the border of Arabia Deserta, the southern boundary of Arabia Deserta, separating the latter from Arabia Felix, runs east-southeast to the Persian Gulf at latitude 29° N., longitude 79° E. On the east Arabia Deserta reaches to the river Euphrates. —

From these statements it is obvious that the boundaries of Arabia Deserta conformed with the configuration of the land. The district of al-Manâẓer forms today the limit between the arable Palmyrena and the steppes of al-Ḥamâd and al-Wudijân (Arabia Deserta). East of the Ḥawrân the western boundary of Arabia Deserta trended along the eastern base of the mountains as far south as the district of aš-Šâma, whence it proceeded across the divide between the Dead Sea and the depression of Sirḥân to the lowland of al-Ğafar and thence along the eastern base of the range of aš-Šera' (or Dusare; Stephen of Byzantium, *Ethnica* [Meineke], p. 237). Thus the western boundary, like the northern, led along the fringe of territory formerly settled. At the southeastern slope of aš-Šera' the boundary turned eastward toward the northern side of the flat-topped range of Ṭubejž al-ʿAfar and toward the northern projections of the rose-colored sand desert of the Nefûd. It followed the edge of the desert to its northeastern end. Here the natural boundary of Arabia Deserta should turn, not eastward toward the Persian Gulf, but northeast between the districts of al-Wudijân and al-Ḥeğera to the Euphrates, ending near al-Kûfa. This natural boundary corresponds with that of Ptolemy (*op. cit.*, V, 18), according to whom the boundary reached the Euphrates and the inner Persian Gulf at longitude 79° E., latitude 30° 10′ N. Ptolemy, as well as the maker of the Peutinger Table, was familiar with the main part of the gulf and with an inner gulf which joined the larger gulf by a narrow channel. According to the Peutinger Table (*Tabula Peutingeriana* [Vienna, 1888], Segm. 11) the inner gulf extended nearly to Babylon; according to Ptolemy, who erroneously placed Babylon almost four degrees too far north, it only extended to latitude 30° 10′ N. Ptolemy also placed the settlement of Iucara (or, more correctly, Ducara: Ḏu Ḳâr, the present Abu Ṛâr) on the Persian Gulf. We may infer that Ptolemy stretched the inner bay of the Persian Gulf nearly to the present an-Neğef, an inference which is confirmed by his definition of the southern boundary of Babylonia (*ibid.*, V, 19). Numerous classical writers were of the opinion that the Chaldean swamps, beginning near the present city of an-Neğef, formed only the extension of the Persian Gulf, which was also called the Maesanian Gulf (Maisanios Kolpos). With this opinion Ptolemy concurs (*ibid.*, VI, 7 : 19). Other classical writers state that the Pallacotas canal and the Chaldean swamps formed the boundary of Arabia Felix.

Arabic writers were of the same opinion. They also held that the swamps near an-Neǧef were directly connected with the Persian Gulf and that seafaring vessels could at one time pass through the channel to the city of al-Ḥîra.

According to Ptolemy, the Cauchabeni (also spelled Chauchabeni) camped in Arabia Deserta near the Euphrates. Their name coincides with that of the Beni Kawkab, or Kawâkbe, a very old Bedouin tribe whose several branches camp today either with the eastern ʿAneze on the Euphrates or with the western ʿAneze in the depression of Sirḥân. Fischer (in Müller's edition of Ptolemy's *Geography*, Vol. 1, Part 2, p. 1012) identifies Chauchabeni with the settlement of al-Ḫašâf west of Bâlis. This is absurd, for al-Ḫašâf is more than 250 kilometers from Arabia Deserta, while the root of the word "Ḫašâf" is wholly at variance with "Chauchab."

Near Syria camped the Batanaei. These in all probability are the tribes which sojourn during July and August in the Syrian district of Batanaea (the present an-Nuḳra) and spend the other months of the year in the inner desert. Even today the Weld ʿAli and the Rwala branches of the ʿAneze divide the year thus. They are called, therefore, the ʿAnezet an-Nuḳra. The spelling "Katanaioi" in Erasmus' *editio princeps* of the Greek text of Ptolemy (Basel, 1533) is accidental. Even if it were justified, these "Katanaioi" could not be identified with the Ḳhaṭân, for the latter never camped upon the Syrian boundary.

Upon the boundary of Arabia Felix dwelt the Agubeni (also Agabeni). They may have been the inhabitants of the large basin al-Ǧûba where Ptolemy's city of Dumatha stood, together with several other settlements.

East from the Agubeni, according to Ptolemy, were the Raabeni. It seems that the Raabeni were the tribe mentioned by Strabo, *Geography*, XVI, 2: 10, under the name Rambaei. It is probable that their name is preserved in the city of ar-Raḥaba (ar-Raḥba), which in the Middle Ages ruled over the central Euphrates and all of Palmyrena.

Near the Persian Gulf Ptolemy places the Orcheni and, between them and the Chauchabeni, the Ausitae. There, by the Chaldean swamps and the Persian Gulf, are also to be sought the Orcheni (belonging to the Chaldeans) mentioned by Strabo, *op. cit.*, XVI, 1: 6, in connection with the Borsippeni (see also Pliny, *Nat. hist.*, VI, 123). The Orcheni should be identified with the inhabitants of the city of Orchoë (Warka) and its vicinity. The situation of this city conforms perfectly with such an identification, for Pliny, *op. cit.*, VI, 130, seeks it on the lower Euphrates.

The Ausitae (also Aiseitae, Aisitae) camped, according to Ptolemy, west of Babylon. Their name recalls the inhabitants of Job's homeland of ʿÛṣ. Aristeas (Alexander Polyhistor, *Fragmenta* [Müller], p. 220) places the district of Ausitis in the mountains of Idumea and Arabia, hence in eastern Edom southeast of the Dead Sea, where the old name ʿÎṣ has been preserved (Musil, *Arabia Petraea*, Vol. 2, Part 1, p. 337; Part 2, p. 242). If Ptolemy's statement that they camped west of Babylon is to be considered, it may be supported by the local name al-ʿAwṣijje in the vicinity of the present settlement of ʿÂna.

Northwest from the Raabeni, Ptolemy seeks the Masani, who are called Masei by Pliny (*op. cit.*, VI, 117).

According to Ptolemy, between the Masani and the Batanaei were the Agraei (or Agrii). According to Eratosthenes (Strabo, *op. cit.*, XVI,

4: 2) a straight line drawn from Petra to Babylonia penetrates the territory of the Chaulotaei and Agraei. Accordingly the Agraei might be sought in the district of al-Ḥeǧera.

Near Babylon also camped the Marteni (or Martini), the Mandani of Pliny (*op. cit.*, VI, 117); Pliny, however, places them in the vicinity of the city of Antiochia-Aribis, which was founded by Nicanor.

Cities and Other Localities in Arabia Deserta According to Ptolemy

Ptolemy records numerous places in Arabia Deserta.

The statement that a city or other place lies on the Euphrates facilitates its identification; but with places in the inner desert this aid is lacking, leaving us to depend solely upon names, their order, and the figures for the latitude and longitude. We may be certain that the latitudes and longitudes were not correctly observed and recorded in most cases, and from the contradictions of various manuscripts we may infer that the original figures have not been preserved unimpaired.

Ptolemy probably fixed positions in Arabia Deserta according to the testimony of nomadic merchants and leaders of caravans. The latter were familiar with the individual stations along the routes which they followed, whereas the former knew the camping places that were regularly used by the various tribes. The caravan leaders were able to state with fair accuracy the direction of routes and the distances; the nomadic merchants guessed at both approximately. According to their testimony, Ptolemy (or his predecessors) drew a map of Arabia Deserta. While at the work he often discovered that the details supplied by the various informants did not agree. It cost him much effort to adjust the apparent disparities and frequently he did not succeed. He failed, for example, near the lower Euphrates and the Persian Gulf. Ptolemy proceeded, however, to determine the latitudes and longitudes of the various points from his sketch. It is easily apparent that they seldom concurred with the facts. Ptolemy was well aware of these defects; hence he designated differently the position of a point determined astronomically and one which had merely been conjectured. While recording the individual places and their situations in his book, Ptolemy disregarded the order of the stations along the roads, preferring the astronomical positions. It is to be expected that many place names have been distorted and that others have been given in incorrect sequence. Likewise it is evident that many writers have not copied Ptolemy's original records accurately. This suffices to prove of what little value the Ptolemaic designations are. Only those few places can be determined with certainty which other writers also have named and located. Beyond these it is necessary to be content with surmise.

If we inspect the accounts of the interior more closely, we shall find that Ptolemy does not record a single settlement within the immense northeastern corner of Arabia between latitude 33° and latitude 35° 5′ N., but that he piles name upon name in the southeast, protracting the map in contradiction to the true outlines of the country in order that he may reach the outer Persian Gulf. At the same time he puts names into this southeastern corner that do not belong there. While he places no settlement between latitude 33° 5′ and latitude 35° 5′ N. (for Rhegana instead of 33° 20′ the text should read 32°20′), there are two on the thirty-second parallel and three between latitude 32° and latitude 33°; three between latitude 31° and latitude 32°; ten between latitude 30° and latitude 31°, and six between latitude 29° and latitude 30°. And yet there used to lead and still lead through the northern part of Arabia Deserta important commercial roads from Syria (Phoenicia) to the Euphrates, with which Ptolemy's informants were surely familiar. In any case, however, it is evident that in inner Arabia there were no *poleis* or true cities (except for Dûma), but rather villages, camp sites, and watering places.

Blau (*Arabien* [1869], p. 574) sought to identify Barathena with the Arabian watering place Baradân, which, however, he erroneously looked for in the proximity of the Ḥawrân range (Asalmanus mons). Spring water wells now flow at a place called Bradân, but this is more than five hundred kilometers southeast of the Ḥawrân and about sixty kilometers west of the Euphrates, whereas Ptolemy's Barathena was on the eastern boundary of the Ḥawrân. The region of the Arabian Baradân according to Ptolemy was inhabited by the Marteni, whose name makes it justifiable for us to connect them with Barathena. The *m* is interchanged in the dialect with the *b*, and *d* is frequently rewritten as *th*. The name Barathena is the equivalent of Berṯen, that being the name of a hill northeast of Dûmat al-Ǧandalijje; still, even the hill stands far from the range of the Ḥawrân. Perhaps Barathena is identical with the rain pond and volcano of al-Mḥarûṭa, past which leads an important transport road near the boundary of Arabia Deserta.

Saue (*var.*, Saua, Gaue) is certainly equivalent to the wells of Suwa' of Arabic writers, the present Swa' at the Sabʿ Bijâr north of al-Mḥarûṭa. Fischer, *op. cit.*, p. 1015, connects Saua with Saf, or as-Safa, but this is unjustifiable since there are no such places in Arabia Deserta.

Choce (*var.*, Coche, Choca) may be sought in the Moḳr Ǧôḥa on the road from Babylonia to Syria.

Gauara (*var.*, Cauara) I find in the basin of al-Ḳaʿara upon the commercial road from Babylonia to Damascus.

Aurana may be identical with the wells of al-Mḥejwer in Wâdi Ḥawrân on the same road.

Rhegana (*var.*, Rheganna, Rhegenna, Begana) suggests the watering places Mḳejrât ar-Rḳejje and Rḳejjân on the old road leading from the lower Euphrates to Syria.

Alata, the next place, we may seek upon the same road in the modern al-Ḫlejṭ (diminutive of al-Ḫalaṭ).

Erupa I would seek in the vicinity of the Tlejl ʿArejfân, south of the range of the Ḥawrân, where there is plenty of water. Fischer (*loc. cit.*) has in mind the lowland of ar-Ruḥbe (ar-Raḥba), but the latter is in Syria north of the Ḥawrân.

Themme, or rather Themne, is placed by Ptolemy far to the east in latitude 31°40′ N., longitude 75°E. Consequently, in determining its situation, we cannot take into account the Themanite pastures on the northeastern boundary of Edom. We are likewise unable to consider the Biblical Têma, because, according to Ptolemy, the latter was in Arabia Felix. In the eastern part of Arabia Deserta are the oases of ʿAjn at-Tamr and aṯ-Ṯmejl. We might look for Themne among them, because the dialect often interchanges the *r*, *l*, and *n*. For our purpose the most suitable would be the situation of ʿAjn at-Tamr, which is a terminal for important roads through the desert.

Luma suggests the rich pasturages at the Ḳârt Lumejma, the site of which approximately agrees with Ptolemy's account.

Thauba (*var.*, Thaua) I would identify with the wells of aṭ-Ṭûba in the valley of al-Radaf. Of course, we should expect it to be spelled with *t* instead of *th*, but the Greeks did not always transcribe the barbarous Arabian names correctly. To identify Thaua with "Ras at-Tobeit," as Fischer (*op. cit.*, p. 1016) does, is wrong, because the name of the latter place is actually Râs aṭ-Ṭubejž (Ṭubejḳ) and it is situated in Arabia Felix.

Seuia is put by Ptolemy in the same latitude as Thauba. Since the places which follow seem to be situated near the depression of Sirḥân, I seek Seuia in the watering place of al-ʿEjsâwijje. Fischer (*loc. cit.*) identifies it with the Suwa of Arabic writers and seeks it in "el-Zefan" (correctly Ṣfân). This is out of the question, for Suwa is situated more than 450 kilometers north-northwest of Ṣfân.

Were it possible to read Dapha (*var.*, Daphna, Sapha) as Capha, we should have the name of the settlement of Kâf (Čâf), which lies beneath a hill near the remains of an old fort in the depression of Sirḥân. Because the transcription Daphna is verified, however, we may identify it with the basin Kâʿ ad-Dâfne. The Dijâf of the Arabic poets (Jâḳût, *Muʿǧam* [Wüstenfeld], Vol. 3, p. 637) is inconceivable because that place is in Syria, in the Ḥawrân. Absolutely untenable is Fischer's identification (*loc. cit.*) of this place with "el-Djôf." Al-Ǧowf cannot be both Dapha and Dumaetha.

Sora, I think, is Ṣwêr (diminutive of Ṣôr), a popular camping site of large caravans. It cannot be the Soractio of Pliny, *Nat. hist.*, VI, 145, as Fischer (*loc. cit.*) contends, because Soractio was situated in Babylonia.

Odagana may be compared with the old wells of Ḥedâǧân at the base of the range of aṭ-Ṭawîl, which offers good pasture. Beside these wells a caravan road still runs southwestward from Dûma.

Tedion is undoubtedly rewritten from Pedion and is identical with the Syrmaion Pedion of Stephen of Byzantium's *Ethnica* (Meineke), p. 593, which formed the eastern Nabataean boundary. As is probably the case here, in Palmyrena also Ptolemy records only Putea, instead of the correct Centum Putea. The Syrmaion Pedion is called by Arabic writers Baṭn as-Sirr (the depression as-Sirr). It forms the northern part of the depression of Sirḥân.

Zagmais is seen by Blau, *Wanderungen* (1868), p. 664, in the name of the old Arabian tribe of Ḍaǧʿâm, the Zocomus of the Christian historians (Sozomenus, *Eccles. hist.* [Migne], col. 1412). As this tribe camped east of Moab (Musil, *Ḳuṣejr ʿAmra*, Vol. 1, p. 130), in the depression Baṭn as-Sirr and its vicinity and as *ḍ* sounds in the dialect like *ẓ*, this identification may be accepted, and a village of the Ẓaǧʿâm in the depression of Sirḥân indicated. Of course, Ptolemy places Zagmais far to the east, but he errs similarly with "Tedion" or Pedion, which we know is not upon the eastern but upon the western boundary of Arabia Deserta.

Obaera (also Obaura) is certainly the same as the old Arabian caravansary of Ubajr, the present Bâjer. From Ubajr evolves in the dialect Bajr; and from Bajr, Bâjer, as Tâjma is derived from Tajma, Tejma.

Artemita (also Artemite) probably denotes a place where *ratam* or *artam* grows. However, as I have never seen *ratam* in Arabia Deserta proper, this place was perhaps situated in the northwestern part of Arabia Deserta, possibly upon the boundary of the Asalmanus mons or the Ḥawrân. Syrian writers knew of a cloister of Artemis beyond Burḳa' Ḥawra', the Arabian Ḳaṣr al-Abjaḍ, in the lowland of ar-Raḥba (Wright, *Catalogue* [1870—1872], p. 710, col. 1). This was probably on the caravan road leading along the western border of Arabia Deserta from Syria southward by way of the Ḫân at-Trâb, the eastern base of the range of the Ḥawrân, Ṛadîr al-Wusâd, and Obaera (Bâjer).

Banatha (*var.*, Banacha; Nachaba in the *editio princeps* [Basel, 1533]) I would change to Nabacha and seek in the oasis of an-Nabk in the depression of Sirḥân. Fischer (*op. cit.*, p. 1016) has in mind the watering place of "Banât" (correctly Banât al-Žên), but the name as well as the situation north and not south of Dûma conforms better with an-Nabk.

Dumaethа (*var.*, Dumetha) is the Arabian Dûmat al-Ǧandal of the early Arabic authorities, the present Dûmat al-Ǧandalijje in the oasis of Ǧûbt al-Ǧowf.

Alata (*var.*, Allata) is missing in some Ptolemaic manuscripts. If it really does belong in the text I identify it with the highland of Lâha on the road from Babylon through the desert to ʿAmmân.

Bere may be identical with the swampy lowland of al-Bḥêra where abundant pasturage is found in autumn.

Calathua (*var.*, Calathusa) suggests Ḳalt Ḫawʿa, or Ḳalt al-Ḥawṣa, on the northeastern boundary of the Nefûd. Here water is abundant. An important road runs eastward and southeastward through these watering places.

Salma we should like to compare with the range of Salma' so greatly renowned among Arabic authors; the latter, however, stands in Arabia Felix. It is possible that Ptolemy's Salma conforms with the "Salmani (et Masei) Arabes" of Pliny, *Nat. hist.*, VI, 118. Perhaps the name has been preserved in the plain of Selmân, which lies along the western border of the district of al-Ḥeǧera at the southeastern edge of Arabia Deserta and on the great road to the lower Euphrates.

APPENDIX IV

THE BOUNDARIES OF ARABIA DESERTA ACCORDING TO THE ARABIC AUTHORS

The Arabic authorities limit and divide Arabia as the classical authors did.

Aš-Šaʿbi (Ibn al-Faḳîh, *Buldân* [de Goeje], p. 128) states that the Ǧezîret al-ʿArab (Peninsula of Arabia) is situated between al-ʿUḏajb (al-

ʿOḏejb) and Ḥaḍramawt, while Abu ʿObejda (*ibid.*) writes that the Ǧezîret al-ʿArab reaches from Ḥafr abi Mûsa to the remotest edge of the Yemen and extends from the sand desert of Jabrîn across to as-Samâwa. — Al-ʿOḏejb is thirty kilometers south of an-Neǧef. The desert of as-Samâwa begins, according to the Arabic writers, in almost the same latitude as al-ʿOḏejb and stretches southwest to the Nefûd, which forms its southern boundary. The records both of aš-Šaʿbi and Abu ʿObejda thus conform in their account of the northern boundary of the Arabian peninsula. Arabia proper, they state, reaches but to al-ʿOḏejb and to the northern boundary of the sand desert of the Nefûd. In other words, the southern boundary of as-Samâwa is identical with the northern boundary of the Arabian peninsula. Therefore the Arabian peninsula is to be regarded as the Arabia Felix of the classic writers.

Al-Iṣṭaḫri, *Masâlik* (De Goeje), p. 13, defines the boundary of Arabia in the administrative district of Ḥomṣ by the settlements of Tadmur and Salamja and in the administrative district of Ḳinnesrîn by the settlements of Ḫunâṣira and Bâlis on the Euphrates; thence by that river and the settlements of ar-Raḳḳa, Ḳarḳîsija', ar-Raḥba, ad-Dâlija, ʿÂna, al-Ḥadîṯa, Hît, al-Anbâr, al-Kûfa, al-Ḥîra, and al-Ḫawarnaḳ. — According to al-Iṣṭaḫri, therefore, Arabia extends north to Salamja, Ḫanâṣer, and Bâlis, east to the Euphrates, and west to a boundary which is not exactly determined.

Abu-l-Feda', *Taḳwîm* (Reinaud and De Slane), p. 77, places the settlement of Ajla in the center of the western boundary of Arabia. The boundary extends thence along the side of Syria and terminates at Bâlis on the Euphrates. The northern boundary trends from Bâlis toward ar-Raḥba, ʿÂna (which is situated about in its center), and al-Kûfa, where the eastern boundary begins. This eastern boundary ends at al-Baṣra. —

Later Arabic geographers therefore consider as Arabia not only Arabia Felix but the whole of Arabia Deserta, the eastern uncultivated part of Arabia Petraea, and almost the whole of Palmyrena and the Chalybonitis of Ptolemy; that is, regions where only Arabs, or nomads, camped during the Abbasside period. Thus it seems that the western and northern boundary of Arabia has corresponded with the boundary of the settled region and has shifted either eastward or westward as the settlers have advanced toward, or retired from, the lands of the nomads. As long as a row of habitable dwellings extended from the port of Ajla to the Ḥawrân, the Sinai peninsula was not considered part of Arabia. However, as soon as the settlers left these settlements, Arabia extended not only to the Sinai peninsula, but also into southern Palestine.

Boundaries of Syria

Northern Arabia was divided, according to the Arabic writers, into the deserts of al-ʿErâḳ (Irak), al-Ǧezîre, and Syria.

Ibn al-Faḳîh, *op. cit.*, pp. 91 f., deduces the name of Syria, Šâm, from the red and black color of the Šâmât hills. Whoever travels from the mountains of Aǧa' and Salma' in the domains of the Ṭajj tribe, until he arrives at Gaza in Palestine, at the Jordan, at Damascus, or at Ḳinnesrîn, passes through the aš-Šâm district (or Syria). Syria spreads from al-Kûfa to ar-Ramle and from Bâlis to Ajla. — The local name aš-Šâma (Šâmât) is quite frequent in northern Arabia. Usually the term is applied to a range composed of roseate or dark yellow rocks upon which is superimposed at places a black crust of lava or slate. The southern boundary of Syria forms, according to Ibn al-Faḳîh, a straight line drawn from al-Kûfa to the sand desert of the Nefûd and thence westward to the Sinai peninsula. The eastern half of this peninsula and the entire territory east of the Jordan appertains to Syria. Ḳinnesrîn lay south-southwest of Aleppo, while Bâlis was almost due east of Aleppo on the right bank of the Euphrates. Therefore Ibn al-Faḳîh joins the whole of Arabia Deserta to Syria.

Al-Iṣṭaḫri, *op. cit.*, p. 15, attributes to the Syrian desert the territory between Bâlis and Ajla. The southern boundary of the desert reaches to the straight line drawn from the district of Madjan through the district of Tebûk to the pasturage of the Ṭajj. — As the entire Nefûd desert belonged in the time of al-Iṣṭaḫri to the Ṭajj tribe, this straight line ought to be projected along the northern fringe of the Nefûd. Al-Iṣṭaḫri does not say that the boundary touches Tebûk itself, but that it penetrates the district of Tebûk. We may conclude that it led from the district of Madjan northeast towards the Nefûd. Thus this southern boundary of Syria approaches the northern boundary of the Arabia Felix of Ptolemy. It would be identical with this boundary along its eastern as well as along its western section, if the district of Tebûk extended in al-Iṣṭaḫri's time to the southern base of the range of aš-Šera', as it does today.

This interpretation is supported by Ibn Ḥawḳal, *Masâlik* (De Goeje), p. 19, and Abu-l-Feda', *op. cit.*, p. 80, according to whom the Syrian desert spreads from Bâlis on the Euphrates to Ajla (al-ʿAḳaba) on the Red Sea, and beyond to the northern boundary of the district of Tebûk. Thus the southern boundary of the Syrian desert would form a straight line running eastward from Ajla along the southern base of the range of aš-Šera'.

Al-Ḳazwîni, *ʿAǧâ'ib* (Wüstenfeld), Vol. 2, p. 137, attributes to Syria the entire region between the Euphrates and al-ʿArîš from the two ranges of the Ṭajj tribe to the Mediterranean Sea. — Al-Ḳazwîni ascribes to the Syrian desert the western half of northern Arabia, for his "between the Euphrates and al-ʿArîš" refers to the region between Bâlis, which forms the northeastern, and al-ʿArîš, which forms the southwestern, limit of Syria. The two ranges, Aǧa' and Salma', are almost in the center of the northern Arabia. Since the settlers were expelled in the thirteenth century from the range of aš-Šera' and nomadic Arabs occupied it, al-Ḳazwîni could also ascribe to the Syrian desert the Sinai peninsula for the reason already explained (see above, p. 509). He does not allege that the ranges of Aǧa' and Salma' belong to Syria. They merely designate the direction of the Syrian boundary.

The Mesopotamian Desert

Ibn Ḥawḳal, *op. cit.*, pp. 17 ff., says that Syria extends from Ajla to Bâlis; that al-Ǧezîre (Mesopotamia) extends from Bâlis to al-Anbâr; and al-ʿErâḳ (Irak) extends from al-Anbâr to ʿAbbâdân. He divides Arabia into al-Ḥeǧâz, with the districts of al-Medîna and Mecca; al-

Jemâma; Neǧd al-Ḥeǧâz, reaching to al-Baḥrejn; and the deserts of al-ʿErâḳ (Irak), al-Ǧezîre (Mesopotamia), and Syria. The Mesopotamian desert extends from Bâlis to al-Anbâr in the direction of the Syrian desert as far as the district of Tejma, the desert of Ḫusâf, the vicinity of Wâdi al-Ḳura', and al-Ḥeǧr. — This definition is very confusing. The desert of Ḫusâf west of Bâlis is placed between Tejma and Wâdi al-Ḳura', by which is meant the large oasis of Dûmat al-Ǧandal. Mindful of these contradictions, we may declare that Ibn Ḥawḳal considers the eastern half of northern Arabia, situated between Bâlis on the north, the oasis of Wâdi al-Ḳura' on the south, and al-Anbâr on the east, as part of the Mesopotamian desert. The western boundary of the Mesopotamian desert follows the divide between the Euphrates watershed on the one side and those of the depression of Sirḥân and the lowland of Manḳaʿ ar-Raḥba on the other. Farther north the Mesopotamian desert is limited by the gap between the mountains of Abu Riǧmên and al-Bišri. This division of the north Arabian desert is based upon the political dependence of the local tribes and is as justified today as it was 1200 years ago, when the entire region known as Mesopotamia belonged to the Taṛleb tribe.

Abu-l-Feda', *op. cit.*, p. 80, repeats the assertion of Ibn Ḥawḳal, but omits al-Ḥeǧr and Ḫusâf. — The boundaries of the Mesopotamian desert at no time stretched from al-Anbâr to Tejma but reached only the district dependent upon Tejma, which extends to the valley of al-Ḳura' (Dûmat al-Ǧandal).

Aš-Šaʿbi (al-Bekri, *Muʿǧam* [Wüstenfeld], p. 6) states that al-ʿErâḳ (Irak) extends from al-Baḥrejn to the sand desert of al-Ḥurr. According to Ibn al-Kalbi (*ibid.*), Irak is bounded by al-Ḥîra, al-Anbâr, Baḳḳa, Hît, ʿAjn at-Tamr, and the edge of the desert as far as al-Ḳumejr, al-Ḳuṭḳuṭâne, and Ḫafijje. — Since the sand desert of al-Ḥurr is identical with the present Nefûd, the entire territory from al-Baḥrejn on the Persian Gulf to the eastern boundary of the Nefûd would belong to Irak. According to Ibn al-Kalbi the settlement of Hît is on the fringe of Irak. Thence the boundary turns southward toward ʿAjn at-Tamr and farther on is marked by al-Ḳuṭḳuṭâne (today aṭ-Ṭuḳṭuḳâne) and Ḫafijje. Baḳḳa is on the Euphrates near Hît. The situation of al-Ḳumejr is unknown to me. It should be sought in the vicinity of ʿAjn at-Tamr or al-Ḳuṭḳuṭâne. The desert of Irak as defined by Ibn al-Kalbi is in fact identical with the border of aṭ-Ṭaff of the Arabic authors, between the tilled Irak and the untilled desert.

According to Ibn Ḥawḳal, *op. cit.*, pp. 18f., and Abu-l-Feda', *loc. cit.*, the desert of Irak extends from ʿAbbâdân on the Persian Gulf to al-Anbâr, borders on Neǧd and the Ḥeǧâz on the west, and forms the pastures of the tribes of Asad, Ṭajj, Tamîm, and clans of the Muḍar. — The desert of Irak as thus defined is much longer than as defined by Ibn al-Kalbi, but not too wide, because between it and the Ḥeǧâz proper lies the territory of Neǧd al-Ḥeǧâz (Neǧd belonging to al-Ḥeǧâz).

As-Samâwa Desert

The early Arabians called Arabia Deserta the desert as-Samâwa.

The boundaries of as-Samâwa followed physiographical features. The northern boundary led through the district of al-Manâẓer, which lies between Palmyrena, which once was and still may be settled, and the southern steppes of al-Wudijân and al-Ḥamâd. East of the Ḥawrân the western boundary followed the eastern fringe of the volcanic regions which were formerly partly settled. Thence it ran along the tilled fields of the northern part of the depression of Sirḥân, which the Arabs called Baṭn as-Sirr. Farther south the boundary was formed by the divide between the watersheds of the depression of Sirḥân on the east and of the Dead Sea and lowland of al-Ǧafar on the west. At the southeastern base of the range of aš-Šera', where the territory that was at one time settled terminates, the southern boundary turned toward the northern fringe of the plateau district of Ṭubejž al-ʿAfar and toward the northern projections of the rose-colored sandy desert of the Nefûd. It followed these projections to the northeastern termination of the Nefûd. Thence the natural boundary of as-Samâwa did not trend eastward towards the Persian Gulf, but northeastward, between the districts of al-Wudijân on the west and al-Ḥeǧera on the east, to the Euphrates, which it reached at the settlement of al-Ḳâdesijje. Aristobulus, Eratosthenes (Strabo, *Geography*, XVI, 1: 11f.; Arrian, *Anabasis*, V, 21 f.), and Herodian, *Ab excessu Divi Marci*, III, 9, thought that the Pallacotas canal, the Chaldean swamps, and the inner extension of the Persian Gulf formed the northeastern boundary of Arabia Felix. The inner extension of the Persian Gulf was called Maisanites Kolpos in distinction to the great Persikos Kolpos (Ptolemy, *Geography*, V, 19, note; Nobbe's edit., VI, 7: 19). Early Arabic writers and, indeed, the present inhabitants believe that a narrow, formerly navigable, inner gulf connected the swamps in the vicinity of an-Neǧef and al-Ḳâdesijje with the Persian Gulf proper.

Even the best Arabic authorities (Ibn Ḫordâḏbeh, *Masâlik* [De Goeje], p. 125) place the northeastern boundary of Neǧd, the old Arabia Felix, at the settlement of al-Ḳâdesijje, and the natives now maintain that the frontier of Neǧd leads from the northeastern end of the sand desert of the Nefûd to the watering places of al-Ḥzûl and al-Ḳâdesijje.

None of the older Arabic writers defines the exact bounds of as-Samâwa.

Al-Iṣṭaḫri, *op. cit.*, p. 23, records that the desert of as-Samâwa extends between Dûmat al-Ǧandal and ʿAjn at-Tamr. — Dûmat al-Ǧandal marked the southern and ʿAjn at-Tamr the eastern boundary of the desert of as-Samâwa.

As-Samâwa is a barren desert between Syria and al-Kûfa, according to al-Bekri, *op. cit.*, p. 783; between Syria and Mosul, according to others cited by al-Bekri. It is the possession of the Kalb tribe. Al-Aṣmaʿi says (*ibid.*) that it is a long, narrow stretch of territory. The poet Ḏu-r-Rumma describes (*ibid.*) mirages (*sarâb*) in the desert of as-Samâwa as images which vary with every step. — It is noteworthy that according to al-Bekri some authors ascribed to the desert of as-Samâwa the region between the middle Euphrates and the Tigris. The similarity of the physiographic formations in the two regions may have given rise to this view. The best Arabic writers, however, assert that the eastern boundary proper was formed by the Euphrates.

Ibn al-Kalbi states (Jâḳût, *op. cit.*, Vol. 3, p. 131) that the name of this desert is as-Samâwa (smooth and level country) because it forms a plain where there are no stones. Jâḳût himself (*ibid.*) holds that, like

Ma' as-Sama', the mother of the King an-No'mân, it derived its name from the watering place of as-Samâwa. As-Sukkari (*ibid.*) calls as-Samâwa a watering place of the Kalb tribe. — As-Samâwa is not without stones, nor is it level everywhere. No other Arabic writer refers to any spring or water called as-Samâwa, but there were, nevertheless, numerous watering places in the desert of as-Samâwa.

According to Ḥaǧǧi Ḫalfa, *Ǧihân numa'* (Constantinople, 1145 A. H.), p. 585, the territory of as-Samâwa, in which there was a place called Ḳurâḳir, extends between Damascus and al-Kûfa. The stones of this region are round and hollow. Broken, such a stone is seen to contain a rosy, ash-colored powder. Ḥaǧǧi Ḫalfa writes (*op. cit.*, p. 465; *Musawwadat Ǧihân numa'* (Codex vindobonensis, No. 1282 [Mxt. 389], fol. 166 v.) that the wide and stony highland of Wâdi as-Samâwa is near al-Kûfa and belongs only to the Beni Kalb. — The stones mentioned by Ḥaǧǧi Ḫalfa are familiar to the natives of the present day, who imagine that gold can be made from the powder, minute quantities of which they contain. As-Samâwa is no *wâdi*. Perhaps Ḥaǧǧi Ḫalfa had heard that the eastern half of this desert is called al-Awdije or al-Wudijân (plural of *wâdi*). The watering place of Ḳurâḳir, famous in Arabic literature, is identical with the present watering place commonly known as Ḳerâžer. It is situated almost on the southern boundary of the Syrmaion Pedion of the Greek writers, or Baṭn as-Sirr, and forms the junction of several important transport roads.

Al-Hamdâni, *Ṣifa* (Müller), p. 129, seeks the watering place of Ḳurâḳir on the frontier of the Kalb and Ḏubjân tribes, near the water of 'Urâ'ir. — The Kalb camped in as-Samâwa; the Ḏubjân in the eastern part of the district of al-Belḳa', which reached as far as the depression of Sirḥân, or Baṭn as-Sirr. This fully conforms with the situation of the present watering place of Ḳerâžer, which also lies on the boundary between the territory of the tribes camping in the region formerly known as al-Belḳa' and those camping in inner Arabia. The watering place of 'Urâ'ir is known to be south of Ḳerâžer. De Goeje, *Mémoire* (1900), p. 47, records that, according to Jâḳût (*Mu'ǧam* [Wüstenfeld], Vol. 2, p. 636, line 4, and Vol. 4, p. 927, line 3) the Taṛleb dwelt by the watering place of Ḳurâḳir which Ḫâled marched by. De Goeje, however, misquotes Jâḳût, who makes no mention of the Taṛleb in this connection. Caetani, *Annali* (1905), Vol. 2, p. 1216, asserts that the watering place of Ḳurâḳir was northwest of 'Ajn at-Tamr. Caetani did not consult Jâḳût. Jâḳût, citing al-Hajṯam, explicitly states in the first passage quoted by De Goeje that Ḳurâḳir was in the territory of the Kalb (not of the Taṛleb); and he adds in the second passage that Wisâde is a place on the road from al-Medîna to Syria, which runs along the spurs of the Ḥawrân range between Jurfu' and Ḳurâḳir. Wisâde is a rain pool called today Ṛadîr al-Wusâd. It is situated among the southeastern spurs of the Ḥawrân on the road leading from Ḳerâžer past Burḳu' to Damascus and northern Syria. In Jâḳût this Burḳu' was erroneously transcribed Jurfu' by a blunder easily committed in Arabic. Jâḳût himself shows that the watering place of Ḳurâḳir is to be sought almost six hundred kilometers west of 'Ajn at-Tamr, on the very frontier of Syria. Al-Hajṯam does not record the Taṛleb at Ḳurâḳir, as this tribe occupied the territory between al-Anbâr and Tadmur in which Caetani seeks Ḳurâḳir.

It is interesting that the sequence of places quoted by al-Hajṯam as given by Jâḳût (*op. cit.*, Vol. 2, p. 636) also confirms us in identifying Ḳurâḳir with Ḳerâžer. Baṭn ar-Rumma (today ar-Rma') is south of the oasis of Fejd. North of the oasis lies Ḥâjel, the capital of the Šammar tribe. North of this town is the watering place of Ḳurâḳir in the territory of the Kalb; and north of Ḳurâḳir is the watering place of Suwa' in the territory of the Taṛleb tribe. — In the time of the poet al-Aḫṭal the Taṛleb camped southwest as well as southeast of Tudmor. It would be possible, therefore, that the watering place of Suwa' was defined as if it were in the Taṛleb territory.

Ḥağği Ḫalfa, *Ǧihân numa'* (Constantinople, 1145 A. H.), p. 531, refers to Ḳurâḳir as a watering place between Dûma and Tejma. ʿAmra is also a watering place east of al-Azraḳ. Šefâr has plenty of water. West from Ḳurâḳir the first valley is called as-Sirr. Ḳajn is a station with water, twenty-four miles from Ḳurâḳir. The watering place of Nabk lies on the road to Neǧd, twenty-two miles (from Šefâr, omitted in the text). — Ḥağği Ḫalfa surely had in mind our watering place of Ḳerâžer, situated in a small eastern projection of the depression of Sirḥân, his Wâdi as-Sirr. It is not, however, between Dûma and Tejma but, instead, is on the road which leads from Syria to the oases of Dûma and Tejma. ʿAmra is identical with the Ḳuṣejr ʿAmra to the northwest of Ḳerâžer. Ḳajn is the same as the wells of al-Žên, which, however, are not twenty-four miles but 250 kilometers distant from Ḳerâžer. Šefâr is obviously an erroneous spelling of Šeṛâr (or Šṛâr), a watering place which lies in the depression of Sirḥân southeast of Ḳerâžer on the Dûma and Tejma road leading from Ḳerâžer past Nabk toward Šeṛâr. No place named Šefâr is known in the vicinity of Ḳerâžer.

APPENDIX V

ANCIENT TRANSPORT ROUTES IN ARABIA DESERTA

So far we have found in the Assyrian and Babylonian records no account of the commerce which flourished in the southern part of Arabia Deserta. Classical writers, however, mention this commerce and the trade routes.

Artemidorus (Strabo, *Geography*, XVI, 4: 18) recorded that trade caravans traveled from Gerrha to Petra.

Pliny, *Nat. hist.*, VI, 144—146, says that the Nabataeans dwell in the city of Petra, 600 Roman miles (*milia passuum*) from the city of Gaza and 135 miles from the Persian Gulf. At Petra the transport road from Syria and Palmyra joins the road from Gaza. From Petra as far as Charax the Omani dwell, and on the bank of the Pasitigris is the city of Forat, belonging to the king of Charax. The route from Petra to Forat leads overland, while the last twelve miles of the journey to Charax are made by water. According to some, boats sailed on the Tigris to the distant cities of Barbatia and Dumatha (Thumatha). The voyage to Dumatha occupied ten days. —

This account, like all that Pliny writes about Arabia, is very obscure. The Omani Arabs dwell, he says, between the cities of Charax and Petra. The latter was a very important commercial center, as three transport roads converged there. For us the road from the city of Forat is of paramount importance, for it led entirely across northern Arabia, touching the oasis of Dûma (Dûmat al-Ǧandal), where I have found Nabataean inscriptions. I identify this oasis with Pliny's city of Dumatha, which, as often with him, has been inaccurately located. From the city of Petra to Dumatha is almost 425 kilometers. This would be a ten days' march for a caravan with such loads as are carried in the desert and would entirely agree with Pliny's report. From Petra the road went through al-Ǧafar to Dumatha and thence past the caravansary of al-Bwejtât and the watering places of al-Ḥazel, Šerâf, and Ḏu Ḳâr, to Forat in the neighborhood of al-Baṣra.

The poet Farazdaḳ (Hell, *Farazdaḳ* [1903] p. 44) knew of a road leading from al-Ǧiwa in al-Baḥrejn through Dûmat al-Ǧandal to the place where al-Walîd ibn Jazîd ibn ʿAbdalmalek lived after he had gone with his friends from the residence of the Caliph Hišâm.—

This road for the greater part of its length must have been identical with the road frequented by caravans going from Gerrha to Petra. Only a day's march northwest of the oasis of Dûma a branch separated from the Gerrha-Petra road and led to Syria through the depression of Sirḥân, in the vicinity of which al-Walîd dwelt.

Another transport route referred to by Pliny is that which led from Gaza on the Mediterranean Sea to Petra, and still another is one which came to Petra from Palmyra. In the first century of our era Palmyra surely enjoyed direct commercial relations with the city of Forat by a route running eastward to the ford called Thapsacus (at the present al-Mijâḏîn) and thence either along the Euphrates or through the adjacent desert. Trade caravans going from Palmyra to Petra did not go directly through the desert but followed the road to Damascus as far as the present ruins of Ḫân at-Trâb, where they turned southward through Burḳuʿ, the Ṛadîr al-Wusâd, Bâjer, and al-Ǧafar.

Pliny does not give correct figures for distances. He writes that it is 600 miles from Gaza to Petra and 135 miles from the Persian Gulf to Petra. In reality from Gaza to Petra, deviations included, is 180-190 kilometers, amounting in all to 135 Roman miles, while from Petra to the northern end of the Persian Gulf is 900 kilometers, making about 600 Roman miles. The distance to the Persian Gulf proper at Forat is 1200 kilometers. It may be seen, then, that Pliny's distances from Gaza to Petra and from the Persian Gulf to Petra have been interchanged. It is likely that he, like other classical and Arabic authorities (see above, p. 503), placed the end of the inner part of the Persian Gulf at the northern extremity of the Chaldean swamps, therefore at the present an-Neǧef.

It seems that the soldiers of Cambyses as well as of Ptolemy Soter (322—283 B. C.) marched over the road from Egypt which runs past the cities of Gaza and Petra and thence through the Arabian desert or through Palmyra to Babylonia. Arrian (*Indica*, 43) writes that both the soldiers of Cambyses, who had arrived safely at Gaza, and the people whom the Lagid Ptolemy had sent to Seleucus Nicator in Babylon, had passed in eight days through a neck of land and then had proceeded through a waterless and desolate region, traveling with the utmost speed upon camels, carrying their water, and moving only at night, since the intense heat of the daytime made it impossible to remain under the open sky. The country beyond the region designated as the neck of land (the Sinai peninsula) is sparsely settled. Even the parts of it farther to the north are desolate and covered with sand.

APPENDIX VI

MEDIEVAL AND MODERN ROUTES IN ARABIA DESERTA

Routes Through Tejma

Through the oasis of Tejma and the abundantly moistened depression Baṭn as-Sirr (the present Wâdi Sirḥân) there led in the Middle Ages important routes from Damascus and Syria to al-Medîna and Irak. The settlements of Boṣra, ʿAmmân, Dûmat al-Ǧandal, Tejma, and Wâdi al-Ḳura' formed the main centers. From the city of Boṣra or ʿAmmân one went either south to Tebûk or southeast to Tejma, passing through the depression of as-Sirr or to the westward of it. From Dûmat al-Ǧandal travel was possible either northeastward to Irak, southeastward to aṯ-Ṯaʿlabijje, or south-southwestward to Tejma. From the last-named oasis traffic went eastward to the oases of the Ṭajj and Asad tribes, or southward to the southern Wâdi al-Ḳura' and al-Medîna.

Aṭ-Ṭabari, *Ta'rîḫ* (De Goeje), Ser. 3, p. 216, mentions in the year 762 A. D. a road from al-Medîna by way of Tejma and Dûmat al-Ǧandal to Damascus.

Al-Hamdâni, *Ṣifa* (Müller), p. 131, knew of a road from Tejma toward the north-northeast. The oases of al-Ḳurejjât on the boundary of the al-Bijâẓ district lay on the left of this road, and the sand desert, frequented by robbers, on the right. The road passed through the territory of the Buḥtur clan of the Ṭajj tribe until it reached, at five marches from al-Kûfa, the territory of the Beni Asad. In the settlements of al-Ḳurejjât dwelt, according to the informant of al-Hamdâni, the members of the Ḏubjân, Buḥtur, and other tribes. — The course of this road is apparent. It probably touched the watering places of Ubejṭ, al-Mrût, aš-Šižîž, al-Bûmijjât, and, at the wells of al-Ḥzûl, within five marches of al-Kûfa, reached the territory of the Beni Asad. It is to be noted that the oasis of Dûmat al-Ǧandal, or al-Ḳurejjât as al-Hamdâni calls it, remained on the left, therefore to the north.

Al-Muḳaddasi, *Aḥsan* (De Goeje), p. 250, refers to three roads from Damascus by way of ʿAmmân and the oasis of Tejma to al-Medîna.

The eastern one passed from ʿAmmân through the depression Baṭn as-Sirr, and was therefore called Ṭarîḳ Baṭn as-Sirr (Road of the Depression of as-Sirr). From ʿAmmân to al-ʿAwnîd was two days' march; to al-Muḥdaṯa half a day; to an-Nabk half a day; to the fresh water among trees, the name of which al-Muḳaddasi forgot, one day; to al-Ǧarba one day; to ʿArfaǧa a day and a half; to Muhri three days; to Tejma four days. — Al-ʿUwajnid (to be read thus instead of al-ʿAwnîd, as printed; al-ʿWejned of today) is eighty kilometers southeast of ʿAmmân, making each day's journey forty kilometers long. The station of al-Muḥdaṯa I identify with the ruins of al-Ḥadîṯa sixty kilometers southeast of al-ʿWejned. This is not a half, but one and a half days' march distant. Thence to an-Nabk (or an-Nabč al-Ṛarbi, as it is called today) is barely twenty kilometers and the march is reported correctly. The next station, the name of which al-Muḳaddasi writes that he had forgotten, may (according to the Constantinople manuscript) be supposed to be some *ṛadîr* with fresh water among trees. *Ṛadîr* signifies a hole containing rain water in a river bed. Such holes are very infrequent in the depression of Sirḥân. The wells there are shallow, often mere small pools containing somewhat salty water. The best water is in the wells of al-Ǧfêrât, the name of which has perhaps been preserved (*ibid.*, p. 250, note n) on the map in the Berlin manuscript, while the map in the Constantinople manuscript repeats the name of the preceding an-Nabk, at a distance of fifty kilometers, or a good day's march. Al-Ǧarba is identical with the watering place of al-Awejseṯ, which is also called Awejseṯ al-Ǧarba, fifty-five kilometers from al-Ǧfêrât. The station of ʿArfaǧa, a day and a half from al-Ǧarba, is eighty kilometers farther to the south-southeast. Hence a day's march between ʿArfaǧa and al-Ǧarba would have to cover about fifty-four kilometers. Near the last-named station the road leaves the depression of Sirḥân, leading off in a southerly direction over the western fringe of the sand desert of the Nefûd to the old watering place Mšâš al-Mowt, almost 140 kilometers distant. I see in this watering place al-Muḳaddasi's well of Muhri. The distance approximates three marches. The marches of the first two days might each cover fifty-five kilometers; that of the third, where a sand desert had to be traversed, only thirty kilometers. The name Muhri (laxative) denotes the action of this water just as today al-Mowt (the death) refers to the same thing. Thence to the oasis of Tejma is a distance of almost 160 kilometers. The road leads over numerous narrow sand drifts, where not more than forty kilometers can be counted upon for one day's march.

The Constantinople manuscript of al-Muḳaddasi's *Aḥsan* (*ibid.*, p. 107, note e) records a road which passed through ʿAmmân, Wubajr, al-Muḥdaṯa, an-Nabk, the water of al-Ǧarba, ʿArfaǧa, Muhri, Tejma, and Ḥeǧr Ṣâleḥ. — In this itinerary Wubajr should be replaced by the correct al-ʿUwajnid, for this route is identical with the one described on page 250 of De Goeje's edition and discussed in the preceding paragraph.

The name of the second road from ʿAmmân to the oasis of Tejma described by al-Muḳaddasi is Ṭarîḳ Wubajr. From ʿAmmân to Wubajr is three marches; thence to al-Aǧwali, four; thence to Ṯaǧr, two; and thence to Tejma, three. — I identify Wubajr (correctly, Ubajr) with the wells and caravansary of Bâjer. In the dialect of the present day the vowel is prolonged in a diphthong. We do not now hear the pronunciation Tajma, but Tâjma; not Ubajẓ, but Bâjeẓ; not Ubajr, but Bâjer. The initial vowel and its carrier, the *hamza*, both disappear in the dialect. From ʿAmmân to Ubajr (Bâjer) is 160 kilometers, or fifty-four kilometers for each day's march. Al-Aǧwali (or, according to *op. cit.*, p. 250, note f, the well of al-Ǧawla) I seek at the ruins of al-Čelwa (al-Kelwa), 170 kilometers south of Bâjer. There are filled-in wells here which are not kept cleaned out by the Bedouins because their water is supposed to be unwholesome. To reach here in four marches from Bâjer it would be necessary to make forty-three kilometers per day. One hundred kilometers south of al-Kelwa the watering place Mšâš az-Zhejrijje in the valley of Feğr is probably identical with the station of Ṯağr. Either Fağr (or Feğr) was wrongly transcribed as Ṯağr by al-Muḳaddasi or the *ṯ* has subsequently been substituted for the *f*, as frequently happens. To Feğr each of the two days' marches would have been fifty kilometers. From Feğr to Tejma, a distance of 110 kilometers, would have required a march of forty kilometers on each of the first two days and of only thirty kilometers on the third day. The first and the last marches are, as a rule, shorter.

The third or western road is in large part identical with the Pilgrim Road via Maʿân to Tebûk, whence it turned toward the oasis of Tejma. From this oasis al-Ḥeğr (or Ḥeğr Ṣâleḥ, as it is written in the Constantinople manuscript, *ibid.*, p. 107, note e) could be reached in three days (*ibid.*, p. 107).

As recorded by al-Muḳaddasi (*ibid.*, p. 250) these were the roads taken to Syria by the aggressive Moslem armies in the times of the first two caliphs, and during the rule of Omayyads the mails from Damascus to al-Medîna were carried over them — in the rainy season over the middle road via Bâjer, in the dry period either by way of Tebûk or through the depression of Sirḥân, where there was much more water than on the middle road. In the time of al-Muḳaddasi these roads were used by Bedouins making the pilgrimage to Mecca. The Bedouins were joined by many settlers from Syria, who congregated in ʿAmmân. In the tenth century safety was guaranteed by the Beni Kilâb, and pilgrims and others traveled in the desert without anxiety (*ibid.*).

Al-Bekri, *Muʿǧam* (Wüstenfeld), pp. 208f., records that according to as-Sakûni there were two roads from al-Medîna to Tejma. The first ran north as far as the southern border of the territory explored by us, then in three marches through the district of al-Ǧenâb and around the mountains of Bard and Ǧudad to the castle of al-Ablaḳ, situated at the southern end of the oasis of Tejma. — The district of al-Ǧenâb belonged to the Ṭajj tribe. It is a plain overlooked by much-eroded hills and bounded on the west by rugged volcanic cliffs and on the east by the sandy desert of the Nefûd and its projections. The hill of Bard (the present Bird) is visible from afar. The extensive hill of Ǧudad, identical with the Ẓelʿ al-Ḳnejm of the present time, is the beacon of all travelers, beckoning them to relaxation in the oasis of Tejma beneath its northern base.

The second road from al-Medîna described by al-Bekri corresponded to the Pilgrim Road as far as the station of al-Ḥeğr, whence it was three marches to the oasis of Tejma.

Al-Bekri, *op. cit.*, p. 209, also described the roads from Tejma to Syria, although he was not careful to discriminate between them. One led through the Ḥawrân to al-Baṯanijje and another through the district of Ḥesmaʾ. — The first would surely seem to be the road through the depression of as-Sirr (Sirḥân) to Ḏerʿât, the most important settlement of the district of al-Baṯanijje on the western base of the Ḥawrân; the second, the road from Tejma running northwest by way of Tebûk and the district of Ḥesmaʾ to Palestine and Egypt.

Al-Idrîsi, *Nuzha*, III, 5, says that Tejma is the nucleus of various roads. He records that from Tejma to al-Ḥeğr it is four marches; from Tejma to Ḫajbar, also four; from Tejma to Dûmat al-Ğandal, four; and from Tejma to the Syrian border, three days. — From Tejma to al-Ḥeğr it is 105 kilometers through rugged country. From Tejma to the oasis of Ḫajbar is 240 kilometers, for the most part through a volcanic district where going is hard. Al-Idrîsi, however, counts this distance four marches, the same as that to Dûmat al-Ğandal; the latter actually is 270 kilometers away and the road thither runs almost two days in sand desert. The distance from Tejma to the Syrian border he places at three days. If we think of the day as the Bedouins do — that is, as a day of intensive riding, on the average of seventy kilometers —, we arrive in three days at the northern boundary of the sand desert of the Nefûd, where the classical authors place the northern boundary of Arabia Felix. This confirmation of the northern boundary of Arabia Felix or the Ḥeğâz accords with Abu Ḥuḏejfa's assertion that Syria begins north of the station of Soraṛ (Jâḳût, *Muʿğam* [Wüstenfeld], Vol. 3, p. 86).

Jâḳût (*op. cit.*, Vol. 1, p. 907; Vol. 4, p. 927) was familiar with the Pilgrim Road from Damascus in Syria to al-Medîna through Burḳuʿ, Wisâde, Ḳurâḳir, and the oasis of Tejma. — Burḳuʿ (not Jurfuʿ, as printed) is identical with the fortress and the reservoirs of Burḳuʿ northeast of the Ḥawrân. Wisâde is today the Ṛadîr al-Wusâd; Ḳurâḳir is the famous watering place of Ḳerâžer. Therefore this road circumvented the range of the Ḥawrân to the east and followed the depression of Sirḥân nearly to the station of ʿArfağa, where it turned toward the oasis of Tejma. Along the northern half of this road the poet al-Mutanabbi hastened from Aleppo to Egypt (*ibid.*, Vol. 2, p. 217; Vol. 3, p. 783).

Through the depression of Sirḥân passed the road of the Ṭajj tribe to Syria (*ibid.*, Vol. 2, p. 46). It was also known as the road of the Arabs or as al-Munaḳḳa (*ibid.*, Vol. 4, p. 669). "Arabs" are nomads.

Ḥağği Ḫalfa, *Ğihân numa'* (Constantinople, 1145 A. H.), p. 540, records a road through the depression of Sirḥân to the oasis of Tejma. It begins at the settlement of Boṣra. Thence it runs to the fort of al-Azraḳ; thence in three marches to Ḳurâḳir through a moist district overgrown with palms; thence in two marches to Ḳalta; thence in two marches to Ṣubajḥa; and thence in three marches to the oasis of Tejma. Thence to the Wâdi aṣ-Ṣawwân and in four marches to al-ʿEla'. This road preserves the most direct course. It has sixteen stations each of twenty-seven miles, but very little water. —

All of Ḥağği Ḫalfa's localities can be identified. Al-Azraḳ is at the northwestern end of the depression of Sirḥân. Ḳurâḳir, or Ḳerâžer, is 130 kilometers southeast thereof. Ḳalta, the name of the next station, signifies merely a small cleft in the rocks, containing rain water. About seventy kilometers southeast of Ḳerâžer rises the hill Tell al-Žalta, difficult of access because a flow of broken lava spreads to the north, while to the south lies a swampy hollow which, during rains, is quite impassable. Easier is the very old highway of al-Mneḳḳa, which runs along the western border of the depression of Sirḥân, where there are several natural reservoirs of the *ḳalta* formation. The station of Ḳalta I should identify with Mṛejrât al-Harma, seventy kilometers southeast of Ḳerâžer. The distance is somewhat short for two marches. The first march, however, leads through a country in some places overlain with lava and in others characterized by salina marshes. The situation of the station of Ṣubajḥa corresponds to that of the watering place of Ṣbâjḥa — this, instead of Ṣubajḥa, being the pronunciation in the dialect of the Rwala — about ninety kilometers southeast of Mṛejrât al-Harma. Here the road leaves the depression of Sirḥân and bears southward. From the watering place of Ṣbâjḥa to the oasis of Tejma is 275 kilometers, which could hardly be covered in three marches. As Ḥağği Ḫalfa himself seems to have allowed forty kilometers for one march, we cannot, therefore, count 275 kilometers as three, but rather as seven marches. It is unfortunate that Ḥağği Ḫalfa does not name a single station between Ṣubajḥa and Tejma. The distance from Tejma to al-ʿEla' is 120 kilometers, which would make either three arduous or four easy marches. It is difficult to determine what Ḥağği Ḫalfa's aṣ-Ṣawwân (the flints) denotes. There is no valley of aṣ-Ṣawwân southwest of Tejma, as the formation of the country leaves room for no such valley. Aṣ-Ṣawwân should follow the station of Ṣubajḥa. Thence the road passes through immense undulating plains covered with flints and called aṣ-Ṣawwân, plains which reach west to the range of aš-Šera' and the district of Ḥesma', and east to the depression of Sirḥân and the sand desert of the Nefûd.

Meḥmed Edîb, *Menâzil* (Constantinople, 1232 A. H.), p. 81, also records a road through the depression of Sirḥân to the oasis of Tejma, but the distances are even more impossible than those of Ḥağği Ḫalfa. From Damascus one march to Boṣra; thence one march to al-Azraḳ; thence three marches to Ḳurâḳir; thence two marches to Ḳalta; thence two marches to Ṣubajḥa; thence two marches to Tejma; and thence four marches through the valley of aṣ-Ṣawwân to al-ʿEla'.

Routes Across as-Samâwa and Through Dûmat al-Ğandal (Seventh to Tenth Centuries)

The transport routes between Syria and Egypt on the one hand and Irak or southern Mesopotamia on the other, made their way either across as-Samâwa or along the Euphrates. Of the roads crossing as-Samâwa the easiest and in part the safest was the road through the depression Baṭn as-Sirr and the oasis of Dûmat al-Ğandal to al-Ḥîra (al-Kûfa). Ḫâled ibn al-Walîd traveled it from al-Ḥîra to Syria. Shorter, though more arduous because of the lack of water, were the roads from the west of the Ḥawrân to Irak. They were called Ṭarîḳ al-Barr (Desert Road), or Ṭarîḳ as-Samâwa (Abu-l-Farağ, *Arâni* [Bûlâḳ, 1285 A. H.], Vol. 20, p. 120). Arabic writers often mention marches from Syria through the desert to Irak or in the opposite direction, yet they seldom record the landmarks by which we may determine the routes taken.

After the Battle of the Camel at al-Baṣra, December 9, 656 A. D., several men went to Damascus, taking the route through the oasis of Dûma in the territory of the Kalb tribe (aṭ-Ṭabari, *Ta'rîḫ* [De Goeje], Ser. 1, p. 3219). — Probably they traveled from al-Baṣra via Selmân and al-Hebeke to Dûmat al-Ğandal — which at the time belonged to the Kalb — and thence through the depression of Sirḥân (Baṭn as-Sirr) and by way of the city of Boṣra to Damascus.

Aṭ-Ṭabari, *op. cit.*, Ser. 1, p. 3410 (see also p. 3408), writes that in the spring of 657 A. D. ʿAli had sent two hundred men from al-Kûfa to Egypt to aid Muḥammad ibn Abi Bekr. Shortly after their departure word of Muḥammad's death reached al-Kûfa, and the reinforcements were recalled within five days. — Moawiyah ruled in Syria; therefore ʿAli's reinforcements from al-Kûfa could not have marched along the Euphrates, but only through the oasis of Dûmat al-Ǧandal directly westward to Egypt.

In the year 658 A. D. (aṭ-Ṭabari, *op. cit.*, Ser. 1, p. 3393) al-Aštar hastened on the order of ʿAli from al-Kûfa to Egypt and was captured there at the port of al-Ḳulzum. — Since this was soon after the fatal battle of Ṣiffîn, al-Aštar could not have followed the Euphrates, making his way to Egypt through Syria, nor could he have gone through Palestine to Egypt, because the cohorts of the Caliph Moawiyah would immediately have captured him. Hence he must have proceeded westward through the desert by way of Dûmat al-Ǧandal. In this direction a road ran to Egypt via al-Ḳulzum. We find this road mentioned by other writers also. Lammens, *Moʿâwia* (1907), p. 113, does not acknowledge that there was a road by way of al-Ḳulzum. He quotes al-Masʿûdi (*Murûǧ* [De Meynard and De Courteille], Vol. 4, p. 423), according to whom al-Aštar went by way of al-ʿArîš. However, the narrative of al-Masʿûdi is very florid and only too likely to be far from the truth. He says that al-Aštar marched with a large army and that there still was a Persian *diḥkân* (mayor, official) in al-ʿArîš. Al-Aštar, however, could only have entered this city either through southern Palestine, where he would have exposed himself to the risk of being captured, or by a long detour. The road to the port of al-Ḳulzum, on the other hand, preserved a straight course and held no danger.

Aṭ-Ṭabari (*op. cit.*, Ser. 1, p. 3447) and Abu-l-Faraǧ (*op. cit.*, Vol. 15, p. 46) record that in the year 660 A. D. the Caliph Moawiyah dispatched aḍ-Ḍaḥḥâk ibn Ḳejs with three thousand men from Damascus to harass the adherents of ʿAli along the Wâḳiṣa road. Aḍ-Ḍaḥḥâk came to this road at the station of aṯ-Ṯaʿlabijje and proceeded to plunder the individual stations and camps and to rob travelers as far as al-Ḳuṭḳuṭâne, where he dispersed a large group of pilgrims. Thereupon ʿAli sent against him an army of four thousand men, which did not overtake him until he reached Tadmur. — Aṯ-Ṯaʿlabijje is on the southeastern edge of the sand desert of the Nefûd. Therefore aḍ-Ḍaḥḥâk went southeast through the depression of Sirḥân, the oasis of Dûma, and the present station of al-Ḥajjânijje to aṯ-Ṯaʿlabijje; he then turned to the north and, at the station of Wâḳṣa, to the northwest until he reached al-Ḳuṭḳuṭâne, or aṭ-Ṭuḳṭuḳâne as it is known today. Thence he fled to Tudmor by way of the watering places of Ḳṭeri, al-Lmât, al-Ḳnêni, aṣ-Ṣaẓri, and Bajjûẓ.

In the year 709 A. D. Jazîd ibn al-Muhalleb, the deposed governor of Khorasan, fled from central Irak to the desert of as-Samâwa and, led by a certain member of the Kalb tribe, traveled the road which ran to Syria and Palestine. In the city of ar-Ramle he was given shelter by Sulejmân ibn ʿAbdalmalek (aṭ-Ṭabari, *op. cit.*, Ser. 2, p. 1211). — This account mentions the Ṭarîḳ aš-Šâm, a road passing through the desert of as-Samâwa to Palestine, but it notes neither its starting point nor its termination.

In the time of the Caliph Hišâm ibn ʿAbdalmalek, a road running from Irak by way of al-Kutkutâne to [Syria, and therefore through the desert of as-Samâwa, is known to have existed (Abu-l-Farağ, *op. cit.*, Vol. 15, p. 115).

In the later part of 743 A. D. the Caliph al-Walîd II sold the deposed governor Ḫâled al-Kasri to his principal enemy, Jûsef ibn ʿOmar. In al-Walîd's camp Ḫâled was put upon a camel and transported to a place called al-Muhdata, one march distant, and thence through the territory of the Kejn tribe to al-Ḥîra (aṭ-Ṭabari, *op. cit.*, Ser. 2, p. 1821). — Al-Muhdata is identical with the ruins of al-Ḥadîta in the depression of Sirḥân. Al-Walîd dwelt at the time west thereof, in al-Radaf. The Kejn were encamped in the depression of Sirḥân. From this it is evident that Ḫâled must have been transported through the depression of Sirḥân to Dûmat al-Ğandal and thence to al-Ḥîra.

In the spring of 744 A. D. the governor Jûsef ibn ʿOmar had to flee from al-Ḥîra through the desert of as-Samâwa to al-Belka' (*ibid.*, Ser. 2, p. 1840). — Doubtless he fled over the same road along which, several months before, al-Walîd had sent poor Ḫâled, for al-Belka' lies to the west of al-Muhdata.

In the last years of the reigns of the Omayyad caliphs the Abbassides and their adherents frequently went from al-Kûfa in Irak through the desert of as-Samâwa and via Dûmat al-Ğandal to the settlement of al-Ḥomejma, situated on the southwestern slope of the range of aš-Šera' northeast of the northern end of the Gulf of ʿAkaba (*ibid.*, Ser. 3, p. 33). — The section of this road between Dûmat al-Ğandal and al-Ḥomejma also formed a part of the road to Egypt by way of al-Kulzum.

The poet Abu-ṭ-Ṭajjeb al-Mutanabbi (*Dîwân* [Dieterici], pp. 699 f.; al-Bekri, *op. cit.*, pp. 589 f.) describes in poetic form his flight in the year 961 A. D. from Egypt to Irak. With a small retinue mounted upon camels he arrived over the road from al-Kolzum by way of Naḫl at the pass of an-Nikâb, whence it is possible to head southeast to Wâdi al-Kura' or northeast to Wâdi al-Mijâh. From Turbân al-Mutanabbi went east to Irak, by the fringe of the Ḥesma over the heights of al-Kefâf and al-Kabd, and past the watering place of al-Bwêra near Wâdi al-Rada'. Through the desert of Busajta, where they had seen numerous ostriches and antelopes, he came to the ʿOkdet al-Ğowf, drank from al-Ğerâwi, passed Ṣawar, aš-Šarûr, al-Ğumejʿi, al-Edâreʿ, ad-Dana', and Aʿkuš, watered his animals in ar-Ruhejme, and rested in al-Kûfa. —

The direction taken by al-Mutanabbi can be determined quite precisely, but it does not seem that he has given the place names in the right order. Naḫl, or an-Naḫl, is a settlement in the middle of the Sinai peninsula. An-Nikâb denotes the passes east of the rift valley of al-ʿAraba, through which roads stretch away into divers corners of Arabia. Turbân is a spring and watering place about forty kilometers north of Ajla (al-ʿAkaba) on the eastern edge of the rift valley. Al-Mutanabbi had to avoid the port of Ajla, because its garrison was Egyptian. Wâdi al-Kura' may mean the Ḥeğâz and al-Medîna, and Wâdi al-Mijâh Mesopotamia, where al-Mutanabbi sought and likely found refuge.

From the Turbân spring it is probable that he went to al-Kwêra in the district of Ḥesma and that this may have been the source of his al-Bwêra. *Raza*, which grows south from al-Kwêra and over the entire

Ḥesma, probably gave rise to his Wâdi al-Ṛaḏa'. East of al-Ḳwêra rises the precipitous slope of the range of aš-Šera', which he certainly avoided, because he would have had to pass the settlement of Maʿân with its garrison. He then crossed the plain of Ḥesma, going around the aš-Šera' range as well as the numerous ridges of al-Kfûf. He must have quenched his thirst in the small wells Mšâš al-Čabd (or, as he writes, al-Kabd). If al-Bwêra is not identical with al-Ḳwêra, it should be sought east of al-Čabd, perhaps in one of the wells of al-Amrar on the northwestern fringe of the desolate plain of al-Bsajṭa (his Busajṭa), in which ostriches and antelopes still roam. ʿOḳdet al-Ǧowf (or al-ʿOḳde) is a deep ravine, half-filled with sand, southeast of the old oasis of Dûmat al-Ǧandal; al-Ǧerâwi is a well and a solitary farm about three kilometers south of the same oasis. Therefore the poet's route must have descended from the desert of al-Busajṭa to run through the ravine ʿOḳdet al-Ǧowf into the basin al-Ǧowf. He probably hastened farther east to Ṣawar, which today bears the name of Ṣwêr. Verily, the commentator al-Wâḥedi identifies this Ṣawar with Ṣawra' (al-Mutanabbi, *loc. cit.*), but neither he nor his informant were proficient in the topography of Arabia, seeking for places at points far removed from their actual situations. Aš-Šaṛûr is the plural of Šṛâr and Šṛajjer, which are the names of watering places northwest of the present settlements of al-Ǧowf. Yet this name might also merely refer to a watering spot to the northeast of Ṣawar, the present Ṣwêr. Al-Ǧumejʿi (Mšâš al-Ǧmejʿi of today) is likewise situated in the same direction, and also al-Eḏâreʿ, or, as the Rwala now refer to it, al-Eẓâreʿ. I have no knowledge of ad-Dana'. Aʿkuš may be sought in the low crests of ʿAkkâš south of the city of an-Neǧef. Ar-Ruhejme is a settlement between ʿAkkâš and an-Neǧef. It is to be regretted that al-Mutanabbi recorded so few names between Ṣwêr and al-Kûfa.

Ibn Ḥawḳal, *Masâlik* (De Goeje), p. 11, also knew of a road leading from Irak straight through the desert of as-Samâwa to the port of al-Ḳulzum in Egypt. The march lasted almost a month. — Perhaps it is the same road as that traveled by al-Mutanabbi.

The oasis of Dûmat al-Ǧandal was situated at the junction of roads to Syria, Irak, al-Medîna, and Egypt (aṭ-Ṭabari, *op. cit.*, Ser. 3, p. 216).

Caetani, *Annali* (1905), Vol. 2, p. 991, writes that there was no road for caravans from al-Ḥîra through the desert of as-Samâwa to the oasis of Dûma. This is refuted by the accounts quoted from the earliest period of Islâm.

Routes from al-Ḥîra (al-Kûfa) to Damascus

The routes from al-Hîra to Damascus and Eḏraʿât (or Ḏerʿât of today) may be determined exactly, although the situation of the individual stations is unsettled.

Ibn Ḫordâḏbeh, *Masâlik* (De Goeje), p. 99, gives fifteen names on the road from al-Ḥîra to Damascus: hence we might divide the distance of 850 kilometers into fifteen marches of fifty-seven kilometers each. Since a camel rider upon a long journey may cover sixty kilometers in eleven hours a day, the fifteen local names mentioned might well signify fifteen equidistant stations. However, the known stations show that the distances between the stations vary. The distance from Ḏerʿât to Manzel (al-Kiswe) is ninety-two kilometers, thence to Damascus only twenty-two kilometers; and from al-Ḥîra to aṭ-Ṭuḳṭuḳâne forty-five kilometers. Therefore the names mentioned probably do not signify caravansaries, but the more important watering places.

From al-Ḥîra the road led to al-Ḳuṭḳuṭâne, al-Buḳʿa, al-Abjaḍ, al-Ḥawši, al-Ǧamʿ, al-Ḫoṭṭi, al-Ǧubba, al-Ḳalûfi, ar-Rawâri, as-Sâʿeda, al-Buḳejʿa, al-Aʿnâk, Edraʿât, Manzel, and Damascus. —

Al-Ḳuṭḳuṭâne is the settlement of aṭ-Ṭuḳṭuḳâne, which is still inhabited. Al-Buḳʿa is not mentioned in the Oxford Codex B (*ibid.*, p. 99, note a) and I am not able to identify it.

Al-Abjaḍ ("white," masculine) I identify with the Ḫašm al-Ṛarra ("white," feminine), beneath which is the abundant well of al-Mačmen.

In the Oxford Codex B (*ibid.*, note b) al-Ǧawši is given instead of al-Ḥawši; I seek this place in the Ḫabra al-Ǧawsijje at the end of the valley of ʿArʿar about fifty kilometers southwest of al-Mačmen.

Al-Ǧamʿ may be the Ṛadîr Ǧamʿân almost sixty kilometers west of al-Ǧawsijje.

Al-Ḫoṭṭi is the Ṛadîr al-Ḫaṭṭ sixty-two kilometers west-northwest of Ǧamʿân.

Instead of al-Ǧubba, Maḥna, which is given in Codex B (*ibid.*, note d), I consider an erroneous spelling of Maǧna, the name of the large rain pond about one hundred kilometers west-northwest of al-Ḫaṭṭ. This is supported by the local legends, according to which a road from Syria to Irak passed al-Maǧna and the mesa of Lâha near by.

This road was also familiar to al-Bekri (*Muʿǧam* [Wüstenfeld], p. 97). He describes in the territory of as-Samâwa of the Kalb tribe a solitary table-shaped elevation called Ilâha, situated on the former border between Syria and the territory of the Taṛleb. In the period of *al-ǧâhilijje* (before Mohammed) a *kâhin* (seer, priest) prophesied to a certain Taṛlebi that he would die in a place called Ilâha. The Taṛlebi at once set out with a small group of camel riders to Syria, whither they arrived without mishap. Upon their return they lost their way and asked a Bedouin which direction to follow. The Bedouin gave them information and told them that they would find their lost road in the neighborhood of the table mountain of Ilâha. Arriving at the table mountain, the Taṛlebi's companions dismounted from their camels, but he remained in the saddle upon his grazing camel. Suddenly a viper bit the camel in her lip. Seeking to throw the viper off, the camel threw her head over and brushed the Taṛlebi's leg. The viper left the lip and bit the rider. Only then was the Taṛlebi reminded of the *kâhin's* prophecy and begged his brother and companions immediately to prepare a grave for him.

Instead of al-Ḳalûfi I read al-ʿAlâwi in the Oxford Codex B (*ibid.*, note e). This probably refers to the present Awdijet al-ʿAlâwijje, although these dry watercourses begin somewhat too far north at ninety-six kilometers west-northwest of al-Maǧna. The next stations, however, and especially that of Ḏerʿât, lay almost on the same parallel of latitude.

Ar-Rawâri is an erroneous transcription of ad-Dawâri (ad-Dwâra of today) or az-Zwâri, which are the names of important rain ponds fifty-eight kilometers west of al-ʿAlâwijje.

As-Sâʿeda must be identical with the spring of Saʿâde which gushes forth about fifty kilometers west of ad-Dawâri (or ad-Dwâra).

Al-Aʿnâk and al-Buḳejʿa are in the Ḥawrân range.

Al-Muḳaddasi, *Aḥsan* (De Goeje), pp. 251f., records three roads from the Euphrates through the desert to Syria. The first of these is discussed here; the second and third on p. 527, below.

The first led from al-Kûfa by way of ar-Ruhejme, an-Naḥît, al-Ḳurâi, al-Ḫanfas, al-Ḥušejje, al-Ṛurajfa, Ḳurâkir, al-Azraḳ, and ʿAmmân; in all eleven short marches. — Al-Kûfa, ʿAmmân, and al-Azraḳ are well known. The station and watering place of Ḳurâkir should be identified with the familiar Ḳurâḳir (Ḳerâžer), for the order of stations places it on the road which led from al-Kûfa to and beyond the present Ḳerâžer. No other Arabic writer spells the name "Ḳurâkir." The substitution of Ḳurâkir for the correct Ḳurâḳir was caused by the palatal pronunciation of the second *ḳ* as *ž*. Al-Muḳaddasi was accustomed in Jerusalem to the palatal pronunciation of the *k* as *č* only, and he thus marked as palatal the pronunciation of the *ḳ*, which was not in his time and is not now so pronounced in Jerusalem. From al-Kûfa the travelers went to the settlement of ar-Ruhejme, which al-Muḳaddasi states is twelve miles from al-Kûfa, the actual distance being thirty kilometers (seventeen miles). The first march is always shorter than the average.

Instead of an-Naḥît I read al-Barrît according to the Berlin and Constantinople Codices (*ibid.*, p. 251, note q). The *ḥ* might have originated through the connection in handwriting of the *r* with the following *î*. Al-Barrît is about 110 kilometers west-southwest of ar-Ruhejme and, since al-Muḳaddasi states that it is two marches from ar-Ruhejme, each march would be fifty-seven kilometers. Instead of Ḳurâi I read al-Ṛurâbi in the Constantinople Codex (*ibid.*, note r), obviously the Ṛadîr al-Ṛurâbi, which lies ninety kilometers farther west of al-Barrît, or at two marches of forty-five kilometers each. The name of the well of al-Ḫanfas has been preserved in an alternative name of the small ruin al-ʿEmâra in the Wâdi al-Obejjeẓ, which is alleged also to be called ʿEmârt al-Ḫnêfes. Not far distant there is an old *ṛadîr*. ʿEmârt al-Ḫnêfes is 102 kilometers from al-Ṛurâbi, or two marches of fifty-one kilometers each. The name of al-Ḥušejje is given more correctly in the Constantinople Codex (*ibid.*, note t) as al-Ḥusejje. Brejčet ummu Ḥsejje is 115 kilometers west of al-Ḫnêfes. The station of al-Ṛurajfa is unknown to me. Perhaps it should be sought in the rain ponds near the volcano of Zellâḳa. The watering place of Ḳerâžer is more easily accessible from the east than any of the other watering places scattered along the east side of the depression of Sirḥân. The limestone formation here projects deeply into the volcanic formation, making it relatively easy for a traveler and his camel to reach the wells. Here the road turned towards the northwest to al-Muḳaddasi's station of al-Azraḳ, which is to be sought not in the fort Ḳaṣr al-Azraḳ but in some large ponds of the same name. The fort lies too far to the right of the direct course from Ḳerâžer to ʿAmmân. The southernmost pond of al-Azraḳ is 110 kilometers from Ḳerâžer, but it may be approached readily. ʿAmmân, ninety kilometers farther west, is likewise easy of access.

Upon this road from al-Kûfa to ʿAmmân, as described by al-Muḳaddasi, there is no spring-water well in the 450 kilometers between al-Barrît and Ḳerâžer. A rider therefore could find the necessary quantity of water only after a heavy rain had filled the numerous ponds, many of which were artificial. Sufficient rain occurs in this region once every four or five years, and even then the fall is local and does not cover the entire area. Before any large company of travelers pass through, they must obtain a scouts' report on the presence of water. Even then it is necessary to take along leather water bags containing several days' supply. The individual day's marches cannot be equalized, because they depend on watering places and the roughness of the terrain.

Route from ʿAjn at-Tamr to the Ḥawrân

Ibn Ḫordâḏbeh records (*op. cit.*, p. 97) a road from ʿAjn at-Tamr via al-Aḫdamijje, al-Ḫafijje, al-Ḫalaṭ, Suwa', al-Uǧajfer, and al-Ṛurraba, to Boṣra in the Ḥawrân.—

The account of the road from ʿAjn at-Tamr to Boṣra is essentially true, though it is embellished with poetic memoirs of the march of Ḫâled ibn al-Walîd, who never went over this road at all. Some camel trader or guide had given information about the main watering places on this road, and these were then connected with Ḫâled's famous march. The poetic expression: "the camels had come by sunrise to ʿAjn at-Tamr, forging their way and tramping over underbrush and ditches," is true only of camel riders cantering from the east westward. Only when approaching ʿAjn at-Tamr from the east do camels walk for any distance across underbrush and ditches.

Al-Aḫdamijje, today al-Ḫadamijje, is the name of a shallow well in the *šeʿîb* of the same name. It is fed by rain water which slowly flows from under the gravel. Al-Ḫalaṭ and al-Ḫafijje should be transposed.

Al-Ḫalaṭ I seek in the Ṛadîr al-Ḫlejṭ 110 kilometers farther west.

The name al-Ḫafijje leads us to the renowned Ḫafâje Lâha, past which, as stated above (p. 524), an old road ran from Syria to Irak.

Keeping the course hitherto followed, we should seek the next station likewise to the west, perhaps at Ḳurâḳir; Ibn Ḫordâḏbeh, however, does not mention Ḳurâḳir and leads us, instead, more than 250 kilometers northwest to the station of Suwa'. This is implied in the following verse: "By Allâh himself, how could the eye of Rafîʿ so keep the trend [of the road] that he came straight from Ḳurâḳir to Suwa'?" Rafîʿ (or Râfeʿ) was Ḫâled's guide from Ḳerâžer to Swa'. Ḳurâḳir, our Ḳerâžer, is the starting point of the road to Suwa', Rafîʿ's ability in following which the poet so admires, for it is very difficult to preserve a straight course over the level Ḥamâd. The informant of Ibn Ḫordâḏbeh surely did not name the station of Suwa', but Ḳurâḳir, after al-Ḫlejṭ and al-Ḫafijje, for it is difficult to understand how a rider could deviate 200 kilometers north-northwest of his route and then return more than 260 kilometers southwest. Ibn Ḫordâḏbeh, not being familiar with the situation of the different stations, omitted the correct Ḳurâḳir and put in its place the Suwa' of the quoted verse.

It is remarkable that the informant did not name any watering place in the 165 kilometers which separate al-Ḫafijje and Ḳurâḳir. Perchance it is here that the station of al-Uǧajfer belongs, some hundred kilometers east-northeast of Ḳerâžer among the wells of the depression of al-Ḫôr on the road from Ḫafâje Lâha to Ḳerâžer. This situation of al-Uǧajfer would facilitate the identification of the following station of al-Ṛurraba. Seventy kilometers west-northwest of Ḳerâžer is the rain pond Umm

Ṛurubât, which is regularly visited by the Bedouins. It is named Umm Ṛurubât (mother of small poplars) because of its thicket of small poplars. Therefore I should read in Ibn Ḫordâḏbeh al-Ṛuraba and not al-Ṛurraba. The latter name, moreover, is very incorrectly preserved in the manuscripts.

In connection with al-Ṛurraba De Goeje (*loc. cit.*, note n) quotes the verse of the poet al-Mutanabbi cited by Jâḳût, *Muʿǧam* (Wüstenfeld), Vol. 3, p. 783, but it has to do with an entirely different region (see above p. 519).

From Umm Ṛurubât to the city of Boṣra in the Ḥawrân is 140 kilometers; water abounds.

Routes from Hît and ar-Raḥba to Damascus

The starting point of the second road described by al-Muḳaddasi (*Aḥsan* [De Goeje], p. 252, note a) as leading from the Euphrates through the desert to Syria (see above, p. 525) was Hît. Its western terminus was not ʿAmmân but Damascus. The stations are not given. According to the Constantinople Codex it took ten days to travel by this road, which means that the distance of 600 kilometers was covered in daily marches of sixty kilometers. This undoubtedly is the road which today is called Darb as-Sâʿi. It leads from the city of Hît to the ruins Ḳṣejr Ḫabbâz about fifty kilometers west-southwest. From here it reaches al-Ḥeǧra, or al-Mḥejwer, 120 kilometers away, or two days of sixty kilometers each. From al-Mḥejwer it is ninety kilometers, or two days, to the watering places Râḥ and al-Mloṣi, and thence 200 kilometers (or three marches of sixty-seven kilometers each) to the spring-water well of Sabʿ Bijâr. Two long marches of sixty kilometers each bring one to the settlement of Ḍmejr, within one short march of Damascus.

Al-Muḳaddasi's third road (*ibid.*) led from ar-Raḥba to Damascus. It is regrettable that we do not know the stations. The Constantinople Codex presents ten stations, indicating that the caravans did not make even as much as fifty kilometers daily. Most probably the first day was taken up by the departure from ar-Raḥba, or the present al-Mijâḏîn, and in the short march of thirty-five kilometers west-southwest to the wells of Ǧibb. The next 125 kilometers in the same direction led to the wells Ḳulbân al-Hejl; one hundred kilometers beyond that lay the big watering place of al-ʿElejjânijje. From al-ʿElejjânijje to Ḍmejr was 136 kilometers without a single spring-water well. Such a march usually takes two days of sixty-eight kilometers, or three of forty-five kilometers, each. Over this road the distance from ar-Raḥba to Damascus could be covered in eight days.

Later Routes across as-Samâwa (After the Eleventh Century)

In the tenth century of our era the Kalb guarded not only the road through the desert from al-Kûfa to Damascus and Tudmor, but the other roads as well, their own camels transporting merchandise over them (aṭ-Ṭabari, *Taʾrîḫ* [De Goeje], Ser. 3, pp. 2217 f.).

In October, 1104 A. D., Biktâš ibn Tutuš joined with the Emir Ajtakîn al-Ḥalabi, the master of the city of Boṣra, and together they marched from the Ḥawrân through the desert to ar-Raḥba (Ibn al-Aṯîr, *Kâmil* [Tornberg], Vol. 10, p. 258). They probably left the vicinity of Boṣra to take a road leading to the northeast toward the watering places of al-Ǧidd and al-Mloṣi and through the valley of aṣ-Ṣwâb to ar-Raḥba, the present al-Mijâḏîn.

Jâḳût, *op. cit.*, Vol. 4, p. 137, gives an account of the road from al-Ḳâdesijje to Syria via ar-Ruhejme, al-Ḳuṭḳuṭâne, Ḳaṣr Muḳâtel, al-Ḳurejjât, and as-Samâwa. — Al-Ḳâdesijje is south of al-Kûfa; ar-Ruhejme and al-Ḳuṭḳuṭâne, the present aṭ-Ṭuḳṭuḳâne, are northwest of al-Ḳâdesijje. Ḳaṣr Muḳâtel evidently is the ancient name of the settlement of Šeṯâṯa. Al-Ḳurejjât denotes the basin Ǧûbt al-Ǧowf, therefore Dûmat al-Ǧandal, to which a road ran through the depression of Sirḥân along the southwestern edge of the desert of as-Samâwa. The situation of the settlements of al-Ḳâdesijje, ar-Ruhejme, al-Ḳuṭḳuṭâne, and Ḳaṣr Muḳâtel proves that these were not stations on any particular road, but the starting places of various roads connecting al-Kûfa and Irak with Dûmat al-Ǧandal. Probably all these roads converged at the watering places of al-Loṣof or aṣ-Ṣammît, whence a single road followed the valley of al-Ḫerr to the wells of al-Hebeke, and thence ran southwest to the rain ponds of al-Bwejtât, which are marked today by the ruins of old huts, and to Dûmat al-Ǧandal. This road does not lack water.

Abu-l-Feda', *Taḳwîm* (Reinaud and De Slane), p. 259, mentions a road called ar-Raṣîf, by which one can journey from the city of Ṣarḫad in the Ḥawrân to Irak in about ten days. — The present population refers to every Roman highway as *ar-raṣîf* (paved road). Such a road leads from Ṣarḫad towards the east-northeast to the spring of Sa'âde and the frontier fortress of Burḳu', where it ends. It is very probable that this road is identical with the one recorded by Ibn Ḫordâḏbeh (see above, pp. 523—525), for it has the same number of marches.

Ḥaǧǧi Ḫalfa, *Ǧihân numa'* (Constantinople, 1145 A.H.), p. 584, likewise knew of a road over which it was possible "in summer" to arrive from the city of Ṣarḫad at Bagdad in ten marches. — Nobody would have taken this route "in summer" because he would have had to take with him water to last ten days. The "summer" period (*aṣ-ṣejf*) originated in Ḥaǧǧi Ḫalfa's text from a misreading of the Arabic word ar-Raṣîf, which was, and still is, the name of the western section of this road. Ḥaǧǧi Ḫalfa, *op. cit.*, p. 470, places the terminus of this road on the Euphrates at the settlement of al-Ambâr (or al-Anbâr); he describes the road from Bagdad to the great ruin of 'Aḳarḳûf as three parasangs in length, and thence on to al-Ambâr as eight parasangs. From al-Ambâr through the desert of as-Samâwa to Damascus he says is ten days' journey.

Routes through the Desert Adjacent to the Euphrates

The Bedouins and traders friendly with them have tended to avoid the settlements on the Euphrates, preferring to go through the desert whenever they are sure that there is water in the wells and in the various natural and artificial reservoirs for rain water.

Aṭ-Ṭabari, *op. cit.*, Ser. 2, pp. 945—948, records that the Syrian army, which at the end of the year 696 A.D. hastened to aid the city of al-Kûfa when it was threatened by the Kharijites, left the Euphrates near Hît and marched via ʿAjn at-Tamr to al-Kûfa. — ʿAjn at-Tamr is situated almost midway between Hît and al-Kûfa, being 110 kilometers from each. The army marched through the desert.

Aṭ-Ṭabari, *op. cit.*, Ser. 1, p. 1379, relates that Jazîd ibn al-Muhalleb fled in the beginning of the year 720 A. D. from Ḫunâṣira, where he had been confined by the Caliph ʿOmar II, and hastened through the desert until he arrived at the settlement of al-Ḳuṭḳuṭâne. Although ʿOmar's soldiers lay in ambush for him at al-ʿOḏejb, he evaded them and took a road through the desert to the city of al-Baṣra. — Ḫunâṣira, the present Ḫanâṣer, is situated almost forty kilometers south of Aleppo. Jazîd could not have gone over the ordinary road along the Euphrates, for it was occupied by military guards; therefore he hastened through the desert. At the beginning of February, when the rains are heaviest, this was comparatively easy, if one secured a dependable guide and protector. Most danger lurked in Palmyrena proper. South of Palmyrena he headed for al-Lmât, the Moḳr Ḳṭeri, and Selmân. Here he went around aṭ-Ṭuḳṭuḳâne and al-ʿOḏejb far to the west and crossed Abu Ṛâr to al-Baṣra.

Abu-l-Farağ, *Aṛâni* (Bûlâḳ, 1285 A. H.), Vol. 15, p. 115, likewise mentions a road which in the time of the Caliph Hišâm ibn ʿAbdalmalek led through aṭ-Ṭuḳṭuḳâne northwestward to Syria.

Jâḳût, *op. cit.*, Vol. 4, p. 137, refers to a road from al-Ḳuṭḳuṭâne by way of ʿAjn at-Tamr and al-Fajjûm to Hît. — Al-Fajjûm may be identified with the oasis of aṯ-Ṯmejl seventy-eight kilometers northwest of ʿAjn at-Tamr and forty-six kilometers south of Hît.

Della Valle (*Viaggi* [Venice, 1664] Vol. 1, pp. 569 ff.) and his men, coming from the settlement of Ḥeḳla, arrived at al-Ḥammâm. After a short march they reached Serija. Then it was two marches to aṭ-Ṭajjibe, three marches to the Euphrates southeast of ar-Rḥaba, and three marches to al-Mešhed near the settlement of ʿÂna. At that point they crossed the Euphrates and, evading the customs officers, marched southeast through the desert to the Tigris, where they appeared at Imâm Mûsa. Here their route turned south to Bagdad. —

Ḥeḳla is forty-three kilometers southeast of Aleppo and al-Ḥammâm, about thirty kilometers almost due south of Ḥeḳla. Thence it is fifty-three kilometers to Serija; 103 kilometers to aṭ-Ṭajjibe; 143 kilometers to aš-Šejḫ ʿAli southeast of ar-Rḥaba, where Della Valle approached the Euphrates; 160 kilometers to al-Mašhad near the settlement of ʿÂna; and thence 260 kilometers to Imâm Mûsa, or, as it is called today, al-Kâẓimên.

On his return trip Della Valle (*op. cit.*, Vol. 4, pp. 598 ff.) passed through the desert by way of al-Aḫejẓer and ʿAjn at-Tamr.

Tavernier, *Voyages* (Paris, 1679), Vol. 1, p. 285, writes that from Bagdad to Anna one had to go four days through the waste which lies between the rivers Euphrates and Tigris. From Anna to Mached-raba was five days, to Taiba an additional five days; from Taiba to Alep not quite three days. This last part of the road, however, was the most dangerous, for nowhere else have so many robbers and thieves lain in ambush. —

The individual marches from Bagdad to ʿÂna were sixty-five kilometers long. They had plenty of water, for spring-water wells are numerous between the Euphrates and the Tigris. Mached-raba is identical with

Mašhed ar-Rḥaba, or aš-Šejḫ ʿAli, as it is called today. Taiba is the old, important station of ʿUrḍ.

Niebuhr in the year 1765 A. D. inquired into the roads leading from Bagdad and al-Baṣra to Syria. He notes (*Reisebeschreibung* [Copenhagen, 1774—1837], Vol. 2, p. 237) that caravans from Bagdad go via ʿAḳarḳûf, al-Hejs, al-Fellûǧe, al-Waḥale, Ummu-r-Rûs, Ṣunejdîž, Hît, al-Muʿêmîre, and ʿAjn al-Arnab, to ʿAḳlat Ḥawrân and thence over the road from al-Baṣra to Aleppo. —

Al-Hejs is unknown to me. From the various errors in the spelling of the names it is evident that Niebuhr himself did not jot down the names of all the stations, but had them written for him by an Arab trader and that, when later he himself copied the Arabic manuscript, he made frequent mistakes. It may be that "al-Hejs" is such a faulty transliteration of the name of the station as-Sêlḥijjîn.

Al-Fellûǧe is a well-known settlement near which the Euphrates is crossed. Al-Waḥale is twenty kilometers to the northwest; Ummu-r-Rûs nine kilometers from al-Waḥale, and aṣ-Ṣnejdîž thirty-four kilometers from Ummu-r-Rûs. The caravans crossed over below Hît to the left bank. Al-Muʿêmîre is a hamlet five kilometers southwest of Hît; ʿAjn al-Arnab is a spring forty kilometers northwest of al-Muʿêmîre; ʿAḳlat Ḥawrân is thirty-five kilometers northwest of ʿAjn al-Arnab.

According to Niebuhr, *op. cit.*, pp. 236 f., the shortest road from al-Baṣra to Aleppo led through the desert. Its real starting point was not al-Baṣra, but the settlement of az-Zubejr. Thence it led past Kwêbde; aš-Šaḳra; al-Ḫneḳe; al-Ḳuṣejr; Wâdi abu-l-Mrîs; ʿAjn Ṣajd; Ummu Ḳrûn, where there was a rain pond established by the wife of a caliph; al-Ṛazâri; al-Ǧirṯmi; al-Ḳâjem, or al-Eṯle; ar-Rhejme; aṭ-Ṭuḳṭuḳâne, or al-Ḥejjâẓijje; al-Ḥesjân; al-Aḫejzer; Râs al-ʿAjn; aṯ-Ṯmejl; al-Kubejsa; ʿAḳlat Ḥawrân; Ṯarab al-Ǧâmûs; al-Mânʿi; ar-Raṯḳa; Baradân; ar-Raḥba, an old fortress by the Euphrates; Ǧibb Ṛanam; al-Ḥamẓ; Ǧebel al-Bišri; al-ʿEḏeme; aṭ-Ṭajjibe, a hill with an adjoining village of the same name which had been utterly demolished twenty or thirty years before; Ḳṣûr al-Eḫwên, two old castles; Ḳâʿ abu-l-Fejjâẓ; ʿAnz ar-Rûṯe; Ṣahârîǧ, near the mountain of Šbêṯ and the range of al-Aḥaṣṣ; Ḥeḳla; ʿAjn Sfîra, or ʿAjn Ḏahab; and Ḥaleb (Aleppo). —

All of these places can be identified. The only fault which may be found with the list is that its sequence is not correct. Wâdi abu-l-Mrîs extends from the wells of Selmân to a spot southwest of the present settlement of as-Samâwa, while ʿAjn Ṣajd lies southeast of as-Samâwa. Ummu Ḳrûn is a familiar station on the Pilgrim Road from an-Neǧef (Mešhed ʿAli) to al-Medîna. Al-Ṛaḏâri is a swampy district thick with reeds, situated about fifty kilometers southeast of al-Ḳâjem. Al-Ǧirṯmi is identical with the well of the same name about forty-five kilometers west of Ummu Ḳrûn. Al-Ḳâjem, or the Ḳaṣr al-Ḳâjem, is the old watering place of Ḫaffân, fifty-two kilometers south of al-Kûfa. Ar-Rhejme is a village thirty kilometers southwest of al-Kûfa. Aṭ-Ṭuḳṭuḳâne is twenty-five kilometers west of ar-Rhejme, and al-Ḥejjâẓijje six kilometers north of the former. Al-Ḥesjân I seek in the Telʿet al-Ḥesjân. Râs al-ʿAjn is a spring at ʿAjn at-Tamr. Caravans went around the swamps near the settlements of Šeṯâṯa and ar-Raḥḥâlijje. Aṯ-Ṯmejl is a spring and al-Kubejsa a village southwest or west of Hît. ʿAḳlat Ḥawrân are shallow rain wells in the channel of the Ḥawrân valley. T̠arab al-Ǧâmûs is the name of a rain water cistern in the rocky bank of the *šeʿîb* of Ḥežlân. Al-Mânʿi is a water in the hills Ẓhûr al-Mânʿi. Ar-Ratḳa is a vigorous spring in a valley of the same name. Baradân is surely identical with the valley and the spring of Bradân, yet it belongs between Râs al-ʿAjn and at-T̠mejl. The station of ar-Rahba really is the active spring that gushes out below the sanctuary of aš-Šejḫ ʿAli. I am not familiar with Ǧibb Ṛanam to the northwest of ar-Rahba. It may, however, be identical with the watering place of Ǧibb south-southwest of ar-Rahba, which is not recorded in its proper place. Al-Ḥamẓ is unknown to me. Al-Bišri denotes the southwestern spurs of the range of that name. Ḳṣûr al-Eḫwên are the Ḳaṣr al-Ḥêr and the Ḳaṣr al-Ḥwêr southeast of aṭ-Ṭajjibe. The Ḳâʿ abu-l-Fejjâẓ is a well of the same name. ʿAnz ar-Rûṯe probably is the Ṭarâḳ al-ʿAnz in the vicinity of which *rûṯe* grows in large quantities. Ṣahârîǧ signify some rocky clefts in the western slope of the mountain of Šbêṯ which catch and store rain water. Al-Aḥaṣṣ is a basalt range north and northwest of Šbêṯ. Ḥeḳla is a village at the southwestern edge of the salina Mâlḥt al-Ǧabbûl. ʿAjn Sfîra is a full stream about a kilometer northwest of the settlement of that name.

When danger lurks near the Euphrates, caravans turn westward and take a route for which they must supply themselves with water for four or five days. Niebuhr, *op. cit.*, Vol. 2, p. 237, records the following stations on this route: from al-Baṣra to Selmân, al-Eṯle, Moḳr Ḳṭeri, al-Bedi, al-Ḥeǧra or al-Mḫejwer, al-Ḳaʿara, Ṣwâb, aṣ-Ṣerâ'em, as-Suḫne, Bîr Ḳdejm, Abu-l-Fejjâẓ, al-Ḥammâm, Ǧebel al-Aḥaṣṣ, Ḥeḳla, Sfîra, Ḥaleb (Aleppo). —

Selmân is about 130 kilometers south of al-Kûfa. With al-Eṯle I am not familiar. Ḳṭeri is the Moḳr Ḳṭeri, a rather shallow pear-shaped rain well situated in a rocky basin in the valley of Tbel. It is about 130 kilometers west of Šeṭâṭa. Al-Bedi is wrongly written for al-Bowli, the name of cisterns in the valley of ʿÂmež. Žaltat al-Ḥeǧra and Ḳulbân al-Mḫejwer are in the valley of Ḥawrân. The place al-Mḫejwer is written "Mhavis" by Niebuhr, which shows that he never had heard the name of this station, but merely copied it from an Arabic manuscript. Al-Ḳaʿara is the Ǧûbt al-Ḳaʿara, and Ṣwâb really is the ʿAḳlat Ṣwâb, a shallow rain well in the valley of the same name. Aṣ-Ṣerâ'em really is the Fejzat aṣ-Ṣerâjeb, in which *b* has been interchanged with *m*. As-Suḫne is written by Niebuhr as it is pronounced, aṣ-Ṣuḫne. Al-Ḥammâm are the cold and warm springs at the southwestern base of the mountain of Šbêṯ.

APPENDIX VII

PAGES FROM THE HISTORY OF THE OASIS OF DÛMAT AL-ǦANDAL

Dûma in Antiquity

According to the Bible (Gen. 25 : 14) Dûma belonged to the descendants of Ishmael. Dûma may also mean Edom, for under the chapter heading "Verdict about Dûma" (Is. 21 : 11) there is a discussion of Seʿîr (in Edom).

We have already seen (above, pp. 480—482) that about the year 688 B. C. Sennacherib launched an expedition against Telḫunu, the queen of the Arabs (Aribi) and priestess of the goddess Dilbat, and defeated her in the desert. The queen thereupon fled with Ḫazâel to the fort of Adumu (Adumat), which stood in the middle of an arid desert, devoid of water. Sennacherib pursued her and laid siege to Adumu. Telḫunu deserted her ally, and Sennacherib then occupied the fort of Adumu in the country of the Aribi, whose gods he carried off to Nineveh, together with Telḫunu and the princess Tabûa.

Esarhaddon (681—668 B. C.) appointed the princess Tabûa as priestess and mistress of the oasis of Adumu, for she had dwelt in his palace for many years (see above, pp. 480, 482, 483).

Pliny, *Nat. hist.*, VI, 157, records that the city of Domata (Domatha) is in Arabia.

Ptolemy, *Geography*, V, 19 : 7, mentions the city of Dumetha, or Dumaetha, in Arabia Deserta.

Glaucus (*Archaeologia* [Müller], p. 409; Stephen of Byzantium, *Ethnica* [Meineke], p. 237) names Dumatha, an Arabian city.

Guidi, *Un nuovo testo* (1891), p. 36, and Nöldeke, *Syrische Chronik* (1893), p. 46, quote a Syriac writer who attributes to Arabia Dûmat Gandal and the land of the Hagareans, where there is an abundance of water, plenty of date palms, and many solid houses. He likewise attributes to Arabia the land of Jemâma in the inner desert. —

The land of the Hagareans denotes the vicinity of the city of Hegra (al-Ḥeǧr) with the fertile and settled Wâdi al-Ḳura'. Jemâma extends south and southeast of Dûmat al-Ǧandal.

Dûmat al-Ǧandal according to the Early Arabic Authorities

Arabic writers refer to the settlement of Dawma or Dûma', or more frequently Dûma. It is popularly referred to as Dûmat al-Ǧandal and poetically as Dûmatu Ḫabten.

Ibn Ḫordâḏbeh, *Masâlik* (De Goeje), p. 129, and Ibn Roste, *A'lâḳ* (De Goeje), p. 177, place Dûmat al-Ǧandal [in the district of al-Medîna and assert that it is thirteen marches from that city, ten from al-Kûfa, and ten from Damascus. The fort in the oasis of Dûma is called Mâred. — This exact measurement of the distances from the oasis of Dûma to the cities of al-Kûfa (al-Ḥîra), al-Medîna, and Damascus indicates that three large commercial roads converged at Dûma and also that a route frequently followed from al-Kûfa to Damascus must have led through Dûmat al-Ǧandal.

Ad-Dînawari, *Aḫbâr* (Guirgass), p. 211, likewise states that Dûmat al-Ǧandal is situated almost midway between Syria and Irak.

Ibn Sa'd, *Ṭabaḳât* (Sachau), Vol. 2, Part 1, p. 44, places Dûmat al-Ǧandal at the entrance to Syria, i. e. five nights from Damascus and fifteen or sixteen nights from al-Medîna.

Al-Ja'ḳûbi, *Ta'rîḫ* (Houtsma), Vol. 1, p. 313, counts the oasis of Dûma among the ten marts which the Arabs annually visited without fear of blood vengeance or robbery, in order to buy their needs. In Dûmat al-Ǧandal a fair was conducted in the first month of Rabî' under the supervision of either the Ghassanian (Ṛassân) or Kalb tribe, whichever was more powerful at the time. — Since we also learn from al-Jaʿḳûbi that the Kalb camping in the vicinity of the oasis of Dûma acquiesced in the supremacy of the Ghassanians, we may infer that the Ghassanians and not the Kalb governed the oasis at this time. Of course, such government prevailed only so long as the Ghassanians were powerful enough to maintain it. As long as they were harassed by the Persian Laḫm, the Kalb were the absolute masters in Dûma. But when, at the end of the sixth century of our era, the strength of the Persian Laḫm was broken, the Ghassanians had virtually no opponents in northern Arabia and, according to Ḥassân ibn Ṯâbet (*Dîwân* [Tûnis, 1281 A. H.], p. 58), they ruled in Dûma as the highest lords and governors. The evidence furnished by al-Jaʿḳûbi excludes indirectly the possibility of even a temporary demolition of the oasis of Dûma. From the accounts of al-Wâḳedi (*Maṛâzi* [Kremer], pp. 174 f.) it may be inferred that in the time of the Prophet Dûma flourished as a center of trade caravans. The discontinuance of its fairs at the beginning of the seventh century is very unlikely. Since these fairs were set for an exact date, the word *rabîʿ* could not in this connection have meant the shifting first month of Rabîʿ, but, rather, the fixed Bedouin season of the first *rabîʿ*, or our March. Very few Bedouins could have come to Dûma when the first month of Rabîʿ fell between July and September. During that time, when there is neither water nor pasture in the inner desert, the Bedouins camp on the boundary of the tilled regions. They could not have reached Dûma with herds for sale or barter.

Muḥammad ibn Ḥabîb (Jâḳût, *Muʿǧam* [Wüstenfeld], Vol. 4, pp. 913—916, and al-Jaʿḳûbi, *op. cit.*, Vol. 1, p. 295) relates that the Wabra clan of the Kalb tribe revered an idol of the deity Wadd, which had been entrusted in Dûmat al-Ǧandal to the family of Ḳarâfṣe ibn al-Aḥwaṣ. Hišâm ibn al-Kalbi (Jâḳût, *op. cit.*, p. 915) learned from his informant that the Bedouins sent sour camel's milk to Wadd. His statue was larger than a tall man. Its outer garments and underclothes were carved, a sword hung suspended on a girdle, a bow and arrows were thrown over its shoulders, and the hand grasped a lance with a pennant. Ḫâled ibn al-Walîd was sent by the Prophet from Tebûk to Dûma to destroy this idol. He encountered, however, the resistance of the ʿAbdwadd and ʿÂmer al-Ǧaddâr families and found it necessary to slay them before he could get the statue.— According to the accounts of al-Wâḳedi (*Maṛâzi* [Kremer], pp. 167 f.) and Ibn Isḥâḳ (Ibn Hišâm, *Sîra* [Wüstenfeld], Vol. 1, p. 903), there fell at the time of Ḫâled's expedition from Tebûk in 630—631 A. D. only Ḥassân, the brother of Okajder, lord of Dûmat al-Ǧandal (see below, p. 539). He perished outside the city. On the other hand, the informant of Hišâm relates that two whole families were annihilated and that Okajder's brother was killed with them. If the idol of the deity Wadd had really been preserved in the Christian city of Dûma as late as the first half of the seventh century, it could not have been destroyed by Ḫâled before his capture of the entire settlement, which occurred during his subsequent expedition from ʿAjn at-Tamr.

Ibn al-Faḳîh, *Buldân* (De Goeje), p. 115, places Dûmat al-Ǧandal on the boundary between Irak and Syria, seven marches from Damascus. — Since it is about 550 kilometers from Dûma to Damascus, one march in this case would have had to cover almost eighty kilometers. Such a distance can be made only by a camel rider who changes his mount at least once.

According to al-Masʿûdi, *Tanbîh* (De Goeje), p. 248, the distance from Dûmat al-Ǧandal to Damascus is five nights, or at least six day's marches. — His estimate therefore would mean a rate of ninety kilometers each day. He too computes from the speed of a fast mail rider instead of from that of an army or of a trade caravan. He counts it from thirteen to fifteen nights from Dûma to al-Medîna, or from fourteen to sixteen marches (at forty-four or fifty kilometers per day). Accordingly he would figure the distance from Dûma to Damascus at from ten to twelve nights, or from eleven to thirteen marches.

Al-Bekri, *Muʿǧam* (Wüstenfeld), p. 353, places Dûmat al-Ǧandal between Birk al-Ṛumâd and Mecca. According to others cited by al-Bekri it lies between al-Ḥeǧâz and aš-Šâm (Syria), ten marches from al-Medîna, ten from al-Kûfa, eight from Damascus, and twelve from Egypt. — Birk al-Ṛumâd is too far away in Yemen to be considered in determining the situation of our Dûmat al-Ǧandal. The distances merely represent rough estimates, for Dûma is almost 700 kilometers from al-Medîna, 500 from al-Kûfa, and 800 from Cairo.

Abu Saʿd says (Jâḳût, *op. cit.*, Vol. 2, pp. 625 f.) that Dûmat al-Ǧandal is in a basin five parasangs long, upon the western slope of which a strong spring flows, irrigating the palm gardens and the fields. The fort in Dûma is called Mâred. Being built of large stones (*ǧandal*), Dûma was called al-Ǧandal. — The basin of the oasis of Dûma is not five, but more than ten, parasangs long. Its western part is almost one parasang (about seven kilometers) wide and several springs irrigate the plain.

Abu ʿObejd as-Sakûni (Jâḳût, *op. cit.*, Vol. 4, p. 76) calls Dûmat al-Ǧandal a fort and several settlements, locating it between Syria and al-Medîna, near the two mountains of the Ṭajj tribe, three or four nights from Tejma. He alleges that in the past the Kinâna clan of the Kalb tribe lived at Dûmat al-Ǧandal. In the oasis are the settlements of Dûma, Skâka, and Ḏu al-Ḳâra. The settlement of Dûma, enclosed in walls, is protected by the strong castle of Mâred, which once belonged to the king Okajder ibn ʿAbdalmalek of the Kinda tribe. In the time of as-Sakûni the castle suffered heavy damage.

Caetani, *Annali* (1905), Vol. 2, p. 261, writes in his translation of this passage that the oasis of Dûmat al-Ǧandal is about five parasangs wide; but Jâḳût did not say this and the statement in any case is contrary to the fact. Caetani further asserts that the ruins of a castle known as Mâred and the base of rigid fortification walls existed in Dûma before the advent of Mohammed. Even Caetani's detail that these had been built of large stones of a peculiar form, however, differs from as-Sakûni's words.

The oasis of Dûma is almost 350 kilometers northwest of the mountains of the Ṭajj tribe, Aǧaʾ and Salma. It is almost 280 kilometers from Tejma to Dûma, a distance which as-Sakûni says it takes three or four nights (i. e. four or five days) to cover. Either seventy or fifty-six kilometers must have been made between them on each march. The settlements of Dûmat al-Ǧandalijje, Skâka, and al-Ḳâra are still inhabited. The remains of the fortification walls may be noted to this day. The castle of Mâred has been newly rebuilt in part and is still so strong that the Rwala captured it in 1909 only after a siege of ten months.

Poetically Dûmat al-Ğandal is called Dûmatu Ḫabten, after the basin in which it is situated. Jâḳût, *op. cit.*, Vol. 2, p. 629, holds that this Dûmatu Ḫabten is different from Dûmat al-Ğandal. He seeks to support this opinion with verses of the poet al-Aḫṭal. However, the content of the poem proves it to have been written about Dûmat al-Ğandal.

Abu-l-Feda', *Taḳwîm* (Reinaud and De Slane), p. 82, records that Dûmat al-Ğandal is on the boundary of Irak and Syria. It is seven marches from Damascus and thirteen marches from al-Medîna.

The First Moslem Expedition Against Dûma (626 A. D.)

This wealthy oasis, controlling the routes to Syria and Irak, was a temptation to Mohammed. He intruded upon it as early as the year 626 A. D. Al-Wâḳedi, *Maġâzi* (Kremer), pp. 174f., relates that Mohammed came from al-Medîna on the fifteenth of the first month of Rabîʿ (626) and that he withdrew on the tenth of the second month of Rabîʿ. He would have liked to gain the oasis of Dûma, which formed the entrance to Syria, in order that by its possession he might intimidate the emperor. He had learned that great crowds gathered there and that their ranks were swollen by various Arabs who had robbed merchants bound for the mart in Dûma and had even contemplated a raid against al-Medîna. Mohammed set out as secretly as possible and sped with a thousand men to attack this multitude. His guide was Maḏkûr of the ʿUḏra tribe. When they had approached to within one march of Dûma, Maḏkûr ascertained where the camels and sheep of the enemy were grazing and the invaders attacked the herds. News of their approach, however, reached the camp and the throngs there dispersed. Mohammed found the tents empty. The scouting detachments which he had dispatched brought in only the captured animals. Muḥammad ibn Maslama alone brought a single prisoner, who was induced to become a Moslem (see aṭ-Ṭabari, *Taʾrîḫ* [De Goeje], Ser. 1, p. 1462; Ibn Hišâm, *Sîra* [Wüstenfeld], Vol. 1, p. 668). —

According to al-Wâḳedi, Mohammed started upon his raid on the fifteenth of the first month of Rabîʿ (August 14) and returned on the tenth of the second month of Rabîʿ (September 8). It seems to me that the earliest record of these events must have placed Mohammed's invasion at the beginning of the fixed Bedouin period of the first *rabîʿ*; a later annotation must have added that the raid lasted twenty-five days; and a final computation, still later, must have changed the meaning of the passage in such a way that the shifting lunar first month of Rabîʿ was understood. Had Mohammed started upon his expedition in the shifting first month of Rabîʿ (about August 14, 626 A. D.), he would have selected the least suitable season. On the dark, undulating plains which lie between the oases of Tejma and Dûma, the coarse gravel offers scant pasture even in spring, the grasses parch by the end of May, and the green wood withers. By the end of August the country is so arid and desolate and the water in the wells gathers so languidly, that to water five camels would often consume half a day. There could not have been a fair in that period at the oasis of Dûma, for access would have been impossible for the caravans of traders from the settled regions, whose camels were accustomed to a better pasture and more frequent drinking. The raisers of sheep and goats would have been unable to bring their herds to sell or to barter.

At the end of July and throughout August Bedouins have never camped, nor do they camp at the present time, in the neighborhood of Dûma. The only pasture for the camels, sheep, and goats of the settlers in Dûma is poor pasture found in the range of aṭ-Ṭawîl one day southwest of the oasis. Water for the animals is drawn either from the wells of al-Žên, or, in years of unusual local precipitation, from the rain wells of Ḥedâǧân, al-Bârde, and al-Mrût. These flocks are guarded only by herdsmen and a few warriors, who flee at the mere sight of an enemy stronger than they. It seems that it was such a camp of herdsmen and warriors that al-Wâḳedi must have had in mind. Had there been women and girls in the camp, such a speedy flight would not have been so easy, because tents would have had to be loaded and the loaded camels driven away. Moreover, sheep and goats never graze farther than fifteen kilometers from a camp. Had Mohammed really come so near Dûma and captured the flocks of sheep, it is strange, indeed, that he was not pursued and that the Arabs failed even to attempt to free their chattel. It is altogether impossible for goats or sheep to cover in August more than thirty kilometers in a day, and al-Wâḳedi omits to state where Mohammed had procured the leather bags for water necessary for these flocks. Moreover, this comment of al-Wâḳedi's inspires yet another doubt.

Mohammed had set out on the fifteenth and returned on the tenth, therefore he was gone twenty-five days. The straight distance between al-Medîna and Dûma is almost 700 kilometers. However, Mohammed could not have kept a straight course. He must have been forced to go around nearly impassable lava tracts and spurs of the sandy Nefûd and to adapt his progress to the condition and positions of the watering places.

Thus, even if we subtract one march from Dûma, we still must consider that the distance was 700 kilometers there and 700 back. No leader of a raiding party would dare to attempt covering 1400 kilometers of arid country in twenty-five summer days. The camels have to graze, and the scantier the pasture, the more time they require for grazing. Between al-Medîna and the oasis of Ḫajbar the road runs for only too much of the way through volcanic country. Thence it leads over sand drifts to Dûma. On long marches across lava and sand not even the best camel can make more than four kilometers an hour. The water between al-Medîna and the oasis of Dûma is salty, failing to abate the camels' thirst for any length of time. The raiders must have been forced to water their mounts every second day. The watering of a thousand camels requires one to two days, since water gathers but languidly. Where camels are watered they cannot graze, for, as a rule, there is not a blade of grass nor a branch of brushwood in the vicinity of a watering place. All is grazed off for ten kilometers around. In short, it is very improbable that Mohammed could have made marches fifty-six kilometers long and it is utterly impossible that he could have driven captured camels and sheep on his return.

Ibn Hišâm does not state the duration of this raid, merely declaring that it was launched in the first month of Rabîʿ. Ibn Isḥâḳ (Ibn Hišâm,

Sîra [Wüstenfeld], Vol. 1, p. 668) does not mention the time. It seems to me that we may rightly surmise that al-Wâḳedi's comment concerned the first half of the fixed *rabîʿ* period of the Bedouins. Such a surmise would clear away, though not explain, many obscurities.

Neither al-Wâḳedi nor Ibn Hišâm assert that Mohammed actually came to the oasis of Dûma itself. Aṭ-Ṭabari, on the other hand, presents al-Wâḳedi's account as if the Prophet had done so.

Al-Masʿûdi, *op. cit.*, p. 248, also writes of the first Moslem raid into the vicinity of Dûma. According to him the name of the lord of the oasis was Okajder ibn ʿAbdalmalek of the Kinda tribe. He was a Christian and conceded the supremacy of the Byzantine emperor Heraclius. Because he harassed caravans bound for al-Medîna, Mohammed intended to punish him. However, Okajder learned of Mohammed's approach and fled with all the inhabitants of the oasis, and Mohammed, having found nobody within, returned frustrated. — This account contains both truth and fancy. Okajder's flight with the entire populace is a fantasy. The oasis has today five thousand warriors; earlier, when northern Arabia was traversed by numerous and wealthy mercantile caravans, there surely were at least as many, if not more. These men in their fortified houses could easily have repelled a thousand Moslems. But Mohammed could not even have thought of a siege, because his return would have been cut off by the hostile Ḳuḍâʿa, Kalb, and Ghassanian tribes, which owned in the oasis numerous houses with their gardens and magazines. The narrative of the capture of the oasis of Dûma is, therefore, a fabrication. Nevertheless, the statement that Okajder was already the lord of the oasis at the time of this first expedition is of interest. It is quite probable that he acknowledged the supremacy of Heraclius, because otherwise the Byzantine officials would have persecuted the caravans bound from Syria or Egypt for Dûma, upon which the prosperity of the town of Dûma depended.

The Second Moslem Expedition Against Dûma
(627—628 A. D.)

After the first ineffectual assault upon Dûma Mohammed mustered a new expedition for the next year.

Al-Wâḳedi, *op. cit.*, pp. 236 f., writes that ʿAbdarraḥmân ibn ʿAwf commanded seven hundred men. Arriving at Dûmat al-Ğandal, he instructed the populace in the tenets of Islâm and to some extent succeeded in converting them. Three days after his arrival, the Christian Prince al-Aṣjaʿ ibn ʿAmr of the Kalb tribe became a Moslem. The commander Ibn ʿAwf informed the Prophet Mohammed of his progress in a letter in which he also expressed his desire to marry a woman of the Kalb tribe. When Mohammed replied by advising him to marry Tumâḍir, the daughter of the Prince, Ibn ʿAwf was delighted. She bore him a son who was given the name Abu Salama. According to another account ʿAbdarraḥmân ibn ʿAwf was sent to the Kalb by Mohammed with orders to take unto himself for wife the daughter of their king, should she consent. Ibn ʿAwf stayed there for a time for the purpose of collecting the *ğizja* (head tax levied on Christians and Jews) and married Tumâḍir, the daughter of King Aṣjaʿ, taking her with him on his return to al-Medîna (aṭ-Ṭabari, *Taʾrîḫ* [De

Goeje], Ser. 1, p. 1556; Ibn Sa'd, *Ṭabaḳât* [Sachau], Vol. 2, Part 1, pp. 64 f.; Vol. 8, p. 218; al-Ja'ḳûbi, *Ta'rîḫ* [Houtsma], Vol. 2, p. 80). —

Ibn 'Awf had undertaken the raid in the month of Ša'bân (December-January), 627—628 A. D., during the rainy season. It is absolutely impossible for seven hundred men to have brought about the capitulation of the fortified settlement of Dûmat al-Ǧandal. They came not only unprepared for a siege, but lacking the support of the neighboring tribes, without which no venture could have succeeded. Probably, however, this expedition was not aimed against the oasis of Dûma, but against the tribes which roamed in its vicinity, an assumption which concurs with al-Wâḳedi's comment relating to al-Aṣja' ibn 'Amr of the Kalb tribe. Mohammed probably wanted to frighten the Kalb, who camped during the rainy season south or southwest of Dûma. The camp of the chief was in all likelihood surrounded by the Moslems, who insisted that the Kalb accept Islâm. Chief Aṣja', or rather Aṣbaṛ, signified his willingness after a short deliberation. By acquiescing he lost nothing and gained much, saving himself and his people from plunder and gaining the friendship of the Moslems, whose sphere of influence was steadily enlarging. The Moslem account refers to him as the "prince" or "king" of the Kalb. Possibly kingship was attributed to him only in the legend of settlers at al-Medîna who had descended from his daughter. None of the north Arabian Bedouin tribes called its chief a king, and the Kalb themselves did not wield much power in those times, having been subjected to the Ghassanian kings, who would have tolerated no title of king among their dependent peoples. But Aṣbaṛ ibn 'Amr could not even have been a prince or head chief of the Kalb, or else the adherents of his son Imrulḳajs (aṭ-Ṭabari, *Ta'rîḫ* [De Goeje], Ser. 1, p. 1872) would have been much more numerous and his influence consequently much weightier (see below, p. 546). Indeed, it is also improbable that the chief Aṣbaṛ bore the title of either "king" or "prince" of the oasis of Dûma. The mightiest family in Dûma were the 'Ulejm ibn Ǧenâb, not the family of 'Abdallâh from which Aṣbaṛ descended.

Caetani, *Annali* (1905), Vol. 2, p. 268, maintains that most of the power among the Kalb was held traditionally within the family of Aṣbaṛ. However, this contradicts all Arabic sources of the period before and after Mohammed. Before the Prophet's time the Kalb were headed by the family of 'Ulejm ibn Ǧenâb; after the Hegira they were led by the Âl Baḥdal, a subdivision of the same family. As long as the Ghassanians were the mightiest tribe of northwestern Arabia, they were also the absolute masters of the oasis of Dûma, where one of their princes resided. No foreign chief could have been appointed resident in the oasis of Dûma before the rise in north Arabia of the Persians and, therefore, of the kings of al-Ḥîra. When such a resident was finally appointed I cannot ascertain that he was selected from among the Kalb tribe camping far to the west of al-Ḥîra. Furthermore, there were no more kings in al-Ḥîra during Mohammed's rule. The power of the Persians had been broken, and the Ghassanians held sway over the western half of north Arabia as far as the Gulf of 'Aḳaba. Therefore it is inconceivable that a Kalbi could have been the prince or king in Dûma at that time. The second Moslem expedition under discussion resulted in the conversion of one Kalb division to Islâm, and the oasis of Dûma was not captured during it. This supposition about

ʿAbdarraḥmân's raid is supported by al-Jaʿḳûbi, who ignores the oasis of Dûma altogether, merely noting that the raid was directed against the Kalb. He does not consider Aṣbaṛ as either a prince or a king, but merely as a *sajjed* (chief).

The Third Moslem Expedition Against Dûma
(630—631 A. D.)

The third campaign against the oasis of Dûma was commanded by Ḫâled ibn al-Walîd, as recorded by al-Wâḳedi, *op. cit.*, pp. 403 ff., and Ibn Hišâm, *Sîra* [Wüstenfeld), Vol. 1, p. 903. In the month of Raǧab, 630 A. D., Mohammed sent Ḫâled from Tebûk with 420 riders against Okajder ibn ʿAbdalmalek, the Christian king of the oasis of Dûmat al-Ǧandal. Wishing to encourage Ḫâled to raid the dangerous territory of the Beni Kalb with so small a company, he predicted to him the outcome of the expedition. On a bright moonlight night the Moslem riders approached the oasis of Dûma. Okajder with his wife ar-Rabâb, daughter of Unejf ibn ʿAmr al-Kindi, was on the roof of his castle drinking and listening to his two chantresses. Suddenly something struck against the castle gate. The Queen peered down and beheld two antelopes rubbing their horns against the gate. Never before had such a ready opportunity to hunt these animals presented itself, and Okajder directed that his horse be brought and rode forth with his brother Ḥassân and two servants. They passed near Ḫâled's riders, whose horses were held motionless and prevented from snorting, in order that the prey might not be warned and escape. Okajder was captured, Ḥassân resisted and fell, and the servants both fled. Ḫâled assured the captive king that his life would be spared and that he would be brought before Mohammed if only he would deliver the fort. Being bound and taken to the front of the gate, Okajder ordered his brother Muẓâd to open. The latter refused and Okajder assured Ḫâled that he could not bring about the capitulation unless freed. Ḫâled made an agreement with him, obliging him to present himself with his brother before Mohammed and to deliver two thousand camels, eight hundred slaves, four hundred suits of armor, and four hundred lances. When he was liberated, he flung wide the gate of the fort and fulfilled the conditions honorably. When he appeared with his brother at al-Medîna, he was courteously received and was bound by a treaty of peace with a specified *ǧizja* tax, Mohammed himself pressing his nail into the hot wax of the seal. Okajder wore a silken robe and a golden cross hung about his neck. —

Caetani, *Annali* (1905), Vol. 2, p. 264, thinks that the presence of Okajder, a descendant of the Kinda tribe from Yemen, as the master of the oasis of Dûmat al-Ǧandal in northern Arabia, must be suspected, because our knowledge of it rests upon authorities too doubtful. Nevertheless Okajder is known to have been in the oasis of Dûma by those best representatives of the al-Medîna school of historians, Ibn Isḥâḳ and al-Wâḳedi, who were highly praised by Caetani, as well as by all the older commentators. The fact that the Kinda camped in Yemen cannot serve as evidence against Okajder's presence at Dûma. Many clans of the Kalb, who divided the possession of north Arabia, dwelt as far away as Yemen, just as the Taṛleb tribe, which pastured its herds in northeastern Arabia and Mesopotamia, included clans which dwelt in remote al-Baḥrejn. When the world's commerce passed through Arabia the relations between the oasis of Dûma and Yemen were brisk and the members of the Kinda tribe ruled over various clans to the east and south of Dûmat al-Ǧandal. However, we have information that Okajder was descended from the Ghassanians (an-Nawawi, *Tahḏîb* [Wüstenfeld], p. 162). His original name was probably al-Akdar, which is also the name by which he was known to different poets. The diminutive was invidiously given to him by the Moslems as in the case of Ṭalḥa, Ṭulejḥa; Maslama, Muṣejlima. Caeṭani (*op. cit.*, Vol. 2, p. 266) is inclined to see in "Okajder" the semblance of the deity al-Oḳajṣer. Since, however, the devout and faithful collectors of legends in al-Medîna detested every semblance of idolatry, they surely would not have fashioned the name upon that of a deity. Moreover, al-Masʿûdi, *Murûǧ* (De Meynard and De Courteille), Vol. 5, p. 205, records that a brave warrior named Okajder ibn al-Ḥamâm fell in the combats with Merwân in Egypt, which proves that Okajder was not a strange name to the Moslems.

According to al-Wâḳedi, Mohammed left al-Medîna in the month of Raǧab (Oct. 14 — Nov. 13), going with a strong army to Tebûk. This march lasted at least fifteen days, so that they could not have arrived in Tebûk before the beginning of November. The direct route from Tebûk to Dûmat al-Ǧandal is about 350 kilometers. Were Ḫâled sent to the oasis of Dûma immediately after Mohammed's arrival in Tebûk, he could have reached it in the middle of November at the earliest. However, the nights in this oasis, 620 meters above sea level, are cold by the middle of November, and the evening entertainment of Okajder under the open sky, as recorded by al-Wâḳedi, is unlikely at this time of year. The comment that the night was bright and moonlit would lead us to the end of November, because the new lunar month began on November 13 and the moonlight nights come between the tenth and the eighteenth of a lunar month. But, as Ḫâled could not have arrived from al-Medîna at Dûma by way of Tebûk in fifteen days, this bright moonlit night would perhaps fit better into the later month of Šaʿbân; in which case, however, Ḫâled would have left Tebûk about the end of Raǧab at the earliest. All these dates, however, are refuted by a later tradition which speaks of a bright, moonlit *summer* night. November, the first rainy month, is never attributed to summer (*aṣ-ṣejf*).

According to the account of al-Wâḳedi, as recorded by al-Belâḏori, *Futûḥ* (De Goeje), p. 63, Mohammed sent Ḫâled to the oasis of Dûma in the month of Šawwâl, therefore in January, 631 A.D. This period is that most suitable for a raid, but hardly warm enough for an entertainment on the roof. Beatrix antelopes, called *baḳar al-maha'* or *baḳar al-waḥš* by the Bedouins, are among the shiest of animals. They shun the vicinity of an oasis within a circumference of forty kilometers. At the oasis of Dûma they would have had to forsake the plateau, descend fifty meters into the basin, and cross the tilled fields which extend along almost its whole length to the palm gardens near Okajder's castle. That antelopes would so venture is absurd. Therefore we find that interwoven into the account of al-Wâḳedi is a legend heedful neither of the topographical nor of the chronological circumstances. In reality the Moslems might have surprised Okajder with his small company on a hunt; al-Wâḳedi, however, records the ceding of the fort to Ḫâled and ascribes circumstances so improbable that we must disbelieve them. The brother of the captured Okajder refused to cede the fort; Okajder asked for freedom and promised to enforce the capitulation of the castle. Had Okajder really been freed and had he really reëntered the castle and got to his brother, as was necessary, it would have been very difficult for him to persuade his brother and the garrison to capitulate. Okajder's brother was free and Ḫâled could not have thought of besieging a strong castle in the land of the hostile Kalb. Mohammed himself, as al-Wâḳedi says, had difficulty in "inducing him even to enter the Beni Kalb territory with so small a band." This remark of al-Wâḳedi shows conclusively that Aṣbar ibn ʿAmr, whom the Moslems converted, could not have been the king or prince of the Kalb. The assertion that Okajder, having regained his freedom, ceded the fort with two thousand camels, eight hundred slaves, four hundred suits of armor, and four hundred lances must also be untrue. Ḫâled would have had to leave a strong garrison in the oasis of Dûma and could not have guarded the camels and the slaves with the remainder, defending the road that for hundreds of kilometers led through a country of no security. It is also doubtful that Okajder presented himself with his brother before Mohammed at al-Medîna. He would thus have given himself into the hands of the Moslems for a second time. We may conclude, therefore with finality that al-Wâḳedi fabricated his narrative of the capture of the fort and of the rich booty.

According to Ibn Isḥâḳ and Ibn Hišâm, Okajder was captured by Ḫâled on a hunt in the neighborhood of the oasis of Dûma and was taken to al-Medîna by his captors, who had not set foot in the oasis. Mohammed spared his life and, after making a treaty of peace with him wherein Okajder pledged himself to pay the *ǧizja* head tax, dismissed him back to Dûma. — Mohammed's action was very shrewd. By giving freedom to Okajder, he won his gratitude and could count upon it that he would never attack the Moslems. He did not compel him to accept Islâm, but would have allowed him to remain a Christian. He had, however, to pay Mohammed the *ǧizja* tax. How large it was and whether Okajder really paid it, we do not know. As long as the tribes camping in the vicinity of the oasis of Dûma were hostile toward the Moslems, Mohammed did not have the power to enforce the tax and, certainly, Okajder was not the only master of the oasis. The settled inhabitants of the great oasis of Dûma which lies between Irak and Syria hail now as they hailed then, from various Babylonian and Syrian cities and tribes. Some are the progeny of a very ancient native stock. The more active and beneficent the commercial intercourse of any city with the oasis of Dûma, the greater the influence of that city upon the oasis. The populace of Dûma live in large settlements or precincts, each of which has its own master. The master of the largest precinct is at the same time the lord or grand master over all the other settlements. Nevertheless, the prince of the most powerful tribe of north Arabia is superior even to the master of the largest precinct. A representative of this prince resides with a force of warriors in the oasis, and whoever would attack the oasis must fight not only the settlers but also the dominant Bedouin tribe.

Ibn Ḳotejba, *Maʿârif* (Wüstenfeld), p. 82, relates that by the will of God Mohammed conquered the oasis of Dûmat al-Ǧandal on his expedition to Tebûk. He sent there Ḫâled ibn al-Walîd, who returned to him bringing as captive the master of Dûma, Okajder. Mohammed then made peace with Okajder, who pledged himself to pay the *ǧizja* tax. — According to this account the chief result of Ḫâled's expedition to Dûma was the capture of Okajder. The conquest of the city is not mentioned, although it is indeed implied by the capture of Okajder.

Al-Masʿûdi, *Tanbîh* (De Goeje), p. 272, says as much. According to him the expedition was not made against the oasis but against its master. The latter was captured and the oasis also fell to Ḫâled.

Al-Belâḏori, *op. cit.*, pp. 61—63, does not mention the capture of the oasis. He relates that Okajder was captured, brought before Mohammed, and released after having become a Moslem. — Al-Belâḏori does not state the source of his report. He alone asserts that Okajder became a Moslem, which is improbable in the light of the other accounts that he paid the *ǧizja* tax, which was levied upon Christians and Jews only. Everything indicates that al-Belâḏori fabricated the treaty of peace, as he gives it. Even the best informant of al-Belâḏori, az-Zuhri (died 741-742 A. D.; see Ibn Saʿd, *Ṭabaḳât* [Sachau], Vol. 2, Part 2, p. 135) knew of no capture of the city of Dûma by Ḫâled. According to him the Prophet sent Ḫâled to the inhabitants of Dûmat al-Ǧandal. Ḫâled captured their prince and released him after he had promised to pay the *ǧizja* tax. The statement that the inhabitants of Dûma belonged to the ʿEbâd from al-Kûfa (really al-Ḥîra) shows that there was not only a commercial but blood relationship between the two commercial centers, Dûma and al-Kûfa (al-Ḥîra). Thus it was and thus it still is. A part of a family may dwell in the oasis and another part in the large commercial centers of the tilled region.

Sejf ibn ʿOmar related (aṭ-Ṭabari, *op. cit.*, Ser. 1, p. 2374) that Mohammed sent Ḫâled from Tebûk to Dûmat al-Ǧandal. The latter by sheer force compelled the oasis to capitulate, took prisoner its king Okajder, and forced him to pay the *ǧizja* tax. — In this account also the cause of the oasis' fall is the capture of Okajder. Had he not been captured, he could have avoided the promise to pay the tax. By this obligation he acknowledged Moslem supremacy over himself and his territory.

Dûmat al-Ǧandal and Dûmat al-Ḥîra

According to al-ʿAbbâs ibn Hišâm al-Kalbi (al-Belâḏori, *op. cit.*, p. 62), Okajder violated the treaty of peace and refused to pay the tax after Mohammed's death. Later he moved from Dûmat al-Ǧandal to al-Ḥîra, where he built a house that was named Dûma after the oasis of Dûmat al-Ǧandal. — This account indicates that Okajder had paid the *ǧizja* tax in 631 A. D. We do not know, however, that he had actually done so and we may hardly suppose that he could have induced the inhabitants of Dûma to pay it. Even had he succeeded at home, his overlords, the Ghassanians, would not have permitted the Moslems to enrich themselves from an oasis tributary to them. Therefore we may believe that the subsequent events ascribed by Ibn Hišâm to the year 632 actually occurred in the year 631. After Mohammed's death it was not necessary for Okajder to move from Dûma; nay, he could not have moved at that time, for the whole of Arabia was in turmoil and the inhabitants of Dûma would not have consented to the departure of their chief with all his property.

It is possible, indeed probable, that the traders from the oasis of Dûma had their own caravansaries and storehouses in al-Ḥîra, for al-Ḥîra was the nearest Babylonian city and the largest city accessible. Trade caravans from southern Persia and Babylonia went through al-Ḥîra; others proceeded from Mesopotamia via ʿAjn at-Tamr to the oasis of Dûma and thence to Petra or Syria. In al-Ḥîra and ʿAjn at-Tamr the merchandise had to be transferred to camels and these were then, and still are, rented by the inhabitants of the oases from the neighboring Bedouin tribes. Merchants from Dûma brought their merchandise to the Syrian border upon camels and returned with Syrian products through Dûma to al-Ḥîra. This trade continues to this day, conducted now upon a smaller scale, because the circulation of the world's trade has turned to other arteries. The merchants from the oasis of al-Ğowf (Dûmat al-Ğandal) today have their own caravansaries and storehouses in the city of al-Meŝhed; in the oasis of Dûma we see today the caravansaries and storehouses of the residents of al-Meŝhed. Al-Meŝhed (Kerbela) is today as important on the western boundary of Irak as al-Ḥîra and ʿAjn at-Tamr were in the seventh century. It is likely that some caravansaries and storehouses in al-Ḥîra and ʿAjn at-Tamr were called Dûma and that this local name was the source of the legend that Okajder, the master of Dûmat al-Ğandal, moved there and built the storehouse. It is not impossible that in the time of the Persian wars Okajder should have had repaired the caravansaries and storehouses that had been demolished after the passing of the kings of al-Ḥîra. In this manner might be explained the Arabian legend which seeks the quarter of Dûma either in ʿAjn at-Tamr or al-Ḥîra. But since this quarter could not possibly have been built within the fifteen months between the death of Mohammed and the conquest of these regions, no motive remains for Okajder's removal from the oasis of Dûma after Mohammed's death. Not only did he remain in the oasis, but he joined his clansmen and with them rebelled against the Moslems of al-Medîna and Mecca.

Al-Belâḏori, *op. cit.*, p. 63, records a legend which circulated in his time in al-Ḥîra. According to this story Okajder lived first with his brothers in the quarter of Dûma in al-Ḥîra. On their mother's side they were related to the Kalb and made frequent trips to visit their uncles, often staying with them for quite a long time. Once they went to hunt with them and discovered a ruined city of which remained but a few walls built of large stones. They restored the city, planted olives and other trees in it, and in distinction from Dûmat al-Ḥîra they called it Dûmat al-Ğandal. — This legend does not take cognizance of the Ghassanians. Therefore it must have first grown up in the period of the Omayyads after the Ghassanians had disappeared and the Kalb had replaced them as the most powerful tribe in northern Arabia. We cannot think of the oasis of Dûma as ever deserted. It stands at the intersection of the most important trade roads, has an abundance of water, and may be effectively defended. Such places were and still are continuously inhabited. It might have been demolished in the wars between the Persians and Byzantines either by the Persian or by the Byzantine Bedouins. Nevertheless, the Byzantines and Ghassanians were the victors and would not have permitted arrivals from al-Ḥîra to usurp so important an oasis as Dûma. Surely the native inhabitants themselves would have returned to the oasis immediately to restore their demolished dwellings. The self-interest of the conqueror demanded that he restore the subjugated oasis in order that its commerce should not suffer. It is unlikely that the new settlers of the oasis would have planted olives there. I spent several weeks at the oasis, yet I cannot recall a single olive tree. The area of olives in the inner desert begins almost four degrees of latitude farther north. On the whole, it seems absurd that the city could have been destroyed and the oasis forgotten, as our legend would have us believe.

According to the legend the new settlement was given a new name. However, the name Dûma is ancient and the cognomen al-Ğandal may be traced more readily to the reigning family than to the large stones, of which, in fact, merely the fort is built. Âl Ğandal (Eben Ğandal) is a very ancient family of Bedouins who camp in northern Arabia.

The legend, however, serves to prove that the relations between Dûma and al-Ḥîra were very intimate and that the inhabitants of al-Ḥîra sojourned in the oasis of Dûma and the Dûma inhabitants in al-Ḥîra, where their district bore the name Dûmat al-Ḥîra. Under no circumstances, however, can we follow Caetani, *op. cit.*, p. 992, in identifying the historical city of Dûmat al-Ğandal with the legendary Dûmat al-Ḥîra, and in seeking the latter near ʿAjn at-Tamr. For not a single geographer or commentator from the earlier period refers to any settlement of Dûma near ʿAjn at-Tamr. Had it been there, its situation would have to be determined in reference to the oasis ʿAjn at-Tamr and not to the city of al-Ḥîra, 120 kilometers distant. Al-Bekri, *Muʿǧam* (Wüstenfeld), p. 354, explicitly states that Dûmat al-Ḥîra is identical with an-Neğef (near al-Ḥîra).

Caetani, *loc. cit.*, introduces the testimony of Jâḳût, *Muʿǧam* (Wüstenfeld), Vol. 2, p. 627 (Caetani cites this erroneously as p. 267): "Thereafter Okajder went back to Dûma. After the death of Mohammed he refused to pay the *ṣadaḳa* (tithe levied on Moslems) tax, left Dûmat al-Ğandal, and took up his residence in the vicinity of al-Ḥîra, where he built a dwelling near ʿAjn at-Tamr and called it Dûma." — What Jâḳût writes is a crude combination of the notes of al-ʿAbbâs ibn Hišâm and of al-Belâḏori. According to Jâḳût Okajder refused to pay the *ṣadaḳa* tax after Mohammed's death and left Dûmat al-Ğandal. Yet, since the tax was refused by the oasis as a whole and by all the tribes camping in its neighborhood, Okajder had no particular reason for leaving the flourishing city. According to Jâḳût, he went from Dûma to al-Ḥîra, or at least to the vicinity of that city, and thence on to the frontier fort of ʿAjn at-Tamr, near which he built himself a new dwelling which he named Dûma. He had, therefore, fifteen months in which to prepare for the migration to al-Ḥîra, to march more than 500 kilometers driving herds, to pause in the neighborhood of al-Ḥîra, to march onward to ʿAjn at-Tamr 120 kilometers farther, to find a fitting place for his new dwelling, and to secure the necessary building materials for erecting it. On the fringe of a desert, however, so much cannot be done in such a short period. How was Okajder to procure the means for erecting his new habitation so rapidly? The citizens of Dûma would not have permitted him to depart with all his relatives and his chattels at such a crucial time. Had he escaped, they surely would have followed him and stormed his new domicile. He might have escaped, but in this case he would not have moved into such an accessible region.

As above stated, none of the old writers places Dûma near ʿAjn at-Tamr. The legend recorded by Jâḳût may bear a relation to the "House of Emigration" of the Carmathians built in the year 882—883 A. D. almost thirty-five kilometers south-southeast of ʿAjn at-Tamr (see above, pp. 366 f.). After the Carmathians had been ousted from Irak and north Arabia, the faithful Moslems sought to destroy them root and branch. In the neighborhood of al-Ḥîra the Carmathian governor of the renowned Oḫajḍer family ruled, living in the "House of Emigration". After his expulsion the faithful Moslems confused his name with that of the famous prince Okajder, ascribed the "House of Emigration" to the latter, and identified it with Dûmat al-Ḥîra.

In this connection Caetani, *op. cit.*, Vol. 2, pp. 263 f., says in commenting upon Jâḳût's report: "The account supported by unreliable witnesses thus appears false... We have an identical account, in a sense quite opposite, that Dûmat al-Ğandal was given its name from Okajder in memory of his native settlement of Dûmat al-Ḥîra. Such mutually opposed accounts impel me to conclude that both are false."

It is difficult to understand, however, how Caetani can here brand Jâḳût's account as false, and elsewhere (*ibid.*, Vol. 2, p. 992) refer to it as if worthy of note (see above, p. 544).

In the various accounts of Dûmat al-Ğandal, Caetani sees first Dûmat al-Ḥîra, then Dûma at Damascus. Thus we read (*ibid.*, Vol. 2, p. 992, note 2): "At-Ṭabari (*Taʾrîḫ* [De Goeje], Ser. 1, p. 2077, line 5) perhaps refers to Dûmat al-Ḥîra and al-Belâḏori (*Futûḥ* [De Goeje], p. III, line 12) to Dûma at Damascus. De Goeje's conclusions (*Mémoire* [1900], pp. 15—16) are identical with ours and we fully concur with them, as opposed to the insufficient conclusions of Wellhausen (*Skizzen* [1899], Vol. 6, p. 47, note 3), according to which Dûmat al-Ḥîra was merely a district in al-Ḥîra."

Dûmat al-Ğandal was not identical with Dûmat al-Ḥîra since the fact that the latter was merely the district occupied by those inhabitants of Dûmat al-Ğandal who sojourned at al-Ḥîra is clearly established by al-Bekri, *op. cit.*, p. 354, where he states that an-Neğef was called Dûmat al-Ḥîra because it was a suburb of al-Ḥîra on the road to Dûmat al-Ğandal. The section from aṭ-Ṭabari to which Caetani alludes reads thus: "Ḫâled marched from al-Ḥîra to ʿAjn at-Tamr and thence to Dûmat al-Ğandal, slew Okajder, took prisoner the daughter of al-Ğûdi, and returned to al-Ḥîra." If, according to Caetani, we substitute Dûmat al-Ḥîra for Dûmat al-Ğandal, it would seem that Ḫâled marched from al-Ḥîra to ʿAjn at-Tamr and thence to Dûmat al-Ḥîra, that in Dûmat al-Ḥîra he slew Okajder and took prisoner the daughter of al-Ğûdi, and that he returned thence to al-Ḥîra. But why did he not slay Okajder immediately after the capture of al-Ḥîra? What is the daughter of the Ghassanian chief al-Ğûdi doing in Dûmat al-Ḥîra?

Caetani (*loc. cit.*) also states that the daughter of al-Ğûdi was captured in Dûma at Damascus. In making this assertion he is obliged to introduce successive corrections in the location of the place. First he eliminates Dûmat al-Ğandal and replaces it with Dûmat al-Ḥîra where he had sent Okajder. Dûmat al-Ḥîra, however, does not harmonize with the daughter of al-Ğûdi. Therefore he substitutes Dûma Dimišḳ for it. Three events, separate both in time and place, are thus brought together. If we read Dûma Dimišḳ instead of Dûmat al-Ğandal in al-Belâḏori, *op.*

cit., p. 111 (not "III" as given by Caetani), we obtain an itinerary fully as absurd as that rendered by al-Belâḏori even when we do not alter his words. At the same time there arises a new difficulty, for Ḫâled has to march by the Ghassanians assembled in Merǵ Râheṭ twice without attacking them or being attacked and he has to go from the closest neighborhood of Damascus in Syria two hundred kilometers into the desert and immediately to turn back to the neighborhood of Damascus to assault the Ghassanians (see below, p. 573). Therefore we cannot replace Dûmat al-Ǧandal with Dûma Dimišḳ. The substitution solves none of our original difficulties, while it raises new ones to plague us. The historical account of Ḫâled does not contain a single proposition that places Dûma either at al-Ḥîra or at Damascus. The interchanging of the known Dûmat al-Ǧandal with the imagined Dûma at Ḥîra and ʿAjn at-Tamr is not justified, nor is it defensible to search for it at Damascus.

In short, therefore, we may conclude that the inhabitants of Dûmat al-Ǧandal had their own quarters at al-Ḥîra and ʿAjn at-Tamr, which Okajder might have built after the disintegration of the al-Ḥîra kingdom, and that after Mohammed's death Okajder joined the opponents of Islâm, though he attained no glory thereby. In this insurrection all the tribes of the vicinity of Dûmat al-Ǧandal participated.

Dûma in the Time of Abu Bekr

According to Sejf (aṭ-Ṭabari, *Taʾrîḫ* [De Goeje], Ser. 1, p. 1872) Mohammed appointed Imrulḳajs ibn Aṣbaṛ of the Kalb tribe as chief of the Ḳuḍâʿa and Kalb tribes. After Mohammed's death the Kalb with their chief Wadîʿa became dissenters, yet Imrulḳajs remained a Moslem and at the order of Abu Bekr was expected to combat Wadîʿa. After the Moslem commander Usâma on his march against the dissenters had arrived at the pastures of the Ḳuḍâʿa tribe, he sent to Imrulḳajs a mounted detail with the demand that he ally himself with Usâma to fight for the sake of their common religion. The dissenters fled from their pastures and sought refuge in Dûma near Chief Wadîʿa.—

This account shows that the chief Imrulḳajs ibn Aṣbaṛ had few adherents among either the Ḳuḍâʿa or the Kalb and that he may originally have been the chief of a small clan of the Kalb, being elevated to the new dignity by the Moslems only, upon whose support he depended. This was also the motive that impelled him to remain faithful to his new religion. He gained little in his wars with the dissenters, and even Usâma's band of reinforcements was of little avail. Sejf's account does not mention what the Kalb did; it says, however, that the dissenting members of the Ḳuḍâʿa tribe took refuge with their herds in the oasis of Dûma; from which it is evident that Dûma was not yet in the Moslem power. It is, therefore, inconceivable how Caetani (*op. cit.*, p. 990, note 2) can express suspicion about al-Ǧûdi's position as chief in Dûmat al-Ǧandal and how he can assert that according to other citations on the authority of Sejf (aṭ-Ṭabari, *op. cit.*, Ser. 1, p. 1872, lines 5 and 8; p. 2083, line 13; Ibn al-Aṯîr, *Usd* [Cairo, 1280 A. H.], Vol. 1, p. 115; see Caetani, *op. cit.*, Vol. 2, p. 583) the chief in Dûma was Imrulḳajs ibn al-Aṣbaṛ and that this is confirmed by the account of the second expedition to Dûmat al-Ǧandal. Caetani assumes that Imrulḳajs was chief in Dûma and that

Sejf's account of Dûmat al-Ğandal is fabricated throughout from false presumptions and errors. Yet Sejf says in none of the accounts recorded by aṭ-Ṭabari that Imrulḳajs was chief in Dûma, but states explicitly that Dûma was a refuge for the enemies of Islâm. Had the Moslem leader ʿAmr ibn al-ʿÂṣ, fighting against Wadîʿa, occupied the oasis of Dûma, the Moslem account surely would not have failed to record the fact. The account given by aṭ-Ṭabari, *op. cit.*, Ser. 1, p. 1872, does not tell whether Wadîʿa actually camped in Dûma. It is certain, however, that the mounted detail of Usâma did not venture to make an unsuccessful attack upon the tribes of Ḳuḍâʿa and Kalb.

Abu Bekr sought to possess Dûma, the greatest oasis of northern Arabia, and thereby to crush the power of the insurgent tribes. According to Sejf (aṭ-Ṭabari, *op. cit.*, Ser. 1, pp. 1921, 1963), al-Aḳraʿ and Šuraḥbîl advanced against the Ḳuḍâʿa who were camping at Dûma, while ʿAmr ibn al-ʿÂṣ was harassing the tribes of Saʿd and Beli. However, neither Šuraḥbîl nor ʿAmr attacked the oasis of Dûma.

After the uprising against the Moslems was downed, some Ḳuḍâʿa clans submitted. Abu Bekr appointed ʿAmr and al-Walîd ibn ʿAḳaba as the overseers of the local tribes (aṭ-Ṭabari, *op. cit.*, Ser. 1, p. 2083). ʿAmr ibn al-ʿÂṣ nominated as his representative and chief of the Ḳuḍâʿa camping in the higher regions a certain ʿAmr of the ʿUḏra tribe (a division of the Ḳuḍâʿa); while al-Walîd designated Imrulḳajs as the chief of the Ḳuḍâʿa camping in the vicinity of Dûma. Both ʿAmr and Imrulḳajs gathered followers, consolidated their power, and obeyed the orders of Abu Bekr. —

According to the accounts just cited both ʿAmr and al-Walîd had to subdue the Ḳuḍâʿa. They failed to subjugate the entire tribe and, having been sent to Syria, left this task to two chiefs, one a member of the ʿUḏra tribe, the other a member of the Kalb tribe (another division of the Ḳuḍâʿa). ʿAmr, with his followers of the ʿUḏra tribe, supported Islâm upon the pastures on the highlands south of Tejma, while the Kalbi, Imrulḳajs ibn Aṣbaṛ, joined the Ḳuḍâʿa between the oases of Tejma and Dûma. That he did not rule this oasis is clearly apparent from the sequel. We may claim that even this account does not consider the oasis of Dûma a Moslem stronghold, or else surely it would have fallen to Imrulḳajs. It is possible that the two chiefs may have gained the Ḳuḍâʿa tribes by clever persuasion rather than by force.

At the order of Abu Bekr the oasis of Dûma was attacked by ʿEjâḍ ibn Ṛanm. When ʿEjâḍ failed, however, Ḫâled ibn al-Walîd of Irak came to his assistance. Various authorities of the al-Medîna and al-Kûfa schools assert this and connect Ḫâled's expedition against Dûmat al-Ğandal with his march to Syria.

According to the account of al-ʿAbbâs ibn Hišâm al-Kalbi (al-Belâḏori, *Futûḥ* [De Goeje], p. 62), Abu Bekr tendered Ḫâled a written order during his stay in ʿAjn at-Tamr directing him to launch an expedition against Okajder. Okajder had left the oasis of Dûma after Mohammed's death, but had returned later. Ḫâled attacked him, slew him, conquered Dûma, and thence went to Syria. —

The Dûma in this account is identical with the oasis of Dûmat al-Ğandal, for the Okajder, who had made a treaty of peace with Mohammed, lived there. Perchance this reference to Okajder's departure from

Dûma is connected with the general uprising of Bedouins against the Moslems and Mohammed. The stronghold of dissent lay several marches south-southeast of Dûma and it would be strange, indeed, if the Christians of Dûma did not use this opportunity to repel the Moslem menace. It does not appear that Okajder joined the dissenters; still, he had to submit to the will of the majority of his countrymen and their allies. From this account it likewise appears that Abu Bekr considered the subjugation of Dûma to be of the utmost importance. Al-Belâḏori's failure to name ʿEjâḍ ibn Ranm cannot be advanced as evidence against that leader's activity in Dûma, for al-Belâḏori's records of events are very condensed.

The assertion that Ḫâled on this occasion went from Dûma direct to Syria is erroneous. As will be shown in the following pages, he returned to al-Ḥîra immediately after the conquest of the oasis of Dûma.

Conquest of Dûma by Ḫâled and ʿEjâḍ

Al-Wâḳedi (al-Belâḏori, *loc. cit.*) also asserts that Ḫâled arrived at and conquered the oasis of Dûmat al-Ǧandal on his march from Irak to Syria. Among the numerous prisoners was Lejla, the daughter of the Ghassanian al-Ǧûdi. Another version has it that Lejla was captured by Ḫâled's mounted band in a Ghassanian village. — Al-Wâḳedi records Ḫâled's actions very incompletely, yet he knew of his march to Dûmat al-Ǧandal. That Ḫâled encountered the Ghassanians there, especially their chieftain al-Ǧûdi, is implied in the mention of the capture of his daughter Lejla. Al-Wâḳedi mentions her because she was the wife of Abu Bekr's son and he wanted to tell the story of her life. He does not mention the fate of her father, as that was outside his purpose. From the presence of the daughter we may, however, infer that the father was also present. The Ghassanians were at that time the mightiest of the tribes of northern Arabia, and the most important oasis of northern Arabia surely was tributary to them. They were the protectors of the oasis, where a member of their reigning family resided. It is hard to fix upon the spot where Lejla was captured, whether at Dûmat al-Ǧandal, where her father was a chieftain and representative of the Ghassanians, or at some other camp or oasis. Nor do the reports agree as to the time of her capture.

Abu-l-Faraǧ, *Arâni* (Bûlâḳ), Vol. 16, pp. 94 f., records several accounts of Lejla. According to one of them, ʿAbdarraḥmân, the son of Abu Bekr, saw Lejla for the first time in Jerusalem. Later the Caliph ʿOmar directed his commander that, after the conquest of Damascus, he deliver Lejla to ʿAbdarraḥmân. According to another account ʿAbdarraḥmân was given Lejla, the daughter of the Damascene prince, by the Caliph ʿOmar. Still another account says that Lejla was the daughter of one of the Syrian kings and that ʿAbdarraḥmân saw her on his way to Syria. When the Moslems at last attained victory and slew her father, they brought Lejla before Abu Bekr, who gave her to his son ʿAbdarraḥmân. According to yet another account, Lejla hailed from Yemen. From these conflicting reports we may surmise that no one knew exactly whether Lejla was captured in Abu Bekr's or ʿOmar's time. Most probably she descended from the reigning family of the Ghassanians and was the daughter of the chieftain al-Ǧûdi. As her father fell in Dûmat al-Ǧandal and many of the prisoners were taken thence to al-Medîna, some have concluded that she likewise was captured in Dûmat al-Ğandal. However, it is probable that she was not taken captive in Dûma, but in one of the settlements tributary to the Ghassanians in the vicinity of Boṣra or al-Ḥawâni, which might have been captured by Ḫâled's riders (*ibid.*, p. 94). The fact that no account recorded in the *Kitâb al-Arâni* names the oasis of Dûma is noteworthy. The royal descent of Lejla was of common interest and, as the Ghassanian kings resided in the vicinity of Damascus, the capture of Lejla was linked with that of the city. How Caetani (*Annali* [1905], Vol. 2, p. 947, note 1) can conclude from the confused accounts in the *Kitâb al-Arâni* that Dûma Dimišḳ is the place of the capture and that the interchange of Dûmat al-Ğandal with Dûma Dimišḳ is quite plain, is beyond my comprehension, for not one of these four accounts mentions Dûma Dimišḳ.

According to Abu Miḫnaf (aṭ-Ṭabari, *op. cit.*, Ser. 1, pp. 2020 f.), Irak was to be attacked from the north and the south upon the written order of Abu Bekr. From the south Ḫâled was to lead the advance, as he returned from the victorious battle at al-Jemâma. ʿEjâḍ ibn Ḳanm was to attack from the north. The latter was then in central Arabia between an-Nbâğ and the Ḥeğâz and was ordered to march to al-Muṣajjaḫ and thence to invade Irak. — An-Nbâğ, the exact situation of which is not given, is identical with the station of an-Nebčijje on the highway to al-Baṣra. Since the eastern boundary of the Ḥeğâz extends southwest from Tejma, ʿEjâḍ's sphere of activity was between an-Nbâğ and the oasis of Tejma. Were he to execute the order of Abu Bekr, he could penetrate to al-Muṣajjaḫ and northern Irak only by way of the oasis of Dûmat al-Ğandal. Therefore he had to attack the oasis with his army and with his Moslem adherents among the Ḳuḍâʿa.

Caetani (*op. cit.*, Vol. 2, p. 955, note 1) writes that the oldest record of the al-Medîna school does not refer to ʿEjâḍ ibn Ḳanm in the year 12 A. H. (633—634 A. D.) and that its silence proves that his participation in the military expedition of 12 A. H. was a mere legend. — I cannot agree with this conclusion. Although the foremost representatives of the al-Medîna school neither knew of nor mentioned Muṯanna ibn Ḥâreṯa, Caetani nevertheless writes (*op. cit.*, p. 953, note 4) that Muṯanna ibn Ḥâreṯa was a personage of real historical importance and the most prominent commander in the early victories in Persia. Yet it is quite true that, according to Abu Miḫnaf and Sejf, ʿEjâḍ did not actually participate in the conquest of Irak during Ḫâled's campaign and that there is no mention of him in the account of the military events in Irak, 12 A. H. There is, however, no reason for believing that he did not take part in the siege of Dûma in the course of these events.

Ḫâled advanced into Irak from the south northward and captured ʿAjn at-Tamr after receiving a letter from ʿEjâḍ ibn Ḳanm (aṭ-Ṭabari, *op. cit.*, Ser. 1, p. 2064) containing a supplication for help. ʿEjâḍ was still in the oasis of Dûmat al-Ğandal, unable to advance. At first he opposed requesting Ḫâled's assistance, but al-Walîd ibn ʿOḳba, who brought him reinforcements from Abu Bekr, finally convinced him of his urgent need of aid. — Until Dûmat al-Ğandal fell, the northern tribes could have cut off every means of connection between Irak and Syria and could have delivered a crushing rear attack upon the Moslems fighting in both regions.

Caetani (*op. cit.*, p. 991) is mistaken when he argues that it would have been far better policy for Abu Bekr to have given Ḫâled an order to take the oasis of Dûmat al-Ǧandal from the settlement of an-Nbâǧ, because a much frequented road is reported to have led directly thence to Dûmat al-Ǧandal. He continues that it was foolish to require Ḫâled's army to make the long and arduous march from ʿAjn at-Tamr (or al-Ḥîra) to Dûma. — According to Caetani it was foolish to take the road from ʿAjn at-Tamr to Dûmat al-Ǧandal, although this road, five hundred kilometers long, has twenty or more watering places and is frequented now, as it was in the past, by trade caravans. Caetani advocates, instead, the road from an-Nbâǧ to Dûma, although it is over seven hundred kilometers long, leads through the unhospitable sand desert of the Nefûd where assured watering places are sometimes two hundred kilometers apart, and was shunned by all merchants. Caetani concerns himself only with the foolishness of Ḫâled's march from ʿAjn at-Tamr to Dûmat al-Ǧandal and ignores the fact that, having marched from an-Nbâǧ to Dûmat al-Ǧandal, he would in any case have had to go on from there to ʿAjn at-Tamr.

On page 990, note 3, of the work cited, after denying ʿEjâḍ's presence in Dûma and maintaining that his expedition never took place, Caetani reasons that a glance at the map and a review of the political situation will show that there was no strategic reason why Ḫâled should have left the Persian border to attack the oasis of Dûma. Such a course, he argues, would have necessitated a march across the immense as-Samâwa desert and an encounter with a strong enemy, while all his return roads might easily have been cut off by Persian armies. — Still, geographical and political reasons did impel Ḫâled to get possession of the oasis of Dûmat al-Ǧandal, for the oasis controlled transport roads throughout northern Arabia and was a stronghold of opponents of Islâm. From the oasis it was possible to interrupt commerce between Syria and al-Medîna, or between al-Ḥîra and al-Medîna. Until Dûma was in the Moslem power, there could be no conquest of the north Arabian tribes. Therefore the expedition to Dûma was imperative because of military and commercial policy. Had Ḫâled failed to capture the oasis of Dûma, he could not have contemplated the march across the desert from Irak to Syria, for on leaving Irak he would have exposed himself to defeat not only by the Persians and by the Byzantines, but also by the north Arabian Bedouins and the inhabitants of the oasis of Dûma.

For these reasons Ḫâled gladly consented to ʿEjâḍ's request and made preparations for an immediate march. Barely had the inhabitants of the oasis of Dûma learned of it (aṭ-Ṭabari, *op. cit.*, Ser. 1, p. 2065), than they sent messengers to all their confederates of the Bahraʾ, Kalb, Ṙassân (Ghassanians), Tanûḫ, and aḍ-Ḍaǧâʿem, asking them for relief. They assaulted ʿEjâḍ ibn Ṙanm, seeking to dispose of him before the arrival of Ḫâled. After the relief forces had arrived, all the defenders of the Dûma oasis placed themselves under the command of two men, Okajder ibn ʿAbdalmalek and al-Ǧûdi ibn Rabîʿa. —

Since the populace of the oasis of Dûma was constantly in touch with that of the oasis of ʿAjn at-Tamr, surely they must have had spies planted to keep them advised as to Ḫâled's activities. A fast messenger on a good trotting camel could arrive from ʿAjn at-Tamr in four days, whereas Ḫâled needed at least two weeks to complete the preparations for such a march. The inhabitants of an oasis are tributary to the various Bedouin clans which camp in its vicinity. Various nomad chiefs own palm gardens in the oasis, which they have acquired either through purchase or misappropriation. Since the clans and their chiefs extort annual tribute from the inhabitants, they find it to their advantage to protect the oasis and to hasten to its aid if the inhabitants are too feeble to repulse an enemy's attack.

All the tribes named by Sejf in this account had their encampments at the time north and west of Dûma along the commercial roads running through the depression of Sirḥân (Baṭn as-Sirr) to Syria and through the bare plain of al-Bsajṭa to Maʿân and Egypt. Hence it is natural that the Dûma traders paid them an annual tribute. Since the Moslems either enlisted or dispersed the tribes camping south and east of Dûma, the inhabitants of the oasis could not seek aid of them. If it is true that the tribes whose aid was asked responded so soon by coming to Dûma, we may conclude that Ḫâled made his expedition during the rainy period, for only then, when every hole and rocky crevice is full of rain water, can the Bedouins travel through the inner desert. At other times they are driven to the desert's fringe by the lack of water.

The presence of two commanders at Dûma may be readily explained. Every larger oasis and every large tribe appoints two heads in times of crisis. One of these is the hereditary chief or prince, the other a military commander who is at the head of the tribe during the period of danger. It is only when the hereditary prince shows a prowess superior to any among the tribe that the tribe does not acknowledge another military chieftain (*ʿažîd al-ḥarb*). We may safely assume that Okajder ibn ʿAbdalmalek was a hereditary prince, the head chief at the oasis, while al-Ǧûdi was merely a military commander appointed by the Ghassanians. The prudent Okajder reasoned quite correctly that, since the inhabitants of the Dûma oasis could not defeat ʿEjâḍ's legion, they must fall an easy prey to the victorious Ḫâled, in spite of the aid of the Arab armies. He proposed that the oasis be surrendered. However, the militant party was preponderant, and Okajder and his followers were forced to leave the oasis. On his march he was overtaken by Ḫâled's soldiers, captured, and, it is alleged, executed on Ḫâled's orders. This execution was justified by the peace treaty which Okajder had drawn up with Mohammed and which he had violated by his opposition to ʿEjâḍ ibn Ṛanm.

Ḫâled surrounded the city of Dûma from the east, ʿEjâḍ from the west. The Arab army of reinforcement camped in Dûma by the fort, where space was too limited to shelter all. Hardly had Ḫâled established his siege operations when he was attacked by al-Ǧûdi and a division of the latter's troops, while another division assaulted ʿEjâḍ. Al-Ǧûdi was defeated and captured, while his panic-stricken followers scampered toward the fort, pursued by Moslems. The fighters took alarm and closed the gate of the fort, while the Moslems cut down both their captives and the defenders grouped before it. Having succeeded in breaking down the gate, Ḫâled massacred all the fighters within. The women and children were sold at market, Ḫâled himself purchasing the pretty daughter of al-Ǧûdi. He then remained in Dûma for some time. On his return journey he sent a part of his soldiers to al-Anbâr, while he himself marched with the rest to al-Ḥîra, where he was accorded a triumphal welcome (aṭ-Ṭabari, *op. cit.*, Ser. 1, pp. 2065 f.). —

This account contains much information that could be known only to a person thoroughly familiar with the oasis of Dûma. The city of Dûma consisted and still consists of numerous solitary groups of houses that are hidden in the palm gardens and are bounded on the north, west, and south by high rocky precipices. It appears that the native populace dwelt in these groups of houses, which are called *ḳṣûr*, castles, while the real fighters and the reinforcement forces occupied the fort of Mâred, situated in the southwestern corner of the oasis. Ḫâled remained on the plain to the east and ʿEjâḍ on that to the west. After the rout and the capture of al-Ǧûdi a furious fight in the vicinity of the fort ensued. The fort is reinforced by high stone walls and is entered by a single small gate. Naturally, much blood was spilt before Ḫâled took possession of the gate. With the fall of the fort all the other oases lost their chief support and had to surrender. Ḫâled got control of the most important roads in northern Arabia, and the remnants of the Arabian relief armies spread the news of his conquest to all the camps.

Later History of Dûmat al-Ǧandal

Under the Moslems the oasis of Dûmat al-Ǧandal lost its prosperity. ʿUmejr ibn al-Ḥabbâb, the chief of the Ḳejs tribe, in the time of the Caliph ʿAbdalmalek attacked the Kalb tribe in al-Iklîl, al-Ǧowf, and as-Samâwa (Abu-l-Faraǧ, *Aṛâni* [Bûlâḳ, 1285 A. H.], Vol. 20, p. 122). —

It is possible that al-Ǧowf is identical with the basin al-Ǧowf, in which is situated the oasis of Dûmat al-Ǧandal. As-Samâwa is surely a watering place or camp site in the desert of as-Sâmawa, which at one time belonged to the Kalb. The situation of al-Iklîl cannot be exactly determined.

Al-Bekri, *Muʿǧam* (Wüstenfeld), p. 95, seeks al-Iklîl in the territory of the Hamdân tribe, while he locates al-Masâni and al-Akâder, which usually are mentioned in conjunction with al-Iklîl, in the territory of the Kalb. —

The waters of al-Akâder are probably identical with the watering places of the family one member of which was Akdar or Okajder, the master of Dûmat al-Ǧandal. The word *al-masâni*, as wells are called when water is drawn from them by camels and cows, points also to Dûmat al-Ǧandal. We should accordingly look for al-Iklîl in the vicinity of Dûma.

Al-Idrîsi, *Nuzha* (Jaubert's transl.), Vol. 1, p. 335, states that there are four marches from Tejma to Dûmat al-Ǧandal, which is a very populous fort offering a safe retreat. Its territory reaches as far as ʿAjn an-Nimr and the Ḥâšeb desert, which is a part of the desert of as-Samâwa. The Ḥâšeb desert spreads to the left of a traveler going from ar-Raḳḳa to Bâlis. —

"ʿAjn an-Nimr" is a faulty transcription of ʿAjn at-Tamr. It seems to me that Ḥâšeb is a faulty transcription of the word "Ḥasâf," which is the name of the steppe west of the Euphrates between ar-Raḳḳa and Bâlis.

Jâḳût, *Muʿǧam* (Wüstenfeld), Vol. 4, p. 389, refers to the fort of Mâred in Dûmat al-Ǧandal; this fort, with al-Ablaḳ, was vainly stormed by Queen az-Zabba.

The oases of Dûmat al-Ǧandal, Ḫajbar, and D̲u al-Merwa are called, according to Jâḳût, *op. cit.*, Vol. 3, p. 277, al-Mašâref (watch grounds) because of their location on the boundary of the settlers' territory.

Ḥaǧǧi Ḫalfa, *Ǧihân numa'* (Constantinople, 1145 A. H.), p. 530, asserts that al-Ǧowf lies between Syria, the Ḥeǧâz, Neǧd, and Irak. It is north of the territory of the Šammar, from which it is separated by the high dunes of the Ḍâḥi desert. The fort of Dûmat al-Ǧandal is built upon a white cliff in al-Ǧowf, and not far from it the spring of ʿAjn at-Tamr gushes out near another stream which springs from under an enormous marble boulder, above which the Ḥimjar D̲û-l-Ḳarnejn had built a dome. In the year 1513 A. D. a great silver treasure was discovered near by. The settlers of al-Ǧowf engage in tillage. Journeys into this area can be made only with good guides. The station of Šubeke is southwest of Dûma on the fringe of the sand desert of aḍ-Ḍâḥi; its water is bad. —

Ḍâḥi is the Nefûd desert. The part of it that lies to the southeast of al-Ǧowf is still known as aẓ-Ẓâḥi. Aš-Šubeke is perhaps the present aš-Šubejče, which, however, is not situated southwest but northwest of Dûmat al-Ǧandal. The fort of Dûmat al-Ǧandal is identical with the ruins of al-Ḥasja.

Niebuhr, *Arabien* (Copenhagen, 1772), p. 344, includes in Neǧd the mountainous region of al-Ǧowf, remarking that near it camp the Âl Sirḥân between the mountains of Šammar and Syria.

Burckhardt, *Syria* (1822), p. 663, writes that the inhabitants of the oasis of al-Ǧowf paid the *zeka* tax to Eben Saʿûd after the year 1790. The head chief was of the family of Eben Derʿ.

Wallin (*Narrative* [1854], pp. 140 f.), who visited al-Ǧowf during 1845, did not hear that the Arabs had ever ascribed this oasis to the Sirḥân clan. According to him the most powerful clan at the time was that of Eben Ḳaʿajjed, but the oldest was the clan of Eben Derʿ, which dwelt in the neighborhood of the fort of Mâred.

From about 1820 to 1853 the inhabitants of the oasis of al-Ǧowf were tributary to the Rwala. Then the oasis was seized by Ṭalâl eben Rašîd. Eben Rašîd remained its master until the spring of 1909, when the oasis reverted to Eben Šaʿlân, head chief of the Rwala tribe. Since 1922 Eben Saʿûd has maintained a regent at al-Ǧowf.

APPENDIX VIII

THE MARCH OF ḪÂLED IBN AL-WALÎD FROM IRAK TO SYRIA

Ibn Isḥâḳ's Version

Ibn Isḥâḳ relates (aṭ-Ṭabari, *Ta'rîḫ* [De Goeje], Ser. 1, pp. 2121-2123) that in the second month of Rabîʿ (13 A. H.) Ḫâled received at al-Ḥîra Abu Bekr's written order to hasten with his picked warriors to aid the Moslems fighting in Syria. Ḫâled forthwith sent all his weaklings and his women to al-Medîna, appointed Chief al-Muṯanna his representative, and departed. First he came to the oasis of ʿAjn at-Tamr, where he attacked and defeated its inhabitants, seized the fort with its garrison of Persians, and ordered the massacre of his prisoners. Many sons of the inhabitants and soldiers of the garrison were sent to Abu Bekr. It was in ʿAjn at-Tamr that Helâl ibn ʿAḳḳa ibn Bišr an-Namari was killed and nailed to a cross on Ḫâled's order.

After that Ḫâled intended to go through the arid desert between the watering place of the Kalb known as Ḳurâḳir and the watering place of the Bahraʾ clan known as Suwaʾ, five nights distant. He sought a dependable guide and his attention was called to Râfeʿ ibn ʿAmîra, a member of the Ṭajj tribe. This man discouraged his project, because death by thirst pursues even the lone camel rider between Ḳurâḳir and Suwaʾ and the danger to Ḫâled with his horses and camels laden with heavy burdens would have been almost insuperable. Nevertheless Ḫâled persevered in his plan, arguing that he must obey the Caliph's explicit order. The guide then acquiesced and ordered the men to take along all the water they could and he bade those who were skilled in doing so to rouse such a desire for water in the camels that their ears would tremble. He requested of Ḫâled twenty large, fat camels that were growing old, the kind that are usually slaughtered. In them he stimulated a great thirst and did not take them to the watering place until they trembled for want of water. After they had satiated their thirst he cut their lips off and tied their mouths so that they could not graze and chew their cuds. Taking all burdens off them, he asked Ḫâled to depart. The horses and the laden camels were urged on. At each camping place four of the original twenty specially treated camels were killed, the water squeezed out of their paunches and given to the horses to drink. In this manner the water contained in the leathern bags was saved for the men only. At the end of the sixth day Ḫâled feared greatly for his men, but Râfeʿ allayed his fears, saying that they would find water.

Upon coming to the two landmarks of the watering place of Suwaʾ, Râfeʿ, whose eyes were sore, asked the men to seek for a small, round *ʿawseǧe* shrub. Since they could not find it Râfeʿ, too, began to lose faith and implored the men to seek more thoroughly and look carefully. Finally they found the stems of the shrub, which had been cut down. Râfeʿ directed them to dig near the roots, and soon they struck spring water which satiated their thirst. Beyond Suwaʾ Ḫâled found both watering places and camp sites. With the dawn he successfully assaulted the camp of the Bahraʾ clan, in which men were still carousing. He then advanced to the Merǧ Râheṭ, where he defeated the Ghassanian tribe in battle. Thence he marched upon the city of Boṣra. —

The order of the Caliph Abu Bekr clearly proves that the Moslem army had been fighting in Syria and had fared badly.

Caetani, *Annali* (1905), Vol. 2, p. 1197, note 2, writes that Ḫâled left Irak for Syria at the time when the other Moslem generals were setting out from al-Medîna to Syria. This assertion contradicts the account preserved for us by Ibn Isḥâḳ, the best representative of the al-Medîna school. The fact that Ḫâled was to hasten to Syria with selected soldiers only shows that they were intended to inspire the Moslems in Syria to greater valor and to enforce Ḫâled's orders. Abu Bekr did not want to enlarge the Moslem army, but desired the seasoned chieftain, Ḫâled, and his loyal troopers to infuse the local army with fresh morale.

We should expect that, in order to fulfill the Caliph's wish, Ḫâled would have taken the least perilous and shortest route to Syria from the city of al-Ḥîra. However, Ibn Isḥâḳ in his account says that Ḫâled went to ʿAjn at-Tamr on the way and besieged the fort. This account precludes a sudden attack, for Ḫâled first fought the inhabitants and afterwards laid siege to the fort itself. This Persian castle had often been attacked by the Bedouins and was strongly fortified and well supplied with water and food. Moreover, its garrison knew very well what to expect from the Moslems and fought with the greatest valor. Various tools and implements of war were necessary in the storming of the castle, and Ḫâled could not have had them, since, according to Ibn Isḥâḳ, the route of his march to Syria was to lie through the desert. He could not reckon with an uprising of the native populace against the Persian garrison, as the latter held the fort while the inhabitants occupied only the city and the gardens. The statement that Helâl ibn ʿAḳḳa, a Bedouin chief, was executed at ʿAjn at-Tamr indicates that the Persians were assisted by the Bedouins and that Ḫâled with his little column would have had to defeat not only the native settlers but also a nomadic army of relief and the Persian garrison. Such a victory would have resulted in heavy casualties among his troopers. We cannot, therefore, believe that Ḫâled, whose foresight and caution we admire, could have acted so injudiciously as to attack ʿAjn at-Tamr on the march to Syria, and we must conclude that he seized the fort before the time of the march. Ibn Isḥâḳ was unquestionably mistaken when he associated the siege with the march.

The first station which Ibn Isḥâḳ mentions on Ḫâled's march to Syria is Ḳurâḳir. This famous watering place of the Kalb has preserved its name in the Ḳulbân Ḳerâžer, situated over 500 kilometers west-southwest of ʿAjn at-Tamr on the eastern boundary of the depression of Sirḥân (the old Baṭn as-Sirr), just where the Arabic geographers and poets sought it. Ibn Isḥâḳ fails to mention anything about the march from ʿAjn at-Tamr to Ḳurâḳir. Hence we may take it for granted that Ḫâled encountered none of the enemy and found water daily for his men and animals. Ibn Isḥâḳ does not explain what caused Ḫâled to forsake the westerly course at Ḳurâḳir and to deviate towards the north. Instead of marching from Ḳurâḳir to the city of Boṣra in three days, traveling through a land abundantly supplied with water and pasture, he crossed the arid desert toward the watering place of Suwaʾ, which is situated over 380 kilometers north of Ḳurâḳir. Why did he do so? Ibn Isḥâḳ gives no answer. Suwaʾ, or as it is now pronounced, Swaʾ, is the name of a height and a *šeʿîb* at the watering place of Sabʿ Bijâr (Seven Wells).

Caetani, *op. cit.*, Vol. 2, p. 1231, says that for small places every new explorer gives names differing from those given by his predecessors. Thus, he alleges, Chesney had found the name Querdi where Peters found Suwe, which might be the Suwa of Ḫâled's march. — Explorers who really act thus deserve severe censure, yet the names misrepresented, according to Caetani, should not be distorted still further. Both Chesney and Peters are right. Al-Werdijje (and not Querdi, as Caetani incorrectly transcribes it) is situated on the left bank of the Euphrates opposite as-Suwe (correctly as-Swêʿijje), on the right bank. How Caetani can connect this place with Suwaʾ and seek it in the vicinity of as-Suẖne (see below, pp. 561f.) is beyond my comprehension.

The wells of Sabʿ Bijâr are in a shallow valley and have no water when there is a drought of several years. All about lies an undulating plain in which it is difficult for a traveler to find his way. The situation of the watering place of Sabʿ Bijâr can be recognized by two small natural domes on which are two cairns of piled stone. There is no other fresh spring water between Ḳurâḳir and Suwaʾ (Sabʿ Bijâr). Ibn Isḥâḳ estimates the distance between these watering places at five nights, which is equivalent to the actual distance of 280 kilometers. Reckoning the distance at five nights means that the traveler reaches his destination on the sixth day, the march on the sixth day possibly being shorter than any of the preceding marches. Caetani, *op. cit.*, Vol. 2, p. 1195, incorrectly translates "five nights" by "five marches."

Ḫâled surely had guides who were thoroughly familiar with the usual transport road from al-Ḥîra to Syria. Since, however, he could not depend on them after departing from it, he sought a new guide. This new guide belonged either to the warriors of the Ṭajj tribe, which accompanied Ḫâled, or to the band of professional guides whom Ḫâled had enlisted. Even today groups of professional guides congregate at the commercial centers on the fringe of the desert. It appears that Râfeʿ was a professional guide, for he was able to keep the course, bore the local topography in mind excellently, and knew the customs of the nomads who rove about a waterless desert. From Ḳurâḳir (or Ḳerâžer) to Suwaʾ, Ḫâled was instructed to take enough water for both the men and the beasts. However, the water bags he had procured at al-Ḥîra were sufficient for water needed by the men for only five or six days. They had to use the water very sparingly, for April, which in my opinion is the month in which the march began, is notorious for the heat that prevails during the day and, whenever the dry southeast wind blows, during the night as well.

Caetani, *op. cit.*, Vol. 2, p. 1219, contends that Ibn Isḥâḳ's statement that Ḫâled was ordered to go from al-Ḥîra to Syria in the second month of Rabîʿ, 13 A. H., is amazingly inaccurate and should be corrected. But it is the correction which is at fault. The statement of Ibn Isḥâḳ is absolutely true and agrees with other accounts of the same events. The word "Rabîʿ," however, does not here refer to the shifting lunar month of the later Moslems, but, rather, to the fixed period of the Bedouins, which must have been meant in the original account followed by Ibn Isḥâḳ.

Before his departure Ḫâled had not thought of the problem of watering the horses. The horses of the nomads endure as much as forty-eight hours without a drink and while Ḫâled was marching over the usual transport road from al-Ḥîra via the oasis of Dûmat al-Ǧandal and on toward the northwest through the depression of Sirḥân as far as Ḳurâḳir, he came to a watering place for his horses every second day. The matter took on a different aspect, however, when, after leaving this road at Ḳurâḳir and heading for Suwaʾ, it became necessary to transport a supply of water for the horses as well as for the men. Had he not carried baggage, he could have sped the march from Ḳurâḳir to Suwa'. As it was, the laden camels could not trot as fast as the untrammeled horses. Had he apportioned the loads of all the camels upon fast riding camels, he would merely have burdened them without attaining a quicker pace. As his companions were averse to parting either with their baggage or with their horses, it was necessary to take along water enough for all.

Since it was found impossible to procure the necessary water bags at Ḳurâḳir, the fat old camels were made to serve as living reservoirs. A strong, fat camel coaxed to drink can hold as much as sixty liters. If he is prevented from grazing and ruminating, he will hold the water in his paunch for several days. In case of necessity he may be slaughtered and the water which is forced out of the paunch will settle in a few hours and become fit for men and animals to drink. The meat of such slaughtered camels provides food for the travelers. The stronger, the fatter, and the larger the camel, the more water he will imbibe and the longer he will be able to survive without grazing. Ḫâled, of course, had many camels which were marked for butchering in order that the army might have fresh meat. If it had rained between Ḳurâḳir and Suwa' that year, the horses could still have found fresh grasses in April, and by grazing on this the amount of water consumed by each horse would have been cut down to an average of six liters per day. If we may judge Ḫâled's force by the strength of present expeditions, he must have had ten horses for every hundred riding camels.

As is explained in greater detail (pp. 570—571), the account of the manner in which water for the horses was procured indicates that Ḫâled imitated the custom of all large nomadic tribes. However, this is not conceded by Caetani, who says (*ibid.*, Vol. 2, p. 1197, note 4) that the entire narrative is fanciful and has been embellished by later commentators, because one camel can carry on his back twenty times the amount of water that can be contained in his paunch. He reasons: why slaughter the camels and drink the water in their paunches when they can carry on their backs twenty times as much water? forgetting that Ḫâled lacked the necessary water bags and had to use, instead, the paunches of his camels. It is inconceivable to Caetani that Ḫâled should act with such cruelty. By such and similar words Caetani proves that he is not acquainted with the desert life. The account of the dangers on the march from Ḳurâḳir to Suwa' was so familiar to the ancient Moslems that there must have been some historical reason for it. Ibn Isḥâḳ is right when he says that there was no fresh spring water between Ḳurâḳir and Suwa', and Caetani's allegation (*loc. cit.*) that his assertion is groundless is itself unsubstantiated. Caetani brings forward (*op. cit.*, Vol. 2, pp. 1216, 1221, etc.) his extensive travels in the Arabian desert and the experiences gained there and professes (*ibid.*, Vol. 2, p. 1221) to know more than half of the road traversed by Ḫâled.

On his march to Syria Ḫâled was guided by the usages of the nomads, just as he followed the roads over which they enter Syria. The Bedouins know two "gates" that lead from inner Arabia to Syria. One gate is southwest of the city of Boṣra and the range of the Ḥawrân; the other, northeast of Damascus between the range of ar-Rawâḳ on the north and the volcanic region of Tlûl al-ʿIjâṯ on the south. West of the first gate the movements of the Bedouins are restricted by the *šeʿibân* of az-Zerḳa' and north of it as far as the second gate by the Ḥawrân district. Ḫâled had originally planned to enter Syria through this first gate, but, since this gate was closed by the enemy (see below, pp. 567–569) he turned to the other. While the first gate is always easy of access, since the depression of Sirḥân contains many watering places, the second can be reached from inner Arabia only after the heavy winter rains have filled the hollows and holes with water. Between these gates the range of the Ḥawrân towers, cut off on the east by that awesome volcanic region the edge of which appears as a black wall trending to the north.

The watering place of Ḳurâḳir is on the road to the first and that of Suwa' (Sabʿ Bijâr) on the road to the second gate. Whoever goes from Ḳerâḳer to Swa' first wends his way northeast for fifty kilometers through a volcanic region and then plods for five days almost due north. For four days he sees on the left a black mass of lava from which rugged individual peaks rise to guide his steps. At the beginning of the fifth day, which is his sixth from Ḳurâḳir, he notes that the lava trends to the northwest toward the second gate. Here he must watch very closely in order to find the shallow valley containing the wells of Sabʿ Bijâr. Every watering place in the desert, particularly if its vicinity is level or undulating, has its mark. These are generally natural eminences upon which are heaped piles of stone. Without such cairns in the desert no one could find his way. The wells of Sabʿ Bijâr are on the edge of a shallow *šeʿîb*. Since they contain water for three or four years only following a heavy winter rain, travelers rarely trust them, seldom visit them, and allow them to become nearly filled with sand.

When, after the four-day march through the dazzling sands of the desert, Râfeʿ's eyes became so sore that he could not see in the distance, he feared that he might not find the watering place of Suwa' and that consequently Ḫâled and his men would perish. Notwithstanding, he did not alter his straight course and brought Ḫâled straight to the two cairns of the watering place. The wells, however, had been filled with sand, and the men could not find them until Râfeʿ — who later explained that while a boy he had once before visited this watering place with his father, — remembered that there grew by the wells a round, small shrub of *ʿawseǧe*. — It is likely that Râfeʿ had been at the watering place of Swa' only once, for the territory of the Ṭajj tribe from which he was descended lay many hundred kilometers to the south and the wells of Swa' probably were then and still are sought only by raiding bands. Hence the narrative of the cut *ʿawseǧe* shrub is quite plausible.

Ibn Isḥâḳ names as the first station from Suwa' the camp of the Ghassanian tribe in the Merǧ Râheṭ. The Merǧ Râheṭ are meadows adjacent to the settlement of ʿAḏra' on the northwest and about 120 kilometers west-southwest from Suwa', on the western side of the second gate from Arabia to Syria. Ḫâled went thither. On the way he attacked a camp of the Bahra' clan, which surely did not camp by the wells of Suwa', which were filled with sand, but west or northwest of them. Because the rains are heavier and more regular in the mountainous regions of Syria and even of Palmyrena than in the level desert, Ḫâled found rain water in the hollows and *šeʿibân* west of Suwa'. He could therefore have reached the camp of the Ghassanian tribe with ease. It is noteworthy that this second gate from inner Arabia to Syria was not guarded, for no one feared attack from a quarter where water was lacking.

Ibn ʿAsâker's Version

Ibn ʿAsâker, *Taʾrîḫ* (Codex Berolinensis, No. 9781 [Spr. 120]), folios 36 r. f., gives an account of Ḫâled's march that purports also to have come from Ibn Isḥâḳ. The account concurs with that known to have been Ibn Isḥâḳ's, but is enlarged to record the names of the places through which Ḫâled marched from Ḳurâḳir: "Thereupon Ḫâled set out from Ḳurâḳir to SWṬH, having the east on his right, and passed al-ḌNʾ. He encamped in FRḲJN, later in al-ḤṢʾD, then in al-ʿRJR, then in SWʾBBL. He said. And he encamped. Sejf ibn ʿAbdallâh ibn Muḫfer points to his informant..."

This text is corrupt and lacks logical sequence. The words "he said," when written in red, are always used to introduce a new subject in this manuscript. That subject should not begin with the words "and he encamped" but rather with the name of the informant. Therefore the words "and he encamped" should either be omitted or put before the "he said" where they belong. One station is missing from the list of camping places, its name, al-ḌNʾ, having been inserted in the wrong place. Furthermore, before "he said" is the local name SWʾBBL, of which no mention is made in other accounts of the march. We should expect to find here the name Suwaʾ, because the road from Ḳurâḳir to Suwaʾ is under discussion and it is customary never to omit the terminal station of an itinerary. Therefore, we may conclude that of the name SWʾBBL only SWʾ should stand in the text, while BBL should be cut out as an error of transcription. Having made these changes, we should have then four stations between Ḳurâḳir and Suwaʾ: al-ḌNʾ, FRḲJN, al-ḤṢʾD, and al-ʿRJR. The place name SWṬH still precedes the list. In the case of this name the ending H has no diacritical marks, although these are written everywhere else. Since the place name SWṬH is absolutely unknown in Arabic literature, it is best to conclude that it also originated in an inaccurate rewriting of the name SWʾ.

The context demands some objective toward which Ḫâled marched from Ḳurâḳir. This goal, however, was not an unknown SWṬH, but the SWʾ known in all Arabic literature. Hence the text must read: "Thereupon Ḫâled set out from Ḳurâḳir to Suwaʾ, having the east on his right." Other accounts of his march begin in this manner. The next part, containing four names of the stations through which Ḫâled marched, is of the utmost importance. By determining their situation we can solve the mystery of Ḫâled's march from Ḳurâḳir to Suwaʾ. It is singular, however, that not a single Arabic writer mentions these stations. Whence has as-Samarḳandi, to whom Ibn ʿAsâker refers, the authority to mention them? It is certain that they could not have been told him except by some person familiar with the region between Ḳurâḳir and Suwaʾ, and indeed it would have been strange if the names of at least a few of these stations north of Ḳurâḳir had not been preserved. In 1908-09 and 1914-15 I explored the region north of Ḳurâḳir and searched for these local names. My search was vain because, as further study has convinced me, they are not to be connected with Ḫâled's march from Irak to Syria at all, but with his raids against the tribe of Tarleb on the right bank of the Euphrates. They are distorted names of places visited before he started on his march to Syria. The informant of Ibn ʿAsâker puts them between Ḳurâḳir and Suwa' for the purpose of determining the four unknown stations. Al-ḌN' is a distortion of the Arabic "al-Ḫanâfes." FS was confused with the following *fanazal* which means "and he encamped." FRḲJN is a faulty transcription of Ḳarḳîṣija'; al-ḤṢ'D is identical with al-Ḥuṣajd; al-ʿRJR with al-ʿAwîr. (Caetani, *Annali*, Vol. 2, p. 1203, writes erroneously Ḥiṣâr instead of ḤṢ'D and Sawâbîl instead of SW'BBL.)

According to as-Samarḳandi (Ibn ʿAsâker, *op. cit.*, fol. 38 r.) Ḫâled on his march found water at the station of Suwa', attacked a camp of the Ghassanian tribe in the Merğ al-ʿAḏra', and went thence to Ḳena' Boṣra to compel the inhabitants of that city to sue for peace and to pay the *ğizja* head tax. —

The Merğ Râheṭ, mentioned in all the other accounts of these events, is called by Ibn ʿAsâker Merğ al-ʿAḏra', after the settlement of ʿAḏra' near which it is situated.

Abu-l-Ḳâsem as-Sahâmi states (Ibn ʿAsâker, *op. cit.*, fol. 34 r.) that Ḫâled was to proceed to Syria with the utmost speed. Having penetrated as far as Suwa', he advanced to Syria via Ḍumejr. The Moslem army, which had preceded him to Syria, camped in al-Ğâbija.

Barhebraeus' Version

Barhebraeus (Ibn al-ʿIbri), *Muḫtaṣar* (Ṣâlḥâni), pp. 169 f., writes that Ḫâled, having gone to Irak, stormed the city of al-Ḥîra and won it without bloodshed. It was his first fight in Irak. Abu Bekr had previously sent to Syria the commander Abu ʿObejda ibn al-Ğarrâḥ with 20,000 men. While Ḫâled was besieging the city of al-Ḥîra, Abu Bekr sent a written order to him to march to join Abu ʿObejda in Syria, and Ḫâled complied. —

Caetani, *op. cit.*, Vol. 2, p. 1202 c and note 1, construes much from the fact that Ḫâled is said to have received the Caliph's order during the time of his siege of al-Ḥîra; he asserts that this date is unique and valuable, because Barhebraeus generally derived his information from the best sources and that there is no reason to doubt his statements. At the same time Caetani points out that Ḫâled could not have started for Syria at the request of the Moslem commanders operating there. — Caetani is not consistent. Barhebraeus states expressly that Abu ʿObejda had been sent to Syria before Ḫâled arrived at al-Ḥîra and that he needed Ḫâled's aid because the Emperor Heraclius was pressing him hard. Caetani refuses to believe this part of the account, although it is confirmed by the best sources; he bases his point wholly on the statement that Ḫâled was ordered to go to Syria just as he was taking possession of the city of al-Ḥîra, although this date is contradicted by the best sources. The statement may be construed loosely as referring merely to the conquest of the district of al-Ḥîra and not to the actual siege of the city. It fails, at any rate, to supply the exact date of Ḫâled's expedition to Irak or that of his departure to Syria.

Versions of al-Madâ'ini and al-Mâwardi

According to the account which was probably preserved by al-Madâ'ini (aṭ-Ṭabari, *Ta'riḫ* [De Goeje], Ser. 1, pp. 2108f.), Abu Bekr sent Ḫâled from Irak to Syria as the commander-in-chief of all the Moslem armies. Ḫâled left the city of al-Ḥîra in the second month of Rabîʿ, 13 A. H., with eight hundred or, according to others, with five hundred men, defeated the enemy at Ṣandawda, al-Muṣajjaḫ, and al-Ḥuṣajd, and advanced through the desert waste from Ḳurâḳir to Suwa', where he attacked a camp in which Ḥurḳûṣ ibn an-Noʿmân al-Bahrâni fell. He then forced a peace upon the inhabitants of the settlements of Arak and Tadmur, defeated the inhabitants of al-Ḳarjatân and Ḥowwârîn, and arrived with much booty at Ḳuṣam, where he concluded peace with the Beni Mašǵaʿa of the Ḳuḍâʿa tribe and on Easter Sunday attacked the camp of the Ghassanian tribe in the Merǵ Râheṭ. —

This account shows clearly that the Moslem armies were fighting in Syria under different commanders before Ḫâled was given the order to go there from Irak. Ḫâled was to unify them and with the aid of his seasoned troops to inspire in them the spirit of conquest. According to a custom that prevails today all of his men rode camels. The horses were tied to the camels and allowed to run along without riders. For five hundred riders upon camels we may count fifty mares; for eight hundred riders eighty mares. Ḫâled left the city of al-Ḥîra in the second period of *rabîʿ* according to the reckoning of the Bedouins, i. e., at the end of March or beginning of April. The road he followed, according to the account of al-Madâ'ini, is in no wise connected with the road to Syria. Al-Madâ'ini did not know the situations of the individual settlements, disregarded the chronological order, and recorded the local names known from the military activities of Ḫâled in Irak just as it suited him to do so. Ḫâled was supposed to hasten to Syria, hence from the city of al-Ḥîra he should have marched west. According to al-Madâ'ini, however, he first traveled to the northwest 150 kilometers to Ṣandawda; then he visited al-Ḥuṣajd; then he covered the 150 kilometers that lead northwest to al-Muṣajjaḫ; and finally he turned southwest toward Ḳurâḳir. It is evident that the skirmishes at Ṣandawda, al-Ḥuṣajd, and al-Muṣajjaḫ belong to some former expedition. The route from al-Muṣajjaḫ to Ḳurâḳir is over 450 kilometers long and leads through a desert. To follow such a road with success would be a more remarkable undertaking than the march of 280 kilometers from Ḳurâḳir to Suwa' which was admired by many Arabic poets. From Suwa' al-Madâ'ini sends Ḫâled not toward the west, to Syria, but toward the northeast, through the desert to the settlement of Arak, which lies 120 kilometers from Suwa'. Caetani, *op. cit.*, Vol. 2, p. 1229, commends this route, saying, that it shows plainly that Suwa' is to be sought at the neighborhood of the settlement of Arak; and, pointing to the map of Kiepert, he places Suwa' in the settlement of as-Suḫne and proceeds to the inference that Ḫâled marched through the desert not northward but southward. This unsupported assumption gives him the basis for a reconstruction of Ḫâled's march to Syria. He seeks the perilous desert between Ḳurâḳir and Suwa' between the range of al-Bišri and the village of as-Suḫne, disregarding the fact that the distance between these places is not more than seventy kilometers; this does not conform with the Arabic accounts which require five nights or six day's marches to reach Suwa' from Ḳurâḳir. Between the range of al-Bišri and the settlement of as-Suḫne there are four abundant watering places in a journey of seventy kilometers, yet Caetani writes that Ḫâled crossed the desert. The settlement of as-Suḫne is often mentioned, yet not a single Arabic writer records that it is identical with the watering place of Suwa' or that Suwa' is anywhere near as-Suḫne.

Arak, Tadmur, al-Ḳarjatân, and Ḥowwârîn were frontier forts, the inhabitants of which could make a defensive stand against Ḫâled and his small body of warriors, just as in the past they had taken the defensive against much stronger groups of nomad raiders. We have accounts that tell of a special expedition sent to Tadmur shortly after Ḫâled's arrival in Syria, which proves that the inhabitants of Tadmur, or Palmyra, had not made peace with Ḫâled.

Muḥammad ibn al-Ḥasan al-Mâwardi records (Ibn ʿAsâker, *op. cit.*, fol. 34 r.) that Ḫâled went to Syria at the order of the Caliph Abu Bekr and, after making an attack upon the Ghassanian tribe in the Merǵ Râheṭ, encamped at Ḳena' Boṣra. The inhabitants of that city made peace with him. It was the first city in Syria conquered by Ḫâled. Ḫâled then made peace with the people of Tadmur and advanced on Ḥowwârîn, where he slew many inhabitants and took captives. — This account takes no cognizance of other treaties of peace known to have been made with different settlements before the conclusion of the peace with the inhabitants of Boṣra; it places the peace with Tadmur and the battle at Ḥowwârîn in a later period.

The account preserved by Sejf (aṭ-Ṭabari, *Ta'rîḫ* [De Goeje], Ser. 1, p. 2154) concurs also with this view. According to this account the chieftain Jazîd ibn Abi Sufjân sent, in the year 13 A. H., Diḥja ibn Ḫalîfa, a member of the Kalb tribe, to subdue Tadmur with a mounted column. The inhabitants of the city made peace with Diḥja on the same terms as the inhabitants of Damascus. —

Had the city of Tadmur capitulated to Ḫâled, Jazîd surely would not have sent a mounted column against it, for all power over Syria lay in Ḫâled's hands. It is also very unlikely that Tadmur, situated in the desert, would have revolted against Ḫâled so soon after its capitulation, especially since it could not have depended upon Byzantine help, while, on the other hand, it might have expected an attack at any time by some new Moslem army.

Caetani, *op. cit.*, Vol. 2, p. 1221, refers to al-Madâ'ini's mention of the city of Tadmur as a major proof that Ḫâled came to Syria from the north. However, the best sources do not refer to Tadmur. Historical novels — as, for instance, the Pseudo-Wâḳedi's *Futûḥ aš-šâm* (Cairo, 1278 A. H.) — cannot be regarded as historical documents. Caetani himself writes (*ibid.*, Vol. 2, p. 1167) that this source is the most recent and the least dependable. However, even the early version of *Futûḥ aš-šâm* contains nothing about the conquest of Tadmur. There is left, then, but one source, al-Madâ'ini, which later authors cite as authority for Ḫâled's coming by way of Tadmur. We may label Ḫâled's deviation from the route to Syria as very improbable and express our conviction that al-Madâ'ini's assertion that Ḫâled subdued the settlements of Arak, Tadmur, al-Ḳarjatân, and Ḥowwârîn has not been authenticated.

However, Caetani, *op. cit.*, Vol. 2, p. 922, note 12, takes the opposite view, one which contradicts his conviction that the concurrent opinions of the two best authorities (in his estimation al-Wâḳedi and Ibn Isḥâḳ) are the most plausible. For neither al-Wâḳedi nor Ibn Isḥâḳ name the settlements of Arak and Tadmur as being on the road by which Ḫâled advanced on Syria and thus do not subscribe to Ḫâled's march from Ṣuwa' to Syria by way of these two places. The reason for al-Madâ'ini's account of the peace concluded between Ḫâled and the settlements of Arak and Tadmur should be sought in the later relations of Ḫâled's descendants in Ḥomṣ with the settlements of Arak and Tadmur, in and about which they owned land.

I seek Ḳuṣam in the Roman station Casama and Casama in the Ḫân al-Manḳûra about sixty-five kilometers west of Swa' on the road over which Ḫâled had to go on his way from Suwa' to the Merǵ Râheṭ.

Of the utmost significance is al-Madâ'ini's assertion that the camp of the Ghassanian tribe was attacked on Easter Sunday. Such information, much better preserved in traditions than are exact dates as fixed by shifting lunar months, we may trust unreservedly. Easter Sunday, 13 A. H., fell on April 24, 634 A. D.; therefore, according to the Bedouin reckoning, at the end of the second period of *rabîʿ*. Since Ḫâled might have departed from al-Ḥîra near the end of the first Bedouin period of *rabîʿ*, we may understand why the tradition confusing the Bedouin periods with the lunar months fluctuates between the first and second lunar months of Rabîʿ as the time of Ḫâled's departure, and yet why the second month (in which he attained Syria) preponderates. The original tradition was to the effect that Ḫâled started his march in *rabîʿ*, i. e., the fixed season of *rabîʿ* which corresponds to our spring and is divided into two halves. This fixed season of *rabîʿ* has nothing to do with the shifting lunar months of Rabîʿ. In any case, the time of Ḫâled's departure from the city of al-Ḥîra as well as the time lost in the desert must be given consideration and part be apportioned to the first and part to the second period of the fixed season of *rabîʿ*.

Al-Hajṯam's Version

Al-Hajṯam ibn ʿAdi relates (Ibn Ḳotejba, *ʿUjûn* [Brockelmann], Vol. 1, pp. 176 f.) that Ḫâled was appointed by Abu Bekr as the commander-in-chief of all the Moslem armies in Syria in place of Abu ʿObejda. Ḫâled penetrated through the desert of as-Samâwa to Ḳurâḳir, intending to go through a waterless country to the watering place of Suwa', six marches distant. Not knowing the road, he engaged as guide a prudent man of the name of Râfeʿ ibn ʿAmîra of the Ṭajj tribe. Râfeʿ advised Ḫâled not to take burdened camels, but his advice was rejected. The guide then warned him that even a lone and courageous camel rider fears death by thirst when he has to pass through that country. Ḫâled, however, persevered in his intention. Whereupon Râfeʿ ordered twenty mature, fat, strong camels, which had been designated for slaughter, to be brought forward, excited in them a craving for water, and sated their thirst. He cut off their lips and bound their muzzles that they might not graze and counseled Ḫâled to have four of these camels slaughtered at each halt, in order that the water from their paunches might be squeezed out and given to the horses, while the men drank the water carried in the leathern bags. So it was. But later when they came into the desolate land where they had had no water, the men and the animals suffered from thirst. At the command of the guide they searched near the road for a shrub of *ʿawseğe*. Upon finding it, they were ordered to dig and thus succeeded in striking water. After Ḫâled had arrived at al-Bišr he found a camp there where the people were making merry at their drink and listening to a chanter. The chanter and his audience were slain and their chattels became the property of the Moslems.—

According to this account, we may infer that the Moslem army was already in Syria, but had achieved no great success. Ḫâled, who was to replace Abu ʿObejda, marched across the desert of as-Samâwa to Ḳurâḳir. No details are given regarding this march of over 600 kilometers. From the omission we might assume that Ḫâled marched over the usual transport road from Irak to Syria, finding enough wells as he advanced. There is no mention of an attack upon a camp near Suwa', although the informant was aware of its presence. This is attested by the story of the feasting Arabs and the roving chanter. Tradition connects this same story with al-Muṣajjaḫ south of the valley of Ḥawrân, with the vicinity of the watering place of Suwa', and with the range of al-Bišr. Al-Hajṯam found it referred to a place beyond Suwa', but he connected it with the range of al-Bišr, utterly disregarding the topographical and chronological sequence. Not a single other account relates that Ḫâled went from Suwa' to the range of al-Bišr; on the contrary, they tell of his sojourn in al-Bišr before his march to Syria at the time of his raid against the camps of the Taṛleb tribe from ʿAjn at-Tamr on the right bank of the Euphrates. The story of the feasting Arabs and of the roving chanter is to be placed much more accurately from the chronological point of view in al-Bišr than in the vicinity of Suwa', where Ḫâled arrived in the lenten period shortly before Easter.

Al-Belâḏori's Version

Al-Belâḏori, *Futûḥ* (De Goeje), p. 111, records an account according to which Ḫâled arrived at the settlement of Dûmat al-Ğandal — which he captured — by way of Araka, where he had forced peace and a stipulated contribution upon the settlement. Thence he marched to Ḳuṣam, where he gave a written guarantee of safety for life and chattels to the Beni Mašğaʿa clan. At Tadmur the inhabitants of the city made a stand for their defense, yet soon sued him to spare their lives and chattels. The inhabitants of the settlement of al-Ḳarjatân made a defense, but were overwhelmed. Ḫâled attacked the flocks of sheep and goats near the settlement of Ḥowwârîn in the range of Sanîr and, despite the help which had come to the inhabitants of Ḥowwârîn from the cities of Baalbek and Boṣra in the Ḥawrân, he won a victory and on Easter Sunday attacked the Christians of the Ghassanian tribe in the Merğ Râheṭ. Thence he marched to the pass of al-ʿOḳâb. —

Events which have no topographical or chronological relation are grouped in this account. Al-Belâḏori does not state unequivocally that all this occurred immediately after Ḫâled's departure from Suwa'. If we admit that these were Ḫâled's activities after leaving the watering place of Suwa', he must have turned northeast from Suwa' to the settlement of Araka, 120 kilometers distant. Araka (ar-Raka), or Raka, is still the name given by the Bedouins to a settlement, the classical name of which was Arak. From Araka he would have had to march over 600 kilometers southward to Dûmat al-Ğandal and thence almost as far to the northwest to Ḳuṣam. From Ḳuṣam he would have had to turn northeast again to Tadmur, then southwest to al-Ḳarjatân, Ḥowwârîn, and the Merğ Râheṭ, and then again toward the northeast to the pass of al-ʿOḳâb. Such a route is absurd.

Caetani's view is quite different, for he says (*Annali*, Vol. 2, p. 1230) that the second half of Ḫâled's itinerary from the settlement of Arak to Damascus is absolutely warranted. It is, says he, an historical event which cannot be denied. The first part of the itinerary from al-Ḥîra to Arak is, he says, as indefensible today as it ever was because of the impossibility of recognizing a single familiar place in the sources which tell the story of Ḫâled's march. — Caetani is mistaken. How can he argue that the second half of a given itinerary is correct when he is unfamiliar with the first half, in spite of its numerous historians? It is plain from Arabic sources that Ḫâled on his way to Syria did not visit the settlement of Arak. Consequently the itinerary of Ḫâled's journey from the settlement of Arak to Damascus is valueless. The sequence of local places recorded upon Ḫâled's march from Suwa' is as absurd chronologically as is the mention of the conquest of Dûmat al-Ğandal beyond the watering place of Suwa'.

Ḫâled's benignant treatment of the inhabitants of Arak and Tadmur is mentioned. They had not surrendered immediately, they had stood in defiance, they had remained Christians, yet he guaranteed them their lives and all their chattels, even exempting them from the annual *ğizja* head tax. It appears, however, as we have already seen, that this assertion is merely a reflection of the later friendship of these settlements with the descendants of Ḫâled.

According to al-Belâḏori's account of these events none of the Byzantine armies was then in Syria, for those who hastened to the aid of Ḥowwârîn were not Byzantine reinforcements but the inhabitants of the cities of Baalbek (almost eighty-five kilometers to the west) and Boṣra (almost 150 kilometers to the south). If Ḫâled were to have joined the Moslem armies in Syria as soon as he could, which the best sources assert that he did, his shortest and most natural road from Suwa' would have led toward the west by way of Ḳuṣam to the Merğ Râheṭ. All raids north and south of this line would have led him from the goal toward which Abu Bekr had directed him and endangered the safety of his army. Just as al-Belâḏori connects the conquest of the settlement of Dûmat al-Ğandal, which must have preceded it, with the march from Suwa' to the Merğ Râheṭ, he also connects with it the conquest of the settlements of Arak as far as Ḥowwârîn, which in reality must have followed it.

The statement that Ḫâled attacked the flocks of the inhabitants of Ḥowwârîn points to the probable origin of the story about the conquest of Arak, Tadmur, al-Ḳarjatân, and Ḥowwârîn. The inhabitants of those settlements at the present time, as was perhaps also the case in the seventh century, own large flocks of goats and sheep which they buy from the nomads and sell in Syria. During the torrid summer season the flocks graze near the settlements and are watered daily in them. Desiring to preserve these convenient pasturages for the summer, the inhabitants during the rainy season pasture their flocks far away, frequently several marches from their respective settlements. Numerous owners of the flocks leave the settlements with their families and camp under tents among their goats and sheep in order to milk them, shear them, and protect them. They lead their goats and sheep to pasturage especially among the hills southwest of Palmyra, for rain recurs there annually, various annuals and aromatic perennials grow in the depressions, and the big marts are relatively close. At the beginning of the winter rains the inhabitants of distant Syrian cities whose principal trade is in live stock also send their flocks to this range. Such cities were, and are, Baalbek between the Lebanon and Antilebanon, and Boṣra on the southwestern boundary of the Ḥawrân. Their flocks graze in the mountainous country as long as they can find sufficient water; and they do not return to their settlements until the end of May when the harvest opens.

It is very probable that Ḫâled needed provisions for his army. Therefore he made a raid from the watering place of Suwa' into the adjacent mountainous country, where he found flocks from the various settlements. Where the owners and shepherds realized that they could not ward off the Moslem band, they surrendered, and the Moslems drove off with as many animals as they cared to. Where the shepherds thought that they were stronger, they resisted the attack. The owners of the flocks from the settlements of Arak and Tadmur were too far from their townsmen, hence they had little hope that reinforcements could be sent them and they surrendered immediately. With the owners from al-Ḳarjatân and Ḥowwârîn the likelihood of support was stronger. Ḫâled probably marched from Suwa' toward the west and stayed in the vicinity of the settlements for some time, where he easily could have been overtaken and attacked by the enemy's reinforcements. This may account for the presence of the inhabitants of Baalbek and Boṣra, who were also in the habit of pasturing their flocks between Tadmur and Damascus and who came to protect them and to render aid to the inhabitants of Ḥowwârîn.

Version of the al-Kûfa School

Probable Date of the March

The account of the al-Kûfa school refers at length to Ḫâled's march to Syria. From various informants, Sejf ibn ʿOmar learned (aṭ-Ṭabari, *Taʾrîḫ* [De Goeje], Ser. 1, pp. 2115 ff.) that after his return from Mecca Ḫâled received a written order to march with half of his men to Syria, while the other half was to remain in Irak with al-Muṯanna. Ḫâled obeyed the command. In the month of al-Muḥarram al-Muṯanna accompanied him to Ḳurâḳir and then returned to the city of al-Ḥîra. —

According to this account, half of the Moslem soldiers from al-Medîna remained in Irak. This detachment had a commander of its own, who, however, ranked under the head chief al-Muṯanna, who had the support of his tribe, the Bekr ibn Wâ'il. The note that al-Muṯanna accompanied Ḫâled as far as Ḳurâḳir arouses interest. We might infer from it that Ḫâled feared an attack, or that al-Muṯanna also had previously intended to march to Syria. Sejf does not say over which road Ḫâled marched from al-Ḥîra to Ḳurâḳir. It cannot be supposed that al-Muṯanna returned to al-Ḥîra in the month of al-Muḥarram. The account associates Ḫâled's departure for Syria with his return from Mecca. It alleges that he started the pilgrimage on the twenty-sixth of Ḏu al-Ḳaʿde — hence on February first — from al-Firâḍ. If he sped as fast as he could, he would have been back in the city of al-Ḥîra at the end of the month of Ḏu al-Ḥiǧǧe (March 6, 634 A. D.). Then he was given the order to march to Syria. Before departing he was to send the women, children, and weaklings to al-Medîna, to arrange all that was necessary for the defense of the conquered parts of Irak, and to provide himself and his men with the indispensable supplies for a journey across the desert. Since he needed at least ten days for these preparations, al-Muṯanna would have had to make the trip of over 1200 kilometers from al-Ḥîra to Ḳurâḳir and back in twenty days if we are to infer that he returned to al-Ḥîra in the month of al-Muḥarram (March 7 to April 5). Ḫâled was aware that he should have to fight upon his arrival in Syria and consequently wanted to spare his men and animals as best he could. We cannot assume, therefore, that he covered more than fifty kilometers a day on his march across the desert. He needed at least twenty days to go from al-Ḥîra to Ḳurâḳir, and he could not have reached that watering place until the last days of al-Muḥarram. From this we must infer that the date al-Muḥarram does not refer to the time of al-Muṯanna's return to al-Ḥîra, but to the time of Ḫâled's departure from al-Ḥîra to Ḳurâḳir. Ḫâled's departure and his march across the desert were much more important and made a deeper impression on the memory than the return of the chief al-Muṯanna to al-Ḥîra, which is not mentioned in any other account. The time of Ḫâled's departure for Syria may therefore be placed in the second half of March, 634 A. D.

Ḫâled's Route by Way of Dûma

Elsewhere (aṭ-Ṭabari, *op. cit.*, Ser. 1, p. 2112) Sejf records that before his march to Syria Ḫâled procured guides and went from the city of al-Ḥîra to the oasis of Dûma and thence across the desert to Ḳurâḳir. There he inquired regarding a road by which he could avoid the Byzantine army. He feared that if he kept his course the latter might block his route and cut off his connection with the other Moslem armies. The guides confirmed the existence of such a road, but declared that it was of no use to warriors and was followed by individual riders only in cases of greatest urgency. No one but Râfeʿ ibn ʿAmîra of the Ṭajj tribe would even consent to guide Ḫâled. At Râfeʿ's request Ḫâled ordered that every man of his army should provide a five-day supply of water for himself and his horse, if he had one. Every guide was to excite a sufficient number of fat and strong camels to crave water, was to give them one drink after another until they were sated, and was to tie their muzzles and block their rectums with sharp stakes so that they could neither excrete dung nor stale. After these preparations they began their march from Ḳurâḳir across the desolate country to Suwa', which is a watering place situated near Syria, north of Ḳurâḳir. They marched during the day and toward the evening of every day squeezed the water from the paunches of ten slaughtered camels, mixed it with camels' milk, and gave each horse a portion. —

This account is very interesting, because it shows the road over which Ḫâled went to Ḳurâḳir and why he turned from there to Suwa'. It also shows that Ḫâled followed the transport road from al-Ḥîra to the oasis of Dûma.

Caetani, *op. cit.*, Vol. 2, p. 1218, in arguing against Ḫâled's route by way of the oasis of Dûma, remarks that there are two other, shorter roads running from al-Ḥîra to Damascus besides the one which he holds that Ḫâled took to Syria, the road, that is, by way of Tadmur; and he refers to Ibn Ḫordâḏbeh, *Masâlik* (De Goeje), p. 97. These two roads, Caetani says, are short, direct, and easy, while the one by way of Tadmur is long and perilous because it leads through regions that were closely inhabited and protected by forts. Ḫâled selected it, notwithstanding. — These deductions are incorrect. The road through Tadmur is a promenade compared with the two roads recorded by Ibn Ḫordâḏbeh, for these can be traveled only after protracted, heavy rains, there being no constant spring for many hundred kilometers. A cavalcade of many horses could not go over them in the spring, summer, or autumn when the rain pools are dry without providing itself with water for a journey of 500 kilometers. Moreover, the Arabic geographers also knew of yet other roads from Irak to Syria (see: al-Muḳaddasi, *Aḥsan* [De Goeje], pp. 251 f.; Ibn Ǧubejr, *Riḥla* [De Goeje, Gibb Memorial], p. 260; Abu-l-Feda', *Taḳwîm* [Reinaud and De Slane], p. 259; Abu-l-Farağ, *Aġâni* [Bûlâḳ, 1285 A. H.], Vol. 15, p. 116; Vol. 20, p. 120, etc.; see also above, pp. 520—528).

Dûma, situated on the road from al-Ḥîra to Ḳurâḳir, cannot be any other than the oasis Dûmat al-Ǧandal. The ancient name of this oasis is Dûma, and various accounts briefly refer to it by that name. Therefore we are not justified in considering a different Dûma unless compelled by reasons of utmost weight. Ḫâled's march presents no such reason, nor does a single account mention a different Dûma, while the oasis of Dûmat al-Ǧandal itself is situated about midway between Syria and Irak and is on the easiest road that connects the two countries. From al-Ḥîra to Dûma the traveler finds water every day, either in spring-water wells or in artificial reservoirs. Many of these wells are about a hundred meters deep and are very old. The reservoirs, mere rain pools, are very numerous, and in the vicinity of nearly all of them are the remains of ancient buildings. Ḫâled could have gone to the oasis of Dûma without great peril, for the oasis already belonged to the Moslems. There he could have supplied himself for the rest of his journey and from there he could have marched northwest over a very old road that led through the depression of Sirḥân to the first gate to Syria at the city of Boṣra.

ʿAbdalwahhâb ibn al-Mubârek (Ibn ʿAsâker, *Ta'rîḫ* [Codex Berolinensis], fol. 36 r.) refers to Ḫâled's march from al-Ḥîra via Dûmat al-Ǧandal to Ḳurâḳir.

Caetani, *op. cit.*, Vol. 2, p. 1219, note 1, who doubts Ḫâled's march by way of the oasis of Dûmat al-Ǧandal, cites Jâḳût, *Muʿǧam* (Wüstenfeld), Vol. 4, p. 137, where he finds mention of Ḫâled's march from al-Ḥîra across the desert to Syria. Had Caetani examined Jâḳût's statement more carefully and had he looked for the individual stations which it mentions, he would have discovered that Jâḳût also knew the road from al-Ḥîra by Dûmat al-Ğandal to Syria, for the station of al-Ḳurejjât, which he mentions, is the name of the group of settlements situated in the oasis which included the town of Dûmat al-Ğandal. This road was traversed not only by Ḫâled, but also by the Moslem reinforcements sent by the Caliph ʿOmar from Syria to al-Ḳâdesijje (al-Belâḏori, *Futûḥ* [De Goeje], p. 261). Caetani (*ibid.*, p. 1217) would have these reinforcement troops go from Damascus directly across the desert to al-Ḳâdesijje, but this is utterly impossible, as there is no spring-water well on the straight line that connects Damascus with al-Ḳâdesijje and ʿOmar could not have requested the Syrian army of relief to provide itself with water sufficient for a march of at least 700 kilometers. The mail road known as Darb as-Sâʿi from Damascus to Hît was not used by horseback riders, as it would be necessary to carry water a distance of 350 kilometers. Caetani is mistaken if he holds that one of the roads recorded by Ibn Ḫordâḏbeh is identical with the present Darb as-Sâʿi (see above, p. 526). Caetani conceived a road across the desert which was unknown either to the Arabic geographers or to the present nomads, while the road by Dûmat al-Ğandal was familiar to all and led to the first gateway from inner Arabia to Syria.

Sejf on Ḫâled's Route from Ḳurâḳir to Suwa'

The first gateway is barely thirty kilometers wide and is bounded on the west by the rugged az-Zerḳa' range and on the east by lava tracts. For its defense the cities of ʿAmmân and Boṣra were fortified and the forts of al-Ḫarâni, al-Azraḳ, and al-Ḥallâbât erected. While it was occupied by Byzantine soldiers and while Christian nomads were in its neighborhood, it was impossible for a Moslem army to penetrate to Syria. Of this Ḫâled must have been informed, for he surely had dependable spies. Ḫâled's apprehension shows that at Ḳurâḳir he already was very near the Byzantine garrisons and that, therefore, we must not seek Ḳurâḳir in the eastern, but in the western half of northern Arabia. Had he advanced with his small band from Ḳurâḳir toward the northwest, he would have found himself among the Byzantine garrisons and could easily have been surrounded and defeated. Since Ḫâled realized his numerical weakness and his inability to cope with these garrisons, he planned to march around them and join his companions in arms in Syria. There must have been no Moslem soldiers in Moab, for Ḫâled could have joined them there in two days. The Moslems therefore must have already reached a position to the west or northwest of Boṣra, whither they could have penetrated without obstruction through the inadequately guarded southern part of Palestine.

Ḫâled's apprehensions, mentioned by our account but ignored by Caetani, *op. cit.*, Vol. 2, pp. 1208 f., throw light on the Syrian situation and show why Ḫâled went to the second gateway into Syria over the perilous road from Ḳurâḳir to Suwa'. The distance from Ḳurâḳir to Suwa' is not given, but it must have been longer than five marches, for the men were ordered by Ḫâled to provide themselves with water for five days and the horses were given drink four times. A Bedouin will water his horse shortly before his departure and does not give him water the following evening if the supply is small. As Ḫâled's men gave drink to their horses four times, the march from Ḳurâḳir to Suwa' lasted more than five days. Caetani, *op. cit.*, Vol. 2, p. 1209, misconstrues the Arabic expression when he says that Ḫâled arrived from Ḳurâḳir at Suwa' in four marches (see above, p. 556).

The different steps in inciting the camels to thirst in order that they should drink and hold the greatest quantity of water possible were not clearly understood even by Sejf and his informants. This accounts for the incongruity of the logical with the chronological sequence of these steps as he describes them. When a Bedouin wants to stimulate a camel's thirst, he takes her near a watering place, binds her, pours water into the receptacle from which the camel is wont to drink, slaps the water with his palm, and coaxes the camel to drink by short songs and a peculiar smacking. The camel sees and hears, but cannot reach the water. In her craving for the water she pricks her ears. Many riding camels are trained to tell from these motions and sounds that they are to go upon a distant journey through the arid desert and to drink more greedily. If they are bound and hear the familiar smacking and songs, they prick their ears in the direction of the water and manifest their craving by a peculiarly beseeching whine. The water is so near, the journey before them so long, and they cannot have water! When the rider does take off their shackles they run to the receptacle and drink in long, deep gulps. The rider adds water as long as they drink. Then he takes them away from the watering place and lets them graze. An hour later he drives them back to the water, binds them, tantalizes them, and excites such a thirst in them that they quiver. Then he lets them drink for a second time. In this manner every fat, strong camel can be forced to drink sixty to seventy liters. Their mouths are then tied to prevent their grazing and ruminating and thus mixing the water in their paunches with food.

To endure any protracted journey without food, a camel must be strong and its hump, on which it lives, must be high and fatty. After several days of meager pasture the hump shrinks and when it has disappeared the animal is generally so weak that it cannot rise with load or rider. If the load is placed upon it while it is standing, or the rider mounts it in the same posture, it walks several days longer.

When Bedouins are returning from a raid with booty and are apprehensive lest the watering places ahead of them be seized and they be forced into the arid desert, if they lack water bags they select several strong, fat camels, stimulate them to drink the greatest amount of water possible, relieve them of all their loads, and drive them ahead just as if the camels were living water bags. Since the animals are destined for slaughter, the Bedouins take all precautions to prevent the contamination and diminution of the water they carry in their animals' paunches. Hence they tie the camels' muzzles so that they cannot ruminate, cut their lips so that they may not even bend for plants, and even block their rectums with wooden stakes to prevent excretion.

Aḫla adbârahen signifies that the camel's hump is left free of the saddle, carrying neither load nor rider. A camel's urethra can be fastened with a sharp stake so that the animal will not stale, and it appears that Sejf had in mind this cruel treatment, for the phrase *ḫalla adbârahen* used by him in this connection is explained by Ibn ʿAsâker, *op. cit.*, fol. 37 r. to mean *li'an lâ jabolna* (in order that they may not stale). According to Sejf's account it was not only the water that was squeezed out of slaughtered camels' paunches, but also the milk and milky particles, and the mixture was given to horses. As much as six hundred liters of water may be obtained from ten slaughtered camels. After it has been cleared and mixed with milk, it suffices for eighty to one hundred horses, especially if they have found fresh annuals.

Sejf had heard from a member of the Bekr ibn Wâ'il tribe that the chieftain Muḥrez ibn Ḥarîš al-Muḥârebi counseled Ḫâled in Ḳurâḳir to place the morning star over his right eyebrow, adding that in this manner he would surely reach Suwa' (aṭ-Ṭabari, *op. cit.*, Ser. 1, p. 2113). — The chieftain advised him to ride from Ḳurâḳir toward the northeast, which was quite correct if Ḫâled wanted to get away from the well-nigh impassable lava into the level desert.

Aṭ-Ṭabari, *loc. cit.*, recounts from various other sources that the guide Râfeʿ directed Ḫâled's men at the watering place of Suwa' to search for two low natural domes similar to breasts. After they had found them and had taken Râfeʿ, whose eyes were sore, to them, he besought them to look for a low, round shrub of *ʿawseǧe*. They found only the stem of the shrub, for it had been cut down; yet they dug near by and soon struck damp sand through which water trickled. Then Râfeʿ divulged that he had been to this place thirty years before with his father. Ḫâled's warriors refreshed themselves and attacked the unsuspecting enemy, who had not the least fear that the Moslems could cross the desert.

Sejf (aṭ-Ṭabari, *op. cit.*, Ser. 1, p. 2114) relates that the Ghassanians assembled in the Merǧ Râheṭ after they had learned of Ḫâled's arrival at Suwa' and of his attack upon al-Muṣajjaḫ. This was disclosed to Ḫâled, who passed by the Byzantine frontier forts situated toward Irak and passed between them and the Jarmûk. Having returned to Suwa' with the prisoners of the Bahra clan, he proceeded onward, encamping on his route near the natural domes of ar-Rummânatân and then at al-Kaṯib; he then marched past Damascus and arrived in the Merǧ aṣ-Ṣuffar, where he found camps of the Ghassanians. He stayed there several days and then proceeded towards Ḳena' Boṣra, which was the first city in Syria to be taken. —

This account, derived by Sejf from ʿAmr ibn Muḥammad, contains much that is chronologically and topographically anomalous. The whole Arabic tradition recognizes it as an historical fact that Ḫâled entered Syria from Suwa'; in order to make his version agree with the tradition, our informant relates that Ḫâled returned from al-Muṣajjaḫ to Suwa'. This is the only explanation of the report of Ḫâled's unnecessary return, for all the accounts affirm the sufficiency of water and pasturage in al-Muṣajjaḫ. If the camp of al-Muṣajjaḫ was situated far to the southeast near the present ʿAjn al-Arnab on the boundary of Irak, as I hold it was, Ḫâled could not have returned thence to Suwa', because he had not come thither from Suwa'. It is certain that Ḫâled stayed several days in Suwa' to rest his men and animals after their last arduous march, and it is likewise certain that small groups of his men plundered the camps or flocks in the vicinity to obtain food. He had no reason for proceeding to the east, to al-Muṣajjaḫ in the desert, instead of to the west, to the Merǧ Râheṭ in Syria, as he was ordered by Abu Bekr. As will be shown in the author's forthcoming volume, *The Middle Euphrates*, Appendix VII, Ḫâled's march on al-Muṣajjaḫ took place before his departure for Syria.

The news of Ḫâled's presence was posted through the territory, and the Ghassanians, who owned the best pasturage and many settlements east and south of Damascus, prepared for defense. They assembled in the Merǧ Râheṭ (near ʿAḏra') at the second gateway from the inner desert toward Damascus. East of the Merǧ Râheṭ is the large Roman fortified camp, Ḍmejr al-ʿAtîže, of which no mention is made and which was perhaps deserted at the time. Or perhaps its garrison had joined the Byzantine army for the defense of the first gateway near Boṣra as well as of Palestine. This is quite probable, because the Persians were defeated and no danger of invasion seemed to threaten from the northeast. Thus we find no Byzantine soldiers at this second gate, and in the Merǧ Râheṭ only the relief forces of the Ghassanian tribe were assembled, whereas their women, girls, and herds were in the Merǧ aṣ-Ṣuffar.

Ḫâled knew of the existence of numerous frontier forts and garrisons to the northeast and he avoided all of them, attacking none. From the context it must be inferred that our informant had in mind the forts of Sergiopolis, Oriza, Arak, and Palmyra (or Tadmur). This supports our theory that Ḫâled went from Suwa' direct to the Merǧ Râheṭ and that the Moslems did not take the settlements of Arak, Tadmur, al-Ḳarjatân, and Ḥowwârîn until later.

As stated explicitly in our account, Ḫâled on his march from Suwa' intended to attack the Ghassanian warriors assembled in the Merǧ Râheṭ; yet it is not stated when and how he accomplished this. Ḫâled could not have circumvented the Ghassanian camp in the Merǧ Râheṭ if he wanted to approach Damascus. The Merǧ Râheṭ is barely twenty-five kilometers from Damascus and is bounded on the north by a high mountain range and on the south by an almost impassable volcanic desert. Even if Ḫâled had left the second gateway of Syria and gone across the mountain range he would have descended through the pass of al-ʿOḳâb into the plain of Merǧ Râheṭ. On the other hand, had he gone through the volcanic desert he would also have emerged at the Merǧ Râheṭ, for the swamps of al-ʿAtejbe, which surely were swollen in the spring, would have prevented his further advance. Ḫâled's movements would have been restricted in the mountain range as well as in the volcanic region and he could easily have been intercepted and surrounded, because the Ghassanian fighters and the settlers knew the terrain far better than Ḫâled and his guides.

Had Ḫâled in some manner avoided the camp of the Ghassanians in the Merǧ Râheṭ and penetrated as far as Damascus itself, he would even then have exposed himself to the danger of being surrounded, for he would have left his enemies behind him at the gate which, if necessary, would provide his only route of escape into the inner desert. Since such imprudence was not characteristic of Ḫâled, we may surmise that he went from Suwa' direct to the Merǧ Râheṭ, attacked and defeated his enemies there, and thus secured the second gateway to Syria. The stations of ar-Rummânatân and al-Kaṯib are hard to fix on the map, because these names are but designations of topographical features. *Rummânatân* denotes two low natural domes and *keṯib*, or rather *keṯîb*, a low solitary mound, particularly of a sandy nature. East of Damascus such features are numerous. It is probable that these stations must be sought west of the Merǧ Râheṭ, for Ḫâled's route past them led onward to Damascus and thence to the Merǧ aṣ-Ṣuffar. As Ḫâled marched westward from Suwa' to Damascus and as the Merǧ aṣ-Ṣuffar was beyond Damascus from Suwa', the Merǧ aṣ-Ṣuffar must have been situated to the south or southwest and not to the east of that city.

Caetani, *op. cit.*, Vol. 2, p. 1209, note 1, unjustly accuses Sejf of errors and, proposing that Merǧ aṣ-Ṣuffarîn be read for Merǧ aṣ-Ṣuffar, proceeds to place it in the neighborhood of the Merǧ Râheṭ. This proposal is contradictory to the context, which implies that the Merǧ aṣ-Ṣuffar is situated beyond Damascus. Caetani would have to grant that Ḫâled, marching from Suwa', made a large semicircle around the Merǧ Râheṭ (near the settlement of ʿAḏra'), approached Damascus, and thence went back toward the east to attack the Ghassanians in the Merǧ aṣ-Ṣuffarîn, near the Merǧ Râheṭ. This circuitous route is, however, rendered impossible by the known location of the Merǧ Râheṭ in the vicinity of the settlement of ʿAḏra' and by the absence of any motive for such a devious advance. Likewise in this case it would become necessary to seek the Merǧ aṣ-Ṣuffar known to the Arabic authors in the vicinity of Damascus. Such a situation is not given by the Arabic geographers, nor is the need of its existence felt by any Arabic historian. If, however, we interpret the account naturally, it leads us to a Merǧ aṣ-Ṣuffar south of Damascus, where Arabic geographers and poets have frequently called it Merǧ aṣ-Ṣuffarîn after a neighboring cloister. Here the Ghassanians suffered a new defeat close upon their losses in the Merǧ Râheṭ, and the victorious Ḫâled marched unopposed upon the city of Boṣra, in order that he might also win the first gate into Syria.

BIBLIOGRAPHY

BIBLIOGRAPHY

Works referred to in this volume only are listed in the bibliography.

Different works by the same ancient or Arabic author are listed together in the same entry and are indicated by Roman numerals. Different works by the same modern author are listed separately.

Of the various names of each Arabic author, the one most frequently used is printed first. Where this has necessitated a transposition of the proper order of the names, the transposition is indicated by a comma (thus: Al-Bekri, Abu ʿObejd ʿAbdallâh ibn ʿAbdalʿazîz *instead of* Abu ʿObejd ʿAbdallâh ibn ʿAbdalʿazîz al-Bekri).

All dates are A.D. except where otherwise indicated.

Abu-l-Faḍâʾil Ṣafiaddîn ʿAbdalmuʾmin ibn ʿAbdalḥaḳḳ (d. 1338). *Marâṣid al-ittilâʿ ʿalaʾ asmâʾi-l-amkina wa-l-biḳâʿ*: edited by T. G. J. Juynboll, 6 vols., Leiden, 1850—1864.

Abu-l-Farağ ʿAli al-Iṣfahâni (d. 967). *Kitâb al-arâni*: 20 vols., Bûlâḳ, 1285 A. H. (1868—1869 A. D.); R. E. Brünnow, editor, *The Twenty-First Volume of the Kitâb al-Aghânî*, Leiden, 1888; *Tables alphabétiques*, edited by I. Guidi, 2 vols., Leiden, 1895—1900.

Abu-l-Fedaʾ Ismâʿîl ibn ʿAli ibn Maḥmûd ibn ʿOmar ibn Šâhanšâh ibn Ajjûb ʿImâdaddîn al-Ajjûbi (1273—1331). I. *Muḫtaṣar taʾrîḫ al-bašar*: edition by J. G. Chr. Adler entitled *Annales muslemici, arabice et latine, opere Jo. Jac. Reiskii sumtibus Pet. Fr. Suhmii*, 5 vols., Copenhagen, 1789—1794. II. *Taḳwîm al-buldân*: edition by (J. T.) Reinaud and W. MacGuckin de Slane entitled *Géographie d'Aboulféda*, Paris, 1840. III. *Tawârîḫ al-ḳadîma min muḫtaṣar fi aḫbâr al-bašar*: edition by H. O. Fleischer entitled *Abulfedae Historia anteislamica*, Leipzig, 1831.

Abu Šâma, Šihâbaddîn Abu-l-Ḳâsim ʿAbdarraḥmân ibn Ismâʿîl (1203-1268). *Kitâb ar-rawdatejn fi aḫbâr ad-dawlatejn*: Cairo, 1287-1288 A. H. (1869—1872 A. D); also edited and translated by Ch. A. C. Barbier de Meynard under the title *Le livre des deux jardins. Histoire de deux règnes, celui de Nour ed-Dîn et celui de Salah ed-Dîn*, constituting *Recueil des historiens des croisades, Historiens orientaux*, Vols. 4 and 5, Paris, 1898, 1906.

Ahlwardt, W. *The Divans of the Six Ancient Arabic Poets Ennābiga, ʾAntara, Tharafa, Zuhair, ʾAlqama and Imruulqais*, London, 1870.

Al-Aḫṭal, Abu Mâlik Ḡijâṯ ibn Ḡawṯ (d. c. 710). I. *Dîwân*: edition by A. Salhani entitled *Dîwân al-Aḫṭal, texte arabe publié pour la première fois d'après le manuscrit de St. Pétersbourg et annoté par* ∾, Beirut, 1891—1892. II. *Naḳâʾiḍ*: edition by A. Salhani entitled *Naqâʾiḍ de Ğarîr et Aḫṭal: recueil de Abou Tammâm*, in *Mélanges de la Faculté orientale*, Vol. 7, Beirut, 1921, pp. 321—381.

Alexander Polyhistor (c. 40 B. C.). Fragments: edited by Carl Müller in his *Fragmenta historicorum graecorum*, Vol. 3, Paris, 1849, pp. 206—244.

Ammianus Marcellinus (d. c. 391). *Rerum gestarum libri* [*qui supersunt*]: edited by V. Gardthausen, 2 vols., Leipzig, 1874—1875.

Arrian (Flavius Arrianus) (d. c. 175). I. *Anabasis*: edited by A. G. Roos, Leipzig, 1907. II. *Historia indica*: edited by Carl Müller in his *Geographi graeci minores*, Vol. 1, Paris, 1861, pp. 306—369.

Asurbanipal. See Streck.

Barhebraeus, Gregorius (Abu-l-Farağ ibn al-ʿIbri) (d. 1286). *Ta'rîḫ muḫtaṣar ad-duwal*: edited by A. Ṣâlḥâni, Beirut, 1890.

Al-Bekri, Abu ʿObejd ʿAbdallâh ibn ʿAbdalʿazîz (d. 1094). *Muʿğam mâ istaʿğama*: edition by Ferdinand Wüstenfeld entitled *Das geographische Wörterbuch des ... el Bekri*, 2 vols., Göttingen, 1876—1877.

Al-Belâḏori, Aḥmad ibn Jaḥja' ibn Ğâbir (d. 892). *Kitâb futûḥ al-buldân*: edition by M. J. De Goeje entitled *Liber expugnationis regionum, auctore.... al-Beládsorí*, Leiden, 1866.

Biblia hebraica, edited by Rudolf Kittel, 2nd edition, 2 vols., Leipzig, 1913.

Blau, O. *Arabien im sechsten Jahrhundert: eine ethnographische Skizze*, in *Zeitschrift der Deutschen Morgenländischen Gesellschaft*, Vol. 23, Leipzig, 1869, pp. 559—592.

Blau, O. *Die Wanderung der sabäischen Völkerstämme im 2. Jahrhundert n. Chr.*, in *Zeitschrift der Deutschen Morgenländischen Gesellschaft*, Vol. 22, Leipzig, 1868, pp. 654—673.

Botta, P. E. and Flandin, E. *Monument de Ninive découvert et décrit par P.E. Botta, mesuré et dessiné par E. Flandin*, 5 vols., Paris, 1846-1850.

British Museum, Department of Egyptian and Assyrian Antiquities. *Cuneiform Texts from Babylonian Tablets, etc., in the British Museum*, London, 1896 ff., 38 parts have appeared (1926).

Burckhardt, J. L. *Travels in Syria and the Holy Land*, London, 1822.

Caetani, Leone (Principe di Teano). *Annali dell'Islām*, Vol. 1, Milan, 1905; Vol. 2, Parts 1 and 2, Milan, 1907.

Cassius Dio Cocceianus (c. 235). *Historiae romanae*: edited by U. P. Boissevain, 3 vols., Berlin, 1895—1901.

De Goeje, M. J., editor. *Bibliotheca geographorum arabicorum*, 8 vols., Leiden, 1870—1894.

De Goeje, M. J. *Mémoire sur la conquête de la Syrie*, constituting *Mémoires d'histoire et de géographie orientales*, No. 2, 2nd edition, Leiden, 1900.

Delitzsch, Friedrich. *Wo lag das Paradies?* Leipzig, 1881.

Dhorme, Paul. *Les pays bibliques et l'Assyrie (suite)*, in *Revue biblique*, New Series, Vol. 7, Paris, 1910, pp. 179—199; Vol. 8, 1911, pp. 198—218.

Dhorme, Paul. *Le pays de Job*, in *Revue biblique*, New Series, Vol. 8, Paris, 1911, pp. 102—107.

Ad-Dînawari, Abu Ḥanîfa Aḥmad ibn Dâ'ûd (d. 895). *Kitâb al-aḫbâr aṭ-ṭiwâl*: edited by Vladimir Guirgass, Leiden, 1888.

Dio, Cassius. See Cassius Dio.

Diodorus Siculus (c. 20 B. C.). *Bibliotheca historica*: Vols. 1—3 edited by Friedrich Vogel, Vols. 4 and 5 edited by C. T. Fischer, in *Bibliotheca scriptorum graecorum et romanorum teubneriana*, Leipzig, 1888—1906.

Farazdaḳ. See Hell.

Fischer. See Ptolemy.

Flügel, G. *Die arabischen, persischen und türkischen Handschriften der K. K. Hofbibliothek*, 3 vols., Vienna, 1863—1867.

Ğarîr. See al-Aḫṭal.

Geographiae expositio compendiaria: edited by Carl Müller in his *Geographi graeci minores*, Vol. 2, Paris, 1861, pp. 494—509.

Glaucus (date unknown). *Archaeologia arabica*: edited by Carl Müller in his *Fragmenta historicorum graecorum*, Vol. 4, Paris, 1851, p. 409.

Goeje, M. J. de. See De Goeje.

Guidi, Ignazio. *Un nuovo testo siriaco sulla storia degli ultimi Sassanidi*, in *Actes du huitième Congrès International des Orientalistes, tenu en 1889 à Stockholm et à Christiania. Section I: Sémitique (B)*, Leiden, 1893, pp. 1—36.

Ḥağği Ḫalfa (or Ḫalîfa), Muṣṭafa ibn ʿAbdallâh Kâtib Čelebi (d. 1658). I. *Ğihân numa'*: Constantinople, 1145 A. H. (1732—1733 A. D.). II. *Musawwadat ğihân numa'*: MS, Codex Vindobonensis, No. 1282 (Mxt. 389), National-Bibliothek, Vienna.

Al-Hamdâni, Abu Muḥammad al-Ḥasan ibn Aḥmad ibn Jaʿḳûb (d. 945). *Ṣifat ğezîrat al-ʿarab*: edited by D. H. Müller, 2 vols., Leiden, 1884—1891.

Ḥamzat ibn Ḥasan al-Iṣfahâni (about 913). *Kitâb ta'rîḫ sini mulûk al-arḍ wa-l-anbijâ'i*: edition by J. M. E. Gottwaldt entitled *Hamzae ispahanensis annalium libri X*, St. Petersburg, 1844.

Ḥassân ibn Ṯâbet (b. c. 563). *Dîwân*: Tunis, 1281 A. H. (1864—1865 A. D.).

Ḥâtem ibn ʿAbdallâh ibn Saʿd aṭ-Ṭâ'i (d. c. 600). *Dîwân*: edited with translation and commentary by Friedrich Schulthess, Leipzig, 1897.

Hebraica, Biblia. See *Biblia hebraica.*

Hell, Joseph, *Das Leben des Farazdaḳ* (640—641 to 732—733) *nach seinen Gedichten und sein Loblied auf al-Walîd ibn Jazîd Dîw. 394*, Leipzig, 1903.

Herodianus (about 250). *Ab excessu Divi Marci libri octo*: edited by L. Mendelssohn, Leipzig, 1883.

Huber, Charles. *Journal d'un voyage en Arabie*, Paris, 1891.

Ibn ʿAsâker aš-Šâfiʿi, Abu-l-Ḳâsim ʿAli ibn al-Ḥasan ibn Hibatallâh Ṯiḳataddîn (1105—1176) *Ta'rîḫ aš-šâm*: MS, Codex Berolinensis, No. 9781 (Spr. 120), Preussische Staatsbibliothek, Berlin.

Ibn al-Aṯîr, ʿAli ibn Muḥammad ʿIzzaddîn (1160—1234). I. *Al-kâmil fi-t-ta'rîḫ*: edition by C. J. Tornberg entitled *Ibn-el-Athir, Chronicon quod perfectissimum inscribitur*, 14 vols., Leiden, 1851—1876. II. *Kitâb usd al-ṛâba fi maʿrifat as-ṣaḥâba*, 5 vols., Cairo, 1280 A. H. (1863-1864 A. D.).

Ibn al-Faḳîh al-Hamaḏâni, Abu Bekr Aḥmad ibn Muḥammad (wrote c. 902). *Kitâb al-buldân*: edited by M. J. De Goeje in his *Bibl. geogr. arab.*, Vol. 5, Leiden, 1885.

Ibn Ğubejr, Abu-l-Ḥusejn Muḥammad ibn Aḥmad (1145—1217). *Riḥla*: edition by M. J. De Goeje entitled *The Travels of Ibn Jubayr*, constituting *E. J. W. Gibb Memorial*, Vol. 5, Leiden, 1907.

Ibn Ḫaldûn, Abu Zajd ʿAbdarraḥmân ibn Muḥammad ibn Muḥammad (1332—1406). I. *Muḳaddima*: edition by Et. Quatremère entitled *Prolégomènes d'Ebn-Khaldoun*, in *Notices et extraits des manuscrits de la Bibliothèque Impériale*, Vols. 16—18 First Parts, Paris, 1858. II. *Kitâb al-ʿibar wa dîwân al-mubtada' wa-l-ḫabar fi ajjâm al-ʿarab wa-l-ʿağam wa-l-berber*, 7 vols., Bûlâḳ, 1284 A. H. (1867—1868 A. D.).

Ibn Ḥawḳal, Abu-l-Ḳâsim (wrote 977). *Kitâb al-masâlik wa-l-mamâlik*: edited by M. J. De Goeje in his *Bibl. geogr. arab.*, Vol. 2, Leiden, 1873.

Ibn Hišâm, ʿAbdalmalik (d. 834). See Ibn Isḥâḳ.

Ibn Ḫordâḏbeh, Abu-l-Ḳâsim ʿObajdallâh ibn ʿAbdallâh (wrote c. 848). *Kitâb al-masâlik wa-l-mamâlik*, edited and translated into French by M. J. De Goeje in his *Bibl. geogr. arab.*, Vol. 6, Leiden, 1889.

Ibn al-ʿIbri, Abu-l-Farağ. See Barhebraeus.

Ibn Isḥâḳ, Muḥammad (d. c. 768). *Kitâb sîrat rasûl allâh* as edited by ʿAbdalmalik ibn Hišâm (d. 834): edition by Ferdinand Wüstenfeld entitled *Das Leben Muhammed's nach Muhammed Ibn Ishâk bearbeitet von Abd el-Malik Ibn Hischâm,* 2 vols. in 3, Göttingen, 1858—1860.

Ibn al-Ḳalânisi, Abu Jaʿli Ḥamzat (d. 1160). *Ḏajl ta'rîḫ dimašḳ*: edition by A. F. Amedroz entitled *History of Damascus, 363—555 A. H.*, Leiden, 1908.

Ibn Ḳotejba, Abu Muḥammad ʿAbdallâh ibn Muslim (d. c. 889) I. *Kitâb al-maʿârif*: edition by F. Wüstenfeld entitled *Ibn Coteiba's Handbuch der Geschichte,* Göttingen, 1850. II. *ʿUjûn al-aḫbâr*: edition by Carl Brockelmann entitled *Ibn Qutaiba's ʿUjûn al Aḫbâr. Nach den Handschriften zu Constantinopel und St. Petersburg herausgegeben von* ∾, constituting supplements to *Zeitschrift für Assyriologie und verwandte Gebiete,* Vols. 15, 17, 19, 21, Berlin and Strassburg, 1900—1908.

Ibn Munḳiḏ, Abu-l-Muẓaffar Usâma ibn Muršid Mağdaddîn Mu'ajjid ad-Dawla (d. 1188). *Kitâb al-iʿtibâr*: edition by Hartwig Derenbourg entitled *Ousâma ibn Mounkidh, un émir syrien au premier siècle des croisades (1095—1188),* Part 2., *Texte arabe de l'autobiographie d'Ousàma publié d'après le manuscrit de l'Escurial,* constituting *Publications de l'École des Langues Orientales Vivantes,* 2nd Series, Vol. 12, Paris, 1889.

Ibn Roste, Abu ʿAli Aḥmad ibn ʿOmar (visited al-Medîna, 903). *Kitâb al-aʿlâḳ an-nafîsa,* edited by M. J. De Goeje in his *Bibl. geogr. arab.*, Vol. 7, Leiden, 1892, pp. 1—229.

Ibn Saʿd ibn Manîʿ az-Zuhri, Abu ʿAbdallâh Muḥammad (d. 845). *Kitâb at-ṭabaḳât al-kebîr*: edition by Eduard Sachau entitled *Biographien Muhammeds, seiner Gefährten und der späteren Träger des Islams bis zum Jahre 230 der Flucht,* 9 vols., Leiden, 1904—1909.

Ibn Serapion (c. 900). *Kitâb ʿağâ'ib al-aḳâlîm as-sabʿa*: edition by Guy le Strange entitled *Description of Mesopotamia and Baghdad, Written About the Year 900 A. D.*, in *Journal of the Royal Asiatic Society,* Vol. 27, London, 1895, pp. 1—76, 225—315.

Al-Idrîsi, Abu ʿAbdallâh Muḥammad ibn Muḥammad ibn ʿAbdallâh ibn Idrîs aš-Šarîf (1100—1166). I. *Kitâb nuzhat al-muštâḳ fi-ḫtirâḳ al-âfâḳ*: French translation by P. A. Jaubert entitled *Géographie d'Édrisi, traduite de l'arabe en français,* constituting *Recueil de voyages et de mémoires, publié par la Société de Géographie,* Vols. 5 and 6, Paris, 1836—1840. II. *Kitâb nuzhat al-muštâḳ fi ḏikr al-amṣâr wa-l-aḳtâr wa-l-buldân wa-l-ğuzur wa-l-madâ'in wa-l-âfâḳ* (a synopsis of I.): Rome 1592.

Imrulḳajs ibn Ḥuğr (d. c. 530). *Dîwân*: edition by (W.) MacGuckin de Slane entitled *Le Diwan d'Amro'lkaïs précédé de la vie de ce poète . . . accompagné d'une traduction et de notes,* Paris, 1837.

Al-Iṣṭaḫri, Abu Isḥâḳ Ibrâhîm ibn Muḥammad al-Fâresi (fl. 951). *Kitâb masâlik al-mamâlik*: edited by M. J. De Goeje in his *Bibl. geogr. arab.*, Vol. 1, Leiden, 1870.

Al-Jaʿḳûbi, Aḥmad ibn abi Jaʿḳûb ibn Wâḍiḥ al-Kâtib (fl. 891). *Ta'rîḫ*: edition by M. Th. Houtsma entitled *Ibn-Wādhih qui dicitur al-Jaʿqubī, Historiae,* 2 vols., Leiden, 1883.

Jâḳût ibn ʿAbdallâh ar-Rûmi (d. 1224). *Kitâb muʿğam al-buldân*: edition by Ferdinand Wüstenfeld entitled *Jacut's geographisches Wörterbuch,* 6 vols., Leipzig, 1866—1873.

Kaiserliche Akademie der Wissenschaften (publisher). *Kuṣejr ʿAmra*, 2 vols., Vol. 1, text; Vol. 2, 51 colored plates, Vienna, 1907.

Al-Ḳazwîni, Zakarija' ibn Muḥammad ibn Maḥmûd (d. 1283). *Cosmography*, consisting of *Kitâb ʿaǧâ'ib al-maḫlûḳât* and *Kitâb âṯâr al-bilâd*: edition by Ferdinand Wüstenfeld entitled *Zakarija Ben Muhammed Ben Mahmud el-Cazwini's Kosmographie*, 2 vols., Göttingen, 1848–1849; *Kitâb ʿaǧâ'ib al-maḫlûḳât*, Cairo, 1321 A. H. (1903—1904 A. D.).

Kemâladdîn Abu-l-Ḳâsim ʿOmar ibn Aḥmad ibn al-ʿAdîm al-ʿOḳajli al-Ḥalabi (d. 1262). *Al-muntaḫab min ta'rîḫ ḥalab*: edition by J. W. Freytag entitled *Selecta ex historia Halebi e codice arabico Bibliothecae Regiae Parisiensis*, Paris, 1819.

Kiepert, H. *Nouvelle carte générale des provinces asiatiques de l'Empire Ottoman*, Berlin, 1884.

Ḳodâma ibn Ǧaʿfar al-Kâtib al-Baġdâdi, Abu-l-Faraǧ (d. 922). *Nabḏ min "kitâb al-ḫarâǧ"*: edited by M. J. De Goeje in his *Bibl. geogr. arab.*, Vol. 6, Leiden, 1889, pp. 184—266.

Königliche Museen in Berlin, Vorderasiatische Abteilung (publisher). *Vorderasiatische Schriftdenkmäler*, 16 vols., Leipzig, 1877 ff.

Kremer, Alfred von. *Über die Gedichte des Labyd*, in *Sitzungsberichte der kaiserlichen Akademie der Wissenschaften*, Philosophisch-historische Classe, Vol. 18, Part 2, Vienna, 1881, pp. 555—605.

Ḳuṣejr ʿAmra. See Kaiserliche Akademie der Wissenschaften; Musil.

Lammens, Henri. *Études sur le règne du Calife Omaiyade Moʿâwia Ier*, Second Series, in *Mélanges de la Faculté Orientale*, Vol. 2, Beirut, 1907, pp. 1—172.

Layard, A. H. *Inscriptions in the Cuneiform Character from Assyrian Monuments*, London, 1882.

Leachman, G. *A Journey through Central Arabia*, in *Journal of the Royal Geographical Society*, Vol. 43, London, 1914, pp. 500—520.

Lebîd, Ibn Rabîʿa abu ʿAḳîl (d. 661 or 680). See Kremer.

Marcianus of Heraclea (c. 400). *Periplus maris exteri*, edited with Latin translation by Carl Müller in his *Geographi graeci minores*, Vol. 1, Paris, 1855, pp. 515—562.

Massignon, Louis. *Mission en Mesopotamie, 1907—1908*, constituting *Mémoires publiées par les membres de l'Institut Français d'Archéologie Orientale*, Vol. 28, Cairo, 1910.

Al-Masʿûdi, Abu-l-Ḥasan ʿAli ibn al-Ḥusejn (d. 956). I. *Murûǧ aḏ-ḏahab wa maʿâdin al-ǧawâhir*: edition and translation by C. Barbier de Meynard and Pavet de Courteille entitled *Les prairies d'or*, 9 vols., Paris, 1861—1877. II. *Kitâb at-tanbîh wa-l-išrâf*: edited by M. J. De Goeje in his *Bibl. geogr. arab.*, Vol. 8, Leiden, 1894.

Meḥmed Edîb ibn Meḥmed Derwîš, Al-Ḥaǧǧ (d. 1801). *Nehǧet al-menâzil*: Constantinople, 1232 A. H. (1817 A. D.).

Mengin, Félix. *Histoire de l'Égypte sous le gouvernement de Mohammed-Aly: ouvrage enrichi de notes par MM. Langlès et Jomard*, 2 vols., Paris, 1823.

Al-Muḳaddasi, Abu ʿAbdallâh Muḥammad ibn Aḥmad (b. 946, wrote 985). *Aḥsan at-taḳâsîm fi maʿrifat al-aḳâlîm*, edited by M. J. De Goeje in his *Bibl. geogr. arab.*, Vol. 3, 2nd edition, Leiden, 1906.

Musil, Alois. *Arabia Petraea*: 3 vols. in 4, Vol. 1, *Moab*; Vol. 2 (in 2 parts), *Edom*; Vol. 3, *Ethnologischer Reisebericht*; Kaiserliche Akademie der Wissenschaften, Vienna, 1907—1908.

Musil, Alois. *Im nördlichen Ḥeǧâz. Vorbericht über die Forschungsreise 1910,* Wien, 1911.

Musil, Alois. *Ḳuṣejr ʿAmra,* in Kaiserliche Akad. der Wiss., *Ḳuṣejr ʿAmra,* Vol. 1, Vienna, 1907, pp. 3—186.

Musil, Alois. *The Northern Ḥeǧâz,* constituting *American Geographical Society, Oriental Explorations and Studies,* No. 1, New York, 1926.

Musil, Alois. *Zur Zeitgeschichte von Arabien,* K.K. Oesterreichische Orient- und Uebersee-Gesellschaft, Vienna, 1918.

Al-Mutanabbi, Abu-ṭ-Ṭajjeb ibn al-Ḥusajn (d. 965). *Dîwân*: edition by F. H. Dieterici entitled *Mutanabbii carmina cum commentario Wâḥidii,* Berlin, 1861.

An-Nâbiṛa aḏ-Ḏubjâni, Zijâd ibn Muʿâwija (c. 600). *Dîwân*: edition by Hartwig Derenbourg entitled *Le Dīwān de Nābiga Dhobyānī ...., texte arabe suivi d'une traduction française par ∾,* in *Journal asiatique,* 6th Series, Vol. 12, Paris, 1868, pp. 197—297, 301—439, 484—515; published separately, Paris, 1869; supplement entitled *Nâbiga Dhobyânî inédit, d'après le ms. arabe 65 de la collection Schefer,* in *Journal asiatique,* Ser. 9, Vol. 13, Paris, 1899, pp. 1—55.

An-Nawawi, Abu Zakarija Jaḥja (d. 1278). *Kitâb tahḏîb al-asmâʾi wa-l-lurât*: edition by Ferdinand Wüstenfeld entitled *The Bibliographical Dictionary of Illustrious Men Chiefly at the Beginning of Islamism,* 2 vols., Göttingen, 1842—1847.

Niebuhr, Carsten. *Beschreibung von Arabien,* Copenhagen, 1772.

Niebuhr, Carsten. *Reisebeschreibung nach Arabien und andern umliegenden Ländern,* 3 vols., Copenhagen and Hamburg, 1774, 1837.

Nöldeke, Theodor. *Die von Guidi herausgegebene syrische Chronik,* in *Sitzungsberichte der kaiserlichen Akademie der Wissenschaften,* Philosophisch-historische Klasse, Vol. 128, Part 9, Vienna, 1893.

Pelly, Lewis. *A Visit to the Wahabee Capital, Central Arabia,* in *Journal of the Royal Geographical Society,* Vol. 35, London 1865, p. 169—191.

Peutinger Table. See *Tabula Peutingeriana.*

Pliny (C. Plinius Secundus) (d. 79). *Naturalis historia*: edited by C. Mayhoff, 2nd edition, 6 vols., Leipzig, 1892—1909; see also D. Detlefsen, editor, *Die geographischen Bücher (II, 242-VI Schluss) der Naturalis historia des C. Plinius Secundus mit vollständigem kritischen Apparat,* constituting *Quellen und Forschungen zur alten Geschichte und Geographie* edited by W. Sieglin, Vol. 9, Berlin, 1904.

Pseudo-Wâḳedi. *Futûḥ aš-šâm*: edition with notes by W. Nassau Lees entitled *The Conquest of Syria Commonly Adscribed to Abou ʿAbdallah Mohammad b. ʿOmar al Wákidí,* 3 vols., in *Bibliotheca indica,* Calcutta, 1854—1862.

Ptolemy (Claudius Ptolemaeus) (c. 150). *Geography*: edited by C. F. A. Nobbe, 3 vols., Leipzig, 1843—1845; bks. i—v edited with Latin translation and atlas, Vol. 1, Part 1, by Carl Müller, Paris, 1884; Vol. 1, Part 2, by C. Th. Fischer, Paris, 1901.

Quatremère, Étienne. *Mémoires géographiques et historiques sur l'Égypte,* 2 vols., Paris, 1811.

Rawlinson, H. C. *Cuneiform Inscriptions of Western Asia,* 5 vols., London, 1861—1884.

Rogers, Robert W. *Two Esarhaddon Texts,* in *Haverford College Studies,* No. 2, Haverford (n. d.), pp. 65—66 and two plates.

Rost, Paul. *Die Keilschrifttexte Tiglat Pileser III, nach den Papierabklatschen und Originalen des Britischen Museums,* 2 vols., Vol. 1, *Einleitung, Transcription und Übersetzung, Wörterverzeichnis und Commentar*; Vol. 2, *Autographierte Texte*; Leipzig, 1893.

(Rousseau, J. B. L. J.) *Description du Pachalik de Bagdad suivie d'une notice historique sur les Wahabis et de quelques autres pièces relatives à l'histoire et à la littérature de l'orient,* Paris, 1809.

Ar-Rukajjât, ʿUbajdallâh ibn Kajs (d. c. 690). *Dîwân*: edition by N. Rhodokanakis, constituting *Sitzungsberichte der Akademie d. Wiss.*, Phil.-hist. Classe, Vol. 144, No. 10, Vienna, 1902.

Sacy, Silvestre de. *Exposé de la religion des Druzes tiré des livres religieux de cette secte,* 2 vols., Paris, 1838.

Sargon. See Winckler, Hugo.

Scheil, V. *Miscelles I. La campagne de Sennachérib contre les Arabes,* in *Orientalistische Literaturzeitung,* Vol. 7, Berlin, 1904, cols. 69—70.

Scheil, V. *Textes élamites-sémitiques,* Series 5, constituting *Mémoires de la Mission Archéologique de Susiane,* Vol. 14, Paris, 1913.

Scheil, V. *Le prisme S d'Assaraddon, roi d'Assyrie 681—668,* constituting *Bibliothèque de l'École des Hautes Études... Sciences philologiques et historiques,* fasc. 208, Paris, 1914.

Schrader, Eberhard, editor. *Keilinschriftliche Bibliothek*: *Sammlung von assyrischen und babylonischen Texten in Umschrift und Uebersetzungen...,* Berlin, Vol. 1, 1889; Vol. 2, 1890; Vol. 3, Part 1, 1892; Vol. 3, Part 2, 1890; Vol. 4, 1896; Vol. 5, 1896; Vol. 6, Part 1, 1900.

Septuagint, The: edition by H. B. Swete entitled *The Old Testament in Greek According to the Septuagint,* 2nd edition, 3 vols., Cambridge, 1891—1895.

Sibṭ ibn al-Ǧawzi, Šamsaddîn Abu-l-Muẓaffar Jûsuf ibn Ḳizuṛlu ibn ʿAbdallâh (d. 1257). *Kitâb mirʾât az-zamân fi taʾrîḫ al-aʿjân*: a selection edited and translated by Ch. A. C. Barbier de Meynard under the title *Extraits du Mirât ez-Zèmân,* in *Recueil des historiens des croisades, Historiens orientaux,* Vol. 3, Paris, 1884, pp. 511—570.

Sixtus of Bourbon of Parma, Prince, and Alois Musil. *In Nordostarabien und Südmesopotamien. Vorbericht über die Forschungsreise 1912,* Vienna, 1913.

Smith, George. *History of Sennacherib,* London, 1878.

Smith, Sidney. *The First Campaign of Sennacherib, King of Assyria, B. C. 705—681,* London, 1921.

Snouck-Hurgronje, C. *Mekka, mit Bilder-Atlas.* Vol. 1, *Die Stadt und ihre Herren*; Vol. 2, *Aus dem heutigen Leben*; The Hague, 1888—1889.

Sozomenus (c. 439). *Ecclesiastica historia,* in: J. P. Migne, *Patrologiae cursus completus..., Series graeca,* Vol. 67, Paris, 1859, cols. 843—1630.

Sprenger, A. *Das Leben und die Lehre des Moḥammad,* 3 vols., Berlin, 1869.

Stephen of Byzantium (c. 600). *Ethnica*: edition by August Meineke entitled *Ethnicorum quae supersunt,* Vol. 1 (only volume published), Berlin, 1879.

Strabo (c. 63 B. C.—c. 19 A. D.). *Geographia*: edited by August Meineke, in *Bibliotheca scriptorum graecorum et romanorum teubneriana,* 3 vols., Leipzig, 1907—1913.

Streck, Maximilian. *Assurbanipal und die letzten assyrischen Könige,* 3 vols., constituting *Vorderasiatische Bibliothek,* No. 7, Leipzig, 1916.

At-Ṭabari, Abu Ǧaʿfar Muḥammad ibn Ǧarîr (d. 923). *Ta'rîḫ ar-rusul wa-l-mulûk*: edition by M. J. De Goeje and others entitled *Annales quos scripsit Abu Djafar Mohammed ibn Djarir at-Tabari*, 3 series in 15 vols., Leiden, 1879—1903.

Tabula Peutingeriana (12th century MS copy of Roman map of time of the Empire): photographic edition in 11 sheets entitled *Peutingeriana Tabula Itineraria . . . nunc primum arte photographica expressa*, Vienna, 1888.

Tavernier, J. B. *Les six voyages... en Turquie, en Perse et aux Indes*, 2 parts, Paris, 1676.

Thevenot, Jean de (1633—1667). *Voyages... en Europe, Asie, et Afrique*, 3 parts in 5 vols., Paris, 1689.

Tiglath Pileser III, Tiglath Pileser IV. See Rost.

Valle, Pietro della. *Viaggi*, 4 vols., Venice, 1664.

Velenovský, J. *Plantae arabicae Musilianae*: constituting *Věstník král. české společnosti nauk. Třída mathematicko-přírodovědecká (Sitzungsberichte der königl. böhm. Gesellschaft der Wissenschaften, Math. naturwiss. Classe)*, 1911, No. 11, Prague, 1912.

Velenovský, J. *Arabské rostliny z poslední cesty Musilovy r. 1915. Plantae arabicae ex ultimo itinere A. Musili a. 1915*: constituting *Věstník král. české společnosti nauk. Třída II. na rok 1921—1922 (Mémoires de la Société Royale des Sciences de Bohême, Classe des Sciences, 1921—1922)*, No. 6, Prague, 1923.

Vorderasiatische Schriftdenkmäler. See Königliche Museen in Berlin, Vorderasiatische Abteilung.

Al-Wâḳedi, Abu ʿAbdallâh Muḥammad ibn ʿOmar (d. 823). *Kitâb al-maġâzi*: edition by Alfred von Kremer entitled *History of Muhammad's Campaigns, by Aboo 'Abd Ollah Mohammad 'bin Omar al-Wákidy*, in *Bibliotheca indica*, Calcutta, 1856; German translation by J. Wellhausen entitled *Muhammed in Medina. Das ist Vakidi's Kitab al-Maghazi in verkürzter deutscher Wiedergabe*, Berlin, 1882.

Wallin, G. A. *Narrative of a Journey from Cairo to Medina and Mecca, by Suez, Arabá, Tawilá, al-Jauf, Jubbe, Háil and Nejd, in 1845*, in *Journal of the Royal Geographical Society*, Vol. 24, London, 1854, pp. 115—207.

Wellhausen, J. *Skizzen und Vorarbeiten*, 6 vols., Berlin, 1884—1889.

Winckler, Hugo. *Die Keilschrifttexte Sargon's nach den Papierabklatschen und Originalen neu herausgegeben*, 2 vols., Vol. 1, *Historisch-sachliche Einleitung, Umschrift und Übersetzung, Wörterverzeichnis;* Vol. 2, *Texte*, transcribed by Dr. Ludwig Abel, Leipzig, 1889.

Winckler, Hugo. *Keilinschriftliches Textbuch zum Alten Testament*, 3rd edition, Leipzig, 1909.

Winckler, Hugo. *Zur Geschichte des alten Arabiens*, in *Altorientalische Forschungen*, Series 1, Vol. 5, Leipzig, 1897, pp. 463—468.

Wright, W. *Catalogue of the Syriac Manuscripts in the British Museum*, 3 vols.. London, 1870—1872.

Wüstenfeld, F. *Fachr ed-dîn der Drusenfürst und seine Zeitgenossen*, constituting *Abhandlungen der K. Gesellschaft der Wissenschaften zu Göttingen*, Vol. 33, Göttingen, 1886.

Az-Zabîdi, Muḥammad Murtaḍa' ibn Muḥammad ibn ʿAbdarrazzâḳ al-Ḥusajni (d. 1791). *Tâǧ al-ʿarûs*, 10 vols., Bûlâḳ, 1307—1308 A. H. (1889—1890).

Zosimus (491-518). *Historia nova*: edited by L. Mendelssohn, Leipzig, 1887.

INDEX

INDEX

The positions of place names occurring on the map of Northern Arabia accompanying this volume are indicated in the index in parentheses by key letters and figures referring to the quadrangles on the map. The reader should also consult the accompanying index map of the author's route and of his topographical descriptions.

The letters SM *refer to the author's map of Southern Mesopotamia which will accompany the author's forthcoming volume* The Middle Euphrates, *to be published in the present series.*

The most important page references are given in italics.

Brief, non-technical characterizations are given in parentheses for the majority of the Arabic botanical terms. The Latin names of such plants as have been identified by J. Velenovský (see Bibliography, p. 584) are also given.

ᶜA. *Abbreviation for* ᶜAjn. *See* proper name
Al-ᶜÂᶜ, 371
Aaron, 496
Ab-. *See* main part of topographical proper name
ᶜAbâdle, 84
Abâʾir, 100, *324*
Abawaʾ, 155
ᶜAbbâdân, 510, 511
Al-ᶜAbbâs ibn Hišâm al-Kalbi, 542, 544, 547
Abbassides, 522
Al-ᶜAbd (m11), 166, 305, *306*, 467
ᶜAbd al-Ǧowf. *See* Al-ᶜAbd (m11)
ᶜAbd al-Maᶜâṣer (k8), 113, 313, 314
Al-ᶜAbd wa Awlâdah (h6—7), 94
ᶜAbdalᶜazîz eben Rašîd, 395, 431
ᶜAbdallâh, Âl, 56
ᶜAbdallâh eben Menfes, 464
ᶜAbdallâh eben Saᶜûd al-Imâm, 248
ᶜAbdallâh eben Ṭalâl, 164, 175, 284, 285, 326
ᶜAbdallâh, family of the Kalb, 538
ᶜAbdallâh, the negro, 11, 13, 283, 446, 459, 460, 464
ᶜAbdalmalek, Caliph, 75, 100, 101, 158, 361, 552
ᶜAbdalwahhâb ibn al-Mubârek, 568
ᶜAbdân eben Dasmân, 231
ᶜAbdarraḥmân eben Rašîd, vice-gerent in Tejma, 143, 178, 180
ᶜAbdarraḥmân ibn Abi Bekr, 548
ᶜAbdarraḥmân ibn ᶜAwf, 537—539
ᶜAbdarraḥmân Pasha Jûsef, Director in Chief of Pilgrimages, 4, 239, 414
ᶜAbde (q13—r16), 445, 449
ᶜAbdelle, 14, 233
Al-ᶜAbderi, 361
Abdul-Hamid, 390
ᶜAbdwadd, 533
Al-ᶜAbed, 113, 313
Abel, 482
Abijate, son of Teʾri, 485—487, 489
Al-Abjaḍ, 243, 524
Al-Abjaḍ, Ḳaṣr, 508
ᶜAbla (subshrub with grayish leaves), 45
Al-Ablaḳ, 518, 553
Abraham, 491, 493, 497
Abraḳ. *See* proper name
ᶜAbs, 55, 101
ᶜAbṭân eben Ǧâzi, 435—437, 440, 441
Abu. *See* main part of topographical proper name
Abu ᶜAmr, 63
Abu-l-ᶜAtâhija, 361
Abu-l-Baḳa aṣ-Ṣaffûri, 378
Abu-l-Baḳar aṭ-Ṭâʾi, 118
Abu Bakr, chief of the Ṣḳûr, 237
Abu Bekr, Caliph, 546—550, 553—555, 560—563, 565, 571
Abu Bekr ibn Kilâb, 138
Abu-l-Faḍâʾil, 13, 37, 55, 76, 125, 270, 359, 362, 364, 577
Abu-l-Faraǧ, 13, 40, 158, 324, 325, 334, 361, 402, 520— 522, 529, 548, 568, 577
Abu-l-Fatḥ ᶜOṯmân ibn Ǧinni, 272
Abu-l-Fedaʾ, 48, 92, 339, 509—511, 528, 535, 568, 577
Abu-l-Hajṯam, 336
Abu Ḥuḏejfa, 519
Abu-l-Ḳâsem as-Saḥâmi, 560
Abu Manṣûr, 336
Abu Miḫnaf, 549
Abu nešr (*Galium ceratopodum*, Boiss.; annual weed with bluish flowers), 301
Abu ᶜObejd as-Sakûni, 534
Abu ᶜObejda, Maᶜmar ibn al-Muṯanna, 509
Abu ᶜObejda ibn al-Ǧarrâḥ, 560, 563, 564
Abu Saᶜd, 534
Abu Šâma, 380, 577
Abu Šâma, chief of the al-Mwâhîb clan, 436
Abu Ṭâher Slîmân ibn al-Ḥasan ibn Behrâm al-Ǧannâbi, 366
Abu Tâjeh, 233, 421, 458

Al-Bowlijjât, Šbn. (e6—7), 34
Bowman, Isaiah, xvii
Al-Bowzeli, 89
Al-Bowzelijjât (f6), 26, 34, 77, 88, 392
Al-Bowzelijje, 82
Bradân (f18), *359*, 506, 531
Al-Brake (g18), 363
Al-Bṛâlijje (g7—8), 91
Bread, prepared in ashes, 218, 219
Al-Brejčât, Ḫabâri (i10), 221, 264
Brejčât al-Mra' (i11), 265, 454
Brejčet ummu Ḥsejje (i11), 265, 525
Al-Bṛejla (h8), 95
Al-Bṛejṭât, Ḫabâri (i7), 100
Al-Brêḳa (d8—9), 40
British, 393, 399. *See also* English, Inklîz
Brukân (*Centaurea camelorum*, Vel.; low, bushy perennial with bristly bracts and yellowish flower heads), 135, 328, 334
Al-Bsajṭa (m8—9), 118, 119, 122, *125*, 126, 131, 167, 437, 523, 551; erosion of, 125
Al-Bsâs (i5), 335
Bṭejjen eben Meršed, 428
Al-Bûb (g18—19), 363
Buda', 483
Buḥtur, 516
Al-Buḳᶜa, 524
Al-Buḳejᶜa, 524, 525
Al-Bûmijjât (o15), 516
Bupleurum semicompositum, L. See *Snejsle*
Burckhardt, J. L., 553, 578
Burial, 169
Burial ground, al-Mǧenne, 142, 144; Nabataean, 272
Burḳ aš-Šaᶜîra, 157, 183, 187
Burḳa' Ḥawra', 508
Burḳuᶜ, Ḳaṣr (g8), 82, 90, *92*, 93, 96, 409, 484, 513, 515, 519, 528
Burrejd (*Bellevalia bracteosa*, Vel.; species of hyacinth), 287
Al-Burᶜûm, 371
Busajṭa, 118, 119, *125*, 130, 522, 523
Al-Buṭmijjât (e6), 382, 384, 385, 389, 390
Al-Buṭum, W. (i5), 334, 337, 343
Bûz, 484
Al-Bwejb (f8), 397
Al-Bwejb, Ḫabâri, 398
Bwejb al-Ḳazwân (l11), 453, 463, 464
Al-Bwejbijje (o9—10), 135, 168, 170
Al-Bwejtât (l13), 206, 209, 214, 296, 298, 515, 528
Al-Bwêr (c5), 388, 389
Al-Bwêra, 522, 523
Al-Bwêrde, Želîb (f17), 70
Bwêẓa (*Paronychia arabica*, L.; low, silver-scaled herb with pinkish flowers), 318
Al-Bwêẓa, Ḫabra (q9), 141
Byzantines, 543, 550
Bzâr as-semen (*Euphorbia Rohlenae*, Vel.; species of spurge), 236

Al-Čaᶜačedi, M. (h13), 247—249, 252, 263
Čabd, Ḥazm (d9—10), 37, 41, 48
Al-Čabd, Mšâš (m4), 523
Čâbde, Fejẓa (i6), 334
Caetani, Leone, 513, 523, 534, 538—540, 544—546, 549, 550, 554—557, 560—563, 565, 568—570, 573, 578
Čâf (j7), 96, 109, 298, 314, 324—327, 388, 395, 396, 406, 441, 484, 507
Čaff al-čalb (*Gymnarrhena micrantha*, Desf.; low annual with scaled stamens bearing yellow heads which stick to the soil and when dried take the shape of a hard spoon), 236, 252
Cafr Chaider, 367
Al-Čahâf (g18), 362
Čahaf Aḥmed eben Hâšem, 363
Cairo, 534
Cakile arabica, Born. Vel. See *Islîḥ*
Calathua, 508
Calathusa, 508
Čalb abu Munṭâr (h13), 246, 248, 249, 254
Čalb al-Čaᶜači (h13—14), 246—249, 252
Calendula aegyptiaca, Desf. See *ᶜEšbet al-ṛurâb* and *Ḥenwa*
Calendula micrantha, Boiss. See *Ḥenwa*
Cambyses, 515
Camels, author is robbed of two, 299, 300; breeding period, 453; conservation of water in, 557, 563, 567, 570, 571; day's journey, 120; dispute about, 319; draw water in the oases, 297, 298; dung marks the road, 155; dunging in drinking water, 305; of ᶜEjâl Turkijje, 320, 321; emaciation prevents rising, 281; fattened with good pasturage, 226; fed with *nejtûl*, 43; fondness for their young, 307; forsaken on the camping ground, 3; frightened easily, 160, 183, 250, 303; gone astray, 247; grazing as they go, 68; grazing on *mḥarût*, 270, 271; in herds, 455; hoof prints in sand mark whence they came, 146, 147; incitement to drink, 570; killed for guests, 177; lack of pasture, 110, 299, 336; lame, 319; liberated, 175; loading of, 303; loads, 453; maladies, 103, 260, 261; milk diluted with water, 56; milk scarce in December, 67; mourning for young ones, 193, 194; need of rest at sunrise, 121; in the Nefûd, 146; pack camels, 453; protected by warriors, 9, 110; reward for lost or stolen, 40, 300, 302, 387; rider on camel does fancy turns, 77; saddling 108; sandstorm and, 19, 159; seven deserted, 39—40; sick, seared with hot iron, 260, 261; silent in the night, 38, 87; stolen, 114, 165; traders, 284; travel across salt marsh, 102, 315; travel in darkness, 307; travel in the sandy desert, 154; wailing for killed young, 193, 194; watering of, 116, 140, 183, 208, 305, 308; white, 55, 480; wounded, 183, 321; young killed, 103
Camping ground, difficulty of choosing, 68, 69; guarding, 49, 71, 333; in arid land, 2; in various seasons, 408, 409; migration to new, 194, 311; order in, 5; scouts look for, 336; scrutiny of abandoned, 80, 81, 253, 254, 329, 402—404; stench near, 2, 3; thief near, 18
Capha, 507
Capparis spinosa, L. See *Šefalleḥ*
Carchemish, 487

Al-Ḥâǧǧ Jâsîn, 190
Ḥaǧǧâǧ, Âl, 84
Al-Ḥaǧǧâǧ, commander of Caliph ʿAbdalmalek, 158, 361
Ḥaǧǧi Ḫalfa, 33, 92, 93, 279, 513, 514, 519, 520, 528, 553, 579
Al-Ḥaǧîra, 380
Al-Haǧm (i10), 263, 415, 418—*420*, 453
Haǧr, Âl, 56
Hagra, 498
Ḥaǧrat Rubbâḫ (i8), 99
Al-Ḥaǧûle (e5), 385
Hailstones, 20
Ḫajappa, 477, 479
Ḫajbar, 84, 172, 173, 176, 339, 519, 536, 553
Ḫajdar, Ḳaṣr, 367
Ḥâjel (q14), xiv, xv, 76, 79, 173, 193, 231, 299, 310, 417, 431, 432, 446, 449, 451, 481, 514
Hâjel eben Fâjez, 414
Ḥajjâč, ʿAjn, 372
Ḥajjâl, Eben, 233
Al-Ḥajjânijje (o16), 449, 521
Hajjâzaʿ, Âl, 52
Al-Hajṯam ibn ʿAdi, 513, 563, 564
Ḥakam al-Ḫuḏri, 233
Al-Ḥakkân, 372
Ḥakše, Âl, 15
Ḥâla, 336
Ḫâla, 63, 336
Al-Ḥâla, 63, 336
Al-Ḫâla, 336
Al-Ḫalâd, Tlûl (i8), 98, 99
Ḫalaf, slave of Sulṭân âl Tajjâr, 388, 390
Ḫalaf eben Iḏen, 240
Halajṯa (or *niḳd*), 328
Al-Ḫalaṭ, 506, 526
Halba (*Zollikoferia mucronata*, Forsk.; bushy annual with long, thin root, gray leaves and longish, yellow flower heads), 200
Al-Halba (e8), 37—39, 79; (l6), 118. *See also* al-Helba
Ḫaldili, 483
Ḥaleb, 8, 438, 440, 530, 531. *See also* Aleppo
Ḫâled al-Ḳasri, 364, 522
Ḫâled eben Saṭṭâm eben Šaʿlân, *206*, 207, 216, 217, 312, 452
Ḫâled ibn al-Walîd, 55, 100, 246, 361, 513, 520, 526, 533, 539—542, 545—569, 571—573
Ḥalfa (*Imperata cylindrica*, L.; a kind of reed-like grass with silky, hairy flower spikes; *see* Figs. 64, 65, 66), 102, 104, 145, 313, 320, *322*, *323*
Ḥalfablatân, 380
Half-*fellâḥîn*, encounter with, 369
Ḫalîfa eben Ṛatjân, 449
Ḥaliǧe, Žalta (h16), 236
Ḫalîl Fattâl, 103
Halimoenemis pilosa, Moq. See *Kalša*
Ḥalîmt al-Ḳâra, 11
Al-Ḫalîže, 233
Al-Ḫall, Darb (r19), 446, 449
Al-Ḥallâbât, Ḳaṣr (h4), 351—*353*, 569
Al-Ḥalli (g11), 261
Ḥalôla (*Leontodon autumnalis*, L.; fall dandelion), 187
Haloxylon articulatum, Cav. See *Rimṯ*
Ḥama' (b5), 48, 359, 391, 485, 499
Al-Ḥamâd (d—e9—f—j10), 63, 70, *73*—75, 80, 91, 122, 180, 202, 211, 213, 231, 254, 255, 259, 263, 265—267, 270, 272, 408, 411, 418, 454, 458, 503, 511, 526
Ḥamad welad Šennûf, 231
Ḥamal, *126*, 130
Ḥamala', 126
Al-Ḥamâʿle, 84
Al-Ḥamâmde, 84
Al-Ḥamâmîd, 15
Al-Ḥamâmijât (m11—12), 193—195, 303
Al-Ḥamar, 126. *See also* Ṭubejž al-Ḥamar
Ḥamaṣ, 248
Ḥamâṭ (*Lithospermum callosum*, Vahl.; hairy perennial with prickly leaves and blue flowers), 132, 135, 145, 149, 155, 200, 246
Al-Ḥamâṭre, 52
Ḥambâẓ (*Rumex vesicarius*, L.; a kind of sorrel), 128, 187, 328
Ḥamd (shrub with long branches and small leaves; resembles *rimṯ*), 238
Ḥamda, Ḫabra (d9—10), 41
Hamdân ibn Ḳarmaṭ, 366
Hamdân, tribe, 552
Ḥamdân walad Ḫaṣi, 136
Al-Hamdâni, 76, 101, 179, 272, 335, 513, 516, 579
Ḥamed, servant of Zejdân eben Ṯamed, 415
Ḥâmed âl Homṭ, 136
Al-Ḥâmel (g10), 403
Ḥâmer, 234, 235
Al-Ḫâmisân, 380
Ḥamma' (*Erucaria Aegiceras*, I. G.; annual with small, pinnate leaves and bunches of red flowers), 182
Ḥamma, Ḳârat (e12), 62
Ḥammad, Âl, 15, 85
Ḥammâdi, 15
Al-Ḥammâm (a7), 529, 531
Ḥammâm ibn ʿOmar, 362
Ḥammâm aṣ-Ṣarrâḥ (h4—5), *348*—*351*
Ḥammâra, the *šwâja*, 223
Ḫamr wâžef (a variety of *semḥ*), 464
Al-Ḥamra', 357, 358
Ḥamṣîṣ (*Rumex lacerus*, Balb.: a kind of sorrel), 287
Al-Ḥamẓ, 530, 531
Ḥamzat al-Iṣfahâni, 324, 351, 579
Ḫân. *See* proper name
Al-Ḥanâfes, 560
Ḫanâṣer (a6), 509, 529
Al-Ḥanâtîš, 56
Al-Ḥanfas, 525
Al-Ḥanûṣ, Riǧlet (j11—12), 244
Ḥanẓal (*Citrullus Colocynthis*, L.; colocynth), 196
Al-Ḥanẓalijjât, Riǧl (k—l12), 201
Haplophyllum rubrum, Vel. See *Frejṯa*
Haplophyllum tuberculatum, Forsk. See *Frejṯa*
Al-Ḫarâb (g18), 365
Al-Ḥarâni (i4), 334, 569
Ḫarar, 490, 493
Ḥarasta (e4), *378*, 380
Ḥarasta at-Tîn, 380
Ḥarb, tribe, 53
Ḥarb abu Tâjeh, 435

ERRATA

p. 40, lines 38 and 39: *for* Ḥabbâb *read* Ḥubâb.
p. 183, line 1: *for* March 2 *read* March 3.
p. 271, line 8: *for* April 13 *read* April 14.
p. 341, Fig. 77: *south is at the top.*
p. 366, line 9: *for* southwest *read* southeast.
p. 552, line 22: *for* Ḥabbâb *read* Ḥubâb.